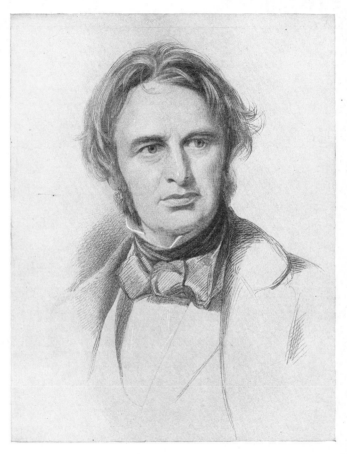

HENRY WADSWORTH LONGFELLOW
From an engraving after the portrait by Lawrence

A

OUTLINES OF
AMERICAN LITERATURE

WITH READINGS

BY

WILLIAM J. LONG

Have the elder races halted?
Do they droop and end their lesson, wearied
over there beyond the seas?
We take up the task eternal, and the burden
and the lesson,
Pioneers! O Pioneers!

GINN AND COMPANY
BOSTON · NEW YORK · CHICAGO · LONDON
ATLANTA · DALLAS · COLUMBUS · SAN FRANCISCO

𝕿𝔥𝔢 𝔄𝔱𝔥𝔢𝔫æ𝔲𝔪 𝔓𝔯𝔢𝔰𝔰

GINN AND COMPANY · PRO-
PRIETORS · BOSTON · U.S.A.

OA

TO MY SISTER

"MILLIE"

IN GRATEFUL REMEMBRANCE OF

A LIFELONG SYMPATHY

PREFACE

(From the preface to " Outlines of English and American Literature ")

The last thing we find in making a book is to
know what to put first. — Pascal

When an author has finished his history, after months or
years of happy work, there comes a dismal hour when he must
explain its purpose and apologize for its shortcomings.

The explanation in this case is very simple and goes back
to a personal experience. When the author first studied the
history of our literature there was put into his hands as a
textbook a most dreary catalogue of dead authors, dead mas-
terpieces, dead criticisms, dead ages ; and a boy who knew
chiefly that he was alive was supposed to become interested
in this literary sepulchre or else have it said that there was
something hopeless about him.   Later he learned that the
great writers of England and America were concerned with
life alone, as the most familiar, the most mysterious, the most
fascinating thing in the world, and that the only valuable or
interesting feature of any work of literature is its vitality.

To introduce these writers not as dead worthies but as companionable men and women, and to present their living subject
as a living thing, winsome as a smile on a human face, —
such was the author's purpose in writing this book.

The apology is harder to frame, as anyone knows who has
attempted to gather the writers of a thousand years into a
single volume that shall have the three virtues of brevity,
readableness and accuracy. That this record is brief in view
of the immensity of the subject is plainly apparent. That it
may prove pleasantly readable is a hope inspired chiefly by the
fact that it was a pleasure to write it, and that pleasure is

contagious. As for accuracy, every historian who fears God or regards man strives hard enough for that virtue; but after all his striving, remembering the difficulty of criticism and the perversity of names and dates that tend to error as the sparks fly upward, he must still trust heaven and send forth his work with something of Chaucer's feeling when he wrote:

> O littel bookë, thou art so unconning,
> How darst thou put thy-self in prees for drede?

Which *may* mean, to one who appreciates Chaucer's wisdom and humor, that having written a little book in what seemed to him an unskilled or "unconning" way, he hesitated to give it to the world for dread of the "prees" or crowd of critics who, even in that early day, were wont to look upon each new book as a camel that must be put through the needle's eye of their tender mercies.

In the selection and arrangement of his material the author has aimed to make a usable book that may appeal to pupils and teachers alike. Because history and literature are closely related (one being the record of man's deed, the other of his thought and feeling) there is a brief historical introduction to every literary period. There is also a review of the general literary tendencies of each age, of the fashions, humors and ideals that influenced writers in forming their style or selecting their subject. Then there is a biography of every important author, written not to offer another subject for hero-worship but to present the man exactly as he was; a review of his chief works, which is intended chiefly as a guide to the best reading; and a critical estimate or appreciation of his writings based partly upon first-hand impressions, partly upon the assumption that an author must deal honestly with life as he finds it and that the business of criticism is, as Emerson said, "not to legislate but to raise the dead." This detailed study of the greater writers of a period is followed by an examination of some of the minor writers and their memorable works. Finally, each chapter concludes with a concise summary of the period under consideration, a list of selections for reading, and a bibliography of works that will be found most useful in acquiring a larger knowledge of the subject.

In its general plan this little volume is modeled on the author's more advanced *English Literature* and *American Literature*; but the material, the viewpoint, the presentation of individual writers, all the details of the work, are entirely new. Such a book is like a second journey through ample and beautiful regions filled with historic associations, a journey that one undertakes with new companions, with renewed pleasure and, it is to be hoped, with increased wisdom. It is hardly necessary to add that our subject has still its unvoiced charms, that it cannot be exhausted or even adequately presented in any number of histories. For literature deals with life; and life, with its endlessly surprising variety in unity, has happily some suggestion of infinity.

Since the prime purpose of any text of literature is to introduce men and women who have a message worth hearing, the greater part of this new edition is given to selections from the work of representative American authors, including those of the present day. These selections have been gathered together with a double motive, — to let each author speak for himself, however briefly, and to encourage the student to form his own judgment, independent of historians or critics. The result should be not only to inspire us to seek a better acquaintance with our elder writers but also to enable us to choose from among the many of our own day the few who by appealing to our particular taste or humor can best minister to our pleasure in reading.

WILLIAM J. LONG

STAMFORD, CONNECTICUT

OA

CONTENTS

PAGE

INTRODUCTION: AN ESSAY OF LITERATURE xiii

CHAPTER I. THE PIONEERS AND NATION-BUILDERS . .   I

Unique Quality of Early American Literature. Two Views of the Pioneers. The Colonial Period. Annalists and Historians. Bradford and Byrd. Puritan and Cavalier Influences. Colonial Poetry. Wigglesworth. Anne Bradstreet. Godfrey. Nature and Human Nature in Colonial Records. The Indian in Literature. Religious Writers. Cotton Mather and Edwards.

The Revolutionary Period. Party Literature. Benjamin Franklin. Revolutionary Poetry. The Hartford Wits. Trumbull's *M'Fingal*. Freneau. Orators and Statesmen of the Revolution. Citizen Literature. James Otis and Patrick Henry. Hamilton and Jefferson. Miscellaneous Writers. Thomas Paine. Crèvecœur. Woolman. Beginning of American Fiction. Charles Brockden Brown. Summary of the Period. Selections for Reading. Bibliography.

CHAPTER II. LITERATURE OF THE NEW NATION . . .   28

Historical Background. Literary Environment. The National Spirit in Prose and Verse. The Knickerbocker School. Halleck, Drake, Willis and Paulding. Southern Writers. Simms, Kennedy, Wilde and Wirt. Various New England Writers. First Literature of the West. Major Writers of the Period. Irving. Bryant. Cooper. Poe. Summary of the Period. Selections for Reading. Bibliography.

CHAPTER III. THE PERIOD OF CONFLICT   75

Political History. Social and Intellectual Changes. Brook Farm and Other Reform Societies. The Transcendental Movement. Literary Characteristics of the Period. The Elder Poets. Longfellow. Whittier. Lowell. Holmes. Lanier. Whitman. The Greater Prose Writers. Emerson. Hawthorne. Some Minor Poets. Timrod, Hayne, Ryan, Stoddard and Bayard Taylor. Secondary Writers of Fiction. Mrs. Stowe, Dana, Herman Melville, Cooke, Eggleston and Winthrop. Juvenile Literature. Louisa M. Alcott. Trowbridge. Miscellaneous Prose. Thoreau. The Historians. Motley, Prescott and Parkman. Summary of the Period. Selections for Reading. Bibliography.

PAGE

CHAPTER IV. THE ALL-AMERICA PERIOD 169

The New Spirit of Nationality. Contemporary History. The Short Story and its Development. Bret Harte. The Local-Color Story and Some Typical Writers. The Novel since 1876. Realism in Recent Fiction. Howells. Mark Twain. Various Types of Realism. Dialect Stories. Joel Chandler Harris. Recent Romances. Historical Novels. Poetry since 1876. Stedman and Aldrich. The New Spirit in Poetry. Joaquin Miller. Dialect Poems. The Poetry of Common Life. Carleton and Riley. Other Typical Poets. Miscellaneous Prose. The Nature Writers. History and Biography. John Fiske. Literary History and Reminiscence. Bibliography.

CHAPTER V. BOOKS AND WRITERS OF THE PRESENT
    DAY 197

The flood of books: outstanding characteristics. Present-Day Authors and Readers. Old Writers and New. Limitations of Our Study.

Present-Day Fiction. A Typical American Novel: *Vandemark's Folly*. Novels of Society. Booth Tarkington. Edith Wharton. The Romance of History. S. Weir Mitchell. Mary Johnston. Winston Churchill. American Types. Influence of *David Harum*. Irving Bacheller. Joseph Lincoln. James Lane Allen. John Fox, Jr. Owen Wister. Gertrude Atherton. Mary Austin. J. Willard Schultz. The Social Novel. Definition. Frank Norris. Later Attempts. The Novel of Adventure. Popularity of the Type. Romance of the North. Jack London and His Followers. Stewart Edward White. Romance of the West. Zane Grey. Typical Yarns.

The Short Story. Qualifications. The Many Short-Story Writers. "O. Henry."

Present-Day Poetry. Sara Teasdale. Edwin Arlington Robinson. Vachel Lindsay. The Classical School. Edith M. Thomas. George Edward Woodberry. Katharine Lee Bates. Poets of the Great War. Outdoor Poets. Robert Frost. Clinton Scollard. Free Verse. Divergent Opinions. Amy Lowell. Carl Sandburg.

The Modern Stage. Three Varieties of Present-Day Drama. The Little Theatre. Typical Plays. Josephine Preston Peabody. David Belasco. Augustus Thomas. Eugene O'Neill. Percy Mackaye. William Vaughn Moody. Booth Tarkington. Edward Knoblauch.

Conclusion: a short cut through present-day literature.

GENERAL BIBLIOGRAPHY 228

LIST OF ILLUSTRATIONS

	PAGE
Henry Wadsworth Longfellow	Frontispiece
Entrance to " Westover," Home of William Byrd	3
Plymouth in 1662. Bradford's House on Right	4
William Byrd	5
New Amsterdam (New York) in 1663	8
Cotton Mather	11
Jonathan Edwards	12
Benjamin Franklin	14
Franklin's Shop	15
Philip Freneau	18
Thomas Jefferson	19
Alexander Hamilton	20
Monticello, the Home of Jefferson in Virginia	21
Charles Brockden Brown	24
William Gilmore Simms	31
John Pendleton Kennedy	32
Washington Irving	34
" Sunnyside," Home of Irving	36
Rip Van Winkle	40
Old Dutch Church, Sleepy Hollow	42
William Cullen Bryant	45
Bryant's Home, at Cummington	49
James Fenimore Cooper	54
Otsego Hall, Home of Cooper	55
Cooper's Cave	59
Edgar Allan Poe	63
West Range, University of Virginia	64
The Building of the *Southern Literary Messenger*	70
" The Man " (Abraham Lincoln)	76
Birthplace of Longfellow at Falmouth (now Portland), Maine	80
Henry Wadsworth Longfellow	82
The Taproom, Wayside Inn, Sudbury	89
Longfellow's Library in Craigie House, Cambridge	91
John Greenleaf Whittier	94
Oak Knoll, Whittier's Home, Danvers, Massachusetts	95
Street in Old Marblehead	98

PAGE

James Russell Lowell 105
Lowell's House, Cambridge, in Winter 109
Oliver Wendell Holmes 112
Old Colonial Doorway 116
Sidney Lanier 118
The Village of McGaheysville, Virginia 121
Walt Whitman 126
Whitman's Birthplace, West Hills, Long Island 131
Ralph Waldo Emerson 134
Emerson's Home, Concord 143
Nathaniel Hawthorne 146
Old Customhouse, Boston 147
"The House of the Seven Gables," Salem (built in 1669) 152
Hawthorne's Birthplace, Salem, Massachusetts 154
Henry Timrod 156
Paul Hamilton Hayne 157
Harriet Beecher Stowe 158
John Esten Cooke 159
Louisa M. Alcott 160
Henry D. Thoreau 161
Francis Parkman 164
Bret Harte 171
George W. Cable 172
Mary E. Wilkins-Freeman 174
William Dean Howells 176
Mark Twain 177
Joel Chandler Harris 180
Edmund Clarence Stedman 184
Thomas Bailey Aldrich 185
Joaquin Miller 187
John Fiske 192
Edward Everett Hale 194

INTRODUCTION

AN ESSAY OF LITERATURE

(Not a Lesson, but an Invitation)

> I sleep, yet I love to be wakened, and love to see
> The fresh young faces bending over me;
> And the faces of them that are old, I love them too,
> For these, as well, in the days of their youth I knew.
>
> " Song of the Well "

What is Literature? In an old English book, written before Columbus dreamed of a westward journey to find the East, is the story of a traveler who set out to search the world for wisdom. Through Palestine and India he passed, traveling by sea or land through many seasons, till he came to a wonderful island where he saw a man plowing in the fields. And the wonder was, that the man was calling familiar words to his oxen, "such wordes as men speken to bestes in his owne lond." Startled by the sound of his mother tongue he turned back on his course "in gret mervayle, for he knewe not how it myghte be." But if he had passed on a little, says the old record, " he would have founden his contree and his owne knouleche."

Facing a new study of literature our impulse is to search in strange places for a definition ; but though we compass a world of books, we must return at last, like the worthy man of *Mandeville's Travels*, to our own knowledge. Since childhood we have been familiar with this noble subject of literature. We have entered into the heritage of the ancient Greeks, who thought that Homer was a good teacher for the nursery; we have made acquaintance with Psalm and Prophecy and Parable, with the knightly tales of Malory, with the fairy stories of Grimm or Andersen, with the poetry of Shakespeare, with the novels of Scott or Dickens, — in short, with some of the best books that the world has ever produced. We know, therefore, what literature is, and that it is an excellent thing which ministers to the joy of living; but when we are asked to define the subject, we are in the position of St. Augustine, who said of time, " If you ask me what time is, I know not; but if you ask me not, then I know." For literature is like happiness, or love, or life itself, in that it can be understood or appreciated but can never be exactly described. It has certain describable qualities, however, and the best place to discover these is our own bookcase.

Here on a shelf are a Dictionary, a History of America, a text on Chemistry, which we read or study for information; **The Tree** on a higher shelf are *As You Like It*, *Hiawatha*, **and the Book** *Lorna Doone*, *The Oregon Trail*, and other works to which we go for pleasure when the day's work is done. In one sense all these and all other books are literature; for the root meaning of the word is " letters," and a letter means a character inscribed or rubbed upon a prepared surface. A series of letters intelligently arranged forms a book, and for the root meaning of " book " you must go to a tree; because the Latin word for book, *liber*, means the inner layer of bark that covers a tree bole, and " book " or " boc " is the old English name for the beech, on whose silvery surface our ancestors carved their first runic letters.

So also when we turn the " leaves " of a book, our mind goes back over a long trail: through rattling printing-shop, and peaceful monk's cell, and gloomy cave with walls covered with picture writing, till the trail ends beside a shadowy forest, where primitive man takes a smooth leaf and inscribes his thought upon it by means of a pointed stick. A tree is the

OA

Adam of all books, and everything that the hand of man has written upon the tree or its products or its substitutes is literature. But that is too broad a definition; we must limit it by excluding what does not here concern us.

Our first exclusion is of that immense class of writings — books of science, history, philosophy, and the rest — to which **Books of Knowledge and of Power** we go for information. These aim to preserve or to systematize the discoveries of men; they appeal chiefly to the intellect, and they are known as the literature of knowledge. There remains another large class of writings, sometimes called the literature of power, consisting of poems, plays, essays, stories of every kind, to which we go treasure-hunting for happiness or counsel, for noble thoughts or fine feelings, for rest of body or exercise of spirit, — for almost everything, in fine, except information. As Chaucer said, long ago, such writings are:

> For pleasaunce high, and for noon other end.

They aim to give us pleasure; they appeal chiefly to our imagination and our emotions; they awaken in us a feeling of sympathy or admiration for whatever is beautiful in nature or society or the soul of man.

The author who would attempt books of such high purpose must be careful of both the matter and the manner of his **The Art of Literature** writing, must give one thought to what he shall say and another thought to how he shall say it. He selects the best or most melodious words, the finest figures, and aims to make his story or poem beautiful in itself, as a painter strives to reflect a face or a landscape in a beautiful way. Any photographer can in a few minutes reproduce a human face, but only an artist can by care and labor bring forth a beautiful portrait. So any historian can write the facts of the Battle of Gettysburg; but only a Lincoln can in noble words reveal the beauty and immortal meaning of that mighty conflict.

OA

To all such written works, which quicken our sense of the beautiful, and which are as a Jacob's ladder on which we mount for higher views of nature or humanity, we confidently give the name "literature," meaning the art of literature in distinction from the mere craft of writing.

Such a definition, though it cuts out the greater part of human records, is still too broad for our purpose, and again **The Passing** we must limit it by a process of exclusion. For **and the Per-** to study almost any period of American letters is to **manent** discover that it produced hundreds of books which served the purpose of literature, if only for a season, by affording pleasure to readers. No sooner were they written than Time began to winnow them over and over, giving them to all the winds of opinion, one generation after another, till the hosts of ephemeral works were swept aside, and only a remnant was left in the hands of the winnower. To this remnant, books of abiding interest, on which the years have no effect save to mellow or flavor them, we give the name of great or enduring literature; and with these chiefly we deal in our present study.

To the inevitable question, What are the marks of great literature? no positive answer can be returned. As a tree is **The Quality** judged by its fruits, so is literature judged not by **of Greatness** theory but by the effect which it produces on human life; and the judgment is first personal, then general. If a book has power to awaken in you a lively sense of pleasure or a profound emotion of sympathy; if it quickens your love of beauty or truth or goodness; if it moves you to generous thought or noble action, then that book is, for you and for the time, a great book. If after ten or fifty years it still has power to quicken you, then for you at least it is a great book forever. And if it affects many other men and women as it affects you, and if it lives with power from one generation to another, gladdening the children as it gladdened the fathers, then surely it is great literature, without further qualification or need of definition. From this viewpoint the greatest poem in the world — greatest in that it abides in most human hearts as a loved and honored guest — is not a mighty *Iliad* or *Paradise Lost* or *Divine Comedy*; it is a familiar little poem of a dozen lines, beginning "The Lord is my Shepherd."

It is obvious that great literature, which appeals to all classes of men and to all times, cannot go far afield for rare subjects, or follow new inventions, or concern itself with fashions that are here to-day and gone to-morrow. Its only subjects are nature and human nature; it deals with common experiences of joy or sorrow, pain or pleasure, that all men understand; it cherishes the unchanging ideals of love, faith, duty, freedom, reverence, courtesy, which were old to the men who kept their flocks on the plains of Shinar, and which will be young as the morning to our children's children.

Such ideals tend to ennoble a writer, and therefore are great books characterized by lofty thought, by fine feeling and, as a rule, by a beautiful simplicity of expression. They have another quality, hard to define but easy to understand, a quality which leaves upon us the impression of eternal youth, as if they had been dipped in the fountain which Ponce de Leon sought for in vain through the New World. If a great book could speak, it would use the words of the Cobzar (poet) in his "Last Song":

> The merry Spring, he is my brother,
> And when he comes this way
> Each year again, he always asks me:
> "Art thou not yet grown gray?"
> But I, I keep my youth forever,
> Even as the Spring his May.

A Definition. Literature, then, if one must formulate a definition, is the written record of man's best thought and feeling, and American literature is the part of that record which belongs to the American people. In its broadest sense literature includes all writing, but as we commonly define the term it excludes

OA

works which aim at instruction, and includes only the works which aim to give pleasure, and which are artistic in that they reflect nature or human life in a way to arouse our sense of beauty. In a still narrower sense, when we study the history of literature we deal chiefly with the great, the enduring books, which may have been written in an elder or a latter day, but which have in them the magic of all time.

One may easily challenge such a definition, which, like most others, is far from faultless. It is difficult, for example, to draw the line sharply between instructive and pleasure-giving works; for many an instructive book of history gives us pleasure, and there may be more instruction on important matters in a pleasurable poem than in a treatise on ethics. There are other objections; but to straighten them all out is to be long in starting, and there is a pleasant journey ahead of us. Chaucer had literature in mind when he wrote:

> Through me men goon into that blisful place
>   Of hertës hele and dedly woundës cure;
> Through me men goon unto the wells of grace,
>   Ther grene and lusty May shal ever endure:
>   This is the wey to al good aventure.

OUTLINES OF
AMERICAN LITERATURE

CHAPTER I

THE PIONEERS AND NATION-BUILDERS

'T was glory once to be a Roman:
She makes it glory now to be a man.
                              Bayard Taylor, " America "

We have this double interest in early American literature,
that it is our own and unlike any other. The literatures of
Europe began with wonder tales of a golden age, with stories
of fairy ships, of kings akin to gods, of heroes who ventured
into enchanted regions and there waged battle with dragons
or the powers of darkness. American literature began with
historical records, with letters of love and friendship, with
diaries or journals of exploration, with elegiac poems lament-
ing the death of beloved leaders or hearth companions, —
in a word, with the chronicles of human experience. In this
respect, of recording the facts and the truth of life as men
and women fronted life bravely in the New World, our early
literature differs radically from that of any other great nation :
it brings us face to face not with myths or shadows but with
our ancestors.

Two Views of the Pioneers. It has become almost a habit
among historians to disparage early American literature, and
nearly all our textbooks apologize for it on the ground that
the forefathers had no artistic feeling, their souls being oppressed by the gloom and rigor of Puritanism.

Even as we read this apology our eyes rest contentedly upon a beautiful old piece of Colonial furniture, fashioned most artistically by the very men who are pitied for their want of art. We remember also that the Puritans furnished only one of several strong elements in early American life, and that wherever the Puritan influence was strongest there books and literary culture did most abound: their private libraries, for example, make our own appear rather small and trashy by comparison.[1] Cotton Mather, disciplined in the strictest of Puritan homes, wrote his poems in Greek, conducted a large foreign correspondence in Latin, read enormously, published four hundred works, and in thousands of citations proved himself intimate with the world's books of poetry and history, science and religion. That the leaders of the colonies, south and north, were masters of an excellent prose style is evident from their own records; that their style was influenced by their familiarity with the best literature appears in many ways, — in the immense collection of books in Byrd's mansion in Virginia, for instance, or in the abundant quotations that are found in nearly all Colonial writings. Before entering college (and there was never another land with so few people and so many colleges as Colonial America) boys of fourteen passed a classical examination which few graduates would now care to face; and the men of our early legislatures produced state papers which for force of reasoning and lucidity of expression have never been surpassed.

Again, our whole conception of American art may be modified by these considerations: that it requires more genius to build a free state than to make a sonnet, and the Colonists were mighty state-builders; that a ship is a beautiful object,

[1] When Plymouth consisted of a score of cabins and a meetinghouse it had at least two excellent libraries. Bradford had over three hundred books, and Brewster four hundred, consisting of works of poetry, philosophy, science, devotion, and miscellanies covering the entire field of human knowledge. In view of the scarcity of books in 1620, one of these collections, which were common in all the New England settlements, was equivalent to a modern library of thirty or forty thousand volumes.

and American ships with their graceful lines and towering clouds of canvas were once famous the world over; that archi-**The Question of Art** tecture is a noble art, and Colonial architecture still charms us by its beauty and utility after three hundred years of experimental building. "Art" is a great word, and we use it too narrowly when we apply it to an

ode of Shelley or a mutilated statue of Praxiteles, but are silent before a Colonial church or a free commonwealth or the Constitution of the United States.

Instead of an apology for our early literature, therefore, we offer this possible explanation: that our forefathers, who set their faces to one of the most heroic tasks ever undertaken by man, were too busy with great deeds inspired by the ideal of liberty to find leisure for the epic or drama

ENTRANCE TO "WESTOVER," HOME OF WILLIAM BYRD

in which the deeds and the ideal should be worthily reflected. They left that work of commemoration to others, and they are still waiting patiently for their poet. Meanwhile we read the straightforward record which they left as their only literary memorial, not as we read the imaginative story of Beowulf or Ulysses, but for the clear light of truth which it sheds upon the fathers and mothers of a great nation.

THE COLONIAL PERIOD (1607–1765)

The Colonial period extends from the first English settlement at Jamestown to the Stamp Act and other measures of "taxation without representation" which tended to unite the colonies and arouse the sleeping spirit of nationality. During this century and a half the Elizabethan dramatists produced their best work; Milton, Bunyan, Dryden and a score of lesser writers were adding to the wealth of English literature; but not a single noteworthy volume crossed the Atlantic to

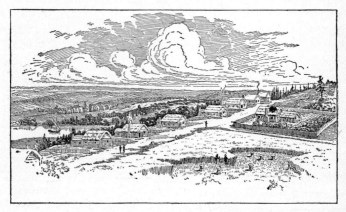

PLYMOUTH IN 1622. BRADFORD'S HOUSE ON RIGHT

reflect in Europe the lyric of the wilderness, the drama of the commonwealth, the epic of democracy. Such books as were written here dealt largely with matters of religion, government and exploration; and we shall hardly read these books with sympathy, and therefore with understanding, unless we remember two facts: that the Colonists, grown weary of ancient tyranny, were determined to write a new page in the world's history; and that they reverently believed God had called them to make that new page record the triumph of freedom and manhood. Hence the historical impulse and the moral or religious bent of nearly all our early writers.

Annalists and Historians. Of the fifty or more annalists of the period we select two as typical of the rest. The first is William Bradford (*cir.* 1590–1657), a noble and learned man, at one time governor of the Plymouth Colony. In collaboration with Winslow he wrote a Journal of the *Mayflower's* voyage (long known as *Mourt's Relation*), and he continued this work independently by writing *Of Plymouth Plantation*, a ruggedly sincere history of the trials and triumph of the Pilgrim Fathers. The second annalist is William Byrd (1674–1744), who, a century after Bradford, wrote his *History of the Dividing Line* and two other breezy Journals that depict with equal ease and gayety the southern society of the early days and the march or campfire scenes of an exploring party in the wilderness.

WILLIAM BYRD

These two writers unconsciously reflected two distinct influences in Colonial literature, which are epitomized in the words "Puritan" and "Cavalier." Bradford, though a Pilgrim (not a Puritan), was profoundly influenced by the puritanic spirit of his age, with its militant independence, its zeal for liberty and righteousness, its confidence in the divine guidance of human affairs. When he wrote his history, therefore, he was in the mood of one to whom the Lord had said, as to Abraham, "Get thee out of thy country, and from thy kindred, and from thy father's house; and I will make of thee a great nation." Byrd, though born and bred in democratic Virginia, had in him something of the aristocrat. He reminds us of the gay Cavaliers who left England to escape the stern discipline of Cromwell and the triumphant Puritans. When he looked forth upon his goodly plantation, or upon the wilderness with its teeming game, he saw them not with the eyes of prophet or evangelist, but as one who remembered that it was written, " And God saw everything that he had made ; and behold it was very good." So he wrote his Journal in an entertaining way, making the best of misfortune, cracking a joke at difficulty or danger, and was well content to reflect this pleasant world without taking it upon his conscience to criticize or reform it.

The same two types of Cavalier and Puritan appear constantly in our own and other literatures as representative of two world-views, two philosophies. Chaucer and Langland were early examples in English poetry, the one with his *Canterbury Tales*, the other with his *Piers Plowman*; and ever since then the same two classes of writers have been reflecting the same life from two different angles. They are not English or American but human types; they appear in every age and in every free nation.

Colonial Poetry. There were several recognized poets in Colonial days, and even the annalists and theologians had a rhyming fancy which often broke loose from the bounds of prose. The quantity of Colonial verse is therefore respectable, but the quality of it suffered from two causes : first, the writers overlooked the feeling of their own hearts (the true source of lyric poetry) and wrote of Indian wars, theology and other unpoetic matters ; second, they wrote poetry not for its own sake but to teach moral or religious lessons.[1] Thus,

---

[1] The above criticism applies only to poetry written in English for ordinary readers. At that time many college men wrote poetry in Greek and Latin, and the quality of it compares favorably with similar poetry written in England during the same period. Several specimens of this "scholars' poetry" are preserved in Mather's *Magnalia*; and there is one remarkable poem, in Greek, which was written in Harvard College by an Indian (one of Eliot's "boys") who a few years earlier had been a whooping savage.

the most widely read poem of the period was *The Day of Doom*, which aimed frankly to recall sinners from their evil ways by holding before their eyes the terrors of the last judgment. It was written by Michael Wigglesworth in 1662. This man, who lived a heroic but melancholy life, had a vein of true poetry in him, as when he wrote his "Dear New England, Dearest Land to Me," and from his bed of suffering sent out the call to his people:

> Cheer on, brave souls, my heart is with you all.

But he was too much absorbed in stern theological dogmas to find the beauty of life or the gold of poesie; and his masterpiece, once prized by an immense circle of readers, seems now a grotesque affair, which might appear even horrible were it not rendered harmless by its jigging, Yankee-Doodle versification.

The most extravagantly praised versifier of the age, and the first to win a reputation in England as well as in America, was Anne Bradstreet (1612–1672), who wrote a book of poems that a London publisher proudly issued under the title of *The Tenth Muse* (1650). The best of Colonial poets was Thomas Godfrey of Philadelphia (1736–1763), whose *Juvenile Poems, with the Prince of Parthia, a Tragedy* contained a few lyrics, odes and pastorals that were different in form and spirit from anything hitherto attempted on this side of the Atlantic. This slender volume was published in 1765, soon after Godfrey's untimely death. With its evident love of beauty and its carefulness of poetic form, it marks the beginning here of artistic literature; that is, literature which was written to please readers rather than to teach history or moral lessons.

Nature and Human Nature. In the literature of the world the two subjects of abiding poetic interest are nature and human nature; but as these subjects appear in Colonial records they are uniformly prosaic, and the reason is very simple. Before nature can be the theme of poets she must assume her winsome mood, must "soothe and heal and bless" the human heart after the clamor of politics, the weariness of trade, the cruel strife of society. To read Wordsworth's "Tintern Abbey" or Bryant's "To a Water-fowl" is to understand the above criticism. But the nature which the Colonists first looked upon seemed wild and strange

NEW AMSTERDAM (NEW YORK) IN 1663

and often terrible. Their somber forests were vast, mysterious, forbidding; and they knew not what perils lurked in them or beyond them. The new climate might give them sunshine or healing rain, but was quite as likely to strike their houses with thunderbolts or harrow their harvests with a cyclone. Meanwhile marauding crows pulled up their precious corn; fierce owls with tufted heads preyed upon their poultry; bears and eagles harried their flocks; the winter wail of the wolf pack or the scream of a hungry panther, sounding through icy, echoless woods, made them shiver in their cabins and draw nearer the blazing fire of pine knots on the hearth.

We can understand, therefore, why there was little poetry of nature in Colonial literature, and why, instead of sonnets to moonbeams or nightingales, we meet quaint and fascinating studies of natural or unnatural history. Such are Josselyn's *New England's Rarities Discovered* and the first part of William Wood's *New England's Prospect*; and such are many chapters of Byrd's *Dividing Line* and other annals that deal with plant or animal life,— books that we now read with pleasure, since the nature that was once wild and strange has become in our eyes familiar and dear.

As for the second subject of poetic interest, human nature, the Colonists had as much of that as any other people ; but human nature as it revealed itself in religious controversy, or became a burden in the immigrants that were unloaded on our shores for the relief of Europe or the enrichment of the early transportation companies, as Bradford and Beverley both tell us,— this furnished a vital subject not for poetry but for prose and protest.

The Indians especially, "the wild men " as they were called, slipping out of the shadows or vanishing into mysterious dis-

The Indians tances, were a source of anxiety and endless specu- lation to the early settlers. European writers like Rousseau, who had never seen an Indian or heard a war- whoop, had been industrious in idealizing the savages, attribut- ing to them all manner of noble virtues ; and the sentimental attitude of these foreign writers was reflected here, after the eastern Indians had well-nigh vanished, in such stories as Mrs. Morton's *Quabi, or The Virtues of Nature*, a romance in verse which was published in 1790. In the same romantic strain are Cooper's *Last of the Mohicans*, Helen Hunt's *Ramona* and some of the early poems of Freneau and Whittier.

The Colonists, on the other hand, had no poetic illusions about the savages. Their enjoyment of this phase of human nature was hardly possible so long as they had to proceed warily on a forest trail, their eyes keen for the first glimpse of a hideously painted face, their ears alert for the twang of a bowstring or the hiss of a feathered arrow. Their deep but practical interest in the Indians found expression in scores of books, which fall roughly into three groups. In the first are the scholarly works of the heroic John Eliot, "the apostle to the Indians"; of Daniel Gookin also, and of a few others who made careful studies of the language and customs of the various Indian tribes. In the second group are the startling experiences of men and women who were carried away by the savages, leaving slaughtered children and burning homes behind them. Such are Mary Rowlandson's *The Sovereignty and Goodness of God* and John Williams's *The Redeemed Captive*, both famous in their day, and still of lively interest. In the third group are the fighting stories, such as John Mason's *History of the Pequot War*. The adventures and hairbreadth escapes recorded as sober facts in these narratives were an excellent substitute for fiction during the Colonial period. Moreover, they furnished a motive and method for the Indian tales and Wild West stories which have since appeared as the sands of the sea for multitude.

Religious Writers. A very large part of our early writings is devoted to religious subjects, and for an excellent reason; namely, that large numbers of the Colonists came to America to escape religious strife or persecution at home. In the New World they sought religious peace as well as freedom of worship, and were determined to secure it not only for themselves but for their children's children. Hence in nearly all their writings the religious motive was uppermost. Hardly were they settled here, however, when they were rudely disturbed by agitators who fomented discord by preaching each his own pet doctrine or heresy. Presently arose a score of controversial writers; and then Anne Hutchinson, Roger Williams and the early Quakers were disciplined or banished, not because of their faith (for the fact is that all the colonies contained men of widely different beliefs who lived peaceably together), but because these unbalanced reformers were obstinately bent upon stirring up strife in a community which had crossed three thousand miles of ocean in search of peace.

Of the theological writers we again select two, not because they were typical, — for it is hard to determine who, among the hundred writers that fronted the burning question of religious tolerance, were representative of their age, — but simply because they towered head and shoulders above their contemporaries. These are Cotton Mather and Jonathan Edwards; the one the most busy man of his age in politics, religion, education and all philanthropic endeavor; the other a profound thinker, who was in the world but not of it, and who devoted the great powers of his mind to such problems as the freedom of the human will and the origin of the religious impulse in humanity.

COTTON MATHER

Cotton Mather (1663–1728) is commonly known by his *Wonders of the Invisible World*, which dealt with the matter

Cotton
Mather

of demons and witchcraft; but that is one of the least of his four hundred works, and it has given a wrong impression of the author and of the age in which he lived. His chief work is the *Magnalia Christi Americana, or the Ecclesiastical History of New England* (1702), which is a strange jumble of patriotism and pedantry, of wisdom and foolishness, written in the fantastic style of Robert Burton's

Anatomy of Melancholy. The most interesting and valuable parts of this chaotic work are the second and third books, which give us the life stories of Bradford, Winthrop, Eliot, Phipps and many other heroic worthies who helped mightily in laying the foundation of the American republic.

The most famous works of Jonathan Edwards (1703–1758) are

JONATHAN EDWARDS

the so-called *Freedom of the Will* and the *Treatise Concerning the Religious Affections*; but these are hard reading, not to be lightly undertaken. It is from the author's minor and neglected works that one receives the impression that he was a very great and noble man, shackled by a terrible theology. By his scholarship, his rare sincerity, his love of truth, his original mind and his transparent style of writing he exercised probably a greater influence at home and abroad than any other writer of the Colonial era. In Whittier's poem "The Preacher" there is a tribute to the tender humanity of Edwards, following this picture of his stern thinking:

> In the church of the wilderness Edwards wrought,
> Shaping his creed at the forge of thought;
> And with Thor's own hammer welded and bent
> The iron links of his argument,
> Which strove to grasp in its mighty span
> The purpose of God and the fate of man.

THE REVOLUTIONARY PERIOD (1765-1800) (1787)

The literary period included in the above term is, in general, the latter half of the eighteenth century; more particularly it extends from the Stamp Act (1765), which united the colonies in opposition to Britain's policy of taxation, to the adoption of the Constitution (1787) and the inauguration of Washington as first president of the new nation.

The writings of this stormy period reflect the temper of two very different classes who were engaged in constant literary warfare. In the tense years which preceded the Revolution the American people separated into two hostile parties: the Tories, or Loyalists, who supported the mother country; and the Whigs, or Patriots, who insisted on the right of the colonies to manage their own affairs, and who furnished the armies that followed Washington in the War of Independence. Then, when America had won a place among the free nations of the world, her people were again divided on the question of the Constitution. On the one side were the Federalists, who aimed at union in the strictest sense; that is, at a strongly centralized government with immense powers over all its parts. On the other side were the Anti-Federalists, or Antis, who distrusted the monarchical tendency of every centralized government since time began, and who aimed to safeguard democracy by leaving the governing power as largely as possible in the hands of the several states. It is necessary to have these distinctions clearly in mind in reading Revolutionary literature, for a very large part of its prose and poetry reflects the antagonistic aims or ideals of two parties which stood in constant and most bitter opposition.

Party Literature

In general, the literature of the Revolution is dominated by political and practical interests; it deals frankly with this present world, aims to find the best way through its difficulties, and so appears in marked contrast with the theological bent and pervasive "other worldliness" of Colonial writings.

Benjamin Franklin. Standing between the two eras, and marking the transition from spiritual to practical interests, is Benjamin Franklin (1706–1790), a "self-made" man, who seems well content with his handiwork. During the latter part of his life and for a century after his death he was held up to young Americans as a striking example of practical wisdom and worldly success.

BENJAMIN FRANKLIN

The narrative of Franklin's patriotic service belongs to political rather than to literary history; for though his pen was busy for almost seventy years, during which time he produced an immense amount of writing, his end was always very practical rather than æsthetic; that is, he aimed to instruct rather than to please his readers. Only one of his works is now widely known, the incomplete *Autobiography*, which is in the form of a letter telling a straightforward story of Franklin's early life, of the disadvantages under which he labored and the industry by which he overcame them. For some reason the book has become a "classic" in our literature, and young Americans are urged to read it; though they often show an independent taste by regarding it askance. As an example of what may be accomplished by perseverance, and as a stimulus to industry in the prosaic matter of getting a living, it doubtless has its value;

but one will learn nothing of love or courtesy or reverence or loyalty to high ideals by reading it; neither will one find in its self-satisfied pages any conception of the moral dignity of humanity or of the infinite value of the human soul. The chief trouble with the *Autobiography* and most other works of Franklin is that in them mind and matter, character and reputation, virtue and pros- perity, are for the most part hopelessly confounded.

On the other hand, there is a sincerity, a plain direct- ness of style in the writings of Franklin which makes them pleasantly readable. Unlike some other apostles of "common sense" he is always courteous and of a friendly spirit; he seems to respect the reader as well as himself and, even in his argumentative or humorous passages, is almost invariably dignified in expression.

Other works of Franklin which were once popular are the maxims of his *Poor Rich- ard's Almanac*, which ap- peared annually from 1732

FRANKLIN'S SHOP

to 1757. These maxims — such as "Light purse, heavy heart," "Diligence is the mother of good luck," "He who waits upon Fortune is never sure of a dinner," "God helps them who help themselves," "Honesty is the best policy," and many others in a similar vein — were widely copied in Colonial and European publications; and to this day they give to Americans abroad a reputation for "Yankee" shrewdness. The best of

OA

them were finally strung together in the form of a discourse
(the alleged speech of an old man at an auction, where people
were complaining of the taxes), which under various titles,
such as "The Way to Wealth" and "Father Abraham's
Speech," has been translated into every civilized language.
Following is a brief selection from which one may judge the
spirit of the entire address :

"It would be thought a hard government that should tax its people one
tenth part of their time, to be employed in its service; but idleness taxes
many of us much more; sloth, by bringing on diseases, absolutely shortens
life. Sloth, like rust, consumes faster than labor wears, while 'The used
key is always bright,' as Poor Richard says. 'But dost thou love life?
Then do not squander time, for that is the stuff life is made of,' as Poor
Richard says. How much more than is necessary do we spend in sleep,
forgetting that the sleeping fox catches no poultry, and that there will be
sleeping enough in the grave, as Poor Richard says. If time be of all
things the most precious, wasting time must be, as Poor Richard says, the
greatest prodigality; since, as he elsewhere tells us, 'Lost time is never
found again,' and what we call time enough always proves little enough.
Let us, then, be up and be doing, and doing to the purpose; so by diligence shall we do more with less perplexity. 'Sloth makes all things difficult, but industry, all easy'; and, 'He that riseth late must trot all day and
shall scarce overtake his business at night'; while 'Laziness travels so
slowly that Poverty soon overtakes him.' 'Drive thy business, let not that
drive thee'; and, 'Early to bed, and early to rise, makes a man healthy,
wealthy and wise,' as Poor Richard says."

Revolutionary Poetry. The poetry of the Revolution, an
abundant but weedy crop, was badly influenced by two factors :
by the political strife between Patriots and Loyalists, and by
the slavish imitation of Pope and other formalists who were
then the models for nearly all versifiers on both sides of the
Atlantic. The former influence appears in numerous ballads
or narrative poems, which were as popular in the days of
Washington as ever they were in the time of Robin Hood.
Every important event of the Revolution was promptly celebrated in verse; but as the country was then sharply divided,
almost every ballad had a Whig or a Tory twist to it. In
consequence we must read two different collections, such as

Moore's *Songs and Ballads of the American Revolution* and Sargent's *Loyalist Poetry of the Revolution*, for supplementary views of the same great struggle.

The influence of Pope and his school is especially notice-able in the work of a group of men called the Hartford **The Hart-** Wits, who at the beginning of our national life had **ford Wits** the worthy ambition to create a national literature. Prominent among these so-called wits were Joel Barlow (1754–1812) and Timothy Dwight (1752–1817). In such ponderous works as Barlow's *Columbiad* and Dwight's *Conquest of Canaan*, both written in mechanical rhymed couplets, we have a reflec-tion not of the glories of American history, as the authors in-tended, but of two aspiring men who, without genius or humor, hoped by industry to produce poems that in size at least should be worthy of a country that stretched between two oceans.

More gifted than either of his fellow "wits" was John Trumbull (1750–1831), who had the instinct of a poet but who was led aside by the strife of Whigs and Tories into the barren field of political satire. His best-known work is *M'Fingal* (1775), a burlesque poem in the doggerel style of Butler's *Hudibras*, which ridiculed a Tory squire and de-scribed his barbarous punishment at the hands of a riotous mob of Whigs. It was the most widely quoted poem of the entire Revolutionary period, and is still interesting as an ex-ample of rough humor and as a reflection of the militant age in which it was produced.

By far the best poet of the Revolution was Philip Freneau (1752–1832). In his early years he took Milton instead of Pope for his poetic master; then, as his independ-**Freneau** ence increased, he sought the ancient source of all poetry in the feeling of the human heart in presence of nature or human nature. In such poems as "The House of Night," "Indian Burying Ground," "Wild Honeysuckle," "Eutaw Springs," "Ruins of a Country Inn" and a few others in which he speaks from his own heart, he anticipated the work of Wordsworth, Coleridge and other leaders of what is now commonly known as the romantic revival in English poetry.

When the Revolution drew on apace Freneau abandoned his poetic dream and exercised a ferocious talent for satiric verse in lashing English generals, native Tories, royal proclamations and other matters far removed from poetry. In later years he wrote much prose also, and being a radical and outspoken democrat he became a thorn in the side of Washington and the Federal party. The bulk of his work, both prose and verse, is a red-peppery kind of commentary on the political history of the age in which he lived.

PHILIP FRENEAU

Orators and Statesmen. For a full century, or from the Stamp Act to the Civil War, oratory was a potent influence in molding our national life ; and unlike other influences, which grow by slow degrees, it sprang into vigorous life in the period of intense agitation that preceded the Revolution. Never before or since has the power of the spoken word been more manifest than during the years when questions of state were debated, not by kings or counselors behind closed doors, but by representative men in open assembly, by farmers and artisans in town halls fronting a village green, by scholarly ministers in the pulpits of churches whose white steeples with their golden vanes spoke silently, ceaselessly, of God and Freedom as the two motives which had inspired the fathers to brave the perils of a savage wilderness.

Among the most famous addresses of the age were the speech of James Otis in the town hall at Boston (1761) and the "Liberty or Death" speech of Patrick Henry to the Virginia burgesses assembled in St. John's church in Richmond (1775). To compare these stirring appeals to patriotism with the parliamentary addresses of a brilliant contemporary, Edmund Burke, is to note a strik-ing difference between English and American oratory of the period, the one charming the ear by its eloquence, the other rousing the will to action like a bugle call.

The statesmen of the Revolution, that glori-ous band whom Wash-ington led, were also voluminous writers and masters of a clear, force-ful style ; but it would probably surprise them now to find themselves included in a history of literature. In truth, they hardly belong there ; for they wrote

THOMAS JEFFERSON

not with any artistic impulse to create a work of beauty that should please their readers ; their practical aim was to inculcate sound political principles or to move their readers to the right action. If we contrast them with certain of their British contemporaries, with Goldsmith and Burns for example, the truth of the above criticism will be evident. Nevertheless, these statesmen produced a body of so-called citizen literature, devoted to the principles and duties of free government, which has never been rivaled in its own field and which is quite as remarkable in its own way as the nature poetry of Bryant or the romances of Cooper or any other purely literary work produced in America.

Hamilton and Jefferson. These two statesmen, who became bitter antagonists during the struggle over the Constitution, may be selected as typical of all the rest. The story of their splendid services in the cause of liberty cannot be told here; such men belong to history rather than to literature; but we may at least note that they deserve more careful and unprejudiced study than rival political parties have thus far given them. Their work has a broad human interest which extends far beyond the borders of America, since they stand for two radically different conceptions of life, one aristocratic, the other democratic, which appear in every age and explain the political and social divisions among free peoples.

ALEXANDER HAMILTON

Hamilton (the Federalist) denied the right and the ability of common men to govern themselves; he was the champion of aristocracy, of class privilege, of centralized power in the hands of the few whom he deemed worthy by birth or talent to govern a nation. The most significant trait of Jefferson (the Anti-Federalist) was his lifelong devotion to democracy. He believed in common men, in their ability to choose the right and their purpose to follow it, and he mightily opposed every tendency to aristocracy or class privilege in America. In the struggle over the Constitution he was fearful that the United States government would become monarchical if given too much authority, and aimed to safeguard democracy by leaving the governing power as largely as possible in the hands of the several states. To readers who are not politicians the most interesting thing concerning these two leaders

MONTICELLO, THE HOME OF JEFFERSON IN VIRGINIA
The westward front

is that Hamilton, the champion of aristocracy, was obscurely born and appeared here as a stranger to make his own way by his own efforts; while Jefferson, the uncompromising democrat, came from an excellent Virginia family and was familiar from his youth with aristocratic society.

The best-known work of Hamilton (to which Madison and Jay contributed liberally) is *The Federalist* (1787). This is a Typical remarkable series of essays supporting the Consti-Writings tution and illuminating the principles of union and federation. The one work of Jefferson which will make his name remembered to all ages is the *Declaration of Independence*.

Besides this document, which is less a state paper than a prose chant of freedom, he wrote a multitude of works, a part of which are now collected in ten large volumes. These are known only to historians ; but the casual reader will find many things of interest in Jefferson's *Letters*, in his *Autobiography* and in his *Summary View of the Rights of America* (1774). The last-named work gave Burke some information and inspiration for his famous oration " On Conciliation with America " and was a potent influence in uniting the colonies in their struggle for independence.

Miscellaneous Works.   In the miscellaneous works of the period may be found more pleasurable reading than in the portly volumes that contain the epics of the Hartford Wits or the arguments of Revolutionary statesmen.   As a type of the forceful political pamphlet, a weapon widely used in England and America in the eighteenth century, there is nothing equal to Thomas Paine's *Common Sense* (1776) and *The Crisis* (1776–1783).   The former hastened on the Declaration of Independence ; the latter cheered the young Patriots in their struggle to make that Declaration valid in the sight of all nations.   Jonathan Carver's *Travels through the Interior Parts of North America* (1778) is an excellent outdoor book dealing with picturesque incidents of exploration in unknown wilds.   The letters of Abigail Adams, Eliza Wilkinson and Dolly Madison portray quiet scenes of domestic life and something of the brave, helpful spirit of the mothers of the Revolution.   Crèvecœur's *Letters from an American Farmer* (1782) draws charming, almost idyllic, pictures of American life during the Revolutionary period, and incidentally calls attention to the " melting pot," in which people of various races are here fused into a common stock.   This mongrel, melting-pot idea (a crazy notion) is supposed to be modern, and has lately occasioned some flighty dramas and novels ; but that it is as old as unrestricted immigration appears plainly in one of Crèvecœur's fanciful sketches :

" What then is the American, this new man? He is either a European or a descendant of a European; hence that strange mixture of blood, which you will find in no other country. I could point out to you a family whose grandfather was an Englishman, whose wife was Dutch, whose son married a French woman, and whose present four sons have now four wives of different nations. *He* is an American who, leaving behind him all his ancient prejudices and manners, receives new ones from the new mode of life he has embraced, the new government he obeys, the new rank he holds. He becomes an American by being received in the broad lap of our great Alma Mater.

" Here individuals of all nations are melted into a new race of men whose labours and posterity will one day cause great changes in the world. Americans are the western pilgrims, who are carrying along with them that great mass of arts, sciences, vigour and industry which began long since in the East; they will finish the great circle. The Americans were once scattered all over Europe; here they are incorporated into one of the finest systems of population which has ever appeared, and which hereafter will become distinct by the power of the different climate they inhabit. The American is a new man, who acts upon new principles; he must therefore entertain new ideas and form new opinions. From involuntary idleness, servile dependence, penury and useless labour he has passed to toils of a very different nature, rewarded by ample subsistence. This is an American."

Finally, there is the *Journal of John Woolman* (1774), written by a gentle member of the society of Friends, which records a spiritual rather than a worldly experience, and which in contrast with the general tumult of Revolutionary literature is as a thrush song in the woods at twilight. It is a book for those who can appreciate its charm of simplicity and sincerity; but the few who know it are inclined to prize it far above the similar work of Franklin, and to unite with Channing in calling it "the sweetest and purest autobiography in the English language."

Beginning of American Fiction. Those who imagine that American fiction began with Irving or Cooper or Poe, as is sometimes alleged, will be interested to learn of Susanna Rowson (daughter of an English father and an American mother), whose later stories, at least, belong to our literature. In 1790 she published *Charlotte Temple*, a romance that was immensely popular in its own day and that has proved far more enduring than any modern "best seller." During the next century the book ran through more than one hundred editions, the last appearing in 1905; and from first to last it has had probably more readers than any novel of Scott or Cooper or Dickens. The reception of this work indicates the widespread interest in fiction here in the late eighteenth century. Moreover, as there were then two types of fiction in England, the sentimentalism of Richardson and the realism of Fielding, so in America the gushing romances of Mrs. Rowson were opposed by the *Female Quixotism* and other alleged realistic stories of Tabitha Tenney. Both schools of fiction had here their authors and their multitudinous readers while Irving and Cooper were learning their alphabet and Poe was yet unborn.

CHARLES BROCKDEN BROWN

Into the crude but hopeful beginnings of American fiction we shall not enter, for the simple reason that our earliest romances are hardly worth the time or patience of any but historical students. At the close of the Revolutionary period, however, appeared a writer whom we may call with some justice the first American novelist. This was Charles Brockden Brown (1771–1810), who is worthy to be remembered on three counts: he was the first in this country to follow literature as a profession; he chose American rather than foreign heroes, and pictured them against an American background; and finally, his use of horrible or grotesque incidents was copied by Poe, his Indian adventures suggested a fruitful theme to Cooper, and his minute analysis of motives and emotions was carried out in a more artistic way by Hawthorne. Hence we may find in Brown's neglected works something of the material and the method of our three greatest writers of fiction.

The six romances of Brown are all dominated by the motive of horror, and are modeled on the so-called Gothic novel with **The Motive of Horror** its sentimental heroine, its diabolical villain, its ghastly mystery, its passages of prolonged agony. If we ask why an American writer should choose this bizarre type, the answer is that agonizing stories were precisely what readers then wanted, and Brown depended upon his stories for his daily bread. At the present time a different kind of fiction is momentarily popular; yet if we begin one of Brown's bloodcurdling romances, the chances are that we shall finish it, since it appeals to that strange interest in morbid themes which leads so many to read Poe or some other purveyor of horrors and mysteries. *Wieland* (1798) is commonly regarded as the best of Brown's works, but is too grotesque and horrible to be recommended. *Edgar Huntly* (1801), with its Indian adventures depicted against a background of wild nature, is a little more wholesome, and may serve very well as a type of the romances that interested readers a century or more ago.

Summary. The Colonial period covers the century and a half from the settlement of Jamestown, in 1607, to the Stamp Act of 1765. The literature of this early age shows two general characteristics, one historical, the other theological. The Colonists believed that they were chosen by God to establish a new nation of freemen; hence their tendency to write annals and to preserve every document that might be of use to the future republic. Moreover, they were for the most part religious men and women; they aimed to give their children sound education and godly character; hence their insistence on schools and universities (seven colleges were quickly founded in the wilderness) for the training of leaders of the people; hence also the religious note which sounds through nearly all their writing.

In our review of the Colonial period we noted four classes of writers: (1) The annalists and historians, of whom Bradford and Byrd were selected as typical of two classes of writers who appear constantly in our own and other literatures. (2) The poets, of whom Wigglesworth, Anne Bradstreet and Godfrey are the most notable. (3) A few characteristic books dealing with nature and the Indians, which served readers of those days in the place of fiction. (4) Theological writers, among whom Cotton Mather and Jonathan Edwards are the most conspicuous.

The Revolutionary period extends from 1765 to the close of the century. A large part of the literature of this period deals, in the early years, with the strife of Loyalists and Patriots or, in the later years, with the wordy wars of Federalists and Anti-Federalists. These are the political parties into which America was divided by the Revolution and by the question of the Constitution. In general, Revolutionary writing has a practical bent, in marked contrast with the theological spirit of Colonial writing.

Our study of Revolutionary literature includes: (1) Benjamin Franklin, who marks the transition from Colonial to Revolutionary times, from spiritual to worldly interests. (2) Revolutionary poetry, with its numerous ballads and political satires; the effort of the Hartford Wits to establish a national literature; and the work of Philip Freneau, who was a romantic poet at heart, but who was led aside by the strife of the age into political and satiric writing. (3) Orators and statesmen, of whom Otis and Henry, Hamilton and Jefferson were selected as typical. (4) Miscellaneous writers, such as Paine, Crèvecœur, Carver, Abigail Adams and John Woolman, who reflected the life of the times from various angles. (5) Charles Brockden Brown, and the beginning of American fiction.

Selections for Reading. Typical selections in Cairns, Selections from Early American Writers; Trent and Wells, Colonial Prose and Poetry; Stedman and Hutchinson, Library of American Literature, and other anthologies (see " Selections " in the General Bibliography). A convenient volume containing a few selections from every important American author is Calhoun and MacAlarney, Readings from American Literature (Ginn and Company).

Bradford's Of Plimoth Plantation and John Smith's Settlement of Virginia, in Maynard's Historical Readings. Chronicles of the Pilgrims, in Everyman's Library. Various records of early American history and literature, in Old South Leaflets (Old South Meeting House, Boston). Franklin's Autobiography, in Standard English Classics, Holt's English Readings and several other school editions (see "Texts " in General Bibliography). Poor Richard's Almanac, in Riverside Literature. The Federalist and Letters from an American Farmer, in Everyman's Library. Woolman's Journal, in Macmillan's Pocket Classics.

Bibliography. For reference works covering the entire field of American history and literature see the General Bibliography. The following works deal with the Colonial and Revolutionary periods.

History. Fisher, The Colonial Era; Thwaite, The Colonies; Fiske, Old Virginia and her Neighbors, Beginnings of New England, Dutch and Quaker Colonies in America.

Winsor, Handbook of the Revolution; Sloane, French War and the Revolution; Fisher, Struggle for American Independence; Fiske, A Critical Period of American History; Hart, Formation of the Union.

Studies of social life in Earle, Home Life in Colonial Days; Fisher, Men, Women and Manners of Colonial Times; Crawford, Romantic Days in the Early Republic.

Literature. Tyler, History of American Literature, 1607–1765, and Literary History of the Revolution; Sears, American Literature of the Colonial and National Periods; Marble, Heralds of American Literature (a few Revolutionary authors); Patterson, Spirit of the American Revolution as Revealed in the Poetry of the Period; Loshe, The Early American Novel (includes a study of Charles Brockden Brown).

Life of Franklin, by Bigelow, 3 vols., by Parton, 2 vols., by McMaster, by Morse, etc. Lives of other Colonial and Revolutionary worthies in American Statesmen, Makers of America, Cyclopedia of American Biography, etc. (see "Biography" in General Bibliography).

Fiction. A few historical novels dealing with Colonial times are: Cooper, Satanstoe, The Red Rover; Kennedy, Rob of the Bowl; Hawthorne, The Scarlet Letter; Motley, Merry Mount; Cooke, The Virginia Comedians; Carruthers, Cavaliers of Virginia; Austin, Standish of Standish; Barr, The Black Shilling; Mary Johnston, To Have and to Hold.

Novels with a Revolutionary setting are: Cooper, The Spy, The Pilot; Simms, The Partisan, Katherine Walton; Kennedy, Horseshoe Robinson; Winthrop, Edwin Brothertoft; Eggleston, A Carolina Cavalier; Maurice Thompson, Alice of Old Vincennes; Mitchell, Hugh Wynne; Churchill, Richard Carvel; Gertrude Atherton, The Conqueror.

CHAPTER II

LITERATURE OF THE NEW NATION (1800–1840)

> Behind him lay the gray Azores,
>   Behind, the gates of Hercules;
> Before him not the ghost of shores,
>   Before him only shoreless seas.
> The good mate said, " Now must we pray,
>   For lo! the very stars are gone:
> Brave Admiral, speak; what shall I say?"
>   " Why say, ' Sail on! sail on! and on!' "
>
> Joaquin Miller, " Columbus "

Historical Background. It was in the early part of the nine-teenth century that America began to be counted among the great nations of the world, and it was precisely at that time that she produced her first national literature, a literature so broadly human that it appealed not only to the whole country but to readers beyond the sea. Irving, Cooper and Bryant are commonly regarded as the first notable New World writers; and we may better understand them and their enthusiastic young contemporaries if we remember that they " grew up with the country"; that they reflected life at a time when America, having won her independence and emerged from a long period of doubt and struggle, was taking her first confident steps in the sun and becoming splendidly conscious of her destiny as a leader among the world's free people.

Indeed, there was good reason for confidence in those early days; for never had a young nation looked forth upon a more **National Enthusiasm** heartening prospect. The primitive hamlets of Colonial days had been replaced by a multitude of substantial towns, the somber wilderness by a prosperous farming country. The power of a thousand rivers was turning the wheels of as many mills or factories, and to the natural wealth of America was added the increase of a mighty commerce with other nations. By the Louisiana Purchase and the acquisition of Florida her territory was vastly increased, and still her sturdy pioneers were pressing eagerly into more spacious lands beyond the Mississippi. Best of all, this enlarging nation, once a number of scattered colonies holding each to its own course, was now the Union; her people were as one in their patriotism, their loyalty, their intense conviction that the brave New World experiment in free government, once scoffed at as an idle dream, was destined to a glorious future. American democracy was not merely a success; it was an amazing triumph. Moreover, this democracy, supposed to be the weakest form of government, had already proved its power; it had sent its navy abroad to humble the insolent Barbary States, and had measured the temper of its soul and the strength of its arm in the second war with Great Britain.

In fine, the New World had brought forth a hopeful young giant of a nation; and its hopefulness was reflected, with more of zeal than of art, in the prose and poetry of its literary men. Just as the enthusiastic Elizabethan spirit reflected itself in lyric or drama after the defeat of the Armada, so the American spirit seemed to exult in the romances of Cooper and Simms; in the verse of Pinckney, Halleck, Drake and Percival; in a multitude of national songs, such as " The American Flag," Warren's Address, " Home Sweet Home" and " The Star-Spangled Banner." We would not venture to liken one set of writings to the other, for we should be on the weak side of an Elizabethan comparison; we simply note that a great national enthusiasm was largely responsible for the sudden appearance of a new literature in the one land as in the other.

Literary Environment. In the works of four writers, Irving, Cooper, Bryant and Poe, we have the best that the early national period produced; but we shall not appreciate these writers until we see them, like pines in a wood, lifting their heads over numerous companions, all drawing their nourishment from the same soil and air. The growth of towns and cities in America had led to a rapid increase of newspapers, magazines and annuals (collections of contemporary prose and verse), which called with increasing emphasis for poems, stories, essays, light or " polite " literature. The rapid growth of the nation set men to singing the old psalm of *Sursum Corda*, and every man and woman who felt the impulse added his story or his verse to the national chorus. When the first attempt at a summary of American literature was made in 1837, the author, Royal Robbins, found more than two thousand living writers demanding his attention.

It was due, one must think, to geography rather than to any spirit of sectionalism, to difficulty of travel between the larger

Knickerbocker School towns rather than to any difference of aim or motive, that the writers of this period associated themselves in a number of so-called schools or literary centers. New York, which now offered a better field for literary work than Boston or Philadelphia, had its important group of writers called the Knickerbocker School, which included Fitz-Greene Halleck and Joseph Rodman Drake, both poets and cheerful satirists of New World society; the versatile Nathaniel Parker Willis, writer of twenty volumes of poems, essays, stories and sketches of travel; and James Kirke Paulding, also a voluminous writer, who worked with Irving in the *Salmagundi* essays and whose historical novels, such as *The Dutchman's Fireside* (1831), are still mildly interesting.[1]

In the South was another group of young writers, quite as able and enthusiastic as their northern contemporaries. Among these we note especially William Gilmore Simms (1806–1870), whose *Yemassee*, *Border Beagles*, *Katherine Walton* and many

---

[1] Irving, Cooper and Bryant are sometimes classed among the Knickerbockers; but the work of these major writers is national rather than local or sectional, and will be studied later in detail.

other historical romances of Colonial and Revolutionary days were of more than passing interest. He was a high-minded Southern and most industrious writer, who produced over forty Writers volumes of poems, essays, biographies, histories and tales; but he is now remembered chiefly by his novels, which won him the title of "the Cooper of the South." At least one of his historical romances should be read, partly for its own sake and partly for a comparison with Cooper's work in the same field. Thus *The Yemassee* (1835), deal-ing with frontier life and Indian warfare, may be read in connection with Cooper's *The Deerslayer* (1841), which has the same general theme; or *The Partisan* (1835), deal-ing with the bitter struggle of southern Whigs and Tories during the Revolution, may well be compared with Coop-er's *The Spy* (1821), which depicts the same struggle in a northern environment.

WILLIAM GILMORE SIMMS

Other notable writers of the South during this period were Richard Henry Wilde the poet, now remembered by the song (from an unfinished opera) beginning, "My life is like the summer rose"; William Wirt, the essayist and biographer; and John Pendleton Kennedy, writer of essays and stories which contain many charming pictures of social life in Virginia and Maryland in the days "before the war."

In New England was still another group, who fortunately avoided the name of any school. Sparks, Prescott, Ticknor, Story, Dana,—the very names indicate how true was Boston to her old scholarly traditions. Meanwhile Connecticut had

OA

its popular poet in James Gates Percival; Maine had its versatile John Neal; and all the northern states were reading **New England and the West** the "goody goody" books of Peter Parley (Samuel Goodrich), the somewhat Byronic *Zophiel* and other emotional poems of Maria Gowen Brooks (whom Southey called "Maria del Occidente"), and the historical romances of Catherine Sedgwick and Sarah Morton.

JOHN PENDLETON KENNEDY

The West also (everything beyond the Alleghenies was then the West) made its voice heard in the new literature. Timothy Flint wrote a very interesting *Journal* from his missionary experiences, and a highly colored romance from his expansive imagination; and James Hall drew some vigorous and sympathetic pictures of frontier life in *Letters from the West, Tales of the Border* and *Wilderness and Warpath.*

There are many other writers who won recognition before 1840, but those we have named are more than enough; for each name is an invitation, and invitations when numerous are simply bothersome. For example, the name of Catherine Sedgwick invites us to read *Hope Leslie* and *The Linwoods*, both excellent in their day, and still interesting as examples of the novels that won fame less than a century ago; or the name of Kennedy leads us to *Swallow Barn* (alluring title!) with its bright pictures of Virginia life, and to *Horseshoe Robinson*, a crude but stirring tale of Revolutionary heroism. The point in naming these minor writers, once as popular as any present-day favorite, is simply this: that the major authors, whom we ordinarily study as typical of the age, were not isolated figures but part of a great romantic movement in literature; that they were influenced on the one hand by European letters, and on the other by a host of native writers who were all intent on reflecting the expanding life of America in the early part of the nineteenth century.

WASHINGTON IRVING (1783–1859)

A very pleasant writer is Irving, a man of romantic and somewhat sentimental disposition, but sound of motive, careful of workmanship, invincibly cheerful of spirit. The genial quality of his work may be due to the fact that from joyous boyhood to serene old age he did very much as he pleased, that he lived in what seemed to him an excellent world and wrote with no other purpose than to make it happy. In summarizing his career an admirer of Irving is reminded of what the Book of Proverbs says of wisdom: "Her ways are ways of pleasantness, and all her paths are peace."

The historian sees another side of Irving's work. Should it be asked, "What did he do that had not been as well or The Man and better done before him?" the first answer is that his Times the importance of any man's work must be measured by the age in which he did it. A schoolboy now knows more about electricity than ever Franklin learned; but that does not detract from our wonder at Franklin's kite. So the work of Irving seems impressive when viewed against the gray literary dawn of a century ago. At that time America had done a mighty work for the world politically, but had added little of value to the world's literature. She read and treasured the best books; but she made no contribution to their number, and her literary impotence galled her sensitive spirit. As if to make up for her failure, the writers of the Knickerbocker, Charleston and other " schools " praised each other's work extravagantly; but no responsive echo came from overseas, where England's terse criticism of our literary effort was expressed in the scornful question, "Who reads an American book?"

Irving answered that question effectively when his *Sketch Book*, *Bracebridge Hall* and *Tales of a Traveller* found a multitude of delighted readers on both sides of the Atlantic. His graceful style was hardly rivaled by any other writer of

the period; and England, at a time when Scott and Byron were playing heroic parts, welcomed him heartily to a place on the literary stage. Thus he united the English and the American reader in a common interest and, as it were, charmed away the sneer from one face, the resentment from the other. He has been called "father of our American letters" for two reasons: because he was the first to win a lasting literary reputation at home and abroad, and

WASHINGTON IRVING

because of the formative influence which his graceful style and artistic purpose have ever since exerted upon our prose writers.

Life. Two personal characteristics appear constantly in Irving's work: the first, that he was always a dreamer, a romance seeker; the second, that he was inclined to close his eyes to the heroic present and open them wide to the glories, real or imaginary, of the remote past. Though he lived in an American city in a day of mighty changes and discoveries, he was far less interested in the modern New York than in the ancient New Amsterdam; and though he was in Europe

at the time of the Napoleonic wars, he apparently saw nothing of
them, being then wholly absorbed in the battles of the long-vanished
Moors. Only once, in his books of western exploration, did he seriously touch the vigorous life of his own times; and critics regard
these books as the least important of all his works.

He was born in New York (1783) when the present colossal city
was a provincial town that retained many of its quaint Dutch characteristics. Over all the straggling town, from the sunny

Boyhood
Battery with its white-winged ships to the Harlem woods
where was good squirrel shooting, Irving rambled at ease on many
a day when the neighbors said he ought to have been at his books.
He was the youngest of the family; his constitution was not rugged,
and his gentle mother was indulgent. She would smile when he told
of reading a smuggled copy of the *Arabian Nights* in school, instead
of his geography; she was silent when he slipped away from family
prayers to climb out of his bedroom window and go to the theater,
while his sterner father thought of him as sound asleep in his bed.

Little harm came from these escapades, for Irving was a merry lad
with no meanness in him; but his schooling was sadly neglected. His
brothers had graduated from Columbia; but on the plea of delicate
health he abandoned the idea of college, with a sigh in which there
was perhaps as much satisfaction as regret. At sixteen he entered a
law office, where he gave less time to studying Blackstone than to
reading novels and writing skits for the newspapers.

This happy indifference to work and learning, this disposition to
linger on the sunny side of the street, went with Irving through life.

Finding
Himself
Experimentally he joined his brothers, who were in the
hardware trade; but when he seemed to be in danger
of consumption they sent him to Europe, where he enjoyed himself
greatly, and whence he returned perfectly well. Next he was sent on
business to England; and there, when the Irving Brothers failed, their
business having been ruined by the War of 1812, Irving manfully
resolved to be no longer a burden on others and turned to literature
for his support. With characteristic love of doing what he liked he
refused a good editorial position (which Walter Scott obtained for him)
and busied himself with his *Sketch Book* (1820). This met with a
generous welcome in England and America, and it was followed by
the equally popular *Bracebridge Hall* and *Tales of a Traveller*. By
these three works Irving was assured not only of literary fame but,
what was to him of more consequence, of his ability to earn his living.

Next we find him in Spain, whither he went with the purpose of translating Navarrete's *Voyages of Columbus*, a Spanish book, in which **Life Abroad** he saw a chance of profit from his countrymen's interest in the man who discovered America. Instead of translating another man's work, however, he wrote his own *Life and Times of Columbus* (1828). The financial success of this book (which is still our most popular biography of the great explorer) enabled Irving to live comfortably in Spain, where he read diligently and accumulated the material for his later works on Spanish history.

"SUNNYSIDE," HOME OF IRVING

By this time Irving's growing literary fame had attracted the notice of American politicians, who rewarded him with an appointment as secretary of the legation at London. This pleasant office he held for two years, but was less interested in it than in the reception which English men of letters generously offered him. Then he apparently grew homesick, after an absence of seventeen years, and returned to his native land, where he was received with the honor due to a man who had silenced the galling question, " Who reads an American book?"

The rest of Irving's long life was a continued triumph. Amazed at first, and then a little stunned by the growth, the hurry, the onward surge of his country, he settled back into the restful past, and was heard with the more pleasure by his countrymen because he seemed to speak to them from a vanished age. Once, inspired by the tide of

life sweeping into the West, he journeyed beyond the Mississippi and found material for his pioneering books; but an active life was far from
His Mellow his taste, and presently he built his house " Sunnyside"
Autumn (appropriate name) at Tarrytown on the Hudson. There he spent the remainder of his days, with the exception of four years in which he served the nation as ambassador to Spain. This honor, urged upon him by Webster and President Tyler, was accepted with characteristic modesty not as a personal reward but as a tribute which America had been wont to offer to the profession of letters.

Chief Works of Irving. A good way to form a general impression of Irving's works is to arrange them chronologically in five main groups. The first, consisting of the *Salmagundi* essays, the *Knickerbocker History* and a few other trifles, we may call the Oldstyle group, after the pseudonym assumed by the author.[1] The second or Sketch-Book group includes the *Sketch Book*, *Bracebridge Hall* and *Tales of a Traveller*. The third or Alhambra group, devoted to Spanish and Moorish themes, includes *The Conquest of Granada*, *Spanish Voyages of Discovery*, *The Alhambra* and certain similar works of a later period, such as *Moorish Chronicles* and *Legends of the Conquest of Spain*. The fourth or Western group contains *A Tour on the Prairies*, *Astoria* and *Adventures of Captain Bonneville*. The fifth or Sunnyside group is made up chiefly of biographies, *Oliver Goldsmith*, *Mahomet and his Successors* and *The Life of Washington*. Besides these are some essays and stories assembled under the titles of *Spanish Papers* and *Wolfert's Roost*.

The *Salmagundi* papers and others of the Oldstyle group would have been forgotten long ago if anybody else had written them. In other words, our interest in them is due not to their intrinsic value (for they are all " small potatoes ") but to the fact that their author became a famous literary man.

---

[1] Ever since Revolutionary days it had been the fashion for young American writers to use an assumed name. Irving appeared at different times as " Jonathan Oldstyle," " Diedrich Knickerbocker " and " Geoffrey Crayon, Gent."

Most candid readers would probably apply this criticism **also**
to the *Knickerbocker History*, had not that grotesque joke
won an undeserved reputation as a work of humor.

The story of the Knickerbocker fabrication illustrates the
happy-go-lucky method of all Irving's earlier work. He had
tired of his *Salmagundi* fooling and was looking
for variety when his eyes lighted on Dr. Mitchill's
Picture of New York, a grandiloquent work written
by a prominent member of the Historical Society. In a light-
headed moment Irving and his brother Peter resolved to burlesque this history and, in the approved fashion of that day,
to begin with the foundation of the world. Then Peter went
to Europe on more important business, and Irving went on
with his joke alone. He professed to have discovered the
notes of a learned Dutch antiquarian who had recently disappeared, leaving a mass of manuscript and an unpaid board-
bill behind him. After advertising in the newspapers for the
missing man, Irving served notice on the public that the profound value of Knickerbocker's papers justified their publication, and that the proceeds of the book would be devoted to
paying the board-bill. Then appeared, in time to satisfy the
aroused curiosity of the Historical Society, to whom the book
was solemnly dedicated, the *History of New York from the
Beginning of the World to the End of the Dutch Dynasty, by
Diedrich Knickerbocker* (1809).

This literary hoax made an instant sensation; it was denounced for its scandalous irreverence by the members of the
Historical Society, especially by those who had Dutch ancestors, but was received with roars of laughter by the rest of
the population. Those who read it now (from curiosity, for its
merriment has long since departed, leaving it dull as any
thrice-repeated joke) are advised to skip the first two books,
which are very tedious fooling, and to be content with an
abridged version of the stories of Wouter van Twiller, William
the Testy and Peter the Headstrong. These are the names of

(margin note:) Knicker-
bocker
History

real Dutch governors of New Amsterdam, and the dates given
are exact dates; but there history ends and burlesque begins.
The combination of fact and nonsense and the strain of gravity
in which absurdities are related have led some critics to place
the *Knickerbocker History* first in time of the notable works
of so-called American humor. That is doubtless a fair classification; but other critics assert that real humor is as purely
human as a smile or a tear, and has therefore no national or
racial limitations.

The *Sketch Book*, chief of the second group of writings, is
perhaps the best single work that Irving produced. We shall
Sketch Book read it with better understanding if we remember
that it was the work of a young man who, having
always done as he pleased, proceeds now to write of whatever
pleasant matter is close at hand. Being in England at the
time, he naturally finds most of his material there; and being
youthful, romantic and sentimental, he colors everything with
the hue of his own disposition. He begins by chatting of the
journey and of the wide sea that separates him from home.
He records his impressions of the beautiful English country,
tells what he saw or felt during his visit to Stratford on Avon,
and what he dreamed in Westminster Abbey, a place hallowed
by centuries of worship and humanized by the presence of the
great dead. He sheds a ready tear over a rural funeral, and
tries to make us cry over the sorrows of a poor widow; then
to relieve our feelings he pokes a bit of fun at John Bull.
Something calls his attention to Isaac Walton, and he writes
a Waltonian kind of sketch about a fisherman. In one chapter
he comments on contemporary literature; then, as if not quite
satisfied with what authors are doing, he lays aside his record
of present impressions, goes back in thought to his home by
the Hudson, and produces two stories of such humor, charm
and originality that they make the rest of the book appear
almost commonplace, as the careless sketches of a painter are
forgotten in presence of his inspired masterpiece.

These two stories, the most pleasing that Irving ever wrote, are "Rip van Winkle" and "The Legend of Sleepy Hollow." They should be read if one reads nothing else of the author's twenty volumes.

The works on Spanish themes appeal in different ways to different readers. One who knows his history will complain (and justly) that Irving is superficial, that he is concerned

RIP VAN WINKLE

with picturesque rather than with important incidents; but one who likes the romance of history, and who reflects that romance **Spanish** plays an important part in the life of any people, **Themes** will find the legends and chronicles of this Spanish group as interesting as fiction. We should remember, moreover, that in Irving's day the romance of old Spain, familiar enough to European readers, was to most Americans still fresh and wondrous. In emphasizing the romantic or picturesque side of his subject he not only pleased his readers but broadened their horizon; he also influenced a whole generation of historians who, in contrast with the scientific or prosaic historians of to-day, did not hesitate to add the element of human interest to their narratives.

The most widely read of all the works of the Spanish group is *The Alhambra* (1832). This is, on the surface, a collection The of semihistorical essays and tales clustering around Alhambra the ancient palace, in Granada, which was the last stronghold of the Moors in Europe; in reality it is a record of the impressions and dreams of a man who, finding himself on historic ground, gives free rein to his imagination. At times, indeed, he seems to have his eye on his American readers, who were then in a romantic mood, rather than on the place or people he was describing. The book delighted its first critics, who called it "the Spanish Sketch Book"; but though pleasant enough as a romantic dream of history, it hardly compares in originality with its famous predecessor.

Except to those who like a brave tale of exploration, and who happily have no academic interest in style, Irving's Western western books are of little consequence. In fact, Stories they are often omitted from the list of his important works, though they have more adventurous interest than all the others combined. *A Tour on the Prairies*, which records a journey beyond the Mississippi in the days when buffalo were the explorers' mainstay, is the best written of the pioneer books; but the *Adventures of Captain Bonneville*, a story of wandering up and down the great West with plenty of adventures among Indians and "free trappers," furnishes the most excitement. Unfortunately this journal, which vies in interest with Parkman's *Oregon Trail*, cannot be credited to Irving, though it bears his name on the title-page.[1]

1 The *Adventures* is chiefly the work of a Frenchman, a daring free-rover, who probably tried in vain to get his work published. Irving bought the work for a thousand dollars, revised it slightly, gave it his name and sold it for seven or eight times what he paid for it. In *Astoria*, the third book of the western group, he sold his services to write up the records of the fur house established by John Jacob Astor, and made a poor job of it.

Of the three biographies *Oliver Goldsmith* (1849) is the best, probably because Irving had more sympathy and affinity

Biographies

with the author of "The Deserted Village" than with Mahomet or Washington. The *Life of Washington* (1855–1859) was plainly too large an undertaking for Irving's limited powers; but here again we must judge the work by the standards of its own age and admit

OLD DUTCH CHURCH, SLEEPY HOLLOW
Mentioned by Irving in "The Legend of Sleepy Hollow"

that it is vastly better than the popular but fictitious biographies of Washington written by Weems and other romancers. Even in Irving's day Washington was still regarded as a demigod; his name was always printed in capitals; and the rash novelist who dared to bring him into a story (as Cooper did in *The Spy*) was denounced for his lack of reverence. In consequence of this false attitude practically all Washington's biographers (with the exception of the judicious Marshall) depicted him as a ponderously dignified creature, stilted, unlovely, unhuman, who must always appear with a halo around his head. Irving was too much influenced by this absurd fashion and by his lack of scholarship to make a trustworthy book; but he gave at least a touch of naturalness and humanity to our first president, and set a new biographical standard by attempting to write as an honest historian rather than as a mere hero-worshiper.

An Appreciation of Irving. The three volumes of the Sketch-Book group and the romantic *Alhambra* furnish an excellent measure of Irving's literary talent. At first glance these books appear rather superficial, dealing with pleasant matters of no consequence; but on second thought pleasant matters are always of consequence, and Irving invariably displays two qualities, humor and sentiment, in which humanity is forever interested. His humor, at first crude and sometimes in doubtful taste (as in his *Knickerbocker History*) grew more refined, more winning in his later works, until a thoughtful critic might welcome it, with its kindness, its culture, its smile in which is no cynicism and no bitterness, as a true example of "American" humor, — if indeed such a specialized product ever existed. His sentiment was for the most part tender, sincere and manly. Though it now seems somewhat exaggerated and at times dangerously near to sentimentality, that may not be altogether a fault; for the same criticism applies to Longfellow, Dickens and, indeed, to most other writers who have won an immense audience by frankly emphasizing, or even exaggerating, the honest sentiments that plain men and women have always cherished both in life and in literature.

The style of Irving, with its suggestion of Goldsmith and Addison (who were his first masters), is deserving of more
Style of unstinted praise. A "charming" style we call it;
Irving and the word, though indefinite, is expressive of the satisfaction which Irving's manner affords his readers. One who seeks the source of his charm may find it in this, that he cherished a high opinion of humanity, and that the friendliness, the sense of comradeship, which he felt for his fellow men was reflected in his writing; unconsciously at first,

perhaps, and then deliberately, by practice and cultivation. In consequence, we do not read Irving critically but sympathetically; for readers are like children, or animals, in that they are instinctively drawn to an author who trusts and understands them.

Thackeray, who gave cordial welcome to Irving, and who called him "the first ambassador whom the New World of letters sent to the Old," was deeply impressed by the fact not that the young American had an excellent prose style but that "his gate was forever swinging to visitors." That is an illuminating criticism; for we can understand the feeling of the men and women of a century ago who, having read the *Sketch Book*, were eager to meet the man who had given them pleasure by writing it. In brief, though Irving wrote nothing of great import, though he entered not into the stress of life or scaled its heights or sounded its deeps, we still read him for the sufficient but uncritical reason that we like him.

In this respect, of winning our personal allegiance, Irving stands in marked contrast to his greatest American contemporary, Cooper. We read the one because we are attracted to the man, the other for the tale he has to tell.

William Cullen Bryant (1794–1878)

Bryant has been called "the father of American song," and the year 1821, when his first volume appeared, is recorded as the natal year of American poetry. Many earlier singers had won local reputations, but he was the first who was honored in all the states and who attained by his poetry alone a dominating place in American letters.

That was long ago; and times have changed, and poets with them. In any collection of recent American verse one may find poems more imaginative or more finely wrought than any that Bryant produced; but these later singers stand in a company and contribute to an already large collection, while Bryant stood alone and made a brave beginning of poetry that we may honestly call native and national. Before he won recognition by his independent work the best that our American singers thought they could do was to copy some English original; but after 1821 they dared to be themselves in poetry, as they had ever been in politics. They had the successful Bryant for a model, and the young Longfellow was one of his pupils. More-over, he stands the hard test of time, and seems to have no successor. He is still our Puritan poet, — a little severe, perhaps, but American to the core, — who reflects better than any other the rugged spirit of that puritanism which had so profoundly influenced our country during the early, formative days of the republic.

WILLIAM CULLEN BRYANT

Life. In the boyhood of Bryant we shall find the inspiration for all his enduring work. He was of Pilgrim stock, and was born (1794) in the little village of Cummington, in western Massachusetts. There, with the Berkshire Hills and the ancient forest forever in sight, he grew to man's stature, working on the farm or attending the district school by day, and reading before the open fire at night. His father was a physician, a scholarly man who directed his son's reading. His mother was a Puritan, one of those quiet, inspiring women who do their work cheerfully, as by God's grace, and who invariably add some sign or patent of nobility to their sons and daughters. There was also in the home a Puritan grandfather who led the family devotions every evening, and whose

prayers with their rich phraseology of psalm or prophecy were
"poems from beginning to end." So said Bryant, who attributed
to these prayers his earliest impulse to write poetry.

Between these two influences, nature without and puritanism
within, the poet grew up; in their shadow he lived and died; little
else of consequence is reflected in the poems that are his best
memorial.

The visible life of Bryant lies almost entirely outside the realm of
poesie. He was fitted for Williams by country ministers, as was
customary in that day; but poverty compelled him to
The Citizen   leave college after two brief terms. Then he studied law,
and for nine or ten years practiced his profession doggedly, unwillingly,
with many a protest at the chicanery he was forced to witness even
in the sacred courts of justice. Grown weary of it at last, he went to
New York, found work in a newspaper office, and after a few years'
apprenticeship became editor of *The Evening Post*, a position which
he held for more than half a century. His worldly affairs prospered;
he became a "leading citizen" of New York, prominent in the social
and literary affairs of a great city; he varied the routine of editorship
by trips abroad, by literary or patriotic addresses, by cultivating a
country estate at Long Island. In his later years, as a literary celebrity,
he loaned his name rather too freely to popular histories, anthologies
and gift books, which better serve their catchpenny purpose if some
famous man can be induced to add "tone" to the rubbish.

And Bryant's poetry? Ah, that was a thing forever apart from his
daily life, an almost sacred thing, to be cherished in moments when,
his day's work done, he was free to follow his spirit and
The Poet   give outlet to the feelings which, as a strong man and a
Puritan, he was wont to restrain. He had begun to write poetry in
childhood, when his father had taught him the value of brevity or
compression and "the difference between poetic enthusiasm and
fustian." Therefore he wrote slowly, carefully, and allowed ample
time for change of thought or diction. So his early "Thanatopsis"
was hidden away for years till his father found and published it, and
made Bryant famous in a day. All this at a time when English critics
were exalting "sudden inspiration," "sustained effort" and poems
"done at one sitting."

Once Bryant had found himself (and the blank verse and simple
four-line stanza which suited his talent) he seldom changed, and he
never improved. His first little volume, *Poems* (1821), contains some

of his best work. In the next fifty years he added to the size but not
to the quality of that volume; and there is little to indicate in such
poems as "Thanatopsis" and "The Flood of Years", that the one
was written by a boy of seventeen and the other by a sage of eighty.
His love of poetry as a thing apart from life is indicated by the fact
that in old age, to forget the grief occasioned by the death of his
wife, he gave the greater part of six years to a metrical translation of
the Greek poet Homer. That he never became a great poet or even
fulfilled his early promise is due partly to his natural limitations, no
doubt, but more largely to the fact that he gave his time and strength
to other things. And a poet is like other men in that he cannot well
serve two masters.

The Poetry of Bryant. Besides the translation of the *Iliad*
and the *Odyssey* there are several volumes of prose to Bryant's
credit, but his fame now rests wholly on a single book of
original poems. The best of these (the result of fifty years of
writing, which could easily be printed on fifty pages) may
be grouped in two main classes, poems of death and poems
of nature; outside of which are a few miscellaneous pieces,
such as "The Antiquity of Freedom," "Planting of the Apple
Tree" and "The Poet," in which he departs a little from his
favorite themes.

Bryant's poems on death reflect something of his Puritan
training and of his personal experience while threatened with

Poems of   consumption; they are also indicative of the poetic
Death   fashion of his age, which was abnormally given to
funereal subjects and greatly influenced by such melancholy
poems as Gray's "Elegy" and Young's "Night Thoughts."
He began his career with "Thanatopsis" (or "View of Death"),
a boyhood piece which astonished America when it was published in 1817, and which has ever since been a favorite with
readers. The idea of the poem, that the earth is a vast sepulcher
of human life, was borrowed from other poets; but the stately
blank verse and the noble appreciation of nature are Bryant's
own. They mark, moreover, a new era in American poetry,
an original era to replace the long imitative period which had

OA

endured since Colonial times. Other and perhaps better poems in the same group are "The Death of the Flowers," "The Return of Youth" and "Tree Burial," in which Bryant goes beyond the pagan view of death presented in his first work.

That death had a strange fascination for Bryant is evident from his returning again and again to a subject which most young poets avoid. Its somber shadow and unanswered question intrude upon nearly all of his nature pieces; so much so that even his "June" portrays that blithe, inspiring month of sunshine and bird song as an excellent time to die. It is from such poems that one gets the curious idea that Bryant never was a boy, that he was a graybeard at sixteen and never grew any younger.

It is in his poems of nature that Bryant is at his best. Even here he is never youthful, never the happy singer whose **Poems of Nature** heart overflows to the call of the winds; he is rather the priest of nature, who offers a prayer or hymn of praise at her altar. And it may be that his noble "Forest Hymn" is nearer to a true expression of human feeling, certainly of primitive or elemental feeling, than Shelley's "Skylark" or Burns's "Mountain Daisy." Thoreau in one of his critical epigrams declared it was not important that a poet should say any particular thing, but that he should speak in harmony with nature; that "the tone of his voice is the main thing." If that be true, Bryant is one of our best poets. He is always in harmony with nature in her prevailing quiet mood; his voice is invariably gentle, subdued, merging into the murmur of trees or the flow of water, — much like Indian voices, but as unlike as possible to the voices of those who go to nature for a picnic or a camping excursion.

Among the best of his nature poems are "To a Waterfowl" (his most perfect single work), "Forest Hymn," "Hymn to the Sea," "Summer Wind," "Night Journey of a River," "Autumn Woods," "To the Fringed Gentian," "Among the Trees," "The Fountain" and "A Rain Dream." To read such poems is to understand the fact, mentioned in our biography, that Bryant's poetry was a thing apart from his daily life. His friends all speak of him as a companionable man, receptive, responsive, abounding in cheerful anecdote, and with a certain "overflowing of strength" in mirth or kindly humor; but one finds absolutely nothing of this genial temper in his verse. There he seems to regard all such bubblings and overflowings as unseemly levity (lo! the Puritan), which he must lay aside in poetry as on entering a church. He is,

BRYANT'S HOME, AT CUMMINGTON

as we have said, the priest of nature, in whom reverence is uppermost; and he who reads aloud the "Forest Hymn," with its solemn organ tone, has an impression that it must be followed by the sublime invitation, "O come, let us worship and bow down; let us kneel before the Lord, our Maker."

Though Bryant is always serious, it is worthy of note that he is never gloomy, that he entirely escapes the pessimism or **In Lighter** despair which seizes upon most poets in times of **Mood** trouble. Moreover, he has a lighter mood, not gay but serenely happy, which finds expression in such poems as "Evening Wind," "Gladness of Nature" and especially "Robert of Lincoln." The exuberance of the last-named, so unlike anything else in Bryant's book of verse, may be explained on the assumption that not even a Puritan could pull a long face in presence of a bobolink. The intense Americanism of the poet appears in nearly all his verse; and occasionally his patriotism rises to a prophetic strain, as in "The Prairie," for example, written when he first saw what was then called "the great American desert." It is said that the honeybee crossed the Mississippi with the first settlers, and Bryant looks with kindled imagination on this little pioneer who

> Fills the savannas with his murmurings,
> And hides his sweets, as in the golden age,
> Within the hollow oak. I listen long
> To his domestic hum, and think I hear
> The sound of that advancing multitude
> Which soon shall fill these deserts. From the ground
> Comes up the laugh of children, the soft voice
> Of maidens, and the sweet and solemn hymn
> Of Sabbath worshippers. The low of herds
> Blends with the rustling of the heavy grain
> Over the dark brown furrows. All at once
> A fresher wind sweeps by, and breaks my dream,
> And I am in the wilderness alone.

Our Pioneer Poet. From one point of view our first national poet is a summary of all preceding American verse and a prophecy of better things to come. To be specific, practically all our early poetry shows the inclination to moralize, to sing a song and then add a lesson to it. This is commonly-attributed to Puritan influence; but in truth it is a universal poetic impulse, a tribute to the early office of the bard, who was the tribal historian and teacher as well as singer. This ancient didactic or moralizing tendency is very strong in Bryant. To his first notable poem, "Thanatopsis," he must add a final "So live"; and to his "Waterfowl" must be appended a verse which tells what steadfast lesson may be learned from the mutable phenomena of nature.

Again, most of our Colonial and Revolutionary poetry was strongly (or weakly) imitative, and Bryant shows the habit of his American predecessors. The spiritual conception of nature revealed in some of his early poems is a New World echo of Wordsworth; his somber poems of death indicate that he was familiar with Gray and Young; his "Evening Wind" has some suggestion of Shelley; we suspect the influence of Scott's narrative poems in the neglected "Stella" and "Little People of the Snow." But though influenced by English writers, the author of "Thanatopsis" was too independent to imitate them; and in his independence, with the hearty welcome which it received from the American public, we have a prophecy of the new poetry.

The originality and sturdy independence of Bryant are clearly shown in his choice of subjects. In his early days **His Origi-** poetry was formal and artificial, after the manner **nality** of the eighteenth century; the romantic movement had hardly gained recognition in England; Burns was known only to his own countrymen; Wordsworth was ridiculed or barely tolerated by the critics; and poets on both sides of the Atlantic were still writing of larks and nightingales, of moonlight in the vale, of love in a rose-covered cottage, of ivy-mantled towers, weeping willows, neglected graves, — a medley of tears and sentimentality. You will find all these and little else in *The Garland, The Token* and many other popular collections of the period; but you will find none of them in Bryant's first or last volume. From the beginning he wrote of Death and Nature; somewhat coldly, to be sure, but with manly sincerity. Then he wrote of Freedom, the watchword of America, not as other singers had written of it but as a Puritan who had learned in bitter conflict the price of his heritage:

> O Freedom! thou art not, as poets dream,
> A fair young girl, with light and delicate limbs,
> And wavy tresses gushing from the cap
> With which the Roman master crowned his slave
> When he took off the gyves. A bearded man,
> Armed to the teeth, art thou; one mailèd hand

> Grasps the broad shield, and one the sword; thy brow,
> Glorious in beauty though it be, is scarred
> With tokens of old wars; thy massive limbs
> Are strong with struggling.

He wrote without affectation of the Past, of Winter, of the North Star, of the Crowded Street, of the Yellow Violet and the Fringed Gentian. If the last-named poems now appear too simple for our poetic taste, remember that simplicity is the hardest to acquire of all literary virtues, and that it was the dominant quality of Bryant. Remember also that these modest flowers of which he wrote so modestly had for two hundred years brightened our spring woods and autumn meadows, waiting patiently for the poet who should speak our appreciation of their beauty. Another century has gone, and no other American poet has spoken so simply or so well of other neglected treasures: of the twin flower, for example, most fragrant of all blooms; or of that other welcome-nodding blossom, beloved of bumblebees, which some call "wild columbine" and others "whippoorwill's shoes."

In a word, Bryant was and is our pioneer poet in the realm of native American poetry. As Emerson said, he was our first original poet, and was original because he dared to be sincere.

JAMES FENIMORE COOPER (1789–1851)

In point of time Cooper is the first notable American novelist. Judging by the booksellers, no other has yet approached him in the sustained interest of his work or the number of his readers.

On first analysis we shall find little in Cooper to account for his abiding popularity. The man himself was not exactly **The Man** lovable; indeed, he had almost a genius for stirring up antagonism. As a writer he began without study or literary training, and was stilted or slovenly in most of his work. He was prone to moralize in the midst of an exciting narrative; he filled countless pages with "wooden" dialogue; he could not portray a child or a woman or a gentleman, though he was confident that he had often done so to perfection. He did not even know Indians or woodcraft, though Indians and woodcraft account for a large part of our interest in his forest romances.

One may enjoy a good story, however, without knowing or caring for its author's peculiarities, and the vast majority of

The Story-teller readers are happily not critical but receptive. Hence if we separate the man from the author, and if we read *The Red Rover* or *The Last of the Mohicans* "just for the story," we shall discover the source of Cooper's power as a writer. First of all, he has a tale to tell, an epic tale of heroism and manly virtue. Then he appeals strongly to the pioneer spirit, which survives in all great nations, and he is a master at portraying wild nature as the background of human life. The vigor of elemental manhood, the call of adventure, the lure of primeval forests, the surge and mystery of the sea, — these are written large in Cooper's best books. They make us forget his faults of temper or of style, and they account in large measure for his popularity with young readers of all nations; for he is one of the few American writers who belong not to any country but to humanity. At present he is read chiefly by boys; but half a century or more ago he had more readers of all classes and climes than any other writer in the world.

Life. The youthful experiences of Cooper furnished him with the material for his best romances. He was born (1789) in New Jersey; but while he was yet a child the family removed to central New York, where his father had acquired an immense tract of wild land, on which he founded the village that is still called Cooperstown. There on the frontier of civilization, where stood the primeval forest that had witnessed many a wild Indian raid, the novelist passed his boyhood amid the picturesque scenes which he was to immortalize in *The Pioneers* and *The Deerslayer*.

Cooper picked up a little " book learning " in a backwoods school, and a little more in a minister's study at Albany. At thirteen he **His Training** entered Yale; but he was a self-willed lad, and was presently dismissed from college. A little later, after receiving some scant nautical training on a merchantman, he entered the navy as midshipman; but after a brief experience in the service he married and resigned his commission. That was in 1811, and the date is significant. It was just before the second war with Great

JAMES FENIMORE COOPER

Britain. The author who wrote so much and so vividly of battles, Indian raids and naval engagements never was within sight of such affairs, though the opportunity was present. In his romances we have the product of a vigorous imagination rather than of observation or experience.

His literary work seems now like the result of whim or accident. One day he flung down a novel that he was reading, declaring to his wife that he could write a better story himself. " Try it," challenged his wife. " I will," said Cooper; and the result was *Precaution*, a romance of English society. He was then a farmer in the Hudson valley, and his knowledge of foreign society was picked up, one must think, from silly novels on the subject.

Strange to say, the story was so well received that the gratified author wrote another. This was *The Spy* (1821), dealing with a Revolutionary hero who had once followed his dangerous calling in the very region in which Cooper was now living. The immense success of this book fairly drove its author into a career. He moved to New York City, and there quickly produced two more successful romances. Thus in four years an unknown man without literary training had become a famous writer, and had moreover produced four different types of fiction: the novel of society in *Precaution*, the historical romance in *The Spy*, and the adventurous romance of forest and of ocean in *The Pioneers* and *The Pilot*.

Cooper now went abroad, as most famous authors do. His books, already translated into several European languages, had made him **Years of** known, and he was welcomed in literary circles; but **Strife** almost immediately he was drawn into squabbles, being naturally inclined that way. He began to write political tirades; and even his romances of the period (*The Bravo, The Heidenmauer, The Headsman*) were devoted to proclaiming the glories of democracy. Then he returned home and proceeded to set his countrymen by the ears (in such books as *Home as Found*) by writing too frankly of their crudity in contrast with the culture of Europe. Then followed long years of controversy and lawsuits, during which our newspapers used Cooper scandalously, and Cooper prosecuted and fined the newspapers. It is a sorry spectacle, of no interest except to those who would understand the bulk of Cooper's neglected works. He was an honest man, vigorous, straightforward, absolutely sincere; but he

OTSEGO HALL, HOME OF COOPER

was prone to waste his strength and embitter his temper by trying to force his opinion on those who were well satisfied with their own. He had no humor, and had never pondered the wisdom of " Who drives fat oxen should himself be fat."

The last years of his life were spent mostly at the old home at Cooperstown, no longer a frontier settlement but a thriving village, from which Natty Bumppo and Chingachgook had long since departed. Before his death (1851) the fires of controversy had sunk to ashes; but Cooper never got over his resentment at the public, and with the idea of keeping forever aloof he commanded that none of his private papers be given to biographers. It is for lack of such personal letters and documents that no adequate life of Cooper has yet been written.

Cooper's Works. There are over sixty volumes of Cooper, but to read them all would savor of penance rather than of pleasure. Of his miscellaneous writings only the *History of the Navy* and *Lives of Distinguished Naval Officers* are worthy of remembrance. Of his thirty-two romances the half, at least, may be ignored; though critics may differ as to whether certain books (*The Bravo* and *Lionel Lincoln*, for example) should be placed in one half or the other. There remain as the measure of Cooper's genius some sixteen works of fiction, which fall naturally into three groups: the historical novels, the tales of pioneer life, and the romances of the sea.

The Spy was the first and probably the best of Cooper's historical romances. Even his admirers must confess that it
The Spy is crudely written, and that our patriotic interest inclines us to overestimate a story which throws the glamor of romance over the Revolution. Yet this faulty tale attempts to do what very few histories have ever done fairly, namely, to present both sides or parties of the fateful conflict; and its unusual success in this difficult field may be explained by a bit of family history. Cooper was by birth and training a stanch Whig, or Patriot; but his wife, to whom he was devotedly attached, was the daughter of an unbending Tory, or Loyalist; and his divided allegiance is plainly apparent in his work. Ordinarily his personal antagonisms, his hatred of "Yankees," Puritans and all politicians of the other party, are dragged into his stories and spoil some of them; but in *The Spy* he puts his prejudices under restraint, tells his tale in an impersonal way, dealing honestly with both Whigs and Tories, and so produces a work having the double interest of a good adventure story and a fair picture of one of the heroic ages of American history.

Aside from its peculiar American interest, *The Spy* has some original and broadly human elements which have caused it, notwithstanding its dreary, artificial style, to be highly appreciated in other countries, in South American countries especially. The secret of its appeal lies largely in this, that in Harvey Birch, a brave man who serves his country without hope or possibility of reward, Cooper has strongly portrayed a type of the highest, the most unselfish patriotism.

The other historical novels differ greatly in value. Prominent among them are *Mercedes of Castile*, dealing with Columbus and the discovery of America; *Satanstoe* and *The Wept of Wish-Ton-Wish*, depicting Colonial life in New York and New England respectively; and *Lionel Lincoln*, which is another story of the Revolution, more labored than *The Spy* and of less sustained interest.

Cooper's first sea story, *The Pilot* (1823), was haphazard enough in both motive and method,[1] but it gave pleasure to a
The Sea multitude of readers, and it amazed critics by show-
Stories ing that the lonely sea could be a place of romantic human interest. Cooper was thus the first modern novelist of the ocean; and to his influence we are partly indebted for the stirring tales of such writers as Herman Melville and Clark Russell. A part of the action of *The Pilot* takes place on land (the style and the characters of this part are wretchedly stilted), but the chief interest of the story lies in the adventures of an American privateer commanded by a disguised hero, who turns out to be John Paul Jones. Cooper could not portray such a character, and his effort to make the dashing young captain heroic by surrounding him with a fog of mystery is like his labored attempt to portray the character of Washington in *The Spy*. On the other hand, he was thoroughly at home on a ship or among common sailors; his sea pictures of gallant craft driven before the gale are magnificent; and Long Tom Coffin

---

[1] The Waverley novels by "the great unknown" were appearing at this time. Scott was supposed to be the author of them, but there was much debate on the subject. One day in New York a member of Cooper's club argued that Scott could not possibly have written *The Pirate* (which had just appeared), because the nautical skill displayed in the book was such as only a sailor could possess. Cooper maintained, on the contrary, that *The Pirate* was the work of a landsman; and to prove it he declared that he would write a sea story as it should be written; that is, with understanding as well as with imagination. *The Pilot* was the result.

is perhaps the most realistic and interesting of all his characters, not excepting even Leatherstocking.

Another and better romance of the sea is *The Red Rover* (1828). In this story the action takes place almost wholly on the deep, and its vivid word pictures of an ocean smiling under the sunrise or lashed to fury by midnight gales are unrivaled in any literature. Other notable books of the same group are *The Water Witch*, *Afloat and Ashore* and *Wing and Wing*. Some readers will prize these for their stories; but to others they may appear tame in comparison with the superb descriptive passages of *The Red Rover*.

When Cooper published *The Pioneers* (1823) he probably had no intention of writing a series of novels recounting the adventures of Natty Bumppo, or Leatherstocking, and his Indian friend Chingachgook; otherwise he would hardly have painted so shabby a picture of these two old heroes, neglected and despised in a land through which they had once moved as masters. Readers were quick to see, however, that these old men had an adventurous past, and when they demanded the rest of the story Cooper wrote four other romances, which are as so many acts in the stirring drama of pioneer life. When these romances are read, therefore, they should be taken in logical sequence, beginning with *The Deerslayer*, which portrays the two heroes as young men on their first war trail, and following in order with *The Last of the Mohicans*, *The Pathfinder*, *The Pioneers* and *The Prairie*. If one is to be omitted, let it be *The Pathfinder*, which is comparatively weak and dull; and if only one is to be read, *The Last of the Mohicans* is an excellent choice.

(margin note: Leatherstocking Tales*)*

After nearly a century of novel writing, these five books remain our most popular romances of pioneer days, and Leatherstocking is still a wingéd name, a name to conjure with, in most civilized countries. Meanwhile a thousand similar works have come and gone and been forgotten. To examine these later books, which attempt to satisfy the juvenile love of

Indian stories, is to discover that they are modeled more or less closely on the original work of the first American novelist.

Cooper's Scenes and Characters. Even in his outdoor romances Cooper was forever attempting to depict human society, especially polite society; but that was the one subject he did not and could not understand. The sea in its grandeur and loneliness; the wild lakes, stretching away to misty, unknown shores or nestling like jewels in their evergreen setting; the forest with its dim trails, its subdued light, its rustlings, whisperings, hints of mystery or peril, — these are his proper scenes, and in them he moves as if at ease in his environment.

In his characters we soon discover the same contrast. If he paints a hero of history, he must put him on stilts to increase his stature. If he portrays a woman, he calls her a "female," makes her a model of decorum, and bores us by her sentimental gabbing. If he describes a social gathering, he instantly

COOPER'S CAVE

Scene of Indian fight in *The Last of the Mohicans*

betrays his unfamiliarity with real society by talking like a book of etiquette. But with rough men or manly men on land or sea, with half-mutinous crews of privateers or disciplined man-of-war's men, with woodsmen, trappers, Indians, adventurous characters of the border or the frontier, — with all these Cooper is at home, and in writing of them he rises almost to the height of genius.

If we seek the secret of this contrast, we shall find it partly in the author himself, partly in a popular, half-baked philoso- **The Return** phy of the period. That philosophy was summed **to Nature** up in the words "the return to nature," and it alleged that all human virtues flow from solitude and all vices from civilization. Such a philosophy appealed strongly to Cooper, who was continually at odds with his fellows, who had been expelled from Yale, who had engaged in many a bitter controversy, who had suffered abuse from newspapers, and who in every case was inclined to consider his opponents as blockheads. No matter in what society he found himself, in imagination he was always back in the free but lawless atmosphere of the frontier village in which his youth was spent. Hence he was well fitted to take the point of view of Natty Bumppo (in *The Pioneers*), who looked with hostile eyes upon the greed and waste of civilization; hence he portrayed his uneducated backwoods hero as a brave and chivalrous gentleman, without guile or fear or selfishness, who owed everything to nature and nothing to society. Europe at that time was ready to welcome such a type with enthusiasm. The world will always make way for him, whether he appears as a hero of fiction or as a man among men.

General Characteristics. The faults of Cooper — his stilted style and slipshod English, his tedious moralizing, his artificial dialogue, his stuffed gentlemen and inane "females," his blunders in woodcraft — all these are so easily discovered by a casual reader that the historian need not linger over them. His virtues are more interesting, and the first of these is that he has a story to tell. Ever since Anglo-Saxon days the "tale-bringer" has been a welcome guest, and that Cooper is a good tale-bringer is evident from his continued popularity at home and abroad. He may not know much about the art of literature, or about psychology, or about the rule that motives must be commensurate with actions; but he knows a good story, and that, after all, is the main thing in a novel.

Again, there is a love of manly action in Cooper and a robustness of imagination which compel attention. He is rather slow in starting his tale; but he always sees a long trail ahead, and knows that every turn of the trail will bring its surprise or adventure. It is only when we analyze and compare his plots that we discover what a prodigal creative power he had. He wrote, let us say, seven or eight good stories; but he spoiled ten times that number by hasty or careless workmanship. In the neglected *Wept of Wish-Ton-Wish*, for example, there is enough wasted material to furnish a modern romancer or dramatist for half a lifetime.

Another fine quality of Cooper is his descriptive power, his astonishing vigor in depicting forest, sea, prairie, — all the **Descriptive** grandeur of wild nature as a background of human **Power** heroism. His descriptions are seldom accurate, for he was a careless observer and habitually made blunders; but he painted nature as on a vast canvas whereon details might be ignored, and he reproduced the total impression of nature in a way that few novelists have ever rivaled. It is this sustained power of creating a vast natural stage and peopling it with elemental men, the pioneers of a strong nation, that largely accounts for Cooper's secure place among the world's fiction writers.

Finally, the moral quality of Cooper, his belief in manhood and womanhood, his cleanness of heart and of tongue, are all **Moral** reflected in his heroes and heroines. Very often he **Quality** depicts rough men in savage or brutal situations; but, unlike some modern realists, there is nothing brutal in his morals, and it is precisely where we might expect savagery or meanness that his simple heroes appear as chivalrous gentlemen "without fear and without reproach." That he was here splendidly true to nature and humanity is evident to one who has met his typical men (woodsmen, plainsmen, lumbermen, lonely trappers or timber-cruisers) in their own environment and experienced their rare courtesy and hospitality. In a word, Cooper knew what virtue is, virtue of white man, virtue of Indian, and he makes us know and respect it. Of a hundred strong scenes which he has vividly pictured there is hardly one that does not leave a final impression as pure and wholesome as the breath of the woods or the sea.

Edgar Allan Poe (1809–1849)

It is a pleasant task to estimate Irving or Bryant, but Poe offers a hard nut for criticism to crack. The historian is baffled by an author who secretes himself in the shadow, or perplexed by conflicting biographies, or put on the defensive by the fact that any positive judgment or opinion of Poe will almost certainly be challenged.

At the outset, therefore, we are to assume that Poe is one of the most debatable figures in our literature. His life may be summed up as a pitiful struggle for a little fame and a little bread. When he died few missed him, and his works were neglected. Following his recognition in Europe came a revival of interest here, during which Poe was absurdly overpraised and the American people berated for their neglect of a genius. Then arose a literary controversy which showed chiefly that our critics were poles apart in their points of view. Though the controversy has long endured, it has settled nothing of importance; for one reader regards Poe as a literary *poseur*, a writer of melodious nonsense in verse and of grotesque horrors in prose; while another exalts him as a double master of poetry and fiction, an artist without a peer in American letters.

Somewhere between these extremes hides the truth; but we shall not here attempt to decide whether it is nearer one side or the other. We note merely that Poe is a writer for such mature readers as can appreciate his uncanny talent. What he wrote of abiding interest or value to young people might be printed in a very small book.

Biographical Sketch. Notwithstanding all that has been written about Poe, we do not and cannot know him as we know most other American authors, whose lives are as an open book. He was always a secretive person, " a lover of mystery and retreats," and such accounts of his life as he gave out are not trustworthy. He came from a good Maryland family, but apparently from one of those offshoots that are not true to type. His father left the study of law to become a strolling actor, and presently married an English actress. It was while the father and mother were playing their parts in Boston that Edgar was born, in 1809.

EDGAR ALLAN POE

Actors led a miserable life in those days, and the Poes were no exception. They died comfortless in Richmond; their three children were separated; and Edgar was adopted by John Allan, a wealthy tobacco merchant. It was in the luxurious Allan home that the boy began the drinking habits which were his bane ever afterwards.

The Allans were abroad on business from 1815 to 1820, and during these years Edgar was at a private school in the suburbs of **Poe's School** London. It was the master of that school who described **Days** the boy as a clever lad spoiled by too much pocket money. The prose tale " William Wilson " has some reflection of these school years, and, so far as known, it is the only work in which Poe introduced any of his familiar experiences.

OA

Soon after his return to Richmond the boy was sent to the University of Virginia, where his brilliant record as a student was marred by his tendency to dissipation. After the first year Mr. Allan, finding that the boy had run up a big gambling debt, took him from college and put him to work in the tobacco house. Whereupon Edgar, always resentful of criticism, quarreled with his foster father and drifted out into the world. He was then, at eighteen, a young man of fine bearing, having the taste and manners of a gentleman; but he had no friend in the world, no heritage of hard work, no means of earning a living.

WEST RANGE, UNIVERSITY OF VIRGINIA

Next we hear vaguely of Poe in Boston, where he published a tiny volume, *Tamerlane and Other Poems, by a Bostonian* (1827). **His Wanderings** Failing to win either fame or money by his poetry, he enlisted in the army under an assumed name and served for about two years. Of his army life we know nothing, nor do we hear of him again until his foster father secured for him an appointment to the military academy at West Point. There Poe made an excellent beginning; but he soon neglected his work, was dismissed, and became an Ishmael again. After trying in vain to secure a political office he went to Baltimore, where he earned a bare living by writing for the newspapers. The popular but mythical account of his life (for which he himself is partly responsible) portrays him at this period in a Byronic rôle, fighting with the Greeks for their liberty.

His literary career began in 1833, when his "Manuscript Found in a Bottle" won for him a prize offered by a weekly newspaper.

The same "Manuscript" brought him to the attention of John Pendleton Kennedy, who secured for him a position on the staff **First** of the *Southern Literary Messenger*. He then settled **Success** in Richmond, and in his grasp was everything that the heart of a young author might desire. He had married his cousin, Virginia Clem, a beautiful young girl whom he idolized; he had a comfortable home and an assured position; Kennedy and other southern writers were his loyal friends; the *Messenger* published his work and gave him a reputation in the literary world of America. Fortune stood smiling beside him, when he quarreled with his friends, left the *Messenger* and began once more his struggle with poverty and despair.

It would require a volume to describe the next few years, and we must pass hurriedly over them. His pen was now his only hope, **A Life of** and he used it diligently in an effort to win recognition **Fragments** and a living. He tried his fortune in different cities; he joined the staffs of various periodicals; he projected magazines of his own. In every project success was apparently within his reach when by some weakness or misfortune he let his chance slip away. He was living in Fordham (a suburb of New York, now called the Bronx) when he did his best work; but there his wife died, in need of the common comforts of life; and so destitute was the home that an appeal was made in the newspapers for charity. One has but to remember Poe's pride to understand how bitter was the cup from which he drank.

After his wife's death came two frenzied years in which not even the memory of a great love kept him from unmanly wooing of other women; but Poe was then unbalanced and not wholly responsible for his action. At forty he became engaged to a widow in Richmond, who could offer him at least a home. Generous friends raised a fund to start him in life afresh; but a little later he was found unconscious amid sordid surroundings in Baltimore. He died there, in a hospital, before he was able to give any lucid account of his last wanderings. It was a pitiful end; but one who studies Poe at any part of his career has an impression of a perverse fate that dogs the man and that insists on an ending in accord with the rest of the story.

The Poetry of Poe. Most people read Poe's poetry for the melody that is in it. To read it in any other way, to analyze or explain its message, is to dissect a butterfly that changes in a moment from a delicate, living creature to a pinch of dust, bright colored but meaningless. It is not for analysis, therefore, but simply for making Poe more intelligible that we record certain facts or principles concerning his verse.

Perhaps the first thing to note is that Poe is not the poet of smiles and tears, of joy and sorrow, as the great poets are, **Theory of Poetry** but the poet of a single mood, — a dull, despairing mood without hope of comfort. Next, he had a theory (a strange theory in view of his mood) that the only object of poetry is to give pleasure, and that the pleasure of a poem depends largely on melody, on sound rather than on sense. Finally, he believed that poetry should deal with beauty alone, that poetic beauty is of a supernal or unearthly kind, and that such beauty is forever associated with melancholy. To Poe the most beautiful imaginable object was a beautiful woman; but since her beauty must perish, the poet must assume a tragic or despairing attitude in face of it. Hence his succession of shadowy Helens, and hence his wail of grief that he has lost or must soon lose them.

All these poetic theories, or delusions, appear in Poe's most widely known work, "The Raven," which has given pleasure **The Raven** to a multitude of readers. It is a unique poem, and its popularity is due partly to the fact that nobody can tell what it means. To analyze it is to discover that it is extremely melodious; that it reflects a gloomy mood; that at the root of its sorrow is the mysterious "lost Lenore"; and that, as in most of Poe's works, a fantastic element is introduced, an "ungainly fowl" addressed with grotesque dignity as "Sir, or Madame," to divert attention from the fact that the poet's grief is not simple or human enough for tears:

And the Raven, never flitting, still is sitting, *still* is sitting
On the pallid bust of Pallas just above my chamber door;
And his eyes have all the seeming of a demon's that is dreaming,
And the lamp-light o'er him streaming throws his shadow on the floor;
And my soul from out that shadow that lies floating on the floor
    Shall be lifted — nevermore!

Equally characteristic of the author are "To One in Paradise," "The Sleeper" and "Annabel Lee," — all melodious, all in hopeless mood, all expressive of the same abnormal idea of poetry. Other and perhaps better poems are "The Coliseum," "Israfel," and especially the second "To Helen," beginning, "Helen, thy beauty is to me."

Young readers may well be content with a few such lyrics, leaving the bulk of Poe's poems to such as may find meaning in their vaporous images. As an example, study these two stanzas from "Ulalume," a work which some may find very poetic and others somewhat lunatic:

> The skies they were ashen and sober;
>   The leaves they were crispèd and sere —
>   The leaves they were withering and sere;
> It was night in the lonesome October
>   Of my most immemorial year;
> It was hard by the dim lake of Auber,
>   In the misty mid region of Weir —
> It was down by the dank tarn of Auber,
>   In the ghoul-haunted woodland of Weir.
>
> Here once, through an alley Titanic
>   Of cypress, I roamed with my soul —
>   Of cypress, with Psyche, my soul.
> These were days when my heart was volcanic
>   As the scoriac rivers that roll —
>   As the lavas that restlessly roll
> Their sulphurous currents down Yaanek,
>   In the ultimate climes of the pole —
> That groan as they roll down Mount Yaanek,
>   In the realms of the boreal pole.

This is melodious, to be sure, but otherwise it is mere word juggling, a stringing together of names and rimes with a total effect of lugubrious nonsense. It is not to be denied that some critics find pleasure in "Ulalume"; but uncritical readers need not doubt their taste or intelligence if they prefer counting-out rimes, "The Jabberwock," or other nonsense verses that are more frankly and joyously nonsensical.

Poe's Fiction. Should it be asked why Poe's tales are nearly all of the bloodcurdling variety, the answer is that they are a triple reflection of himself, of the fantastic romanticism of his age, and of the taste of readers who were then abnormally fond of ghastly effects in fiction. Let us understand these elements clearly; for otherwise Poe's horrible stories will give us nothing beyond the mere impression of horror.

To begin with the personal element, Poe was naturally inclined to morbidness. He had a childish fear of darkness
The Man and and hobgoblins; he worked largely "on his nerves";
his Times   he had an abnormal interest in graves, ghouls and the terrors which preternatural subjects inspire in superstitious minds. As a writer he had to earn his bread; and the fiction most in demand at that time was of the "gothic" or *Mysteries of Udolpho* kind, with its diabolical villain, its pallid heroine in a haunted room, its medley of mystery and horror.[1] At the beginning of the century Charles Brockden Brown had made a success of the "American gothic" (a story of horror modified to suit American readers), and Poe carried on the work of Brown with precisely the same end in view, namely, to please his audience. He used the motive of horror partly because of his own taste and training, no doubt, but more largely because he shrewdly "followed the market" in fiction. Then as now there were many readers who enjoyed, as Stevenson says, being "frightened out of their boots," and to such readers he appealed. His individuality and, perhaps, his chief excellence as a story-writer lay in his use of strictly logical methods, in his ability to make the most impossible yarn seem real by his reasonable way of telling it. Moreover, he was a discoverer, an innovator, a maker of new types, since he was the first to introduce in his stories the blend of calm, logical science and

---

[1] As Richardson suggests, the popular novels of Poe's day are nearly all alike in that they remind us of the fat boy in *Pickwick*, who "just wanted to make your flesh creep." Jane Austen (and later, Scott and Cooper) had written against this morbid tendency, but still the "gothic" novel had its thousands of shuddering readers on both sides of the Atlantic.

wild fancy of a terrifying order; so he served as an inspiration as well as a point of departure for Jules Verne and other
writers of the same pseudo-scientific school.

Poe's numerous tales may be grouped in three or four
classes. Standing by itself is "William Wilson," a story of
Groups of   double personality (one good and one evil genius in
Stories   the same person), to which Stevenson was indebted
in his *Strange Case of Dr. Jekyll and Mr. Hyde*. Next are the
tales of pseudo-science and adventure, such as "Hans Pfaall"
and the "Descent into the Maelstrom," which represent a
type of popular fiction developed by Jules Verne, H. G. Wells
and many others, all of whom were more or less influenced
by Poe. A third group may be called the ingenious-mystery
stories. One of the most typical of these is "The Gold Bug,"
a tale of cipher-writing and buried treasure, which contains the
germ, at least, of Stevenson's *Treasure Island*. To the same
group belong "The Murders in the Rue Morgue" and other
stories dealing with the wondrous acumen of a certain Dupin, who
is the father of "Old Sleuth," "Sherlock Holmes" and other
amateur detectives who do such marvelous things in fiction, —
to atone, no doubt, for their extraordinary dullness in real life.

Still another group consists of phantom stories, — ghastly
yarns that serve no purpose but to make the reader's spine
creep. The mildest of these horrors is "The Fall of the
House of Usher," which some critics place at the head of
Poe's fiction. It is a "story of atmosphere"; that is, a story
in which the scene, the air, the vague "feeling" of a place
arouse an expectation of some startling or unusual incident.
Many have read this story and found pleasure therein; but
others ask frankly, "Why bother to write or to read such
palpable nonsense?" With all Poe's efforts to make it real,
Usher's house is not a home or even a building in which
dwells a man; it is a vacuum inhabited by a chimera. Of
necessity, therefore, it tumbles into melodramatic nothingness
the moment the author takes leave of it.

If it be asked, "What shall one read of Poe's fiction?" the answer must depend largely upon individual taste. "The **What to Read** Gold Bug" is a good story, having the adventurous interest of finding a pirate's hidden gold; at least, that is how most readers regard it, though Poe meant us to be interested not in the gold but in his ingenious cryptogram or secret writing. The allegory of "William Wilson" is per-

THE BUILDING OF THE *SOUTHERN LITERARY MESSENGER*

haps the most original of Poe's works; and for a thriller "The House of Usher" may be recommended as the least repulsive of the tales of horror. To the historian the chief interest of all these tales lies in the influence which they have exerted on a host of short-story writers at home and abroad.

An Estimate of Poe. Any summary of such a difficult subject is unsatisfactory and sub-ject to challenge. We shall try here simply to outline Poe's aim and method, leaving the student to supply from his own reading most of the details and all the exceptions.

Poe's chief purpose was not to tell a tale for its own sake or to portray a human character; he aimed to produce an effect or impression in the reader's mind, an impression of unearthly beauty in his poems and of unearthly horror in his prose. Some writers (Hawthorne, for example) go through life as in a dream; but if one were to judge Poe by his work, one might think that he had suffered a long nightmare. Of his familiar experience, his youth, his army training, his meeting with other men, his impressions of nature or humanity, there is hardly a trace in his work; of despair, terror and hallucinations there is a plethora.

His method was at once haphazard and carefully elaborated, — a paradox, it seems, till we examine his work or read his records thereof. In his poetry words appealed to **His Method** him, as they appeal to some children, not so much for their meaning as for their sound. Thus the word "nevermore," a gloomy, terrible word, comes into his mind, and he proceeds to brood over it. The shadow of a great loss is in the word, and loss meant to Poe the loss of beauty in the form of a woman; therefore he invents "the lost Lenore" to rime with his "nevermore." Some outward figure of despair is now needed, something that will appeal to the imagination; and for that Poe selects the sable bird that poets have used since Anglo-Saxon times as a symbol of gloom or mystery. Then carefully, line by line, he hammers out "The Raven," a poem which from beginning to end is built around the word "nevermore" with its suggestion of pitiless memories.

Or again, Poe is sitting at the bedside of his dead wife when another word suddenly appeals to him. It is Shakespeare's

> Duncan is in his grave;
> After life's fitful fever he sleeps well.

And from that word is born "For Annie," with an ending to the first stanza which is an epitome of the poem, and which Longfellow suggested as a fitting epitaph for Poe's tomb:

> And the fever called "Living"
> Is conquered at last.

He reads Coleridge's "Rime of the Ancient Mariner," and his "Manuscript Found in a Bottle" is the elaborated result of his chance inspiration. He sees Cooper make a success of a sea tale, and Irving of a journal of exploration; and, though he knows naught of the sea or the prairie, he produces his hair-raising *Arthur Gordon Pym* and his *Journal of Julius Rodman*. Some sailor's yarn of a maelstrom in the North Sea comes to his ears, and he fabricates a story of a man who went into the whirlpool. He sees a newspaper account of a premature burial, and his "House of Usher" and several other stories reflect the imagined horror of such an experience. The same criticism applies to his miscellaneous thrillers, in which with rare cunning he uses phantoms, curtains, shadows, cats, the moldy odor of the grave, — and all to make a gruesome tale inspired by some wild whim or nightmare.

In fine, no other American writer ever had so slight a human basis for his work; no other ever labored more patiently or more carefully. The unending controversy over Poe commonly reduces itself to this deadlock: one reader asks, "What did he do that was worth a man's effort in the doing?" and another answers, "What did he do that was not cleverly, skillfully done?"

Summary. The early part of the nineteenth century (sometimes called the First National period of American letters) was a time of unusual enthusiasm. The country had recently won its independence and taken its place among the free nations of the world; it had emerged triumphant from a period of doubt and struggle over the Constitution and the Union; it was increasing with amazing rapidity in territory, in population and in the wealth which followed a successful commerce; its people were united as never before by noble pride in the past and by a great hope for the future. It is not surprising, therefore, that our first really national literature (that is, a literature which was read by practically the whole country, and which represented America to foreign nations) should appear in this expansive age as an expression of the national enthusiasm.

The four chief writers of the period are: Irving, the pleasant essayist, story-teller and historian; Bryant, the poet of primeval nature; Cooper, the novelist, who was the first American author to win world-wide fame; and Poe, the most cunning craftsman among our early writers, who wrote a few melodious poems and many tales of mystery or horror. Some critics would include also among the major writers William Gilmore Simms (sometimes called "the Cooper of the South"), author of many adventurous romances dealing with pioneer life and with Colonial and Revolutionary history.

Chief Writers

The numerous minor writers of the age are commonly grouped in local schools. The Knickerbocker school, of New York, includes the poets Halleck and Drake, the novelist Paulding, and one writer of miscellaneous prose and verse, Nathaniel P. Willis, who was for a time more popular than any other American writer save Cooper. In the southern school (led by Poe and Simms) were Wilde, Kennedy and William Wirt. The West was represented by Timothy Flint and James Hall. In New England were the poets Percival and Maria Brooks, the novelists Sarah Morton and Catherine Sedgwick, and the historians Sparks and Bancroft. The writers we have named are merely typical; there were literally hundreds of others who were more or less widely known in the middle of the last century.

The first common characteristic of these writers was their patriotic enthusiasm; the second was their romantic spirit. The romantic movement in English poetry was well under way at this time, and prac-

Foreign Influence tically all our writers were involved in it. They were strongly influenced, moreover, by English writers of the period or by settled English literary traditions. Thus, Irving modeled his style closely on that of Addison; the early poetry of Bryant shows the influence of Wordsworth; the weird tales of Poe and his critical essays were both alike influenced by Coleridge; and the quickening influence of Scott appears plainly in the romances of Cooper. The minor writers were even more subject to foreign influences, especially to German and English romanticism. There was, however, a sturdy independence in the work of most of these writers which stamps it as original and unmistakably American. The nature poetry of Bryant with its rugged strength and simplicity, the old Dutch legends and stories of Irving, the pioneer romances of Cooper and Simms, the effective short stories of Poe, — these have hardly a counterpart in foreign writings of the period. They are the first striking expressions of the new American spirit in literature.

Selections for Reading. Irving's Sketch Book, in Standard English Classics and various other school editions (see "Texts" in General Bibliography); The Alhambra, in Ginn and Company's Classics for Children; parts of Bracebridge Hall, in Riverside Literature; Conquest of Granada and other works, in Everyman's Library.

Selections from Bryant, in Riverside Literature and Pocket Classics.

Cooper's Last of the Mohicans, in Standard English Classics and other school editions; the five Leatherstocking tales, in Everyman's Library; The Spy, in Riverside Literature.

Selections from Poe, prose and verse, in Standard English Classics, Silver Classics, Johnson's English Classics, Lake English Classics.

Simms's The Yemassee, in Johnson's English Classics. Typical selections from minor authors of the period, in Readings from American Literature and other anthologies (see "Selections" in General Bibliography).

Bibliography. For works covering the whole field of American history and literature see the General Bibliography. The following are recommended for a special study of the early part of the nineteenth century.

History. Adams, History of the United States, 1801–1817, 9 vols.; Von Holst, Constitutional and Political History, 1787–1861, 8 vols.; Sparks, Expansion of the American People; Low, The American People; Expedition of Lewis and Clarke, in Original Narratives Series (Scribner); Page, The Old South; Drake, The Making of the West.

Literature. There is no good literary history devoted to this period. Critical studies of the authors named in the text may be found in Richardson's American Literature and other general histories. For the lives of minor authors see Adams, Dictionary of American Authors, or Appleton's Cyclopedia of American Biography.

Irving. Life and Letters, by P. M. Irving, 4 vols., in Crayon edition of Irving's works. Life by Warner, in American Men of Letters; by Hill, in American Authors; by Boynton (brief), in Riverside Biographies.

Essays by Brownell, in American Prose Masters; by Payne, in Leading American Essayists; by Perry, in A Study of Prose Fiction; by Curtis, in Literary and Social Addresses.

Bryant. Life, by Godwin, 2 vols.; by Bigelow, in American Men of Letters; by Curtis. Wilson, Bryant and his Friends.

Essays, by Stedman, in Poets of America; by Curtis, in Orations and Addresses; by Whipple, in Literature and Life; by Burton, in Literary Leaders.

Cooper. Life, by Lounsbury, in American Men of Letters; by Clymer (brief), in Beacon Biographies.

Essays, by Erskine, in Leading American Novelists; by Brownell, in American Prose Masters; by Matthews, in Gateways to Literature.

Poe. Life, by Woodberry, in American Men of Letters; by Trent, in English Men of Letters; Life and Letters, 2 vols., by Harrison.

Essays, by Stedman, in Poets of America; by Brownell, in American Prose Masters; by Burton, in Literary Leaders; by Higginson, in Short Studies of American Authors; by Andrew Lang, in Letters to Dead Authors; by Gates, in Studies and Appreciations; by Gosse, in Questions at Issue.

Simms. Life, by Trent, in American Men of Letters. Critical studies by Moses, in Literature of the South; by Link, in Pioneers of Southern Literature; by Wauchope, in Writers of South Carolina.

Fiction. A few novels dealing with the period are: Brown, Arthur Merwyn; Kennedy, Swallow Barn; Paulding, Westward Ho; Mrs. Stowe, The Minister's Wooing; Cooke, Leather Stocking and Silk; Eggleston, The Circuit Rider, The Hoosier Schoolmaster; Winthrop, John Brent.

CHAPTER III

THE PERIOD OF CONFLICT (1840–1876)

The muffled drum's sad roll has beat
   The soldier's last tattoo ;
No more on Life's parade shall meet
   That brave and fallen few.
On Fame's eternal camping-ground
   Their silent tents are spread,
And Glory guards, with solemn round,
   The bivouac of the dead.

         O'Hara, " The Bivouac of the Dead "

Political History. To study the history of America after 1840 is to have our attention drawn as by a powerful lodestone to the Civil War. It looms there in the middle of the nineteenth century, a stupendous thing, dominating and dwarfing all others. To it converge many ways that then seemed aimless or wandering, the unanswered questions of the Constitution, the compromises of statesmen, the intrigues of politicians, the clamor of impatient reformers, the silent degradation of the slave. And from it, all its passion and suffering forgotten, its heroism remembered, proceed the unexpected blessings of a finer love of country, a broader sense of union, a surer faith in democracy, a better understanding of the spirit of America, more gratitude for her glorious past, more hope for her future. So every thought or mention of the mighty conflict draws us onward, as the first sight of the Rockies, massive and snow crowned, lures the feet of the wanderer on the plains.

We shall not attempt here to summarize the war between the South and the North or even to list its causes and consequences. The theme is too vast. We note only that the main issues of the conflict, state rights and slavery, had been debated for the better part of a century, and might still have found peaceful solution had they not been complicated by the minor issues of such an age of agitation as America never saw before and, as we devoutly hope, may never see again.

Such agitation was perhaps inevitable in a country that had grown too rapidly for its government to assimilate the new possessions. By **The Age of** the Oregon treaty, the war with Mexico and the annexa-**Agitation** tion of Texas vast territories had suddenly been added to the Union, each with its problem that called for patient and wise deliberation, but that a passionate and half-informed Congress was expected to settle overnight. With the expansion of territory in the West came a marvelous increase of trade and wealth in the North,

"THE MAN"

and a corresponding growth in the value of cotton and slave labor in the South. Then arose an economic strife; the agricultural interests of one part of the country clashed with the manufacturing interests of another (in such matters as the tariff, for example), and in the tumult of party politics it was impossible to reach any harmonious adjustment. Finally, the violent agitation of the slave question forced it to the front not simply as a moral or human but as a political issue; for the old "balance of power" between the states was upset when the North began to outstrip the South in population, and every state was then fiercely jealous of its individual rights and obligations in a way that we can now hardly comprehend.

As a result of these conflicting interests and the local or sectional passions which they aroused, there was seldom a year after 1840 when the country did not face a situation of extreme difficulty or danger. Indeed, even while Webster was meditating his prophetic oration with its superb climax of "Liberty and Union, now and forever, one and inseparable," many of the most thoughtful minds, south and north, believed that Congress faced a problem beyond its power to solve; that no single government was wise enough or strong enough to meet the situation, especially a government divided against itself.

In the midst of the political tumult, which was increased by the clamor of agitators and reformers, came suddenly the secession of a state from the Union, an act long threatened, long feared, but which arrived at last with the paralyzing effect of a thunderbolt. Then the clamor ceased; minor questions were swept aside as by a tempest, and the main issues were settled not by constitutional rights, not by orderly process of law or the ballot, but by the fearful arbitrament of the sword. And even as the thunderbolt fell and the Union trembled, came also unheralded one gaunt, heroic, heaven-sent man to lead the nation in its hour of peril:

The Wind and the Whirlwind

> Oh, slow to smite and swift to spare,
>   Gentle and merciful and just!
> Who in the fear of God didst bear
>   The sword of power, a nation's trust!

Such is an outline of the period of conflict, an outline to which the political measures or compromises of the time, its sectional antagonism, its score of political parties, its agitators, reformers, and all other matters of which we read confusedly in the histories, are but so many illuminating details.

Social and Intellectual Changes. The mental ferment of the period was almost as intense as its political agitation. Thus, the antislavery movement, which aimed to rescue the negro from his servitude, was accompanied by a widespread communistic attempt to save the white man from the manifold evils of our competitive system of industry. Brook Farm [1] was the most famous of these communities; but there were more than thirty others scattered over the country, all holding property in common, working on a basis of mutual helpfulness, aiming at a nobler life and a better system of labor than that which now separates the capitalist and the workingman.

This brave attempt at human brotherhood, of which Brook Farm was the visible symbol, showed itself in many other ways: in the projection of a hundred social reforms; in the establishment of lyceums throughout the country, where every man with a message might find a hearing. In education our whole school system was changed by applying the methods of Pestalozzi, a Swiss reformer; for the world had suddenly become small, thanks to

Widening Horizons

---

[1] This was a Massachusetts society, founded in 1841 by George Ripley. It included Hawthorne, Dana and Curtis in its large membership, and it had the support of Emerson, Greeley, Channing, Margaret Fuller and a host of other prominent men and women.

steam and electricity, and what was spoken in a corner the newspapers immediately proclaimed from the housetops. In religious circles the Unitarian movement, under Channing's leadership, gained rapidly in members and in influence; in literature the American horizon was broadened by numerous translations from the classic books of foreign countries; in the realm of philosophy the western mind was stimulated by the teaching of the idealistic system known as Transcendentalism.

Emerson was the greatest exponent of this new philosophy, which made its appearance here in 1836. It exalted the value of the indi-

Transcendentalism vidual man above society or institutions; and in dealing with the individual it emphasized his freedom rather than his subjection to authority, his soul rather than his body, his inner wealth of character rather than his outward possessions. It taught that nature was an open book of the Lord, in which he who runs may read a divine message; and in contrast with eighteenth-century philosophy (which had described man as a creature of the senses, born with a blank mind, and learning only by experience), it emphasized the divinity of man's nature, his inborn ideas of right and wrong, his instinct of God, his passion for immortality, — in a word, his higher knowledge which transcends the knowledge gained from the senses, and which is summarized in the word "Transcendentalism."

We have described this in the conventional way as a new philosophy, though in truth it is almost as old as humanity. Most of the great thinkers of the world, in all ages and in all countries, have been transcendentalists; but in the original way in which the doctrine was presented by Emerson it seemed like a new revelation, as all fine old things do when they are called to our attention, and it exercised a profound influence on our American life and literature.

Literature of the Period. The violent political agitation and the profound social unrest of the period found expression in multitudinous works of prose or verse; but the curious fact is that these are all minor works, and could without much loss be omitted from our literary records. They are mostly sectional in spirit, and only what is national or human can long endure.

To illustrate our criticism, the terrible war that dominates the period never had any worthy literary expression; there are thousands of writings but not a single great poem or story or

essay or drama on the subject. The antislavery movement likewise brought forth its poets, novelists, orators and essayists ;

Minor Works some of the greater writers were drawn into its
whirlpool of agitation, and Whittier voiced the conviction that the age called for a man rather than a poet in a
cry which was half defiance and half regret :

> Better than self-indulgent years
> The outflung heart of youth,
> Than pleasant songs in idle ears
> The tumult of the truth !

That was the feeling in the heart of many a promising young
southern or northern poet in midcentury, just as it was in
1776, when our best writers neglected literature for political
satires against Whigs or Tories. Yet of the thousand works
which the antislavery agitation inspired we can think of only
one, Mrs. Stowe's *Uncle Tom's Cabin*, which lives with power
to our own day ; and there is something of universal human
nature in that famous book, written not from knowledge or
experience but from the imagination, which appeals broadly to
our human sympathy, and which makes it welcome in countries
where slavery as a political or a moral issue has long since
been forgotten.

Though the ferment of the age produced no great books,
it certainly influenced our literature, making it a very differ-
General ent product from that of the early national period.
Character- For example, nearly every political issue soon became
istics a moral issue ; and there is a deep ethical earnestness in the essays of Emerson, the poems of Longfellow and
the novels of Hawthorne which sets them apart, as of a
different spirit, from the works of Irving, Poe and Cooper.

Again, the mental unrest of the period showed itself in a
passion for new ideas, new philosophy, new prose and poetry.
We have already spoken of the transcendental philosophy, but
even more significant was the sudden broadening of literary
interest. American readers had long been familiar with the

OA

best English poets; now they desired to know how our common life had been reflected by poets of other nations. In answer to that desire came, first, the establishment of professorships of *belles-lettres* in our American colleges; and then a flood of translations from European and oriental literatures. As we shall presently see, every prominent writer from Emerson to Whitman was influenced by new views of life as reflected in the world's poetry. Longfellow is a conspicuous example; with his songs inspired by Spanish or German or Scandinavian originals he is at times more like an echo of Europe than a voice from the New World.

BIRTHPLACE OF LONGFELLOW, AT FALMOUTH (NOW PORTLAND), MAINE

Finally, this period of conflict was governed more largely than usual by ideals, by sentiment, by intense feeling. Witness the war, with the heroic sentiments which it summoned up south and north. As the deepest human feeling cannot be voiced in prose, we confront the strange phenomenon of an American age of poetry. This would be remarkable enough to one who remembers that the genius of America had hitherto appeared practical and prosaic, given to action rather than speech, more concerned to "get on" in life than to tell what life means; but it is even more remarkable in view of the war, which covers the age with its frightful shadow. As Lincoln, sad and overburdened, found the relief of tears in the beautiful ending of Longfellow's "Building of the Ship," so, it seems, the heart of America, torn by the sight of her sons in conflict, found blessed relief in songs of

An Age of Poetry

love, of peace, of home, of beauty, — of all the lovely and immortal ideals to which every war offers violent but impotent contradiction. And this may be the simple explanation of the fact that the most cherished poems produced by any period of war are almost invariably its songs of peace.

THE GREATER POETS

HENRY WADSWORTH LONGFELLOW (1807–1882)

When Longfellow sent forth his *Voices of the Night*, in 1839, that modest little volume met with a doubly warm reception. Critics led by Poe pounced on the work to condemn its sentimentality or moralizing, while a multitude of readers who needed no leader raised a great shout of welcome.

Now as then there are diverse critical opinions of Longfellow, and unfortunately these opinions sometimes obscure the more interesting facts : that Longfellow is still the favorite of the American home, the most honored of all our elder poets ; that in foreign schools his works are commonly used as an introduction to English verse, and that he has probably led more young people to appreciate poetry than any other poet who ever wrote our language. That strange literary genius Lafcadio Hearn advised his Japanese students to begin the study of poetry with Longfellow, saying that they might learn to like other poets better in later years, but that Longfellow was most certain to charm them at the beginning.

The reason for this advice, given to the antipodes, was probably this, that young hearts and pure hearts are the same the world over, and Longfellow is the poet of the young and pure in heart.

Life. The impression of serenity in Longfellow's work may be explained by the gifts which Fortune offered him in the way of endowment, training and opportunity. By nature he was a gentleman ; his home training was of the best ; to his college education four years of foreign study were added, a very unusual thing at that time; and no sooner was he ready for his work than the way opened as if the magic *Sesame* were on his lips. His own college gave him a chair of modern languages and literature, which was the very thing he wanted; then Harvard offered what seemed to him a wider field, and finally his country called him from the professor's chair to teach the love of poetry to the whole nation. Before his long and beautiful life ended he had enjoyed for half a century the two rewards that all poets desire, and the most of them in vain; namely, fame and love. The first may be fairly won; the second is a free gift.

HENRY WADSWORTH LONGFELLOW

Longfellow was born (1807) in the town of Falmouth, Maine, which has since been transformed into the city of Portland. Like Bryant he was descended from Pilgrim stock; but where the older poet's training had been strictly puritanic, Longfellow's was more liberal and broadly cultured. Bryant received the impulse to poetry from his grandfather's prayers, but Longfellow seems to have heard his first call in the sea wind. Some of his best lyrics sing of the ocean; his early book of essays was called *Driftwood*, his last volume of poetry *In the Harbor*; and in these lyrics and titles we have a reflection of his boyhood impressions in looking forth from the beautiful Falmouth headland, then a wild, wood-fringed pasture but now a formal park:

> I remember the black wharves and the slips,
>   And the sea tides tossing free,
> And Spanish sailors with bearded lips,
> And the beauty and mystery of the ships,
>   And the magic of the sea.

This first call was presently neglected for the more insistent summons of literature; and thereafter Longfellow's inspiration was at **The Call of** second hand, from books rather than from nature or **Books** humanity. Soon after his graduation from Bowdoin (1825) he was offered a professorship in modern languages on condition that he prepare himself for the work by foreign study. With a glad heart he abandoned the law, which he had begun to study in his father's office, and spent three happy years in France, Spain and Italy. There he steeped himself in European poetry, and picked up a reading knowledge of several languages. Strangely enough, the romantic influence of Europe was reflected by this poet in a book of prose essays, *Outre Mer*, modeled on Irving's *Sketch Book*.

For five years Longfellow taught the modern languages at Bowdoin, and his subject was so new in America that he had to prepare his **Years of** own textbooks. Then, after another period of foreign **Teaching** study (this time in Denmark and Germany), he went to Harvard, where he taught modern languages and literature for eighteen years. In 1854 he resigned his chair, and for the remainder of his life devoted himself whole-heartedly to poetry.

His literary work began with newspaper verses, the best of which appear in the "Earlier Poems" of his collected works. Next he attempted prose in his *Outre Mer*, *Driftwood Essays* and the romances *Hyperion* and *Kavanagh*. In 1839 appeared his first volume of poetry, *Voices of the Night*, after which few years went by without some notable poem or volume from Longfellow's pen. His last book, *In the Harbor*, appeared with the news of his death, in 1882.

Aside from these "milestones" there is little to record in a career so placid that we remember by analogy "The Old Clock on the **His Serenity** Stairs." For the better part of his life he lived in Cambridge, where he was surrounded by a rare circle of friends, and whither increasing numbers came from near or far to pay the tribute of gratitude to one who had made life more beautiful by his singing. Once only the serenity was broken by a tragedy, the death of the poet's wife, who was fatally burned before his eyes, — a tragedy which occasioned his translation of Dante's *Divina Commedia* (by which work he strove to keep his sorrow from overwhelming him) and the exquisite "Cross of Snow." The latter seemed too sacred for publication; it was found, after the poet's death, among his private papers.

Reading Longfellow's poems one would never suspect that they were produced in an age of turmoil. To be sure, one finds a few **His Work and Influence** poems on slavery (sentimental effusions, written on shipboard to relieve the monotony of a voyage), but these were better unwritten since they added nothing to the poet's song and took nothing from the slave's burden. Longfellow has been criticized for his inaction in the midst of tumult, but possibly he had his reasons. When everybody's shouting is an excellent time to hold your tongue. He had his own work to do, a work for which he was admirably fitted; that he did not turn aside from it is to his credit and our profit. One demand of his age was, as we have noted elsewhere, to enter into the wealth of European poetry; and he gave thirty years of his life to satisfying that demand. Our own poetry was then sentimental, a kind of " sugared angel-cake "; and Longfellow, who was sentimental enough but whose sentiment was balanced by scholarship, made poetry that was like wholesome bread to common men. Lowell was a more brilliant writer, and Whittier a more inspired singer; but neither did a work for American letters that is comparable to that of Longfellow, who was essentially an educator, a teacher of new ideas, new values, new beauty. His influence in broadening our literary culture, in deepening our sympathy for the poets of other lands, and in making our own poetry a true expression of American feeling is beyond measure.

Minor Poems. It was by his first simple poems that Longfellow won the hearts of his people, and by them he is still most widely and gratefully remembered. To name these old favorites (" The Day is Done," " Resignation," " Ladder of St. Augustine," " Rainy Day," " Footsteps of Angels," " Light of Stars," " Reaper and the Flowers," " Hymn to the Night," " Midnight Mass," " Excelsior," " Village Blacksmith," " Psalm of Life ") is to list many of the poems that are remembered and quoted wherever in the round world the English language is spoken.

Ordinarily such poems are accepted at their face value as a true expression of human sentiment; but if we examine them critically, remembering the people for whom they were written, we may discover the secret of their popularity. The

Anglo-Saxons are first a busy and then a religious folk; when their day's work is done their thoughts turn naturally **Vesper** to higher matters; and any examination of Long-**Songs** fellow's minor works shows that a large proportion of them deal with the thoughts or feelings of men at the close of day. Such poems would be called *Abendlieder* in German; a good Old-English title for them would be "Evensong"; and both titles suggest the element of faith or worship. In writing these poems Longfellow had, unconsciously perhaps, the same impulse that leads one man to sing a hymn and another to say his prayers when the day is done. Because he expresses this almost universal feeling simply and reverently, his work is dear to men and women who would not have the habit of work interfere with the divine instinct of worship.

Further examination of these minor poems shows them to be filled with sentiment that often slips over the verge of sentimentality. The sentiments expressed are not of the exalted, imaginative kind; they are the sentiments of plain people who feel deeply but who can seldom express their feeling. Now, most people are sentimental (though we commonly try to hide the fact, more's the pity), and we are at heart grateful to the poet who says for us in simple, musical language what we are unable or ashamed to say for ourselves. In a word, the popularity of Longfellow's poems rests firmly on the humanity of the poet.

Besides these vesper songs are a hundred other short poems, among which the reader must make his own selection. The **Typical** ballads should not be neglected, for Longfellow **Poems** knew how to tell a story in verse. If he were too prone to add a moral to his tale (a moral that does not speak for itself were better omitted), we can overlook the fault, since his moral was a good one and his readers liked it. The "occasional" poems, also, written to celebrate persons or events (such as "Building of the Ship," "Hanging of the Crane," "Morituri Salutamus," "Bells of Lynn," "Robert

Burns," " Chamber over the Gate ") well deserved the welcome which the American people gave them. And the sonnets (such as " Three Friends," " Victor and Vanquished," " My Books," " Nature," " Milton," " President Garfield," " Giotto's Tower ") are not only the most artistic of Longfellow's works but rank very near to the best sonnets in the English language.

American Idyls. In the same spirit in which Tennyson wrote his *English Idyls* the American poet sent forth certain works reflecting the beauty of common life on this side of the ocean ; and though he never collected or gave them a name, we think of them as his " American Idyls." Many of his minor poems belong to this class, but we are thinking especially of *Evangeline, Miles Standish* and *Hiawatha*. The last-named, with its myths and legends clustering around one heroic personage, is commonly called an epic ; but its songs of Chibiabos, Minnehaha, Nokomis and the little Hiawatha are more like idyllic pictures of the original Americans.

Evangeline: a Tale of Acadie (1847) met the fate of Longfellow's earlier poems in that it was promptly attacked by

Evangeline a few critics while a multitude of people read it with delight. Its success may be explained on four counts. First, it is a charming story, not a " modern " or realistic but a tender, pathetic story such as we read in old romances, and such as young people will cherish so long as they remain young people. Second, it had a New World setting, one that was welcomed in Europe because it offered readers a new stage, more vast, shadowy, mysterious, than that to which they were accustomed ; and doubly welcomed here because it threw the glamor of romance over familiar scenes which deserved but had never before found their poet. Third, this old romance in a new setting was true to universal human nature ; its sentiments of love, faith and deathless loyalty were such as make the heart beat faster wherever true hearts are found. Finally, it was written in an unusual verse form, the unrimed hexameter, which Longfellow handled as well, let

us say, as most other English poets who have tried to use
that alluring but difficult measure. For hexameters are like the
Italian language, which is very easy to "pick up," but which
few foreigners ever learn to speak with the rhythm and
melody of a child of Tuscany.

Longfellow began his hexameters fairly well, as witness the
opening lines of *Evangeline* :

> This is the forest primeval. The murmuring pines and the hemlocks,
> Bearded with moss, and in garments green, indistinct in the twilight,
> Stand like Druids of eld, with voices sad and prophetic,
> Stand like harpers hoar, with beards that rest on their bosoms.
> Loud from its rocky caverns the deep-voiced neighboring ocean
> Speaks, and in accents disconsolate answers the wail of the forest.

Occasionally also he produced a very good but not quite
perfect line or passage :

> And as the voice of the priest repeated the service of sorrow,
> So with a mournful sound, like the voice of a vast congregation,
> Solemnly answered the sea, and mingled its roar with the dirges.

One must confess, however, that such passages are exceptional,
and that one must change the proper stress of a word too
frequently to be enthusiastic over Longfellow's hexameters.
Some of his lines halt or hobble, refusing to move to the
chosen measure, and others lose all their charm when
spoken aloud :

> When she had passed it seemed like the ceasing of exquisite music.

That line has been praised by critics, but one must believe
that they never pronounced it. To voice its sibilant hissing
is to understand the symbol for a white man in the Indian
sign language ; that is, two fingers of a hand extended before
the face, like the fork of a serpent's tongue.[1] On the whole,
Longfellow's verse should be judged not by itself but as a part

---

[1] This curious symbol, a snake's tongue to represent an Englishman, was invented
by some Indian whose ears were pained by a language in which the *s* sounds occur too
frequently. Our plurals are nearly all made that way, unfortunately ; but Longfellow was
able to make a hissing line without the use of a single plural.

of the tale he was telling. Holmes summed up the first impression of many readers by saying that he found these
"brimming lines" an excellent medium for a charming story.

That is more than one can truthfully say of the next important idyl, *The Courtship of Miles Standish* (1858). The
story is a good one and, more than all the histories, has awakened a romantic interest in the Pilgrims; but its unhappy
hexameters go jolting along, continually upsetting the musical
rhythm, until we wish that the tale had been told in either
prose or poetry.

The Song of Hiawatha (1855) was Longfellow's greatest
work, and by it he will probably be longest remembered as a
world poet. The materials for this poem, its musical names, its primitive traditions, its fascinating
folklore, were all taken from Schoolcraft's books about the
Ojibway Indians; its peculiar verse form, with its easy rhythm
and endless repetition, was copied from the *Kalevala*, the
national epic of Finland. Material and method, the tale and
the verse form, were finely adapted to each other; and though
Longfellow showed no originality in *Hiawatha*, his poetic talent
or genius appears in this: that these tales of childhood are
told in a childlike spirit; that these forest legends have the
fragrance of hemlock in them; and that as we read them,
even now, we seem to see the wigwam with its curling smoke,
and beyond the wigwam the dewy earth, the shining river, and
the blue sky with its pillars of tree trunks and its cloud of
rustling leaves. The simplicity and naturalness of primitive
folklore is in this work of Longfellow, who of a hundred
writers at home and abroad was the first to reveal the poetry
in the soul of an Indian.

As the poem is well known we forbear quotation; as it is
too long, perhaps, we express a personal preference in naming
"Hiawatha's Childhood," his "Friends," his "Fishing" and
his "Wooing" as the parts most likely to please the beginner.
The best that can be said of *Hiawatha* is that it adds a new

tale to the world's storybook. That book of the centuries has only a few stories, each of which portrays a man from birth to death, fronting the problems of this life, meeting its joy or sorrow in man fashion, and then setting his face bravely to " Ponemah," the Land of the Hereafter. That Longfellow added a chapter to the volume which preserves the stories of Ulysses, Beowulf, Arthur and Roland is undoubtedly his best or most endur- ing achievement.

His Experimental Works. Unless the student wants to encourage a sentimental mood by reading *Hyperion*, Longfellow's prose works need not detain us. Much more valuable and readable are his translations from various European languages, and of these his metrical

THE TAPROOM, WAYSIDE INN, SUDBURY

version of *The Divine Comedy* of Dante is most notable. He attempted also several dramatic works, among which *The Spanish Student* (1843) is still readable, though not very convincing. In *Christus : a Mystery* he attempted a miracle play of three acts, dealing with Christianity in the apostolic, medieval and modern eras ; but not even his admirers were satisfied with the result. " The Golden Legend " (one version of which Caxton printed on the first English press, and which a score of different poets have paraphrased) is the only part of *Christus* that may interest young readers by its romantic portrayal of the Middle Ages. To name such works is to suggest Longfellow's

varied interests and his habit of experimenting with any subject
or verse form that attracted him in foreign literatures.

The *Tales of a Wayside Inn* (1863–1873) is the most popular
of Longfellow's miscellaneous works.   Here are a score of
stories from ancient or modern sources, as told by a circle
of the poet's friends in the Red Horse Inn, at Sudbury.   The
title suggests at once the *Canterbury Tales* of Chaucer; but
it would be unwise to make any comparison between the two
works or the two poets.   The ballad of " Paul Revere's Ride "
is the best known of the *Wayside Inn* poems; the Viking
tales of " The Saga of King Olaf " are the most vigorous;
the mellow coloring of the Middle Ages appears in such
stories as " The Legend Beautiful " and " The Bell of Atri."

Characteristics of Longfellow.   The broad sympathy of
Longfellow, which made him at home in the literatures of
a dozen nations, was one of his finest qualities.   He lived in
Cambridge ; he wrote in English ; he is called the poet of the
American home; but had he lived in Finland and written in
a Scandinavian tongue, his poems must still appeal to us.
Indeed, so simply did he reflect the sentiments of the human
heart that Finland or any other nation might gladly class him
among its poets.

For example, many Englishmen have written about their
Wellington, but, as Hearn says, not even Tennyson's poem on
A Poet of all the subject is quite equal to Longfellow's " Warden
Peoples   of the Cinque Ports."   The spirit of the Spanish
missions, with their self-sacrificing monks and their soldiers
" with hearts of fire and steel," is finely reflected in " The
Bells of San Blas."   The half-superstitious loyalty of the
Russian peasant for his hereditary ruler has never been better
reflected than in " The White Czar."   The story of Belisarius
has been told in scores of histories and books of poetry; but
you will feel a deeper sympathy for the neglected old Roman
soldier in Longfellow's poem than in anything else you may
find on the same theme.   And there are many other foreign

heroes or brave deeds that find beautiful expression in the verse of our American poet. Of late it has become almost a critical habit to disparage Longfellow; but no critic has pointed out another poet who has reflected with sympathy and understanding the feelings of so many widely different peoples.

Naturally such a poet had his limitations. In comparison with Chaucer, for example, we perceive instantly that Longfellow knew only one side of life, the better side. Unhappy or rebellious or turbulent souls were beyond his ken. He wrote only for those who work by day and sometimes go to evensong at night, who hopefully train their children or reverently bury their dead, and who cleave to a writer that speaks for them the fitting word of faith or cheer or consolation on every proper occasion. As humanity is largely made of such men and women, Longfellow will always be a popular poet. For him, with his serene outlook, there were not nine Muses

LONGFELLOW'S LIBRARY IN CRAIGIE HOUSE, CAMBRIDGE

but only three, and their names were Faith, Hope and Charity.

Concerning his faults, perhaps the most illuminating thing that can be said is that critics emphasize and ordinary readers

Poetic Faults ignore them. The reason for this is that every poem has two elements, form and content: a critic looks chiefly at the one, an ordinary reader at the other. Because the form of Longfellow's verse is often faulty it is easy ᴄᴏ criticize him, to show that he copies the work of others, that he lacks originality, that his figures are often forced or questionable; but the reader, the young reader especially, may be too much interested in the charm of the poet's story or the truth of his sentiment to dissect his poetic figures. Thus, in the best-known of his earlier poems, "A Psalm of Life," he uses the famous metaphor of "footprints on the sands of time." That is so bad a figure that to analyze is to reject it; yet it never bothers young people, who would understand the poet and like him just as well even had he written "signboards" instead of "footprints." The point is that Longfellow is so obviously a true and pleasant poet that his faults easily escape attention unless we look for them. There is perhaps no better summary of our poet's qualities than to record again the simple fact that he is the poet of young people, to whom sentiment is the very breath of life. Should you ask the reason for his supremacy in this respect, the answer is a paradox. Longfellow was not an originator; he had no new song to sing, no new tale to tell. He was the poet of old heroes, old legends, old sentiments and ideals. Therefore he is the poet of youth.

John Greenleaf Whittier (1807–1892)

The strange mixture of warrior and peace lover in Whittier has led to a strange misjudgment of his work. From the obscurity of a New England farm he emerged as the champion of the Abolitionist party, and for thirty tumultuous years his poems were as war cries. By such work was he judged as "the trumpeter of a cause," and the judgment stood between him and his audience when he sang not of a cause but of a country. Even at the present time most critics speak of Whittier as "the antislavery poet." Stedman, for example, focuses our attention on certain lyrics of reform which he calls "words wrung from the nation's heart"; but the plain fact is that only a small part of the nation approved these lyrics or took any interest in the poet who wrote them.

Such was Whittier on one side, a militant poet of reform, sending forth verses that had the brattle of trumpets and the waving of banners in them:

> Lift again the stately emblem on the Bay State's rusted shield,
> Give to Northern winds the Pine Tree on our banner's tattered field.
> Sons of men who sat in council with their Bibles round the board,
> Answering England's royal missive with a firm, " Thus saith the Lord ! "
> Rise again for home and freedom ! set the battle in array !
> What the fathers did of old time we their sons must do to-day.

On the other side he was a Friend, or Quaker, and the peaceful spirit of his people found expression in lyrics of faith that have no equal in our poetry. He was also a patriot to the core. He loved America with a profound love ; her ideals, her traditions, her epic history were in his blood, and he glorified them in ballads and idyls that reflect the very spirit of brave Colonial days. To judge Whittier as a trumpeter, therefore, is to neglect all that is important in his work ; for his reform poems merely awaken the dying echoes of party clamor, while his ballads and idyls belong to the whole American people, and his hymns of faith to the wider audience of humanity.

Life. The span of Whittier's life was almost the span of the nineteenth century. He was born (1807) in the homestead of his ancestors at Haverhill, Massachusetts, and spent his formative years working in the fields by day, reading beside the open fire at night, and spending a few terms in a " deestrict " school presided over by teachers who came or went with the spring. His schooling was, therefore, of the scantiest kind ; his real education came from a noble home, from his country's history, from his toil and outdoor life with its daily contact with nature. The love of home and of homely virtues, the glorification of manhood and womanhood, the pride of noble traditions, and always a background of meadow or woodland or sounding sea, — these were the subjects of Whittier's best verse, because these were the things he knew most intimately.

It was a song of Burns that first turned Whittier to poetry; but hardly had he begun to write songs of his own when Garrison, the **First Verses** antislavery agitator, turned his thought from the peaceful farm to the clamoring world beyond. Attracted by certain verses (Whittier's sister Elizabeth had sent them secretly to Garrison's paper) the editor came over to see his contributor and found to his surprise a country lad who was in evident need of education. Instead of asking for more poetry, therefore, Garrison

JOHN GREENLEAF WHITTIER

awakened the boy's ambition. For two terms he attended the Haverhill Academy, supporting himself meanwhile by making shoes. Then his labor was needed at home; but finding his health too delicate for farm work he chose other occupations and contributed manfully to the support of his family.

For several years thereafter Whittier was like a man trying to find himself. He did factory work; he edited newspapers; he showed a talent for political leadership; he made poems which he sold at a price to remind him of what he had once received for making shoes. While poetry and politics both called to him alluringly a crisis arose; Garrison summoned him; and with a sad heart, knowing that he left all hope of political or literary success behind, he went over to the Abolitionist party. That was in 1833, when Whittier was twenty-six years old. At that time the Abolitionists were detested in the North as well as in the South, and to join them was to become an outcast.

Then came the militant period of Whittier's life. He became editor of antislavery journals; he lectured in the cause; he was stoned for his utterances; his printing shop was burned by a mob. Meanwhile his poems were sounding abroad like trumpet blasts, making friends, making enemies. It was a passionate age, when political enemies were hated like Hessians, but Whittier was always chivalrous with his opponents. Read his "Randolph of Roanoke" **Storm and** for a specific example. His "Laus Deo" (1865), a chant **Stress** of exultation written when he heard the bells ringing the news of the constitutional amendment prohibiting slavery, was the last poem of this period of storm and stress.

In the following year Whittier produced *Snow-Bound*, his masterpiece. Though he had been writing for half a century, he had never won either fame or money by his verse; but the publication of this

OAK KNOLL, WHITTIER'S HOME, DANVERS, MASSACHUSETTS

beautiful idyl placed him in the front rank of American poets. Thereafter he was a national figure, and the magazines which once scorned his verses were now most eager to print them. So he made an end of the poverty which had been his portion since childhood.

For the remainder of his life he lived serenely at Amesbury, for the most part, in a modest house presided over by a relative. He **Peaceful** wrote poetry now more carefully, for a wider audience, **Years** and every few years saw another little volume added to his store: *Ballads of New England, Miriam and Other Poems, Hazel Blossoms, Poems of Nature, St. Gregory's Quest, At Sundown.* When he died (1892) he was honored not so widely perhaps as Longfellow, but more deeply, as we honor those whose peace has been won

OA

through manful strife. Holmes, the ready poet of all occasions, expressed a formal but sincere judgment in the lines:

> Best loved and saintliest of our singing train,
>   Earth's noblest tributes to thy name belong:
> A lifelong record closed without a stain,
>   A blameless memory shrined in deathless song.

Earlier Works.[1] In Whittier's poetry we note three distinct stages, and note also that he was on the wrong trail until he followed his own spirit. His earliest work was inspired by Burns, but this was of no consequence. Next he fell under the spell of Scott and wrote "Mogg Megone" and "The Bridal of Pennacook." These Indian romances in verse are too much influenced by Scott's border poems and also by sentimental novels of savage life, such as Mrs. Child's *Hobomok*; they do not ring true, and in this respect are like almost everything else in literature on the subject of the Indians.

In *Voices of Freedom* (1849) and other poems inspired by the antislavery campaign Whittier for the first time came close **Reform Poems** to his own age. He was no longer an echo but a voice, a man's voice, shouting above a tumult. He spoke not for the nation but for a party; and it was inevitable that his reform lyrics should fall into neglect with the occasions that called them forth. They are interesting now not as poems but as sidelights on a critical period of our history. Their intensely passionate quality appears in "Faneuil Hall," "Song of the Free," "The Pine Tree," "Randolph of Roanoke" and "The Farewell of an Indian Slave Mother."

There is a fine swinging rhythm in these poems, in "Massachusetts to Virginia" especially, which recalls Macaulay's "Armada"; and two of them at least show astonishing power and vitality. One is "Laus Deo," to which we have referred in our story of the poet's life. The other is "Ichabod" (1850),

---

[1] Though we are concerned here with Whittier's poetry, we should at least mention certain of his prose works, such as *Legends of New England, Leaves from Margaret Smith's Journal* and *Old Portraits and Modern Sketches*. The chief value of these is in their pictures of Colonial life.

written after the "Seventh of March Speech" of Webster, when that statesman seemed to have betrayed the men who elected and trusted him. Surprise, anger, scorn, indignation, sorrow, — all these emotions were loosed in a flood after Webster's speech; but Whittier waited till he had fused them into one emotion, and when his slow words fell at last they fell with the weight of judgment and the scorching of fire upon their victim. If words could kill a man, these surely are the words. "Ichabod" is the most powerful poem of its kind in our language; but it is fearfully unjust to Webster. Those who read it should read also "The Lost Occasion," written thirty years later, which Whittier placed next to "Ichabod" in the final edition of his poems. So he tried to right a wrong (unfortunately after the victim was dead) by offering generous tribute to the statesman he had once misjudged.

Ballads and American Idyls. Whittier's manly heart and his talent for flowing verse made him an excellent ballad writer; but his work in this field is so different from that of his predecessors that he came near to inventing a new type of poetry. Thus, many of the old ballads celebrate the bravery that mounts with fighting; but Whittier always lays emphasis on the higher quality that we call moral courage. "Barclay of Ury" will illustrate our criticism: the verse has a martial swing; the hero is a veteran who has known the lust of battle; but his courage now appears in self-mastery, in the ability to bear in silence the jeers of a mob. Again, the old ballad aims to tell a story, nothing else, and drives straight to its mark; but Whittier portrays the whole landscape and background of the action. He deals largely with Colonial life in New England, and his descriptions of place and people are unrivaled in our poetry. Read one of his typical ballads, "The Wreck of Rivermouth" or "The Witch's Daughter" or "The Garrison of Cape Ann" or "Skipper Ireson's Ride," and see how closely he identifies himself with the place and time of his story.

There is one quality, however, in which our Quaker poet resembles the old ballad makers; namely, his intense patriotism; **Patriotic Quality** and this recalls the fact that ballads were the first histories, the first expression not only of brave deeds but of the national pride which the deeds symbolized. Though Whittier keeps himself modestly in the background, as a story-teller ought to do, he can never quite repress the love of his native land or the quickened heartbeats that set

STREET IN OLD MARBLEHEAD
Skipper Ireson's home on extreme right

his verse marching as if to the drums. This patriotism, though intense, was never intolerant but rather sympathetic with men of other lands, as appears in "The Pipes at Lucknow," a ballad dealing with a dramatic incident of the Sepoy Rebellion. The Scotsman who could read that ballad unmoved, without a kindling of the eye or a stirring of the heart, would be unworthy of his clan or country.

Even better than Whittier's ballads are certain narrative poems reflecting the life of simple people, to which we give the name of idyls. "Telling the Bees," "In School Days," "My Playmate," "Maud Muller," "The Barefoot Boy," — there are no other American poems quite like these, none so tender, none written with such perfect sympathy. Some of them are like photographs; and the lens that gathered them was not a glass but a human heart. Others sing the emotion of love as only Whittier, the Galahad of poets, could have sung it,— as in this stanza from "A Sea Dream":

> Draw near, more near, forever dear!
> Where'er I rest or roam,
> Or in the city's crowded streets,
> Or by the blown sea foam,
> The thought of thee is home!

Snow-Bound. The best of Whittier's idyls is *Snow-Bound* (1866), into which he gathered a boy's tenderest memories. In naming this as the best poem in the language on the subject of home we do not offer a criticism but an invitation. Because all that is best in human life centers in the ideal of home, and because Whittier reflected that ideal in a beautiful way, *Snow-Bound* should be read if we read nothing else of American poetry. There is perhaps only one thing to prevent this idyl from becoming a universal poem: its natural setting can be appreciated only by those who live within the snow line, who have seen the white flakes gather and drift, confining every family to the circle of its own hearth fire in what Emerson calls "the tumultuous privacy of storm."

The plan of the poem is simplicity itself. It opens with a description of a snowstorm that thickens with the December night. The inmates of an old farmhouse gather about the open fire, and Whittier describes them one by one, how they looked to the boy (for *Snow-Bound* is a recollection of boyhood), and what stories they told to reveal their interests. The rest of the poem is a reverie, as of one no longer a boy, who looks into his fire and sees not the fire-pictures but those other scenes or portraits that are graved deep in every human heart.

To praise such a work is superfluous, and to criticize its artless sincerity is beyond our ability. Many good writers have **Charm of** explained the poem; yet still its deepest charm **Snow-Bound** escapes analysis, perhaps because it has no name. The best criticism that the present writer ever heard on the subject came from a Habitant farmer in the Province of Quebec, a simple, unlettered man, who was a poet at heart but who would have been amazed had anyone told him so. His children, who were learning English literature through the happy medium of *Evangeline* and *Snow-Bound*, brought the latter poem home from school, and the old man would sit smoking his pipe and listening to the story. When they read of the winter scenes, of the fire roaring its defiance up the chimney-throat at the storm without, —

> What matter how the night behaved?
> What matter how the north-wind raved?
> Blow high, blow low, not all its snow
> Could quench our hearth-fire's ruddy glow, —

then he would stir in his chair, make his pipe glow fiercely, and blow a cloud of smoke about his head. But in the following scene, with its memories of the dead and its immortal hope, he would sit very still, as if listening to exquisite music. When asked why he liked the poem his face lighted: "W'y I lak heem, M'sieu Whittier? I lak heem 'cause he speak de true. He know de storm, and de leetle *cabane*, and heart of de boy an' hees moder. *Oui, oui*, he know de man also."

Nature, home, the heart of a boy and a man and a mother,— the poet who can reflect such elemental matters so that the simple of earth understand and love their beauty deserves the critic's best tribute of silence.

Poems of Faith and Nature. Aside from the reform poems it is hard to group Whittier's works, which are all alike in that they portray familiar scenes against a natural background. In his *Tent on the Beach* (1867) he attempted a collection of tales in the manner of Longfellow's *Wayside Inn*, but of these only one or two ballads, such as "Abraham Davenport" and "The Wreck of Rivermouth," are now treasured. The best part of the book is the " Prelude," which pictures the poet among his friends and records his impressions of sky and sea and shore.

The outdoor poems of Whittier are interesting, aside from their own beauty, as suggesting two poetic conceptions of nature which have little in common. The earlier regards nature as a mistress to be loved or a divinity to be worshiped for her own sake; she has her own laws or mercies, and man is but one of her creatures. The Anglo-Saxon scops viewed nature in this way; so did Bryant, in whose "Forest Hymn" is the feeling of primitive ages. Many modern poets (and novelists also, like Scott and Cooper) have outgrown this conception; they regard nature as a kind of stage for the drama of human life, which is all-important.

Two Views of Nature

Whittier belongs to this later school; he portrays nature magnificently, but always as the background for some human incident, sad or tender or heroic, which appears to us more real because viewed in its natural setting. Note in " The Wreck of Rivermouth," for example, how the merry party in their sailboat, the mowers on the salt marshes, the " witch " mumbling her warning, the challenge of a careless girl, the skipper's fear, the river, the breeze, the laughing sea, — everything is exactly as it should be. It is this humanized view of the natural world which makes Whittier's ballads unique and which gives deeper meaning to his " Hampton Beach," " Among the Hills," " Trailing Arbutus," " The Vanishers " and other of his best nature poems.

Our reading of Whittier should not end until we are familiar with " The Eternal Goodness," " Trust," " My Soul and I," " The Prayer of Agassiz " and a few more of his hymns of faith. Our appreciation of such hymns will be more sympathetic if we remember, first, that Whittier came of ancestors whose souls approved the opening proposition of the Declaration of Independence; and second,

Whittier's Creed

that he belonged to the Society of Friends, who believed that God revealed himself directly to every human soul (the "inner light" they called it), and that a man's primal responsibility was to God and his own conscience. The creed of Whittier may therefore be summarized in two articles: "I believe in the Divine love and in the equality of men." The latter article appears in all his poems; the former is crystallized in "The Eternal Goodness," a hymn so trustful and reverent that it might well be the evensong of humanity.

Characteristics of Whittier. One may summarize Whittier in the statement that he is the poet of the home and the hills, and of that freedom without which the home loses its chief joy and the hill its inspiration. In writing of such themes Whittier failed to win the highest honors of a poet; and the failure was due not to his lack of culture, as is sometimes alleged (for there is no other culture equal to right living), but rather to the stern conditions of his life, to his devotion to duty, to his struggle for liberty, to his lifelong purpose of helping men by his singing. Great poems are usually the result of seclusion, of aloofness, but Whittier was always a worker in the world.

His naturalness is perhaps his best poetic virtue. There is in his verse a spontaneous "singing" quality which leaves A Natural   the impression that poetry was his native language. Singer   It is easy to understand why Burns first attracted him, for both poets were natural singers who remind us of what Bede wrote of Cædmon: "He learned not the art of poetry from men." Next to his spontaneity is his rare simplicity, his gift of speaking straight from a heart that never grew old. Sometimes his simplicity is as artless as that of a child, as in "Maud Muller"; generally it is noble, as in his modest "Proem" to *Voices of Freedom*; occasionally it is passionate, as in the exultant cry of "Laus Deo"; and at times it rises to the simplicity of pure art, as in "Telling the Bees." The last-named poem portrays an old Colonial custom which provided that when death came to a farmhouse the bees must be told and their hives draped in mourning. It portrays also, as a perfect, natural background, the path to Whittier's home and his sister's old-fashioned flower garden, in which the daffodils still bloom where she planted them long ago.

That Whittier was not a great poet, as the critics assure us, may be frankly admitted. That he had elements of greatness

The Man and the Poet is also without question; and precisely for this reason, because his power is so often manifest in noble or exquisite passages, there is disappointment in reading him when we stumble upon bad rimes, careless workmanship, mishandling of his native speech. Our experience here is probably like that of Whittier's friend Garrison. The latter had read certain poems that attracted him; he came quickly to see the poet; and out from under the barn, his clothes sprinkled with hayseed, crawled a shy country lad who explained bashfully that he had been hunting hens' nests. Anything could be forgiven after that; interest in the boy would surely temper criticism of the poet.

Even so our present criticism of Whittier's verse must include certain considerations of the man who wrote it: that he smacked of his native soil; that his education was scanty and hardly earned; that he used words as his father and mother used them, and was not ashamed of their rural accent. His own experience, moreover, had weathered him until he seemed part of a rugged landscape. He knew life, and he loved it. He had endured poverty, and glorified it. He had been farm hand, shoemaker, self-supporting student, editor of country newspapers, local politician, champion of slaves, worker for reform, defender of a hopeless cause that by the awful judgment of war became a winning cause. And always and everywhere he had been a man, one who did his duty as he saw it, spake truth as he believed it, and kept his conscience clean, his heart pure, his faith unshaken. All this was in his verse and ennobled even his faults, which were part of his plain humanity. As Longfellow was by study of European literatures the poet of books and culture, so Whittier was by experience the poet of life. The homely quality of his verse, which endears it to common men, is explained on the ground that he was nearer than any other American poet to the body and soul of his countrymen.

JAMES RUSSELL LOWELL (1819–1891)

The work of Lowell is unusual and his rank or position hard to define. Though never a great or even a popular writer, he was regarded for a considerable part of his life as the most prominent man of letters in America. At the present time his reputation is still large, but historians find it somewhat easier to praise his works than to read them. As poet, critic, satirist, editor and teacher he loomed as a giant among his contemporaries, overtopping Whittier and Longfellow at one time; but he left no work comparable to *Snow-Bound* or *Hiawatha,* and one is puzzled to name any of his poems or essays that are fairly certain to give pleasure. To read his volumes is to meet a man of power and brilliant promise, but the final impression is that the promise was not fulfilled, that the masterpiece of which Lowell was capable was left unwritten.

Biographical Sketch. Lowell came from a distinguished family that had "made history" in America. His father was a cultured clergyman; he grew up in a beautiful home, "Elmwood," in the college town of Cambridge; among his first companions were the noble books that filled the shelves of the family library. From the beginning, therefore, he was inclined to letters; and though he often turned aside for other matters, his first and last love was the love of poetry.

At fifteen he entered Harvard, where he read almost everything, he said, except the books prescribed by the faculty. Then he studied law and opened an office in Boston, where he found few clients, being more interested in writing verses than in his profession. With his marriage in 1844 the first strong purpose seems to have entered his

indolent life. His wife was zealous in good works, and presently
Lowell, who had gayly satirized all reformers, joined in the antislavery
campaign and proceeded to make as many enemies as friends by his
reform poems.

Followed then a period of hard, purposeful work, during which he
supported himself by editing *The Pennsylvania Freeman* and by writing
Varied   for the magazines. In 1848, his banner year, he published
Tasks   his best volume of *Poems, Sir Launfal, A Fable for
Critics* and the first series of
The Biglow Papers. It was
not these volumes, however,
but a series of brilliant lectures on the English poets
that caused Lowell to be
called to the chair in Harvard which Longfellow had
resigned. He prepared for
this work by studying abroad,
and for some twenty years
thereafter he gave courses
in English, Italian, Spanish
and German literatures. For
a part of this time he was
also editor in turn of *The
Atlantic Monthly* and *The
North American Review.*

In the simpler days of the
republic, when the first question asked of a
Life Abroad

JAMES RUSSELL LOWELL

diplomat was not whether he had money enough to
entertain society in a proper style, the profession of letters was
honored by sending literary men to represent America in foreign
courts, and Lowell's prominence was recognized by his appointment
as ambassador to Spain (1877) and to England (1880). It was in this
patriotic service abroad that he won his greatest honors. In London
especially he made his power felt as an American who loved his
country, as a democrat who believed in democracy, and as a cultured
gentleman who understood Anglo-Saxon life because of his familiarity
with the poetry in which that life is most clearly reflected. Next to
keeping silence about his proper business, perhaps the chief requirement

of an ambassador is to make speeches about everything else, and no other foreign speaker was ever listened to with more pleasure than the witty and cultured Lowell. One who summed up his diplomatic triumph said tersely that he found the Englishmen strangers and left them all cousins.

He was recalled from this service in 1885. The remainder of his life was spent teaching at Harvard, writing more poetry and editing his numerous works. His first volume of poems, *A Year's Life*, was published in 1841; his last volume, *Heartsease and Rue*, appeared almost half a century later, in 1888. That his death occurred in the same house in which he was born and in which he had spent the greater part of his life is an occurrence so rare in America that it deserves a poem of commemoration.

Lowell's Poetry. There are golden grains everywhere in Lowell's verse but never a continuous vein of metal. In other words, even his best work is notable for occasional lines rather than for sustained excellence. As a specific example study the "Commemoration Ode," one of the finest poems inspired by the Civil War. The occasion of this ode, to commemorate the college students who had given their lives for their country, was all that a poet might wish; the brilliant audience that gathered at Cambridge was most inspiring; and beyond that local audience stood a nation in mourning, a nation which had just lost a million of its sons in a mighty conflict. It was such an occasion as Lowell loved, and one who reads the story of his life knows how earnestly he strove to meet it. When the reading of his poem was finished his audience called it "a noble effort," and that is precisely the trouble with the famous ode; it is too plainly an effort. It does not sing, does not overflow from a full heart, does not speak the inevitable, satisfying word. In consequence (and perhaps this criticism applies to most ambitious odes) we are rather glad when the "effort" is at an end. Yet there are excellent passages in the poem, notably the sixth and the last stanzas, one with its fine tribute to Lincoln, the other expressive of deathless loyalty to one's native land.

The best of Lowell's lyrics may be grouped in two classes, the first dealing with his personal joy or grief, the second with the feelings of the nation. Typical of the former are "The First Snowfall" and a few other lyrics reflecting the poet's sorrow for the loss of a little daughter, — simple, human poems, in refreshing contrast with most others of Lowell, which strive for brilliancy. The best of the national lyrics is "The Present Crisis" (1844). This was at first a party poem, a ringing appeal issued during the turmoil occasioned by the annexation of Texas; but now, with the old party issues forgotten, we can all read it with pleasure as a splendid expression of the American heart and will in every crisis of our national history.

Lyrics

In the nature lyrics we have a double reflection, one of the external world, the other of a poet who could not be single-minded, and who was always confusing his own impressions of nature or humanity with those other impressions which he found reflected in poetry. Read the charming "To the Dandelion," for example, and note how Lowell cannot be content with his

> Dear common flower that grow'st beside the way,
> Fringing the dusty road with harmless gold,

but must bring in Eldorado and twenty other poetic allusions to glorify a flower which has no need of external glory. Then for comparison read Bryant's "Fringed Gentian" and see how the elder poet, content with the flower itself, tells you very simply how its beauty appeals to him. Or read "An Indian-Summer Reverie" with its scattered lines of gold, and note how Lowell cannot say what he feels in his own heart but must search everywhere for poetic images; and then, because he cannot find exactly what he seeks or, more likely, because he finds a dozen tempting allusions where one is plenty, he goes on and on in a vain quest that ends by leaving himself and his reader unsatisfied.

The most popular of Lowell's works is *The Vision of Sir
Launfal* (1848), in which he invents an Arthurian kind of
legend of the search for the Holy Grail. Most of
his long poems are labored, but this seems to have
been written in a moment of inspiration. The "Prelude"
begins almost spontaneously, and when it reaches the charming passage "And what is so rare as a day in June?" the
verse fairly begins to sing, — a rare occurrence with Lowell.
Critical readers may reasonably object to the poet's moralizing,
to his imperfect lines and to his setting of an Old World
legend of knights and castles in a New World landscape ; but
uncritical readers rejoice in a moral feeling that is fine and
true, and are content with a good story and a good landscape
without inquiring whether the two belong together. Moreover,
Sir Launfal certainly serves the first purpose of poetry in that it
gives pleasure and so deserves its continued popularity among
young readers.

Two satiric poems that were highly prized when they were
first published, and that are still formally praised by historians
who do not read them, are *A Fable for Critics*
and *The Biglow Papers*. The former is a series
of doggerel verses filled with grotesque puns and quips
aimed at American authors who were prominent in 1848.
The latter, written in a tortured, "Yankee" dialect, is
made up of political satires and conceits occasioned by the
Mexican and Civil wars. Both works contain occasional
fine lines and a few excellent criticisms of literature or
politics, but few young readers will have patience to sift out
the good passages from the mass of glittering rubbish in
which they are hidden.

Much more worthy of the reader's attention are certain
neglected works, such as Lowell's sonnets, his "Prometheus,"
"Columbus," "Agassiz," "Portrait of Dante," "Washers of
the Shroud," "Under the Old Elm" (with its noble tribute
to Washington) and "Stanzas on Freedom." It is a pity that

Sir Launfal

Satires

such poems, all of which contain memorable lines, should be kept from the wide audience they deserve, and largely because of the author's digressiveness. To examine them is to conclude that, like most of Lowell's works, they are not simple enough in feeling to win ordinary readers, like the poetry of Longfellow, and not perfect enough in form to excite the admiration of critics, like the best of Poe's melodies.

LOWELL'S HOUSE, CAMBRIDGE, IN WINTER

Lowell's Prose. In brilliancy at least Lowell has no peer among American essayists, though others excel him in the better qualities of originality or charm or vigor. The best of his prose works are the scintillating essays collected in *My Study Windows* and *Among My Books*. In his political essays he looked at humanity with his own eyes, but the titles of the volumes just named indicate his chief interest as a prose writer, which was to interpret the world's books rather than the world's throbbing life. For younger readers the most pleasing of the prose works are the comparatively simple sketches, "My Garden Acquaintance," "Cambridge Thirty Years Ago" and "On a Certain Condescension in Foreigners." In these sketches we meet the author at his best, alert, witty and so widely read that he cannot help giving a literary flavor to whatever he writes. Among the best of his essays on literary subjects are those on Chaucer, Dante, Keats, Walton and Emerson.

One who reads a typical collection of Lowell's essays is apt to be divided between open admiration and something akin to **Quality of** resentment. On the one hand they are brilliant, **the Essays** stimulating, filled with "good things"; on the other they are always digressive, sometimes fantastic and too often self-conscious; that is, they call our attention to the author rather than to his proper subject. When he writes of Dante he is concerned to reveal the soul of the Italian master; but when he writes of Milton he seems chiefly intent on showing how much more he knows than the English editor of Milton's works. When he presents Emerson he tries to make us know and admire the Concord sage; but when he falls foul of Emerson's friends, Thoreau and Carlyle, his personal prejudices are more in evidence than his impersonal judgment. In consequence, some of the literary essays are a better reflection of Lowell himself than of the men he wrote about.

An author must be finally measured, however, by his finest work, by his constant purpose rather than by his changing mood; and the finest work of Lowell, his critical studies of the elder poets and dramatists, are perhaps the most solid and the most penetrating that our country has to show. He certainly kept "the great tradition" in criticism, a tradition which enjoins us, in simple language, to seek only the best and to reverence it when we find it. As he wrote:

> Great truths are portions of the soul of man;
> Great souls are portions of eternity;
> Each drop of blood that e'er through true heart ran
> With lofty message, ran for thee and me.

Oliver Wendell Holmes (1809-1894)

It is a sad fate for a writer to be known as a humorist; nobody will take him seriously ever afterward. Even a book suffers from such a reputation, the famous *Don Quixote* for example, which we read as a type of extravagant humor but which is in reality a tragedy, since it portrays the disillusionment of a man who believed the world to be like his own heart, noble and chivalrous, and who found it filled with villainy. Because Holmes (who was essentially a moralist and a preacher) could not repress the bubbling wit that was part of his nature, our historians must set him down as a humorist and name the "One-Hoss Shay" as his most typical work. Yet his best poems are as pathetic as "The Last Leaf," as sentimental as "The Voiceless," as patriotic as "Old Ironsides," as worshipful as the "Hymn of Trust," as nobly didactic as "The Chambered Nautilus"; his novels are studies of the obscure problems of heredity, and his most characteristic prose work, *The Autocrat of the Breakfast Table*, is an original commentary on almost everything under the sun.

Evidently we prize a laugh above any other product of literature, and because there is a laugh or a smile hidden in many a work of Holmes he must still keep the place assigned to him as an "American" humorist. Even so, he is perhaps our most representative writer in this field; for he is as thoroughly American as a man can be, and his rare culture and kindness are in refreshing contrast to the crude horseplay or sensationalism that is unfortunately trumpeted abroad as New World humor.

A Placid Life. Though Holmes never wrote a formal autobiography he left a very good reflection of himself in his works, and it is in these alone that we become acquainted with him, — a genial, witty, observant, kind-hearted and pure-hearted man whom it is good to know.

He belonged to what he called "the Brahmin caste" of intellectual aristocrats (as described in his novel *Elsie Venner*), for he came from

OA

an old New England family extending back to Anne Bradstreet and the governors of the Bay Colony. He was born in Cambridge; he was educated at Andover and Harvard; he spent his life in Boston, a city which satisfied him so completely that he called it " the hub of the solar system." Most ambitious writers like a large field with plenty of change or variety, but Holmes was content with a small and very select circle with himself at the center of it.

OLIVER WENDELL HOLMES

For his profession he chose medicine and studied it four years, the latter half of the time in Paris. At that period his foreign training was as rare in medicine as was Longfellow's in poetry. He practiced his profession in Boston and managed to make a success of it, though patients were a little doubtful of a doctor who wrote poetry and who opened his office with the remark that " small fevers " would be " gratefully received." Also he was for thirty-five years professor of anatomy at the Harvard Medical School. What with healing or teaching or learning, this doctor might have been very busy; but he seems to have found plenty of leisure for writing, and the inclination was always present. " Whoso has once tasted type," he said, " must indulge the taste to the end of his life."

His literary work began at twenty-one, when he wrote " Old Ironsides " in protest against the order to dismantle the frigate *Constitution*, which had made naval history in the War of 1812. That first poem, which still rings triumphantly in our ears, accomplished two things: it saved the glorious old warship, and it gave Holmes a hold on public attention which he never afterward lost. During the next twenty-five years he wrote poetry,

The Writer

and was so much in demand to furnish verses for special occasions that he was a kind of poet-laureate of his college and city. He was almost fifty when the *Atlantic Monthly* was projected and Lowell demanded, as a condition of his editorship, that Holmes be engaged as the first contributor. Feeling in the mood for talk, as he commonly did, Holmes responded with *The Autocrat.* Thereafter he wrote chiefly in prose, making his greatest effort in fiction but winning more readers by his table talk in the form of essays. His last volume, *Over the Teacups,* appeared when he was past eighty years old.

We have spoken of the genial quality of Holmes as revealed in his work, but we would hardly be just to him did we fail to note his **Pet** pet prejudices, his suspicion of reformers, his scorn of **Prejudices** homeopathic doctors, his violent antipathy to Calvinism. Though he had been brought up in the Calvinistic faith (his father was an old-style clergyman), he seemed to delight in clubbing or satirizing or slinging stones at it. The very mildest he could do was to refer to " yon whey-faced brother " to express his opinion of those who still clung to puritanic doctrines. Curiously enough, he still honored his father and was proud of his godly ancestors, who were all stanch Puritans. The explanation is, of course, that Holmes never understood theology, not for a moment; he only disliked it, and was consequently sure that it must be wrong and that somebody ought to put an end to it. In later years he mellowed somewhat. One cannot truthfully say that he overcame his prejudice, but he understood men better and was inclined to include even reformers and Calvinists in what he called " the larger humanity into which I was born so long ago."

Works of Holmes. In the field of " occasional " poetry, written to celebrate births, dedications, feasts and festivals of every kind, Holmes has never had a peer among his countrymen. He would have made a perfect poet-laureate, for he seemed to rise to every occasion and have on his lips the right word to express the feeling of the moment, whether of patriotism or sympathy or sociability. In such happy poems as " The Boys," " Bill and Jo," " All Here " and nearly forty others written for his class reunions he reflects the spirit of college men who gather annually to live the " good old days " over again.[1]   He wrote also some seventy other poems for special occasions, the quality of which may be judged from "Old Ironsides," "Under the Violets," "Grandmother's Story" and numerous appreciations of Lowell, Burns, Bryant, Whittier and other well-known poets.

Among poems of more general interest the best is "The Chambered Nautilus," which some read for its fine moral lesson and others for its beautiful symbolism or almost perfect workmanship.   Others that deserve to be remembered are "The Last Leaf" (Lincoln's favorite), "Nearing the Snow Line," "Meeting of the Alumni," "Questions and Answers" and "The Voiceless," — none great poems but all good and very well worth the reading.

"The Deacon's Masterpiece, or the Wonderful One-Hoss Shay" is the most popular of the humorous poems.   Many **Humorous Poems** readers enjoy this excellent skit without thinking what the author meant by calling it "a logical story."   It is, in fact, the best pebble that he hurled from his sling against his *bête noire*; for the old "shay" which went to pieces all at once was a symbol of Calvinistic theology. That theology was called an iron chain of logic, every link so perfectly forged that it could not be broken at any point. Even so was the "shay" built, unbreakable in every single part; but when the deacon finds himself sprawling and dumfounded in the road beside the wrecked masterpiece the poet concludes :

> End of the wonderful one-hoss shay.
> Logic is logic. That's all I say.

Other typical verses of the same kind are "The Height of the Ridiculous," "Daily Trials," "The Comet" and "Contentment."   In the last-named poem Holmes may have been poking fun at the Brook Farmers and other enthusiasts who

---

[1] It may add a bit of interest to these poems if we remember that among the members of the Class of '29 was Samuel Smith, author of "America," a poem that now appeals to a larger audience than the class poet ever dreamed of.

were preaching the simple life. Poets and preachers of this gospel in every age are apt to insist that to find simplicity one must return to nature or the farm, or else camp in the woods and eat huckleberries, as Thoreau did; but Holmes remembered that some people must live in the city, while others incomprehensibly prefer to do so, and wrote his " Contentment " to express their idea of the simple life:

> Little I ask; my wants are few;
>   I only wish a hut of stone
> (A *very plain* brown stone will do)
>   That I may call my own;
> And close at hand is such a one,
> In yonder street that fronts the sun.
>
> I care not much for gold or land;
>   Give me a mortgage here and there,
> Some good bank-stock, some note of hand,
>   Or trifling railroad share.
> I only ask that Fortune send
> A *little* more than I shall spend.

The most readable of the prose works is *The Autocrat of the Breakfast Table* (1858), a series of monologues in which Holmes, who was called the best talker of his age, transferred his talk in a very charming way to paper. As the book professes to record the conversation at the table of a certain Boston boarding-house, it has no particular subject; the author rambles pleasantly from one topic to another, illuminating each by his wisdom or humor or sympathy. Other books of the same series are *The Professor at the Breakfast Table, The Poet at the Breakfast Table* and *Over the Teacups*. Most critics consider *The Autocrat* the best and *The Poet* second best of the series; but there is a tender vein of sentiment and reminiscence in the final volume which is very attractive to older readers.

The slight story element in the breakfast-table books probably led Holmes to fiction, and he straightway produced three novels, *Elsie Venner*, *The Guardian Angel* and *A Mortal Antipathy*. These are studies of heredity, of the physical element in morals, of the influence of mind over matter and other subjects more suitable for essays than for fiction; but a few mature readers who care less for a story than for an observation or theory of life will find *The Guardian Angel* an interesting novel. And some will surely prize *Elsie*

OLD COLONIAL DOORWAY
Holmes's birthplace, at Cambridge

Venner for its pictures of New England life, its description of boarding school or evening party or social hierarchy, at a time when many a New England family had traditions to which it held as firmly and almost as proudly as any European court.

The Quality of Holmes. The intensely personal quality of the works just mentioned is their most striking characteristic; for Holmes always looks at a subject with his own eyes, and measures its effect on the reader by a previous effect produced upon himself. " If I like this," he says in substance, "why, you must like it too; if it strikes me as absurd, you cannot take any other attitude; for are we not both human and therefore just alike?" It never occurred to Holmes that anybody could differ with him and still be normal; those who ventured to do so found the Doctor looking keenly at them to discover their symptoms. In an ordinary egoist or politician or theologian this would be insufferable;

but strange to say it is one of the charms of Holmes, who is so witty and pleasant-spoken that we can enjoy his dogmatism without the bother of objecting to it. In one of his books he hints that talking to certain persons is like trying to pet a squirrel; if you are wise, you will not imitate that frisky little beast but assume the purring-kitten attitude while listening to the Autocrat.

Another interesting quality of Holmes is what we may call his rationalism, his habit of taking nothing for granted, of **First-Hand** judging every matter by observation rather than **Impressions** by tradition or sentiment or imagination; and herein he is in marked contrast with Longfellow and other romantic writers of the period. We shall enjoy him better if we remember his bent of mind. As a boy he was fond of tools and machinery; as a man he was interested in photography, safety razors, inventions of every kind; as a physician he rebelled against drugs (then believed to have almost magical powers, and imposed on suffering stomachs in horrible doses) and observed his patients closely to discover what mentally ailed them; and as boy or man or physician he cared very little for books but a great deal for his own observation of life. Hence there is always a surprise in reading Holmes, which comes partly from his flashes of wit but more largely from his independent way of looking at things and recording his first-hand impressions. His *Autocrat* especially is a treasure and ranks with Thoreau's *Walden* among the most original books of American literature.

SIDNEY LANIER (1842–1881)

The name of Lanier is often associated with that of Timrod, and the two southern poets were outwardly alike in that they struggled against physical illness and mental depression; but where we see in Timrod the tragedy of a poet broken by pain and neglect, the tragedy of Lanier's life is forgotten in our wonder at his triumph. It is doubtful if any other poet ever raised so pure a song of joy out of conditions that might well have occasioned a wail of despair.

The joyous song of Lanier is appreciated only by the few. He is not popular with either readers or critics, and the difficulty of assigning him a place or rank may be judged from recent attempts. One history of American literature barely mentions Lanier in a slighting reference to " a small cult of poetry in parts of America " ;[1] another calls him the only southern poet who had a national horizon, and accords his work ample criticism ;[2] a third describes him as " a true artist " having " a lyric power hardly to be found in any other American," but the brief record ends with the cutting criticism that his work is " hardly national." [3] And so with all other histories, one dismisses him as the author

SIDNEY LANIER

of a vague rhapsody called " The Marshes of Glynn," another exalts him as a poet who rivals Poe in melody and far surpasses him in thought or feeling. Evidently there is no settled criticism of Lanier, as of Bryant or Longfellow; he is not yet secure in his position among the elder poets, and what we record here is such a personal appreciation as any reader may formulate for himself.

[1] Trent, *History of American Literature* (1913), p. 471.
[2] Moses, *Literature of the South* (1910), pp. 358–383.
[3] Wendell, *Literary History of America* (1911), pp. 495–498.

Life. America has had its Puritan and its Cavalier writers, but seldom one who combines the Puritan's stern devotion to duty with the Cavalier's joy in nature and romance and music. Lanier was such a poet, and he owed his rare quality to a mixed ancestry. He was descended on his mother's side from Scotch-Irish and Puritan forbears, and on his father's side from Huguenot (French) exiles who were musicians at the English court. One of his ancestors, Nicholas Lanier, is described as "a musician, painter and engraver" for Queen Elizabeth and King James, and as the composer of music for some of Ben Jonson's masques.

His boyhood was spent at Macon, Georgia, where he was born in 1842. A study of that boyhood reveals certain characteristics which **Early Traits** reappear constantly in the poet's work. One was his rare purity of soul; another was his brave spirit; a third was his delight in nature; a fourth was his passion for music. At seven he made his first flute from a reed, and ever afterwards, though he learned to play many instruments, the flute was to him as a companion and a voice. With it he cheered many a weary march or hungry bivouac; through it he told all his heart to the woman he loved; by it he won a place when he had no other means of earning his bread. Hence in "The Symphony," a poem which fronts one of life's hard problems, it is the flute that utters the clearest and sweetest note.

Lanier had finished his course in Oglethorpe University (a primitive little college in Midway, Georgia) and was tutoring there when **In War Time** the war came, and the college closed its doors because teachers and students were away at the first call to join the army. For four years he was a Confederate soldier, serving in the ranks with his brother and refusing the promotion offered him for gallant conduct in the field. There was a time during this period when he might have sung like the minstrels of old, for romance had come to him with the war. By day he was fighting or scouting with his life in his hand; but when camp fires were lighted he would take his flute and slip away to serenade the girl who "waited for him till the war was over."

We mention these small incidents with a purpose. There is a delicacy of feeling in Lanier's verse which might lead a reader to assume that the poet was effeminate, when in truth he was as manly as any Norse scald or Saxon scop who ever stood beside his chief in battle. Of the war he never sang; but we find some reflection of the girl who waited in the poem "My Springs."

Lanier was at sea, as signal officer on a blockade runner, when his ship was captured by a Federal cruiser and he was sent to the mili-**War's** tary prison at Point Lookout (1864). A hard and bitter **Aftermath** experience it was, and his only comfort was the flute which he had hidden in his ragged sleeve. When released the following year he set out on foot for his home, five hundred miles away, and reached it more dead than alive; for consumption had laid a heavy hand upon him. For weeks he was desperately ill, and during the illness his mother died of the same wasting disease; then he rose and set out bravely to earn a living, — no easy matter in a place that had suffered as Georgia had during the war.

We shall not enter into his struggle for bread, or into his wanderings in search of a place where he could breathe without pain. He **The Gleam** was a law clerk in his father's office at Macon when, knowing that he had but a slender lease of life, he made his resolve. To the remonstrances of his father he closed his ears, saying that music and poetry were calling him and he must follow the call. The superb climax of Tennyson's " Merlin and the Gleam " was in his soul:

> O young mariner,
> Down to the haven
> Call your companions,
> Launch your vessel
> And crowd your canvas,
> And, ere it vanishes
> Over the margin,
> After it, follow it,
> Follow the Gleam!

Thus bravely he went northward to Baltimore, taking his flute with him. He was evidently a wonderful artist, playing not by the score but making his instrument his voice, so that his audience seemed to hear a soul speaking in melody. His was a magic flute. Soon he was supporting himself by playing in the Peabody Orchestra, living joyously meanwhile in an atmosphere of music and poetry and books; for he was always a student, determined to understand as well as to practice his art. He wrote poems, stories, anything to earn an honest dollar; he gave lectures on music and literature; he planned a score of books that he did not and could not write, for he was living in a fever of mind and body. Music and poetry were surging within him for expression; but his strength was failing, his time short.

In 1879 he was appointed lecturer at Johns Hopkins University, and for the first time he had an assured income, small, indeed, but **The Struggle** very heartening since it was enough to support his family. He began teaching with immense enthusiasm; but presently he was speaking in a whisper from an invalid's chair. Under such circumstances were uttered some of our most cheering words on art and poetry. Two years later he died in a tent among the hills, near Asheville, North Carolina, whither he had gone in a vain search for health.

THE VILLAGE OF McGAHEYSVILLE, VIRGINIA

Near here Lanier spent his summers during the last years of his life

There is in all Lanier's verse a fragmentariness, a sense of something left unsaid, which we may understand better if we remember that his heart was filled with the noblest emotions, but that when he strove to write them his pen failed for weariness. Read the daily miracle of dawn in " Sunrise," for example, and find there the waiting oaks, the stars, the tide, the marsh with its dreaming pools, light, color, fragrance, melody, — everything except that the hand which wrote the poem was too weak to guide the pencil. The rush of impressions and memories in " Sunrise," its tender beauty and vague incompleteness, as of something left unsaid, may be explained by the fact that it was Lanier's last song.

Works of Lanier. Many readers have grown familiar with Lanier's name in connection with *The Boy's Froissart, The Boy's King Arthur, The Boy's Mabinogion* and *The Boy's Percy*, four books in which he retold in simple language some of the old tales that are forever young. His chief prose works, *The English Novel* and *The Science of English Verse*, are of interest chiefly to critics; they need not detain us here except to note that the latter volume is devoted to Lanier's pet theory that music and poetry are governed by the same laws. Of more general interest are his scattered "Notes," which contain suggestions for many a poem that was never written, intermingled with condensed criticisms. Of the poet Swinburne he says, "He invited me to eat; the service was silver and gold, but no food therein except salt and pepper." One might say less than that with more words, or read a whole book to arrive at this summary of Whitman's style and bottomless philosophy: "Whitman is poetry's butcher; huge raw collops slashed from the rump of poetry, and never mind the gristle, is what he feeds our souls with. . . . His argument seems to be that because the Mississippi is long, therefore every American is a god."

Those who read Lanier's poems should begin with the simplest, with his love songs, "My Springs" and "In Ab-

His Best Poems   sence," or his "Ballad of Trees and the Master," or his outdoor poems, such as "Tampa Robins," "Song of the Chattahoochee," "Mocking Bird," and "Evening Song." In the last-named lyrics he began the work (carried out more fully in his later poems) of interpreting in words the harmony which his sensitive ear detected in the manifold voices of nature.

Next in order are the poems in which is hidden a thought or an ideal not to be detected at first glance; for to Lanier poetry was like certain oriental idols which when opened are found to be filled with exquisite perfumes. "The Stirrup Cup" is one of the simplest of these allegories. It was a custom in olden days when a man was ready to journey, for one who loved him to bring a glass of wine which he drank in the saddle; and this was called the stirrup or parting cup. In the cup offered Lanier was a rare cordial, filled with "sweet herbs from all antiquity," and the name of the cordial was Death:

> Then, Time, let not a drop be spilt:
> Hand me the cup whene'er thou wilt;
> 'T is thy rich stirrup cup to me;
> I 'll drink it down right smilingly.

In four stanzas of "Night and Day" he compresses the tragedy of *Othello*, not the tragedy that Shakespeare wrote but the tragedy that was in the Moor's soul when Desdemona was gone. In "Life and Song" he sought to express the ideal of a poet, and the closing lines might well be the measure of his own heroic life:

> His song was only living aloud,
> His work a singing with his hand.

In "How Love Looked for Hell" the lesson is hidden deeper; for the profound yet simple meaning of the poem is that, search high or low, Love can never find hell because he takes heaven with him wherever he goes. Another poem of the same class, but longer and more involved, is "The Symphony." Here Lanier faces one of the greatest problems of the age, the problem of industrialism with its false standards and waste of human happiness, and his answer is the same that Tennyson gave in his later poems; namely, that the familiar love in human hearts can settle every social question when left to its own unselfish way:

> Vainly might Plato's brain revolve it,
> Plainly the heart of a child might solve it.

The longer poems of Lanier are of uneven merit and are all more or less fragmentary. The chief impression from reading the "Psalm of the West," for example, is that it is the prelude to some greater work that was left unfinished. More finely wrought and more typical of Lanier's mood and **Marshes of Glynn** method is "The Marshes of Glynn," his best-known work. It is a marvelous poem, one of the most haunting in our language; yet it is like certain symphonies in that it says nothing, being all feeling, — vague, inexpressible feeling. Some readers find no meaning or satisfaction in it; others hail it as a perfect interpretation of their own mood or emotion when they stand speechless before the sunrise or the afterglow or a landscape upon which the very spirit of beauty and peace is brooding.

The Quality of Lanier. In order to sympathize with Lanier, and so to understand him, it is necessary to keep in mind that he was a musician rather than a poet in our ordinary understanding of the term. In his verse he used words, exactly as he used the tones of his flute, not so much to express ideas as to call up certain emotions that find no voice save in music. As he said, "Music takes up the thread that language drops," which explains that beautiful but puzzling line which closes "The Symphony":

> Music is Love in search of a word.

We have spoken of "The Symphony" as an answer to the problem of industrial waste and sorrow, but it contains also **Music and Poetry** Lanier's confession of faith; namely, that social evils arise among men because of their lack of harmony; and that spiritual harmony, the concord of souls which makes strife impossible, may be attained through music. The same belief appears in *Tiger Lilies* (a novel written by Lanier in his early days), in which a certain character makes these professions:

"To make a *home* out of a household, given the raw materials—to wit, wife, children, a friend or two and a house — two other things are necessary. These are a good fire and good music. And inasmuch as we can do without the fire for half the year, I may say music is the one essential."

" Late explorers say they have found some nations that have no God; but I have not read of any that had no music." " Music means harmony, harmony means love, love means — God ! "

One may therefore summarize Lanier by saying that he was a poet who used verbal rhythm, as a musician uses harmonious chords, to play upon our better feelings. His poems of nature give us no definite picture of the external world but are filled with murmurings, tremblings, undertones, — all the vague impressions which one receives when alone in the solitudes, as if the world were alive but inarticulate:

Ye marshes, how candid and simple and nothing-withholding and free
Ye publish yourselves to the sky and offer yourselves to the sea!
Tolerant plains, that suffer the sea and the rains and the sun,
Ye spread and span like the catholic man that hath mightily won
God out of knowledge and good out of infinite pain
And sight out of blindness and purity out of a stain.

His poems of life have similar virtues and weaknesses: they are melodious; they are nobly inspired; they appeal to our finest feelings; but they are always vague in that they record no definite thought and speak no downright message.

The criticism may be more clear if we compare Lanier with Whittier, a man equally noble, who speaks a language that all
Lanier and men understand. The poems of the two supplement
Whittier each other, one reflecting the reality of life, the other its mysterious dreams. In Whittier's poetry we look upon a landscape and a people, and we say, " I have seen that rugged landscape with my own eyes; I have eaten bread with those people, and have understood and loved them." Then we read Lanier's poetry and say, " Yes, I have had those feelings at times; but I do not speak of them to others because I cannot tell what they mean to me." Both poets are good, and both fail of greatness in poetry, Whittier because he has no exalted imagination, Lanier because he lacks primitive simplicity and strength. One poet sings a song to cheer the day's labor, the other makes a melody to accompany our twilight reveries.

"WALT" WHITMAN (1819–1892)

Since Whitman insisted upon being called "Walt" instead of Walter, so let it be. The name accords with the free-and-easy style of his verse. If you can find some abridged selections from that verse, read them by all means; but if you

WALT WHITMAN

must search the whole of it for the passages that are worth reading, then pass it cheerfully by; for such another vain display of egotism, vulgarity and rant never appeared under the name of poetry. Whitman was so absurdly fond of his "chants" and so ignorant of poetry that he preserved the whole of his work in a final edition, and his publishers still insist upon printing it, rubbish and all. The result is that the few rare verses which stamp him as a poet are apt to be over-looked in the multitudinous gabblings which, of themselves, might mark him as a mere freak or "sensation" in our modest literature.

Biographical Sketch. Ordinarily when we read poetry we desire to know something of the man who wrote it, of his youth, his training, the circumstance of his work and the personal ideals which made him view life steadily in one light rather than in another. In dealing with Whitman it is advisable to leave such natural curiosity unsatisfied, and for two reasons: first, the man was far from admirable or upright, and to meet him at certain stages is to lose all desire to read his poetry; and second, he was so extremely secretive about himself, while professing boundless good-fellowship with all men, that we can seldom trust his own record, much less that of his admirers. There are great blanks in the story of his life; his real biography has not yet been written; and in the jungle of controversial writings which has grown up around him one loses sight of Whitman in a maze of extravagant or contradictory opinions.[1]

Let it suffice then to record, in catalogue fashion, that Whitman was born (1819) on Long Island, of stubborn farmer stock; that he **Traits and** spent his earliest years by the sea, which inspired his **Incidents** best verse; that he grew up in the streets of Brooklyn and was always fascinated by the restless tide of city life, as reflected in such poems as "Crossing Brooklyn Ferry"; that his education was scanty and of the "picked up" variety; that to the end of his life, though ignorant of what literary men regard as the *a-b-c* of knowledge, he was supremely well satisfied with himself; that till he was past forty he worked irregularly at odd jobs, but was by choice a loafer; that he was a man of superb physical health and gloried in his body, without much regard for moral standards; that his strength was broken by nursing wounded soldiers during the war, a beautiful and unselfish service; that he was then a government clerk in Washington until partly disabled by a paralytic stroke, and that the remainder of his life was spent at Camden, New Jersey. His *Leaves of Grass* (published first in 1855, and republished with additions many times) brought him very little return in money, and his last years were spent in a state of semipoverty, relieved by the gifts of a small circle of admirers.

Whitman's Verse. In a single book, *Leaves of Grass*, Whitman has collected all his verse. This book would be a chaos even had he left his works in the order in which they were written; but that is precisely what he did not do. Instead, he enlarged and rearranged the work ten different times, mixing up his worst and his best verses, so that it is now

[1] Of the many biographies of Whitman perhaps the best for beginners is Perry's *Walt Whitman* (1906), in American Men of Letters Series.

very difficult to trace his development as a poet. We may, however, tentatively arrange his work in three divisions : his early shouting to attract attention (as summarized in the line " I sound my barbaric yawp over the roofs of the world "), his war poems, and his later verse written after he had learned something of the discipline of life and poetry.

The quality of his early work may be judged from a few disjointed lines of his characteristic " Song of Myself ":

Has any one supposed it lucky to be born?
I hasten to inform him or her that it is just as lucky to die, and I know it.

I pass death with the dying and birth with the new-wash'd babe, and am
    not contain'd between my hat and boots,
And peruse manifold objects, no two alike, and every one good,
The earth good and the stars good, and their adjuncts all good.

The big doors of the country barn stand open and ready,
The dried grass of the harvest-time loads the slow-drawn wagon,
The clear light plays on the brown, gray and green intertinged,
The armfuls are pack'd to the sagging mow.
I am there, I help, I came stretch'd atop of the load,
I felt its soft jolts, one leg reclined on the other,
I jump from the cross-beams and seize the clover and timothy,
And roll head over heels and tangle my hair full of wisps.

The boatmen and clam-diggers arose early and stopt for me,
I tuck'd my trowser ends in my boots and went and had a good time;
You should have been with us that day round the chowder-kettle.

Thus he rambles on, gabbing of every place or occupation or newspaper report that comes into his head. When he ends this grotesque " Song of Myself " after a thousand lines or more, he makes another just like it. We read a few words here and there, amazed that any publisher should print such rubbish ; and then, when we are weary of Whitman's conceit or bad taste, comes a flash of insight, of imagination, of poetry :

Afoot and light-hearted I take to the open road,
Healthy, free, the world before me,
The long brown path before me leading wherever I choose.

These yearnings why are they? these thoughts in the darkness why
    are they?
Why are there men and women that while they are nigh me the sunlight
    expands my blood?
Why when they leave me do my pennants of joy sink flat and lank?
Why are there trees I never walk under but large and melodious thoughts
    descend upon me?

There are, in short, hundreds of pages of such "chanting"
with its grain of wheat hid in a bushel of chaff. We refer
to it here not because it is worth reading but to record the
curious fact that many European critics hail it as typical
American poetry, even while we wonder why anybody should
regard it as either American or poetic.

The explanation is simple. Europeans have not yet rid
themselves of the idea that America is the strange, wild land
Foreign of Cooper's *Pioneers*, and that any poetry produced
Opinion here must naturally be uncouth, misshapen, defiant
of all poetic laws or traditions. To such critics Whitman's
crudity seems typical of a country where one is in nightly
danger of losing his scalp, where arguments are settled by
revolvers, and where a hungry man needs only to shoot a
buffalo or a bear from his back door. Meanwhile America,
the country that planted colleges and churches in a wilderness,
that loves liberty because she honors law, that never saw a
knight in armor but that has, even in her plainsmen and
lumberjacks, a chivalry for woman that would adorn a Bayard,
— that real America ignores the bulk of Whitman's work
simply because she knows that, of all her poets, he is the
least representative of her culture, her ideals, her heroic and
aspiring life.

The second division of Whitman's work is made up chiefly
of verses written in war time, to some of which he gave the
significant title, *Drum Taps*. In such poems as
Drum Taps "Beat, Beat, Drums," "Cavalry Crossing a Ford"
and "By the Bivouac's Fitful Flame" he reflected the emotional excitement of '61 and the stern days that followed.

Note, for example, the startling vigor of " Ethiopia Saluting the Colors," which depicts an old negro woman by the road-side, looking with wonder on the free flag which she sees for the first time aloft over marching men :

> Who are you, dusky woman, so ancient, hardly human,
> With your woolly-white and turban'd head and bare bony feet?
> Why, rising by the roadside here, do you the colors greet?

Another side of the war is reflected in such poems as " Come up from the Fields, Father," an exquisite picture of an old mother and father receiving the news of their son's death on the battlefield. In the same class belong two fine tributes, " O Captain, My Captain " and " When Lilacs Last in the Dooryard Bloomed," written in moments of noble emotion when the news came that Lincoln was dead. The former tribute, with its rhythmic swing and lyric refrain, indicates what Whitman might have done in poetry had he been a more patient workman. So also does " Pioneers," a lyric that is wholly American and Western and exultant :

> Have the elder races halted?
> Do they droop and end their lesson, wearied over there beyond the seas?
> We take up the task eternal, and the burden and the lesson,
> Pioneers! O Pioneers!

In the third class of Whitman's works are the poems written late in life, when he had learned to suppress his **Later Poems** blatant egotism and to pay some little attention to poetic form and melody. Though his lines are still crude and irregular, many of them move to a powerful rhythm, such as the impressive " With Husky-Haughty Lips, O Sea," which suggests the surge and beat of breakers on the shore. In others he gives finely imaginative expression to an ideal or a yearning, and his verse rises to high poetic levels. Note this allegory of the spider, an insect that, when adrift or in a strange place, sends out delicate filaments on the air currents until one thread takes hold of some solid substance and is used as a bridge over the unknown :

A noiseless patient spider,
I mark'd where on a little promontory it stood isolated,
Mark'd how to explore the vacant vast surrounding
It launch'd forth filament, filament, filament out of itself,
Ever unreeling them, ever tirelessly speeding them.

And you, O my soul, where you stand,
Surrounded, detached, in measureless oceans of space,
Ceaselessly musing, venturing, throwing, seeking the spheres to
    connect them,
Till the bridge you will need be form'd, till the ductile anchor hold,
Till the gossamer thread you fling catch somewhere, O my soul.

WHITMAN'S BIRTHPLACE, WEST HILLS, LONG ISLAND

Among the best of Whitman's works are his poems on
death. "Joy, Shipmate, Joy," "Death's Valley," "Darest
Thou Now, O Soul," "Last Invocation," "Good-Bye, My
Fancy," — in such haunting lyrics he reflects the natural view
of death, not as a terrible or tragic or final event but as a
confident going forth to meet new experiences. Other notable poems that well repay the reading are "The Mystic
Trumpeter," "The Man-of-War Bird," "The Ox Tamer,"
"Thanks in Old Age" and "Aboard at a Ship's Helm."

In naming the above works our purpose is simply to lure
the reader away from the insufferable Whitmanesque "chant"

and to attract attention to a few poems that sound a new note in literature, a note of freedom, of joy, of superb confidence, which warms the heart when we hear it. When these poems are known others will suggest themselves : " Rise, O Days, from Your Fathomless Deeps," " I Hear America Singing," " There was a Boy Went Forth," " The Road Unknown," " Out of the Cradle Endlessly Rocking." There is magic in such names ; but unfortunately in most cases the reader will find only an alluring title and a few scattered lines of poetry ; the rest is Whitman.

The author of the " Song of Myself " proclaimed himself the poet of democracy and wrote many verses on his alleged

Democracy subject ; but those who read them will soon tire of one whose idea of democracy was that any man is as good, as wise, as godlike as any other. Perhaps his best work in this field is " Thou Mother with Thy Equal Brood," a patriotic poem read at " Commencement" time in Dartmouth College (1872). There is too much of vainglorious boasting in the poem (for America should be modest, and can afford to be modest), but it has enough of prophetic vision and exalted imagination to make us overlook its unworthy spread-eagleism.

As a farewell to Whitman one should read what is perhaps his noblest single work, " The Prayer of Columbus." The

Prayer of Columbus poem is supposed to reflect the thought of Columbus when, as a worn-out voyager, an old man on his last expedition, he looked out over his wrecked ships to the lonely sea beyond ; but the reader may see in it another picture, that of a broken old man in his solitary house at Camden, writing with a trembling hand the lines which reflect his unshaken confidence :

> My terminus near,
> The clouds already closing in upon me,
> The voyage balk'd, the course disputed, lost,
> I yield my ships to Thee.

My hands, my limbs grow nerveless,
My brain feels rack'd, bewilder'd;
Let the old timbers part, I will not part,
I will cling fast to Thee, O God, though the waves buffet me,
Thee, Thee at least I know.

Is it the prophet's thought I speak, or am I raving?
What do I know of life? what of myself?
I know not even my own work past or present;
Dim ever-shifting guesses of it spread before me,
Of newer better worlds, their mighty parturition,
Mocking, perplexing me.

And these things I see suddenly, what mean they?
As if some miracle, some hand divine, unseal'd my eyes,
Shadowy vast shapes smile through the air and sky,
And on the distant waves sail countless ships,
And anthems in new tongues I hear saluting me.

THE PROSE WRITERS

RALPH WALDO EMERSON (1803–1882)

Emerson is the mountaineer of our literature; to read him
is to have the impression of being on the heights. It is
solitary there, far removed from ordinary affairs; but the air
is keen, the outlook grand, the heavens near. Our companions are the familiar earth by day or the mysterious stars
by night, and these are good if only to recall the silent
splendor of God's universe amid the pother of human inventions. There also the very spirit of liberty, which seems to
have its dwelling among the hills, enters into us and makes
us sympathize with Emerson's message of individual freedom.

It is still a question whether Emerson should be classed
with the poets or prose writers, and our only reason for
placing him with the latter is that his "Nature" seems more
typical than his "Woodnotes," though in truth both works
convey precisely the same message. He was a great man

who used prose or verse as suited his mood at the moment; but he was never a great poet, and only on rare occasions was he a great prose writer.

Life. Emerson has been called "the wingéd Franklin," "the Yankee Shelley" and other contradictory names which strive to express the union of shrewd sense and lofty idealism that led him

to write "Hitch your wagon to a star" and many another aphorism intended to bring heaven and earth close together. We shall indicate enough of his inheritance if we call him a Puritan of the Puritans, a moralist descended from seven generations of heroic ministers who had helped to make America a free nation, and who had practiced the love of God and man and country before preaching it to their congregations.

The quality of these ancestors entered into Emerson and gave him the granite steadfastness that is one of his marked characteristics. Meeting him in his serene old age one

RALPH WALDO EMERSON

would hardly suspect him of heroism; but to meet him in childhood is to understand the kind of man he was, and must be. If you would appreciate the quality of that childhood, picture to yourself a bare house with an open fire and plenty of books, but little else of comfort. There are a mother and six children in the house, desperately poor; for the father is dead and has left his family nothing and everything, — nothing that makes life rich, everything in the way of ideals and blessed memories to make life wealthy. The mother works as only a poor woman can from morning till night. The children go to school by day; but instead of playing after school-hours they run errands

for the neighbors, drive cows from pasture, shovel snow, pick huckleberries, earn an honest penny. In the evening they read together
before the open fire. When they are hungry, as they often are, a
Puritan aunt who shares their poverty tells them stories of human
endurance. The circle narrows when an older brother goes to college;
the rest reduce their meals and spare their pennies in order to help
him. After graduation he teaches school and devotes his earnings to
giving the next brother his chance. All the while they speak courteously to each other, remember their father's teaching that they are
children of God, and view their hard life steadily in the light of that
sublime doctrine.

The rest of the story is easily told. Emerson was born in Boston,
then a straggling town, in 1803. When his turn came he went to
The College Harvard, and largely supported himself there by such
Boy odd jobs as only a poor student knows how to find.
Wasted time he called it; for he took little interest in college discipline or college fun and was given to haphazard reading, "sinfully
strolling from book to book, from care to idleness," as he said. Later
he declared that the only good thing he found in Harvard was a
solitary chamber.

After leaving college he taught school and shared his earnings,
according to family tradition. Then he began to study for the
The ministry; or perhaps we should say "read," for Emerson
Preacher never really studied anything. At twenty-three he was
licensed to preach, and three years later was chosen pastor of the
Second Church in Boston. It was the famous Old North Church in
which the Mathers had preached, and the Puritan divines must
have turned in their graves when the young radical began to utter
his heresies from the ancient pulpit. He was loved and trusted by
his congregation, but presently he differed with them in the matter
of the ritual and resigned his ministry.

Next he traveled in Europe, where he found as little of value as
he had previously found in college. The old institutions, which roused
the romantic enthusiasm of Irving and Longfellow, were to him only
relics of barbarism. He went to Europe, he said, to see two men,
and he found them in Wordsworth and Carlyle. His friendship with
the latter and the letters which passed between "the sage of Chelsea"
and "the sage of Concord" (as collected and published by Charles
Eliot Norton in his *Correspondence of Carlyle and Emerson*) are the
most interesting result of his pilgrimage.

On his return he settled in the village of Concord, which was to be his home for the remainder of his long life. He began to lecture, **The Lecturer** and so well was the " Lyceum " established at that time that he was soon known throughout the country. For forty years this lecturing continued, and the strange thing about it is that in all that time he hardly met one audience that understood him or that carried away any definite idea of what he had talked about. Something noble in the man seemed to attract people; as Lowell said, they did not go to hear what Emerson said but to hear Emerson.

Meanwhile he was writing prose and poetry. His literary work began in college and consisted largely in recording such thoughts **The Writer** or quotations as seemed worthy of preservation. In his private *Journal* (now published in several volumes) may be found practically everything he put into the formal works which he sent forth from Concord. These had at first a very small circle of readers; but the circle widened steadily, and the phenomenon is more remarkable in view of the fact that the author avoided publicity and had no ambition for success. He lived contentedly in a country village; he cultivated his garden and his neighbors; he spent long hours alone with nature; he wrote the thoughts that came to him and sent them to make their own way in the world, while he himself remained, as he said, " far from fame behind the birch trees."

The last years of his life were as the twilight of a perfect day. His mental powers failed slowly; he seemed to drift out of the present world into another of pure memories; even his friends became spiritualized, lost the appearance of earth and assumed their eternal semblance. When he stood beside the coffin of Longfellow, looking intently into the poet's face, he was heard to murmur, " A sweet, a gracious personality, but I have forgotten his name." To the inevitable changes (the last came in 1882) he adapted himself with the same serenity which marked his whole life. He even smiled as he read the closing lines of his " Terminus " :

> As the bird trims her to the gale,
> I trim myself to the storm of time,
> I man the rudder, reef the sail,
> Obey the voice at eve obeyed at prime:
> " Lowly faithful, banish fear,
> Right onward drive unharmed;
> The port, well worth the cruise, is near,
> And every wave is charmed."

Emerson's Poetry. There is a ruggedness in Emerson's verse which attracts some readers while it repels others by its unmelodious rhythm. It may help us to measure that verse if we recall the author's criticism thereof. In 1839 he wrote:

" I am naturally keenly susceptible to the pleasures of rhythm, and cannot believe but one day I shall attain to that splendid dialect, so ardent is my wish; and these wishes, I suppose, are ever only the buds of power; but up to this hour I have never had a true success in such attempts."

One must be lenient with a poet who confesses that he cannot attain the " splendid dialect," especially so since we are inclined to agree with him. In the following passage from " Each and All" we may discover the reason for his lack of success:

> Little thinks, in the field, yon red-cloaked clown
> Of thee from the hill-top looking down;
> The heifer that lows in the upland farm,
> Far-heard, lows not thine ear to charm;
> The sexton, tolling his bell at noon,
> Deems not that great Napoleon
> Stops his horse, and lists with delight,
> Whilst his files sweep round yon Alpine height;
> Nor knowest thou what argument
> Thy life to thy neighbor's creed has lent.
> All are needed by each one;
> Nothing is fair or good alone.
> I thought the sparrow's note from heaven,
> Singing at dawn on the alder bough;
> I brought him home in his nest at even;
> He sings the song, but it cheers not now,
> For I did not bring home the river and sky:
> He sang to my ear; they sang to my eye.
> The delicate shells lay on the shore;
> The bubbles of the latest wave
> Fresh pearls to their enamel gave,
> And the bellowing of the savage sea
> Greeted their safe escape to me.
> I wiped away the weeds and foam,
> I fetched my sea-born treasures home;
> But the poor, unsightly, noisome things
> Had left their beauty on the shore
> With the sun and the sand and the wild uproar.

Our first criticism is that the poem contains both fine and faulty lines, and that the total impression is an excellent one. Next, we note that the verse is labored; for Emerson was not a natural singer, like Whittier, and was hampered by his tendency to think too much instead of giving free expression to his emotion.[1] Finally, he is didactic; that is, he is teaching the lesson that you must not judge a thing by itself, as if it had no history or connections, but must consider it in its environment, as a part of its own world.

• As in "Each and All" so in most of his verse Emerson is too much of a teacher or moralist to be a poet. In "The Rhodora," one of his most perfect poems, he proclaims that "Beauty is its own excuse for being"; but straightway he forgets the word and devotes his verse not to beauty but to some ethical lesson. Very rarely does he break away from this unpoetic habit, as when he interrupts the moralizing of his "World Soul" to write a lyric that we welcome for its own sake:

> Spring still makes spring in the mind
>   When sixty years are told;
> Love wakes anew this throbbing heart,
>   And we are never old.
> Over the winter glaciers
>   I see the summer glow,
> And through the wide-piled snowdrift
>   The warm rosebuds below.

The most readable of Emerson's poems are those in which he reflects his impressions of nature, such as "Seashore," **Typical** "The Humble-Bee," "The Snow-Storm," "Days," **Poems** "Fable," "Forbearance," "The Titmouse" and "Woodnotes." In another class are his philosophical poems devoted to transcendental doctrines. The beginner will do well to skip these, since they are more of a puzzle than a

---

[1] Most good poems are characterized by both thought and feeling, and by a perfection of form that indicates artistic workmanship. With Emerson the thought is the main thing; feeling or emotion is subordinate or lacking, and he seldom has the patience to work over his thought until it assumes beautiful or perfect expression.

source of pleasure. In a third class are poems of more personal interest, such as the noble "Threnody," a poem of grief written after the death of Emerson's little boy; "Good-Bye," in which the poet bids farewell to fame as he hies him to the country; "To Ellen," which half reveals his love story; "Written in Rome," which speaks of the society he found in solitude; and the "Concord Hymn," written at the dedication of Battle Monument, with its striking opening lines:

> By the rude bridge that arched the flood,
> Their flag to April's breeze unfurled,
> Here once the embattled farmers stood,
> And fired the shot heard round the world.

Prose Works. Perhaps the most typical of Emerson's prose works is his first book, to which he gave the name *Nature* (1836). In this he records not his impressions of bird or beast or flower, as his neighbor Thoreau was doing in *Walden*, but rather his philosophy of the universe. "Nature always wears the colors of the spirit"; "Every animal function, from the sponge up to Hercules, shall hint or thunder to man the laws of right and wrong, and echo the ten commandments"; "The foundations of man are not in matter but in spirit, and the element of spirit is eternity," — scores of such expressions indicate that Emerson deals with the soul of things, not with their outward appearance. Does a flower appeal to him? Its scientific name and classification are of no consequence; like Wordsworth, he would understand what thought of God the flower speaks. To him nature is a mirror in which the Almighty reflects his thought; again it is a parable, a little story written in trees or hills or stars; frequently it is a living presence, speaking melodiously in winds or waters; and always it is an inspiration to learn wisdom at first hand:

"Our age is retrospective. It builds the sepulchres of the fathers. It writes biographies, histories, criticisms. The foregoing generations beheld God and Nature face to face; we, through their eyes. Why should not we also enjoy an original relation to the universe? Why should not we have a poetry and philosophy of insight, and not of tradition?"

The last quotation might well be an introduction to Emerson's second work, *The American Scholar* (1837), which was a plea for laying aside European models and fronting life as free men in a new world. Holmes called this work "our intellectual Declaration of Independence," and it was followed by a succession of volumes — *Essays, Representative Men, Conduct of Life, Society and Solitude* and several others — all devoted to the same two doctrines of idealism and individuality.

Among these prose works the reader must make his own selection. All are worth reading; none is easy to read; even the best of them is better appreciated in brief instalments, since few can follow Emerson long without wearying. *English Traits* is a keen but kindly criticism of "our cousins" overseas, which an American can read with more pleasure than an Englishman. *Representative Men* is a series of essays on Plato, Shakespeare, Napoleon and other world figures, which may well be read in connection with Carlyle's *Heroes and Hero Worship*, since the two books reflect the same subject from widely different angles. Carlyle was in theory an aristocrat and a force-worshiper, Emerson a democrat and a believer in ideals. One author would relate us to his heroes in the attitude of slave to master, the other in the relation of brothers and equals.

(margin note: Representative Men)

Of the shorter prose works, collected in various volumes of *Essays*, we shall name only a few in two main groups, which we may call the ideal and the practical. In the first group are such typical works as "The Over-Soul," "Compensation," "Spiritual Laws" and "History"; in the latter are "Heroism," "Self-Reliance," "Literary Ethics" (an address to young collegians), "Character" and "Manners."

(margin note: The Essays)

It is difficult to criticize such writings, which have a daring originality of thought and a springlike freshness of expression that set them apart from all other essays ancient or modern. They are the most quotable, the fittest to "point a moral or adorn a tale" that have ever appeared in our literature; but they are also disjointed, oracular, hard to follow; and the explanation is found in the manner of their production. When Emerson projected a new lecture or essay he never thought his subject out or ordered it from beginning to end. That would have been another man's way of doing it. He collected from his notebooks such thoughts as seemed to bear upon his subject, strung them together, and made an end when he had enough. The connection or relation between his thoughts is always frail and often invisible; some compare it with the thread which holds the pearls of a necklace together; others quote with a smile the epigram of Goldwin Smith, who said that he found an Emersonian essay about as coherent as a bag of marbles. And that suggests a fair criticism of all Emerson's prose; namely, that it is a series of expressions excellent in themselves but having so little logical sequence that a paragraph from one essay may be placed at the beginning, middle or end of any other, where it seems to be equally at home.

The Doctrine of Emerson. Since we constantly hear of "idealism" in connection with Emerson, let us understand the word if we can; or rather the fact, for idealism is the most significant quality of humanity. The term will be better understood if we place it beside "materialism," which expresses an opposite view of life. The difference may be summarized in the statement that the idealist is a man of spirit, or idea, in that he trusts the evidence of the soul; while the materialist is a man of flesh, or sense, in that he believes only what is evident to the senses. One judges the world by himself; the other judges himself by the world.

To illustrate our meaning: the materialist, looking outward, sees that the world is made up of force-driven matter, of gas, carbon and mineral; and he says, "Even so am I made up." He studies an object, sees that it has its appointed cycle of growth and decay, and concludes, "Even so do I appear and vanish." To him the world is the only reality, and the world perishes, and man is but a part of the world.

The idealist, looking first within, perceives that self-consciousness is the great fact of life, and that consciousness expresses itself in words or deeds; then he looks outward, and is aware of another Consciousness that expresses itself in the lowly grass or in the stars of heaven. Looking inward he finds that he is governed by ideas of truth, beauty, goodness and duty; looking outward he everywhere finds evidence of truth and beauty and moral law in the world. He sees, moreover, that while his body changes constantly his self remains the same yesterday, to-day and forever; and again his discovery is a guide to the outer world, with its seedtime and harvest, which is but the symbol or garment of a Divine Self that abides without shadow of change in a constantly changing universe. To him the only reality is spirit, and spirit cannot be harmed by fire or flood; neither can it die or be buried, for it is immortal and imperishable.

The Idealist

Such, in simple words, was the idealism of Emerson, an idealism that was born in him and that governed him long before he became involved in transcendentalism, with its scraps of borrowed Hindu philosophy. It gave message or meaning to his first work, *Nature*, and to all the subsequent essays or poems in which he pictured the world as a symbol or visible expression of a spiritual reality. In other words, nature was to Emerson the Book of the Lord, and the chief thing of interest was not the book but the idea that was written therein.

Having read the universe and determined its spiritual quality, Emerson turned his eyes on humanity. Presently he announced that a man's chief glory is his individuality; that he is a free being, different from every other; that his business is to obey his individual genius; that he should, therefore, ignore the Past with its traditions, and learn directly "from the Divine Soul which inspires all men." Having announced that doctrine, he spent the rest of his life in illustrating or enlarging it; and the sum of his teaching was, " Do not follow

The Individualist

me or any other master; follow your own spirit. Never mind
what history says, or philosophy or tradition or the saints and
sages. The same inspiration which led the prophets is yours
for the taking, and you have your work to do as they had
theirs. Revere your own soul; trust your intuition; and
whatever you find in your heart to do, do it without doubt or
fear, though all the world thunder in your ears that you must
do otherwise. As for the voice of authority, 'Let not a man
quit his belief that a popgun is a popgun, though the anointed
and honorable of the earth affirm it to be the crack of doom.'"

Such was Emer-
son's pet doctrine
of individualism. It
appeared with star-
tling vigor in *The
American Scholar*
at a time when our
writers were prone
to imitate English
poetry, German sen-
timentality or some
other imported prod-
uct. It came also

EMERSON'S HOME, CONCORD

with good grace from one whose life was noble, but it had a
weak or dangerous or grotesque side that Emerson over-
looked. Thus, every crank or fanatic or rainbow-chaser is
also an individualist, and most of them believe as strongly as
Emerson in the Over-Soul. The only difference is that they
do not have his sense or integrity or humor to balance their
individualism. While Emerson exalted individual liberty he
seemed to forget that America is a country devoted to "liberty
under law," and that at every period of her history she has
had need to emphasize the law rather than the liberty. Moreover, individualism is a quality that takes care of itself, being
finest in one who is least conscious of his own importance;

and to study any strongly individual character, a Washington or
a Lincoln for example, is to discover that he strove to be true to
his race and traditions as well as to himself. Hence Emerson's
doctrine, to live in the Present and have entire confidence in
yourself, needs to be supplemented by another : to revere the Past
with its immortal heroes, who by their labor and triumph have
established some truths that no sane man will ever question.

There are other interesting qualities of Emerson, his splendid optimism, for instance, which came partly from his spiritual
**A New
World
Writer**
view of the universe and partly from his association
with nature; for the writer who is in daily contact
with sunshine or rain and who trusts his soul's ideals
of truth and beauty has no place for pessimism or despair ; even
in moments of darkness he looks upward and reads his lesson :

> Teach me your mood, O patient stars,
>   Who climb each night the ancient sky,
> Leaving on space no shade, no scars,
>   No trace of age, no fear to die !

Though he was and still is called a visionary, there is a practical quality in his writing which is better than anything you
will find in *Poor Richard's Almanac*. Thus the burden of
Franklin's teaching was the value of time, a lesson which the
sage of Concord illuminates as with celestial light in his poem
" Days," and to which he brings earth's candle in his prose
essay " Work and Days." [1] Indeed, the more one reads Emerson the more is one convinced that he is our typical New
World writer, a rare genius who combines the best qualities
of Franklin and Edwards, having the practical sense of the
one and the spiritual insight of the other.[2] With his idealism

[1] The two works should be read in connection as an interesting example of Emerson's
use of prose and verse to reflect the same idea. Holmes selects the same two works to
illustrate the essential difference between prose and poetry. See Holmes, *Ralph Waldo
Emerson*, p. 310.

[2] In 1830 Channing published an essay, " National Literature," in which he said
that Benjamin Franklin and Jonathan Edwards were the only writers up to that time
who had worthily presented the American mind, with its practical and ideal sides, to
foreign readers.

and individuality, his imagination that soars to heaven but is equally at home on solid earth, his sound judgment to balance his mysticism, his forceful style that runs from epigram to sustained eloquence, his straight-fibered manhood in which criticism finds nothing to pardon or regret, — with all these sterling qualities he is one of the most representative writers that America has ever produced.

NATHANIEL HAWTHORNE (1804–1864)

Some great writers belong to humanity, others to their own land or people. Hawthorne is in the latter class apparently, for ever since Lowell rashly characterized him as "the greatest imaginative genius since Shakespeare" our critics commonly speak of him in superlatives. Meanwhile most European critics (who acclaim such unequal writers as Cooper and Poe, Whitman and Mark Twain) either leave Hawthorne unread or else wonder what Americans find in him to stir their enthusiasm.

The explanation is that Hawthorne's field was so intensely local that only those who are familiar with it can appreciate him. Almost any reader can enjoy Cooper, since he deals with adventurous men whom everybody understands; but Hawthorne deals with the New England Puritan of the seventeenth century, a very peculiar hero, and to enjoy the novelist one must have some personal or historic interest in his subject. Moreover, he alienates many readers by presenting only the darker side of Puritanism. He is a man who never laughs and seldom smiles in his work; he passes over a hundred normal and therefore cheerful homes to pitch upon some gloomy habitation of sin or remorse, and makes that the burden of his tale. In no other romancer do we find genius of such high order at work in so barren a field.

Life. There is an air of reserve about Hawthorne which no biography has ever penetrated. A schoolmate who met him daily once said, "I love Hawthorne; I admire him; but I do not know him. He lives in a mysterious world of thought and imagination which he never permits me to enter." That characterization applies as well to-day as when it was first spoken, almost a century ago. To his family and to a very few friends Hawthorne was evidently a genial man;[1] but from the world and its affairs he always held aloof, wrapped in his mantle of mystery.

A study of his childhood may help us to understand the somber quality of all his work. He was descended from the Puritans who

came to Boston with John Winthrop, and was born in the seaport of Salem, Massachusetts, in 1804. He was only four years old when his father, a sea captain, died in a foreign port; whereupon the mother draped herself in weeds, retired from the sight of neighbors, and for the next forty years made life as funereal as possible. Besides the little boy there were two sisters in the family, and the elder took her meals in her own room, as did the mother. The others went about the darkened house on tiptoe, or peeped out at the world through closed shutters.

NATHANIEL HAWTHORNE

The shadow of that unnatural home was upon Hawthorne to the end of his life; it accounts in part for his shyness, his fear of society, his lack of interest in his own age or nation.

At seventeen Hawthorne went to Bowdoin College, where Longfellow was his classmate and Franklin Pierce (later President of the United States) one of his friends. His college life seems to have been happy, even gay at times; but when he graduated (1825) and his classmates scattered to find work in the world he returned to his Salem home and secluded himself as if he

Seclusion at Salem

---

[1] Intimate but hardly trustworthy pictures of Hawthorne and his family are presented by his son, Julian Hawthorne, in *Nathaniel Hawthorne and his Wife*. A dozen other memoirs have appeared; but Hawthorne did not want his biography written, and there are many unanswered questions in the story of his life.

had no interest in humanity. It was doubtful, he said afterwards, whether a dozen people knew of his existence in as many years.

All the while he was writing, gathering material for his romances or patiently cultivating his fine style. For days he would brood over a subject; then he would compose a story or parable for the magazines. The stamp of originality was on all these works, but they were seldom accepted. When they returned to him, having found no appreciative editor, he was apt to burn them and complain that he was neglected. Studying the man as he reveals himself at this time in his *Note-Books* (published in a garbled edition by the Hawthorne family), one has the impression that he was a shy, sensitive genius, almost morbidly afraid of the world. From a distance he sent out his stories as "feelers"; when these were ignored he shrank into himself more deeply than before.

OLD CUSTOMHOUSE, BOSTON
Where Hawthorne worked

Love brought him out of his retreat, as it has accomplished many another miracle. When he became engaged his immediate thought was to find work, and one of his friends secured a position for him in the Boston customhouse, where he weighed coal until he was replaced by a party spoilsman.[1] There were no civil-service rules in those days. Hoping to secure a home, he invested his savings in Brook Farm, worked there for a time with the reformers, detested them, lost his money and gained the experience which he used later in his *Blithedale Romance.* Then he married, and lived in poverty and great happiness for four years in the "Old Manse" at Concord. Another friend obtained for him political appointment as surveyor of the Salem

[1] Hawthorne profited three times by the spoils system. When his Boston experience was repeated at Salem he took his revenge in the opening chapter of *The Scarlet Letter,* which ridicules those who received political jobs from the other party.

customhouse; again he was replaced by a spoilsman, and again he complained bitterly. The loss proved a blessing, however, since it gave him leisure to write *The Scarlet Letter*, a novel which immediately placed Hawthorne in the front rank of American writers.

He was now before an appreciative world, and in the flush of fine feeling that followed his triumph he wrote *The House of the Seven Gables*, *A Wonder Book* and *The Snow Image*. Literature was calling him most hopefully when, at the very prime of life, he turned his back on fortune. His friend Pierce had been nominated by the Democrats (1852), and he was asked to write the candidate's biography for campaign purposes. It was hardly a worthy task, but he accepted it and did it well. When Pierce was elected he " persuaded " Hawthorne to accept the office of consul at Liverpool. The emoluments, some seven thousand dollars a year, seemed enormous to one who had lived straitly, and in the four years of Pierce's administration our novelist saved a sum which, with the income from his books, placed him above the fear of want. Then he went for a long vacation to Italy, where he collected the material for his *Marble Faun*. But he wrote nothing more of consequence.

Farewell Greatness

The remainder of his life was passed in a pleasant kind of hermitage in Emerson's village of Concord. His habits of solitude and idleness (" cursed habits," he called them) were again upon him; though he began several romances — *Dr. Grimshawe's Secret*, *Septimius Felton*, *The Ancestral Footstep* and *The Dolliver Romance* — he never made an end of them. In his work he was prone to use some symbol of human ambition, and the symbol of his own later years might well have been the unfinished manuscript which lay upon the coffin when his body was laid under the pines in the old Concord burying ground (1864). His friend Longfellow has described the scene in his beautiful poem " Hawthorne."

The Unfinished Story

Short Stories and Sketches. Many young people become familiar with Hawthorne as a teller of bedtime stories long before they meet him in the rôle of famous novelist. In his earlier days he wrote *Grandfather's Chair* (modeled on a similar work by Scott), dealing with Colonial legends, and broadened his field in *Biographical Stories for Children*. Other and better works belonging to the same juvenile class are *A Wonder Book* (1851) and *Tanglewood Tales* (1853), which are modern versions of the classic myths and stories that Greek mothers used to tell their children long ago.

The best of Hawthorne's original stories are collected in *Twice-Told Tales, Mosses from an Old Manse* and *The* **Pictures of** *Snow Image and Other Twice-Told Tales*. As the **the Past** bulk of this work is rather depressing we select a few typical tales, arranging them in three groups. In the first are certain sketches, as Hawthorne called them, which aim not to tell a story but to give an impression of the past. "The Old Manse" (in *Mosses from an Old Manse*) is an excellent introduction to this group. Others in which the author comes out from the gloom to give his humor a glimpse of pale sunshine are "A Rill from the Town Pump," "Main Street," "Little Annie's Ramble," "Sights from a Steeple" and, as suggestive of Hawthorne's solitary outings, "Footprints on the Seashore."

In the second group are numerous allegories and symbolical stories. To understand Hawthorne's method of allegory [1] read **Allegories** "The Snow Image," which is the story of a snowy figure that became warm, living and companionable to some children until it was spoiled by a hard-headed person, without imagination or real sense, who forgot that he was ever a child himself or that there is such a beautiful and precious thing as a child-view of the universe.

In his constant symbolism (that is, in his use of an outward sign or token to represent an idea) Hawthorne reflected a trait that is common to humanity in all ages. Thus, every nation has its concrete symbol, its flag or eagle or lion; a great religion is represented by a cross or a crescent; in art and poetry

---

[1] An allegory is a figure of speech (in rhetoric) or a story (in literature) in which an external object is described in such a way that we apply the description to our own inner experience. Many proverbs, such as "People who live in glass houses should not throw stones," are condensed allegories. So also are fables and parables, such as the fable of the fox and the grapes, or the parable of the lost sheep. Bunyan's famous allegory, *The Pilgrim's Progress*, describes a journey from one city to another, but in reading it we are supposed to think of a Christian's experience in passing through this world to the next.

the sword stands for war and the dove for peace ; an individual has his horseshoe or rabbit's foot or " mascot " as the simple expression of an idea that may be too complex for words. Among primitive people such symbols were associated with charms, magic, baleful or benignant influences ; and Hawthorne accepted this superstitious idea in many of his works, though he was apt to hint, as in " Lady Eleanore's Mantle," that the magic of his symbol might have a practical explanation. In this story the lady's gorgeous mantle is a symbol of pride ; its blighting influence *may* be due to the fact that, — but to tell the secret is to spoil the story, and that is not fair to Hawthorne or the reader.

Some of these symbolic tales are too vague or shadowy to be convincing ; in others the author makes artistic use of some **The Black** simple object, such as a flower or an ornament, to **Veil** suggest the mystery that broods over every life. In " The Minister's Black Veil," for example, a clergyman startles his congregation by appearing with a dark veil over his face. The veil itself is a familiar object ; on a woman or a bonnet it would pass unnoticed ; but on the minister it becomes a portentous thing, at once fascinating and repellent. Yesterday they knew the man as a familiar friend ; to-day he is a stranger, and they fear him with a vague, nameless fear. Forty years he wears the mysterious thing, dies and is buried with it, and in all that time they never have a glimpse of his face. Though there is a deal of nonsense in the story, and a hocus-pocus instead of a mystery, we must remember that veil as a striking symbol of the loneliness of life, of the gulf that separates a human soul from every other.

Another and better symbolic tale is " The Great Stone Face," which appeals strongly to younger readers, especially to those who have lived much out of doors and who cherish the memory of some natural object, some noble tree or mossy cliff or singing brook, that is forever associated with their thoughts of childhood. To others the tale will have added interest in that it is supposed to portray the character of Emerson as Hawthorne knew him.

In the third group are numerous stories dealing with Colonial history, and of these "The Gray Champion" and **Legendary** "The Gentle Boy" are fairly typical. Hawthorne **Tales** has been highly praised in connection with these tales as "the artist who created the Puritan in literature." Most readers will gladly recognize the "artist," since every tale has its line or passage of beauty; but some will murmur at the "creation." The trouble with Hawthorne was that in creating his Puritan he took scant heed of the man whom the Almighty created. He was not a scholar or even a reader; his custom was to brood over an incident of the past (often a grotesque incident, such as he found in Winthrop's old *Journal*), and from his brooding he produced an imaginary character, some heartless fanatic or dismal wretch who had nothing of the Puritan except the label. Of the real Puritan, who knew the joy and courtesy as well as the stern discipline of life, our novelist had only the haziest notion. In consequence his "Gentle Boy" and parts also of his *Scarlet Letter* leave an unwarranted stain on the memory of his ancestors.[1]

The Four Romances. The romances of Hawthorne are all studies of the effects of sin on human development. If but one of these romances is to be read, let it be *The House of the Seven Gables* (1851), which is a pleasanter story than Hawthorne commonly tells, and which portrays one character that he knew by experience rather than by imagination. Many of

---

[1] Occasionally, as in "The Gray Champion" and "Endicott and the Red Cross," Hawthorne paints the stern courage of the Puritan, but never his gentle or humane qualities. His typical tale presents the Puritan in the most unlovely guise. In "The Maypole of Merrymount," for example, Morton and his men are represented as inoffensive, art-loving people who were terrorized by the "dismal wretches" of a near-by colony of Puritans. Nothing could be farther from the truth. Morton's crew were a lawless set and a scandal to New England; but they were tolerated until they put all the settlements in danger by debauching the Indians and selling them rum, muskets and gunpowder. The "dismal wretches" were the Pilgrims of Plymouth,—gentle, heroic men, lovers of learning and liberty, who profoundly influenced the whole subsequent history of America.

Hawthorne's stories run to a text, and the text here is, "The fathers have eaten sour grapes, and the children's teeth are set on edge." The characters are represented as "under a curse";[1] that is, they are bearing the burden and sorrow of some old iniquity committed before they were born; but the affliction is banished in a satisfactory way without leaving us in the haze of mystery that envelops so much of Hawthorne's work. His humor is also in evidence, his interest in life overcomes for a

"THE HOUSE OF SEVEN GABLES," SALEM (BUILT IN 1669)

time his absorption in shadowy symbols, and his whole story is brightened by his evident love of Phœbe Pyncheon, the most natural and winsome of all his characters.

The other romances deal with the same general theme, the blighting effect of sin, but vary greatly in their scenes and characters. The *Marble Faun* (published in England as *Transformation*, 1860) is the most popular, possibly because its scene is laid in Rome, a city to which all travelers go, or aspire to go, before they die; but though it moves in "an atmosphere of art," among the studios of "the eternal city," it is the least

---

[1] This is a reflection of a family tradition. An ancestor of Hawthorne was judge at the Salem witch trials, in 1692. One of the poor creatures condemned to death is said to have left a curse on the judge's family. In his *Note-Books* Hawthorne makes mention of the traditional curse, and analyzes its possible effect on his own character.

artistic of all the author's works.[1] In *The Blithedale Romance*
(1852) Hawthorne deals with the present rather than the past
and apparently makes use of his observation, since his scenes
and characters are strongly suggestive of the Brook Farm community of reformers, among whom he spent one critical and
unhappy year. *The Scarlet Letter* (1850) is not only the most
original and powerful of the romances but is commonly ranked
by our critics at the head of American fiction. The scene is
laid in Boston, in the old Puritan days ; the main characters
are vividly drawn, and the plot moves to its gloomy but impressive climax as if Wyrd or Fate were at the bottom of it.

Characteristics of Hawthorne. Almost the first thing we
notice in Hawthorne is his style, a smooth, leisurely, " classic "
style which moves along, like a meadow brook, without hurry
or exertion. Gradually as we read we become conscious of the
novelist's characters, whom he introduces with a veil of mystery
around them. They are interesting, as dreams and other mysterious things always are, but they are seldom real or natural
or lifelike. At times we seem to be watching a pantomime of
shadows, rather than a drama of living men and women.

The explanation of these shadowy characters is found in
Hawthorne's method of work, as revealed by the *Note-Books*
Method of   in which he stored his material. Here is a typical
Work   record, which was occasioned, no doubt, by the
author's meeting with some old nurse, whom he straightway
changed from her real semblance to a walking allegory :

" Change from a gay young girl to an old woman. Melancholy events,
the effects of which have clustered around her character. . . . Becomes a
lover of sick chambers, taking pleasure in receiving dying breaths and laying
out the dead. Having her mind full of funeral reminiscences, and possessing
more acquaintances beneath the turf than above it."

[1] The *Marble Faun* ends in a fog, as if the author did not know what to do with his
characters. It has the amateurish fault of halting the narrative to talk with the reader ;
and it moralizes to such an extent that the heroine (who is pictured as of almost angelic
virtue) eventually becomes a prig and a preacher, — two things that a woman must never
be. Nevertheless, the romance has a host of enthusiastic readers, and to criticize it
adversely is to bring a storm about one's ears.

This is enough of a story in itself; we need not read "Edward Fane's Rosebud" to see how Hawthorne filled in the details. The strange thing is that he never studied or questioned the poor woman to discover whether she was anything like what he imagined her to be. On another page we read:

"A snake taken into a man's stomach and nourished there from fifteen to thirty-five years, tormenting him most horribly." [Then follows the inevitable moral:] "Type of envy or some other evil passion."

HAWTHORNE'S BIRTHPLACE, SALEM, MASSACHUSETTS

There are many such story-records in the *Note-Books*, but among them you will find no indication that the story-teller ever examined the facts with a purpose to discover whether a snake could survive thirty-five years, or minutes, in the acids of a human stomach, or how long a Puritan church would tolerate a minister who went about with a veil on his face, or whether any other of his symbols had any vital connection with human experience. In a word, Hawthorne was prone to make life conform to his imagination, instead of making his imagination conform to life. Living as he did in the twilight, between the day and the night, he seems to have missed the chief lesson of each, the urge of the one and the repose of the other; and especially did he miss the great fact of cheerfulness. The deathless courage of man, his invincible hope that springs to life under the most adverse circumstances, like the cyclamen abloom under the snows of winter, — this primal and blessed fact seems to have escaped his notice. At times he hints at it, but he never gives it its true place at the beginning, middle and end of human life.

Thus far our analysis has been largely negative, and Hawthorne was a very positive character. He had the feeling of **Artist and Moralist** an artist for beauty; and he was one of the few romancers who combine a strong sense of art with a puritanic devotion to conscience and the moral law. Hence his stories all aim to be both artistic and ethical, to satisfy our sense of beauty and our sense of right. In his constant moralizing he was like George Eliot; or rather, to give the figure its proper sequence, George Eliot was so exclusively a moralist after the Hawthornesque manner that one suspects she must have been familiar with his work when she began to write. Both novelists worked on the assumption that the moral law is the basis of human life and that every sin brings its inevitable retribution. The chief difference was that Hawthorne started with a moral principle and invented characters to match it, while George Eliot started with a human character in whose experience she revealed the unfolding of a moral principle.

The individuality of Hawthorne becomes apparent when we attempt to classify him, — a vain attempt, since there is no **A Solitary Genius** other like him in literature. In dealing with almost any other novelist we can name his models, or at least point out the story-tellers whose methods influenced his work; but Hawthorne seems to have had no predecessor. Subject, style and method were all his own, developed during his long seclusion at Salem, and from them he never varied. From his *Twice-Told Tales* to his unfinished *Dolliver Romance* he held steadily to the purpose of portraying the moral law against a background of Puritan history.

Such a field would have seemed very narrow to other American writers, who then, as now, were busy with things too many or things too new; but to Hawthorne it was a world in itself, a world that lured him as the Indies lured Columbus. In imagination he dwelt in that somber Puritan world, eating at its long-vanished tables or warming himself at its burnt-out fires, until the impulse came to reproduce it in literature. And he did reproduce it, powerfully, single-heartedly, as only genius could have done it. That his portrayal was inaccurate is perhaps a minor consideration; for one writer must depict life as he meets it on the street or in books, while another is confined to what Ezekiel calls "the chambers of imagery." Hawthorne's liberties with the facts may be pardoned on the ground that he was not an historian but an artist. The historian tells what life has accomplished, the artist what life means.

HENRY TIMROD

Secondary Writers of Prose or Verse

The Poets. Among the fifty or more poets of the period of conflict Henry Timrod, Paul Hamilton Hayne and Abram J. Ryan are notable for this reason, that their fame, once local, seems to widen with the years. They are commonly grouped as southern poets because of the war lyrics in which they voiced the passionate devotion of the South to its leaders; but what makes them now interesting to a larger circle of readers are their poems of an entirely different kind, — poems that reflect in a tender and beautiful way the common emotions of men in all places and in all ages. Two other prominent singers of the southern school are Theodore O'Hara and James Ryder Randall.

In another group are such varied singers as Richard Henry Stoddard, George H. Boker, Henry Howard Brownell, Thomas B. Read, John G. Saxe, J. G. Holland and Bayard Taylor. These were all famous poets in their own day, and some of them were prolific writers, Holland and Taylor especially. The latter produced thirty volumes of poems, essays, novels and sketches of travel ; but, with the exception of his fine translation of Goethe's *Faust* and a few of his original lyrics, the works which he sent forth so abundantly are now neglected. He is typical of a hundred writers who answer the appeal of to-day and win its applause, and who are forgotten when to-morrow comes with its new interests and its new favorites.

PAUL HAMILTON HAYNE

Fiction Writers. Comparatively few novels were written during this period, perhaps because the terrible shadow of war was over the country and readers were in no mood for fiction. The most popular romance of the age, and one of the most widely read books that America has ever produced, was *Uncle Tom's Cabin* (1852), which has been translated and dramatized into so many tongues that it is known all over the earth. The author, Harriet Beecher Stowe (1811–1896), wrote several other stories, all characterized by humor, kindness and intense moral earnestness. Some of these, such as *Oldtown Folks, The Minister's Wooing, The Pearl of Orr's Island* and *Oldtown Fireside Stories* have decidedly more literary charm than her famous story of slavery.

The mid-century produced some very good sea stories, and in these we see the influence of Cooper, who was the first to **Tales of the Sea** use the ocean successfully as a scene of romantic interest. Dana's *Two Years before the Mast* (1840) was immensely popular when our fathers were boys. It contained, moreover, such realistic pictures of sailor life that it was studied by aspirants for the British and American navies

in the days when the flag rippled proudly over the beautiful old sailing ships. This excellent book is largely a record of personal experience; but in the tales of Herman Melville (1819–1891) we have the added elements of imagination and adventure. *Typee, White Jacket, Moby Dick,* — these are capital tales of the deep, the last-named especially.

Typee (a story well known to Stevenson, evidently) is remarkable for its graphic pictures of sailor life afloat and ashore in the Marquesas Islands, a new field in

HARRIET BEECHER STOWE

those days. The narrative is continued in *White Jacket*, which tells of the return from the South Pacific aboard a man-of-war. In *Moby Dick* we have the real experience of a sailorman and whaler (Melville himself) and the fictitious wanderings of a stout captain, a primeval kind of person, who is at times an interesting lunatic and again a ranting philosopher. In the latter we have an echo of Carlyle, who was making a stir in America in 1850, and who affected Melville so strongly that the latter soon lost his bluff, hearty, sailor fashion of writing, which everybody liked, and assumed a crotchety style that nobody cared to read.

A few other novels of the period are interesting as showing the sudden change from romance to realism, a change for
From Romance to Realism
which the war was partly responsible, and which will be examined more closely in the following chapter. John Esten Cooke (1830–1886) may serve as a concrete example of the two types of fiction. In his earlier romances, notably in *Leather Stocking and Silk* and *The Virginia Comedians* (1854), he aimed to do for the Cavalier society of the South what Hawthorne was doing for the old Puritan régime in New England ; but his later stories, such as *Surrey of Eagle's Nest,* are chiefly notable for their realistic pictures of the great war.

JOHN ESTEN COOKE

The change from romance to realism is more openly apparent in Theodore Winthrop and Edward Eggleston, whose novels deal frankly with pioneers of the Middle West ; not such pioneers as Cooper had imagined in *The Prairie,* but such plain men and women as one might meet anywhere beyond the Alleghenies in 1850. Winthrop's *John Brent* (1862) and Eggleston's *The Hoosier Schoolmaster* and *The Circuit Rider* (1874) are so true to a real phase of American life that a thoughtful reader must wonder why they are not better known. They are certainly refreshing to one who tires of our present so-called realism with its abnormal or degenerate characters.

OA

More widely read than any of the novelists just mentioned are certain others who appeared in answer to the increasing demand of young people for a good story. It is doubtful if any American writer great or small has given more pleasure to young readers than Louisa M. Alcott with her *Little Women* (1868) and other stories for girls, or John T. Trowbridge,

author of *Cudjo's Cave, Jack Hazard, A Chance for Himself* and several other juveniles that once numbered their boy readers by tens of thousands.

Thoreau. Among the many secondary writers of the period the most original and most neglected was Henry D. Thoreau (1817–1862), a man who differed greatly from other mortals in almost every respect, but chiefly in

LOUISA M. ALCOTT

this, that he never was known to "go with the crowd," not even on the rare occasions when he believed the crowd to be right. He was one of the few persons who select their own way through life and follow it without the slightest regard for the world's opinion.

Numerous examples of Thoreau's oddity might be given, but we note here only his strange determination to view life with his own eyes. This may appear a simple matter until we reflect that most men measure life by what others have said or written concerning life's values. They accept the standards of

their ancestors or their neighbors; they conform themselves to
a world in which governments and other long-established insti-
His
Originality   tutions claim their allegiance; they are trained to
win success in such a world by doing one thing well,
and to measure their success by the fame or money or office
or social position which they achieve by a lifetime of labor
and self-denial.

Thoreau sharply chal-
lenged this whole concep-
tion of life, which, he said,
was more a matter of habit
than of reason or convic-
tion. He saw in our social
institutions as much of
harm as of benefit to the
individual. He looked with
distrust on all traditions,
saying that he had listened
for thirty years without
hearing one word of sound
advice from his elders.
He was a good workman
and learned to do several
things passing well; but
he saw no reason why a

HENRY D. THOREAU

free man should repeat himself daily in a world of infinite
opportunities. Also he was a scholar, versed in classical lore
and widely read in oriental literature; but unlike his friend
Emerson he seldom quoted the ancients, being more concerned with his own thoughts of life than by the words of phi-
losophers, and more fascinated by the wild birds that ate crumbs
from his table than by all the fabled gods of mythology. As
for success, the fame or money for which other men toiled
seemed to him but empty bubbles; the only wealth he prized
was his soul's increase in love and understanding : " If the day

and the night are such that you greet them with joy, and life emits a fragrance like sweet-scented herbs — is more elastic, starry and immortal — that is your success."

There are other interesting matters in Thoreau's philosophy, but these will appear plainly enough to one who reads his own record. His best-known work is *Walden* (1854), a **Walden** journal in which he recorded what he saw or thought or felt during the two years when he abandoned society to live in a hut on the shore of Walden Pond, near his native village of Concord. If there be any definite lesson in the book, it is the proof of Thoreau's theory that simplicity is needed for happiness, that men would be better off with fewer possessions, and that earning one's living should be a matter of pleasure rather than of endless toil and anxiety. What makes *Walden* valuable, however, is not its theories but its revelation of an original mind fronting the facts of life, its gleams of poetry and philosophy, its startling paradoxes, its first-hand impressions of the world, its nuggets of sense or humor, and especially its intimate observation of the little wild neighbors in feathers or fur who shared Thoreau's solitude. It is one of the few books in American literature that successive generations have read with profit to themselves and with increasing respect for the original genius who wrote it.

The Historians. The honored names of Bancroft, Sparks, Prescott, Motley and Parkman are indicative of the importance attached to history-writing in America ever since Colonial days, and of the remarkably fine and sometimes heroic quality of American historians. Another matter suggested by these names is the changing standard or ideal of historical writing. In an earlier time history was a dry chronicle of important events, or of such events as seemed important to the chronicler; at the present day it threatens to degenerate into an equally dry chronicle of economic forces; and between these thirsty extremes are various highly colored records glorifying kings or conquerors or political parties as the chief things of history.

These American historians had a different standard. They first consulted all available records to be sure of the facts or **The Epic** events. Then they closely examined the scene in **of History** which the event had come to pass, knowing that environment is always a factor in human history. Finally they studied historical personages, not as others had described them but as they revealed themselves in letters, diaries, speeches, — personal records revealing human motives that all men understand, because man is everywhere the same. From such a combination of event, scene and characters our historians wrote a dramatic narrative, giving it the heroic cast without which history, the prose epic of liberty, is little better than a dull catalogue. Another very important matter was that they cultivated their style as well as their knowledge ; they were literary men no less than historians, and in the conviction that the first object of literature is to give pleasure they produced works that have charmed as well as instructed a multitude of readers. There are chapters in Prescott's *Conquest of Mexico* and *Conquest of Peru* over which one must sit up late, as over a novel of Scott; in Motley's *Rise of the Dutch Republic* and *History of the United Netherlands* there are scores of glowing passages dealing with great characters or great events which stir the reader like a tale of gallant adventure.

Prescott deals with force in action, and the action at times seems to be an exaltation of violence and cruelty. Motley also delights in action ; but he is at heart an apostle of liberty, or perhaps we should say, of the American ideal of liberty, and his narrative often assumes the character of a partisan chant of freedom.

To the native, at least, Francis Parkman (1823–1893) is probably the most interesting of our historians, partly because of his lucid style and partly because of his Ameri- **Parkman** can theme. Early in life he selected his subject (the Old French Wars) and spent the best part of forty years in making himself familiar not only with what occurred during the struggle between France and England for possession of the New World, but also with the primeval scene and all the motley characters of the fateful drama. It is doubtful if any other historian ever had a more minute knowledge of his subject; and the astonishing, the heroic part of the matter is that he attained this vast knowledge in spite of the handicap of almost constant suffering and blindness. In a dozen volumes he tells his story, — volumes crowded with action or adventure, and written in such a vividly convincing style that one has the impression that Parkman must have been an eye-witness of the events which he describes.

FRANCIS PARKMAN

Among these volumes the second part of *Pioneers of France in the New World* and *La Salle and the Discovery of the Great West* are recommended to the beginner. The former deals with the career of Champlain, who opened the way for future settlements in the North; the latter with one of the most adventurous, lion-hearted men that ever cheerfully faced toil and endless danger. Standing apart from Parkman's main theme is a single volume, *The California and Oregon Trail* (1849), which recounts the picturesque incidents of the author's trip through the Northwest, then an unknown country, with a tribe of unspoiled Indians. Those who like a tale of adventure need not go to fiction to find it, for it is here in Parkman's narrative, — a tale of care-free wandering amid plains or mountains and, what is historically more important, a picture of a vanished life that will never be seen here again.

Summary. The period of conflict has no definite limits on either side, but for convenience we may think of it as included between the years 1840 and 1876. Its earlier years were filled with an ever-increasing agitation of the questions of slavery and state rights ; its center was the Civil War ; its close was the Centennial Exposition at Philadelphia, which we have selected as an outward symbol of a reunited country.

The most noticeable feature of the age, apart from the great war, was its ceaseless political turmoil. Of deeper significance to the student of literature was the profound mental unrest which showed itself in reform movements, in various communistic societies like Brook Farm, in an eager interest in the poetry of other nations, in the establishment of college professorships of foreign literatures, in the philosophical doctrine of transcendentalism, and in many other efforts of mid-century Americans to enlarge their mental horizon.

A host of minor writings of the period reflect the sectional passions or interests that stirred our people deeply at the time, but that are now almost forgotten. The comparatively small body of major literature was concerned with the permanent ideals of America or with the simple human feelings that have no age or nationality. In general, it was a time of poetry rather than of prose, being distinguished above all other periods of American literature by the number and quality of its poets.

Our detailed study of the age includes : (1) The major or so-called elder poets, Longfellow, Whittier, Lowell, Holmes, Lanier and Whitman. (2) The life and work of Emerson, who was both poet and prose writer. (3) The career of Hawthorne, the novelist of Puritanism, who is commonly ranked at the head of American fiction-writers. (4) A brief review of the secondary writers of prose and verse. (5) An examination of the work of Thoreau, the most individualistic writer in an age of individualism, and of Parkman, whom we have selected as representative of the American historians.

Selections for Reading. Typical selections from minor writers of the period in Calhoun and MacAlarney, Readings from American Literature ; Stedman and Hutchinson, Library of American Literature, and various other collections. Important works of all major writers are published in inexpensive editions for school use, a few of which are named below.

Longfellow's short poems, Evangeline, parts of Hiawatha and of Tales of a Wayside Inn, in Riverside Literature ; selections from the narrative poems in Lake English Classics ; selected poems in various other school series.

Whittier's Snow Bound and selected short poems, in Riverside Literature, Maynard's English Classics, etc.

Lowell's Sir Launfal, selected short poems and selected essays, in Riverside Literature, Maynard's English Classics.

Holmes's poems, selected, in Maynard's English Classics; The Autocrat, in Everyman's Library; selected prose and verse, in Riverside Literature.

Lanier's poems, with selections from Timrod and Hayne, in Pocket Classics, Maynard's English Classics, etc.

Whitman's poems, brief selections, in Maynard's English Classics; Triggs, Selections from the Prose and Poetry of Walt Whitman.

Emerson's poems, in Riverside Literature; Representative Men and selected essays, in Pocket Classics; Nature and various essays, in Everyman's Library.

Hawthorne's House of the Seven Gables and selected short stories, in Pocket Classics; Twice-Told Tales and other selections, in Riverside Literature.

Thoreau's Walden, in Everyman's Library; Walden and selections from other works, in Riverside Literature.

Bibliography. For extended works covering the field of American history and literature see the General Bibliography. The following works are useful in a special study of the period of conflict.

History. Rhodes, History of the United States 1850–1877, 7 vols.; Wilson, Division and Reunion; Stephens, War between the States; Paxson, the Civil War; Rhodes, Lectures on the Civil War; Hart, Romance of the Civil War (supplementary reading for young people). Lives of notable characters in American Statesmen, Great Commanders and other series. Grant, Personal Memoirs; Gordon, Reminiscences of the Civil War; Alexander Stephens, Recollections; Hoar, Autobiography; Blaine, Twenty Years in Congress; Greeley, Recollections; Booker Washington, Up from Slavery.

Literature. The great period of American letters is still awaiting its historian. Brief chapters are found in Richardson, Trent, Cairns, Wendell and other general histories of our literature. Good essays on individual authors of the period in Stedman, Poets of America; Brownell, American Prose Masters; Erskine, Leading American Novelists; Vincent, American Literary Masters; Burton, Literary Leaders of America.

Frothingham's Transcendentalism in New England will throw light on the so-called Concord school. Howells's Literary Friends and Acquaintance is a fine appreciation of the Cambridge writers. Wauchope's Writers of South Carolina contains excellent studies of Timrod, Hayne, Simms and other writers of the Palmetto state. Moses' Literature of the South and Henneman's Literary and Intellectual Life of the South are among the best works devoted to southern authors exclusively.

Longfellow. Life, by Higginson, in American Men of Letters; by Carpenter (brief), in Beacon Biographies; by Robertson, in Great Writers; by S. Longfellow, 3 vols. (the standard biography). Essays by Stedman, in Poets of America; by Mrs. Fields, in Authors and Friends; by Curtis, in Literary and Social Essays; by Higginson, in Old Cambridge; by Howells, in Literary Friends and Acquaintance.

Whittier. Life, by Pickard, 2 vols.; by Carpenter, in American Men of Letters; by Higginson, in English Men of Letters; by Burton (brief), in Beacon Biographies; by Perry, by Underwood. Mrs. Claflin, Personal Recollections of Whittier; Hawkins, the Mind of Whittier; Fowler, Whittier: Prophet, Seer and Man; Pickard, Whittier Land. Essays, by Woodberry, in Makers of Literature; by Stedman, in Poets of America; by Higginson, in Contemporaries; by Hazeltine, in Chats about Books; by Mrs. Fields, in Authors and Friends.

Lowell. Life, by Greenslet; by Scudder, 2 vols.; by Hale (brief), in Beacon Biographies; by Underwood. Edward Everett Hale, James Russell Lowell and his Friends. Essays, by Higginson, in Old Cambridge; by Woodberry, in Makers of Literature; by Stedman, in Poets of America.

Holmes. Life, by Morse, 2 vols.; by Crothers, in American Men of Letters. Essays, by Stedman, in Poets of America; by Haweis, in American Humorists; by Noble, in Impressions and Memories; by Stearns, in Cambridge Sketches; by L. Stephen, in Studies of a Biographer.

Lanier. Life, by Mims, in American Men of Letters; by West; by Ward, in Preface to Lanier's Poems (1884). Essays, by Baskerville, in Southern Writers; by Higginson, in Contemporaries; by Gilman, in South Atlantic Quarterly (1905); by Ward, in Century Magazine (1888); by Northrup, in Lippincott's (1905).

Whitman. Life, by Perry; by Carpenter, in English Men of Letters; by Platt (brief), in Beacon Biographies; by Binns, by Bucke. Essays, by Stedman, in Poets of America; by Stevenson, in Familiar Studies of Men and Books; by Dowden, in Studies in Literature; by Santayana, in Interpretations of Poetry and Religion.

Emerson. Life, by Woodberry; by Cabot (Memoir of Emerson, 2 vols.); by O. W. Holmes, in American Men of Letters; by Garnett, in Great Writers; by Sanborn (brief), in Beacon Biographies. E. W. Emerson, Emerson in Concord; Conway, Emerson at Home. Essays, by Stedman, in Poets of America; by Mrs. Fields, in Authors and Friends; by Lowell, in Literary Essays; by Stearns, in Sketches from Concord and Appledore; by Everett, in Essays Theological and Literary; by Beers, in Points at Issue; by Chapman, in Emerson and Other Essays.

Hawthorne. Life, by Woodberry, in American Men of Letters; by Henry James, in English Men of Letters; by Fields (brief), in Beacon Biographies; by Conway, in Great Writers. A more intimate but doubtful biography is Julian Hawthorne's Nathaniel Hawthorne and his Wife.

Bridge, Personal Recollections of Hawthorne. Essays, by Brownell, in American Prose Masters; by Perry, in A Study of Prose Fiction; by Gates, in Studies and Appreciations; by L. Stephen, in Hours in a Library; by Higginson, in Short Studies of American Authors.

Thoreau. Life, by Salt, in Great Writers; by Sanborn, in American Men of Letters. Page, Thoreau: his Life and Aims. Essays by Higginson, in Short Studies of American Authors; by Stevenson, in Familiar Studies of Men and Books; by Lowell, in Literary Essays.

Parkman. Life, by Fiske; by Farnham; by Sedgwick. Essays, by Fiske, in introduction to Parkman's works and in A Century of Science and Other Essays; by Vedder, in American Writers of To-day; by Whipple, in Recollections of Eminent Men.

CHAPTER IV

THE ALL–AMERICA PERIOD

Thou Mother with thy equal brood,
Thou varied chain of different States, yet one identity only,
A special song before I go I'd sing o'er all the rest:
For thee, the Future.

Whitman, "Thou Mother"

Some critics find little or no American literature of a distinctly national spirit prior to 1876, and they explain the lack of it on the assumption that Americans were too far apart and too much occupied with local or sectional interests for any author to represent the nation. It was even said at the time of the Centennial Exposition that our countrymen had never met, save on the battlefields of the Civil War, until the common interest in Jubilee Year drew men and women from the four quarters of America "around the old family altar at Philadelphia."

Whatever exaggeration there may be in that fine poetic figure, it is certain that our literature, once confined to a few schools or centers, began in the decade after 1870 to be broadly representative of the whole country. Miller's *Songs of the Sierras*, Hay's *Pike-County Ballads*, Harte's *Tales of the Argonauts*, Cable's *Old Creole Days*, Mark Twain's *Tom Sawyer*, Miss Jewett's *Deephaven*, Stockton's *Rudder Grange*, Harris's *Uncle Remus*, — a host of surprising books suddenly appeared with the announcement that America was too large for any one man or literary school to be its spokesman. It is because of these new voices, coming from North, South, East or West and heard with delight by the whole nation, that we venture to call the years after 1876 the all-America period of our literature.

We are still too near that period to make a history of it, for the simple reason that a true history implies distance and **Contempo-** perspective. No historian could read, much less **rary History** measure and compare, a tenth part of the books that have won recognition since 1876. In such works as he might select as typical he must be governed by his own taste or judgment; and the writer was never born who could by such personal standards forecast the judgment of time and of humanity. In a word, contemporary or "up-to-date" histories are vain attempts at the impossible; save in the unimportant matter of chronicling names or dates they are all alike untrustworthy. The student should bear in mind, therefore, that the following summary of our recent literature is based largely upon personal opinion; that it selects a few authors by way of illustration, omitting many others who may be of equal or greater importance. We are confronted by a host of books that serve the prime purpose of literature by giving pleasure; but what proportion of them are enduring books, or what few of them will be known to readers of the next century as the *Sketch Book* and *Snow-Bound* are known to us, — these are questions that only Father Time can answer.

The Short Story. The period after 1876 has been called the age of fiction, but "the short-story age" might be a better name for it, since the short story is apparently more popular than any other form of literature and since it has been developed here more abundantly than in any other land, — possibly because America offers such an immense and ever-surprising field to an author in search of a strange or picturesque tale. Readers of the short story demand life and variety, and here are all races and tribes and conditions of men, living in all kinds of "atmosphere" from the trapper's hut to the steel skyscraper and from the crowded city slums to the vast open places where one's companionship is with the hills or the stars. Hence a double tendency in our recent stories, to make them expressive of New World life and to make each story a reflection of some peculiar type of Americanism, — one of the many types that here meet in a common citizenship.

The truth of the above criticism may become evident by reviewing the history of the short story in America. Irving began with mere hints or outlines of stories (sketches he called them) and added a few legendary tales of the Dutch settlers on the Hudson. Then came Poe, dealing with the phantoms of his own brain rather than with human life or endeavor. Next appeared Hawthorne, who dealt largely in moral allegories and whose tales are always told in an atmosphere of mystery and twilight shadows. Finally, after the war, came a multitude of writers who insisted on dealing with our American life as

BRET HARTE

it is, with miners, immigrants, money kings, mountaineers, planters, cowboys, woodsmen, — a host of varied characters, each speaking the speech and typifying the customs or ideals of his particular locality. It was these *post-bellum* writers who invented the so-called story of local color (a story true to a certain place or a certain class of men), which is America's most original contribution to the world's literature.

Francis Bret Harte (1839–1902) is generally credited with the invention of the local-color story; but he was probably indebted to earlier works of the same kind, notably to Longstreet's *Georgia Scenes* (1836) and Baldwin's *Flush Times of Alabama and Mississippi* (1853). He had followed the "forty-niners" to California in a headlong

Bret Harte

GEORGE W. CABLE

search for gold when, finding himself amid the picturesque scenes and characters of the early mining camps, it suddenly occurred to him that he had before his eyes a literary gold mine such as no other modern romancer had discovered. Thereupon he wrote "The Luck of Roaring Camp" (first published in *The Overland Monthly*, 1868), and followed it with "The Outcasts of Poker Flat" and "Tennessee's Partner."

These stories took the literary world by storm, and almost overnight Harte became a celebrity. Following up his advantage he proceeded to write some thirty volumes of the same general kind, which were widely read and promptly forgotten. Though he was plainly too sentimental and sensational, there was a sense of freshness or originality in his early stories and poems which made them wonderfully attractive. His first three tales were probably his best, and they are still worth reading, — not for their literary charm or truth but as interesting early examples of the local-color story.

The interest aroused by the mining-camp tales influenced other American writers to discover the neglected literary wealth of their several localities; but they were fortunately on guard against Harte's exaggerated sentimentality and related their stories with more art and more truth to nature. As a specific example read Cable's *Old Creole Days* and *Madame Delphine* with their exquisite pictures of life in the old French city of New Orleans. These are romances or creations of fancy, to be sure; but in their lifelike characters, their natural scenes and soft Creole dialect they are as realistic (that is, as true to a real type of American life) as anything that can be found in literature. They are, in fact, studies as well as stories, such minute and affectionate studies of old people, old names and old customs as the great French novelist Balzac made in preparation for his work. Though time holds its own secrets, one can hardly avoid the conviction that *Old Creole Days* and *Madame Delphine* are not books of a day but permanent additions to American fiction.

Cable

Cable was accompanied by so many other good writers that it would require a volume to do them justice. We name only, by way of indicating the wide variety that awaits the reader, the charming stories of Grace King and Kate Chopin dealing with plantation life; the New England stories, powerful or brilliant or somber, of Sarah Orne Jewett, Rose Terry Cooke and Mary E. Wilkins; the tender and cheery southern stories of Thomas Nelson Page; the impressive stories of mountaineer life by Mary Noailles Murfree (Charles Egbert Craddock); the humorous, *Alice-in-Wonderland* kind of stories told by Frank Stockton; and a bewildering miscellany of other works, of which the names Thomas Bailey Aldrich, Hamlin Garland, Alice French (Octave Thanet), Rowland Robinson, Frank Norris and Henry C. Bunner are as a brief but inviting index.

Typical Story-Writers

It would be unjust at the present time to discriminate among these writers or to compare them with others, perhaps equally good, whom we have not named. Occasionally in the flood of short stories appears one that compels attention. Aldrich's " Marjorie Daw," Edward Everett Hale's " The Man without a Country," Stockton's " The Lady or the Tiger," — each of these impresses us so forcibly by its delicate artistry or appeal to patriotism or whimsical ending that we hail it as

MARY E. WILKINS FREEMAN

a new classic, forgetting that the term "classic" carries with it the implication of something old and proved, safe from change or criticism. Undoubtedly a few of our recent stories deserve the name; they will be more widely known a century hence than they are now, and may finally rank above " Rip Van Winkle" or " The Gold Bug " or " The Snow Image " ; but until the perfect tale is sifted from the thousand that are almost perfect, every ambitious critic is free to make his own prophecy.

Some Recent Novelists. There is a difference between our earlier and later fiction which becomes apparent when we compare specific examples. As a type of the earlier novel take Cooper's *The Spy* or Longfellow's *Hyperion* or Hawthorne's *The House of the Seven Gables* or Simms's *Katherine Walton* or Cooke's *The Virginia Comedians*, and read it in connection with a recent novel, such as Howells's *Annie Kilburn* or Miss Jewett's *Deephaven* or Harold Frederick's *Illumination*

or James Lane Allen's *The Reign of Law* or Frank Norris's
The Octopus. Disregarding the important element of style, we
note that the earlier novels have a distant background in time
or space; that their chief interest lies in the story they have
to tell; that they take us far away from present reality into
regions where people are more impressive and sentiments more
exalted than in our familiar, prosaic world. The later novels
interest us less by the story than by the analysis of character;
they deal with human life as it is here and now, not as we
imagine it to have been elsewhere or in a golden age. In a
word, our later novels are realistic in purpose, and in this respect they are in marked contrast with our novels of an earlier
age, which are nearly all of the romantic kind.[1]

The realistic movement in American fiction began, as we
have noted, with the short-story writers; and presently the
most talented of these writers, having learned the value of real
scenes and characters, turned to the novel and produced works
having the double interest of romance and realism; that is,
they told an old romantic tale of love or heroism and set it
amid scenes or characters that were typical of American life.
Miss Jewett's novels of northern village life, for example, are
even finer than her short stories in the same field. The same
criticism applies to Miss Murfree with her novels of mountaineer life in Tennessee, to James Lane Allen with his novels of
his native Kentucky, and to many another recent novelist who
tells a brave tale of his own people. We call these, in the
conventional way, novels of New England or the South or
the West; in reality they are novels of humanity, of the old
unchanging tragedies or comedies of human life, which seem
more true or real to us because they appear in a familiar setting.

There is another school of realism which subordinates the
story element, which avoids as untrue all unusual or heroic

---

[1] In the above comparison we have ignored a large number of recent novels that
are quite as romantic as any written before the war. Romance is still, as in all past ages,
more popular than realism: witness the millions of readers of Lew Wallace, E. P. Roe
and other modern romancers.

incidents and deals with ordinary men or women ; and of this
school William Dean Howells is a conspicuous example. Judging him by his novels alone it would be difficult to determine
his rank ; but judging him by his high aim and distinguished
style (a style remarkable for its charm and purity in an age
too much influenced by newspaper slang and smartness) he is
certainly one of the best of our recent prose writers. Since his

first modest volume ap-
peared in 1860 he has
published many poems,
sketches of travel, appreciations of literature, parlor
comedies, novels, — an immense variety of writings ;
but whatever one reads of
his sixty-odd books, whether
Venetian Life or *A Boys'
Town*, one has the im-
pression of an author who
lives for literature, who
puts forth no hasty or
unworthy work, and who
aims steadily to be true
to the best traditions of
American letters.

WILLIAM DEAN HOWELLS

In middle life Howells turned definitely to fiction and wrote,
among various other novels, *A Woman's Reason, The Minister's Charge, A Modern Instance* and *The Rise of Silas Lapham.* These are all realistic in that they deal frankly with
contemporary life ; but in their plots and conventional endings
they differ but little from the typical romance.[1] Then Howells

---

[1] Several of Howells's earlier novels deal with New England life, but superficially
and without understanding. However minutely they depict its manners or mannerisms
they seldom dip beneath the surface. If the reader wants not the body but the soul
of New England, he must go to some other fiction writer, to Sarah Orne Jewett, for
example, or to Rose Terry Cooke.

fell under the influence of Tolstoi and other European realists, and his later novels, such as *Annie Kilburn, A Hazard of New Fortunes* and *The Quality of Mercy*, are rather aimless studies of the speech, dress, mannerisms and inanities of American life with precious little of its ideals, — which are the only things of consequence, since they alone endure. He appears here as the photographer rather than the painter of American life, and his work has the limited interest of another person's family album.

MARK TWAIN

Another realist of a very different kind is Samuel L. Clemens (1835–1910), who is more widely known by his pseudonym of Mark Twain. He grew up, he tells us, in "a loafing, down-at-the-heels town in Missouri"; he was educated "on the river," and in most of his work he attempted to deal with the rough-and-ready life which he knew intimately at first hand. His *Life on the Mississippi*, a vivid delineation of river scenes and characters, is perhaps his best work, or at least the most true to his aim and his experience. *Roughing It* is another volume from his store of personal observation, this time in the western mining camps; but here his realism goes as far astray from truth as any old romance in that it exaggerates even the sensational elements of frontier life.

The remaining works of Mark Twain are, with one or two exceptions, of very doubtful value. Their great popularity for a time was due largely to the author's reputation as a humorist, — a strange reputation it begins to appear, for he was at heart a pessimist, an iconoclast, a thrower of stones, and with the exception of his earliest work, *The Celebrated Jumping Frog* (1867), which reflected some rough fun or horseplay, it is questionable whether the term "humorous" can properly be applied to any of his books. Thus the blatant *Innocents Abroad* is not a work of humor but of ridicule (a very different matter), which jeers at travelers who profess admiration for the scenery or institutions of Europe, — an admiration that was a sham to Mark Twain because he was incapable of understanding it. So with the grotesque capers of *A Connecticut Yankee at King Arthur's Court*, with the sneering spirit of *The Man that Corrupted Hadleyburg*, with the labored attempts to be funny of *Adam's Diary* and with other alleged humorous works; readers of the next generation may ask not what we found to amuse us in such works but how we could tolerate such crudity or cynicism or bad taste in the name of American humor.

The most widely read of Mark Twain's works are *Tom Sawyer* and *Huckleberry Finn*. The former, a glorification of a liar and his dime-novel adventures, has enough descriptive power to make the story readable, but hardly enough to disguise its sensationalism, its lawlessness, its false standards of boy life and American life. In *Huckleberry Finn*, a much better book, the author depicts the life of the Middle West as seen by a homeless vagabond. With a runaway slave as a companion the hero, Huck Finn, drifts down the Mississippi on a raft, meeting with startling experiences at the hands of quacks and imposters of every kind. One might suppose, if one took this picaresque record seriously, that a large section of our country was peopled wholly by knaves and fools. The adventures are again of a sensational kind; but the characters are powerfully drawn, and the vivid pictures of the mighty river by day or night are among the best examples of descriptive writing in our literature.

Still another type of realism is suggested by the names
Stephen Crane and Frank Norris. These young writers, in-
Crane and   fluenced by the French novelist Zola, condemned
Norris   the old romance as false and proclaimed, somewhat
grandly at first, that they would tell the truth, the whole truth
and nothing but the truth. Then they straightway forgot that
health and moral sanity are the truth of life, and proceeded to
deal with degraded or degenerate characters as if these were
typical of humanity. Their earlier works are studies of brutality, miscalled realism; but later Crane wrote his *Red Badge
of Courage* (a rather wildly imaginative story of the Civil War),
and Norris produced works of real power in *The Octopus* and
The Pit, one a prose epic of the railroad, the other of a grain
of wheat from the time it is sown in the ground until it becomes a matter of good food or of crazy speculation. There
is an impression of vastness, of continental breadth and sweep,
in these two novels which sets them apart from all other fiction
of the period.

The flood of dialect stories which appeared after 1876 may
seem at first glance to be mere variations of Bret Harte's local-
color stories, but they are something more and better than
that. The best of them — such, for example, as Page's *In Ole
Virginia* or Rowland Robinson's *Danvis Folk* — are written
on the assumption that we can never understand a man, that
is, the soul of a man, unless we know the very language in
which he expresses his thought or feeling. These dialect
stories, therefore, are intimate studies of American life rather
than of local speech or manners.

Joel Chandler Harris (1848–1908) is not our best writer of
dialect stories but only the happy and most fortunate man who
Harris   wrote *Uncle Remus* (1880), and wrote it, by the
              way, as part of his day's work as a newspaper man,
without a thought that it was a masterpiece, a work of genius.
The first charm of the book is that it fascinates children with
its frolicsome adventures of Brer Rabbit, Brer Tarrypin, Brer

B'ar, Brer Fox and the wonderful Tar Baby; the second, that it combines in a remarkable way a primitive or universal with a local and intensely human interest. Thus, almost everybody is interested in folklore, especially in the animal stories which are part of the tradition of every primitive tribe; but folklore, as commonly written, is not a branch of fiction but of science. Before it can enter the golden door of literature it must find

JOEL CHANDLER HARRIS

or create some human character who interests us not by his stories but by his humanity; and Harris furnished this character in the person of Uncle Remus, a very lovable old plantation negro, drawn with absolute fidelity to life.

Other novelists have portrayed a negro in fiction, but Harris did a more original work by creating his Brer Rabbit. In the adventures of this happy-go-lucky creature, with his childishness and humor, we have the symbol not of any one negro but of the whole race of negroes as the author knew them intimately in a condition of servitude. The creation of these two original characters, as real as Poor Richard or Natty Bumppo and far more fascinating, is one of the most notable achievements of American fiction.

Aside from the realistic movement, our recent fiction is like a river flowing sluggishly over hidden bowlders: the surface is so broken by whirlpools, eddies and aimless flotsam that it is difficult to determine the main current. Here our attention is attracted by clever stories of "society in the making," there

Problem Novels by somber problem-novels dealing with city slums, lonely farms, department stores, political rings, business corruption, religious creeds, social injustice, — with every conceivable matter that can furnish a novelist not with a story but with a cry for reform. The propaganda novel is evidently a favorite in America; but whether it has any real influence in reforming abuses, as the novels of Dickens led to better schools and prisons in England, is yet to be determined.

Occasionally appears a reform novel great enough to make us forget the reform, such as Helen Hunt Jackson's *Ramona* (1884). This famous story began as an attempt to plead the cause of the oppressed Indian, to do for him what *Uncle Tom's Cabin* was supposed to have done for the negro; it ended in an idyllic story so well told that readers forgot to cry, "Lo, the poor Indian," as the author intended. At the present time *Ramona* is not classed with the problem-novels but with the most readable of American romances.

While the new realistic novel occupied the attention of critics the old romance had, as usual, an immensely larger

Popular Romances number of readers. Moral romances with a happy ending have always been popular, and of these E. P. Roe furnished an abundance. His *Barriers Burned Away*, *A Face Illumined*, *Opening of a Chestnut Burr* and *Nature's Serial Story* depict American characters in an American landscape, and have a wholesome atmosphere of manliness and cleanness that makes them eminently "safe" reading. Unfortunately they are melodramatic and sentimental, and critics commonly sneer or jeer at them; but that is not a rational criticism. Romances that won instant welcome from a host of readers and that are still widely known after half a century have at least "the power to live"; and vitality, the quality that makes a character or a story endure, is always one of the marks of a good romance.

Another romancer untouched by the zeal for realism was Marion Crawford, who in a very interesting essay, *The Novel*, proclaimed with some show of reason that the novel was simply a "pocket theater," a convenient stage whereon the reader could enjoy by himself any comedy or tragedy that pleased him. That Crawford lived abroad the greater part of his life and was familiar with society in a dozen countries may explain the fact that his forty-odd novels are nearly all of the social kind. His Roman novels, *Saracinesca, Sant' Ilario* and a dozen others, are perhaps his best work. They are good stories; they take us among cultured foreign people and give us glimpses of a life that is hidden from most travelers; but they are superficial and leave the impression that the author was a man without much heart, that he missed the deeper meanings of life because he had little interest in them. His characters are as puppets that are sent through a play for our amusement and for no other reason. In this, however, he remained steadily true to his own ideal of fiction as a convenient substitute for the theater. Moreover, he was a good workman; his stories were for the most part well composed and very well written.

More popular even than the romances of Roe and Crawford are the stories with a background of Colonial or Revolutionary history, a type to which America has ever given hearty welcome. Ford's *Janice Meredith*, Mitchell's *Hugh Wynne*, Mary Johnston's *To Have and to Hold*, Maurice Thompson's *Alice of Old Vincennes*, Churchill's *Richard Carvel*, — the reader can add to the list of recent historical romances almost indefinitely; but no critic can now declare which shall be called great among them. To the same interesting group of writers belong Lew Wallace, whose enormously popular *Ben Hur* has obscured his better story, *The Fair God*, and Mary Hartwell Catherwood, whose *Lady of Fort St. John* and other stirring tales of the Northwest have the same savage wilderness background against which Parkman wrote his histories.

For other romances of the period we have no convenient term except to call them old-fashioned. Such, for instance, are Blanche Willis Howard's *One Summer* and Arthur Sherburne Hardy's *Passe Rose* and *But Yet a Woman*, — pleasant, leisurely, exquisitely finished romances, which belong to no particular time or place and which deserve the fine old name of romance, because they seem to grow young rather than old with the passing years.

Poetry since 1876. It is commonly assumed that the last half century has been almost exclusively an age of prose. The student of literature knows, on the contrary, that one difficulty of judging our recent poetry lies in the amount and variety of it. Since 1876 more poetry has been published here than in all the previous years of our history; and the quality of it, if one dare judge it as a whole, is surprisingly good. The designation of "the prose age," therefore, should not blind us to the fact that America never had so many poets as at present. Whether a future generation will rank any of these among our elder poets is another question. Of late years we have had no singer to compare with Longfellow, to be sure; but we have had a dozen singers who reflect the enlarging life of America in a way of which Longfellow never dreamed. He lived mostly in the past and was busy with legends, folklore, songs of the night; our later singers live in the present and write songs of the day. And this suggests the chief characteristic of recent poetry; namely, that it aims to be true to life as it is here and now rather than to life as it was romantically supposed to be in classic or medieval times.[1]

This emancipation of our poetry from the past, with the loss and gain which such a change implies, was not easily accomplished, and the terrible reality of the great war was

[1] The above characterization applies only to the best, or to what most critics deem best, of our recent poetry. It takes no account of a large mass of verse which leaves an impression of faddishness in the matter of form or phrase or subject. Such verse appeals to the taste of the moment, but Time has an effective way of dealing with it and with all other insincerities in literature.

perhaps the decisive factor in the struggle. Before the war
our poetry was largely conventional, imitative, sentimental;
and even after the war, when Miller's *Songs of the Sierras*
and John Hay's *Pike-County Ballads* began to sing, however
crudely, of vigorous life, the acknowledged poets and critics of
the time were scandalized. Thus, to read the letters of Bayard
Taylor is to meet a poet who bewails the lack of poetic
material in America and who "hungers," as he says, for the

EDMUND CLARENCE STEDMAN

romance and beauty of other
lands. He writes *Songs of
the Orient, Lars : a Pas-
toral of Norway, Prince
Deukalion* and many other
volumes which seem to in-
dicate that poetry is to be
found everywhere save at
home. Even his "Song of
the Camp" is located in
the Crimea, as if heroism
and tenderness had not recently bloomed on a hun-
dred southern battlefields.
So also Stedman wrote his
Alectryon and *The Blame-
less Prince*, and Aldrich
spent his best years in making artificial nosegays (as Holmes
told him frankly) when he ought to have been making poems.
These and many other poets said proudly that they belonged to
the classic school ; they all read Shelley and Keats, dreamed
of medieval or classic beauty, and in unnumbered reviews
condemned the crudity of those who were trying to find
beauty at their own doors and to make poetry of the stuff of
American life.

   It was the war, or rather the new American spirit that
issued from the war, which finally assured these poets and

critics that mythology and legend were, so far as America was concerned, as dead as the mastodon, and that life itself **Stedman and** was the only vitally interesting subject of poetry. **Aldrich** Edmund Clarence Stedman (1833–1908), after writing many "finished" poems that were praised and forgotten, manfully acknowledged that he had been following the wrong trail and turned at last to the poetry of his own people. His *Alice of Monmouth,* an idyl of the war, and a few short pieces, such as " Wanted : a Man," are the only parts of his poetical works that are now remembered. Thomas Bailey Aldrich (1836–1907) went through the same transformation. He had a love of formal beauty, and in the exquisite finish of his verse has had few rivals in American poetry ; but he spent the great part of his life in making pretty trifles. Then he seemed to waken to the meaning of poetry as a noble expression of

THOMAS BAILEY ALDRICH

the truth or beauty of this present life, and his last little book of *Songs and Sonnets* contains practically all that is worth remembering of his eight or nine volumes of verse.

One of the first in time of the new singers was Cincinnatus Heine Miller or, as he is commonly known, Joaquin Miller **Joaquin** (1841–1912). His *Songs of the Sierras* (1871) **Miller** and other poems of the West have this advantage, that they come straight from the heart of a man who has shared the stirring life he describes and who loves it with an

overmastering love. To read his *My Own Story* or the preface
to his *Ship in the Desert* is to understand from what fullness
of life came lines like these:

> Room! room to turn round in, to breathe and be free,
> To grow to be giant, to sail as at sea
> With the speed of the wind on a steed with his mane
> To the wind, without pathway or route or a rein.
> Room! room to be free, where the white-bordered sea
> Blows a kiss to a brother as boundless as he;
> Where the buffalo come like a cloud on the plain,
> Pouring on like the tide of a storm-driven main,
> And the lodge of the hunter to friend or to foe
> Offers rest, and unquestioned you come or you go.
> My plains of America! seas of wild lands! . . .
> I turn to you, lean to you, lift you my hands.

Indeed, there was a splendid promise in Miller, but the
promise was never fulfilled. He wrote voluminously, feeling
that he must express the lure and magic of the boundless
West; but he wrote so carelessly that the crude bulk of his
verse obscures the originality of his few inspired lines. To read
the latter is to be convinced that he was a true poet who
might have accomplished a greater work than Whitman, since
he had more genius and manliness than the eastern poet
possessed; but his personal oddities, his zeal for reforms, his
love of solitude, his endless quest after some unnamed good
which kept him living among the Indians or wandering between Mexico and the ends of Alaska, — all this hindered his
poetic development. It may be that an Indian-driven arrow,
which touched his brain in one of his numerous adventures,
had something to do with his wanderings and his failure.

There is a poetry of thought that can be written down in
words, and there is another poetry of glorious living, keenly
felt in the winds of the wilderness or the rush of a splendid
horse or the flight of a canoe through the rapids, for which
there is no adequate expression. Miller could feel superbly this
poetry of the mountaineer, the plainsman and the voyageur;

that he could even suggest or half reveal it to others makes him worthy to be named among our most original singers.

The hundred other poets of the period are too near for criticism, too varied even for classification ; but we may at least note two or three significant groupings. In one **Irwin Russell** group are the dialect poets, who attempt to make poetry serve the same end as fiction of the local-color school.

Irwin Russell, with his gay negro songs tossed off to the twanging accompaniment of his banjo, belongs in this group. His verses are notable not for their dialect (others have done that better) but for their fidelity to the negro character as Russell had observed it in the old plantation days. There is little of poetic beauty in his work ; it is chiefly remarkable for its promise, for its opening of a new field of poesie ; but unfortunately the promise was spoiled by the author's fitful life and his untimely death.

JOAQUIN MILLER

Closely akin to the dialect group in their effective use of the homely speech of country people are several popular poets, of **Carleton and Riley** whom Will Carleton and James Whitcomb Riley are the most conspicuous. Carleton's " Over the Hills to the Poorhouse " and other early songs won him a wide circle of readers ; whereupon he followed up his advantage with *Farm Ballads* and other volumes filled with rather crude but sincere verses of home and childhood. For half a century these sentimental poems were as popular as the early works of Longfellow, and they are still widely read by people who like homely themes and plenty of homely sentiment in their poetry.

Riley won an even larger following with his *Old Swimmin' Hole, Rhymes of Childhood Days* and a dozen other volumes that aimed to reflect in rustic language the joys and sorrows of country people. Judged by the number of his readers he would be called the chief poet of the period; but judged by the quality of his work it would seem that he wrote too much, and wrote too often "with his eye on the gallery." He was primarily an entertainer, a platform favorite, and in his impersonation of country folk was always in danger of giving his audience what he thought they would like, not what he sincerely felt to be true. Hence the impression of the stage and a "make-up" in a considerable part of his work. At times, however, Riley could forget the platform and speak from the heart as a plain man to plain men. His work at such moments has a deeper note, more simple and sincere, and a few of his poems will undoubtedly find a permanent place in American letters. The best feature of his work is that he felt no need to go far afield, to the Orient or to mythology, but found the beauty of fine feeling at his door and dared to call one of his collections *Poems Here at Home*.

In a third group of recent poets are those who try to reflect the feeling of some one type or race of the many that make up the sum total of American life. Such are Emma Lazarus, speaking finely for the Jewish race, and Paul Lawrence Dunbar, voicing the deeper life of the negro, — not the negro of the old plantation but the negro who was once a slave and must now prove himself a man. In the same group we are perhaps justified in placing Lucy Larcom, singing for the mill girls of New England, and Eugene Field, who shows what fun and sentiment may brighten the life of a busy newspaper man in a great city.

Finally come a larger number of poets who cannot be grouped, who sing each of what he knows or loves best:

Celia Thaxter, of the storm-swept northern ocean; Madison Cawein, of nature in her more tender moods; Edward Rowland Sill, of the aspirations of a rare Puritan soul. More varied in their themes are Edith Thomas, Emily Dickinson, Henry C. Bunner, Richard Watson Gilder, George Edward Woodberry, William Vaughn Moody, Richard Hovey, and several others who are perhaps quite as notable as any of those whom we have too briefly reviewed. They all sing of American life in its wonderful complexity and have added poems of real merit to the book of recent American verse. And that is a very good book to read, more inspiring and perhaps more enduring than the popular book of prose fiction.

Miscellaneous Prose. The historian who is perplexed by our recent poetry or fiction must be overwhelmed by the flood of miscellaneous works covering every field of human endeavor. As one who wanders through a forest has no conception of the forest itself but only of individual trees, so the reader of latter-day literature can form no distinct impression of it as a whole but must linger over the individual authors who happen to attract his attention. Hence in all studies of contemporary literature we have the inevitable confusion of what is important with what merely seems so because of its nearness or newness or appeal to our personal interests. The reader is amused by a *David Harum*, or made thoughtful by a *Looking Backward*, or wonderstruck by a *Life of Lincoln* as big as a ten-volume history; and he thinks, "This is surely a book to live." But a year passes and *David Harum* is eclipsed by a more popular hero of fiction, *Looking Backward* is relegated to the shelf of forgotten tracts, and Nicolay and Hay's "monumental" biography becomes a source book, which someone, it is to be hoped, will some day use in making a life of Lincoln that will be worthy of the subject and of the name of literature.

There is one feature in our recent literature, however, which attracts the attention of all critics; namely, the number of nature writers who have revealed to us the beauty of our

natural environment, as Ruskin awakened his readers to the
beauty of art and Joaquin Miller to the unsung glory of the
Nature   pioneers. In this respect, of adding to our enjoy-
Writers   ment of human life by a new valuation of all life,
our nature literature has no parallel in any age or nation.

To be specific, one must search continental literatures carefully to find even a single book that belongs unmistakably
to the outdoor school. In English literature we find several
poets who sing occasionally of the charms of nature, but only
two books in fourteen centuries of writing that deal frankly
with the great outdoors for its own sake: one is Isaac Walton's
Complete Angler (1653), the other Gilbert White's *Natural
History of Selborne* (1789).[1] In American literature the story
is shorter but of the same tenor until recent times. From the
beginning we have had many journals of exploration; but
though the joy of wild nature is apparent in such writings,
they were written to increase our knowledge, not our pleasure
in life. Josselyn's *New England's Rarities* (1672), Alexander
Wilson's *American Ornithology* (1801), Audubon's *Birds of
America* (1827), — these were our nearest approach to nature
books until Thoreau's *Walden* (1854) called attention to the
immense and fascinating field which our writers had so long
overlooked.

Thoreau, it will be remembered, was neglected by his own
generation; but after the war, when writers began to use the
picturesque characters of plantation or mining camp as the
material for a new American literature, then the living world
of nature seemed suddenly opened to their vision. Bradford
Torrey, himself a charming nature writer, edited Thoreau's
journals, and lo! these neglected chronicles became precious
because the eyes of America were at last opened. Maurice
Thompson wrote as a poet and scholar in the presence of

---

[1] There were other works of a scientific nature, and some of exploration, but no real
nature books until the first notable work of Richard Jefferies (one of the best of nature
writers) appeared in 1878. By that time the nature movement in America was well
under way.

nature, John Muir as a reverent explorer, and William Hamilton Gibson as an artist with an eye single to beauty; then in rapid succession came Charles Abbott, Rowland Robinson, John Burroughs, Olive Thorne Miller, Florence Bailey, Frank Bolles, and a score more of a somewhat later generation. Most of these are frankly nature writers, not scientists; they aim not simply to observe the shy, fleeting life of the woods or fields but to reflect that life in such a way as to give us a new pleasure by awakening a new sense of beauty.

It is a remarkable spectacle, this rediscovery of nature in an age supposed to be given over to materialism, and its influence appears in every branch of our literature. The nature writers have evidently done a greater work than they knew; they have helped a multitude of people to enjoy the beauty of a flower without pulling it to pieces for a Latin name, to appreciate a living bird more than a stuffed skin, and to understand what Thoreau meant when he said that the *anima* of an animal is the only interesting thing about him. Because they have given us a new valuation of life, a new sense of its sacredness and mystery, their work may appeal to a future generation as the most original contribution to recent literature.

Another interesting feature of recent times is the importance attached to historical and biographical works, which have History and increased so rapidly since 1876 that there is now Biography no period of American life and no important character or event that lacks its historian. The number of such works is astonishing, but their general lack of style and broad human interest places them outside of the field of literature. The tendency of recent historical writing, for example, is to collect facts *about* persons or events rather than to reproduce the persons or events so vividly that the past lives again before our eyes. The result of such writing is to make history a puppet show in which dead figures are moved about by unseen economic forces; meanwhile the only record that lives in literature is the one that represents history as it really was in the making; that is, as a drama of living, self-directing men.

There is at least one recent historian, however, whose style gives distinction to his work and makes it worthy of especial notice. This is John Fiske (1842–1901), whose field and method are both unusual. He began as a student of law and philosophy, and his first notable book, *Outlines of Cosmic Philosophy*, attracted in-

stant attention in England and America by its literary style and rare lucidity of statement. It was followed by a series of essays, such as *The Idea of God*, *The Destiny of Man* and *The Origin of Evil*, which were so far above others of their kind that for a time they were in danger of becoming popular. Of a thousand works occasioned by the theory of evolution, when that theory was a nine days' wonder, they are among the very few that stand the test of time by affording as much pleasure and surprise as when they were first written.

JOHN FISKE

It was comparatively late in life that our philosopher turned historian, and his first work in this field, *American Political Ideas Viewed from the Standpoint of Universal History*, announced that here at last was a writer with broad horizons, who saw America not as an isolated nation making a strange experiment but as adding a vital chapter to the great world's history. It was a surprising work, unlike any other in the field of American history, and it may fall to another generation to appreciate its originality. Finally Fiske took up the study of particular periods or epochs, viewed them with the same deep insight, the same broad sympathy, and reflected them in a series of brilliant narratives : *Old Virginia and her Neighbors*, *The Beginnings of New England*, *Dutch and Quaker Colonies in America* and a few others, the series ending chronologically with *A Critical Period of American History*, the "critical" period being the time of doubt and struggle over the Constitution. These narratives, though not unified, form a fairly complete history from the Colonial period to the formation of the Union.

To read any of these books is to discover that Fiske is concerned not chiefly with events but with the meaning or philosophy of events ; that he has a rare gift of delving below the surface, of seeing in the endeavors of a handful of men at Jamestown or Plymouth or Philadelphia a profoundly significant chapter of universal history. Hence we seem to read in his pages not the story of America but the story of Man. Moreover, he had enthusiasm ; which means that his heart was young and that he could make even dull matters vital and interesting. Perhaps the best thing that can be said of his work is that it is a pleasure to read it, — a criticism which is spoken for mature or thoughtful readers rather than for those who read history for its dramatic or heroic interest.

Another feature of our recent prose is the number of books devoted to the study of American letters ; and that, like the study of nature, is a phenomenon which is without Literary precedent. Notwithstanding Emerson's plea for independence in *The American Scholar* (1837), our critics were busy long after that date with the books of other lands, thinking that there was no American literature worthy of their attention. In the same year that Emerson made his famous address Royal Robbins made what was probably the first attempt at a history of American literature.[1] It consisted of a few tag-ends attached to a dry catalogue of English writers, and the scholarly author declared that, as there was only one poor literary history then in existence (namely, Chambers'), he must depend largely on his own memory for correcting the English part of the book and creating a new American part.

EDWARD EVERETT HALE

Nor were conditions improved during the next forty years.

After the war, however, the viewpoint of our historians was changed. They began to regard American literature with increasing respect as an original product, as a true reflection of human life in a new field and under the stimulus of new incentives to play the fine old game of "life, liberty and the pursuit of happiness." In 1878 appeared Tyler's *History of American Literature 1607–1765* in two bulky volumes that surprised readers by revealing a mass of important writings in a period supposed to be barren of literary interest; and the surprise increased when the same author produced two more volumes dealing with the literature of the Revolution. In 1885 came Stedman's *Poets of America*,

---

[1] *Chambers' History of the English Language and Literature, to which is added A History of American Contributions to the English Language and Literature, by Royal Robbins (Hartford, 1837).* It is interesting to note that the author complained of the difficulty of his task in view of the fact that there were at that time over two thousand living American authors.

an excellent critical study of New World poetry; and two years later Richardson published the first of his two splendid volumes of *American Literature*. These good beginnings were followed by a host of biographies dealing with every important American author, until we now have choice of a large assortment of literary material where Royal Robbins had none at all.

Such formal works are for the student, but the reader who goes to books for recreation has also been remembered. Edward Everett Hale's *James Russell Lowell and his Friends*, Higginson's *Old Cambridge*, Howells's *Literary Friends and Acquaintance*, Trowbridge's *My Own Story*, Mrs. Field's *Authors and Friends*, Stoddard's *Homes and Haunts of our Elder Poets*, Curtis's *Homes of American Authors*, Mitchell's *American Lands and Letters*, — these are but few of many recent books of reminiscences, all bearing witness to the fact that American literature has a history and tradition of its own. It is no longer an appendix to English literature but an original record, to be cherished as we cherish any other precious national heritage, and to stand or fall among the literatures of the world as it shall be found true or false to the fundamental ideals of American life.

Bibliography. The best work on our recent literature is Pattee, A History of American Literature since 1870 (Century Co., 1915), which deals with two hundred or more writers. A more sketchy attempt at a contemporaneous history is Vedder, American Writers of To-day (Silver, 1894, revised 1910), devoted to nineteen writers whom the author regards as most important.

From a multitude of books dealing with individual authors or with special types of literature we have selected the following brief list, which is suggestive rather than critical.

Study of Fiction. Henry James, The Art of Fiction; Howells, Criticism in Fiction; Crawford, The Novel: What It Is; Smith, The American Short Story; Canby, The Short Story in English.

Biography. Life of Harriet Beecher Stowe, by C. E. Stowe. Life of Bret Harte, by Pemberton, or by Merwin, or by Boynton. Life of Bayard Taylor, by Marie Taylor and Horace Scudder; or by Smyth, in American Men of Letters. Life of Stedman, by Laura Stedman and G. M. Gould.

Life of Thomas Bailey Aldrich, by Greenslet. Letters of Sarah Orne Jewett, edited by Annie Fields. Life of Edward Rowland Sill, by Parker. Thompson's Eugene Field. Mrs. Field's Charles Dudley Warner. Grady's Joel Chandler Harris. Life of Mark Twain, by Paine, 3 vols.

Historical and Reminiscent. Page, The Old South; Nicholson, The Hoosiers; Howells, My Literary Passions; Henry James, Notes of a Son and Brother; Stoddard, Recollections Personal and Literary, edited by Hitchcock; Elizabeth Stuart Phelps, Chapters from a Life; Trowbridge, My Own Story.

CHAPTER V

BOOKS AND WRITERS OF THE PRESENT DAY

> I'm going out to fetch the little calf
> That's standing by the mother. It's so young,
> It totters when she licks it with her tongue.
> I sha'n't be gone long — You come too.
>
> Robert Frost, "The Pasture"[1]

In contrast with the literature of a past age, which is easily apprehended because generations of readers have sifted out for us the few works of enduring interest, the literature of the present offers a baffling problem. As we approach the subject, note well its outstanding characteristics.

The first is vastness, as of a moving flood. Between five and six thousand new books are now published in America every year, far more than one meets in a history covering all the centuries of English literature. Granting that half of this annual product may be dismissed as works of instruction, there remain between two and three thousand books and a corresponding multitude of authors, all at once demanding our attention. Before we could examine these, at the rate of two or three books each week, twenty years would come and go, leaving fifty thousand more books as a contribution to present-day literature.

The second characteristic, undefined but real as a fog, is a bewildering vagueness. This is so pronounced that one may question whether present literature be not as illusory as the present moment. We are told that, of all moments, the present only is ours; but there is never a present moment. While we think of it, lo! our moment is passed and another is passing. So with the flood of books that go by us continually: we call

[1] From Robert Frost's *North of Boston* (Henry Holt and Company).

them present-day literature, ignoring the fact that true literature has a timeless or permanent quality, meaning that it appears but does not pass, remaining with us forever.

For example, there came recently from our press, without any trumpet of announcement, a little novel by Louis Hémon, a French writer domiciled in Canada, and its name was *Maria Chapdelaine*. It portrayed the lives of village people in the province of Quebec, in our own day; but it was a work of pure genius in that it reflected faithful-hearted people of any province of earth in any age since man became civilized. No sooner was it here than it seemed to have been always with us, so beautiful it was, and so natural, and so human. One followed the story as one might listen to a church organ softly playing, or as one might watch the twilight with a star hanging over it and a wood-thrush singing. Beyond question this unpretentious novel is literature with its eternal quality; but if you ask, What recent American books should be so classed? there is no man wise enough to give answer. Literature must be sifted by time and humanity before one can know what books are passing and what are permanent.

With this introduction, let it be specified that present-day books will here be regarded as those of the last fifteen or twenty years. During this period some two thousand writers have claimed a place in American literature. The difficulty of adjusting their claim is manifest in the work of historians who wrestle with the subject. Thus, in 1915 appeared a history of recent literature dealing with about three hundred " prominent " or " promising " authors, and omitting many more. Most of the three hundred are still writing; yet in 1922 appeared another record of " prominent " or " promising " authors, and hardly a dozen of those emphasized in the first book are emphasized in the second, though both historians deal as faithfully as they can with the material at hand. Moreover, you might search both records without finding the writer that seems to you most finely representative of the present day.

Authors and Readers. In explanation of this phenomenon of criticism one needs but to recall the fact that a score or more of promising new writers appear every year. Occasionally the first book of such a writer is as good, apparently, as the best work of authors who have long been conspicuous on the literary stage, or it may be decidedly better. Very often the writer's first book is his best book. Indeed, it may be the only book of his that is worth reading; but he follows his market (for writers are human, like other folk) and continues to write long after he has anything to say. Meanwhile the older writers are all busy, each producing a book every year or two, though one who reads their later work must wonder how it was that many of them so easily won a reputation which they so hardly keep.

The answer is simple : every new author is like a pleasant new visitor in that he forms a circle of acquaintances who like him or believe in him. If the circle be large enough, his literary success is assured, because publishers will print any dull book he may write, trusting his circle of readers to accept the offering. This is true of nearly all writers who have recently been prominent, and who suggest a curious literary contrast between the present and an earlier age.

Old Writers and New. Our elder writers, from Poe to Longfellow and from Irving to Emerson, all followed practically the same literary course, which is the course still commonly followed by the best writers of European countries. They began modestly; they won a place with more or less difficulty; they steadily developed their talent; and by works of increasing power they widened their audience, their influence, their reputation. In the end they became national figures, each standing for some manifestation of the American spirit; and they have more readers now, both at home and abroad, than ever they had during their lifetime.

The story of our younger writers is different, especially the story of our favorites during the past forty years. As a rule, they begin boldly with an original or striking work ; they win a large audience easily; but for some unexplained reason they seldom develop or fulfil their early promise. In consequence they fail to become national figures, as Longfellow and Emerson were national; nor have they won recognition abroad to compare with that of Poe or Cooper or Whitman. Nearly every one of to-day's prominent writers, after his first success, has produced much ordinary work; yet so widespread is the interest in new literature, and so vast our country, that an author who once wins recognition is upheld by his circle of readers so long as he continues to write. Outside that circle your well-known writer who appears prominently in the literary reviews is a mere name, and may rightly be regarded as inferior to a score of writers who are not well known.

In fine, the tendency of present-day writers as a class, and with few individual exceptions, is to be too much absorbed in the present; that is, they reflect a passing interest or humor or novelty rather than the enduring truths of nature or of human nature. Such a generalization is open to challenge, and doubtless has its proportion of error; but it suggests, at least, an explanation of the common literary phenomenon of a writer who is enormously successful to-day, only to be forgotten when to-morrow brings forth its new interests, with new writers to make the most of their opportunity. Wordsworth's sonnet beginning "The world is too much with us" may be an excellent summary of the matter.

Limitations of our Study. Facing such conditions, it would be vain to pretend that one can write a trustworthy history or criticism of present-day literature. Aside from the vastness and vagueness of the subject, fair history and fair criticism of the present are both impossible. The sole purpose of this or of any similar chapter is, happily, to serve as a temporary guide for those who are bewildered by too many books.

If you conclude, after reading, that the selection of authors and types is too much governed by personal taste, you are probably right. If you ask, Why are not such and such favorite authors included? the only answer is that "favorite" has a rather personal meaning, and that a hundred million Americans have more favorites than any one American can understand. At every point in the narrative, therefore, you may have reason to differ from the opinion expressed, and you certainly have the right to follow your own taste. Lest our pleasant study become "like sweet bells jangled, out of tune and harsh," let two harmonious principles be understood: first, that we must omit the so-called younger writers who are supposed to be blazing a new trail through the old field of literature, because such trails commonly peter out in a squirrel track and end in a tree; and second, that there is ample room here for every personal impression that is modestly so expressed, but no room whatever for dogmatic judgment.

THE NOVELISTS

Because the novel is the most impressive form of modern literature, some have used it as a practical instrument of progress or reform; hence the problem novel and the novel of set purpose. There are scores of such, each aiming at reform of business or religion or politics or society. A few are well done, and may be effective by calling attention to this or that need or cry; but they are excluded from this study, because the moment you devote a novel to any other than its sole or proper purpose it becomes, in our imagination at least, a kind of tract or propaganda, and should be so classed. The first and last purpose of fiction is to give pleasure, and the purpose is accomplished by portraying certain types of men and women or certain human experiences in a way which, however colored by imagination or humor or emotion, still gives the impression of truth, as if we were dealing with real men and real experiences.

One American Novel. For more than a century now — ever since the day of Charles Brockden Brown — our people have been talking about "the great American novel" and confidently expecting its appearance. Such an expectation might possibly be realized in England or France, each with its ancient folk-lore, its settled tradition, its native population; but it is an idle dream in America, for the reason that our country is too vast, with too many and too varied races of men and types of character, for any one novel to reflect it with even a semblance of truth.

Meanwhile a multitude of novelists are portraying life in this or that section, under this or that urge or handicap; and one of these furnishes an admirable start for our study of present-day fiction. This is *Vandemark's Folly* (1922), one of the best American novels of this or any other period. The scene is laid along the Erie Canal and on the lonely Iowa prairies, at a time when the canal was a pioneer highway over which passed all sorts and conditions of men, lured by the call of land in the West. Into that westward-moving multitude comes a boy, a waif, who is molded into manhood by two influences; namely, responsiveness to the vigorous life about him and loyalty to the memory of his mother. There is nothing strange or forced or foreign in the story; the narrative develops as naturally as life itself and becomes intensely real, intensely American,— real in that it pictures life as it is, or was, and American in that the action might well have occurred in Iowa or Kansas or any one of a score of our states, but could not have occurred in any other land on earth.

The author of the novel, Herbert Quick, cannot have lived the life which he portrays; but he certainly knows those who have lived it, or else he has a most excellent imagination. He enters with the understanding of sympathy into the rough but essentially healthy spirit of the frontier; his portrayal of the moving throng that thins out as it moves westward, until only a solitary driver is seen rising in his "schooner" over the prairie swells, like a ship alone on a vast sea, is marvelous in its fidelity to pioneer experience. Into the story come good men and bad, fine women and foolish, all portrayed with truth, with humor, with charity; and through the story runs a little romance, as naturally, as inevitably, as a brook winds its way through shade and sunshine to the waiting sea.

In sum, here is, if not a great novel, at least a good human and national novel, a type of what the American novel should be but seldom is. Almost simultaneously appeared *The Covered Wagon*, by Emerson Hough, a story of the Oregon Trail, having the same pioneer theme as *Vandemark's Folly*, the same wide horizon and the same epic quality. Both novels are uncommonly good reflections of our moving frontier, the most stirring scene in the American national drama. Many more such are waiting to be discovered by the Connecticut and the Ohio, by the Cumberland Road and the Santa Fé Trail, by every one of the pioneer highways over which a free people passed in their conquest of a continent.

Novels of Society. Among many novelists who deal each with a section of American society, North or South or East or West, two are here selected, not because they are the best, for that cannot justly be said, but because it is better to read two, any two, than to regard a hundred without reading.

One such portrayer of the people of a section is Booth Tarkington, who aims to reflect the Middle West, and whose novels of young life and the " gawky " age, *Penrod*, *Gentle Julia*, and *Seventeen*, have been widely welcomed. Of his more ambitious works *The Magnificent Ambersons* (1918) is perhaps the best. After reading these books one has an impression that the author has lost the child's imaginative view of life and has not yet attained the man's view. He has a clever knack of writing, but the knack has not developed since he published *Monsieur Beaucaire* in 1900. Concerning the quality of his work there are two opinions. His circle of readers and some critics declare that he reflects youth truthfully, as he sees it; that he not only reveals youth to itself, but gives age more sympathy in dealing with the folly of children who have too little work and too much liberty for their own good. That is surely one phase of American society, and as such, a novelist must deal with it. Other critics think that Tarkington's idea of youth appears to be a mannerless cub of a boy and an impertinent girl, both badly brought up by stupid relatives in an atmosphere of sham culture, and that by portraying such types as representative he unconsciously gives a false impression of a whole society. And such critics are disappointed that one who can write well should be content with a superficial portrayal of silly experiences, without ever facing the big things of life, or reflecting the indomitable will and mighty achievement of the Middle West, or thinking out a plot to its logical conclusion, or following the development of a character as molded by steadfast ideal and changing circumstance.

Mrs. Edith Wharton portrays a different section in a different way. Her mind is mature; her talent is carefully cultivated; she aims to reflect from a cosmopolitan viewpoint one phase of that vast complexity which we call America. Her field is small and, it must be confessed, a little snobbish: she deals with " society," and confines herself to that corner of society which complacently regards itself as the best. In consequence there are no wide horizons in her books, which are distinctly of the indoor variety. In her method she has been influenced by Henry James, a novelist who has an impressive way of picking at petty things as if he would conjure something important out of a nut. So, though her work is carefully planned and more carefully labored, her every novel is marred (or improved, as some think) by analytical details that seldom repay a reader for the lack of action. Her short stories, on the other hand, are very finely done, are indeed models of the short-story art. *The Age of Innocence* (1920) gives a good impression of this author's style and quality, but many think that *The House of Mirth* (1905) is a better novel.

The Romance of History. Writers of historical romances are numerous. When upon rare occasion one of them writes a story that helps us to visualize our heroic past, the instant and hearty response indicates that this type of novel is quite as popular as ever it was in the day of Scott or Cooper. For example, a writer whose name was recently a household word among literary folk is S. Weir Mitchell, who ended his labors in 1914. He has to his credit over thirty literary works; but his *Hugh Wynne, Free Quaker*, an excellent novel of the War of Independence, has probably more readers than all his other books combined and is now practically his only book that is widely known.

Mary Johnston, a Southern writer with a charmingly Southern attitude, has given us one stirring romance of Colonial days in *To Have and to Hold*, and another of our Civil War in *The Long Roll*. Her works are few; for which we may be grateful, since she cultivates her talent, apparently, and when her work finally appears it rewards us for the waiting. Among all our writers of historical romance there is none that tells a better tale or tells it in a more satisfactory way.

At the present time, probably the best known of our historical novelists is Winston Churchill, who for over twenty years has devoted himself to portraying the stirring periods of American history. His most popular and, as many think, his best novel is *Richard Carvel* (1899), a story of the War of Independence, with the naval hero John Paul Jones as one of the characters. His novel of Civil War days, *The Crisis*, might well be read with Miss Johnston's *The Long Roll*, since one portrays the romance of the war from the Union and the other from the Confederate side. Though these works appeared earlier than the period which we have specified as the present, they are here recommended for the reason that, like most American writers of the past half-century, the novelist does not fulfil his splendid early promise by works of increased power. *The Inside of the Cup* (1913) is perhaps the best of his later romances.

Types of Character. A score of novelists are devoted to the portrayal of different types of American character, especially types that begin to appear now as survivals of a simpler and more heroic age.

To this kind of novel a mighty impetus was given by *David Harum*, written by Edward Noyes Westcott near the beginning of the present century. Aside from its human interest, which is large, or its literary value, which is debatable, this homely story furnishes a commentary on critical publishers and uncritical readers. Our publishers are keen men ; they are alert to discover new writers ; each employs trained readers and, occasionally, a famous critic to examine manuscripts with the one purpose of finding a work that is worth printing ; they make it their chief concern to know what the public wants, and to supply it as attractively and as cheaply as possible, for such is the *business* of publishing. Yet these experienced men were as blind as moles to the human appeal of *David Harum*, which went begging from one to another, while critics could see nothing in it that was worth the small risk of publication. Then one publisher "took a chance," as he supposed, after suggesting certain changes to which the author agreed ; and hardly was the book out when readers welcomed it by the hundred thousand. Its popular success was tremendous, and few critics would now deny that its success was deserved. The story smacked of the soil. There was humor and kindness and unchanging human nature in it. One or two of the characters were as real in a literary sense as if they had stepped out of the pages of Dickens, and as real in the American sense as if we had known them about the stove of a country grocery store. The writer died before his story was published, and he remains, perhaps fortunately, a man of one book.

Working in the same field, Irving Bacheller has given us one excellent type of countryman in *Eben Holden* (1900), a readable novel that well deserved the welcome with which readers received it. Since then he has written several more novels, which show a falling off rather than a development of literary power. Another worker in the field is Joseph Lincoln, who, lured by that undefinable call of the near-sea which draws visitors to Cape Cod, has reflected in a dozen novels his idea of old-time characters with the tang of the brine in them. Read *Mary-'Gusta* (1916), which is perhaps his best work, or *The Portygee* (1920) or *Fair Harbor* (1922), not because they are particularly good novels but because they exemplify a type in which readers are interested. It is a mistake to assume that the writers of this or of any other age make literature. Some do — working apart in solitude; but the great majority merely supply a demand that is created by readers. Nor does this apply to minor literature only: Homer's poems and Shakespeare's plays were both alike the response to a popular demand.

A different type of character appears in the work of James Lane Allen, whose field is the Bluegrass region of Kentucky. A good novel in which to become acquainted with this writer's style and method is *The Mettle of the Pasture* (1903). If a later work is desired, because it is more of the present day, try *The Kentucky Warbler* (1918). In a neighboring field John Fox, Jr., portrays a unique type, the so-called Mountain White or American Highlander; and it is an interesting study to compare his happy romances with those of the more studious-minded Allen. His reputation was made by *The Little Shepherd of Kingdom Come* (1903). A later and more popular romance is his *Trail of the Lonesome Pine* (1908). The falling off which is characteristic of most American novelists is evident in *Erskine Dale, Pioneer* (1920), which is readable enough, but which has little to distinguish it from the work of a hundred amateurs.

The great West offers many human types: the Friar, the Don, the Plainsman, the Indian, the Peon, the Rancher, and, " cutting circles " around them all, the Cowboy, who is our most picturesque character since Leatherstocking. Here on the last frontier is a splendid field for fiction; but the field is not well cultivated for the reason that, by apparently irresistible attraction, writers of Western fiction produce not a novel of character but a yarn of adventure. *The Virginian* of Owen Wister is an attempt, and almost the sole recent attempt in this field, to combine the novel of character with the popular adventure story.

Gertrude Atherton is of the West by birth and training; but not content with this ample field, she goes from California to New York and overseas to England in her search for material, becoming a cosmopolitan in her journeying. Her work is less a study of types than of social or political conditions which are supposed to mold the type. Her fifteen novels are of very uneven merit, some being excellently done, while others are best characterized by "smartness." *The Splendid Idle Forties*, dealing with the West, and *The Conqueror*, reflecting the political turmoil that centered in Alexander Hamilton, are regarded as her best works. Her latest and most popular novel is *Black Oxen* (1923), in which the heroine is a woman, once a "reigning beauty" in New York society, who returns after thirty years and a surgical operation as young and bewitching as ever. As literature the book is rather trashy; but it is an excellent example of the writer's power to hold her circle of readers by a portrayal of novel incidents enlivened by a brilliant style and society manners.

Very different is Mary Austin, who lived for years on the edge of the Mohave Desert,— lived as an Indian woman lives, and so entered into the desert secrets. You will know whether or not you want to read more of this rare writer's works, as some do, if you begin with her fanciful tales for children in *The Basket Woman*. The most remarkable work that has ever been done in the Western field with the Indian as a character appears in the little books of J. Willard Schultz, who is ignored by literary critics because he writes only adventure stories for boys. Would that those who write for men and women had the secret of his method! The heroes of all his tales are a white boy, the son of a fur trader, and his "almost brother" Pitamakan, a young Blackfoot Indian. The adventures and escapes of these two are a marvelous reflection of the habits and beliefs of savage riders of the Plains in the days of the buffalo. Schultz's way of telling a story — simple, straightforward, with constant action and dramatic dialogue — is near perfection, and was evidently learned by listening to Indian tale-tellers while he was a member of the tribe. Of all our writers, early or late, he is the only one who comes near to knowing the soul of an Indian.

The Social Novel. An extreme type of modern fiction is the so-called social novel, meaning one in which the chief character is not so much an individual as a whole class of men and women who give (to the novelist) an impression of being governed by economic law or industrial habit rather than by free will. In dealing with this peculiar type one should note, first, that the writers who gave it impetus were all young journalists (Stephen Crane, Frank Norris, Harold Frederic) accustomed to continuous excitement, which is not wholesome, and to snap judgments of men or events, which are very seldom right; and second, that they all selected Zola for their model, with the result that their earliest fiction was characterized by frequent brutality or bad taste, which they imagined was realism.

The most striking novel of this type was written by Frank Norris after he was done with realism of the Zola kind. Then he planned a trilogy of novels of the wheat, each being an allegory of industrial America. Thus *The Octopus*, which was intended to make the locomotive symbolic of its hero or villain, portrays the grain-grower in a losing war against the transportation trust, with its power and greed and alleged selfishness. The whole story, and the author's peculiar notion of railroads, is condensed into the episode of an engine plowing at full speed through a flock of sheep. The second of the trilogy, *The Pit*, deals with the financial manipulation of grain, as reflected by a deal in the Chicago wheat pit; and the third, *The Wolf* (never written), was planned to follow our American grain in its last journey to a starving community in Europe. The first novel was undoubtedly strong and original, but showed the journalistic craving for excitement. The second was weaker, with excitement more artificial; and it may be as well that the third was not written. The writer's plan was greater than his power to accomplish.

Norris, though outside our specified limits, is nevertheless selected because he was the greatest of a modern group, and because later novelists who make an allegory of the farm or the factory or the stockyard or of industry itself have all alike failed to give their themes reality, and have either entered other fields (as Crane wrote his *Red Badge of Courage*) or else have resorted in their novels to "stunts" more characteristic of the sensation-loving journalist than of the balance and restraint of the true novelist. Apparently the social novel is too big and too impersonal for satisfactory treatment, or else the right man has not yet appeared, to master it. If you doubt the criticism, select any social novel of recent days and put it to the test. The only approach to artistic success in this field since Norris wrote *The Octopus* appears in a very different novel, *The Reign of Law*, by James Lane Allen, in which we are only half persuaded that the hemp fields of Kentucky may govern the life of a community.

The Novel of Adventure. While literary critics are busy with such writers as we have named, a multitude of readers blithely follow their own taste, which leads them to the novel of adventure, — now as in all times the most popular form of fiction. Rafael Sabatini writes his *Captain Blood*, for example, and readers care not a whit what reviewers say or think, because they are satisfied with a well-told story of buccaneers and treasure and love and brave adventure.

The North is a favorite scene of such fiction, and a score of writers since Jack London have exploited it; but all follow the same false trail, striving for "brutal" characters or incidents and drawing a grossly perverted picture of both nature and human nature. Not one of them has his eye on the truth of life; their work is, in consequence, of no interest save to the many who like dime novels. Stewart Edward White made a much better beginning with his *Blazed Trail*, *Conjuror's House* and *Silent Places*; but presently he rambled off into other fields of fiction, without once taking his work or his reader seriously.

The West has long been the favorite location for outdoor adventure, and for a simple reason: it was our last frontier. The type of Western story is ever the same. There must be a cowboy hero, a girl in danger or distress, a gunman or bad man, and a band of rustlers or outlaws, the whole scrambled together with plenty of shooting and such varied humor and adventure as the writer finds in his unfettered imagination. The only departure from type appears when a writer, striving for novelty, begins with a Western scene and then produces a "gold brick" by making a conventional detective story, to be solved by the clock, or by using as his heroes and villains a band of "movie" actors who go through the motions of wild-west adventure in their usual flashy way.

Numerous writers are busily producing the romance of Western adventure; but it would be unfair to discriminate among them, since all are doing the same thing in about the same way. Zane Grey is for the moment the most popular writer in this field, and occasionally he tells a very good tale, as in *The Man of the Forest*; but he has no humor, and his work is very uneven, — extremely crude in stories of the Ohio frontier, or rather hysteric in *The Wanderer of the Wasteland*, or given over to wordy descriptions besprinkled with purple adjectives. If you must have a specific example of the "real thing" in Western fiction, try Mulford's *The Man from Bar-20* and White's *Lynch Lawyers*, with their zest and humor and riding and shooting, and no pretense whatever save of pleasing you with a good, impossible yarn.

Such adventure stories (which are scoffed at by literary critics) represent the oldest type of fiction. They have always appealed to the most readers, for the reason that every proper man longs to get out of the humdrum into the adventurous life; and they still furnish entertainment to uncounted readers who ask only that a novel hold to its first purpose of giving wholesome pleasure.

THE SHORT STORY

to here

The modern short story, which is very different from the ancient tale, is America's peculiar contribution to literary types. In its present form it originated here and, encouraged by our many magazines, rose swiftly to its present leading place. In its material it covers every type and character and incident of our enormously varied life; in its method it is bound by cast-iron rules, and must meet rigid tests prescribed by magazine editors. That these artificial tests might be "more honored in the breach than in the observance" is aside from the question: we are dealing with the short story as it is, not as it might better be.

Qualifications. Among the many prescribed tests are: (1) Originality, or at least ingenuity. In this the short story differs from the novel, which may follow old ways or old plots that have been used for ages. (2) Unity, as distinct from complexity of theme or treatment. The story must deal with a single incident or situation; it must plan the one impression which is to be made, and work steadily at that impression without halt or digression. (3) Something must happen; in other words, there must be constant action, as in a dialogue or play. The writer must have a moving tale to tell, and his matter is of much more consequence than his style or manner. (4) The tale must be modern, up to date or up to the minute, and must conform to the rule for visitors written over the door of Cotton Mather's study, "Be short!"

There are other qualifications of the short story, as magazines now demand it; but these four — originality, unity, action and up-to-dateness — are the essentials. If it can be adorned by a brilliant style or enlivened by the play of humor, so much the better. In form and structure the story should be as compact as the steel frame of a skyscraper, but this rule needs no emphasis. Nature has decreed that the skeleton of a thing is all-important and that it should be concealed.

Short-Story Writers. The surprising thing is that scores of writers are producing as many varieties of this far-from-easy type of fiction every year. To discriminate among them, measuring their relative place or value, would be very difficult because they change constantly, new favorites appearing while the old turn away to other work. The latest to attain a leading position in the crowded field was "O. Henry" (William Sydney Porter), who finished his work in 1910. No other has taken his place in our magazines or in our journalistic periodicals that strive to increase their huge circulation by printing something amazing every week.

One's first impression of this writer, so enormously popular and so bepraised by critics, is that ordinarily he has little truth in his work or sincerity in his method. He tells a mere anecdote, as any drummer or after-dinner speaker might tell it, with no other plan or purpose than to produce a laugh or a shock at the end. In this last he is as ingeniously surprising as a mousetrap baited with toasted cheese. His "art" is that of the vaudeville stage; he pleases his audience by pulling a rabbit or something more startling out of a hat. His stories fall into two main groups: one reflects his rambling among tramps, escaped convicts and other misunderstood folk; the other, his literary acrobatics in a Sunday newspaper.

Standing apart from the bulk of "O. Henry's" work, as of better quality, are some of the earlier stories, such as are collected in *The Four Million*. They reveal the author not as a mere entertainer, but as viewing soberly the complex life of a modern city, detecting the gleams of truth or beauty above the passing show, and reflecting something of the eternally heroic adventure of humanity. A few of these stories will undoubtedly find a permanent place in our literature.

There are many short-story writers who regularly do better work than "O. Henry" ever did; but none of them has won such a prominent place, perhaps because no one has his knack of surprising "Mr. Everybody," for whom, he said, he wrote.

Of late the short story, which began with Irving as a type of literature, tends to become more and more journalistic, with the result that our best writers drop it for the novel or the drama or some other work that is less mechanical and more artistic. To get acquainted with our short-story craftsmen read the annual *Best Short Stories* or some other of the collections named in the bibliography at the end of the chapter.

POETRY

A recent history (1923) deals with over a hundred poets who are called prominent, in comparison with a larger number who are hopeful of winning recognition. If you would begin well in such a multitude and have pleasure in the beginning, let Sara Teasdale be your introduction to present-day poetry. What her relative place may be is of no consequence : she writes good poetry, and that is enough to say of any modern singer. Moreover, if you are wont to compare to-day's verse with the little songs of yesterday that have a place in your memory, she is one of the few can stand the comparison. Her poems are practically all lyrics ; they have the long virtue of shortness ; there are no strange words or obscure references to distract attention ; the style is limpid, so clear that it suggests the figure of still water in which images are reflected ; almost without exception the lines have a musical or singing quality, which to old-fashioned folk marks the difference between real and imitation poetry. Read first the *Love Songs* (1917), which was not Miss Teasdale's first book but the first to arouse the hope that a poet had come. Then, for a reflection of more thoughtful moods, read *Flame and Shadow* (1920). Before you have finished either volume you will probably say, Here is one who can reflect the beauty, the wonder, the mystery and the reverence of life in poems that are short and simple and always finely done.

When you have estimated these poems it would be well, for

a pleasant comparison, to read *Factories and Other Poems* (1915) or *The Old Road to Paradise* (1918) or *Cross-Currents* (1921), which are little books of verse by Margaret Widdemer. The two singers won recognition at about the same time, and you will have more benefit from comparing their works for yourself than from reading the second-hand criticism of any historian.

Most critics, but not most readers, would probably place Edwin Arlington Robinson first among present-day poets. He has carefully kept out of the limelight and labored in scholarly fashion to reflect the truth of life as he sees it. To him life appears rather fearfully austere, and his first volume, *Children of the Night*, is as depressing as a down-east fog. That has beauty, if one cares to search it out; but most readers prefer to come in by the fire. In later volumes he emerges from the gray; yet still he does not sing the joy of life, only its stern truth or duty. His craftsmanship is excellent; no slipshod or hasty work escapes from him; he seems to think, with Chaucer,

> Ther n' is no werkman, whatsoever he be,
> That may both werkë wel et hastily.

The Town Down the River (1910) is a good volume in which to make this poet's acquaintance. *The Man Against the Sky* (1916) has some pages of better poetry, but more that are rather heavy reading. *Collected Poems* (1921) contains all the poet's earlier or later work that he thinks worthy of preservation, and with this volume in hand the reader can take the best possible way with any new poet, — go "skipping through," with liberty to linger wherever one likes. Two different types of poem appear in the collection: those that reflect the author's observation of life and those that echo his study of history or literature. For a beginning, if you have no other guide, try "The Poor Relative" or "Octaves" or "The Master" (a study of Lincoln) or "Ben Jonson Entertains a Man from Stratford." But don't look for joyous singing in Robinson's verse; the best you can expect is the monotone of the sea.

A Modern Minstrel. In every way different from the poet last named is Vachel Lindsay, a carefree rambler through our West and Southwest, who recites his way along and makes a camp meeting of every assembly, waving his arms to his verse as if he were a drum major. He is what we never expected to see in America, a minstrel, a troubadour, born out of time, out of place. To understand his poetry one should first read his prose, especially *A Handy Guide for Beggars* and *Adventures While Preaching the Gospel of Beauty.*

There is something of the reformer in our minstrel, something also of the buffoon. He has one streak of pure poetry and another of freakishness; which of the two will appear is always uncertain. He has no poetic model or master, imitates nobody, and dares to be himself without affectation. His verse is sometimes crude and sometimes splendid. Typical of the latter is "Abraham Lincoln Walks," one of the finest poems written during the Great War. Another is "General Booth Enters Heaven," written on the death of the Salvation Army leader; but here we have a suggestion of tambourines and glory-hallelujah shouting, as if the old hero of the faith must take his familiar audience with him into heaven.

Typical of Lindsay's "jazz" style, with its freakishness and rollicking measure, is his "Song of the Congo," which should be chanted rather than read, with a camp-meeting tune for the Mumbo Jumbo refrain. The short poem "Niagara" will suggest others that show the poet in his rôle of reformer or prophet. Of poems that may be read with dramatic or ventriloquial accompaniment "Two Old Crows" and "The Potato Dance" are good examples. Of his several collected works try first *The Congo and Other Poems* (1914), then *The Chinese Nightingale and Other Poems* (1917) and *The Golden Whales of California* (1920).

The Classical School. Among our so-called poets of culture is Edith M. Thomas, who has for many years produced poetry of uniform and excellent quality. She is a dreamer and, at times, a thinker whose work would seem more appropriate to the clear classical age of Greece than to the smoky industrial age of America. Any one of her dozen books of poetry will serve as an introduction to one who is well worth knowing, the earlier *Lyrics and Sonnets*, for example, or the later *Cassia and Other Verse*.

George Edward Woodberry is another good example of the same classical school of American poetry. He has written many books of prose (essays, criticisms, literary appreciations) and a few books of poetry, all alike rather remote from life and all characterized by thought and scholarship rather than by emotion. *The Roamer and Other Poems* (1920) is one of his latest volumes.

Almost as well known to critics, and perhaps better known to ordinary readers, is Katharine Lee Bates, who gave excellent promise as a poet, but whose work as a college teacher has always prevented her, she says, from following her heart longer than for a brief poetic holiday. Her patriotic poems are uncommonly good (note that the best poems of the Great War were nearly all written by women), and one of her lyrics, "America the Beautiful," is already so widely accepted that it bids fair to take a permanent place with Julia Ward Howe's "Battle Hymn of the Republic" as a national song. It would be well to begin acquaintance with this poet in *Fairy Gold*, which was written, and very well written, for children; then for work of increasing power read *America the Beautiful and Other Poems, The Retinue* and *Yellow Clover*.

Poets of the War. Two poets of the Great War who are read largely because of their death on the battlefield are Alan Seeger and Joyce Kilmer. Both had made a beginning of poetry before the war; but whether they showed a promise greater than that of many others is not yet known, for the reason that we refuse to judge. Their work is cherished, like that of the young English poet Rupert Brooke, because of their sacrifice. Seeger's one memorable poem is "I Have a Rendezvous with Death," which proved prophetic. Kilmer's best poem is that which gives title to his tiny volume *Trees and Other Poems* (1915). For further reading the best work is *Joyce Kilmer* (1918), a book of poems, essays and letters published after the author's death.

Outdoor Poets. Most critics would probably agree that one of the most notable of recent poets is Robert Frost, who finds his poetry out of doors, either in the face of the fields or the faces of men who are in daily contact with the elemental realities of earth and sky. There are no joyous lyrics in his work, but only narrative, meditative and descriptive verse. Of him more than of any other recent poet the word "realistic" may be used in its best sense. He describes a scene or an incident in a way that makes you see what he sees, — a thing that few descriptive writers ever accomplish. Read "The Birches," for example, and see the graceful trees bending under the weight of a winter storm. So in all his work, he invents nothing; he is rather sternly accurate in picturing things as they are; any book of his gives the total impression of a winter landscape, gaunt, bare, cheerless, with sharp outlines and chilly blue shadows. His style is casual, often conversational or dramatic, and always terse, — the repressed style of an outdoor man, accustomed to silence, who wastes never a word. With all this matter-of-factness our poet is still a poet, one who sees beauty where others see only wood or stubble.

Frost began his poetic career in England with *A Boy's Will* (1913), which Englishmen welcomed as the work of a "truly American" poet, meaning one totally different from their own. The next year he settled on a New Hampshire farm and proceeded to put the farm into poetry, much as Charles A. Stevens (a writer for young people) put a Maine farm into prose with his Old Squire stories. "The Woodpile," "Christmas Trees," "After Apple Picking," "Mending Wall," "Putting in the Seed," — such poems are crystallized bits of life; anyone who has worked on a northern farm will recognize them as such,

with memories of a time when the woodpile meant a bucksaw,
a tired back, a cold bath in a cold room, — anything but poetry.
Two small but excellent volumes for the beginner are *North of
Boston* (1914) and *Mountain Interval* (1916).

An outdoor singer of contrasting type is Clinton Scollard,
who has published more than thirty books of verse. That is too
many, — at least, one fears so ; yet there is nothing hurried or
careless in the poet's work, though his mood be that of a linnet.
His verse is always graceful, often pleasing, and it has the
singing quality. The future may know more about him than
does the present. One of the earlier volumes, *With Reed and
Lyre*, for example, or *Hills of Song*, may give a better first
impression of Scollard's joyously lyrical quality than some of
the volumes published in more recent years.

Free Verse. Any examination of present-day poetry must
include free verse, or *vers libre*, as the writers thereof call it for
some odd reason, — perhaps to show that they have " taken "
freshman French. They are the " imagists," the " colorists,"
the " futurists," the " revolutionaries " of literature, and they
have ingenious explanations of themselves and their formless
verse. One theory is that, being artists, they must have complete freedom from rules and conventions ; another, that the
modern world needs a more adequate expression than old poets
have ever given it. Therefore do they speak with images or
symbols rather than with words, sending forth thoughts in the
mass or ideas in the birth or figures dimly shaped, as it were,
in the rough marble, leaving the reader to grasp the main idea
and fill in all details for himself. Especially do these writers
insist that the new voice must speak as freely as the new soul
thinks or feels.

There are two opinions of such new souls and voices. One
is that they are really doing something rare and making an
important contribution to our literature, as they themselves
think. The other is that they are victims of an old delusion,
which appears as frequently as a new cure or a new religion ;

that their easy and childish verse forms are an excuse to escape from the patient labor which finished verse demands ; that they do not write poetry but a poor substitute, which they would have us believe is " just as good " or even better.

Such are the opposing criticisms, both strongly held. If you would decide for yourself which is more nearly right, try any volume written by a modern apostle of free verse, avoiding the extremists, who are merely clownish in their attempt to be more irregular than others. Amy Lowell is, for the time being, the chief exponent of the new poetry. She has written seven volumes of verse, and many essays in explanation thereof. *A Dome of Many-Coloured Glass* (1912) is the most readable of her works, not because it is good poetry but because it is at least rhythmical, and so spares the reader the jolting gait of her later volumes. Though all free-verse makers think that they follow Whitman, very few of them have noticed that he commonly uses a chanting, rhythmic prose that falls pleasantly on the ear. More characteristic of Miss Lowell's fixed style and method are her later volumes; such, for example, as *Pictures of the Floating World* (1919) or *Legends* (1921).

If, or when, you weary of such verse, you may find something that is perhaps better, certainly more vigorous and original, in Carl Sandburg's crude hunks of poetry. Try his *Slabs of the Sunburnt West* (1922) or his earlier *Chicago Poems*. There are several more who easily write free verse ; but two are enough for a beginning. Some may find them too much.

THE DRAMA

Three different varieties of drama now occupy our stage. The first is made exclusively for acting ; often it is made for some particular actress or actor ; always, for better effect, it is made over by producer or manager until the author hardly recognizes his original work, the prime object being to draw a crowd and leave money in the box office. This is the commercialized play, sometimes good, more often sensational or sentimental or verging on the brink of indecency. Whether good, bad or indifferent, literature has nothing to do with such plays, since one never thinks of reading them. They must be seen on the stage or they have no existence.

The second kind of play is the dramatization of a popular novel, one which has had so many readers that the alert dramatist's attention is called to it as a probable money-maker on the stage. This also is commercialized, and with it literature has nothing to do; especially not since the dramatized story is commonly a *Pollyanna* or a *Lightnin'* or some other accident of popular taste that is hardly worth consideration either as play or novel.

The third kind of play is what is becoming known as the literary and artistic drama, which places the portrayal of truth or beauty above all other considerations. Literature is concerned with this form of drama because it can be read with pleasure, apart from the stage with its always distressful glitter and frequently distressful acting. It is noteworthy that Jacinto Benavente, who is at the head of his craft in Spain (a land of great dramatists) and whose plays have been acted over most of the civilized world, has recently announced (1923) that he has abandoned the theater and will henceforth write plays for the *reading* public. Among his reasons are that, what with salaries and costumes and scenery, the expense of producing a play is now enormous; that for a play to fail on the stage, after such expense, may be disastrous; that, in consequence, the playwright no less than the producer must forever keep his eye on his audience rather than on the truth of life; that, finally, the actors of a play commonly give a totally different impression from what the maker of the play intended. And he adds, with the conviction of experience, that only one who reads a drama as the author wrote it can appreciate its true value as a reflection of life.

The Little Theater. Until recent years the artistic drama had small chance of being either staged or read in America.

Suddenly appeared the so-called Little Theater (1911), and the response showed that many had been waiting for better plays than producers had thus far given them. The first aim of the Little Theater was to free the drama from commercialism ; the second, to give any dramatist of ability an audience and a fair hearing. The new impulse spread rapidly, powerfully, until within the space of ten years the Provincetown Players, the Washington Square Players, the Wisconsin Players, and fifty other organized groups as far south as New Orleans and as far west as Los Angeles offer to our dramatists not only the chance but the encouragement to do original and artistic work.

It is not meant by the above that our " regular " theaters deliberately discourage good work ; on the contrary, they are mostly eager for original plays, taking the best they can get and making them over in face of the stern alternative of pleasing an audience or losing money. The fact is, according to a dramatic critic who has been acquainted with the New York theater for twenty-odd years, that most playwrights have been quite as commercial as producers or managers in that they copy any trashy or sentimental model with a hopeful eye on the financial returns. Then came the Little Theater, saying, " The play's the thing ! " and frankly inviting good work for the work's sake. Whether this is but another fad or whether it will bring the American stage nearer to the European stage, with its more artistic plays and better acting, remains for the future to say.

Typical Plays. As an introduction to the modern literary and poetic drama, read *The Piper* by Josephine Preston Peabody. This is one of the many prize plays of recent years; it had its successful day on the stage, and after the footlights are out it is still good reading. The story is the old legend of the Pied Piper of Hamelin, who piped the rats out of a city into the river, and then, when the city refused to pay, piped its children away by his music. If you read more plays by this author (*Marlowe* and *The Wolf of Gubbio*) or by others who attempt the artistic drama, you must notice this disappointing quality, that they commonly search other lands and distant times for a theme. This is plainly a weakness or blindness of our dramatists; for yesterday appeared an Englishman named Drinkwater, and his impressive *Abraham Lincoln* showed the kind of dramatic material which our own writers have long neglected.

Between the older and the newer dramatists stand two whose work is well worth examining, especially by one who is interested in the technique of playwriting. These are David Belasco and Augustus Thomas, who have to their credit several works that are distinctly better than the ordinary commercialized drama. *The Return of Peter Grimm* by Belasco and *The Witching Hour* by Thomas are, on the whole, the best works of those now called the older dramatists because, so rapidly do we change favorites, they produced their chief works before 1912.

Most promising of present-day dramatists is Eugene O'Neill, one of the Provincetown Players, who is associated with the Little Theater movement. He has originality, force, imagination and, above all, sincerity. Recognition came quickly to him because of his striking plays of the sea; such, for example, as *Anna Christie* and *The Moon of the Caribbees*. The best of all his plays is *Beyond the Horizon* (1920). His astonishing variety appears in *The Emperor Jones*, which portrays a negro ex-convict who imposes on the credulity of some West Indian natives to make himself monarch of the tribe. When they discover the fraud, the "emperor" flees by night to the forest, where he is beset by ghosts, hoodoos, hobgoblins, all the hallucinations begotten of a superstitious mind and a misspent life. Such a night! To see it even in pantomime is to remember Clarence, in *King Richard the Third*:

> O, I have passed a miserable night,
> So full of ugly sights, of ghastly dreams,
> That, as I am a Christian faithful man,
> I would not spend another such a night,
> Though 'twere to buy a world of happy days,
> So full of dismal terror was the time!

OA

Contrasting with the vigor and originality of O'Neill is Percy Mackaye, who has written a dozen conventional plays, seven masques, or pageants, and three operas. He stands for the civic theater to replace the commercialized stage; at times he writes with the hope of influencing a town to take part in a drama, thus going back to the community idea that produced the miracle plays of the Middle Ages. *Caliban,* written to celebrate the tercentenary of the death of Shakespeare, is his best masque; the *Canterbury Pilgrims* (note the foreign material) is his best comedy; *The Immigrants* (now printed as a "lyric drama" but originally written as an opera) is his only dramatic work that shows originality. All these were intended to be seen on the stage to the accompaniment of music, lights, pageantry, and they give an inadequate or disappointing impression in the reading.

William Vaughn Moody is a more forceful dramatist, especially when he reflects the conflict of Puritan ideals with the growing freedom of the West, in which some of the Puritan's descendants now find themselves, — an American theme surely. His best play is *The Great Divide.* Booth Tarkington may well be selected as typical of the many authors who, having won success in other fields, are lured away by the theater. He has written several plays which, with one exception, give the same impression as his novels. The exception is *Clarence* (1919), his best drama and, as some judge, the finest of all his works. Edward Knoblauch writes for stage effects chiefly, and his work is characterized by novelty. Thus, in *My Lady's Dress*, while the heroine sleeps, five dreamlike scenes (plays within a play) portray the care of silkworms in Italy, the weaving of silk in France, the making of lace in Holland, the manufacture of artificial flowers in London, and the trapping of furs in Siberia. Here is a veritable "movie" drama. It is mentioned here as an excellent example of the feminine appeal which attracts the modern woman (who is in the majority in almost every audience) and of the novelty which lures the playgoing man, the American man especially, who is ready to be amused or surprised after his day's work, but does not want to think if he can avoid it.

We have considered only a few typical novelists, poets and dramatists, to the exclusion of our many essayists, humorists, critics, historians and nature writers. To name them all briefly would be to make a mere catalogue; to select those most worthy of remembrance is not yet possible. Undoubtedly, for every book or author here mentioned, ten or twenty that may be quite as good have been passed over in silence, the reason being that no historian could read enough of their collective work to make fair estimate of their relative values. The best that can be done within the limits of a chapter is to make, as it were, a short cut through the middle of present-day litera-ture. To compass the whole field would mean a long life's lesson — and a chaotic big book at the end.

Bibliography. *General History.* Cambridge History of American Literature, Vols. III and IV (Putnam, 1917–1921); a good miscellany by many authors, each dealing with one phase or type of literature. Pattee, History of Ameri-can Literature since 1870 (Century Co., 1915); an excellent summary and criticism of the period from 1870 to 1900; chief writers from 1900 to 1915 briefly mentioned. Manly and Rickert, Contemporary American Literature (Harcourt, Brace and Company, 1923); a very condensed account of about two hundred writers; less a history than a good catalogue; valuable for its bibliographies, including studies and reviews of various authors that have appeared in recent magazines.

General Criticism. Perry, The American Spirit in Literature (1918). Sher-man, On Contemporary Literature (1917). Hackett (editor) On American Books (1920); personal impressions of recent literature by five critics. More, Shelburne Essays, 11 vols. (1904–1921). Canby, Benet and Loveman, Satur-day Papers (1921). Brooks, Letters and Leadership (1918). Mencken, Book of Prefaces, 1 vol. (1917); Prejudices, 2 vols. (1919–1920). Eliot, The Sacred Wood: Essays on Poetry and Criticism (1920). Underwood, Literature and Insurgency (1914).

The Novel. Van Doren, The American Novel (1921). Overton, Women Who Make Our Novels (1918). Gordon, Men Who Make Our Novels (1919). Cooper, Some American Story Tellers (1911). Phelps, The Advance of the English Novel in the Twentieth Century (1916).

The Short Story. Pattee, The Development of the American Short Story (Harper, 1923); latest on the subject, scholarly and readable. Baker, The Contemporary Short Story (1916). Lieberman, The American Short Story (1912). Canby, The Short Story in English (1909). Smith, The American Short Story (1912). Cross, The Short Story (1914). Books dealing with technique and aiming to tell the beginner how to write, are Barrett, Short Story Writing (1898); Esenwein, Writing the Short Story (1909); Williams, Handbook on Story Writing (1917).

Poetry. Cook, Our Poets of To-day (1918; revised by additions, 1920). Wilkinson, New Voices (1919). Peckham, Present-Day American Poetry (1917). Untermeyer, The New Era in American Poetry (1919). Lowes, Convention and Revolt in Poetry (1919). Amy Lowell, Tendencies in Modern American Poetry (1917). Aiken, Skepticisms: Notes on Contemporary Poetry (1919).

The Drama. Matthews, A Book about the Theatre (1916). Clark, British and American Drama of Today (1921). Phelps, The Twentieth Century Theatre (1918); Essays on Modern Dramatists (1920). Moses, The American Dramatist (1917). Chandler, Aspects of Modern Drama (1914). Cheney, The New Movement in the Theatre (1914); The Art Theatre (1917); The Open Air Theatre (1918). Eaton, The American Stage of Today (1908); Plays and Players (1916). Burton, The New American Drama (1913). Andrews, The Drama Today (1913). Lewisohn, The Drama and the Stage (1922). Nathan, The Critic and the Drama (1922). Goldberg, The Drama of Transition (1922). Constance Mackay, The Little Theatre in the United States (1917). Percy Mackaye, The Civic Theatre (1912); The Community Drama (1917). Beegle and Crawford, Community Drama and Pageantry (1916). Baker, Technique of the Drama (1915). Lewis, Technique of the One-Act Play (1918). Hamilton, Studies in Stagecraft (1914); Problems of the Playwright (1917).

Collections of Short Stories. Best Short Stories, edited by O'Brien, 8 vols., each containing the alleged best stories published during a year (Small, Maynard, 1916–1922). Law, Modern Short Stories (Century Co., 1918). Laselle, Short Stories of the New America (Holt, 1919). Heydrick, Americans All (Harcourt, 1920). Williams, Our Short Story Writers (Moffatt, Yard, 1920).

Anthologies. Cooper, Poems of Today, prepared for high-school use (Ginn and Company, 1923). Braithwaite, Anthology of Magazine Verse and Yearbook of American Poetry, annual volumes; Golden Treasury of Magazine Verse (Small, Maynard). Untermeyer, Modern American Poetry (Harcourt, 1921). Le Gallienne, Modern Book of American Verse (Boni and Liveright, 1919). Miscellany of American Poetry (Harcourt, 1920). Monroe and Henderson, The New Poetry (Macmillan, 1920). Richards, High Tide; Melody of Earth; Star Points, 3 vols. (Houghton, 1920). Rittenhouse, Little Book of Modern Verse; Second Book of Modern Verse, 1913, 1919, 2 vols. (Houghton). Stork, Contemporary Verse Anthology, 1916–1920 (Dutton). Clarke, Treasury of War Poetry, 2 vols. (Houghton). From the Front (Appleton, 1918). Erskine, American Humor in Verse (Duffield, 1917). Some Imagist Poets, 3 vols. (Houghton, 1915–1917). Cronyn, The Path on the Rainbow, Indian songs (Boni and Liveright, 1918).

Collections of Plays. Mantle, Best Plays, annual volumes (1920-) (Small, Maynard). Moses, Representative Plays by American Dramatists, 1918–1921, 4 vols. (Dutton). Mayorga, Representative One-Act Plays by American Authors, 24 plays by as many authors (Little, Brown, 1919). Knickerbocker, Plays for Classroom Interpretation (Holt, 1921). Cohen, One Act Plays by Modern Authors, Mackaye, Peabody, Rogers, Tarkington, and Young (Harcourt, 1921). Baker, Modern American Plays, by Belasco, Sheldon, and Thomas (Harcourt, 1920). Quinn, Representative American Plays, by Crothers, Mackaye, Sheldon, and Thomas (Century Co., 1917). Cook and Shay, Provincetown Plays, 1916, 1921, 4 vols. (Stewart Kidd). Dickinson, Wisconsin Plays, 1914, 1918, 2 vols. (Huebsch). Washington Square Plays, Drama League Series (Doubleday, 1916). Baker, Harvard Plays, written by students : Plays of the 47 Workshop, 2 vols. ; Plays of the Harvard Dramatic Club, 2 vols. (Brentano, 1918, 1920).

Collections of Essays. Atlantic Classics, 2 vols. (Atlantic Monthly Press). Kilmer, Literature in the Making (Harper, 1917). Morley, Modern Essays (Harcourt, 1920).

GENERAL BIBLIOGRAPHY

Books dealing with individual writers and with limited periods are named elsewhere, in the special bibliographies that supplement each of the preceding chapters. The following works, selected from a much larger number, will be found useful for reference during the entire course of study.

American Literature. There is unfortunately no series of scholarly volumes covering the whole field, and nothing that approaches a standard history of the subject. One of the best general surveys is Richardson, American Literature, 2 vols. (Putnam, 1887). This is a critical work, containing no biographical material, and the historical sequence is broken by studying each type of literature (fiction, poetry, etc.) by itself. Other general surveys, containing a small amount of biography sadly interwoven with critical matter, are Trent, American Literature (Appleton); Cairn, History of American Literature (Oxford University Press); Wendell, Literary History of America (Scribner); and the Cambridge American Literature, 2 vols. (announced, 1916, Putnam). There are also a score of textbooks dealing briefly with the subject.

Among histories dealing with selected authors in groups or with the writers of some particular section of the country are National Studies in American Letters (Macmillan), which includes Higginson's Old Cambridge, Nicholson's The Hoosiers, Addison's The Clergy in American Letters, etc.; Fulton, Southern Life in Southern Literature; Moses, Literature of the South; Holliday, History of Southern Literature; Wauchope, Writers of North Carolina; Lawton, The New England Poets; Painter, Poets of Virginia; Venable, Beginnings of Literary Culture in the Ohio Valley.

Poetry. Stedman, Poets of America; Onderdonck, History of American Verse; Collins, Poetry and Poets of America.

Fiction. Loshe, The Early American Novel; Erskine, Leading American Novelists; Smith, The American Short Story; Baldwin, American Short Stories; Perry, A Study of Prose Fiction; Howells,

Criticism in Fiction; James, The Art of Fiction; Crawford, The Novel: What It Is.

Miscellaneous Types. Jameson, History of Historical Writing in America; Payne, Leading American Essayists; Brownell, American Prose Masters; Haweis, American Humorists; Payne, American Literary Criticisms; Sears, History of Oratory; Fuller and Trueblood, British and American Eloquence; Seilhamer, History of the American Theater; Hudson, Journalism in the United States; Thomas, History of Printing in America.

A very useful little book is Whitcomb, Chronological Outlines of American Literature (Macmillan), in which all important works are arranged, first, in chronological order, year by year, and then according to authors.

Biography. The best series of literary biographies is American Men of Letters (Houghton). A few American authors are included in English Men of Letters, Great Writers, the brief Beacon Biographies and other series. Biographical collections are Adams, Dictionary of American Authors; Cyclopedia of American Biography, 6 vols. (Appleton); Allibone, Dictionary of English Literature and British and American Authors, 6 vols. (Lippincott); Howes, American Bookmen; Fields, Biographical Notes and Personal Sketches.

Selections. Calhoun and MacAlarney, Readings from American Literature, containing selections from all important authors in one volume (Ginn and Company); Stedman and Hutchinson, Library of American Literature, 11 vols. (Webster); Duyckinck, Cyclopedia of American Literature, 2 vols. (Scribner); Bronson, American Poems and American Prose, 2 vols. (University of Chicago Press); Lounsbury, American Poems (Yale University Press); Stedman, An American Anthology, supplementing the same author's Poets of America (Houghton); Page, Chief American Poets, with very full selections from our nine elder poets (Houghton); The Humbler Poets, newspaper and magazine verse, 2 vols. (McClurg); Golden Treasury of American Songs and Lyrics (Macmillan); Rittenhouse, Little Book of Modern Verse (Houghton); Carpenter, American Prose (Macmillan); Johnson, American Orations, 3 vols. (Putnam); Harding, Select Orations (Macmillan).

Library of Southern Literature, 16 vols., a monumental work, edited under supervision of the University of Virginia (Martin and Holt Co., Atlanta); Trent, Southern Writers; Mims and Payne, Southern Poetry; Kent, Southern Poets.

School Texts. For the works of minor writers some of the anthologies named above are necessary; but the major authors may be read to better advantage in various inexpensive texts edited for class use. Such, for example, are Standard English Classics (Ginn and Company); Riverside Literature (Houghton); Pocket Classics (Macmillan); Lake Classics (Scott); Maynard's English Classics (Merrill); Silver Classics (Silver, Burdett); Johnson's English Classics (Johnson); English Readings (Holt); Eclectic Classics (American Book Co.); Everyman's Library (Dutton). There are nearly a score more of these handy little editions, lists of which may be obtained by writing to the various publishing houses, especially to those that make a specialty of schoolbooks.

American History. In studying our literature a good textbook of history should always be at hand; such as Montgomery, Student's American History, or Muzzey, American History, or Channing, Students' History of the United States. More extended works are much better, if the student has time or inclination to consult them.

A useful reference work in connection with our early literature is American History Told by Contemporaries, edited by Hart, 4 vols. (Macmillan). The American History Series, 6 vols. (Scribner), tells the story of America by epochs, the different epochs being treated by different authors. Another good history of the same kind is Epochs of American History, 3 vols. (Longmans). The most complete history is The American Nation, 27 vols. (Harper).

Political and party history in Stanwood, History of the Presidency (Houghton), and Johnston, American Political History, 2 vols. (Putnam).

Biographies of notable characters in American Statesmen (Houghton), Makers of America (Dodd), Great Commanders (Appleton), True Biographies (Lippincott), and various other series. National Cyclopedia of American Biography, 15 vols. (White).

Bibliography of the subject in Channing, Hart and Turner, Guide to the Study and Reading of American History, revised to 1912 (Ginn and Company); and in Andrews, Gambrill and Tall, Bibliography of History (Longmans).

READINGS IN AMERICAN
LITERATURE

ACKNOWLEDGMENT

The selections from Longfellow, Whittier, Lowell, Holmes, Emerson, Hawthorne, Thoreau, Harriet Beecher Stowe, Bret Harte, Lucy Larcom, E. C. Stedman, Thomas Bailey Aldrich, Celia Thaxter, Edward Rowland Sill, John Fiske, Amy Lowell, and Josephine Preston Peabody are used by permission of, and by special arrangement with, Houghton Mifflin Company, the authorized publishers.

CONTENTS

THE COLONIAL PERIOD

PAGE

BRADFORD, WILLIAM. Of Plymouth Plantation [Extracts from Book II] 1

BYRD, WILLIAM. The History of the Dividing Line [Extracts] . 3

WIGGLESWORTH, MICHAEL. God's Controversy with New England [Conclusion] 7

BRADSTREET, ANNE. Some Verses upon the Burning of our House 8

GODFREY, THOMAS. The Prince of Parthia [Bethas Speaks] . 9

WILLIAMS, JOHN. The Redeemed Captive [Extracts] . . . 10

MATHER, COTTON. Magnalia : Life of John Winthrop [Extracts] 13

EDWARDS, JONATHAN. A Farewell Sermon [Extracts] . . . 15

THE REVOLUTIONARY PERIOD

FRANKLIN, BENJAMIN. Autobiography [Extracts] 19

FRENEAU, PHILIP
Death's Epitaph [From "The House of Night"] 25
The Indian Burying Ground 26
Wild Honeysuckle 27

OTIS, JAMES. Introduction to Speech on Writs of Assistance . 28

HENRY, PATRICK. Conclusion of Speech on Arming the Colony 30

HAMILTON, ALEXANDER. The Federalist, No. LXX 31

JEFFERSON, THOMAS. Autobiography [Extracts] 35

PAINE, THOMAS. The Crisis, No. XV 38

WILKINSON, ELIZA. Letter from Charleston, 1781 40

ADAMS, ABIGAIL
Letters : To John Adams, 1778 43
         To Mrs. Smith, 1800 45

WOOLMAN, JOHN. Journal : Visits to the Indians at Wehaloosing, 1763 47

BROWN, CHARLES BROCKDEN. Edgar Huntly [Across Country] 54

LITERATURE OF THE NEW NATION

PAGE

HALLECK, FITZ-GREENE. Marco Bozzaris   59
DRAKE, JOSEPH RODMAN. The Culprit Fay [Extract] . . .   62
SIMMS, WILLIAM GILMORE. The Yemassee [Harrison's Inter-
    view with Sanutee]   63
WILDE, RICHARD HENRY. The Summer Rose   65
KENNEDY, JOHN PENDLETON. Swallow Barn [The Mill] . .   66
IRVING, WASHINGTON. The Legend of Sleepy Hollow . . .   68
BRYANT, WILLIAM CULLEN
    The Return of Youth   93
    A Forest Hymn   94
    To a Waterfowl   98
    Robert of Lincoln   99
    To the Fringed Gentian   101
COOPER, JAMES FENIMORE. The Red Rover [The Hurricane] .   102
POE, EDGAR ALLAN
    Israfel   110
    To One in Paradise   112
    To Helen   113
    A Descent into the Maelström [Extract]   113

THE PERIOD OF CONFLICT

LONGFELLOW, HENRY WADSWORTH
    A Psalm of Life   121
    Giotto's Tower   122
    The Rainy Day   123
    The Building of the Ship [The Launching]   123
    The Song of Hiawatha : Hiawatha's Friends   127
    The White Czar   133
WHITTIER, JOHN GREENLEAF
    The Pipes at Lucknow   134
    Telling the Bees   137
    Snow-Bound [Abridged]   139
    All's Well   150
    The Trailing Arbutus   150
    Hampton Beach [Extract]   151
LOWELL, JAMES RUSSELL
    Under the Old Elm [Extracts]   152

CONTENTS

PAGE

To the Dandelion 154
Sonnet IV, "For this true nobleness I seek in vain" . . 156
My Garden Acquaintance [Extract] 156

HOLMES, OLIVER WENDELL
Old Ironsides 158
Hymn of Trust 159
The Last Leaf 160
The Chambered Nautilus 161
The Height of the Ridiculous 162
The Autocrat of the Breakfast Table [Extract] 164

LANIER, SIDNEY
Tampa Robins 165
Night and Day 166
In Absence, IV 167
Evening Song 167

WHITMAN, WALT
Cavalry Crossing a Ford 168
By the Bivouac's Fitful Flame 168
To the Man-of-War Bird 169
Aboard at a Ship's Helm 169
O Captain! My Captain! 170
Joy, Shipmate, Joy! 171

EMERSON, RALPH WALDO
The Titmouse 171
Forbearance 174
The Snow-Storm 175
The Rhodora 175
The Humble-Bee 175
Good-Bye 177
Days 178
Works and Days [Extracts] 179
The American Scholar [Extracts] 180
Literary Ethics [Conclusion of address of July 24, 1838] . 183

HAWTHORNE, NATHANIEL
The Old Manse [Abridged] 185
Lady Eleanore's Mantle 193

TIMROD, HENRY
The Arctic Voyager 207
Hark to the Shouting Wind 208

PAGE

HAYNE, PAUL HAMILTON
   The Ax and the Pine 209
   The Tempter in the House 210
RYAN, ABRAM J. Lines, "The death of men is not the death" . 210
TAYLOR, BAYARD
   Bedouin Song , ... 211
   The National Ode [Extract] 212
STOWE, HARRIET BEECHER. The Pearl of Orr's Island, Chapter XXXV 213
MELVILLE, HERMAN. Moby Dick, Chapter CXXXIII . . . 217
COOKE, JOHN ESTEN. Leather Stocking and Silk, Chapter XVIII 227
THOREAU, HENRY DAVID. Walden : The Ponds 229
PARKMAN, FRANCIS. La Salle and the Discovery of the Great West [Extracts] 235

THE ALL-AMERICA PERIOD

HARTE, FRANCIS BRET. Tennessee's Partner 239
CABLE, GEORGE WASHINGTON. Madame Délicieuse [Extract] 249
PAGE, THOMAS NELSON. In Ole Virginia : Meh Lady [Extract] 254
JACKSON, HELEN HUNT. Ramona, Chapter XIV [Alessandro's Return] 266
FREEMAN, MARY E. WILKINS. The Debtor, Chapter II [A Formal Call] 278
GARLAND, HAMLIN. A Son of the Middle Border : Wheat and the Harvest 288
ALLEN, JAMES LANE. The Reign of Law, Chapter XV [Gabriella's History] 292
MARK TWAIN
   Life on the Mississippi, Chapter IX 299
   Huckleberry Finn, Chapter IX [The Cavern] 306
STEDMAN, EDMUND CLARENCE. Alice of Monmouth [Extract] 308
ALDRICH, THOMAS BAILEY
   Sonnets : XX, Books and Seasons 310
          XXI, Outward Bound 310
MILLER, JOAQUIN
   Songs of the Sierras : Dawn at San Diego [Extract] . . 311
             Vaquero 312
RILEY, JAMES WHITCOMB. When the Frost is on the Punkin . 313

CONTENTS

PAGE

THAXTER, CELIA
    Chanticleer 314
    The Sandpiper 315
SILL, EDWARD ROWLAND. The Fool's Prayer 316
DICKINSON, EMILY
    The Storm 317
    A Book 318
LAZARUS, EMMA. Venus of the Louvre 318
LARCOM, LUCY
    When the Woods turn Brown 319
    The Water-Lily 320
FIELD, EUGENE
    The Singing in God's Acre 320
    The Explorer's Wooing 321
CRAWFORD, F. MARION. Via Crucis, Chapter X [An Ambush] 322
THOMPSON, MAURICE. A Marsh-land Incident 331
GIBSON, WILLIAM HAMILTON. Pastoral Days : Spring [Extracts] 337
FISKE, JOHN. American Political Ideas : The Town-Meeting 342
HOWELLS, WILLIAM DEAN. Literary Friends and Acquaintance
    [Extract] 347

BOOKS AND WRITERS OF THE PRESENT DAY

WHARTON, EDITH. The Debt, Part III (with synopsis of Parts
    I and II) 355
O. HENRY. A Service of Love 363
TEASDALE, SARA
    A Prayer 369
    Pierrot 369
    The Garden 370
    Red Maples 370
    The Coin 371
WIDDEMER, MARGARET
    Old Books 371
    To Youth after Pain 373
ROBINSON, EDWIN ARLINGTON
    Octaves, I 374
    The Wilderness 374
LINDSAY, VACHEL
    Abraham Lincoln walks at Midnight 376

PAGE

Niagara 377
The Light o' the Moon : The Beggar Speaks 379
THOMAS, EDITH M. "Cleave to Thine Acre" 380
WOODBERRY, GEORGE EDWARD. Albert of Belgium 380
BATES, KATHARINE LEE. Yellow Warblers 380
SEEGER, ALAN. I have a Rendezvous with Death 381
FROST, ROBERT
Mending Wall 383
After Apple-Picking 384
LOWELL, AMY. The Coal Picker 385
PEABODY, JOSEPHINE PRESTON. Men Have Wings at Last . . 387
KILMER, JOYCE. Holy Ireland 390

NOTES 401

INDEX 425

THE COLONIAL PERIOD

WILLIAM BRADFORD

OF PLYMOUTH PLANTATION

[Extracts from Book II]

All this while the Indians came skulking about them, and
would sometimes show themselves aloof off, but when any
approached near them, they would run away; and once they
stole away their tools where they had been at work and were
gone to dinner. But about the 16 of March a certain Indian ₅
came boldly amongst them, and spoke to them in broken
English, which they could well understand, but marveled
at it. At length they understood by discourse with him, that
he was not of these parts, but belonged to the eastern parts
where some English ships came to fish, with whom he was ₁₀
acquainted, and could name sundry of them by their names,
amongst whom he had got his language. He became profitable to them in acquainting them with many things concerning the state of the country in the east parts where he lived,
which was afterwards profitable unto them; as also of the ₁₅
people here, of their names, number and strength, of their
situation and distance from this place, and who was chief
amongst them. His name was Samoset; he told them also of
another Indian whose name was Squanto, a native of this
place, who had been in England and could speak better Eng- ₂₀
lish than himself. Being, after some time of entertainment
and gifts, dismissed, a while after he came again, and five
more with him, and they brought again all the tools that were
stolen away before, and made way for the coming of their
great Sachem, called Massasoit; who about four or five ₂₅

1

days after came with the chief of his friends and other attendance, with the aforesaid Squanto. With whom after
friendly entertainment, and some gifts given him, they made
a peace with him (which hath now continued this twenty-
5 four years).

. . . .

Afterwards they (as many as were able) began to plant
their corn, in which service Squanto stood them in great
stead, showing them both the manner how to set it, and after
how to dress and tend it. Also he told them except they got
10 fish and set with it (in these old grounds) it would come to
nothing, and he showed them that in the middle of April
they should have store enough come up the brook, by which
they began to build, and taught them how to take it, and
where to get other provisions necessary for them; all which
15 they found true by trial and experience. Some English seed
they sowed, as wheat and peas, but it came not to good,
either by the badness of the seed, or lateness of the season
or both, or some other defect.

In this month of April, whilst they were busy about their
20 seed, their Governor (Mr. John Carver) came out of the field
very sick, it being a hot day; he complained greatly of his
head, and lay down, and within a few hours his senses failed,
so as he never spoke more till he died, which was within a
few days after. Whose death was much lamented, and caused
25 great heaviness and loss amongst them, as there was cause.
He was buried in the best manner that they could, with some
volleys of shot by all that bore arms; and his wife, being a
weak woman, died within five or six weeks after him.

. . . .

Only I shall remember one passage more, rather of mirth
30 than of weight. On the day called Christmas-day, the Governor called them out to work (as was used); but the most
of this new company excused themselves, and said it went
against their consciences to work on that day. So the Governor told them that if they made it a matter of conscience,

he would spare them till they were better informed; so he
led away the rest and left them; but when they came home
at noon from their work, he found them in the street at play
openly, some pitching the bar, and some at stool-ball, and
such like sports. So he went to them, and took away their 5
implements, and told them that was against his conscience,
that they should play, and let others work; if they made the
keeping of it matter of devotion, let them keep their houses,
but there should be no gaming, or reveling in the streets.
Since which time nothing hath been attempted that way, at 10
least openly.

WILLIAM BYRD

THE HISTORY OF THE DIVIDING LINE

[Extracts]

The Sabbath happened very opportunely to give some ease
to our jaded people, who rested religiously from every work
but that of cooking the kettle. We observed very few corn-
fields in our walks, and those very small, which seemed the 15
stranger to us, because we could see no other tokens of husbandry or improvement. But, upon further inquiry, we were
given to understand people only made corn for themselves,
and not for their stocks, which know very well how to get
their own living. Both cattle and hogs ramble into the 20
neighboring marshes and swamps, where they maintain themselves the whole winter long, and are not fetched home till
the spring. Thus these indolent wretches, during one half
of the year, lose the advantage of the milk of their cattle, as
well as their dung, and many of the poor creatures perish in 25
the mire into the bargain, by this ill management. Some, who
pique themselves more upon industry than their neighbors,
will, now and then, in compliment to their cattle, cut down
a tree whose limbs are loaded with the moss afore-mentioned.
The trouble would be too great to climb the tree in order to 30

gather this provender, but the shortest way (which in this country is always counted the best) is to fell it, just like the lazy Indians, who do the same by such trees as bear fruit, and so make one harvest for all.

.   .   .   .

5   The soil of our landlord's plantation, though none of the best, seemed more fertile than any thereabouts, where the ground is near as sandy as the deserts of Africa, and consequently barren. The road leading from thence to Edenton, being in distance about twenty-seven miles, lies upon a ridge
10 called Sandy Ridge, which is so wretchedly poor that it will not bring potatoes. The pines in this part of the country are of a different species from those that grow in Virginia: their bearded leaves are much longer and their cones much larger. Each cell contains a seed of the size and figure
15 of a black-eye pea, which, shedding in November, is very good mast for hogs, and fattens them in a short time. The smallest of these pines are full of cones, which are eight or nine inches long, and each affords commonly sixty or seventy seeds. This kind of mast has the advantage of all other, by
20 being more constant, and less liable to be nipped by the frost, or eaten by the caterpillars. The trees also abound more with turpentine, and consequently yield more tar, than either the yellow or the white pine; and for the same reason make more durable timber for building. The inhabitants hereabouts pick
25 up knots of lightwood in abundance, which they burn into tar, and then carry it to Norfolk or Nansemond for a market. The tar made in this method is the less valuable, because it is said to burn the cordage, though it is full as good for all other uses, as that made in Sweden or Muscovy. Surely there
30 is no place in the world where the inhabitants live with less labor than in North Carolina. It approaches nearer to the description of Lubberland than any other, by the great felicity of the climate, the easiness of raising provisions, and the slothfulness of the people. Indian corn is of so great increase
35 that a little pains will subsist a very large family with bread,

and then they may have meat without any pains at all, by the help of the low grounds, and the great variety of mast that grows on the high land. The men, for their parts, just like the Indians, impose all the work upon the poor women. They make their wives rise out of their beds early in the morning, at the same time that they lie and snore, till the sun has risen one third of his course, and dispersed all the unwholesome damps. Then, after stretching and yawning for half an hour, they light their pipes, and, under the protection of a cloud of smoke, venture out into the open air; though, if it happens to be never so little cold, they quickly return shivering into the chimney corner. When the weather is mild, they stand leaning with both their arms upon the cornfield fence, and gravely consider whether they had best go and take a small heat at the hoe, but generally find reasons to put it off till another time.

.   .   .   .

Betwixt this and Edenton there are many whortleberry slashes, which afford a convenient harbor for wolves and foxes. The first of these wild beasts is not so large and fierce as they are in other countries more northerly. He will not attack a man in the keenest of his hunger, but run away from him as from an animal more mischievous than himself.

The foxes are much bolder, and will sometimes not only make a stand, but likewise assault anyone that would balk them of their prey. The inhabitants hereabouts take the trouble to dig abundance of wolf-pits, so deep and perpendicular that, when a wolf is once tempted into them, he can no more scramble out again than a husband who has taken the leap can scramble out of matrimony.

Most of the houses in this part of the country are log-houses, covered with pine or cypress shingles three feet long and one broad. They are hung upon laths with pegs, and their doors too turn upon wooden hinges, and have wooden locks to secure them, so that the building is finished without nails or other iron work. They also set up their pales without

any nails at all, and indeed more securely than those that are nailed. There are three rails mortised into the posts: the lowest of this serves as a sill with a groove in the middle, big enough to receive the end of the pales; the middle part of the
5 pale rests against the inside of the next rail, and the top of it is brought forward to the outside of the uppermost. Such wreathing of the pales in and out makes them stand firm, and much harder to unfix than when nailed in the ordinary way.

. . . .

We hurried away the surveyors about nine this morning,
10 who extended the line seven miles and a hundred and sixty poles, notwithstanding the ground was exceedingly uneven. At the distance of five miles we forded a stream to which we gave the name of Bluewing Creek, because of the great number of those fowls that then frequented it. About two and a
15 half miles beyond that, we came upon Sugar-tree Creek, so called from the many trees of that kind that grow upon it. By tapping this tree, in the first warm weather in February, one may get from twenty to forty gallons of liquor, very sweet to the taste and agreeable to the stomach. This may
20 be boiled into molasses first, and afterwards into very good sugar, allowing about ten gallons of the liquor to make a pound. There is no doubt, too, that a very fine spirit may be distilled from the molasses, at least as good as rum. The sugar tree delights only in rich ground, where it grows very
25 tall, and by the softness and sponginess of the wood should be a quick grower. Near this creek we discovered likewise several spice trees, the leaves of which are fragrant, and the berries they bear are black when dry, and of a hot taste, not much unlike pepper. The low grounds upon the creek are
30 very wide, sometimes on one side, sometimes on the other; though most commonly upon the opposite shore the high land advances close to the bank, only on the north side of the line it spreads itself into a great breadth of rich low ground on both sides of the creek for four miles together,
35 as far as this stream runs into Hico River, whereof I shall

presently make mention. One of our men spied three buf-
faloes, but his piece being loaded only with goose-shot, he
was able to make no effectual impression on their thick hides;
however, this disappointment was made up by a brace of
bucks, and as many wild turkeys, killed by the rest of the 5
company. Thus Providence was very bountiful to our endeavors, never disappointing those that faithfully rely upon
it, and pray heartily for their daily bread.

MICHAEL WIGGLESWORTH

GOD'S CONTROVERSY WITH NEW ENGLAND

WRITTEN IN THE TIME OF THE GREAT DROUGHT ANNO 1662
BY A LOVER OF NEW ENGLAND'S PROSPERITY

[Conclusion]

Ah dear New England! dearest land to me;
   Which unto God hast hitherto been dear,   10
And mayst be still more dear than formerly,
   If to his voice thou wilt incline thine ear.

Consider well and wisely what the rod,
   Wherewith thou art from year to year chastised,
Instructeth thee. Repent, and turn to God,   15
   Who will not have his nurture be despised.

Thou still hast in thee many praying saints,
   Of great account, and precious with the Lord,
Who daily pour out unto him their plaints,
   And strive to please him both in deed and word.   20

Cheer on, brave souls, my heart is with you all,
   And shall be with you, mauger Satan's might:
And wheresoe'er this body be a thrall,
   Still in New England shall be my delight.

ANNE BRADSTREET

SOME VERSES UPON THE BURNING OF OUR HOUSE

July 10, 1666

In silent night when rest I took,
For sorrow near I did not look.
I wakened was with thundering noise
And piteous shrieks of dreadful voice.
5   That fearful sound of "Fire!" and "Fire!"
Let no man know, is my desire.

I, starting up, the light did spy,
And to my God my heart did cry
To strengthen me in my distress,
10   And not to leave me succorless;
Then coming out, beheld apace
The flame consume my dwelling-place.

And when I could no longer look
I blest His name that gave and took,
15   That laid my goods now in the dust;
Yea, so it was, and so 'twas just—
It was His own; it was not mine.
Far be it that I should repine.

He might of all justly bereft,
20   But yet sufficient for us left.
When by the ruins oft I passed
My sorrowing eyes aside did cast,
And here and there the places spy
Where oft I sat, and long did lie.

25   Here stood that trunk and there that chest;
There lay that store I counted best;

My pleasant things in ashes lie,
And them behold no more shall I.
Under thy roof no guest shall sit,
Nor at thy table eat a bit;

No pleasant tale shall e'er be told, 5
Nor things recounted done of old,
No candle e'er shall shine in thee,
Nor bridegroom's voice e'er heard shall be,
In silence ever thou shalt lie.
Adieu, adieu; all's vanity. 10

. . . .

THOMAS GODFREY

THE PRINCE OF PARTHIA

[Bethas Speaks]

True, I am fallen, but glorious was my fall,
The day was bravely fought, we did our best,
But victory's of heaven. Look o'er yon field,
See if thou findest one Arabian back
Disfigured with dishonorable wounds. 15
No, here, deep on their bosoms, are engraved
The marks of honor! 'twas through here their souls
Flew to their blissful seats. Oh! why did I
Survive the fatal day? To be this slave,
To be the gaze and sport of vulgar crowds, 20
Thus, like a shackled tiger, stalk my round,
And grimly lower upon the shouting herd.
Ye Gods! —

. . . .

Welcome my dungeon, but more welcome death.
Trust not too much, vain Monarch, to your power, 25
Know fortune places all her choicest gifts

On ticklish heights, they shake with every breeze,
And oft some rude wind hurls them to the ground.
Jove's thunder strikes the lofty palaces,
While the low cottage, in humility,
5   Securely stands, and sees the mighty ruin.
What king can boast, to-morrow as to-day,
Thus, happy will I reign? The rising sun
May view him seated on a splendid throne,
And, setting, see him shake the servile chain.

.   .   .   .

JOHN WILLIAMS

THE REDEEMED CAPTIVE

[Extracts]

10   The enemies who entered the house were all of them Indians and Maquas, insulted over me awhile, holding up
hatchets over my head, threatening to burn all I had; but
yet God beyond expectation made us to be pitied: for though
some were so cruel and barbarous as to take and carry to the
15 door two of my children and murder them, as also a negro
woman; yet they gave me liberty to put on my clothes, keeping me bound with a cord on one arm, till I put my clothes on
the other, and then changing my cord, they let me dress
myself, and then pinioned me again. Gave liberty to my
20 dear wife to dress herself and our children. About sun an
hour high, we were all carried out of the house for a march,
and saw many houses of my neighbors in flames, perceiving
the whole fort, one house excepted, to be taken. Who can
tell what sorrows pierced our souls when we saw ourselves
25 carried away from God's sanctuary, to go into a strange land,
exposed to so many trials, the journey being at least three
hundred miles we were to travel, the snow up to our knees
and we never inured to such hardships and fatigues.

.   .   .   .

After this we went up the mountain, and saw the smoke of
the fires in the town, and beheld the awful desolation in our
town; and before we marched any farther they killed a
sucking child of the English. There were slain by the enemy
of the inhabitants of our town to the number of thirty-eight 5
besides nine of the neighboring towns. We traveled not far
the first day; God made the heathen so to pity our children
that, though they had several wounded persons of their own
to carry upon their shoulders for thirty miles before they
came to the river, yet they carried our children, uncapable 10
of traveling, in their arms and upon their shoulders. When
we came to our lodging place, the first night, they dug away
the snow and made some wigwams, cut down some of the
small branches of the spruce trees to lie down on, and gave
the prisoners somewhat to eat; but we had but little appetite. 15
I was pinioned and bound down that night, and so I was every
night whilst I was with the army. Some of the enemy who
brought drink with them out of the town fell to drinking,
and in their drunken fit they killed my negro man, the only
dead person I either saw at the town or in the way. 20

In the night an Englishman made his escape; in the morning I was called for and ordered by the General to tell the
English that if any more made their escape they would burn
the rest of the prisoners. He that took me was unwilling to
let me speak with any of the prisoners as we marched; but 25
on the morning of the second day, he being appointed to
guard the rear, I was put into the hands of my other master,
who permitted me to speak to my wife when I overtook her
and to walk with her and help her in her journey.

.   .   .   .

I was made to wade over a small river, and so were all the 30
English, the water above knee-deep, the stream very swift,
and after that to travel up a small mountain; my strength
was almost spent before I came to the top of it: no sooner
had I overcome the difficulty of that ascent, but I was permitted to sit down and be unburdened of my pack; I sat 35

pitying those who were behind, and entreated my master to
let me go down and help my wife; but he refused, and would
not let me stir from him. I asked each of the prisoners (as
they passed by me) after her, and heard that passing through
5 the aforesaid river, she fell down, and was plunged over head
and ears in the water; after which she traveled not far, for
at the foot of the mountain the cruel and blood-thirsty savage
who took her slew her with his hatchet at one stroke.

   .   .   .   .

When we came to our lodging-place, an Indian captain
10 from the eastward spake to my master about killing me and
taking off my scalp. I lifted up my heart to God, to implore
his grace and mercy in such a time of need; and afterwards
I told my master, if he intended to kill me, I desired he would
let me know of it, assuring him that my death, after a promise
15 of quarter, would bring the guilt of blood upon him. He told
me he would not kill me. We laid down and slept, for God
sustained and kept us.

   .   .   .   .

My master returned on the evening of the Sabbath
(March 12) and told me, he had killed five moose. The next
20 day (Monday, March 13) we were removed to the place
where he killed them. We tarried there three days, till we
had roasted and dried the meat. My master made me a pair
of snow-shoes, for (said he) you cannot possibly travel without them, the snow being knee deep. We parted from thence
25 heavy laden; I traveled with a burden on my back, with
snow-shoes twenty-five miles the first day of wearing them,
and again the next day till afternoon; and then we came to
the French river.

COTTON MATHER

MAGNALIA CHRISTI AMERICANA: OR THE ECCLE-SIASTICAL HISTORY OF NEW ENGLAND

NEHEMIAS AMERICANUS. THE LIFE OF JOHN WINTHROP, ESQ. GOVERNOR OF THE MASSACHUSETTS COLONY

[Extracts]

Being made, at the unusually early age of eighteen, a justice of peace, his virtues began to fall under a more general observation; and he not only so bound himself to the behavior of a Christian, as to become exemplary for a conformity to the laws of Christianity in his own conversation, 5 but also discovered a more than ordinary measure of those qualities which adorn an officer of humane society. His justice was impartial, and used the balance to weigh not the cash, but the case of those who were before him . . . his wisdom did exquisitely temper things according to the art of 10 governing, which is a business of more contrivance than the seven arts of the schools . . . his courage made him dare to do right, and fitted him to stand among the lions that have sometimes been the supporters of the throne: all which virtues he rendered the more illustrious by emblazoning them 15 with the constant liberality and hospitality of a gentleman. This made him the terror of the wicked, and the delight of the sober, the envy of the many, but the hope of those who had any hopeful design in hand for the common good of the nation, and the interests of religion. 20

Accordingly when the noble design of carrying a colony of chosen people into an American wilderness was by some eminent persons undertaken, this eminent person was, by the consent of all, chosen for the Moses, who must be the leader of so great an undertaking: and indeed nothing but a Mosaic 25 spirit could have carried him through the temptations to which either his farewell to his own land or his travel in a

strange land must necessarily expose a gentleman of his
education.

.   .   .   .

To teach the frugality necessary for those times, he
abridged himself of a thousand comfortable things which he
5 had allowed himself elsewhere: his habit was not that soft
raiment which would have been disagreeable to a wilderness; his table was not covered with the superfluities that
would have invited unto sensualities; water was commonly
his own drink, though he gave wine to others. But at the
10 same time his liberality unto the needy was even beyond
measure generous; and therein he was continually causing
the blessing of him that was ready to perish to come upon
him, and the heart of the widow and the orphan to sing for
joy. . . . Once it was observable that, on Feb. 5, 1630, when
15 he was distributing the last handful of the meal in the
barrel unto a poor man distressed by the wolf at the door,
at that instant they spied a ship arrived at the harbor's
mouth laden with provisions for them all. Yea, the governor
sometimes made his own private purse to be the public, not
20 by sucking into it, but by squeezing out of it; for when the
public treasure had nothing in it, he did himself defray the
charges of the public. . . . 'Twas his custom also to send some
of his family upon errands unto the houses of the poor about
their meal time, on purpose to spy whether they wanted;
25 and if it were found that they wanted, he would make that the
opportunity of sending supplies unto them. And there was
one passage of his charity that was perhaps a little unusual:
in an hard and long winter, when wood was very scarce at
Boston, a man gave him a private information that a needy
30 person in the neighborhood stole wood sometimes from his
pile; whereupon the governor in a seeming anger did reply,
"Does he so? I'll take a course with him; go, call that man
to me, I'll warrant you I'll cure him of stealing!" When the
man came, the governor considering that if he had stolen, it
35 was more out of necessity than disposition, said unto him,

"Friend, it is a severe winter, and I doubt you are but meanly provided for wood; wherefore I would have you supply yourself at my wood-pile till this cold season be over." And he then merrily asked his friends, Whether he had not effectually cured this man of stealing his wood? 5

JONATHAN EDWARDS

A FAREWELL SERMON

NORTHAMPTON, JUNE 22, 1750

[Extracts]

Now I am taking my leave of this people I would apply myself to such among them as I leave in a Christless, graceless condition; and would call on such seriously to consider of that solemn day when they and I must meet before the Judge of the world. 10

My parting with you is in some respects in a peculiar manner a melancholy parting; inasmuch as I leave you in most melancholy circumstances; because I leave you in the gall of bitterness, and bond of iniquity, having the wrath of God abiding on you, and remaining under condemnation to everlasting misery and destruction. Seeing I must leave you, it would have been a comfortable and happy circumstance of our parting if I had left you in Christ, safe and blessed in that sure refuge and glorious rest of the saints. But it is otherwise. I leave you far off, aliens and strangers, wretched subjects and captives of sin and Satan, and prisoners of vindictive justice, without Christ, and without God in the world. 20

Your consciences bear me witness that, while I had opportunity, I have not ceased to warn you, and set before you your danger. I have studied to represent the misery and necessity of your circumstances in the clearest manner possible. I have tried all ways that I could think of tending to awaken your consciences, and make you sensible of the necessity of your 25

improving your time, and being speedy in flying from the wrath to come, and thorough in the use of means for your escape and safety. I have diligently endeavored to find out and use the most powerful motives to persuade you to take
5 care for your own welfare and salvation. I have not only endeavored to awaken you, that you might be moved with fear, but I have used my utmost endeavors to win you: I have sought out acceptable words, that if possible I might prevail upon you to forsake sin, and turn to God, and accept
10 of Christ as your Savior and Lord. I have spent my strength very much in these things. But yet, with regard to you whom I am now speaking to, I have not been successful; but have this day reason to complain in those words, Jer. vi. 29: "The bellows are burnt, the lead is consumed of the fire, the
15 founder melteth in vain, for the wicked are not plucked away." It is to be feared that all my labors, as to many of you, have served no other purpose but to harden you, and that the word which I have preached, instead of being a savor of life unto life, has been a savor of death unto death.
20 Though I shall not have any account to give for the future of such as have openly and resolutely renounced my ministry, as of a betrustment committed to me, yet remember you must give account for yourselves, of your care of your own souls, and your improvement of all means past and future,
25 through your whole lives. God only knows what will become of your poor perishing souls, what means you may hereafter enjoy, or what disadvantages and temptations you may be under. May God in his mercy grant that, however all past means have been unsuccessful, you may have future
30 means which may have a new effect; and that the word of God, as it shall be hereafter dispensed to you, may prove as the fire and the hammer that breaketh the rock in pieces. However, let me now at parting exhort and beseech you not wholly to forget the warnings you have had while under my
35 ministry. When you and I shall meet at the day of judgment, then you will remember them: the sight of me, your

former minister, on that occasion, will soon revive them to
your memory, and that in a very affecting manner. O do
not let that be the first time that they are so revived.

. . . .

As you would seek the future prosperity of this society it
is of vast importance that you should avoid contention.   5

A contentious people will be a miserable people. The contentions which have been among you, since I first became
your pastor, have been one of the greatest burdens I have
labored under in the course of my ministry,—not only the
contentions you have had with me, but those which you have 10
had one with another, about your lands and other concerns,—
because I knew that contention, heat of spirit, evil speaking,
and things of the like nature, were directly contrary to the
spirit of Christianity, and did in a peculiar manner tend to
drive away God's Spirit from a people, and to render all 15
means of grace ineffectual, as well as to destroy a people's
outward comfort and welfare.

Let me therefore earnestly exhort you, as you would seek
your own future good, hereafter to watch against a contentious spirit. "If you would see good days, seek peace, and 20
ensue it." 1 Pet. iii. 10. 11. Let the contention which has
lately been about the terms of Christian communion, as it
has been the greatest of your contentions, so be the last of
them. I would, now I am preaching my farewell sermon,
say to you, as the Apostle to the Corinthians, 2 Cor. xiii. 11: 25
"Finally, brethren, farewell. Be perfect, be of one mind,
live in peace; and the God of love and peace shall be
with you."

And here I would particularly advise those that have ad-
hered to me in the late controversy to watch over their spirits, 30
and avoid all bitterness towards others. Your temptations
are, in some respects, the greatest, because what has been
done lately is grievous to you. But however wrong you may
think others have done, maintain, with great diligence and
watchfulness, a Christian meekness and sedateness of spirit; 35

and labor, in this respect, to excel others who are of the contrary part. And this will be the best victory: For "he that rules his spirit, is better than he that takes a city." Therefore let nothing be done through strife or vain glory. Indulge
5 no revengeful spirit in any wise; but watch and pray against it; and, by all means in your power, seek the prosperity of this town. And never think you behave yourselves as becomes Christians but when you sincerely, sensibly, and fervently love all men of whatever party or opinion, and whether
10 friendly or unkind, just or injurious, to you or your friends, or to the cause and kingdom of Christ.

. . . .

Having briefly mentioned these important articles of advice, nothing remains but that I now take my leave of you, and bid you all *farewell*, wishing and praying for your best
15 prosperity. I would now commend your immortal souls to Him who formerly committed them to me, expecting the day when I must meet you before Him, who is the Judge of quick and dead. I desire that I may never forget this people, who have been so long my special charge, and that I may never
20 cease fervently to pray for your prosperity. May God bless you with a faithful pastor, one that is well acquainted with His mind and will, thoroughly warning sinners, wisely and skillfully searching professors, and conducting you in the way to eternal blessedness. May you have truly a burning
25 and shining light set up in this candlestick; and may you, not only for a season, but during his whole life, and that a long life, be willing to rejoice in his light.

And let me be remembered in the prayers of all God's people that are of a calm spirit, and are peaceable and faith-
30 ful in Israel, of whatever opinion they may be with respect to terms of church communion.

And let us all remember, and never forget our future solemn meeting on that great day of the Lord; the day of infallible decision, and of the everlasting and unalterable
35 sentence. AMEN.

THE REVOLUTIONARY PERIOD

BENJAMIN FRANKLIN

AUTOBIOGRAPHY

[Extracts]

I now took a fancy to poetry, and made some little pieces;
my brother, thinking it might turn to account, encouraged
me, and put me on composing occasional ballads. One was
called *The Lighthouse Tragedy* and contained an account of
the drowning of Captain Worthilake, with his two daughters: 5
the other was a sailor's song, on the taking of *Teach* (or
Blackbeard) the pirate. They were wretched stuff, in the
Grub-street-ballad style; and when they were printed he
sent me about the town to sell them. The first sold wonderfully, the event, being recent, having made a great noise. 10
This flattered my vanity; but my father discouraged me by
ridiculing my performances, and telling me verse-makers
were generally beggars. So I escaped being a poet, most probably a very bad one; but as prose writing has been of great
use to me in the course of my life, and was a principal means 15
of my advancement, I shall tell you how, in such a situation,
I acquired what little ability I have in that way.

There was another bookish lad in the town, John Collins
by name, with whom I was intimately acquainted. We
sometimes disputed, and very fond we were of argument, and 20
very desirous of confuting one another, which disputatious
turn, by the way, is apt to become a very bad habit, making
people often extremely disagreeable in company by the contradiction that is necessary to bring it into practice; and
thence, besides souring and spoiling the conversation, is pro- 25

ductive of disgusts and perhaps enmities where you may
have occasion for friendship. I had caught it by reading my
father's books of dispute about religion. Persons of good
sense, I have since observed, seldom fall into it, except law-
5 yers, university men, and men of all sorts that have been bred
at Edinburgh.

A question was once, somehow or other, started between
Collins and me, of the propriety of educating the female sex
in learning, and their abilities for study. He was of opinion
10 that it was improper, and that they were naturally unequal
to it. I took the contrary side, perhaps a little for dispute's
sake. He was naturally more eloquent, had a ready plenty
of words; and sometimes, as I thought, bore me down more
by his fluency than by the strength of his reasons. As we
15 parted without settling the point, and were not to see one
another again for some time, I sat down to put my arguments
in writing, which I copied fair and sent to him. He answered,
and I replied. Three or four letters of a side had passed,
when my father happened to find my papers and read them.
20 Without entering into the discussion, he took occasion to talk
to me about the manner of my writing; observed that, though
I had the advantage of my antagonist in correct spelling and
pointing (which I owed to the printing-house), I fell far short
in elegance of expression, in method and in perspicuity, of
25 which he convinced me by several instances. I saw the justice
of his remarks, and thence grew more attentive to the manner
in writing, and determined to endeavor at improvement.

About this time I met with an odd volume of the *Spectator*.
It was the third. I had never before seen any of them. I
30 bought it, read it over, and was much delighted with it. I
thought the writing excellent, and wished, if possible, to
imitate it. With this view, I took some of the papers, and
making short hints of the sentiments in each sentence, laid
them by a few days, and then, without looking at the book,
35 tried to complete the papers again, by expressing each hinted
sentiment at length, and as fully as it had been expressed

before, in any suitable words that should come to hand. Then I compared my *Spectator* with the original, discovered some of my faults, and corrected them. But I found I wanted a stock of words, or a readiness in recollecting and using them, which I thought I should have acquired before that time if I had gone on making verses; since the continual occasion for words of the same import, but of different length, to suit the measure, or of different sound for the rhyme, would have laid me under a constant necessity of searching for variety, and also have tended to fix that variety in my mind, and make me master of it. Therefore, I took some of the tales and turned them into verse; and after a time, when I had pretty well forgotten the prose, turned them back again. I also sometimes jumbled my collections of hints into confusion, and after some weeks endeavored to reduce them into the best order, before I began to form the full sentences and complete the paper. This was to teach me method in the arrangement of thoughts. By comparing my work afterwards with the original, I discovered many faults and amended them; but I sometimes had the pleasure of fancying that, in certain particulars of small import, I had been lucky enough to improve the method or the language, and this encouraged me to think I might possibly in time come to be a tolerable English writer, of which I was extremely ambitious. My time for these exercises, and for reading, was at night, after work, or before it began, in the morning, or on Sundays, when I contrived to be in the printing-house alone, evading as much as I could the common attendance on public worship which my father used to exact of me when I was under his care, and which, indeed, I still thought a duty, though I could not, as it seemed to me, afford time to practice it.

．　．　．　．　．　．　．　．　．

While I was intent on improving my language, I met with an English grammar (I think it was Greenwood's), at the end of which there were two little sketches of the arts of rhetoric and logic, the latter finishing with a specimen of a dispute in

the Socratic method; and soon after I procured Xenophon's *Memorable Things of Socrates*, wherein there are many instances of the same method. I was charmed with it, adopted it, dropped my abrupt contradiction and positive argumenta-
5 tion, and put on the humble inquirer and doubter. . . . I found this method safest for myself and very embarrassing to those against whom I used it; therefore I took a delight in it, practiced it continually, and grew very artful and expert in drawing people, even of superior knowledge, into conces-
10 sions, the consequences of which they did not foresee, entangling them in difficulties out of which they could not extricate themselves, and so obtaining victories that neither myself nor my cause always deserved. I continued this method some few years, but gradually left it, retaining only
15 the habit of expressing myself in terms of modest diffidence; never using, when I advanced anything that may possibly be disputed, the words *certainly, undoubtedly,* or any others that give the air of positiveness to an opinion; but rather say, I conceive or apprehend a thing to be so and so; it appears to
20 me, or *I should think it so or so,* for such and such reasons; or *I imagine it to be so;* or *it is so, if I am not mistaken.* This habit, I believe, has been of great advantage to me when I have had occasion to inculcate my opinions, and persuade men into measures that I have been from time to time
25 engaged in promoting; and, as the chief ends of conversation are to *inform* or to be *informed,* to *please* or to *persuade,* I wish well-meaning, sensible men would not lessen their power of doing good by a positive assuming manner, that seldom fails to disgust, tends to create opposition, and to defeat every
30 one of those purposes for which speech was given to us, to wit, giving or receiving information or pleasure. For, if you would inform, a positive and dogmatical manner in advancing your sentiments may provoke contradiction and prevent a candid attention. If you wish information and improvement
35 from the knowledge of others, and yet at the same time express yourself as firmly fixed in your present opinions,

modest, sensible men, who do not love disputation, will probably leave you undisturbed in the possession of your error.
And by such a manner, you can seldom hope to recommend
yourself in *pleasing* your hearers, or to persuade those whose
concurrence you desire. Pope says, judiciously: 5

> "*Men should be taught as if you taught them not,*
> *And things unknown propos'd as things forgot;*"

. . . .

And now I set on foot my first project of a public nature,
that for a subscription library. I drew up the proposals, got
them put into form by our great scrivener, Brockden, and, 10
by the help of my friends in the Junto, procured fifty subscribers of forty shillings each to begin with, and ten shillings
a year for fifty years, the term our company was to continue.
We afterwards obtained a charter, the company being increased to one hundred: this was the mother of all the North 15
American subscription libraries, now so numerous. It is become a great thing itself, and continually increasing. These
libraries have improved the general conversation of the Americans, made the common tradesmen and farmers as intelligent
as most gentlemen from other countries, and perhaps have 20
contributed in some degree to the stand so generally made
throughout the colonies in defense of their privileges. .

On this little fund we began. The books were imported;
the library was opened one day in the week for lending to
the subscribers, on their promissory notes to pay double the 25
value if not duly returned. The institution soon manifested
its utility, was imitated by other towns, and in other prov-
inces. The libraries were augmented by donations; reading
became fashionable; and our people, having no public amuse-
ments to divert their attention from study, became better 30
acquainted with books, and in a few years were observed by
strangers to be better instructed and more intelligent than
people of the same rank generally are in other countries.

. . . .

The objections and reluctances I met with in soliciting the subscriptions, made me soon feel the impropriety of presenting one's self as the proposer of any useful project, that might be supposed to raise one's reputation in the smallest degree
5 above that of one's neighbors, when one has need of their assistance to accomplish that project. I therefore put myself as much as I could out of sight, and stated it as a scheme of a *number of friends*, who had requested me to go about and propose it to such as they thought lovers of reading. In this
10 way my affair went on more smoothly, and I ever after practiced it on such occasions; and, from my frequent successes, can heartily recommend it. The present little sacrifice of your vanity will afterwards be amply repaid. If it remains a while uncertain to whom the merit belongs, someone more
15 vain than yourself will be encouraged to claim it, and then even envy will be disposed to do you justice by plucking those assumed feathers, and restoring them to their right owner.

This library afforded me the means of improvement by constant study, for which I set apart an hour or two each
20 day, and thus repaired in some degree the loss of the learned education my father once intended for me. Reading was the only amusement I allowed myself. I spent no time in taverns, games, or frolics of any kind; and my industry in my business continued as indefatigable as it was necessary. I was
25 indebted for my printing-house; I had a young family coming on to be educated, and I had to contend for business with two printers, who were established in the place before me. My circumstances, however, grew daily easier. My original habits of frugality continuing, and my father having, among
30 his instructions to me when a boy, frequently repeated a proverb of Solomon, "Seest thou a man diligent in his calling, he shall stand before kings, he shall not stand before mean men," I from thence considered industry as a means of obtaining wealth and distinction, which encouraged me, though
35 I did not think that I should ever literally *stand before kings*, which, however, has since happened; for I have stood before

five, and even had the honor of sitting down with one, the King of Denmark, to dinner.

We have an English proverb that says, "*He that would thrive, must ask his wife.*" It was lucky for me that I had one as much disposed to industry and frugality as myself. 5 She assisted me cheerfully in my business, folding and stitching pamphlets, tending shop, purchasing old linen rags for the paper-makers, etc., etc. We kept no idle servants, our table was plain and simple, our furniture of the cheapest. For instance, my breakfast was a long time bread and milk 10 (no tea), and I ate it out of a twopenny earthen porringer, with a pewter spoon. But mark how luxury will enter families, and make a progress, in spite of principle: being called one morning to breakfast, I found it in a china bowl, with a spoon of silver! They had been bought for me with- 15 out my knowledge by my wife, and had cost her the enormous sum of three-and-twenty shillings, for which she had no other excuse or apology to make, but that she thought *her* husband deserved a silver spoon and china bowl as well as any of his neighbors. This was the first appearance of plate and china 20 in our house, which afterward, in a course of years, as our wealth increased, augmented gradually to several hundred pounds in value.

PHILIP FRENEAU

DEATH'S EPITAPH

From "The House of Night"

Death in this tomb his weary bones hath laid,
Sick of dominion o'er the human kind— 25
Behold what devastations he hath made,
Survey the millions by his arm confined.

Six thousand years has sovereign sway been mine,
None but myself can real glory claim;

Great Regent of the world I reigned alone,
And princes trembled when my mandate came.

Vast and unmatched throughout the world, my fame
Takes place of gods, and asks no mortal date—
No; by myself, and by the heavens, I swear
Not Alexander's name is half so great.

Nor swords nor darts my prowess could withstand,
All quit their arms, and bowed to my decree,—
Even mighty Julius died beneath my hand,
For slaves and Cæsars were the same to me!

Traveler, wouldst thou his noblest trophies seek,
Search in no narrow spot obscure for those;
The sea profound, the surface of all land
Is molded with the myriads of his foes.

THE INDIAN BURYING GROUND

In spite of all the learned have said,
  I still by old opinion keep;
The posture that we give the dead
  Points out the soul's eternal sleep.

Not so the ancients of these lands—
  The Indian, when from life released,
Again is seated with his friends,
  And shares again the joyous feast.

His imaged birds, and painted bowl,
  And venison, for a journey dressed,
Bespeak the nature of the soul,
  Activity, that wants no rest.

His bow for action ready bent,
  And arrows with a head of stone,
Can only mean that life is spent,
  And not the old ideas gone.

Thou, stranger, that shall come this way,
   No fraud upon the dead commit,—
Observe the swelling turf, and say,
   They do not lie, but here they sit.

Here still a lofty rock remains,   5
   On which the curious eye may trace
(Now wasted half by wearing rains)
   The fancies of a ruder race.

Here still an aged elm aspires,
   Beneath whose far projecting shade   10
(And which the shepherd still admires)
   The children of the forest played.

There oft a restless Indian queen
   (Pale Shebah with her braided hair),
And many a barbarous form is seen   15
   To chide the man that lingers there.

By midnight moons, o'er moistening dews,
   In habit for the chase arrayed,
The hunter still the deer pursues,
   The hunter and the deer—a shade!   20

And long shall timorous Fancy see
   The painted chief, and pointed spear,
And Reason's self shall bow the knee
   To shadows and delusions here.

THE WILD HONEYSUCKLE

Fair flower, that dost so comely grow,   25
   Hid in this silent, dull retreat,
Untouched thy honied blossoms blow,
   Unseen thy little branches greet:
     No roving foot shall crush thee here,
     No busy hand provoke a tear.   30

By Nature's self in white arrayed,
　　She bade thee shun the vulgar eye,
And planted here the guardian shade,
　　And sent soft waters murmuring by;
5　　　　Thus quietly thy summer goes,
　　　　Thy days declining to repose.

Smit with those charms, that must decay,
　　I grieve to see your future doom;
They died—nor were those flowers more gay,
10　　The flowers that did in Eden bloom;
　　　　Unpitying frosts and Autumn's power
　　　　Shall leave no vestige of this flower.

From morning suns and evening dews
　　At first thy little being came;
15　If nothing once, you nothing lose,
　　　For when you die you are the same;
　　　　The space between is but an hour,
　　　　The frail duration of a flower.

JAMES OTIS

INTRODUCTION TO SPEECH ON WRITS OF ASSISTANCE

May it please your honors,

20　　I was desired by one of the court to look into the books and consider the question now before them concerning Writs of Assistance. I have accordingly considered it, and now appear not only in obedience to your order, but likewise in behalf of the inhabitants of this town, who have presented another 25 petition, and out of regard to the liberties of the subject. And I take this opportunity to declare that, whether under a fee or not (for in such a cause as this I despise a fee), I will to my dying day oppose with all the powers and faculties God has given me all such instruments of slavery on the one hand, 30 and villainy on the other, as this writ of assistance is.

It appears to me the worst instrument of arbitrary power, the most destructive of English liberty and the fundamental principles of law, that ever was found in an English law book. I must therefore beg your honors' patience and attention to the whole range of an argument, that may perhaps appear uncommon in many things, as well as to points of learning that are more remote and unusual: that the whole tendency of my design may the more easily be perceived, the conclusions better descend, and the force of them be better felt. I shall not think much of my pains in this cause, as I engaged in it from principle. I was solicited to argue this cause as Advocate General; and because I would not, I have been charged with desertion from my office. To this charge I can give a very sufficient answer. I renounced that office, and I argue this cause from the same principle; and I argue it with the greater pleasure, as it is in favor of British liberty, at a time when we hear the greatest monarch upon earth declaring from his throne that he glories in the name of Briton, and that the privileges of his people are dearer to him than the most valuable prerogatives of his crown; and it is in opposition to a kind of power, the exercise of which in former periods of English history, cost one King of England his head, and another his throne. I have taken more pains in this cause than I ever will take again, although my engaging in this and another popular cause has raised much resentment. But I think I can sincerely declare that I cheerfully submit myself to every odious name for conscience' sake: and from my soul I despise all those, whose guilt, malice, or folly has made them my foes. Let the consequences be what they will, I am determined to proceed. The only principles of public conduct that are worthy of a gentleman or a man are to sacrifice estate, ease, health, and applause, and even life, to the sacred calls of his country.

These manly sentiments, in private life, make the good citizen; in public life, the patriot and the hero. I do not say that when brought to the test, I shall be invincible. I pray

God I may never be brought to the melancholy trial; but if I ever should, it will be then known how far I can reduce to practice principles which I know to be founded in truth. In the meantime, I will proceed to the subject of this writ.

PATRICK HENRY

CONCLUSION OF SPEECH ON ARMING THE COLONY

5   They tell us, sir, that we are weak—unable to cope with so formidable an adversary. But when shall we be stronger? Will it be the next week, or the next year? Will it be when we are totally disarmed, and when a British guard shall be stationed in every house? Shall we gather strength by ir-
10 resolution and inaction? Shall we acquire the means of effectual resistance by lying supinely on our backs, and hugging the delusive phantom of Hope, until our enemies shall have bound us hand and foot? Sir, we are not weak, if we make a proper use of those means which the God of nature hath
15 placed in our power. Three millions of people, armed in the holy cause of liberty, and in such a country as that which we possess, are invincible by any force which our enemy can send against us. Besides, sir, we shall not fight our battles alone. There is a just God who presides over the destinies
20 of nations, and who will raise up friends to fight our battles for us. The battle, sir, is not to the strong alone; it is to the vigilant, the active, the brave. Besides, sir, we have no election. If we were base enough to desire it, it is now too late to retire from the contest. There is no retreat, but in sub-
25 mission and slavery! Our chains are forged, their clanking may be heard on the plains of Boston! The war is inevitable —and let it come!! I repeat it, sir, let it come!!!

It is in vain, sir, to extenuate the matter. Gentlemen may cry, peace, peace—but there is no peace. The war is actually
30 begun! The next gale that sweeps from the north will bring to our ears the clash of resounding arms! Our brethren are

already in the field! Why stand we here idle? What is it that gentlemen wish? what would they have? Is life so dear, or peace so sweet, as to be purchased at the price of chains and slavery? Forbid it, Almighty God! I know not what course others may take; but as for me, give me liberty, or 5 give me death!

X ALEXANDER HAMILTON

THE FEDERALIST, NO. LXX

There is an idea, which is not without its advocates, that a vigorous executive is inconsistent with the genius of republican government. The enlightened well-wishers to this species of government must at least hope that the supposition is 10 destitute of foundation, since they can never admit its truth without, at the same time, admitting the condemnation of their own principles. Energy in the executive is a leading character in the definition of good government. It is essential to the protection of the community against foreign at- 15 tacks. It is not less essential to the steady administration of the laws, to the protection of property against those irregular and high-handed combinations which sometimes interrupt the ordinary course of justice, to the security of liberty against the enterprises and assaults of ambition, of faction, 20 and of anarchy. Every man, the least conversant in Roman story, knows how often that republic was obliged to take refuge in the absolute power of a single man, under the formidable title of dictator, as well against the intrigues of ambitious individuals who aspired to the tyranny, and the 25 seditions of whole classes of the community whose conduct threatened the existence of all government, as against the invasions of external enemies who menaced the conquest and destruction of Rome.

There can be no need, however, to multiply arguments or 30 examples on this head. A feeble executive implies a feeble

execution of the government. A feeble execution is but another phrase for a bad execution; and a government ill executed, whatever it may be in theory, must be, in practice, a
bad government.

5   Taking it for granted, therefore, that all men of sense will
agree in the necessity of an energetic executive, it will only
remain to inquire, what are the ingredients which constitute
this energy? How far can they be combined with those other
ingredients which constitute safety in the republican sense?
10 And how far does this combination characterize the plan
which has been reported by the convention?

The ingredients which constitute energy in the executive
are unity, duration, an adequate provision for its support,
competent powers.

15   The ingredients which constitute safety in the republican
sense are a due dependence on the people, a due responsibility.

Those politicians and statesmen who have been the most
celebrated for the soundness of their principles and for the
justness of their views, have declared in favor of a single
20 executive and a numerous legislature. They have, with great
propriety, considered energy as the most necessary qualification of the former, and have regarded this as most applicable
to power in a single hand; while they have, with equal propriety, considered the latter as best adapted to deliberation
25 and wisdom, and best calculated to conciliate the confidence
of the people and to secure their privileges and interests.

That unity is conducive to energy will not be disputed.
Decision, activity, secrecy, and dispatch will generally characterize the proceedings of one man in a much more eminent
30 degree than the proceedings of any greater number; and in
proportion as the number is increased, these qualities will be
diminished.

This unity may be destroyed in two ways: either by vesting the power in two or more magistrates of equal dignity
35 and authority, or by vesting it ostensibly in one man, subject,
in whole or in part, to the control and coöperation of others,

in the capacity of counselors to him. Of the first, the two consuls of Rome may serve as an example; of the last, we shall find examples in the constitutions of several of the states. New York and New Jersey, if I recollect right, are the only states which have intrusted the executive author- 5 ity wholly to single men. Both these methods of destroying the unity of the executive have their partisans; but the votaries of an executive council are the most numerous. They are both liable, if not to equal, to similar objections, and may in most lights be examined in conjunction. 10

. . . .

Wherever two or more persons are engaged in any common enterprise or pursuit, there is always danger of difference of opinion. If it be a public trust or office, in which they are clothed with equal dignity and authority, there is peculiar danger of personal emulation and even animosity. From 15 either, and especially from all these causes, the most bitter dissensions are apt to spring. Whenever these happen, they lessen the respectability, weaken the authority, and distract the plans and operations of those whom they divide. If they should unfortunately assail the supreme magistracy of a 20 country, consisting of a plurality of persons, they might impede or frustrate the most important measures of the government in the most critical emergencies of the state. And what is worse still, they might split the community into violent and irreconcilable factions, adhering differently to the differ- 25 ent individuals who composed the magistracy.

Men often oppose a thing merely because they have had no agency in planning it, or because it may have been planned by those whom they dislike. But if they have been consulted, and have happened to disapprove, opposition then be- 30 comes, in their estimation, an indispensable duty of self-love. They seem to think themselves bound in honor and by all motives of personal infallibility to defeat the success of what has been resolved upon contrary to their sentiments. Men of upright and benevolent tempers have too many opportunities 35

of remarking with horror to what desperate lengths this disposition is sometimes carried, and how often the great interests of society are sacrificed to the vanity, to the conceit, and to the obstinacy of individuals who have credit enough to
5 make their passions and their caprices interesting to mankind. Perhaps the question now before the public may, in its consequences, afford melancholy proofs of the effects of this despicable frailty, or rather detestable vice in the human character.

. . . .

10   But one of the weightiest objections to a plurality in the executive, which lies as much against the last as the first plan, is that it tends to conceal faults, and destroy responsibility. Responsibility is of two kinds, to censure and to punishment. The first is the most important of the two, especially
15 in an elective office. Men in public trust will much oftener act in such a manner as to render them unworthy of being any longer trusted than in such a manner as to make them obnoxious to legal punishment. But the multiplication of the executive adds to the difficulty of detection in either case.
20 It often becomes impossible, amidst mutual accusations, to determine on whom the blame or the punishment of a pernicious measure, or series of pernicious measures, ought really to fall. It is shifted from one to another with so much dexterity, and under such plausible appearances, that the public
25 opinion is left in suspense about the real author. The circumstances which may have led to any national miscarriage or misfortune are sometimes so complicated that where there are a number of actors who may have had different degrees and kinds of agency, though we may clearly see upon
30 the whole that there has been mismanagement, yet it may be impracticable to pronounce to whose account the evil which may have been incurred is truly chargeable. "I was overruled by my council. The council were so divided in their opinions that it was impossible to obtain any better resolu-
35 tion on the point." These and similar pretexts are constantly

at hand, whether true or false. And who is there that will either take the trouble or incur the odium of a strict scrutiny into the secret springs of the transaction? Should there be found a citizen zealous enough to undertake the unpromising task, if there happen to be a collusion between the parties concerned, how easy is it to clothe the circumstances with so much ambiguity as to render it uncertain what was the precise conduct of any of those parties.

. . . .

It is evident from these considerations that the plurality of the executive tends to deprive the people of the two greatest securities they can have for the faithful exercise of any delegated power: *first*, the restraints of public opinion, which lose their efficacy as well on account of the division of the censure attendant on bad measures among a number as on account of the uncertainty on whom it ought to fall; and *secondly*, the opportunity of discovering with facility and clearness the misconduct of the persons they trust, in order either to their removal from office, or to their actual punishment, in cases which admit of it.

THOMAS JEFFERSON

AUTOBIOGRAPHY

[Extracts]

The remissness of Congress, and their permanent session, began to be a subject of uneasiness; and even some of the legislatures had recommended to them intermissions and periodical sessions. As the Confederation had made no provision for a visible head of the government during vacations of Congress, and such a one was necessary to superintend the executive business, to receive and communicate with foreign ministers and nations, and to assemble Congress on sudden and extraordinary emergencies, I proposed, early in April, the appointment of a committee, to be called the "Committee of the States," to consist of a member from each State, who should remain in session during the recess of Congress: that the functions of Congress should be divided into executive and legislative, the latter to be reserved, and the former, by a general resolution, to be delegated to that Committee. This proposition was afterwards agreed to; a Committee appointed, who entered on duty on the subsequent adjournment of Congress, quarreled very soon, split into two parties, abandoned their post, and left the government without any visible head until the next meeting in Congress. We have since seen the same thing take place in the Directory of France; and I believe it will forever take place in any Executive consisting of a plurality. Our plan best, I believe, combines wisdom and practicability, by providing a plurality of counselors but a single arbiter for ultimate decision. I was in France when we heard of this schism and separation of our Committee, and, speaking with Dr. Franklin of this singular disposition of men to quarrel and divide into parties, he gave his sentiments, as usual, by way of apologue. He mentioned the Eddystone lighthouse in the British Channel, as being built on a rock in the mid-channel, totally inaccessible in winter from the boisterous character of that sea in that season; that, therefore, for the two keepers employed to keep up the lights all provisions for the winter were necessarily carried to them in the autumn, as they could never be visited again till the return of the milder season; that on the first practicable day in the spring a boat put off to them with fresh supplies. The boatmen met at the door one of the keepers, and accosted him with a "How goes it, friend? Very well. How is your companion? I do not know. Don't know? Is not he here? I can't tell. Have you not seen him to-day? No. When did you see him? Not since last fall. You have killed him? Not I, indeed." They were about to lay hold of him, as having certainly murdered his companion; but he desired them to go upstairs and examine for themselves. They went up, and there found the other keeper. They had quarreled, it seems, soon after being left there, had divided into two parties, assigned the cares below to one, and those above to the other, and had never spoken to, or seen, one another since.

.   .   .   .

Our body was little numerous, but very contentious. Day after day was wasted on the most unimportant questions. A member, one of those afflicted with the morbid rage of debate, of an ardent mind, prompt imagination, and copious flow of words, who heard with impatience any logic which was not his own, sitting near me on some occasion of a trifling but wordy debate, asked me how I could sit in silence, hearing so much false reasoning which a word should refute? I observed to him that to refute indeed was easy, but to silence was impossible; that in measures brought forward by myself I took the laboring oar, as was incumbent on me, but that in general I was willing to listen; that if every sound argument or objection was used by some one or other of the numerous debaters, it was enough; if not, I thought it sufficient to suggest the omission, without going into a repetition of what had already been said by others; that this was a waste and abuse of the time and patience of the House which could not be justified. And I believe that if the members of deliberate bodies were to observe this course generally they would do in a day what takes them a week; and it is really more questionable than may at first be thought whether Bonaparte's dumb legislature, which said nothing and did much, may not be preferable to one which talks much and does nothing. I served with General Washington in the legislature of Virginia before the Revolution, and during it with Dr. Franklin in Congress. I never heard either of them speak ten minutes at a time, nor to any but the main point, which was to decide the question. They laid their shoulders to the great points, knowing that the little ones would follow of themselves. If the present Congress errs in too much talking, how can it be otherwise in a body to which the people send one hundred and fifty lawyers, whose trade it is to ques-

tion everything, yield nothing, and talk by the hour? That
one húndred and fifty lawyers should do business together
ought not to be expected.

. . . .

And here I cannot leave this great and good country without expressing my sense of its preëminence of character
among the nations of the earth. A more benevolent people I
have never known, nor greater warmth and devotedness in
their select friendships. Their kindness and accommodation
to strangers is unparalleled; and the hospitality of Paris is
beyond anything I had conceived to be practicable in a large
city. Their eminence, too, in science, the communicative dis-
positions of their scientific men, the politeness of the general
manners, the ease and vivacity of their conversation, give a
charm to their society to be found nowhere else. In a comparison of this with other countries, we have the proof of pri-
macy which was given to Themistocles, after the battle of
Salamis. Every general voted to himself the first reward of
valor, and the second to Themistocles. So, ask the traveled
inhabitant of any nation, in what country on earth would
you rather live? Certainly in my own, where are all my
friends, my relations, and the earliest and sweetest affections
and recollections of my life. Which would be your second
choice? France.

THOMAS PAINE

THE CRISIS, NO. XV

APRIL 19, 1783

"The times that tried men's souls" are over—and the
greatest and completest revolution the world ever knew,
gloriously and happily accomplished.

But to pass from the extremes of danger to safety—from
the tumult of war to the tranquillity of peace—though sweet
in contemplation, requires a gradual composure of the senses

to receive it. Even calmness has the power of stunning when it opens too instantly upon us. The long and raging hurricane that should cease in a moment would leave us in a state rather of wonder than enjoyment; and some moments of recollection must pass before we could be capable of tasting the felicity of repose. There are but few instances in which the mind is fitted for sudden transitions: it takes in its pleasures by reflection and comparison; and those must have time to act before the relish for new scenes is complete.

In the present case—the mighty magnitude of the object —the various uncertainties of fate it has undergone—the numerous and complicated dangers we have suffered or escaped—the eminence we now stand on, and the vast prospect before us, must all conspire to impress us with contemplation.

To see it in our power to make a world happy—to teach mankind the art of being so—to exhibit on the theater of the universe a character hitherto unknown—and to have, as it were, a new creation intrusted to our hands, are honors that command reflection, and can neither be too highly estimated nor too gratefully received.

In this pause then of recollection—while the storm is ceasing and the long agitated mind vibrating to a rest—let us look back on the scenes we have passed, and learn from experience what is yet to be done.

Never, I say, had a country so many openings to happiness as this. Her setting out in life, like the rising of a fair morning, was unclouded and promising.

.   .   .   .

The remembrance, then, of what is past, if it operates rightly, must inspire her with the most laudable of all ambition, that of adding to the fair fame she began with. The world has seen her great in adversity, struggling, without a thought of yielding, beneath accumulated difficulties, bravely, nay proudly, encountering distress, and rising in resolution as the storm increased. All this is justly due to her, for her fortitude has merited the character. Let, then, the world see that she can bear prosperity, and that her honest virtue in time of peace is equal to the bravest virtue in time of war.

She is now descending to the scenes of quiet and domestic life, not beneath the cypress shade of disappointment, but to
5 enjoy in her own land and under her own vine the sweet of her labors and the reward of her toil. In this situation may she never forget that a fair national reputation is of as much importance as independence, that it possesses a charm that wins upon the world, and makes even enemies civil, that it
10 gives a dignity which is often superior to power, and commands reverence where pomp and splendor fail.

.   .   .   .

With the blessings of peace, independence, and an universal commerce, the states, individually and collectively, will have leisure and opportunity to regulate and establish
15 their domestic concerns, and to put it beyond the power of calumny to throw the least reflection on their honor. Character is much easier kept than recovered; and that man, if any such there be, who, from sinister views or littleness of soul, lends unseen his hand to injure it, contrives a wound it
20 will never be in his power to heal.

ELIZA WILKINSON

LETTERS

MRS. WILKINSON VISITS CHARLESTON, 1781

Yonge's Island, July 14th

Well, I have been to town, and seen all my friends and quarreled with my enemies. I went on board the prison ship, too, and drank coffee with the prisoners; the dear fellows
25 were in high spirits, and expecting to be speedily exchanged; indeed, they were so before I left town. I saw the last vessel sail, and a number of ladies with them of our acquaintance, who have sailed from their native land.

.   .   .   .

One day Kitty and I were going to take a walk on the Bay to get something we wanted. Just as we had got our hats on, up ran one of the Billets into the dining-room, where we were,—

"Your servant, ladies,"—   5

"Your servant, sir."

"Going out, ladies?"

"Only to take a little walk."

He immediately turned about and ran down stairs, I guessed for what.   10

"Kitty, Kitty, let us hurry off, child; he is gone for his hat and sword, as sure as you are alive, and means to accompany us." We immediately caught up our silk gowns to keep them from rustling, and flew down stairs as light as we could, to avoid being heard. Out of the street door we went, and I 15 believe ran near two hundred yards, and then walked very fast. Looking behind, we saw him at some distance walking at a great rate. We hurried down another street, and went in a half-run until we came to Bedon's Alley, and, turning . that, we walked on leisurely to rest ourselves. It was near 20 an hour after, being in a store in Broad Street, that we saw him pass, in company with five or six other officers, with one of whom he was hooking arms. Kitty spied him out, and, pointing to him and looking at me, we ran behind the door to hide ourselves; but he got a glimpse of us before we could do 25 so and, quitting his companions, came immediately into the store and seemed quite transported to find us. Foolish fellow! I could not help pitying him for his good-nature and behaving *mighty civil* to him. Had he been one of your impudent, blustering red-coats, who think nothing bad enough 30 they can say of the *rebels*, I should have discarded him that moment and driven him from my presence, but he accosted us so smilingly, and with such an air of diffidence that I could not find in my heart one spark of ill-nature towards him; so I smiled too, and away we walked. He offered me 35 his hand, or arm rather, to lean on.

"Excuse me, sir," said I; "I will support myself, if you please."

"No, Madam, the pavements are very uneven—you may get a fall; do accept my arm."

5   "Pardon me, I cannot."

"Come, you do not know what your condescension may do—I will turn rebel!"

"Will you?" said I, laughing—"turn rebel first, and then offer your arm."

10   We stopped in another store, where were several British officers; after asking for articles which I wanted, I saw a broad roll of ribbon, which appeared to be of black and white stripes.

"Go," said I to the officer that was with us, "and reckon 15 the stripes of that ribbon; see if they are *thirteen*!" (with an emphasis I spoke the word—and he went too!)

"Yes, they are thirteen, upon my word, Madam."

"Do hand it me." He did so; I took it, and found that it was narrow black ribbon, carefully wound round a broad 20 white. I returned it to its place on the shelf.

"Madam," said the merchant, "you can buy the black and white, too, and tack them in stripes."

"By no means, sir; I would not have them *slightly tacked*, but *firmly united*." The above-mentioned officers sat on the 25 counter kicking their heels;—how they gaped at me when I said this! but the merchant laughed heartily.

Well, I have composed a long letter out of nothing; pardon the subject. I am on this lonely island and have nothing to inspire my pen. Let me hear from you, but I would rather 30 see you, if you would think it worth while to favor me with a visit. Come, my dear, I have a thousand little things to whisper in your ear, of *who*, and *what*, and *how*. If you have but the tenth part of that curiosity ascribed to your sex, you will fly to Yonge's Island, to *enjoy* these promised tête-35 à-têtes.—Not one word more.

Eliza W.

ABIGAIL ADAMS

LETTERS

To John Adams

25 October, 1778

The morning after I received your very short letter, I determined to devote the day to writing to my friend; but I had only just breakfasted, when I had a visit from Monsieur Rivière, an officer on board the *Languedoc*, who speaks English well, the captain of the *Zara*, and six or eight other officers from on board another ship. The first gentleman dined with me and spent the day, so that I had no opportunity of writing that day. The gentlemen officers have made me several visits, and I have dined twice on board, at very elegant entertainments. Count d'Estaing has been exceedingly polite to me. Soon after he arrived here, I received a message from him requesting that I would meet him at Colonel Quincy's, as it was inconvenient leaving his ship for any long time. I waited upon him, and was very politely received. Upon parting, he requested that the family would accompany me on board his ship and dine with him the next Thursday, with any friends we chose to bring; and his barge should come for us. We went, according to the invitation, and were sumptuously entertained with every delicacy that this country produces and the addition of every foreign article that could render our feast splendid. Music and dancing for the young folks closed the day.

The temperance of these gentlemen, the peaceable, quiet disposition both of officers and men, joined to many other virtues which they have exhibited during their continuance with us, are sufficient to make Europeans, and Americans too, blush at their own degeneracy of manners. Not one officer has been seen the least disguised with liquor since their arrival. Most that I have seen appear to be gentlemen of family and education. I have been the more desirous to

take notice of them, as I cannot help saying, that they have
been neglected in the town of Boston. Generals Heath and
Hancock have done their part, but very few, if any, private
families have any acquaintance with them. Perhaps I feel
5 more anxious to have them distinguished on account of the
near and dear connections I have among them. It would
gratify me much, if I had it in my power, to entertain every
officer in the fleet.

In the very few lines I have received from you not the least
10 mention is made that you have ever received a line from me.
I have not been so parsimonious as my friend,—perhaps I
am not so prudent; but I cannot take my pen, with my
heart overflowing, and not give utterance to some of the
abundance which is in it. Could you, after a thousand fears
15 and anxieties, long expectation, and painful suspense, be
satisfied with my telling you that I was well, that I wished
you were with me, that my daughter sent her duty, that I
had ordered some articles for you which I hoped would arrive, etc. etc.? By Heaven, if you could, you have changed
20 hearts with some frozen Laplander, or made a voyage to a region that has chilled every drop of your blood; but I will restrain a pen already, I fear, too rash, nor shall it tell you how
much I have suffered from this appearance of—inattention.

The articles sent by Captain Tucker have arrived safe,
25 and will be of great service to me. Our money is very little
better than blank paper. It takes forty dollars to purchase
a barrel of cider; fifty pounds lawful for a hundred of sugar,
and fifty dollars for a hundred of flour; four dollars per day
for a laborer, and find him, which will amount to four more.
30 You will see, by bills drawn before the date of this, that I
had taken the method which I was happy in finding you had
directed me to. I shall draw for the rest as I find my situation requires. No article that can be named, foreign or
domestic, but what costs more than double in hard money
35 what it once sold for. In one letter I have given you an account of our local situation, and of every thing I thought

you might wish to know. Four or five sheets of paper, written to you by the last mail, were destroyed when the vessel was taken. Duplicates are my aversion, though I believe I should set a value upon them, if I were to receive them from a certain friend, a friend who never was deficient in testifying his regard and affection to his

Portia

To Mrs. Smith

Washington, 21 November, 1800

My dear Child,

I arrived here on Sunday last and without meeting with any accident worth noticing, except losing ourselves when we left Baltimore and going eight or nine miles on the Frederick road, by which means we were obliged to go the other eight through woods, where we wandered two hours without finding a guide or the path. Fortunately, a straggling black came up with us, and we engaged him as a guide, to extricate us out of our difficulty; but woods are all you see from Baltimore until you reach *the city*, which is only so in name. Here and there is a small cot, without a glass window, interspersed amongst the forests, through which you travel miles without seeing any human being. In the city there are buildings enough, if they were compact and finished, to accommodate Congress and those attached to it; but as they are, and scattered as they are, I see no great comfort for them. The river, which runs up to Alexandria, is in full view of my window; and I see the vessels as they pass and repass. The house is upon a grand and superb scale, requiring about thirty servants to attend and keep the apartments in proper order and perform the ordinary business of the house and stables; an establishment very well proportioned to the President's salary. The lighting the apartments, from the kitchen to parlors and chambers, is a tax indeed; and the fires we are obliged to keep to secure us from daily agues is another very cheering comfort. To as-

sist us in this great castle, and render less attendance necessary, bells are wholly wanting, not one single one being hung
through the whole house; and promises are all you can obtain. This is so great an inconvenience that I know not what
5 to do, or how to do. The ladies from Georgetown and in the
city have many of them visited me. Yesterday I returned
fifteen visits,—but such a place as Georgetown appears,—
why, our Milton is beautiful! But no comparisons;—if they
will put me up some bells, and let me have wood enough to
10 keep fires, I design to be pleased. I could content myself almost anywhere three months; but, surrounded with forests,
can you believe that wood is not to be had, because people
cannot be found to cut and cart it! Briesler entered into a
contract with a man to supply him with wood. A small
15 part, a few cords only, has he been able to get. Most of that
was expended to dry the walls of the house before we came
in; and yesterday the man told him it was impossible for
him to procure it to be cut and carted. He has had recourse
to coals, but we cannot get grates made and set. We have,
20 indeed, come into a *new country*.

You must keep all this to yourself and, when asked how I
like it, say that I write you the situation is beautiful, which
is true. The house is made habitable, but there is not a
single apartment finished; and all withinside, except the
25 plastering, has been done since Briesler came. We have not
the least fence, yard, or other convenience, without; and the
great unfinished audience-room I make a drying-room of, to
hang up the clothes in. The principal stairs are not up, and
will not be this winter. Six chambers are made comfortable;
30 two are occupied by the President and Mr. Shaw; two lower
rooms, one for a common parlor, and one for a levee-room.
Up stairs there is the oval room, which is designed for the
drawing-room and has the crimson furniture in it. It is a
very handsome room now; but when completed it will be
35 beautiful. If the twelve years in which this place has been
considered as the future seat of government had been im-

proved, as they would have been if in New England, very many of the present inconveniences would have been removed. It is a beautiful spot, capable of every improvement; and the more I view it, the more I am delighted with it.

Since I sat down to write, I have been called down to a servant from Mount Vernon with a billet from Major Custis and a haunch of venison and a kind, congratulatory letter from Mrs. Lewis upon my arrival in the city, with Mrs. Washington's love, inviting me to Mount Vernon, where, health permitting, I will go before I leave this place.

The Senate is much behindhand. No Congress has yet been made. 'Tis said —— —— is on his way, but travels with so many delicacies in his rear that he cannot get on fast lest some of them should suffer.

Thomas comes in and says a House is made; so to-morrow, though Saturday, the President will meet them. Adieu, my dear. Give my love to your brother, and tell him he is ever present upon my mind.

Affectionately your mother,
A. Adams

JOHN WOOLMAN

JOURNAL

VISITS TO THE INDIANS AT WEHALOOSING ON THE RIVER SUSQUEHANNA, 1763

[Extracts]

Tenth of sixth month.—We set out early this morning and crossed the western branch of Delaware, called the Great Lehie, near Fort Allen. The water being high, we went over in a canoe. Here we met an Indian, had friendly conversation with him, and gave him some biscuit; and he, having killed a deer, gave some of it to the Indians with us. After traveling some miles, we met several Indian men and women with a cow and horse and some household goods, who were lately come from their dwelling at Wyoming and were going to settle at another place. We made them some small presents; and, as some of them understood English, I told them my motive for coming into their country, with which they appeared satisfied. One of our guides talking awhile with an ancient woman concerning us, the poor old woman came to my companion and me and took her leave of us with an appearance of sincere affection. We pitched our tent near the banks of the same river, having labored hard in crossing some of those mountains called the Blue Ridge. The roughness of the stones and the cavities between them, with the steepness of the hills, made it appear dangerous. But we were preserved in safety, through the kindness of Him whose works in these mountainous deserts appeared awful, and towards whom my heart was turned during this day's travel.

Near our tent, on the sides of large trees peeled for that purpose, were various representations of men going to and returning from the wars, and of some being killed in battle. This was a path heretofore used by warriors, and as I walked about viewing those Indian histories, which were painted mostly in red or black, and thinking on the innumerable afflictions which the proud, fierce spirit produceth in the world, also on the toils and fatigues of warriors in traveling over mountains and deserts; on their miseries and distresses when far from home and wounded by their enemies; of their bruises and great weariness in chasing one another over the rocks and mountains; of the restless, unquiet state of mind of those who live in this spirit, and of the hatred which mutually grows up in the minds of their children,—the desire to cherish the spirit of love and peace among these people arose very fresh in me. This was the first night that we lodged in the woods, and being wet with traveling in the rain, as were also our blankets, the ground, our tent, and the bushes under which we purposed to lay, all looked discouraging; but I believed that it was the Lord who had thus far brought me forward, and that he would dispose of me as he saw good, and so I felt easy. We kindled a fire, with our tent open to it, then laid some bushes next the ground, and put our blankets upon them for our bed, and, lying down, got some sleep. In the morning, feeling a little unwell, I went into the river; the water was cold, but soon after I felt fresh and well. . . . 5

Twelfth of sixth month being the first of the week and a rainy day, we continued in our tent, and I was led to think of the nature of the exercise which hath attended me. Love was the first motion, and thence a concern arose to spend some time with the Indians, that I might feel and understand 10 their life and the spirit they live in, if haply I might receive some instruction from them, or they might be in any degree helped forward by my following the leadings of truth among them; and as it pleased the Lord to make way for my going at a time when the troubles of war were increasing, and 15 when, by reason of much wet weather, traveling was more difficult than usual at that season, I looked upon it as a more favorable opportunity to season my mind, and to bring me into a nearer sympathy with them. As mine eye was to the great Father of Mercies, humbly desiring to learn his will 20 concerning me, I was made quiet and content.

Our guide's horse strayed, though hoppled, in the night, and after searching some time for him his footsteps were discovered in the path going back, whereupon my kind companion went off in the rain, and after about seven hours re- 25 turned with him. Here we lodged again, tying up our horses before we went to bed, and loosing them to feed about break of day.

Thirteenth of sixth month.—The sun appearing, we set forward, and as I rode over the barren hills my meditations 30 were on the alterations in the circumstances of the natives of this land since the coming in of the English. The lands near the sea are conveniently situated for fishing; the lands near the rivers, where the tides flow, and some above, are in many places fertile, and not mountainous, while the changing 35 of the tides makes passing up and down easy with any kind of traffic. The natives have in some places, for trifling considerations, sold their inheritance so favorably situated, and in other places have been driven back by superior force; their way of clothing themselves is also altered from what it was, and they being far removed from us have to pass over mountains, swamps, and barren deserts, so that traveling is very troublesome in bringing their skins and furs to trade with us. By the extension of the English settlements, and partly by the increase of English hunters, the wild beasts on which the natives chiefly depend for subsistence are not so plentiful as they were; and people too often, for the sake of gain, induce them to waste their skins and furs in purchasing a liquor which tends to the ruin of them and their families.

.   .   .   .

On reaching the Indian settlement at Wyoming, we were told that an Indian runner had been at that place a day or two before us and brought news of the Indians having taken an English fort westward and destroyed the people, and that they were endeavoring to take another; also that another Indian runner came there about the middle of the previous night from a town about ten miles from Wehaloosing, and brought the news that some Indian warriors from distant parts came to that town with two English scalps and told the people that it was war with the English.

Our guides took us to the house of a very ancient man. Soon after we had put in our baggage, there came a man from another Indian house some distance off. Perceiving there was a man near the door I went out; the man had a tomahawk wrapped under his matchcoat out of sight. As I approached him he took it in his hand; I went forward, and, speaking to him in a friendly way, perceived he understood some English. My companion joining me, we had some talk with him concerning the nature of our visit in these parts; he then went into the house with us, and, talking with our guides, soon appeared friendly, sat down and smoked his pipe. Though taking his hatchet in his hand at the instant

I drew near him had a disagreeable appearance, I believe he had no other intent than to be in readiness in case any violence were offered to him.

. . . .

Fifteenth of sixth month.—We proceeded forward till the afternoon, when, a storm appearing, we met our canoe at an appointed place and stayed all night, the rain continuing so heavy that it beat through our tent and wet both us and our baggage. The next day we found abundance of trees blown down by the storm yesterday, and had occasion reverently to consider the kind dealings of the Lord, who provided a safe place for us in a valley while this storm continued. We were much hindered by the trees which had fallen across our path, and in some swamps our way was so stopped that we got through with extreme difficulty. I had this day often to consider myself as a sojourner in this world. A belief in the all-sufficiency of God to support his people in their pilgrimage felt comfortable to me, and I was industriously employed to get to a state of perfect resignation.

We seldom saw our canoe but at appointed places, by reason of the path going off from the river. This afternoon Job Chilaway, an Indian from Wehaloosing, who talks good English and is acquainted with several people in and about Philadelphia, met our people on the river. Understanding where we expected to lodge, he pushed back about six miles, and came to us after night; and in a while our own canoe arrived, it being hard work pushing up the stream. Job told us that an Indian came in haste to their town yesterday and told them that three warriors from a distance lodged in a town above Wehaloosing a few nights past, and that these three men were going against the English at Juniata. . . .

Parting from Job Chilaway on the 17th, we went on and reached Wehaloosing about the middle of the afternoon. The first Indian that we saw was a woman of a modest countenance, with a Bible, who spoke first to our guide, and then with an harmonious voice expressed her gladness at seeing us, having before heard of our coming. By the direction of our guide we sat down on a log while he went to the town to tell the people we were come. My companion and I, sitting thus together in a deep inward stillness, the poor woman came and sat near us; and, great awfulness coming over us, we rejoiced in a sense of God's love manifested to our poor souls. After a while we heard a conch-shell blow several times, and then came John Curtis and another Indian man, who kindly invited us into a house near the town, where we found about sixty people sitting in silence. After sitting with them a short time I stood up, and in some tenderness of spirit acquainted them, in a few short sentences, with the nature of my visit, and that a concern for their good had made me willing to come thus far to see them; which some of them understanding interpreted to the others and there appeared gladness among them. I then showed them my certificate, which was explained to them; and the Moravian who overtook us on the way, being now here, bade me welcome. But the Indians knowing that this Moravian and I were of different religious societies, and as some of their people had encouraged him to come and stay a while with them, they were, I believe, concerned that there might be no jarring or discord in their meetings; and having, I suppose, conferred together, they acquainted me that the people, at my request, would at any time come together and hold meetings. They also told me that they expected the Moravian would speak in their settled meetings, which are commonly held in the morning and near evening. So finding liberty in my heart to speak to the Moravian, I told him of the care I felt on my mind for the good of these people, and my belief that no ill effects would follow if I sometimes spake in their meetings when love engaged me thereto, without calling them together at times when they did not meet of course. He expressed his good-will towards my speaking at any time all that I found in my heart to say.

.   .   .   .

We expected only two Indians to be of our company, but
when we were ready to go we found many of them were going
to Bethlehem with skins and furs, and chose to go in company with us. So they loaded two canoes in which they desired us to go, telling us that the waters were so raised with 5
the rains that the horses should be taken by such as were
better acquainted with the fording-places. We, therefore,
with several Indians, went in the canoes, and others went on
horses, there being seven besides ours. We met with the
horsemen once on the way by appointment, and at night we 10
lodged a little below a branch called Tankhannah, and some
of the young men, going out a little before dusk with their
guns, brought in a deer.

.   .   .   .

Twenty-fourth of sixth month.—This day we passed Fort
Allen and lodged near it in the woods. We forded the west- 15
erly branch of the Delaware three times, which was a shorter
way than going over the top of the Blue Mountains called
the Second Ridge. In the second time of fording where the
river cuts through the mountain, the waters being rapid and
pretty deep, my companion's mare being a tall, tractable 20
animal, was sundry times driven back through the river,
being laden with the burdens of some small horses which
were thought unable to come through with their loads. The
troubles westward, and the difficulty for Indians to pass
through our frontier, was, I apprehend, one reason why so 25
many came, expecting that our being in company would
prevent the outside inhabitants being surprised. We reached
Bethlehem on the 25th, taking care to keep foremost, and to
acquaint people on and near the road who these Indians
were. This we found very needful, for the frontier inhab- 30
itants were often alarmed at the report of the English being
killed by Indians westward. Among our company were some
whom I did not remember to have seen at meeting, and
some of these at first were very reserved; but we being
several days together, and behaving in a friendly manner 35

towards them, and making them suitable return for the services they did us, they became more free and sociable.

Twenty-sixth of sixth month.—Having carefully endeavored to settle all affairs with the Indians relative to our jour-
5 ney, we took leave of them, and I thought they generally parted from us affectionately. We went forward to Richland and had a very comfortable meeting among our friends, it being the first day of the week. . . . Between the English settlements and Wehaloosing we had only a narrow path,
10 which in many places is much grown up with bushes, and interrupted by abundance of trees lying across it. These, together with the mountain swamps and rough stones, make it a difficult road to travel, and the more so because rattlesnakes abound here, of which we killed four. People who
15 have never been in such places have but an imperfect idea of them; and I was not only taught patience, but also made thankful to God, who thus led about and instructed me, that I might have a quick and lively feeling of the afflictions of my fellow-creatures whose situation in life is difficult.

CHARLES BROCKDEN BROWN

EDGAR HUNTLY

[Across Country]

20   There were two ways before me. One lay along the interior base of the hill, over a sterile and trackless space, and exposed to the encounter of savages, some of whom might possibly be lurking here. The other was the well frequented road, on the outside and along the river, which was to be
25 gained by passing over this hill. The practicability of the passage was to be ascertained by inquiries made to my hostess. She pointed out a path that led to the rocky summit and down to the river's brink. The path was not easy to be kept in view or to be trodden, but it was undoubtedly to be
30 preferred to any other.

A route, somewhat circuitous, would terminate in the river road. Thenceforward the way to Solebury was level and direct; but the whole space which I had to traverse was not less than thirty miles. In six hours it would be night, and to perform the journey in that time would demand the agile boundings of a leopard and the indefatigable sinews of an elk.

My frame was in miserable plight. My strength had been assailed by anguish, and fear, and watchfulness; by toil, and abstinence, and wounds. Still, however, some remnant was left; would it not enable me to reach my home by nightfall? I had delighted from my childhood in feats of agility and perseverance. In roving through the maze of thickets and precipices, I had put my energies, both moral and physical, frequently to the test. Greater achievements than this had been performed; and I disdained to be outdone in perspicacity by the lynx, in his sure-footed instinct by the roe, or in patience under hardship and contention with fatigue by the Mohawk. I have ever aspired to transcend the rest of animals in all that is common to the rational and brute, as well as in all by which they are distinguished from each other.

I likewise burned with impatience to know the condition of my family, to dissipate at once their tormenting doubts and my own, with regard to our mutual safety. The evil that I feared had befallen them was too enormous to allow me to repose in suspense; and my restlessness and ominous forebodings would be more intolerable than any hardship or toils to which I could possibly be subjected during this journey.

I was much refreshed and invigorated by the food that I had taken and by the rest of an hour. With this stock of recruited force I determined to scale the hill. After receiving minute directions, and returning many thanks for my hospitable entertainment, I set out.

.   .   .   .

Presently the treading of many feet was heard, and several figures were discovered, following each other in that straight

and regular succession which is peculiar to the Indians.
They kept along the brow of the hill joining the promontory.
I distinctly marked seven figures in succession.

My resolution was formed. Should anyone cast his eye
5 hither, suspect or discover an enemy, and rush towards me,
I determined to start upon my feet, fire on my foe as he advanced, throw my piece on the ground, and then leap into
the river.

Happily, they passed unobservant and in silence. I re-
10 mained in the same posture for several minutes. At length,
just as my alarms began to subside, the halloos, before heard,
arose, and from the same quarter as before. This convinced
me that my perils were not at an end. This now appeared to
be merely the vanguard, and would speedily be followed by
15 others, against whom the same caution was necessary to be
taken.

My eye, anxiously bent the only way by which anyone
could approach, now discerned a figure, which was indubi-
tably that of a man armed; none other appeared in company,
20 but doubtless others were near. He approached, stood still,
and appeared to gaze steadfastly at the spot where I lay.

The optics of a Lennilennapee I knew to be far keener
than my own. A log or a couched fawn would never be mistaken for a man, nor a man for a couched fawn or a log. Not
25 only a human being would be instantly detected, but a decision be unerringly made whether it were friend or foe.
That my prostrate body was the object on which the attention of this vigilant and steadfast gazer was fixed, could not
be doubted. Yet, since he continued an inactive gazer, there
30 was ground for a possibility to stand upon, that I was not
recognized. My fate, therefore, was still in suspense.

The interval was momentary. I marked a movement,
which my fears instantly interpreted to be that of level-
ing a gun at my head. This action was sufficiently conform-
35 able to my prognostics. Supposing me to be detected, there
was no need for him to change his post. Aim might be too

fatally taken, and his prey be secured, from the distance at which he now stood.

These images glanced upon my thought, and put an end to my suspense. A single effort placed me on my feet. I fired with precipitation that precluded the certainty of hitting my mark, dropped my piece upon the ground, and leaped from this tremendous height into the river. I reached the surface, and sunk in a moment to the bottom.

Plunging endlong into the water, the impetus created by my fall from such a height would be slowly resisted by this denser element. Had the depth been less, its resistance would not perhaps have hindered me from being mortally injured against the rocky bottom. Had the depth been greater, time enough would not have been allowed me to regain the surface. Had I fallen on my side, I should have been bereaved of life or sensibility by the shock which my frame would have received. As it was, my fate was suspended on a thread. To have lost my presence of mind, to have forborne to counteract my sinking for an instant after I had reached the water, would have made all exertions to regain the air fruitless. To so fortunate a concurrence of events was thy friend indebted for his safety!

Yet I only emerged from the gulf to encounter new perils. Scarcely had I raised my head above the surface and inhaled the vital breath, when twenty shots were aimed at me from the precipice above. A shower of bullets fell upon the water. Some of them did not fall further than two inches from my head. I had not been aware of this new danger, and now that it assailed me continued gasping the air and floundering at random. The means of eluding it did not readily occur. My case seemed desperate and all caution was dismissed.

This state of discomforting surprise quickly disappeared. I made myself acquainted at a glance with the position of surrounding objects. I conceived that the opposite bank of the river would afford me most security, and thither I tended with all the expedition in my power.

Meanwhile, my safety depended on eluding the bullets that continued incessantly to strike the water at an arm's length from my body. For this end I plunged beneath the surface, and only rose to inhale fresh air. Presently the
5 firing ceased, the flashes that lately illuminated the bank disappeared, and a certain bustle and murmur of confused voices gave place to solitude and silence.

X

LITERATURE OF THE NEW NATION

FITZ-GREENE HALLECK

MARCO BOZZARIS

At midnight, in his guarded tent,
  The Turk was dreaming of the hour
When Greece, her knee in suppliance bent,
  Should tremble at his power:
In dreams, through camp and court, he bore   5
The trophies of a conqueror;
  In dreams his song of triumph heard;
Then wore his monarch's signet ring:
Then pressed that monarch's throne—a king;
As wild his thoughts, and gay of wing,   10
  As Eden's garden bird.

At midnight, in the forest shades,
  Bozzaris ranged his Suliote band,
True as the steel of their tried blades,
  Heroes in heart and hand.   15
There had the Persian's thousands stood,
There had the glad earth drunk their blood
  On old Platæa's day;
And now there breathed that haunted air
The sons of sires who conquered there,   20
With arm to strike and soul to dare,
  As quick, as far as they.

An hour passed on—the Turk awoke;
  That bright dream was his last;
He woke—to hear his sentries shriek,   25
"To arms! they come! the Greek! the Greek!"

He woke—to die midst flame, and smoke,
And shout, and groan, and saber-stroke,
    And death-shots falling thick and fast
As lightnings from the mountain-cloud;
5 And heard, with voice as trumpet loud,
    Bozzaris cheer his band:
"Strike—till the last armed foe expires;
Strike—for your altars and your fires;
Strike—for the green graves of your sires;
10   God—and your native land!"

They fought—like brave men, long and well;
    They piled that ground with Moslem slain,
They conquered—but Bozzaris fell,
    Bleeding at every vein.
15 His few surviving comrades saw
His smile when rang their proud hurrah,
    And the red field was won;
Then saw in death his eyelids close
Calmly, as to a night's repose,
20   Like flowers at set of sun.

Come to the bridal-chamber, Death!
    Come to the mother's, when she feels,
For the first time, her first-born's breath;
    Come when the blessed seals
25 That close the pestilence are broke,
And crowded cities wail its stroke;
Come in consumption's ghastly form,
The earthquake shock, the ocean storm;
Come when the heart beats high and warm
30   With banquet-song and dance, and wine;
And thou art terrible—the tear,
The groan, the knell, the pall, the bier,
And all we know, or dream, or fear
    Of agony, are thine.

But to the hero, when his sword
  Has won the battle for the free,
Thy voice sounds like a prophet's word;
And in its hollow tones are heard
  The thanks of millions yet to be.   5
Come, when his task of fame is wrought—
Come, with her laurel-leaf, blood-bought—
  Come in her crowning hour—and then
Thy sunken eye's unearthly light
To him is welcome as the sight   10
  Of sky and stars to prisoned men;
Thy grasp is welcome as the hand
Of brother in a foreign land;
Thy summons welcome as the cry
That told the Indian isles were nigh   15
  To the world-seeking Genoese,
When the land wind, from woods of palm,
And orange-groves, and fields of balm,
  Blew o'er the Haytian seas.

Bozzaris! with the storied brave   20
  Greece nurtured in her glory's time,
Rest thee—there is no prouder grave,
  Even in her own proud clime.
She wore no funeral-weeds for thee,
  Nor bade the dark hearse wave its plume   25
Like torn branch from death's leafless tree
In sorrow's pomp and pageantry,
  The heartless luxury of the tomb;
But she remembers thee as one
Long loved and for a season gone;   30
For thee her poet's lyre is wreathed,
Her marble wrought, her music breathed;
For thee she rings the birthday bells;
Of thee her babe's first lisping tells;

For thine her evening prayer is said
At palace-couch and cottage-bed;
Her soldier, closing with the foe,
Gives for thy sake a deadlier blow;
His plighted maiden, when she fears
For him the joy of her young years,
Thinks of thy fate, and checks her tears;
    And she, the mother of thy boys,
Though in her eye and faded cheek
Is read the grief she will not speak,
    The memory of her buried joys,
And even she who gave thee birth
Will, by their pilgrim-circled hearth,
    Talk of thy doom without a sigh;
For thou art Freedom's now, and Fame's:
One of the few, the immortal names,
    That were not born to die.

JOSEPH RODMAN DRAKE

THE CULPRIT FAY

[Extract]

Up, Fairy! quit thy chickweed bower,
The cricket has called the second hour,
Twice again, and the lark will rise
To kiss the streaking of the skies—
Up! thy charmèd armor don,
Thou'lt need it ere the night be gone.

He put his acorn helmet on;
It was plumed of the silk of the thistledown;
The corselet plate that guarded his breast
Was once the wild bee's golden vest;
His cloak, of a thousand mingled dyes,
Was formed of the wings of butterflies;

His shield was the shell of a ladybug queen,
Studs of gold on a ground of green;
And the quivering lance which he brandished bright,
Was the sting of a wasp he had slain in fight.
Swift he bestrode his firefly steed;   5
   He bared his blade of the bent grass blue;
He drove his spurs of the cockle seed,
   And away like a glance of thought he flew,
To skim the heavens and follow far
The fiery trail of the rocket star.   10

WILLIAM GILMORE SIMMS

THE YEMASSEE

[Harrison's Interview with Sanutee]

The Englishman again addressed Sanutee, and proposed
returning with him to Pocota-ligo. His anxiety on this point
was clearly enough manifest to the Indian, who replied
sternly.

"The chief will go alone. He wants not that the Coosaw- 15
killer should darken the lodge of Matiwan. Let Harrison"
—and as he addressed the Englishman by his name, he placed
his hand kindly upon his shoulder, and his tones were more
conciliatory—"let Harrison go down to his ships—let him go
with the palefaces to the other lands. Has he not a mother 20
that looks for him at evening?"

"Sanutee," said Harrison, fixing his eye upon him curiously — "wherefore should the English go upon the
waters?"

"The Yemassees would look on the big woods, and call 25
them their own. The Yemassees would be free."

"Old chief—" exclaimed the Englishman, in a stern but
low tone, while his quick, sharp eye seemed to explore the
very recesses of the Indian's soul—"Old chief—thou hast
spoken with the Spaniard."   30

The Indian paused for an instant, but showed no signs of emotion or consciousness at a charge which, at that period and under the then existing circumstances, almost involved the certainty of his hostility towards the Carolinians, with whom the Spaniards of Florida were perpetually at war. He replied, after an instant's hesitation, in a calm, fearless manner:—

"Sanutee is a man—he is a father—he is a chief—the great chief of the Yemassee. Shall he come to the Coosaw-killer, and ask when he would loose his tongue? Sanutee, when the swift hurricane runs along the woods, goes into the top of the tall pine, and speaks boldly to the Manneyto—shall he not speak to the English—shall he not speak to the Spaniard? Does Harrison see Sanutee tremble, that his eye looks down into his bosom? Sanutee has no fear."

"I know it, chief—I know it—but I would have you without guile also. There is something wrong, chief, which you will not show me. I would speak to you of this, therefore I would go with you to Pocota-ligo."

"Pocota-ligo is for the Manneyto—it is holy ground—the great feast of the green corn is there. The white man may not go when the Yemassee would be alone."

"But white men are in Pocota-ligo—is not Granger there, the fur trader?"

"He will go," replied the chief, evasively, and turning away, as he did so, to depart; but suddenly, with an air of more interest, returning to the spot where Harrison stood, seemingly meditating deeply, he again touched his arm, and spoke—

"Harrison will go down to the great lakes with his people. Does the Coosaw-killer hear? Sanutee is the wise chief of Yemassee."

"I am afraid the wise chief of Yemassee is about to do a great folly. But, for the present, Sanutee, let there be no misunderstanding between us and our people. Is there anything of which you complain?"

"Did Sanutee come on his knees to the English? He begs not bread—he asks for no blanket."

"True, Sanutee—I know all that—I know your pride, and that of your people; and because I know it, if you have had wrong from our young men, I would have justice done you." 5

"The Yemassee is not a child—he is strong, he has knife and hatchet—and his arrow goes straight to the heart. He begs not for the justice of the English—"

"Yet, whether you beg for it or not, what wrong have they done you, that they have not been sorry?" 10

"Sorry—will sorry make the dog of Sanutee to live?"

"There you are wrong, Sanutee; the dog assaulted the stranger, and though he might have been more gentle and less hasty, what he did seems to have been done in self-defense. The deer was his game." 15

"Ha, does Harrison see the arrow of Sanutee?" and he pointed to the broken shaft still sticking in the side of the animal.

"True, that is your mark, and would have been fatal after a time, without the aid of gunshot. The other was more 20 immediate in effect."

"It is well. Sanutee speaks not for the meat, nor for the dog. He begs no justice from the English, and their braves may go to the far lands in their canoes, or they may hold fast to the land which is the Yemassee's. The sun and the storm 25 are brothers—Sanutee has said."

RICHARD HENRY WILDE

THE SUMMER ROSE: OR THE LAMENT
OF THE CAPTIVE

My life is like the Summer Rose,
   That opens to the morning sky;
But, ere the shades of evening close,
   Is scattered on the ground—to die: 30

But on the rose's humble bed
   The sweetest dews of night are shed;
As if she wept such waste to see:
   But none shall weep a tear for me.

5   My life is like the autumn leaf,
   That trembles in the moon's pale ray;
Its hold is frail, its date is brief,
   Restless, and soon to pass away:

Yet, ere that leaf shall fall and fade,
10   The parent tree shall mourn its shade;
The winds bewail the leafless tree:
   But none shall breathe a sigh for me.

My life is like the print which feet
   Have left on Tampa's desert strand;
15   Soon as the rising tide shall beat,
   This track will vanish from the sand:

Yet still, as grieving to efface
   All vestige of the human race,
On that lone shore loud moans the sea:
20   But none shall e'er lament for me.

JOHN PENDLETON KENNEDY

SWALLOW BARN

[The Mill]

The first thing he did was to send an order to Bristol, (for he never had any opinion of the mechanics at home) for a complete set of mill machinery; and the second, to put up a house of pine weather-boards, for the mill. Contempo-
25 raneously with this last operation, he set about the dam; and, in the course of one summer, he had a huge breastwork of logs thrown across the path of the modest, diminutive

Apple-pie, which would have terrified the stream even if it
had been a giant.

.   .   .   .

In a few days, with the help of one or two rains, the pool
was completely full; and, to the infinite pleasure of my grand
uncle, a thin thread of water streamed over one corner of the   5
dam,—the most beautiful little cascade in the world; it
looked like a glossy streamer of delicate white ribbon. My
grand uncle was delighted. "There, my boy," said he to
Walter, "there is Tivoli for you! We shall have our mill
a-going in a week."   10
Sure enough, that day week, off went the mill. All the
corn of the farm was brought down to this place; and, for an
hour or two that morning, the mill clattered away as if it had
been filled with a thousand iron-shod devils, all dancing a
Scotch reel. My great uncle thumped his cane upon the floor   15
with a look of triumph, whilst his eyes started from his head,
as he frequently exclaimed to the people about him, "I told
you so; this comes of energy and foresight; this shows the
use of a man's faculties, my boy!"
It was about an hour and a half, or perhaps two hours,—   20
as my authority affirms,—after the commencement of this
racket and clatter in the mill, that my grand uncle, and all
the others who were intent upon the operation, were a little
surprised to discover that the millstone began to slacken in
its speed; the bolting cloth was manifestly moving lazily,   25
and the wheels were getting tired. Presently, a dismal
screech was heard, that sounded like all the trumpets of
Pandemonium blown at once; it was a prolonged, agonizing,
diabolical note that went to the very soul.
"In the name of all the imps of Tartarus,—(a famous in-   30
terjection of my grand uncle) what is that?" "It's only the
big wheel stopped as chock as a tombstone," said the miller,
"and it naturally screeches, because, you see, the gudgeon is
new, and wants grease." Hereupon a court of inquiry was
instituted; and, leading the van, followed by the whole troop, 35

out went my grand uncle to look at the head-gate. Well, not
a thing was to be seen there but a large solitary bull-frog,
squatted on his hams at the bottom of the race, and looking
up at his visitors with the most piteous and imploring counte-
5 nance, as much as to say, "I assure you, gentlemen, I am
exceedingly astonished at this extraordinary convulsion myself, which has left me, as you perceive, naked and dry."
Then the court proceeded upon their investigation towards
the dam, to observe how that came on.

       .   .   .   .

10   "It seems to me, master," said an arch-looking negro, who
was gaping over the flood-gate upon the muddy waste, "that
the mill's run out of water."

    "Who asked you for your opinion, you scoundrel?" said
my grand uncle in a great fury,—for he was now beginning
15 to fret,—"get out of my sight, and hold your tongue!"

    "The fellow is right," said the miller, "we have worked out
the water, that's clear!"

    "It's a two-hour mill," added the negro, in a voice scarcely
audible, taking the risk of my grand uncle's displeasure, and
20 grinning saucily but good-humoredly, as he spoke.

WASHINGTON IRVING

THE LEGEND OF SLEEPY HOLLOW[1]

In the bosom of one of those spacious coves which indent
the eastern shore of the Hudson, at that broad, expansion
of the river denominated by the ancient Dutch navigators
the Tappan Zee, and where they always prudently shortened
25 sail and implored the protection of St. Nicholas when they
crossed, there lies a small market town or rural port, which
by some is called Greensburgh, but which is more generally
and properly known by the name of Tarry Town. This name
was given, we are told, in former days, by the good house-

[1] Somewhat abridged.

wives of the adjacent country, from the inveterate propensity
of their husbands to linger about the village tavern on market
days. Be that as it may, I do not vouch for the fact, but
merely advert to it, for the sake of being precise and authentic. Not far from this village, perhaps about two miles, there 5
is a little valley or rather lap of land among high hills, which
is one of the quietest places in the whole world. A small
brook glides through it, with just murmur enough to lull one
to repose; and the occasional whistle of a quail or tapping of
a woodpecker is almost the only sound that ever breaks in 10
upon the uniform tranquillity.

From the listless repose of the place, and the peculiar character of its inhabitants, who are descendants from the original Dutch settlers, this sequestered glen has long been known
by the name of Sleepy Hollow, and its rustic lads are called 15
the Sleepy Hollow Boys throughout all the neighboring country. A drowsy, dreamy influence seems to hang over the
land, and to pervade the very atmosphere. Some say that
the place was bewitched by a high German doctor, during the
early days of the settlement; others, that an old Indian chief, 20
the prophet or wizard of his tribe, held his pow-wows there
before the country was discovered by Master Hendrick Hudson. Certain it is, the place still continues under the sway
of some witching power, that holds a spell over the minds of
the good people, causing them to walk in a continual reverie. 25
They are given to all kinds of marvelous beliefs; are subject
to trances and visions; and frequently see strange sights, and
hear music and voices in the air. The whole neighborhood
abounds with local tales, haunted spots, and twilight superstitions; stars shoot and meteors glare oftener across the 30
valley than in any other part of the country, and the nightmare, with her whole nine-fold, seems to make it the favorite
scene of her gambols.

The dominant spirit, however, that haunts this enchanted
region, and seems to be commander-in-chief of all the powers 35
of the air, is the apparition of a figure on horseback without

a head. It is said by some to be the ghost of a Hessian trooper, whose head had been carried away by a cannon-ball, in some nameless battle during the Revolutionary War, and who is ever and anon seen by the country folk, hurrying along in the gloom of night, as if on the wings of the wind. His haunts are not confined to the valley, but extend at times to the adjacent roads, and especially to the vicinity of a church at no great distance. Indeed, certain of the most authentic historians of those parts, who have been careful in collecting and collating the floating facts concerning this specter, allege that the body of the trooper having been buried in the church-yard, the ghost rides forth to the scene of battle in nightly quest of his head, and that the rushing speed with which he sometimes passes along the Hollow, like a midnight blast, is owing to his being belated, and in a hurry to get back to the churchyard before daybreak.

Such is the general purport of this legendary superstition, which has furnished materials for many a wild story in that region of shadows; and the specter is known at all the country firesides, by the name of the Headless Horseman of Sleepy Hollow.

In this by-place of nature, there abode, in a remote period of American history, that is to say, some thirty years since, a worthy wight of the name of Ichabod Crane, who sojourned, or, as he expressed it, "tarried," in Sleepy Hollow, for the purpose of instructing the children of the vicinity. He was a native of Connecticut, a State which supplies the Union with pioneers for the mind as well as for the forest, and sends forth yearly its legions of frontier woodmen and country schoolmasters. The cognomen of Crane was not inapplicable to his person. He was tall, but exceedingly lank, with narrow shoulders, long arms and legs, hands that dangled a mile out of his sleeves, feet that might have served for shovels, and his whole frame most loosely hung together. His head was small, and flat at top, with huge ears, large green glassy eyes, and a long snipe nose, so that it looked like a weather-

cock perched upon his spindle neck, to tell which way the wind
blew. To see him striding along the profile of a hill on a
windy day, with his clothes bagging and fluttering about him,
one might have mistaken him for the genius of famine descending upon the earth, or some scarecrow eloped from a 5
cornfield.

His schoolhouse was a low building of one large room,
rudely constructed of logs; the windows partly glazed, and
partly patched with leaves of old copy-books. It was most
ingeniously secured at vacant hours, by a withe twisted in 10
the handle of the door, and stakes set against the window
shutters; so that though a thief might get in with perfect
ease, he would find some embarrassment in getting out,—an
idea most probably borrowed by the architect, Yost Van
Houten, from the mystery of an eelpot. The schoolhouse 15
stood in a rather lonely but pleasant situation, just at the
foot of a woody hill, with a brook running close by, and a
formidable birch-tree growing at one end of it. From hence
the low murmur of his pupils' voices, conning over their lessons, might be heard in a drowsy summer's day, like the hum 20
of a beehive; interrupted now and then by the authoritative
voice of the master, in the tone of menace or command; or,
peradventure, by the appalling sound of the birch, as he urged
some tardy loiterer along the flowery path of knowledge.
Truth to say, he was a conscientious man, and ever bore in 25
mind the golden maxim, "Spare the rod and spoil the child."
Ichabod Crane's scholars certainly were not spoiled.

When school-hours were over, he was the companion and
playmate of the larger boys; and, on holiday afternoons,
would convoy some of the smaller ones home, who happened 30
to have pretty sisters or good housewives for mothers noted
for the comforts of the cupboard. Indeed, it behooved him
to keep on good terms with his pupils. The revenue arising
from his school was small and would have been scarcely
sufficient to furnish him with daily bread, for he was a 35
huge feeder, and, though lank, had the dilating powers of an

anaconda; but to help out his maintenance, he was, according to country custom in those parts, boarded and lodged at the houses of the farmers, whose children he instructed. With these he lived successively a week at a time; thus going the rounds of the neighborhood, with all his worldly effects tied up in a cotton handkerchief.

In addition to his other vocations, he was the singing-master of the neighborhood, and picked up many bright shillings by instructing the young folks in psalmody. It was a matter of no little vanity to him on Sundays, to take his station in front of the church gallery, with a band of chosen singers; where, in his own mind, he completely carried away the palm from the parson. Certain it is, his voice resounded far above all the rest of the congregation; and there are peculiar quavers still to be heard in that church, and which may even be heard half a mile off, quite to the opposite side of the mill-pond, on a still Sunday morning, which are said to be legitimately descended from the nose of Ichabod Crane. Thus, by divers little makeshifts in that ingenious way which is commonly denominated "by hook and by crook," the worthy pedagogue got on tolerably enough, and was thought, by all who understood nothing of the labor of headwork, to have a wonderfully easy life of it.

From his half itinerant life, also, he was a kind of traveling gazette, carrying the whole budget of local gossip from house to house: so that his appearance was always greeted with satisfaction. He was, moreover, esteemed by the women as a man of great erudition, for he had read several books quite through, and was a perfect master of Cotton Mather's *History of New England Witchcraft*, in which, by the way, he most firmly and potently believed.

He was, in fact, an odd mixture of small shrewdness and simple credulity. His appetite for the marvelous, and his powers of digesting it, were equally extraordinary; and both had been increased by his residence in this spell-bound region. No tale was too gross or monstrous for his capacious swallow.

It was often his delight, after his school was dismissed in the afternoon, to stretch himself on the rich bed of clover bordering the little brook that whimpered by his schoolhouse, and there con over old Mather's direful tales, until the gathering dusk of evening made the printed page a mere mist before 5 his eyes.

Another of his sources of fearful pleasure was, to pass long winter evenings with the old Dutch wives, as they sat spinning by the fire, with a row of apples roasting and splutterirg along the hearth, and listen to their marvelous 10 tales of ghosts and goblins, and haunted fields, and haunted brooks, and haunted bridges, and haunted houses, and particularly of the headless horseman, or Galloping Hessian of the Hollow, as they sometimes called him. He would delight them equally by his anecdotes of witchcraft, and of the dire- 15 ful omens and portentous sights and sounds in the air, which prevailed in the earlier times of Connecticut; and would frighten them woefully with speculations upon comets and shooting stars, and with the alarming fact that the world did absolutely turn round, and that they were half the time 20 topsy-turvy!

But if there was a pleasure in all this, while snugly cuddling in the chimney-corner of a chamber that was all of a ruddy glow from the crackling wood-fire, and where, of course, no specter dared to show his face, it was dearly pur- 25 chased by the terrors of his subsequent walk homewards. What fearful shapes and shadows beset his path amidst the dim and ghastly glare of a snowy night! With what wistful look did he eye every trembling ray of light streaming across the waste fields from some distant window! How often was 30 he appalled by some shrub covered with snow, which, like a sheeted specter, beset his very path! How often did he shrink with curdling awe at the sound of his own steps on the frosty crust beneath his feet; and dread to look over his shoulder, lest he should behold some uncouth being tramping 35 close behind him! and how often was he thrown into complete dismay by some rushing blast, howling among the trees, in the idea that it was the Galloping Hessian on one of his nightly scourings!

Among the musical disciples who assembled, one evening in each week, to receive his instructions in psalmody, was Katrina Van Tassel, the daughter and only child of a substantial Dutch farmer. She was a blooming lass of fresh eighteen; plump as a partridge; ripe and melting and rosy-cheeked as one of her father's peaches, and universally famed, not merely for her beauty, but her vast expectations. She was withal a little of a coquette, as might be perceived even in her dress, which was a mixture of ancient and modern fashions, as most suited to set off her charms. She wore the ornaments of pure yellow gold, which her great-great-grandmother had brought over from Saardam; the tempting stomacher of the olden time; and withal a provokingly short petticoat, to display the prettiest foot and ankle in the country round.

Ichabod Crane had a soft and foolish heart toward the sex; and it is not to be wondered at that so tempting a morsel soon found favor in his eyes; more especially after he had visited her in her paternal mansion. Old Baltus Van Tassel was a perfect picture of a thriving, contented, liberal-hearted farmer. He seldom, it is true, sent either his eyes or his thoughts beyond the boundaries of his own farm; but within those everything was snug, happy, and well-conditioned. He was satisfied with his wealth, but not proud of it; and piqued himself upon the hearty abundance rather than the style in which he lived. His stronghold was situated on the banks of the Hudson, in one of those green, sheltered, fertile nooks in which the Dutch farmers are so fond of nestling. A great elm-tree spread its broad branches over it; at the foot of which bubbled up a spring of the softest and sweetest water, in a little well formed of a barrel; and then stole sparkling away through the grass, to a neighboring brook, that bubbled along among alders and dwarf willows. Hard

by the farm-house was a vast barn, that might have served
for a church; every window and crevice of which seemed
bursting forth with the treasures of the farm; the flail was
busily resounding within it from morning till night; swallows
and martins skimmed twittering about the eaves; and rows 5
of pigeons, some with one eye turned up, as if watching the
weather, some with their heads under their wings, or buried
in their bosoms, and others swelling, and cooing, and bowing
about their dames, were enjoying the sunshine on the roof.
Sleek unwieldy porkers were grunting in the repose and 10
abundance of their pens; whence sallied forth, now and then,
troops of sucking pigs, as if to snuff the air. A stately squadron of snowy geese were riding in an adjoining pond, convoy-
ing whole fleets of ducks; regiments of turkeys were gobbling
through the farm-yard, and Guinea fowls fretting about it, 15
like ill-tempered housewives, with their peevish, discontented
cry. Before the barn door strutted the gallant cock, that
pattern of a husband, a warrior, and a fine gentleman, clap-
ping his burnished wings and crowing in the pride and gladness of his heart,—sometimes tearing up the earth with his 20
feet, and then generously calling his ever-hungry family of
wives and children to enjoy the rich morsel which he had
discovered.

The pedagogue's mouth watered as he looked upon this
sumptuous promise of luxurious winter fare. In his devour- 25
ing mind's eye, he pictured to himself every roasting-pig
running about with a pudding in his belly, and an apple in
his mouth; the pigeons were snugly put to bed in a comfortable pie, and tucked in with a coverlet of crust; the geese
were swimming in their own gravy; and the ducks pairing 30
cosily in dishes, like snug married couples, with a decent com-
petency of onion sauce. In the porkers he saw carved out the
future sleek side of bacon, and juicy relishing ham; not a
turkey but he beheld daintily trussed up, with its gizzard under its wing, and, peradventure, a necklace of savory sau- 35
sages; and even bright chanticleer himself lay sprawling on

his back, in a side dish, with uplifted claws, as if craving that quarter which his chivalrous spirit disdained to ask while living.

When he entered the house, the conquest of his heart was
5 complete. It was one of those spacious farm-houses, with high-ridged, but lowly-sloping roofs, built in the style handed down from the first Dutch settlers; the low projecting eaves forming a piazza along the front, capable of being closed up in bad weather. Under this were hung flails, harness, various
10 utensils of husbandry, and nets for fishing in the neighboring river. Benches were built along the sides for summer use; and a great spinning-wheel at one end, and a churn at the other, showed the various uses to which this important porch might be devoted. From this piazza the wondering Ichabod
15 entered the hall, which formed the center of the mansion and the place of usual residence. Here, rows of resplendent pewter, ranged on a long dresser, dazzled his eyes. In one corner stood a huge bag of wool ready to be spun; in another a quantity of linsey-woolsey just from the loom; ears of Indian
20 corn and strings of dried apples and peaches, hung in gay festoons along the walls, mingled with the gaud of red peppers; and a door left ajar gave him a peep into the best parlor, where the claw-footed chairs and dark mahogany tables shone like mirrors; and irons, with their accompany-
25 ing shovel and tongs, glistened from their covert of asparagus tops; mock-oranges and conch-shells decorated the mantelpiece; strings of various-colored birds' eggs were suspended above it; a great ostrich egg was hung from the center of the room, and a corner cupboard, knowingly left open, displayed
30 immense treasures of old silver and well-mended china.

From the moment Ichabod laid his eyes upon these regions of delight, the peace of his mind was at an end, and his only study was how to gain the affections of the peerless daughter of Van Tassel. In this enterprise, however, he had more real
35 difficulties than generally fell to the lot of a knight-errant of yore, who seldom had anything but giants, enchanters, fiery

dragons, and such like easily conquered adversaries, to contend with; and had to make his way merely through gates of iron and brass, and walls of adamant to the castle keep, where the lady of his heart was confined; all which he achieved as easily as a man would carve his way to the center of a Christmas pie; and then the lady gave him her hand as a matter of course. Ichabod, on the contrary, had to win his way to the heart of a country coquette, beset with a labyrinth of whims and caprices, which were forever presenting new difficulties and impediments; and he had to encounter a host of fearful adversaries of real flesh and blood, the numerous rustic admirers, who beset every portal to her heart, keeping a watchful and angry eye upon each other, but ready to fly out in the common cause against any new competitor.

Among these the most formidable was a burly, roaring, roistering blade, of the name of Abraham, or, according to the Dutch abbreviation, Brom Van Brunt, the hero of the country round, which rang with his feats of strength and hardihood. He was broad-shouldered and double-jointed, with short curly black hair, and a bluff, but not unpleasant countenance, having a mingled air of fun and arrogance. From his Herculean frame and great powers of limb, he had received the nickname of Brom Bones, by which he was universally known. He was famed for great knowledge and skill in horsemanship, being as dexterous on horseback as a Tartar. He was foremost at all races and cock-fights; and, with the ascendancy which bodily strength acquires in rustic life, was the umpire in all disputes, setting his hat on one side, and giving his decisions with an air and tone admitting of no gainsay or appeal. He was always ready for either a fight or a frolic; but had more mischief than ill-will in his composition; and, with all his overbearing roughness, there was a strong dash of waggish good humor at bottom.

This rantipole hero had for some time singled out the blooming Katrina for the object of his uncouth gallantries, and though his amorous toyings were something like the

gentle caresses and endearments of a bear, yet it was whispered that she did not altogether discourage his hopes. Certain it is, his advances were signals for rival candidates to
retire, who felt no inclination to cross a lion in his amours;
5 insomuch, that when his horse was seen tied to Van Tassel's
paling, on a Sunday night, a sure sign that his master was
courting, or, as it is termed, "sparking," within, all other
suitors passed by in despair, and carried the war into other
quarters.

10   Such was the formidable rival with whom Ichabod Crane
had to contend, and, considering all things, a stouter man
than he would have shrunk from the competition, and a wiser
man would have despaired. He had, however, a happy mixture of pliability and perseverance in his nature; he was in
15 form and spirit like a supple-jack—yielding, but tough;
though he bent, he never broke; and though he bowed beneath the slightest pressure, yet, the moment it was away—
jerk! he was as erect, and carried his head as high as ever.

He who wins a thousand common hearts is therefore en-
20 titled to some renown; but he who keeps undisputed sway
over the heart of a coquette, is indeed a hero. Certain it is,
this was not the case with the redoubtable Brom Bones; and
from the moment Ichabod Crane made his advances, the interests of the former evidently declined; his horse was no
25 longer seen tied at the palings on Sunday nights, and a deadly
feud gradually arose between him and the preceptor of Sleepy
Hollow.

Brom, who had a degree of rough chivalry in his nature,
would fain have carried matters to open warfare and have
30 settled their pretensions to the lady, according to the mode
of those most concise and simple reasoners, the knights-
errant of yore,—by single combat; but Ichabod was too conscious of the superior might of his adversary to enter the lists
against him; he had overheard a boast of Bones, that he
35 would "double the schoolmaster up, and lay him on a shelf
of his own schoolhouse," and he was too wary to give him an

opportunity. There was something extremely provoking in this obstinately pacific system; it left Brom no alternative but to draw upon the funds of rustic waggery in his disposition, and to play off boorish practical jokes upon his rival. Ichabod became the object of whimsical persecution to Bones 5 and his gang of rough riders. They harried his hitherto peaceful domains, smoked out his singing-school by stopping up the chimney, broke into the schoolhouse at night, in spite of its formidable fastenings of withe and window stakes, and turned everything topsy-turvy, so that the poor schoolmaster 10 began to think all the witches in the country held their meetings there. But what was still more annoying, Brom took all opportunities of turning him into ridicule in presence of his mistress, and had a scoundrel dog whom he taught to whine in the most ludicrous manner, and introduced as a rival of 15 Ichabod's, to instruct her in psalmody.

In this way matters went on for some time, without producing any material effect on the relative situations of the contending powers. On a fine autumnal afternoon, Ichabod, in pensive mood, sat enthroned on the lofty stool from whence 20 he usually watched all the concerns of his little literary realm. In his hand he swayed a ferule, that scepter of despotic power; the birch of justice reposed on three nails behind the throne, a constant terror to evil doers; while on the desk before him might be seen sundry contraband articles 25 and prohibited weapons, detected upon the persons of idle urchins, such as half-munched apples, popguns, whirligigs, fly-cages, and whole legions of rampant little paper gamecocks. Apparently there had been some appalling act of justice recently inflicted, for his scholars were all busily in- 30 tent upon their books, or slyly whispering behind them with one eye kept upon the master; and a kind of buzzing stillness reigned throughout the schoolroom. It was suddenly interrupted by the appearance of a negro in tow-cloth jacket and trousers, a round-crowned fragment of a hat, like the cap of 35 Mercury, and mounted on the back of a ragged, wild, half-

broken colt, which he managed with a rope by way of halter. He came clattering up to the school-door with an invitation to Ichabod to attend a merry-making or "quilting-frolic," to be held that evening at Mynheer Van Tassel's; and having
5 delivered his message with that air of importance and effort at fine language which a negro is apt to display on petty embassies of the kind, he dashed over the brook, and was seen scampering away up the Hollow, full of the importance and hurry of his mission.

10   The gallant Ichabod spent at least an extra half hour at his toilet, brushing and furbishing up his best, and indeed only suit of rusty black, and arranging his locks by a bit of broken looking-glass, that hung up in the schoolhouse. That he might make his appearance before his mistress in the true
15 style of a cavalier, he borrowed a horse from the farmer with whom he was domiciliated, a choleric old Dutchman, of the name of Hans Van Ripper, and, thus gallantly mounted, issued forth, like a knight-errant in quest of adventures. But it is meet I should, in the true spirit of romantic story, give
20 some account of the looks and equipments of my hero and his steed. The animal he bestrode was a broken-down plow-horse, that had outlived almost everything but his vicious-ness. He was gaunt and shagged, with a ewe neck and a head like a hammer; his rusty mane and tail were tangled and
25 knotted with burrs; one eye had lost its pupil, and was glaring and spectral; but the other had the gleam of a genuine devil in it. Still he must have had fire and mettle in his day, if we may judge from the name he bore of Gunpowder. He had, in fact, been a favorite steed of his master's, the choleric
30 Van Ripper, who was a furious rider, and had infused, very probably, some of his own spirit into the animal; for, old and broken-down as he looked, there was more of the lurking devil in him than in any young filly in the country.

Ichabod was a suitable figure for such a steed. He rode
35 with short stirrups, which brought his knees nearly up to the pommel of the saddle; his sharp elbows stuck out like grass-

hoppers'; he carried his whip perpendicularly in his hand, like a scepter, and as his horse jogged on, the motion of his arms was not unlike the flapping of a pair of wings. A small wool hat rested on the top of his nose, for so his scanty strip of forehead might be called, and the skirts of his black coat fluttered out almost to the horse's tail. Such was the appearance of Ichabod and his steed as they shambled out of the gate of Hans Van Ripper, and it was altogether such an apparition as is seldom to be met with in broad daylight.

It was toward evening that Ichabod arrived at the castle of the Herr Van Tassel, which he found thronged with the pride and flower of the adjacent country. Old farmers, a spare leathern-faced race, in homespun coats and breeches, blue stockings, huge shoes, and magnificent pewter buckles. Their brisk, withered little dames, in close crimped caps, long-waisted short-gowns, homespun petticoats, with scissors and pin-cushions, and gay calico pockets hanging on the outside. Buxom lasses, almost as antiquated as their mothers, excepting where a straw hat, a fine ribbon, or perhaps a white frock, gave symptoms of city innovation. The sons, in short square-skirted coats with rows of stupendous brass buttons, and their hair generally queued in the fashion of the times, especially if they could procure an eel-skin for the purpose, it being esteemed, throughout the country, as a potent nourisher and strengthener of the hair.

Brom Bones, however, was the hero of the scene, having come to the gathering on his favorite steed, Daredevil, a creature, like himself, full of mettle and mischief, and which no one but himself could manage. He was, in fact, noted for preferring vicious animals, given to all kinds of tricks, which kept the rider in constant risk of his neck, for he held a tractable well-broken horse as unworthy of a lad of spirit.

Fain would I pause to dwell upon the world of charms that burst upon the enraptured gaze of my hero, as he entered the state parlor of Van Tassel's mansion. Not those of the bevy of buxom lasses, with their luxurious display of red and

white, but the ample charms of a genuine Dutch country
tea-table, in the sumptuous time of autumn. Such heaped-up
platters of cakes of various and almost indescribable kinds,
known only to experienced Dutch housewives! There was
5 the doughty doughnut, the tenderer oly koek, and the crisp
and crumbling cruller; sweet cakes and short cakes, ginger-
cakes and honey-cakes, and the whole family of cakes. And
then there were apple-pies and peach-pies and pumpkin-pies;
besides slices of ham and smoked beef; and moreover delec-
10 table dishes of preserved plums, and peaches, and pears, and
quinces; not to mention broiled shad and roasted chickens;
together with bowls of milk and cream, all mingled higgledy-
piggledy, pretty much as I have enumerated them, with the
motherly teapot sending up its clouds of vapor from the
15 midst—Heaven bless the mark! I want breath and time to
discuss this banquet as it deserves, and am too eager to get
on with my story. Happily, Ichabod Crane was not in so
great a hurry as his historian, but did ample justice to every
dainty.

20   And now the sound of the music from the common room, or
hall, summoned to the dance. The musician was an old gray-
headed negro, who had been the itinerant orchestra of the
neighborhood for more than half a century. His instrument
was as old and battered as himself. The greater part of the
25 time he scraped on two or three strings, accompanying every
movement of the bow with a motion of the head; bowing
almost to the ground, and stamping with his foot whenever
a fresh couple were to start.

    Ichabod prided himself upon his dancing as much as upon
30 his vocal powers. Not a limb, not a fiber about him was idle;
and to have seen his loosely hung frame in full motion, and
clattering about the room, you would have thought Saint
Vitus himself, that blessed patron of the dance, was figuring
before you in person. He was the admiration of all the
35 negroes; who, having gathered, of all ages and sizes, from the
farm and the neighborhood, stood forming a pyramid of shin-

ing black faces at every door and window, gazing with delight at the scene, rolling their white eye-balls, and showing grinning rows of ivory from ear to ear. How could the flogger of urchins be otherwise than animated and joyous? the lady of his heart was his partner in the dance, and smiling graciously in reply to all his amorous oglings; while Brom Bones, sorely smitten with love and jealousy, sat brooding by himself in one corner.

When the dance was at an end, Ichabod was attracted to a knot of the sager folks, who, with old Van Tassel, sat smoking at one end of the piazza, gossiping over former times, and drawing out long stories about the war.

There was the story of Doffue Martling, a large bluebearded Dutchman, who had nearly taken a British frigate with an old iron nine-pounder from a mud breastwork, only that his gun burst at the sixth discharge. And there was an old gentleman who shall be nameless, being too rich a mynheer to be lightly mentioned, who, in the battle of White-Plains, being an excellent master of defense, parried a musket-ball with a small sword, insomuch that he absolutely felt it whiz round the blade, and glance off at the hilt; in proof of which he was ready at any time to show the sword, with the hilt a little bent. There were several more that had been equally great in the field, not one of whom but was persuaded that he had a considerable hand in bringing the war to a happy termination.

But all these were nothing to the tales of ghosts and apparitions that succeeded. The neighborhood is rich in legendary treasures of the kind. Local tales and superstitions thrive best in these sheltered, long-settled retreats; but are trampled under foot by the shifting throng that forms the population of most of our country places. Besides, there is no encouragement for ghosts in most of our villages, for they have scarcely had time to finish their first nap and turn themselves in their graves, before their surviving friends have traveled away from the neighborhood; so that when they turn out at night to walk their rounds, they have no acquaintance left to call upon. This is perhaps the reason why we so seldom hear of ghosts except in our long-established Dutch communities.

The immediate cause, however, of the prevalence of super-
5 natural stories in these parts, was doubtless owing to the vicinity of Sleepy Hollow. There was a contagion in the very air that blew from that haunted region; it breathed forth an atmosphere of dreams and fancies infecting all the land. Several of the Sleepy Hollow people were present at Van
10 Tassel's, and, as usual, were doling out their wild and wonderful legends. Many dismal tales were told about funeral trains, and mourning cries and wailings heard and seen about the great tree where the unfortunate Major André was taken, and which stood in the neighborhood. Some mention was
15 made also of the woman in white, that haunted the dark glen at Raven Rock, and was often heard to shriek on winter nights before a storm, having perished there in the snow. The chief part of the stories, however, turned upon the favorite specter of Sleepy Hollow, the headless horseman, who had
20 been heard several times of late, patrolling the country; and, it was said, tethered his horse nightly among the graves in the churchyard.

The sequestered situation of this church seems always to have made it a favorite haunt of troubled spirits. It stands
25 on a knoll, surrounded by locust-trees and lofty elms, from among which its decent whitewashed walls shine modestly forth, like Christian purity beaming through the shades of retirement. A gentle slope descends from it to a silver sheet of water, bordered by high trees, between which peeps may
30 be caught at the blue hills of the Hudson. To look upon its grass-grown yard, where the sunbeams seem to sleep so quietly, one would think that there at least the dead might rest in peace. On one side of the church extends a wide woody dell, along which raves a large brook among broken
35 rocks and trunks of fallen trees. Over a deep black part of the stream, not far from the church, was formerly thrown a

wooden bridge; the road that led to it, and the bridge itself,
were thickly shaded by overhanging trees, which cast a gloom
about it, even in the daytime, but occasioned a fearful darkness at night. This was one of the favorite haunts of the
headless horseman; and the place where he was most fre- 5
quently encountered. The tale was told of old Brouwer, a
most heretical disbeliever in ghosts, how he met the horseman returning from his foray into Sleepy Hollow, and was
obliged to get up behind him; how they galloped over bush
and brake, over hill and swamp, until they reached the 10
bridge; when the horseman suddenly turned into a skeleton,
threw old Brouwer into the brook, and sprang away over the
tree-tops with a clap of thunder.

This story was immediately matched by a thrice marvelous adventure of Brom Bones, who made light of the 15
Galloping Hessian as an arrant jockey. He affirmed that on
returning one night from the neighboring village of Sing Sing,
he had been overtaken by this midnight trooper; that he had
offered to race with him for a bowl of punch, and should have
won it too, for Daredevil beat the goblin horse all hollow, 20
but just as they came to the church bridge, the Hessian
bolted, and vanished in a flash of fire.

All these tales, told in that drowsy undertone with which
men talk in the dark, the countenances of the listeners only
now and then receiving a casual gleam from the glare of a 25
pipe, sank deep in the mind of Ichabod. He repaid them in
kind with large extracts from his invaluable author, Cotton
Mather, and added many marvelous events that had taken
place in his native State of Connecticut, and fearful sights
which he had seen in his nightly walks about Sleepy Hollow. 30

The revel now gradually broke up. The old farmers gathered together their families in their wagons, and were heard
for some time rattling along the hollow roads, and over the
distant hills. Some of the damsels mounted on pillions behind their favorite swains, and their light-hearted laughter, 35
mingling with the clatter of hoofs, echoed along the silent

woodlands, sounding fainter and fainter, until they gradually died away,—and the late scene of noise and frolic was all silent and deserted. Ichabod only lingered behind, according to the custom of country lovers, to have a tête-à-tête with the
5 heiress; fully convinced that he was now on the high road to success. What passed at this interview I will not pretend to say, for in fact I do not know. Something, however, I fear me, must have gone wrong, for he certainly sallied forth, after no very great interval, with an air quite desolate and chop-
10 fallen.—Oh, these women! these women! Could that girl have been playing off any of her coquettish tricks?—Was her encouragement of the poor pedagogue all a mere sham to secure her conquest of his rival?—Heaven only knows, not I!—Let it suffice to say, Ichabod stole forth with the air of
15 one who had been sacking a hen-roost rather than a fair lady's heart. Without looking to the right or left to notice the scene of rural wealth on which he had so often gloated, he went straight to the stable, and with several hearty cuffs and kicks, roused his steed most uncourteously from the com-
20 fortable quarters in which he was soundly sleeping, dreaming of mountains of corn and oats, and whole valleys of timothy and clover.

It was the very witching time of night that Ichabod, heavy-hearted and crestfallen, pursued his travels homewards,
25 along the sides of the lofty hills which rise above Tarry Town, and which he had traversed so cheerily in the after-noon. The hour was as dismal as himself. Far below him the Tappan Zee spread its dusky and indistinct waste of waters, with here and there the tall mast of a sloop, riding
30 quietly at anchor under the land. In the dead hush of mid-night, he could even hear the barking of the watch-dog from the opposite shore of the Hudson; but it was so vague and faint as only to give an idea of his distance from this faithful companion of man. Now and then, too, the long-drawn crow-
35 ing of a cock, accidentally awakened, would sound far, far off, from some farm-house away among the hills—but it was

like a dreaming sound in his ear. No signs of life occurred near him, but occasionally the melancholy chirp of a cricket, or perhaps the guttural twang of a bull-frog from a neighboring marsh, as if sleeping uncomfortably and turning suddenly in his bed. 5

All the stories of ghosts and goblins that he had heard in the afternoon now came crowding upon his recollection. The night grew darker and darker; the stars seemed to sink deeper in the sky, and driving clouds occasionally hid them from his sight. He had never felt so lonely and dismal. He 10 was, moreover, approaching the very place where many of the scenes of the ghost stories had been laid. In the center of the road stood an enormous tulip-tree, which towered like a giant above all the other trees of the neighborhood, and formed a kind of landmark. Its limbs were gnarled and fan- 15 tastic, large enough to form trunks for ordinary trees, twisting down almost to the earth, and rising again into the air. It was connected with the tragical story of the unfortunate André, who had been taken prisoner hard by; and was universally known by the name of Major André's tree. The 20 common people regarded it with a mixture of respect and superstition, partly out of sympathy for the fate of its ill-starred namesake, and partly from the tales of strange sights and doleful lamentations told concerning it.

As Ichabod approached this fearful tree, he began to 25 whistle: he thought his whistle was answered—it was but a blast sweeping sharply through the dry branches. As he approached a little nearer, he thought he saw something white hanging in the midst of the tree—he paused and ceased whistling; but on looking more narrowly, perceived that it 30 was a place where the tree had been scathed by lightning, and the white wood laid bare. Suddenly he heard a groan—his teeth chattered and his knees smote against the saddle: it was but the rubbing of one huge bough upon another, as they were swayed about by the breeze. He passed the tree in 35 safety, but new perils lay before him.

About two hundred yards from the tree a small brook crossed the road, and ran into a marshy and thickly wooded glen, known by the name of Wiley's swamp. A few rough logs, laid side by side, served for a bridge over this stream. On that side of the road where the brook entered the wood, a group of oaks and chestnuts, matted thick with wild grapevines, threw a cavernous gloom over it. To pass this bridge was the severest trial. It was at this identical spot that the unfortunate André was captured, and under the covert of those chestnuts and vines were the sturdy yeomen concealed who surprised him. This has ever since been considered a haunted stream, and fearful are the feelings of the schoolboy who has to pass it alone after dark.

As he approached the stream, his heart began to thump; he summoned up, however, all his resolution, gave his horse half a score of kicks in the ribs, and attempted to dash briskly across the bridge; but instead of starting forward, the perverse old animal made a lateral movement, and ran broadside against the fence. Ichabod, whose fears increased with the delay, jerked the reins on the other side, and kicked lustily with the contrary foot: it was all in vain; his steed started, it is true, but it was only to plunge to the opposite side of the road into a thicket of brambles and alder bushes. The schoolmaster now bestowed both whip and heel upon the starveling ribs of old Gunpowder, who dashed forward, snuffling and snorting, but came to a stand just by the bridge, with a suddenness that had nearly sent his rider sprawling over his head. Just at this moment a plashy tramp by the side of the bridge caught the sensitive ear of Ichabod. In the dark shadow of the grove, on the margin of the brook, he beheld something huge, misshapen, black and towering. It stirred not, but seemed gathered up in the gloom, like some gigantic monster ready to spring upon the traveler.

The hair of the affrighted pedagogue rose upon his head with terror. What was to be done? To turn and fly was now too late; and besides, what chance was there of escaping ghost or goblin, if such it was, which could ride upon the wings of the wind? Summoning up, therefore, a show of courage, he demanded in stammering accents, "Who are you?" He received no reply. He repeated his demand in a still more agitated voice. Still there was no answer. Once more he cudgeled the sides of the inflexible Gunpowder, and, shutting his eyes, broke forth with involuntary fervor into a psalm tune. Just then the shadowy object of alarm put itself in motion, and with a scramble and a bound stood at once in the middle of the road. Though the night was dark and dismal, yet the form of the unknown might now in some degree be ascertained. He appeared to be a horseman of large dimensions, and mounted on a black horse of powerful frame. He made no offer of molestation or sociability, but kept aloof on one side of the road, jogging along on the blind side of old Gunpowder, who had now got over his fright and waywardness.

Ichabod, who had no relish for this strange midnight companion, and bethought himself of the adventure of Brom Bones with the Galloping Hessian, now quickened his steed in hopes of leaving him behind. The stranger, however, quickened his horse to an equal pace. Ichabod pulled up, and fell into a walk, thinking to lag behind,—the other did the same. His heart began to sink within him; he endeavored to resume his psalm tune, but his parched tongue clove to the roof of his mouth, and he could not utter a stave. There was something in the moody and dogged silence of this pertinacious companion that was mysterious and appalling. It was soon fearfully accounted for. On mounting a rising ground, which brought the figure of his fellow-traveler in relief against the sky, gigantic in height, and muffled in a cloak, Ichabod was horror-struck on perceiving that he was headless! but his horror was still more increased on observing that the head, which should have rested on his shoulders, was carried before him on the pommel of his saddle! His terror rose to desperation; he rained a shower of kicks and blows upon Gunpowder, hoping by a sudden movement to give his companion the slip; but the specter started full jump with him. Away, then, they dashed through thick and thin; stones flying and sparks flashing at every bound. Ichabod's flimsy garments fluttered in the air, as he stretched his long lank body away over his horse's head, in the eagerness of his flight.

They had now reached the road which turns off to Sleepy Hollow; but Gunpowder, who seemed possessed with a demon, instead of keeping up it, made an opposite turn, and plunged headlong down hill to the left. This road leads through a sandy hollow, shaded by trees for about a quarter of a mile, where it crosses the bridge famous in goblin story; and just beyond swells the green knoll on which stands the whitewashed church.

As yet the panic of the steed had given his unskillful rider an apparent advantage in the chase; but just as he had got halfway through the hollow, the girths of the saddle gave way, and he felt it slipping from under him. He seized it by the pommel, and endeavored to hold it firm, but in vain; and had just time to save himself by clasping old Gunpowder round the neck, when the saddle fell to the earth, and he heard it trampled underfoot by his pursuer. For a moment the terror of Hans Van Ripper's wrath passed across his mind —for it was his Sunday saddle; but this was no time for petty fears; the goblin was hard on his haunches; and (unskillful rider that he was!) he had much ado to maintain his seat; sometimes slipping on one side, sometimes on another, and sometimes jolted on the high ridge of his horse's backbone, with a violence that he verily feared would cleave him asunder.

An opening in the trees now cheered him with the hopes that the church-bridge was at hand. The wavering reflection of a silver star in the bosom of the brook told him that he was not mistaken. He saw the walls of the church dimly glaring under the trees beyond. He recollected the place where Brom Bones's ghostly competitor had disappeared. "If I can but

reach that bridge," thought Ichabod, "I am safe." Just then
he heard the black steed panting and blowing close behind
him; he even fancied that he felt his hot breath. Another
convulsive kick in the ribs, and old Gunpowder sprang upon
the bridge; he thundered over the resounding planks; he 5
gained the opposite side; and now Ichabod cast a look behind
to see if his pursuer should vanish, according to rule, in a
flash of fire and brimstone. Just then he saw the goblin rising in his stirrups, and in the very act of hurling his head at
him. Ichabod endeavored to dodge the horrible missile, but 10
too late. It encountered his cranium with a tremendous
crash,—he was tumbled headlong into the dust, and Gunpowder, the black steed, and the goblin rider, passed by like
a whirlwind.

The next morning the old horse was found without his 15
saddle, and with the bridle under his feet, soberly cropping
the grass at his master's gate. Ichabod did not make his
appearance at breakfast; dinner-hour came, but no Ichabod.
The boys assembled at the schoolhouse, and strolled idly
about the banks of the brook; but no schoolmaster. Hans 20
Van Ripper now began to feel some uneasiness about the fate
of poor Ichabod, and his saddle. An inquiry was set on foot,
and after diligent investigation they came upon his traces.
In one part of the road leading to the church was found the
saddle trampled in the dirt; the tracks of horses' hoofs deeply 25
dented in the road, and evidently at furious speed, were
traced to the bridge, beyond which, on the bank of a broad
part of the brook, where the water ran deep and black, was
found the hat of the unfortunate Ichabod, and close beside it
a shattered pumpkin. 30

The brook was searched, but the body of the schoolmaster
was not to be discovered. Hans Van Ripper, as executor of
his estate, examined the bundle which contained all his
worldly effects. They consisted of two shirts and a half;
two stocks for the neck; a pair or two of worsted stockings; 35
an old pair of corduroy small-clothes; a rusty razor; a book

of psalm-tunes, full of dogs' ears, and a broken pitch-pipe.
As to the books and furniture of the schoolhouse, they belonged to the community, excepting Cotton Mather's *History of Witchcraft*, a *New England Almanac*, and a book
5 of dreams and fortune-telling; in which last was a sheet of
foolscap much scribbled and blotted in several fruitless attempts to make a copy of verses in honor of the heiress of
Van Tassel. These magic books and the poetic scrawl were
forthwith consigned to the flames by Hans Van Ripper; who
10 from that time forward determined to send his children no
more to school; observing that he never knew any good
come of this same reading and writing. Whatever money
the schoolmaster possessed, and he had received his quarter's
pay but a day or two before, he must have had about his
15 person at the time of his disappearance.

The mysterious event caused much speculation at the
church on the following Sunday. Knots of gazers and gossips were collected in the churchyard, at the bridge, and at
the spot where the hat and pumpkin had been found. The
20 stories of Brouwer, of Bones, and a whole budget of others,
were called to mind; and when they had diligently considered
them all, and compared them with the symptoms of the
present case, they shook their heads, and came to the conclusion that Ichabod had been carried off by the galloping
25 Hessian. As he was a bachelor, and in nobody's debt, nobody
troubled his head any more about him. The school was removed to a different quarter of the hollow, and another pedagogue reigned in his stead.

It is true, an old farmer, who had been down to New York
30 on a visit several years after, and from whom this account of
the ghostly adventure was received, brought home the intelligence that Ichabod Crane was still alive; that he had left the
neighborhood, partly through fear of the goblin and Hans
Van Ripper, and partly in mortification at having been sud-
35 denly dismissed by the heiress; that he had changed his
quarters to a distant part of the country; had kept school

and studied law at the same time, had been admitted to the
bar, turned politician, electioneered, written for the newspapers, and finally had been made a justice of the Ten Pound
Court. Brom Bones too, who shortly after his rival's disappearance conducted the blooming Katrina in triumph to the 5
altar, was observed to look exceedingly knowing whenever
the story of Ichabod was related, and always burst into a
hearty laugh at the mention of the pumpkin; which led some
to suspect that he knew more about the matter than he
chose to tell. 10

WILLIAM CULLEN BRYANT

THE RETURN OF YOUTH

My friend, thou sorrowest for thy golden prime,
　For thy fair youthful years too swift of flight;
Thou musest, with wet eyes, upon the time
　Of cheerful hopes that filled the world with light,—
Years when thy heart was bold, thy hand was strong, 15
　And quick the thought that moved thy tongue to speak,
And willing faith was thine, and scorn of wrong
　Summoned the sudden crimson to thy cheek.

Thou lookest forward on the coming days,
　Shuddering to feel their shadow o'er thee creep; 20
A path, thick-set with changes and decays,
　Slopes downward to the place of common sleep;
And they who walked with thee in life's first stage,
　Leave one by one thy side, and, waiting near,
Thou seest the sad companions of thy age— 25
　Dull love of rest, and weariness and fear.

Yet grieve thou not, nor think thy youth is gone,
　Nor deem that glorious season e'er could die.
Thy pleasant youth, a little while withdrawn,
　Waits on the horizon of a brighter sky; 30

Waits, like the morn, that folds her wing and hides,
  Till the slow stars bring back her dawning hour;
Waits, like the vanished spring, that slumbering bides
  Her own sweet time to waken bud and flower.

5   There shall he welcome thee, when thou shalt stand
      On his bright morning hills, with smiles more sweet
    Than when at first he took thee by the hand,
      Through the fair earth to lead thy tender feet.
    He shall bring back, but brighter, broader still,
10   Life's early glory to thine eyes again,
    Shall clothe thy spirit with new strength, and fill
      Thy leaping heart with warmer love than then.

    Hast thou not glimpses, in the twilight here,
      Of mountains where immortal morn prevails?
15   Comes there not, through the silence, to thine ear
      A gentle rustling of the morning gales;
    A murmur, wafted from that glorious shore,
      Of streams that water banks forever fair,
    And voices of the loved ones gone before,
20   More musical in that celestial air?

A FOREST HYMN

    The groves were God's first temples.
        Ere man learned
    To hew the shaft, and lay the architrave,
    And spread the roof above them—ere he framed
25   The lofty vault, to gather and roll back
    The sound of anthems; in the darkling wood,
    Amid the cool and silence, he knelt down,
    And offered to the Mightiest solemn thanks
    And supplication. For his simple heart
30   Might not resist the sacred influences
    Which, from the stilly twilight of the place,
    And from the gray old trunks that high in heaven

Mingled their mossy boughs, and from the sound
Of the invisible breath that swayed at once
All their green tops, stole over him, and bowed
His spirit with the thought of boundless power
And inaccessible majesty. Ah, why   5
Should we, in the world's riper years, neglect
God's ancient sanctuaries, and adore
Only among the crowd, and under roofs
That our frail hands have raised? Let me, at least,
Here, in the shadow of this aged wood,   10
Offer one hymn—thrice happy, if it find
Acceptance in His ear.
                    Father, thy hand
Hath reared these venerable columns, thou
Didst weave this verdant roof. Thou didst look down
Upon the naked earth, and, forthwith, rose   15
All these fair ranks of trees. They, in thy sun,
Budded, and shook their green leaves in thy breeze,
And shot toward heaven. The century-living crow,
Whose birth was in their tops, grew old and died
Among their branches, till, at last, they stood,   20
As now they stand, massy, and tall, and dark,
Fit shrine for humble worshiper to hold
Communion with his Maker. These dim vaults,
These winding aisles, of human pomp or pride
Report not. No fantastic carvings show   25
The boast of our vain race to change the form
Of thy fair works. But thou art here—thou fill'st
The solitude. Thou art in the soft winds
That run along the summit of these trees
In music; thou art in the cooler breath   30
That from the inmost darkness of the place
Comes, scarcely felt; the barky trunks, the ground,
The fresh moist ground, are all instinct with thee.
Here is continual worship;—Nature, here,
In the tranquillity that thou dost love,   35

Enjoys thy presence. Noiselessly, around,
From perch to perch, the solitary bird
Passes; and yon clear spring, that, midst its herbs,
Wells softly forth and wandering steeps the roots
Of half the mighty forest, tells no tale
Of all the good it does. Thou hast not left
Thyself without a witness, in the shades,
Of thy perfections. Grandeur, strength, and grace
Are here to speak of thee. This mighty oak—
By whose immovable stem I stand and seem
Almost annihilated—not a prince,
In all that proud old world beyond the deep,
E'er wore his crown as loftily as he
Wears the green coronal of leaves with which
Thy hand has graced him. Nestled at his root
Is beauty, such as blooms not in the glare
Of the broad sun. That delicate forest flower,
With scented breath and look so like a smile,
Seems, as it issues from the shapeless mold,
An emanation of the indwelling Life,
A visible token of the upholding Love,
That are the soul of this great universe.
     My heart is awed within me when I think
Of the great miracle that still goes on,
In silence round me—the perpetual work
Of thy creation, finished, yet renewed
Forever. Written on thy works I read
The lesson of thy own eternity.
Lo! all grow old and die—but see again,
How on the faltering footsteps of decay
Youth presses—ever gay and beautiful youth
In all its beautiful forms. These lofty trees
Wave not less proudly than their ancestors
Molder beneath them. Oh, there is not lost
One of earth's charms: upon her bosom yet,
After the flight of untold centuries,

The freshness of her far beginning lies
And yet shall lie. Life mocks the idle hate
Of his arch-enemy Death—yea, seats himself
Upon the tyrant's throne—the sepulcher,
And of the triumphs of his ghastly foe ·   5
Makes his own nourishment. For he came forth
From thine own bosom, and shall have no end.
   There have been holy men who hid themselves
Deep in the woody wilderness, and gave
Their lives to thought and prayer, till they outlived   10
The generation born with them, nor seemed
Less aged than the hoary trees and rocks
Around them;—and there have been holy men
Who deemed it were not well to pass life thus.
But let me often to these solitudes   15
Retire, and in thy presence reassure
My feeble virtue. Here its enemies,
The passions, at thy plainer footsteps shrink
And tremble and are still. O God! when thou
Dost scare the world with tempest, set on fire   20
The heavens with falling thunderbolts, or fill
With all the waters of the firmament,
The swift dark whirlwind that uproots the woods
And drowns the villages; when, at thy call,
Uprises the great deep and throws himself   25
Upon the continent, and overwhelms
Its cities—who forgets not, at the sight
Of these tremendous tokens of thy power,
His pride, and lays his strifes and follies by?
Oh, from these sterner aspects of thy face   30
Spare me and mine, nor let us need the wrath
Of the mad unchained elements to teach
Who rules them. Be it ours to meditate,
In these calm shades, thy milder majesty,
And to the beautiful order of thy works   35
Learn to conform the order of our lives.

TO A WATERFOWL

Whither, midst falling dew,
While glow the heavens with the last steps of day,
Far, through their rosy depths, dost thou pursue
    Thy solitary way?

5   Vainly the fowler's eye
Might mark thy distant flight to do thee wrong,
As, darkly limned upon the crimson sky,
    Thy figure floats along.

Seek'st thou the plashy brink
10 Of weedy lake, or marge of river wide,
Or where the rocking billows rise and sink
    On the chafed ocean-side?

There is a Power whose care
Teaches thy way along that pathless coast—
15 The desert and illimitable air—
    Lone wandering, but not lost.

All day thy wings have fanned,
At that far height, the cold, thin atmosphere,
Yet stoop not, weary, to the welcome land,
20   Though the dark night is near.

And soon that toil shall end;
Soon shalt thou find a summer home, and rest,
And scream among thy fellows; reeds shall bend,
    Soon, o'er thy sheltered nest.

25   Thou'rt gone, the abyss of heaven
Hath swallowed up thy form; yet, on my heart
Deeply hath sunk the lesson thou hast given,
    And shall not soon depart.

He who, from zone to zone,
Guides through the boundless sky thy certain flight,
In the long way that I must tread alone,
   Will lead my steps aright.

ROBERT OF LINCOLN

Merrily swinging on brier and weed,   5
  Near to the nest of his little dame,
Over the mountainside or mead,
   Robert of Lincoln is telling his name:
      Bob-o'-link, bob-o'-link,
      Spink, spank, spink;   10
Snug and safe is that nest of ours,
Hidden among the summer flowers.
      Chee, chee, chee.

Robert of Lincoln is gayly drest,
  Wearing a bright black wedding-coat;   15
White are his shoulders and white his crest.
   Hear him call in his merry note:
      Bob-o'-link, bob-o'-link,
      Spink, spank, spink;
Look, what a nice new coat is mine,   20
Sure there was never a bird so fine.
      Chee, chee, chee.

Robert of Lincoln's Quaker wife,
  Pretty and quiet, with plain brown wings,
Passing at home a patient life,   25
   Broods in the grass while her husband sings:
      Bob-o'-link, bob-o'-link,
      Spink, spank, spink;
Brood, kind creature; you need not fear
Thieves and robbers while I am here.   30
      Chee, chee, chee.

Modest and shy as a nun is she;
 One weak chirp is her only note.
Braggart and prince of braggarts is he,
 Pouring boasts from his little throat:
5
  Bob-o'-link, bob-o'-link,
  Spink, spank, spink;
Never was I afraid of man;
Catch me, cowardly knaves, if you can!
  Chee, chee, chee.

10
Six white eggs on a bed of hay,
 Flecked with purple, a pretty sight!
There as the mother sits all day,
 Robert is singing with all his might:
  Bob-o'-link, bob-o'-link,
15
  Spink, spank, spink;
Nice good wife, that never goes out,
Keeping house while I frolic about.
  Chee, chee, chee.

Soon as the little ones chip the shell,
20
 Six wide mouths are open for food;
Robert of Lincoln bestirs him well,
 Gathering seeds for the hungry brood.
  Bob-o'-link, bob-o'-link,
  Spink, spank, spink;
25
This new life is likely to be
Hard for a gay young fellow like me.
  Chee, chee, chee.

Robert of Lincoln at length is made
 Sober with work, and silent with care;
30
Off is his holiday garment laid,
 Half forgotten that merry air:
  Bob-o'-link, bob-o'-link,
  Spink, spank, spink;

Nobody knows but my mate and I
Where our nest and our nestlings lie.
                Chee, chee, chee.

Summer wanes; the children are grown;
    Fun and frolic no more he knows;
Robert of Lincoln's a humdrum crone;
    Off he flies, and we sing as he goes:
            Bob-o'-link, bob-o'-link,
            Spink, spank, spink;
When you can pipe that merry old strain,
Robert of Lincoln, come back again.
                Chee, chee, chee.

TO THE FRINGED GENTIAN

Thou blossom bright with autumn dew,
And colored with the heaven's own blue,
That openest when the quiet light
Succeeds the keen and frosty night,

Thou comest not when violets lean
O'er wandering brooks and springs unseen,
Or columbines, in purple dressed,
Nod o'er the ground-bird's hidden nest.

Thou waitest late and com'st alone,
When woods are bare and birds are flown,
And frost and shortening days portend
The aged year is near his end.

Then doth thy sweet and quiet eye
Look through its fringes to the sky,
Blue—blue—as if that sky let fall
A flower from its cerulean wall.

I would that thus, when I shall see
The hour of death draw near to me,
Hope, blossoming within my heart,
May look to heaven as I depart.

JAMES FENIMORE COOPER

THE RED ROVER

[The Hurricane]

Wilder made a swift turn or two on the quarter-deck, turning his quick glances from one quarter of the heavens to another; from the black and lulling water on which his vessel was rolling, to the sails; and from his silent and profoundly
5 expectant crew, to the dim lines of spars that were waving above his head, like so many pencils tracing their curvilinear and wanton images over the murky volumes of the superincumbent clouds.

"Lay the after-yards square!" he said, in a voice which
10 was heard by every man on deck, though his words were apparently spoken but little above his breath. The creaking of the blocks, as the spars came slowly and heavily round to the indicated positions, contributed to the imposing character of the moment, sounding like notes of fearful preparation.

15 "Haul up the courses!" resumed Wilder with the same eloquent calmness of manner. Then, taking another glance at the threatening horizon, he added slowly but with emphasis, "Furl them—furl them both. Away aloft, and hand your courses!" he continued in a shout; "roll them up,
20 cheerily; in with them, boys, cheerily; in!"

The conscious seamen took their impulses from the tones of their commander. In a moment, twenty dark forms were leaping up the rigging, with the alacrity of so many quadrupeds. In another minute, the vast and powerful sheets of
25 canvas were effectually rendered harmless, by securing them in tight rolls to their respective spars. The men descended as swiftly as they had mounted to the yards; and then succeeded another breathing pause. At this appalling moment, a candle would have sent its flame perpendicularly towards
30 the heavens. The ship, missing the steadying power of the wind, rolled heavily in the troughs of the seas, which began

to lessen at each instant, as if the startled element was recalling into the security of its own vast bosom that portion of its particles which had so lately been permitted to gambol madly over its surface. The water washed sullenly along the side of the ship, or, as she laboring rose from one of her frequent falls into the hollows of the waves, it shot back into the ocean from her decks in glittering cascades. Every hue of the heavens, every sound of the element, and each dusky and anxious countenance, helped to proclaim the intense interest of the moment. In this brief interval of expectation and inactivity, the mates again approached their commander.

"It is an awful night, Captain Wilder!" said Earing, presuming on his rank to be the first to speak.

"I have known far less notice given of a shift of wind," was the answer.

"We have had time to gather in our kites, 'tis true, sir; but there are signs and warnings that come with this change which the oldest seaman must dread!"

"Yes," continued Knighthead, in a voice that sounded hoarse and powerful, even amid the fearful accessories of that scene; "yes, it is no trifling commission that can call people that I shall not name out upon the water in such a night as this. It was in just such weather that I saw the *Vesuvius* ketch go to a place so deep, that her own mortar would not have been able to have sent a bomb into the open air, had hands and fire been there fit to let it off!"

"Ay; and it was in such a time that the *Greenlandman* was cast upon the Orkneys, in as flat a calm as ever lay on the sea."

"Gentlemen," said Wilder, with a peculiar and perhaps an ironical emphasis on the word, "what would ye have? There is not a breath of air stirring, and the ship is naked to her topsails!"

It would have been difficult for either of the two malcontents to give a very satisfactory answer to this question. Both were secretly goaded by mysterious and superstitious apprehensions, that were powerfully aided by the more real and intelligible aspect of the night; but neither had so far forgotten his manhood, and his professional pride, as to lay bare the full extent of his own weakness, at a moment when he was liable to be called upon for the exhibition of qualities of a more positive and determined character. The feeling that was uppermost betrayed itself in the reply of Earing, though in an indirect and covert manner.

"Yes, the vessel is snug enough now," he said, "though eyesight has shown us it is no easy matter to drive a freighted ship through the water as fast as one of those flying craft aboard which no man can say who stands at the helm, by what compass she steers, or what is her draught!"

"Ay," resumed Knighthead, "I call the _Caroline_ fast for an honest trader. There are few square-rigged boats who do not wear the pennants of the king, that can eat her out of the wind on a bowline, or bring her into their wake with studding-sails set. But this is a time and an hour to make a seaman think. Look at yon hazy light, here in with the land, that is coming so fast down upon us, and then tell me whether it comes from the coast of America, or whether it comes from out of the stranger who has been so long running under our lee, but who has got, or is fast getting, the wind of us at last, while none here can say how, or why. I have just this much, and no more, to say: give me for consort a craft whose captain I know, or give me none!"

"Such is your taste, Mr. Knighthead," said Wilder, coldly; "mine may, by some accident, be different."

"Yes, yes," observed the more cautious and prudent Earing, "in time of war, and with letters of marque aboard, a man may honestly hope the sail he sees should have a stranger for her master; or otherwise he would never fall in with an enemy. But, though an Englishman born myself, I should rather give the ship in that mist a clear sea, seeing that I neither know her nation nor her cruise. Ah, Captain Wilder, this is an awful sight for the morning watch! Often and

often have I seen the sun rise in the east, and no harm done;
but little good can come of a day when the light first breaks
in the west. Cheerfully would I give the owners the last
month's pay, hard as it has been earned, did I but know under
what flag the stranger sails."

"Frenchman, Don, or Devil, yonder he comes!" cried
Wilder. Then, turning towards the attentive crew, he shouted,
in a voice that was appalling by its vehemence and warning,
"Let run the after-halyards! round with the fore-yard; round
with it, men, with a will!"

These were cries that the startled crew but too well understood. Every nerve and muscle were exerted to execute the
orders, to be in readiness for the tempest. No man spoke;
but each expended the utmost of his power and skill in direct
and manly efforts. Nor was there, in verity, a moment to
lose, or a particle of human strength expended here, without
a sufficient object.

The lurid and fearful-looking mist, which, for the last
quarter of an hour, had been gathering in the northwest, was
driving down upon them with the speed of a race-horse. The
air had already lost the damp and peculiar feeling of an
easterly breeze; and little eddies were beginning to flutter
among the masts—precursors of the coming squall. Then, a
rushing, roaring sound was heard moaning along the ocean,
whose surface was first dimpled, next ruffled, and finally
covered with a sheet of clear, white, and spotless foam. At
the next moment, the power of the wind fell upon the inert
and laboring Bristol trader.

While the gust was approaching, Wilder had seized the
slight opportunity afforded by the changeful puffs of air to
get the ship as much as possible before the wind; but the
sluggish movement of the vessel met neither the wishes of
his own impatience nor the exigencies of the moment. Her
bows slowly and heavily fell off from the north, leaving her
precisely in a situation to receive the first shock on her broadside. Happy it was, for all who had life at risk in that

defenseless vessel, that she was not fated to receive the whole
weight of the tempest at a blow. The sails fluttered and
trembled on their massive yards, bellying and collapsing
alternately for a minute, and then the rushing wind swept
5 over them in a hurricane.

The *Caroline* received the blast like a stout and buoyant
ship as she was, yielding to its impulse until her side lay
nearly incumbent on the element; and then, as if the fearful
fabric were conscious of its jeopardy, it seemed to lift its
10 reclining masts again, struggling to work its way through
the water.

"Keep the helm a-weather! Jam it a-weather, for your
life!" shouted Wilder, amid the roar of the gust.

The veteran seaman at the wheel obeyed the order with
15 steadiness, but in vain did he keep his eyes on the margin of
his head sail, to watch the manner in which the ship would
obey its power. Twice more, in as many moments, the giddy
masts fell towards the horizon, waving as often gracefully
upward, and then they yielded to the mighty pressure of the
20 wind, until the whole machine lay prostrate on the water.

"Be cool!" said Wilder, seizing the bewildered Earing by
the arm, as the latter rushed madly up the steep side of the
deck; "it is our duty to be calm: bring hither an ax."

Quick as the thought which gave the order, the admonished
25 mate complied, jumping into the mizzen-channels of the ship,
to execute with his own hands the mandate that he knew
must follow.

"Shall I cut?" he demanded, with uplifted arms, and in a
voice that atoned for his momentary confusion, by its steadi-
30 ness and force.

"Hold!—Does the ship mind her helm at all?"

"Not an inch, sir."

"Then cut," Wilder clearly and calmly added.

A single blow sufficed for the discharge of this important
35 duty. Extended to the utmost powers of endurance, by the
vast weight it upheld, the lanyard struck by Earing no sooner

parted, than each of its fellows snapped in succession, leaving
the mast dependent on its wood for the support of all the
ponderous and complicated hamper it upheld. The cracking
of the spar came next; and the whole fell, like a tree that had
been snapped at its foundation.   5

"Does she fall off?" called Wilder, to the observant seaman at the wheel.

"She yielded a little, sir; but this new squall is bringing
her up again."

"Shall I cut?" shouted Earing from the main-rigging, whither 10
he had leaped, like a tiger who had bounded on his prey.

"Cut."

A louder and more imposing crash succeeded this order,
though not before several heavy blows had been struck into
the massive mast itself. As before, the sea received the   15
tumbling maze of spars, rigging, and sails; the vessel surging,
at the same instant, from its recumbent position, and rolling
far and heavily to windward.

"She rights! she rights!" exclaimed twenty voices which
had been mute, in a suspense that involved life and death.   20

"Keep her dead away!" added the calm but authoritative
voice of the young commander. "Stand by to furl the fore-
topsail—let it hang a moment to drag the ship clear of the
wreck—cut, cut—cheerily, men—hatchets and knives—cut
with all, and cut *off* all!"   25

As the men now worked with the vigor of hope, the ropes
that still confined the fallen spars to the vessel were quickly
severed; and the *Caroline*, by this time dead before the gale,
appeared barely to touch the foam that covered the sea. The
wind came over the waste in gusts that rumbled like distant   30
thunder, and with a power that seemed to threaten to lift the
ship from its proper element. As a prudent and sagacious
seaman had let fly the halyards of the solitary sail that remained, at the moment the squall approached, the loosened
but lowered topsail was now distended in a manner that   35
threatened to drag after it the only mast which still stood.

Wilder saw the necessity of getting rid of the sail, and he also saw the utter impossibility of securing it. Calling Earing to his side, he pointed out the danger, and gave the necessary order.

5   "The spar cannot stand such shocks much longer," he concluded; "should it go over the bows, some fatal blow might be given to the ship at the rate she is moving. A man or two must be sent aloft to cut the sail from the yards."

"The stick is bending like a willow whip," returned the
10 mate, "and the lower mast itself is sprung. There would be great danger in trusting a hand in that top, while these wild squalls are breathing around us."

"You may be right," returned Wilder, with a sudden conviction of the truth of what the other had said. "Stay you
15 then here; if anything befall me, try to get the vessel into port as far north as the Capes of Virginia, at least;—on no account attempt Hatteras, in the present condition of—"

"What would you do, Captain Wilder?" interrupted the mate, laying his hand on the shoulder of his commander, who
20 had already thrown down his sea-cap on the deck, and was preparing to divest himself of some of his outer garments.

"I go aloft to ease the mast of that topsail, without which we lose the spar, and possibly the ship."

"I see that plain enough, sir; but, shall it be said that an-
25 other did the duty of Edward Earing? It is your business to carry the vessel into the Capes of Virginia, and mine to cut the topsail adrift. If harm comes to me, why, put it in the log, with a word or two about the manner in which I played my part. That is the most proper epitaph for a sailor."

30   Wilder made no resistance. He resumed his watchful and reflecting attitude, with the simplicity of one who had been too long trained to the discharge of certain obligations himself, to manifest surprise that another should acknowledge their imperative character. In the meantime, Earing pro-
35 ceeded steadily to perform what he had just promised. Passing into the waist of the ship, he provided himself with a

suitable hatchet, and then, without speaking a syllable to any of the mute but attentive seamen, he sprang into the fore-rigging, every strand and rope-yarn of which was tightened by the strain nearly to snapping. The understanding eyes of his observers comprehended his intention; and with precisely the same pride of station as had urged him to the dangerous undertaking, four or five of the oldest mariners jumped upon the rattlings, to mount into an air that apparently teemed with a hundred hurricanes.

"Lie down out of that fore-rigging," shouted Wilder, through a deck trumpet; "lie down; all, but the mate, lie down!" His words were borne past the inattentive ears of the excited and mortified followers of Earing, but for once they failed of their effect. Each man was too earnestly bent on his purpose to listen to the sounds of recall. In less than a minute, the whole were scattered along the yards, prepared to obey the signal of their officer. The mate cast a look about him; perceiving that the time was comparatively favorable, he struck a blow upon the large rope that confined one of the lower angles of the distended and bursting sail to the yard. The effect was much the same as would be produced by knocking away the keystone of an ill-cemented arch. The canvas broke from its fastenings with a loud explosion, and, for an instant, it was seen sailing in the air ahead of the ship, as if it were sustained on wings. The vessel rose on a sluggish wave—the lingering remains of the former breeze—and settled heavily over the rolling surge, borne down alike by its own weight and the renewed violence of the gusts. At this critical instant, while the seamen aloft were still gazing in the direction in which the little cloud of canvas had disappeared, a lanyard of the lower rigging parted, with a crack that reached the ears of Wilder.

"Lie down!" he shouted wildly through his trumpet; "down by the backstays; down for your lives; every man of you, down!"

A solitary individual profited by the warning, gliding to the deck with the velocity of the wind. But rope parted after rope, and the fatal snapping of the wood followed. For a moment, the towering mass tottered, seeming to wave
5 towards every quarter of the heavens; and then, yielding to the movements of the hull, the whole fell, with a heavy crash, into the sea. Cord, lanyard, and stay snapped like thread, as each received in succession the strain of the ship, leaving the naked and despoiled hull of the *Caroline* to drive before the
10 tempest, as if nothing had occurred to impede its progress.

A mute and eloquent pause succeeded the disaster. It seemed as if the elements themselves were appeased by their work, and something like a momentary lull in the awful rushing of the winds might have been fancied. Wilder sprang to
15 the side of the vessel, and distinctly beheld the victims, who still clung to their frail support. He even saw Earing waving his hand in adieu with a seaman's heart, like a man who not only felt how desperate was his situation, but who knew how to meet it with resignation. Then the wreck of spars, with
20 all who clung to it, was swallowed up in the body of the frightful, preternatural-looking mist which extended on every side of them, from the ocean to the clouds.

EDGAR ALLAN POE

ISRAFEL

And the angel Israfel, whose heart-strings are a lute, and who has the sweetest voice of all God's creatures.—The Koran

25   In Heaven a spirit doth dwell
            Whose heart-strings are a lute;
        None sing so wildly well
        As the angel Israfel,
        And the giddy stars (so legends tell),
30   Ceasing their hymns, attend the spell
            Of his voice, all mute.

Tottering above
  In her highest noon,
  The enamored moon
Blushes with love,
  While, to listen, the red levin   5
  (With the rapid Pleiads, even,
  Which were seven)
  Pauses in Heaven.

And they say (the starry choir
  And the other listening things)   10
That Israfeli's fire
Is owing to that lyre
  By which he sits and sings,
The trembling living wire
  Of those unusual strings.   15

But the skies that angel trod,
  Where deep thoughts are a duty,
Where Love's a grown-up God,
  Where the Houri glances are
Imbued with all the beauty   20
  Which we worship in a star.

Therefore thou art not wrong,
  Israfeli, who despisest
An unimpassioned song;
To thee the laurels belong,   25
  Best bard, because the wisest:
Merrily live, and long!

The ecstasies above
  With thy burning measures suit:
Thy grief, thy joy, thy hate, thy love,   30
  With the fervor of thy lute:
  Well may the stars be mute!

Yes, Heaven is thine; but this
　　Is a world of sweets and sours;
　　Our flowers are merely—flowers,
And the shadow of thy perfect bliss
5　　Is the sunshine of ours.

If I could dwell
Where Israfel
　　Hath dwelt, and he where I,
He might not sing so wildly well
10　　A mortal melody,
While a bolder note than this might swell
　　From my lyre within the sky.

TO ONE IN PARADISE

Thou wast all that to me, love,
　　For which my soul did pine:
15　A green isle in the sea, love,
　　A fountain and a shrine
All wreathed with fairy fruits and flowers,
　　And all the flowers were mine.

Ah, dream too bright to last!
20　　Ah, starry Hope, that didst arise
But to be overcast!
　　A voice from out the Future cries,
"On! on!"—but o'er the Past
　　(Dim gulf!) my spirit hovering lies
25　Mute, motionless, aghast.

For, alas! alas! with me
　　The light of Life is o'er!
　　No more—no more—no more—
(Such language holds the solemn sea
30　　To the sands upon the shore)
Shall bloom the thunder-blasted tree,
　　Or the stricken eagle soar.

And all my days are trances,
   And all my nightly dreams
Are where thy gray eye glances,
   And where thy footstep gleams—
In what ethereal dances,   5
   By what eternal streams.

TO HELEN

Helen, thy beauty is to me
   Like those Nicæan barks of yore,
That gently, o'er a perfumed sea,
   The weary, wayworn wanderer bore   10
   To his own native shore.

On desperate seas long wont to roam,
   Thy hyacinth hair, thy classic face,
Thy Naiad airs, have brought me home
   To the glory that was Greece   15
And the grandeur that was Rome.

Lo! in yon brilliant window-niche
   How statue-like I see thee stand,
   The agate lamp within thy hand!
Ah, Psyche, from the regions which   20
   Are Holy Land!

A DESCENT INTO THE MAELSTRÖM

[Extract]

[The Norwegian fisherman who tells this story had just been caught in
a terrific hurricane which tore the masts out of his boat and swept his
younger brother into the sea.]

Well, so far we had ridden the swells very cleverly; but
presently a gigantic sea happened to take us right under the
counter, and bore us with it as it rose—up—up—as if into
the sky. I would not have believed that any wave could rise 25

so high. And then down we came with a sweep, a slide, and a plunge, that made me feel sick and dizzy, as if I was falling from some lofty mountain-top in a dream. But while we were up I had thrown a quick glance around—and that one
5 glance was all sufficient. I saw our exact position in an instant. The Moskoe-ström whirlpool was about a quarter of a mile dead ahead—but no more like the every-day Moskoe-ström, than the whirl as you now see it is like a mill-race. If I had not known where we were, and what we had to expect,
10 I should not have recognized the place at all. As it was, I involuntarily closed my eyes in horror. The lids clenched themselves together as if in a spasm.

It could not have been more than two minutes afterwards until we suddenly felt the waves subside, and were enveloped
15 in foam. The boat made a sharp half turn to larboard, and then shot off in its new direction like a thunderbolt. At the same moment the roaring noise of the water was completely drowned in a kind of shrill shriek—such a sound as you might imagine given out by the water-pipes of many thousand
20 steam-vessels, letting off their steam all together. We were now in the belt of surf that always surrounds the whirl; and I thought, of course, that another moment would plunge us into the abyss—down which we could only see indistinctly on account of the amazing velocity with which we were borne
25 along. The boat did not seem to sink into the water at all, but to skim like an air-bubble upon the surface of the surge. Her starboard side was next the whirl, and on the larboard arose the world of ocean we had left. It stood like a huge writhing wall between us and the horizon.

30 It may appear strange, but now, when we were in the very jaws of the gulf, I felt more composed than when we were only approaching it. Having made up my mind to hope no more, I got rid of a great deal of that terror which unmanned me at first. I suppose it was despair that strung my nerves.
35 It may look like boasting—but what I tell you is truth— I began to reflect how magnificent a thing it was to die in such

a manner, and how foolish it was in me to think of so paltry a
consideration as my own individual life, in view of so wonderful a manifestation of God's power. I do believe that I
blushed with shame when this idea crossed my mind. After
a little while I became possessed with the keenest curiosity 5
about the whirl itself. I positively felt a *wish* to explore its
depths, even at the sacrifice I was going to make; and my
principal grief was that I should never be able to tell my old
companions on shore about the mysteries I should see. These,
no doubt, were singular fancies to occupy a man's mind in 10
such extremity—and I have often thought, since, that the
revolutions of the boat around the pool might have rendered
me a little light-headed.

There was another circumstance which tended to restore
my self-possession; and this was the cessation of the wind, 15
which could not reach us in our present situation—for, as
you saw yourself, the belt of surf is considerably lower than
the general bed of the ocean, and this latter now towered
above us, a high, black, mountainous ridge. If you have
never been at sea in a heavy gale, you can form no idea of the 20
confusion of mind occasioned by the wind and spray together.
They blind, deafen, and strangle you, and take away all
power of action or reflection. But we were now, in a great
measure, rid of these annoyances—just as death-condemned
felons in prison are allowed petty indulgences, forbidden 25
them while their doom is yet uncertain.

How often we made the circuit of the belt it is impossible
to say. We careered round and round for perhaps an hour,
flying rather than floating, getting gradually more and more
into the middle of the surge, and then nearer and nearer to its 30
horrible inner edge. All this time I had never let go of the
ring-bolt. My brother was at the stern, holding on to a small
empty water-cask which had been securely lashed under the
coop of the counter, and was the only thing on deck that had
not been swept overboard when the gale first took us. As we 35
approached the brink of the pit he let go his hold upon this,

and made for the ring, from which, in the agony of his terror, he endeavored to force my hands, as it was not large enough to afford us both a secure grasp. I never felt deeper grief than when I saw him attempt this act—although I knew he
5 was a madman when he did it—a raving maniac through sheer fright. I did not care, however, to contest the point with him. I knew it could make no difference whether either of us held on at all; so I let him have the bolt, and went astern to the cask. This there was no great difficulty in do-
10 ing; for the smack flew round steadily enough, and upon an even keel—only swaying to and fro, with the immense sweeps and swelters of the whirl. Scarcely had I secured myself in my new position, when we gave a wild lurch to starboard, and rushed headlong into the abyss. I muttered a
15 hurried prayer to God, and thought all was over.

As I felt the sickening sweep of the descent, I had instinctively tightened my hold upon the barrel, and closed my eyes. For some seconds I dared not open them—while I expected instant destruction, and wondered that I was not already in
20 my death-struggles with the water. But moment after moment elapsed. I still lived. The sense of falling had ceased; and the motion of the vessel seemed much as it had been before, while in the belt of foam, with the exception that she now lay more along. I took courage and looked once again
25 upon the scene.

Never shall I forget the sensations of awe, horror, and admiration with which I gazed about me. The boat appeared to be hanging, as if by magic, midway down, upon the interior surface of a funnel vast in circumference, prodigious in depth,
30 and whose perfectly smooth sides might have been mistaken for ebony, but for the bewildering rapidity with which they spun around, and for the gleaming and ghastly radiance they shot forth, as the rays of the full moon, from that circular rift amid the clouds, which I have already described, streamed in
35 a flood of golden glory along the black walls, and far away down into the inmost recesses of the abyss.

At first I was too much confused to observe anything accurately. The general burst of terrific grandeur was all that I beheld. When I recovered myself a little, however, my gaze fell instinctively downward. In this direction I was able to obtain an unobstructed view, from the manner in which the 5 smack hung on the inclined surface of the pool. She was quite upon an even keel—that is to say, her deck lay in a plane parallel with that of the water—but this latter sloped at an angle of more than forty-five degrees, so that we seemed to be lying upon our beam-ends. I could not help observing, never- 10 theless, that I had scarcely more difficulty in maintaining my hold and footing in this situation, than if we had been upon a dead level; and this, I suppose, was owing to the speed at which we revolved.

The rays of the moon seemed to search the very bottom 15 of the profound gulf; but still I could make out nothing distinctly, on account of a thick mist in which everything there was enveloped, and over which there hung a magnificent rainbow, like that narrow and tottering bridge which Mussulmans say is the only pathway between Time and Eternity. This 20 mist, or spray, was no doubt occasioned by the clashing of the great walls of the funnel, as they all met together at the bottom—but the yell that went up to the heavens from out of that mist, I dare not attempt to describe.

Our first slide into the abyss itself, from the belt of foam 25 above, had carried us to a great distance down the slope; but our farther descent was by no means proportionate. Round and round we swept—not with any uniform movement but in dizzying swings and jerks, that sent us sometimes only a few hundred yards—sometimes nearly the complete circuit 30 of the whirl. Our progress downward, at each revolution, was slow, but very perceptible.

Looking about me upon the wide waste of liquid ebony on which we were thus borne, I perceived that our boat was not the only object in the embrace of the whirl. Both above and 35 below us were visible fragments of vessels, large masses of

building timber and trunks of trees, with many smaller
articles, such as pieces of house furniture, broken boxes, barrels, and staves. I have already described the unnatural
curiosity which had taken the place of my original terrors. It
5 appeared to grow upon me as I drew nearer and nearer to my
dreadful doom. I now began to watch, with a strange interest, the numerous things that floated in our company. I
must have been delirious—for I even sought *amusement* in
speculating upon the relative velocities of their several de-
10 scents toward the foam below. "This fir tree," I found myself
at one time saying, "will certainly be the next thing that
takes the awful plunge and disappears,"—and then I was disappointed to find that the wreck of a Dutch merchant ship
overtook it and went down before. At length, after making
15 several guesses of this nature, and being deceived in all—this
fact—the fact of my invariable miscalculation, set me upon
a train of reflection that made my limbs again tremble, and
my heart beat heavily once more.

It was not a new terror that thus affected me, but the
20 dawn of a more exciting *hope*. This hope arose partly from
memory, and partly from present observation. I called to
mind the great variety of buoyant matter that strewed the
coast of Lofoden, having been absorbed and then thrown
forth by the Moskoe-ström. By far the greater number of
25 the articles were shattered in the most extraordinary way—
so chafed and roughened as to have the appearance of being
stuck full of splinters—but then I distinctly recollected that
there were *some* of them which were not disfigured at all.
Now I could not account for this difference except by sup-
30 posing that the roughened fragments were the only ones
which had been *completely absorbed*—that the others had
entered the whirl at so late a period of the tide, or, from some
reason, had descended so slowly after entering, that they did
not reach the bottom before the turn of the flood came, or of
35 the ebb, as the case might be. I conceived it possible, in
either instance, that they might thus be whirled up again to

the level of the ocean, without undergoing the fate of those
which had been drawn in more early or absorbed more rapidly. I made, also, three important observations. The first
was, that as a general rule, the larger the bodies were, the
more rapid their descent; the second, that, between two 5
masses of equal extent, the one spherical, and the other *of
any other shape*, the superiority in speed of descent was with
the sphere; the third, that, between two masses of equal size,
the one cylindrical, and the other of any other shape, the
cylinder was absorbed the more slowly. Since my escape, I 10
have had several conversations on this subject with an old
schoolmaster of the district; and it was from him that I
learned the use of the words "cylinder" and "sphere." He explained to me—although I have forgotten the explanation—
how what I observed was, in fact, the natural consequence of 15
the forms of the floating fragments, and showed me how it
happened that a cylinder, swimming in a vortex, offered more
resistance to its suction, and was drawn in with greater difficulty, than an equally bulky body, of any form whatever.

There was one startling circumstance which went a great 20
way in enforcing these observations, and rendering me anxious to turn them to account, and this was that, at every revolution, we passed something like a barrel, or else the yard or
the mast of a vessel, while many of these things, which had
been on our level when I first opened my eyes upon the won- 25
ders of the whirlpool, were now high up above us, and seemed
to have moved but little from their original station.

I no longer hesitated what to do. I resolved to lash myself securely to the water cask upon which I now held, to cut
it loose from the counter, and to throw myself with it into the 30
water. I attracted my brother's attention by signs, pointed
to the floating barrels that came near us, and did everything
in my power to make him understand what I was about to
do. I thought at length that he comprehended my design—
but, whether this was the case or not, he shook his head 35
despairingly, and refused to move from his station by the

ring-bolt. It was impossible to reach him; the emergency admitted of no delay; and so, with a bitter struggle, I resigned him to his fate, fastened myself to the cask by means of the lashings which secured it to the counter, and precipi-
5 tated myself with it into the sea, without another moment's hesitation.

The result was precisely what I had hoped it might be. As it is myself who now tell you this tale—as you see that I *did* escape—and as you are already in possession of the mode
10 in which this escape was effected, and must therefore anticipate all that I have farther to say—I will bring my story quickly to conclusion. It might have been an hour, or thereabout, after my quitting the smack, when, having descended to a vast distance beneath me, it made three or four wild
15 gyrations in rapid succession, and, bearing my loved brother with it, plunged headlong, at once and forever, into the chaos of foam below. The barrel to which I was attached sunk very little farther than half the distance between the bottom of the gulf and the spot at which I leaped overboard, before
20 a great change took place in the character of the whirlpool. The slope of the sides of the vast funnel became momently less and less steep. The gyrations of the whirl grew, gradually, less and less violent. By degrees, the froth and the rainbow disappeared, and the bottom of the gulf seemed
25 slowly to uprise. The sky was clear, the winds had gone down, and the full moon was setting radiantly in the west, when I found myself on the surface of the ocean, in full view of the shores of Lofoden, and above the spot where the pool of the Moskoe-ström *had been.*

THE PERIOD OF CONFLICT

HENRY WADSWORTH LONGFELLOW

A PSALM OF LIFE

WHAT THE HEART OF THE YOUNG MAN SAID TO THE PSALMIST

Tell me not, in mournful numbers,
   Life is but an empty dream!
For the soul is dead that slumbers,
   And things are not what they seem.

Life is real! Life is earnest!   5
   And the grave is not its goal;
Dust thou art, to dust returnest,
   Was not spoken of the soul.

Not enjoyment, and not sorrow,
   Is our destined end or way;   10
But to act, that each to-morrow
   Find us farther than to-day.

Art is long, and Time is fleeting,
   And our hearts, though stout and brave,
Still, like muffled drums, are beating   15
   Funeral marches to the grave.

In the world's broad field of battle,
   In the bivouac of Life,
Be not like dumb, driven cattle!
   Be a hero in the strife!   20

Trust no Future, howe'er pleasant!
    Let the dead Past bury its dead!
Act,—act in the living Present!
    Heart within, and God o'erhead!

5   Lives of great men all remind us
        We can make our lives sublime,
    And, departing, leave behind us,
        Footprints on the sands of time;—

    Footprints, that perhaps another,
10   Sailing o'er life's solemn main,
    A forlorn and shipwrecked brother,
        Seeing, shall take heart again.

    Let us, then, be up and doing,
        With a heart for any fate;
15   Still achieving, still pursuing,
        Learn to labor and to wait.

GIOTTO'S TOWER

How many lives, made beautiful and sweet
    By self-devotion and by self-restraint,
    Whose pleasure is to run without complaint
20   On unknown errands of the Paraclete,
Wanting the reverence of unshodden feet,
    Fail of the nimbus which the artists paint
    Around the shining forehead of the saint,
    And are in their completeness incomplete!
25   In the old Tuscan town stands Giotto's tower,
    The lily of Florence blossoming in stone,—
    A vision, a delight, and a desire,—
The builder's perfect and centennial flower,
    That in the night of ages bloomed alone,
30   But wanting still the glory of the spire.

THE RAINY DAY

The day is cold, and dark, and dreary;
It rains, and the wind is never weary;
The vine still clings to the moldering wall,
But at every gust the dead leaves fall,
   And the day is dark and dreary.   5

My life is cold, and dark, and dreary;
It rains, and the wind is never weary;
My thoughts still cling to the moldering Past,
But the hopes of youth fall thick in the blast,
   And the days are dark and dreary.   10

Be still, sad heart! and cease repining;
Behind the clouds is the sun still shining;
Thy fate is the common fate of all,
Into each life some rain must fall,
   Some days must be dark and dreary.   15

THE BUILDING OF THE SHIP

[The Launching]

All is finished! and at length
Has come the bridal day
Of beauty and of strength.
To-day the vessel shall be launched!
With fleecy clouds the sky is blanched,   20
And o'er the bay,
Slowly, in all his splendors dight,
The great sun rises to behold the sight.

The ocean old,
Centuries old,   25
Strong as youth, and as uncontrolled,
Paces restless to and fro,
Up and down the sands of gold.

His beating heart is not at rest;
And far and wide,
With ceaseless flow,
His beard of snow
Heaves with the heaving of his breast.
He waits impatient for his bride.
There she stands,
With her foot upon the sands,
Decked with flags and streamers gay,
In honor of her marriage day,
Her snow-white signals fluttering, blending,
Round her like a veil descending,
Ready to be
The bride of the gray old sea.

On the deck another bride
Is standing by her lover's side.
Shadows from the flags and shrouds,
Like the shadows cast by clouds,
Broken by many a sunny fleck,
Fall around them on the deck.

The prayer is said,
The service read,
The joyous bridegroom bows his head;
And in tears the good old Master
Shakes the brown hand of his son,
Kisses his daughter's glowing cheek
In silence, for he cannot speak,
And ever faster
Down his own the tears begin to run.
The worthy pastor—
The shepherd of that wandering flock,
That has the ocean for its wold,
That has the vessel for its fold,
Leaping ever from rock to rock—

Spake, with accents mild and clear,
Words of warning, words of cheer,
But tedious to the bridegroom's ear.
He knew the chart
Of the sailor's heart,   5
All its pleasures and its griefs,
All its shallows and rocky reefs,
All those secret currents, that flow
With such resistless undertow,
And lift and drift, with terrible force,   10
The will from its moorings and its course.
Therefore he spake, and thus said he:—
"Like unto ships far off at sea,
Outward or homeward bound, are we.
Before, behind, and all around,   15
Floats and swings the horizon's bound,
Seems at its distant rim to rise
And climb the crystal wall of the skies,
And then again to turn and sink,
As if we could slide from its outer brink.   20
Ah! it is not the sea,
It is not the sea that sinks and shelves,
But ourselves
That rock and rise
With endless and uneasy motion,   25
Now touching the very skies,
Now sinking into the depths of ocean.
Ah! if our souls but poise and swing
Like the compass in its brazen ring,
Ever level and ever true   30
To the toil and the task we have to do,
We shall sail securely, and safely reach
The Fortunate Isles, on whose shining beach
The sights we see, and the sounds we hear,
Will be those of joy and not of fear!"   35

Then the Master,
With a gesture of command,
Waved his hand;
And at the word,
Loud and sudden there was heard,
All around them and below,
The sound of hammers, blow on blow,
Knocking away the shores and spurs.
And see! she stirs!
She starts,—she moves,—she seems to feel
The thrill of life along her keel,
And, spurning with her foot the ground,
With one exulting, joyous bound,
She leaps into the ocean's arms!

And lo! from the assembled crowd
There rose a shout, prolonged and loud,
That to the ocean seemed to say,
"Take her, O bridegroom, old and gray,
Take her to thy protecting arms,
With all her youth and all her charms!"

How beautiful she is! How fair
She lies within those arms, that press
Her form with many a soft caress
Of tenderness and watchful care!
Sail forth into the sea, O ship!
Through wind and wave, right onward steer!
The moistened eye, the trembling lip,
Are not the signs of doubt or fear.

Sail forth into the sea of life,
O gentle, loving, trusting wife,
And safe from all adversity
Upon the bosom of that sea
Thy comings and thy goings be!

For gentleness and love and trust
Prevail o'er angry wave and gust;
And in the wreck of noble lives
Something immortal still survives!

Thou, too, sail on, O Ship of State!   5
Sail on, O Union, strong and great!
Humanity, with all its fears,
With all the hopes of future years,
Is hanging breathless on thy fate!
We know what Master laid thy keel,   10
What Workmen wrought thy ribs of steel,
Who made each mast, and sail, and rope,
What anvils rang, what hammers beat,
In what a forge and what a heat
Were shaped the anchors of thy hope!   15
Fear not each sudden sound and shock;
'Tis of the wave and not the rock;
'Tis but the flapping of the sail,
And not a rent made by the gale!
In spite of rock and tempest's roar,   20
In spite of false lights on the shore,
Sail on, nor fear to breast the sea!
Our hearts, our hopes, are all with thee,
Our hearts, our hopes, our prayers, our tears,
Our faith, triumphant o'er our fears,   25
Are all with thee,—are all with thee!

THE SONG OF HIAWATHA

HIAWATHA'S FRIENDS

Two good friends had Hiawatha,
Singled out from all the others,
Bound to him in closest union,
And to whom he gave the right hand   30
Of his heart, in joy and sorrow;

Chibiabos, the musician,
And the very strong man, Kwasind.
  Straight between them ran the pathway,
Never grew the grass upon it;
Singing birds, that utter falsehoods,
Story-tellers, mischief-makers,
Found no eager ear to listen,
Could not breed ill-will between them,
For they kept each other's counsel,
Spake with naked hearts together,
Pondering much and much contriving
How the tribes of men might prosper.
  Most beloved by Hiawatha
Was the gentle Chibiabos,
He the best of all musicians,
He the sweetest of all singers.
Beautiful and childlike was he,
Brave as man is, soft as woman,
Pliant as a wand of willow,
Stately as a deer with antlers.
  When he sang, the village listened;
All the warriors gathered round him,
All the women came to hear him;
Now he stirred their souls to passion,
Now he melted them to pity.
  From the hollow reeds he fashioned
Flutes so musical and mellow,
That the brook, the Sebowisha,
Ceased to murmur in the woodland,
That the wood-birds ceased from singing,
And the squirrel, Adjidaumo,
Ceased his chatter in the oak-tree,
And the rabbit, the Wabasso,
Sat upright to look and listen.
  Yes, the brook, the Sebowisha,
Pausing, said, "O Chibiabos,

Teach my waves to flow in music,
Softly as your words in singing!"
   Yes, the bluebird, the Owaissa,
Envious, said, "O Chibiabos,
Teach me tones as wild and wayward,   5
Teach me songs as full of frenzy!"
   Yes, the robin, the Opechee,
Joyous, said, "O Chibiabos,
Teach me tones as sweet and tender,
Teach me songs as full of gladness!"   10
   And the whippoorwill, Wawonaissa,
Sobbing, said, "O Chibiabos,
Teach me tones as melancholy,
Teach me songs as full of sadness!"
   All the many sounds of nature   15
Borrowed sweetness from his singing;
All the hearts of men were softened
By the pathos of his music;
For he sang of peace and freedom,
Sang of beauty, love, and longing;   20
Sang of death, and life undying
In the Islands of the Blessed,
In the kingdom of Ponemah,
In the land of the Hereafter.
   Very dear to Hiawatha   25
Was the gentle Chibiabos,
He the best of all musicians,
He the sweetest of all singers;
For his gentleness he loved him,
And the magic of his singing.   30
   Dear, too, unto Hiawatha
Was the very strong man, Kwasind,
He the strongest of all mortals,
He the mightiest among many;
For his very strength he loved him,   35
For his strength allied to goodness.

Idle in his youth was Kwasind,
Very listless, dull, and dreamy,
Never played with other children,
Never fished and never hunted,
Not like other children was he;
But they saw that much he fasted,
Much his Manito entreated,
Much besought his Guardian Spirit.
"Lazy Kwasind!" said his mother,
"In my work you never help me!
In the Summer you are roaming
Idly in the fields and forests;
In the Winter you are cowering
O'er the firebrands in the wigwam:
In the coldest days of Winter
I must break the ice for fishing;
With my nets you never help me!
At the door my nets are hanging,
Dripping, freezing with the water;
Go and wring them, Yenadizze!
Go and dry them in the sunshine!"
Slowly, from the ashes, Kwasind
Rose, but made no angry answer;
From the lodge went forth in silence,
Took the nets, that hung together,
Dripping, freezing at the doorway,
Like a wisp of straw he wrung them,
Like a wisp of straw he broke them,
Could not wring them without breaking,
Such the strength was in his fingers.
"Lazy Kwasind!" said his father,
"In the hunt you never help me;
Every bow you touch is broken,
Snapped asunder every arrow;
Yet come with me to the forest,
You shall bring the hunting homeward."

Down a narrow pass they wandered,
Where a brooklet led them onward,
Where the trail of deer and bison
Marked the soft mud on the margin,
Till they found all further passage   5
Shut against them, barred securely
By the trunks of trees uprooted,
Lying lengthwise, lying crosswise,
And forbidding further passage.

"We must go back," said the old man,   10
"O'er these logs we cannot clamber;
Not a woodchuck could get through them,
Not a squirrel clamber o'er them!"
And straightway his pipe he lighted,
And sat down to smoke and ponder.   15
But before his pipe was finished,
Lo! a path was cleared before him;
All the trunks had Kwasind lifted,
To the right hand, to the left hand,
Shot the pine-trees swift as arrows,   20
Hurled the cedars light as lances.

"Lazy Kwasind!" said the young men,
As they sported in the meadow:
"Why stand idly looking at us,
Leaning on the rock behind you?   25
Come and wrestle with the others,
Let us pitch the quoit together!"

Lazy Kwasind made no answer,
To their challenge made no answer,
Only rose, and, slowly turning,   30
Seized the huge rock in his fingers,
Tore it from its deep foundation,
Poised it in the air a moment,
Pitched it sheer into the river,
Sheer into the swift Pauwating,   35
Where it still is seen in Summer.

Once as down that foaming river,
Down the rapids of Pauwating,
Kwasind sailed with his companions,
In the stream he saw a beaver,
Saw Ahmeek, the King of Beavers,
Struggling with the rushing currents,
Rising, sinking in the water.

Without speaking, without pausing,
Kwasind leaped into the river,
Plunged beneath the bubbling surface,
Through the whirlpools chased the beaver,
Followed him among the islands,
Stayed so long beneath the water,
That his terrified companions
Cried, "Alas! good-by to Kwasind!
We shall never more see Kwasind!"
But he reappeared triumphant,
And upon his shining shoulders
Brought the beaver, dead and dripping,
Brought the King of all the Beavers.

And these two, as I have told you,
Were the friends of Hiawatha,
Chibiabos, the musician,
And the very strong man, Kwasind.
Long they lived in peace together,
Spake with naked hearts together,
Pondering much and much contriving
How the tribes of men might prosper.

THE WHITE CZAR

The White Czar is Peter the Great. *Batyushka*, "father dear," and *gosudar*, "sovereign," are titles the Russian people are fond of giving to the Czar in their popular songs.

Dost thou see on the rampart's height
That wreath of mist, in the light   5
Of the midnight moon? O, hist!
It is not a wreath of mist;
It is the Czar, the White Czar,
    Batyushka! Gosudar!

He has heard, among the dead,   10
The artillery roll o'erhead;
The drums and the tramp of feet
Of his soldiery in the street;
He is awake! the White Czar,
    Batyushka! Gosudar!   15

He has heard in the grave the cries
Of his people: "Awake! arise!"
He has rent the gold brocade
Whereof his shroud was made;
He is risen! the White Czar,   20
    Batyushka! Gosudar!

From the Volga and the Don
He has led his armies on,
Over river and morass,
Over desert and mountain pass;   25
The Czar, the Orthodox Czar,
    Batyushka! Gosudar!

He looks from the mountain-chain
Toward the seas, that cleave in twain

The continents; his hand
Points southward o'er the land
Of Roumili! O Czar,
        Batyushka! Gosudar!

And the words break from his lips:
"I am the builder of ships,
And my ships shall sail these seas
To the Pillars of Hercules!
I say it; the White Czar,
        Batyushka! Gosudar!

"The Bosphorus shall be free;
It shall make room for me;
And the gates of its water-streets
Be unbarred before my fleets.
I say it; the White Czar,
        Batyushka! Gosudar!

"And the Christian shall no more
Be crushed as heretofore,
Beneath thine iron rule,
O Sultan of Istamboul!
I swear it; I the Czar,
        Batyushka! Gosudar!"

JOHN GREENLEAF WHITTIER

THE PIPES AT LUCKNOW

Pipes of the misty moorlands,
    Voice of the glens and hills;
The droning of the torrents,
    The treble of the rills!
Not the braes of broom and heather,
    Nor the mountains dark with rain,
Nor maiden bower, nor border tower,
    Have heard your sweetest strain!

Dear to the Lowland reaper,
   And plaided mountaineer,—
To the cottage and the castle
   The Scottish pipes are dear;—
Sweet sounds the ancient pibroch   5
   O'er mountain, loch, and glade;
But the sweetest of all music
   The pipes at Lucknow played.

Day by day the Indian tiger
   Louder yelled, and nearer crept;   10
Round and round the jungle-serpent
   Near and nearer circles swept.
"Pray for rescue, wives and mothers,—
   Pray to-day!" the soldier said;
"To-morrow, death's between us   15
   And the wrong and shame we dread."

Oh, they listened, looked, and waited,
   Till their hope became despair;
And the sobs of low bewailing
   Filled the pauses of their prayer.   20
Then up spake a Scottish maiden,
   With her ear unto the ground:
"Dinna ye hear it?—dinna ye hear it?
   The pipes o' Havelock sound!"

Hushed the wounded man his groaning;   25
   Hushed the wife her little ones;
Alone they heard the drum-roll
   And the roar of Sepoy guns.
But to sounds of home and childhood
   The Highland ear was true;—   30
As her mother's cradle-crooning
   The mountain pipes she knew.

Like the march of soundless music
　　Through the vision of the seer,
More of feeling than of hearing,
　　Of the heart than of the ear,
5　She knew the droning pibroch,
　　She knew the Campbell's call:
"Hark! hear ye no' MacGregor's,—
　　The grandest o' them all!"

Oh, they listened, dumb and breathless,
10　And they caught the sound at last;
Faint and far beyond the Goomtee
　　Rose and fell the piper's blast!
Then a burst of wild thanksgiving
　　Mingled woman's voice and man's;
15　"God be praised!—the march of Havelock!
　　The piping of the clans!"

Louder, nearer, fierce as vengeance,
　　Sharp and shrill as swords at strife,
Came the wild MacGregor's clan-call,
20　Stinging all the air to life.
But when the far-off dust-cloud
　　To plaided legions grew,
Full tenderly and blithesomely
　　The pipes of rescue blew!

25　Round the silver domes of Lucknow,
　　Moslem mosque and Pagan shrine,
Breathed the air to Britons dearest,
　　The air of Auld Lang Syne.
O'er the cruel roll of war-drums
30　Rose that sweet and homelike strain;
And the tartan clove the turban,
　　As the Goomtee cleaves the plain.

Dear to the corn-land reaper
  And plaided mountaineer,—
To the cottage and the castle
  The piper's song is dear.
Sweet sounds the Gaelic pibroch   5
  O'er mountain, glen, and glade;
But the sweetest of all music
  The Pipes at Lucknow played!

TELLING THE BEES

Here is the place; right over the hill
  Runs the path I took;   10
You can see the gap in the old wall still,
  And the stepping stones in the shallow brook.

There is the house, with the gate red-barred,
  And the poplars tall;
And the barn's brown length, and the cattle-yard, 15
  And the white horns tossing above the wall.

There are the beehives ranged in the sun;
  And down by the brink
Of the brook are her poor flowers, weed-o'errun,
  Pansy and daffodil, rose and pink.   20

A year has gone, as the tortoise goes,
  Heavy and slow;
And the same rose blows, and the same sun glows,
  And the same brook sings of a year ago.

There's the same sweet clover-smell in the breeze; 25
  And the June sun warm
Tangles his wings of fire in the trees,
  Setting, as then, over Fernside farm.

I mind me how with a lover's care
    From my Sunday coat
I brushed off the burrs, and smoothed my hair,
    And cooled at the brookside my brow and throat.

5   Since we parted, a month had passed,—
    To love, a year;
Down through the beeches I looked at last
    On the little red gate and the well-sweep near.

I can see it all now,—the slantwise rain
10   Of light through the leaves,
The sundown's blaze on her window-pane,
    The bloom of her roses under the eaves.

Just the same as a month before,—
    The house and the trees,
15   The barn's brown gable, the vine by the door,—
    Nothing changed but the hives of bees.

Before them, under the garden wall,
    Forward and back,
Went drearily singing the chore-girl small,
20   Draping each hive with a shred of black.

Trembling, I listened: the summer sun
    Had the chill of snow;
For I knew she was telling the bees of one
    Gone on the journey we all must go!

25   Then I said to myself, "My Mary weeps
    For the dead to-day:
Haply her blind old grandsire sleeps
    The fret and the pain of his age away."

But her dog whined low; on the doorway sill,
30   With his cane to his chin,
The old man sat; and the chore-girl still
    Sung to the bees stealing out and in.

And the song she was singing ever since
　　In my ear sounds on:—
"Stay at home, pretty bees, fly not hence!
　　Mistress Mary is dead and gone!"

SNOW–BOUND

The sun that brief December day   5
Rose cheerless over hills of gray,
And, darkly circled, gave at noon
A sadder light than waning moon.
Slow tracing down the thickening sky
Its mute and ominous prophecy,   10
A portent seeming less than threat,
It sank from sight before it set.
A chill no coat, however stout,
Of homespun stuff could quite shut out,
A hard, dull bitterness of cold,   15
　　That checked, mid-vein, the circling race
　　Of life-blood in the sharpened face,
The coming of the snow-storm told.
The wind blew east; we heard the roar
Of Ocean on his wintry shore,   20
And felt the strong pulse throbbing there
Beat with low rhythm our inland air.

Meanwhile we did our nightly chores,—
Brought in the wood from out of doors,
Littered the stalls, and from the mows   25
Raked down the herd's-grass for the cows:
Heard the horse whinnying for his corn;
And, sharply clashing horn on horn,
Impatient down the stanchion rows
The cattle shake their walnut bows;   30
While, peering from his early perch
Upon the scaffold's pole of birch,

The cock his crested helmet bent
And down his querulous challenge sent.

Unwarmed by any sunset light
The gray day darkened into night,
5 A night made hoary with the swarm
And whirl-dance of the blinding storm,
As zigzag wavering to and fro
Crossed and recrossed the wingèd snow:
And ere the early bedtime came
10 The white drift piled the window-frame,
And through the glass the clothes-line posts
Looked in like tall and sheeted ghosts.

So all night long the storm roared on:
The morning broke without a sun;
15 In tiny spherule traced with lines
Of Nature's geometric signs,
In starry flake and pellicle
All day the hoary meteor fell;
And, when the second morning shone,
20 We looked upon a world unknown,
On nothing we could call our own.
Around the glistening wonder bent
The blue walls of the firmament,
No cloud above, no earth below,—
25 A universe of sky and snow!
The old familiar sights of ours
Took marvelous shapes; strange domes and towers
Rose up where sty or corn-crib stood,
Or garden-wall, or belt of wood;
30 A smooth white mound the brush-pile showed,
A fenceless drift what once was road;
The bridle-post an old man sat
With loose-flung coat and high cocked hat;
The well-curb had a Chinese roof;
35 And even the long sweep, high aloof,

In its slant splendor, seemed to tell
Of Pisa's leaning miracle.

A prompt, decisive man, no breath
Our father wasted: "Boys, a path!"
Well pleased, (for when did farmer boy   5
Count such a summons less than joy?)
Our buskins on our feet we drew;
    With mittened hands, and caps drawn low
    To guard our necks and ears from snow,
We cut the solid whiteness through.   10
And, where the drift was deepest, made
A tunnel walled and overlaid
With dazzling crystal: we had read
Of rare Aladdin's wondrous cave,
And to our own his name we gave,   15
With many a wish the luck were ours
To test his lamp's supernal powers.
We reached the barn with merry din,
And roused the prisoned brutes within.
The old horse thrust his long head out,   20
And grave with wonder gazed about;
The cock his lusty greeting said,
And forth his speckled harem led;
The oxen lashed their tails, and hooked,
And mild reproach of hunger looked;   25
The hornèd patriarch of the sheep,
Like Egypt's Amun roused from sleep,
Shook his sage head with gesture mute,
And emphasized with stamp of foot.

All day the gusty north-wind bore   30
The loosening drift its breath before;
Low circling round its southern zone,
The sun through dazzling snow-mist shone,
No church-bell lent its Christian tone

To the savage air, no social smoke
Curled over woods of snow-hung oak.
A solitude made more intense
By dreary-voicèd elements,
5   The shrieking of the mindless wind,
The moaning tree-boughs swaying blind,
And on the glass the unmeaning beat
Of ghostly finger-tips of sleet.
Beyond the circle of our hearth
10   No welcome sound of toil or mirth
Unbound the spell, and testified
Of human life and thought outside.
We minded that the sharpest ear
The buried brooklet could not hear,
15   The music of whose liquid lip
Had been to us companionship,
And, in our lonely life, had grown
To have an almost human tone.

As night drew on, and, from the crest
20   Of woodèd knolls that ridged the west,
The sun, a snow-blown traveler, sank
From sight beneath the smothering bank,
We piled with care our nightly stack
Of wood against the chimney-back,—
25   The oaken log, green, huge, and thick,
And on its top the stout back-stick;
The knotty forestick laid apart,
And filled between with curious art
The ragged brush; then, hovering near,
30   We watched the first red blaze appear,
Heard the sharp crackle, caught the gleam
On whitewashed wall and sagging beam,
Until the old, rude-furnished room
Burst, flower-like, into rosy bloom;

While radiant with a mimic flame
Outside the sparkling drift became,
And through the bare-boughed lilac-tree
Our own warm hearth seemed blazing free.
The crane and pendent trammels showed,   5
The Turk's heads on the andirons glowed;
While childish fancy, prompt to tell
The meaning of the miracle,
Whispered the old rhyme: "*Under the tree,*
When fire outdoors burns merrily,   10
There the witches are making tea."

.   .   .   .

Shut in from all the world without,
We sat the clean-winged hearth about,
Content to let the north-wind roar
In baffled rage at pane and door,   15
While the red logs before us beat
The frost-line back with tropic heat;
And ever, when a louder blast
Shook beam and rafter as it passed,
The merrier up its roaring draught   20
The great throat of the chimney laughed,
The house-dog on his paws outspread
Laid to the fire his drowsy head,
The cat's dark silhouette on the wall
A couchant tiger's seemed to fall;   25
And, for the winter fireside meet,
Between the andirons' straddling feet,
The mug of cider simmered slow,
The apples sputtered in a row,
And, close at hand, the basket stood   30
With nuts from brown October's wood.

What matter how the night behaved?
What matter how the north-wind raved?

Blow high, blow low, not all its snow
Could quench our hearth-fire's ruddy glow.

   .   .   .   .   .   .

We sped the time with stories old,
Wrought puzzles out, and riddles told,
Or stammered from our school-book lore
"The chief of Gambia's golden shore."

   .   .   .   .   .   .

Our father rode again his ride
On Memphremagog's wooded side;
Sat down again to moose and samp
In trapper's hut and Indian camp;
Lived o'er the old idyllic ease
Beneath St. François' hemlock-trees;
Again for him the moonlight shone
On Norman cap and bodiced zone;
Again he heard the violin play
Which led the village dance away,
And mingled in its merry whirl
The grandam and the laughing girl.
Or, nearer home, our steps he led
Where Salisbury's level marshes spread
Mile-wide as flies the laden bee;
  Where merry mowers, hale and strong,
  Swept, scythe on scythe, their swaths along
The low green prairies of the sea.
We shared the fishing off Boar's Head,
  And round the rocky Isles of Shoals
  The hake-broil on the driftwood coals;
The chowder on the sand-beach made,
Dipped by the hungry, steaming hot,
With spoons of clam-shell from the pot.
We heard the tales of witchcraft old,
And dream and sign and marvel told
To sleepy listeners as they lay
Stretched idly on the salted hay,

Adrift along the winding shores,
  When favoring breezes deigned to blow
  The square sail of the gundelow,
And idle lay the useless oars.

Our mother, while she turned her wheel   5
Or run the new-knit stocking heel,
Told how the Indian hordes came down
At midnight on Cocheco town,
And how her own great-uncle bore
His cruel scalp-mark to fourscore.   10
Recalling, in her fitting phrase,
  So rich and picturesque and free
  (The common unrhymed poetry
Of simple life and country ways),
The story of her early days,—   15
She made us welcome to her home;
Old hearths grew wide to give us room;
We stole with her a frightened look
At the gray wizard's conjuring-book,
The fame whereof went far and wide   20
Through all the simple country-side;
We heard the hawks at twilight play,
The boat-horn on Piscataqua,
The loon's weird laughter far away;
We fished her little trout-brook, knew   25
What flowers in wood and meadow grew,
What sunny hillsides autumn-brown
She climbed to shake the ripe nuts down,
Saw where in sheltered cove and bay
The ducks' black squadron anchored lay,   30
And heard the wild geese calling loud
Beneath the gray November cloud.

    .   .   .   .

Brisk wielder of the birch and rule,
The master of the district school

Held at the fire his favored place;
Its warm glow lit a laughing face
Fresh-hued and fair, where scarce appeared
The uncertain prophecy of beard.
5 He teased the mitten-blinded cat,
Played cross-pins on my uncle's hat,
Sang songs, and told us what befalls
In classic Dartmouth's college halls.
Born the wild Northern hills among,
10 From whence his yeoman father wrung
By patient toil subsistence scant,
Not competence and yet not want,
He early gained the power to pay
His cheerful, self-reliant way;
15 Could doff at ease his scholar's gown
To peddle wares from town to town;
Or through the long vacation's reach
In lonely lowland districts teach,
Where all the droll experience found
20 At stranger hearths in boarding round,
The moonlit skater's keen delight,
The sleigh-drive through the frosty night,
The rustic party, with its rough
Accompaniment of blind-man's-buff,
25 And whirling plate, and forfeits paid,
His winter task a pastime made.
Happy the snow-locked homes wherein
He tuned his merry violin,
Or played the athlete in the barn,
30 Or held the good dame's winding yarn,
Or mirth-provoking versions told
Of classic legends rare and old,
Wherein the scenes of Greece and Rome
Had all the commonplace of home,
35 And little seemed at best the odds
'Twixt Yankee peddlers and old gods;

Where Pindus-born Arachthus took
The guise of any grist-mill brook,
And dread Olympus at his will
Became a huckleberry hill.

    .   .   .   .   .

At last the great logs, crumbling low,   5
Sent out a dull and duller glow,
The bull's-eye watch that hung in view,
Ticking its weary circuit through,
Pointed with mutely-warning sign
Its black hand to the hour of nine.   10
That sign the pleasant circle broke:
My uncle ceased his pipe to smoke,
Knocked from its bowl the refuse gray,
And laid it tenderly away;
Then roused himself to safely cover   15
The dull red brands with ashes over.
And while, with care, our mother laid
The work aside, her steps she stayed
One moment, seeking to express
Her grateful sense of happiness   20
For food and shelter, warmth and health,
And love's contentment more than wealth,
With simple wishes (not the weak,
Vain prayers which no fulfillment seek,
But such as warm the generous heart,   25
O'er-prompt to do with Heaven its part)
That none might lack, that bitter night,
For bread and clothing, warmth and light.

    .   .   .   .   .

Next morn we wakened with the shout
  Of merry voices high and clear;   30
   And saw the teamsters drawing near
To break the drifted highways out.
Down the long hillside treading slow
We saw the half-buried oxen go,

Shaking the snow from heads uptost,
Their straining nostrils white with frost.
Before our door the straggling train
Drew up, an added team to gain.
The elders threshed their hands a-cold,
    Passed, with the cider-mug, their jokes
    From lip to lip; the younger folks
Down the loose snow-banks, wrestling, rolled,
Then toiled again the cavalcade
    O'er windy hill, through clogged ravine,
    And woodland paths that wound between
Low drooping pine-boughs winter-weighed.
From every barn a team afoot,
At every house a new recruit,
Where, drawn by Nature's subtlest law,
Haply the watchful young men saw
Sweet doorway pictures of the curls
And curious eyes of merry girls,
Lifting their hands in mock defense
Against the snow-balls' compliments,
And reading in each missive tost
The charm with Eden never lost.

We heard once more the sleigh-bells' sound;
    And, following where the teamsters led,
The wise old Doctor went his round,
Just pausing at our door to say
In the brief autocratic way
Of one who, prompt at Duty's call,
Was free to urge her claim on all,
    That some poor neighbor sick abed
At night our mother's aid would need.
For, one in generous thought and deed,
    What mattered in the sufferer's sight
    The Quaker matron's inward light,
The Doctor's mail of Calvin's creed?

All hearts confess the saints elect
   Who, twain in faith, in love agree,
And melt not in an acid sect
   The Christian pearl of charity!

So days went on: a week had passed   5
Since the great world was heard from last.
The Almanac we studied o'er,
Read and reread our little store
Of books and pamphlets, scarce a score;
One harmless novel, mostly hid   10
From younger eyes, a book forbid,
And poetry, (or good or bad,
A single book was all we had,)
Where Ellwood's meek, drab-skirted Muse,
   A stranger to the heathen Nine,   15
   Sang, with a somewhat nasal whine,
The wars of David and the Jews.
At last the floundering carrier bore
The village paper to our door.
Lo! broadening outward as we read,   20
To warmer zones the horizon spread;
In panoramic length unrolled
We saw the marvels that it told.
Before us passed the painted Creeks,
   And daft McGregor on his raids   25
   In Costa Rica's everglades.
   And up Taygetus winding slow
Rode Ypsilanti's Mainote Greeks,
   A Turk's head at each saddle bow!
Welcome to us its week-old news,   30
Its corner for the rustic Muse,
   Its monthly gauge of snow and rain,
Its record, mingling in a breath
The wedding knell and dirge of death;

Jest, anecdote, and love-lorn tale,
The latest culprit sent to jail;
Its hue and cry of stolen and lost,
Its vendue sales and goods at cost,
    And traffic calling loud for gain.
We felt the stir of hall and street,
The pulse of life that round us beat;
The chill embargo of the snow
Was melted in the genial glow;
Wide swung again our ice-locked door,
And all the world was ours once more!

.   .   .   .

ALL'S WELL

The clouds, which rise with thunder, slake
    Our thirsty souls with rain;
The blow most dreaded falls to break
    From off our limbs a chain;
And wrongs of man to man but make
    The love of God more plain.
As through the shadowy lens of even
The eye looks farthest into heaven
On gleams of star and depths of blue
The glaring sunshine never knew!

THE TRAILING ARBUTUS

I wandered lonely where the pine-trees made
Against the bitter East their barricade,
    And, guided by its sweet
Perfume, I found, within a narrow dell,
The trailing spring flower tinted like a shell
    Amid dry leaves and mosses at my feet.

From under dead boughs, for whose loss the pines
Moaned ceaseless overhead, the blossoming vines
   Lifted their glad surprise,
While yet the bluebird smoothed in leafless trees
His feathers ruffled by the chill sea-breeze,   5
   And snow-drifts lingered under April skies.

As, pausing, o'er the lonely flower I bent,
I thought of lives thus lowly, clogged and pent,
   Which yet find room,
Through care and cumber, coldness and decay,   10
To lend a sweetness to the ungenial day,
   And make the sad earth happier for their bloom.

HAMPTON BEACH

[Extract]

Good-by to pain and care! I take
   Mine ease to-day:
Here where these sunny waters break,   15
And ripples this keen breeze, I shake
All burdens from the heart, all weary thoughts away.

I draw a freer breath—I seem
   Like all I see—
Waves in the sun—the white-winged gleam   20
Of sea-birds in the slanting beam—
And far-off sails which flit before the south-wind free.

So when Time's veil shall fall asunder,
   The soul may know
No fearful change, nor sudden wonder,   25
Nor sink the weight of mystery under,
But with the upward rise, and with the vastness grow.

And all we shrink from now may seem
  No new revealing;
Familiar as our childhood's stream,
Or pleasant memory of a dream
5 The loved and cherished Past upon the new life stealing.

Serene and mild the untried light
  May have its dawning;
And, as in summer's northern night
The evening and the dawn unite,
10 The sunset hues of Time blend with the soul's new morning.

JAMES RUSSELL LOWELL

UNDER THE OLD ELM

POEM READ AT CAMBRIDGE ON THE HUNDREDTH ANNIVERSARY
OF WASHINGTON'S TAKING COMMAND OF THE AMERICAN ARMY,
3D JULY, 1775

V. (3)

Soldier and statesman, rarest unison;
High-poised example of great duties done
Simply as breathing, a world's honors worn
As life's indifferent gifts to all men born;
15 Dumb for himself, unless it were to God,
But for his barefoot soldiers eloquent,
Tramping the snow to coral where they trod,
Held by his awe in hollow-eyed content;
Modest, yet firm as Nature's self; unblamed
20 Save by the men his nobler temper shamed;
Never seduced through show of present good
By other than unsetting lights to steer
New-trimmed in Heaven, nor than his steadfast mood
More steadfast, far from rashness as from fear;

Rigid, but with himself first, grasping still
In swerveless poise the wave-beat helm of will;
Not honored then or now because he wooed
The popular voice, but that he still withstood;
Broad-minded, higher-souled, there is but one   5
Who was all this and ours, and all men's—WASHINGTON.

.   .   .   .

VI. (1)

The longer on this earth we live
And weigh the various qualities of men,
Seeing how most are fugitive,
Or fitful gifts, at best, of now and then,   10
Wind-wavered corpse-lights, daughters of the fen,
The more we feel the high stern-featured beauty
Of plain devotedness to duty,
Steadfast and still, nor paid with mortal praise,
But finding amplest recompense   15
For life's ungarlanded expense
In work done squarely and unwasted days.
For this we honor him, that he could know
How sweet the service and how free
Of her, God's eldest daughter here below,   20
And choose in meanest raiment which was she.

(2)

Placid completeness, life without a fall
From faith or highest aims, truth's breachless wall,
Surely if any fame can bear the touch,
His will say "Here!" at the last trumpet's call,   25
The unexpressive man whose life expressed so much.

VII. (2)

That lifted blade transformed our jangling clans,
Till then provincial, to Americans,
And made a unity of wildering plans;

Here was the doom fixed: here is marked the date
When this New World awoke to man's estate,
Burnt its last ship and ceased to look behind:
Nor thoughtless was the choice; no love or hate
5 Could from its poise move that deliberate mind,
Weighing between too early and too late
Those pitfalls of the man refused by Fate:
His was the impartial vision of the great
Who see not as they wish, but as they find.
10 He saw the dangers of defeat, nor less
The incomputable perils of success;
The sacred past thrown by, an empty rind;
The future, cloud-land, snare of prophets blind;
The waste of war, the ignominy of peace;
15 On either hand a sullen rear of woes,
Whose garnered lightnings none could guess,
Piling its thunder-heads and muttering "Cease!"
Yet drew not back his hand, but gravely chose
The seeming-desperate task whence our new nation rose.

TO THE DANDELION

20 Dear common flower, that grow'st beside the way,
Fringing the dusty road with harmless gold,
First pledge of blithesome May,
Which children pluck, and, full of pride uphold,
High-hearted buccaneers, o'erjoyed that they
25 An Eldorado in the grass have found,
Which not the rich earth's ample round
May match in wealth, thou art more dear to me
Then all the prouder summer-blooms may be.

Gold such as thine ne'er drew the Spanish prow
30 Through the primeval hush of Indian seas,
Nor wrinkled the lean brow
Of age, to rob the lover's heart of ease;

'Tis the Spring's largess, which she scatters now
To rich and poor like, with lavish hand,
Though most hearts never understand
   To take it at God's value, but pass by
    The offered wealth with unrewarded eye.   5

  Thou art my tropics and mine Italy;
To look at thee unlocks a warmer clime;
   The eyes thou givest me
Are in the heart, and heed not space or time:
   Not in mid June the golden cuirassed bee   10
Feels a more summer-like warm ravishment
In the white lily's breezy tent,
   His fragrant Sybaris, than I, when first
   From the dark green thy yellow circles burst.

  Then think I of deep shadows on the grass,   15
Of meadows where in sun the cattle graze,
   Where, as the breezes pass,
The gleaming rushes lean a thousand ways,
   Of leaves that slumber in a cloudy mass,
Or whiten in the wind, of waters blue   20
That from the distance sparkle through
   Some woodland gap, and of a sky above,
   Where one white cloud like a stray lamb doth move.

  My childhood's earliest thoughts are linked with thee;
The sight of thee calls back the robin's song,   25
   Who, from the dark old tree
Beside the door, sang clearly all day long,
   And I, secure in childish piety,
Listened as if I heard an angel sing
With news from heaven, which he could bring   30
   Fresh every day to my untainted ears
   When birds and flowers and I were happy peers.

How like a prodigal doth nature seem,
When thou, for all thy gold, so common art!
   Thou teachest me to deem
More sacredly of every human heart,
5   Since each reflects in joy its scanty gleam
Of heaven, and could some wondrous secret show
Did we but pay the love we owe,
    And with a child's undoubting wisdom look
    On all these living pages of God's book.

SONNET IV

10   "For this true nobleness I seek in vain,
In woman and in man I find it not;
I almost weary of my earthly lot,
My life-springs are dried up with burning pain."
Thou find'st it not? I pray thee look again,
15   Look *inward* through the depths of thine own soul.
How is it with thee? Art thou sound and whole?
Doth narrow search show thee no earthly stain?
Be noble! and the nobleness that lies
In other men, sleeping, but never dead,
20   Will rise in majesty to meet thine own;
Then wilt thou see it gleam in many eyes,
Then will pure light around thy path be shed,
And thou wilt nevermore be sad or lone.

MY GARDEN ACQUAINTANCE[1]

[Extract]

The return of the robin is commonly announced by the
25 newspapers, like that of eminent or notorious people to a
watering-place, as the first authentic notification of spring.
And such his appearance in the orchard and garden undoubtedly is. But, in spite of his name of migratory thrush,

[1] From *My Study Windows*. Reprinted by permission of Houghton
Mifflin Company, publishers.

he stays with us all winter, and I have seen him when the
thermometer marked fifteen degrees below zero of Fahrenheit,
armed impregnably within, like Emerson's Titmouse, and as
cheerful as he. The robin has a bad reputation among people
who do not value themselves less for being fond of cherries. 5
There is, I admit, a spice of vulgarity in him, and his song is
rather of the Bloomfield sort, too largely ballasted with prose.
His ethics are of the Poor Richard school, and the main
chance which calls forth all his energy is altogether of the
belly. He never has those fine intervals of lunacy into which 10
his cousins, the catbird and the mavis, are apt to fall. But
for a' that and twice as muckle's a' that, I would not exchange him for all the cherries that ever came out of Asia
Minor. With whatever faults, he has not wholly forfeited
that superiority which belongs to the children of nature. He 15
has a finer taste in fruit than could be distilled from many
successive committees of the Horticultural Society, and he
eats with a relishing gulp not inferior to Dr. Johnson's. He
feels and freely exercises his right of eminent domain. His is
the earliest mess of green peas; his all the mulberries I had 20
fancied mine. But if he get also the lion's share of the rasp-
berries, he is a great planter, and sows those wild ones in the
woods, that solace the pedestrian and give a momentary calm
even to the jaded victims of the White Hills. He keeps a
strict eye over one's fruit, and knows to a shade of purple 25
when your grapes have cooked long enough in the sun. During the severe drought a few years ago, the robins wholly
vanished from my garden. I neither saw nor heard one for
three weeks. Meanwhile a small foreign grape-vine, rather
shy of bearing, seemed to find the dusty air congenial, and, 30
dreaming perhaps of its sweet Argos across the sea, decked
itself with a score or so of fair bunches. I watched them
from day to day till they should have secreted sugar enough
from the sunbeams, and at last made up my mind that I
would celebrate my vintage the next morning. But the robins 35
too had somehow kept note of them. They must have sent

out spies, as did the Jews into the promised land, before I was
stirring. When I went with my basket, at least a dozen of
these winged vintagers bustled out from among the leaves,
and alighting on the nearest trees interchanged some shrill
5 remarks about me of a derogatory nature. They had fairly
sacked the vine. Not Wellington's veterans made cleaner
work of a Spanish town; not Federals or Confederates were
ever more impartial in the confiscation of neutral chickens.
I was keeping my grapes a secret to surprise the fair Fidele
10 with, but the robins made them a profounder secret to her
than I meant. The tattered remnant of a single bunch was all
my harvest-home. How paltry it looked at the bottom of my
basket,—as if a humming-bird had laid her egg in an eagle's
nest! I could not help laughing; and the robins seemed to
15 join heartily in the merriment. There was a native grape-
vine close by, blue with its less refined abundance, but my
cunning thieves preferred the foreign flavor. Could I tax
them with want of taste?

OLIVER WENDELL HOLMES

OLD IRONSIDES

Ay, tear her tattered ensign down!
20   Long has it waved on high,
And many an eye has danced to see
    That banner in the sky;
Beneath it rung the battle shout,
    And burst the cannon's roar;—
25 The meteor of the ocean air
    Shall sweep the clouds no more!

Her decks, once red with heroes' blood,
    Where knelt the vanquished foe,
When winds were hurrying o'er the flood,
30   And waves were white below,

No more shall feel the victor's tread,
  Or know the conquered knee; —
The harpies of the shore shall pluck
  The eagle of the sea!

Oh, better that her shattered hulk   5
  Should sink beneath the wave;
Her thunders shook the mighty deep,
  And there should be her grave;
Nail to the mast her holy flag,
  Set every threadbare sail,   10
And give her to the god of storms,
  The lightning and the gale!

HYMN OF TRUST

O Love Divine, that stooped to share
  Our sharpest pang, our bitterest tear,
On Thee we cast each earth-born care,   15
  We smile at pain while Thou art near!

Though long the weary way we tread,
  And sorrow crown each lingering year,
No path we shun, no darkness dread,
  Our hearts still whispering, Thou art near!   20

When drooping pleasure turns to grief,
  And trembling faith is changed to fear,
The murmuring wind, the quivering leaf,
  Shall softly tell us, Thou art near!

On Thee we fling our burdening woe,   25
  O Love Divine, forever dear,
Content to suffer while we know,
  Living and dying, Thou art near!

THE LAST LEAF

I saw him once before,
As he passed by the door,
    And again
The pavement stones resound,
As he totters o'er the ground
    With his cane.

They say that in his prime,
Ere the pruning-knife of Time
    Cut him down,
Not a better man was found
By the Crier on his round
    Through the town.

But now he walks the streets,
And he looks at all he meets
    Sad and wan,
And he shakes his feeble head,
That it seems as if he said,
    "They are gone."

The mossy marbles rest
On the lips that he has prest
    In their bloom,
And the names he loved to hear
Have been carved for many a year
    On the tomb.

My grandmamma has said—
Poor old lady, she is dead
    Long ago—
That he had a Roman nose,
And his cheek was like a rose
    In the snow.

But now his nose is thin,
And it rests upon his chin
    Like a staff,
And a crook is in his back,
And a melancholy crack   5
    In his laugh.

I know it is a sin
For me to sit and grin
    At him here;
But the old three-cornered hat,   10
And the breeches, and all that,
    Are so queer!

And if I should live to be
The last leaf upon the tree
    In the spring,—   15
Let them smile, as I do now,
At the old forsaken bough
    Where I cling.

THE CHAMBERED NAUTILUS

This is the ship of pearl, which, poets feign,
  Sails the unshadowed main,—   20
  The venturous bark that flings
On the sweet summer wind its purpled wings
In gulfs enchanted, where the Siren sings,
  And coral reefs lie bare,
Where the cold sea-maids rise to sun their streaming hair. 25

Its webs of living gauze no more unfurl;
  Wrecked is the ship of pearl!
  And every chambered cell,

Where its dim dreaming life was wont to dwell,
As the frail tenant shaped his growing shell,
   Before thee lies revealed,—
Its irised ceiling rent, its sunless crypt unsealed!

5 Year after year beheld the silent toil
   That spread his lustrous coil;
   Still, as the spiral grew,
He left the past year's dwelling for the new,
Stole with soft step its shining archway through,
10   Built up its idle door,
Stretched in his last-found home, and knew the old no more.

Thanks for the heavenly message brought by thee,
   Child of the wandering sea,
   Cast from her lap, forlorn!
15 From thy dead lips a clearer note is born
Than ever Triton blew from wreathèd horn!
   While on mine ear it rings,
Through the deep caves of thought I hear a voice that sings:—

Build thee more stately mansions, O my soul,
20   As the swift seasons roll!
   Leave thy low-vaulted past!
Let each new temple, nobler than the last,
Shut thee from heaven with a dome more vast,
   Till thou at length art free,
25 Leaving thine outgrown shell by life's unresting sea!

THE HEIGHT OF THE RIDICULOUS

I wrote some lines once on a time
   In a wondrous merry mood,
And thought, as usual, men would say
   They were exceeding good.

They were so queer, so very queer,
   I laughed as I would die;
Albeit, in the general way,
   A sober man am I.

I called my servant, and he came;   5
   How kind it was of him,
To mind a slender man like me,
   He of the mighty limb!

"These to the printer," I exclaimed,
   And, in my humorous way,   10
I added, (as a trifling jest,)
   "There'll be the devil to pay."

He took the paper, and I watched,
   And saw him peep within;
At the first line he read, his face   15
   Was all upon the grin.

He read the next; the grin grew broad,
   And shot from ear to ear;
He read the third, a chuckling noise
   I now began to hear.   20

The fourth; he broke into a roar;
   The fifth; his waistband split;
The sixth; he burst five buttons off,
   And tumbled in a fit.

Ten days and nights, with sleepless eye,   25
   I watched that wretched man,
And since, I never dare to write
   As funny as I can.

THE AUTOCRAT OF THE BREAKFAST TABLE[1]

[Extract from "The Professor's Paper"]

For the past nine years I have rowed about, during a good part of the summer, on fresh or salt water. My present fleet on the river Charles consists of three row-boats. 1. A small flat-bottomed skiff of the shape of a flat-iron, kept mainly to
5 lend to boys. 2. A fancy "dory" for two pairs of sculls, in which I sometimes go out with my young folks. 3. My own particular water-sulky, a "skeleton" or "shell" race-boat, twenty-two feet long, with huge out-riggers, which boat I pull with ten-foot sculls,—alone, of course, as it holds but
10 one, and tips him out, if he doesn't mind what he is about. In this I glide around the Back Bay, down the stream, up the Charles to Cambridge and Watertown, up the Mystic, round the wharves, in the wake of steamboats, which leave a swell after them delightful to rock upon; I linger under the bridges,
15 —those "caterpillar bridges," as my brother professor so happily called them; rub against the black sides of old wood-schooners; cool down under the overhanging stern of some tall Indiaman; stretch across to the Navy Yard, where the sentinel warns me off from the *Ohio*,—just as if I should hurt
20 her by lying in her shadow; then strike out into the harbor, where the water gets clear and the air smells of the ocean,— till all at once I remember, that, if a west wind blows up of a sudden, I shall drift along past the islands, out of sight of the dear old State-house,—plate, tumbler, knife and fork all
25 waiting at home, but no chair drawn up at the table,—all the dear people waiting, waiting, waiting, while the boat is slid-ing, sliding, sliding into the great desert, where there is no tree and no fountain. As I don't want my wreck to be washed up on one of the beaches in company with devil's aprons,
30 bladder-weeds, dead horse-shoes, and bleached crab-shells, I turn about and flap my long, narrow wings for home. When

---

[1] Reprinted by permission of Houghton Mifflin Company, publishers.

the tide is running out swiftly, I have a splendid fight to
get through the bridges, but always make it a rule to beat,—
though I have been jammed up into pretty tight places at
times, and was caught once between a vessel swinging round
and the pier, until our bones (the boat's, that is) cracked as 5
if we had been in the jaws of Behemoth. Then back to my
moorings at the foot of the Common, off with the rowing-
dress, dash under the green translucent wave, return to the
garb of civilization, walk through my Garden, take a look at
my elms on the Common, and, reaching my habitat, in con- 10
sideration of my advanced period of life, indulge in the
Elysian abandonment of a huge recumbent chair.

When I have established a pair of well-pronounced
feathering-calluses on my thumbs, when I am in training so
that I can do my fifteen miles at a stretch without coming to 15
grief in any way, when I can perform my mile in eight minutes or a little more, then I feel as if I had old Time's head
in chancery, and could give it to him at my leisure.

SIDNEY LANIER

TAMPA ROBINS[1]

The robin laughed in the orange-tree:
"Ho, windy North, a fig for thee: 20
While breasts are red and wings are bold
And green trees wave us globes of gold,
    Time's scythe shall reap but bliss for me
    —Sunlight, song, and the orange-tree.

Burn, golden globes in leafy sky,   25
My orange-planets: crimson I
Will shine and shoot among the spheres
(Blithe meteor that no mortal fears)
    And thrid the heavenly orange-tree
    With orbits bright of minstrelsy.   30

[1] Reprinted by permission of Charles Scribner's Sons, publishers.

If that I hate wild winter's spite—
The gibbet trees, the world in white,
The sky but gray wind over a grave—
Why should I ache, the season's slave?
5   I'll sing from the top of the orange-tree
   Gramercy, winter's tyranny.

I'll south with the sun, and keep my clime;
My wing is king of the summer-time;
My breast to the sun his torch shall hold;
10 And I'll call down through the green and gold
   "Time, take thy scythe, reap bliss for me,
   Bestir thee under the orange-tree."

NIGHT AND DAY[1]

The innocent, sweet Day is dead.
Dark Night hath slain her in her bed.
15 Oh, Moors are as fierce to kill as to wed!
   —Put out the light, said he.

A sweeter light than ever rayed
From star of heaven or eye of maid
Has vanished in the unknown Shade.
20   —She's dead, she's dead, said he.

Now, in a wild, sad after-mood
The tawny Night sits still to brood
Upon the dawn-time when he wooed.
   —I would she lived, said he.

25 Star-memories of happier times,
Of loving deeds and lovers' rhymes,
Throng forth in silvery pantomimes.
   —Come back, O Day! said he.

[1] Reprinted by permission of Charles Scribner's Sons, publishers.

IN ABSENCE[1]

IV

Let no man say, *He at his lady's feet*
  Lays worship that to Heaven alone belongs;
Yea, swings the incense that for God is meet
  In flippant censers of light lover's songs.
Who says it, knows not God, nor love, nor thee;   5
  For love is large as is yon heavenly dome:
In love's great blue, each passion is full free
  To fly his favorite flight and build his home.
Did e'er a lark with skyward-pointing beak
  Stab by mischance a level-flying dove?   10
Wife-love flies level, his dear mate to seek:
  God-love darts straight into the skies above.
    Crossing, the windage of each other's wings
    But speeds them both upon their journeyings.

EVENING SONG[1]

Look off, dear Love, across the sallow sands,   15
  And mark yon meeting of the sun and sea,
How long they kiss in sight of all the lands.
    Ah! longer, longer, we.

Now in the sea's red vintage melts the sun,
  As Egypt's pearl dissolved in rosy wine,   20
And Cleopatra night drinks all. 'Tis done,
    Love, lay thine hand in mine.

Come forth, sweet stars, and comfort heaven's heart;
  Glimmer, ye waves, round else unlighted sands.
O night! divorce our sun and sky apart   25
    Never our lips, our hands.

[1] Reprinted by permission of Charles Scribner's Sons, publishers.

WALT WHITMAN

CAVALRY CROSSING A FORD[1]

A line in long array where they wind betwixt green islands,
They take a serpentine course, their arms flash in the sun—
    hark to the musical clank,
Behold the silvery river, in it the splashing horses. loitering
    stop to drink,
Behold the brown-faced men, each group, each person a
    picture, the negligent rest in saddles,
5 Some emerge on the opposite bank, others are just entering
    the ford—while,
Scarlet and blue and snowy white,
The guidon flags flutter gayly in the wind.

BY THE BIVOUAC'S FITFUL FLAME[1]

By the bivouac's fitful flame,
A procession winding around me, solemn and sweet and slow
    —but first I note
10 The tents of the sleeping army, the fields' and woods' dim
    outline,
The darkness, lit by spots of kindled fire, the silence,
Like a phantom far or near an occasional figure moving,
The shrubs and trees, (as I lift my eyes they seem to be
    stealthily watching me,)
While wind in procession thoughts, O tender and wondrous
    thoughts,
15 Of life and death, of home and the past and loved, and of
    those that are far away;
A solemn and slow procession there as I sit on the ground,
By the bivouac's fitful flame.

---

[1] From *Drum Taps*, by permission of Doubleday, Page & Company,
publishers.

TO THE MAN–OF–WAR BIRD[1]

Thou who hast slept all night upon the storm,
Waking renew'd on thy prodigious pinions,
(Burst the wild storm? above it thou ascended'st,
And rested on the sky, thy slave that cradled thee,)
Now a blue point, far, far in heaven floating,   5
As to the light emerging here on deck I watch thee,
(Myself a speck, a point on the world's floating vast.)

Far, far at sea,
After the night's fierce drifts have strewn the shore with
        wrecks,
With re-appearing day as now so happy and serene,   10
The rosy and elastic dawn, the flashing sun,
The limpid spread of air cerulean,
Thou also re-appearest.

Thou born to match the gale, (thou art all wings,)
To cope with heaven and earth and sea and hurricane,   15
Thou ship of air that never furl'st thy sails,
Days, even weeks untired and onward, through spaces, realms
        gyrating,
At dusk that look'st on Senegal, at morn America,
That sport'st amid the lightning-flash and thunder-cloud,
In them, in thy experiences, had'st thou my soul,   20
What joys! what joys were thine!

ABOARD AT A SHIP'S HELM[1]

Aboard at a ship's helm,
A young steersman steering with care.

Through fog on a sea-coast dolefully ringing,
An ocean-bell—O a warning bell, rocked by the waves.   25

[1] From *Leaves of Grass*, by permission of Doubleday, Page & Company,
publishers.

O you give good notice indeed, you bell by the sea-reefs
ringing,
Ringing, ringing, to warn the ship from its wreck-place.

For as on the alert, O steersman, you mind the loud
admonition,
The bows turn, the freighted ship tacking speeds away under
her gray sails,
5 The beautiful and noble ship with all her precious wealth
speeds away gayly and safe.

But O the ship, the immortal ship! O ship aboard the ship!
Ship of the body, ship of the soul, voyaging, voyaging,
voyaging.

O CAPTAIN! MY CAPTAIN![1]

O Captain! my Captain! our fearful trip is done,
The ship has weathered every rack, the prize we sought is won,
10 The port is near, the bells I hear, the people all exulting,
While follow eyes the steady keel, the vessel grim and daring;
But O heart! heart! heart!
O the bleeding drops of red,
Where on the deck my Captain lies,
15 Fallen cold and dead.

O Captain! my Captain! rise up and hear the bells;
Rise up—for you the flag is flung—for you the bugle trills,
For you bouquets and ribbon'd wreaths—for you the shores
a-crowding;
For you they call, the swaying mass, their eager faces turning;
20 Here Captain! dear father!
This arm beneath your head!
It is some dream that on the deck,
You've fallen cold and dead.

[1] From *Leaves of Grass*, by permission of Doubleday, Page & Company,
publishers.

My Captain does not answer, his lips are pale and still,
My father does not feel my arm, he has no pulse nor will,
The ship is anchor'd safe and sound, its voyage closed and
      done,
From fearful trip the victor ship comes in with object won;
  Exult O shores, and ring O bells!   5
    But I with mournful tread,
      Walk the deck my Captain lies,
        Fallen cold and dead.

JOY, SHIPMATE, JOY![1]

  Joy, shipmate, joy!
  (Pleased to my soul at death I cry,)   10
  Our life is closed, our life begins,
  The long, long anchorage we leave,
  The ship is clear at last, she leaps!
  She swiftly courses from the shore,
  Joy, shipmate, joy!   15

RALPH WALDO EMERSON

THE TITMOUSE

You shall not be overbold
When you deal with arctic cold,
As late I found my lukewarm blood
Chilled wading in the snow-choked wood.
How should I fight? my foeman fine   20
Has million arms to one of mine:
East, west, for aid I looked in vain,
East, west, north, south, are his domain.
Miles off, three dangerous miles, is home;
Must borrow his winds who there would come.   25

[1] From *Leaves of Grass*, by permission of Doubleday, Page & Company,
publishers.

Up and away for life! be fleet!—
The frost-king ties my fumbling feet,
Sings in my ears, my hands are stones,
Curdles the blood to the marble bones,
Tugs at the heart-strings, numbs the sense,
And hems in life with narrowing fence.
Well, in this broad bed lie and sleep,—
The punctual stars will vigil keep,—
Embalmed by purifying cold;
The winds shall sing their dead-march old,
The snow is no ignoble shroud,
The moon thy mourner, and the cloud.

Softly,—but this way fate was pointing,
'Twas coming fast to such anointing,
When piped a tiny voice hard by,
Gay and polite, a cheerful cry,
Chic-chicadeedee! saucy note
Out of sound heart and merry throat,
As if it said, 'Good day, good sir!
Fine afternoon, old passenger!
Happy to meet you in these places,
Where January brings few faces.'

This poet, though he live apart,
Moved by his hospitable heart,
Sped, when I passed his sylvan fort,
To do the honors of his court,
As fits a feathered lord of land;
Flew near, with soft wing grazed my hand,
Hopped on the bough, then, darting low,
Prints his small impress on the snow,
Shows feats of his gymnastic play,
Head downward, clinging to the spray.

Here was this atom in full breath,
Hurling defiance at vast death;

This scrap of valor just for play
Fronts the north-wind in waistcoat gray,
As if to shame my weak behavior;
I greeted loud my little savior,
'You pet! what dost here? and what for?   5
In these woods, thy small Labrador,
At this pinch, wee San Salvador!
What fire burns in that little chest
So frolic, stout and self-possest?
Henceforth I wear no stripe but thine;   10
Ashes and jet all hues outshine.
Why are not diamonds black and gray,
To ape thy dare-devil array?
And I affirm, the spacious North
Exists to draw thy virtue forth.   15
I think no virtue goes with size;
The reason of all cowardice
Is, that men are overgrown,
And, to be valiant, must come down
To the titmouse dimension.'   20

    'Tis good-will makes intelligence,
And I began to catch the sense
Of my bird's song: 'Live out of doors
In the great woods, on prairie floors.
I dine in the sun; when he sinks in the sea,   25
I too have a hole in a hollow tree;
And I like less when Summer beats
With stifling beams on these retreats,
Than noontide twilights which snow makes
With tempest of the blinding flakes.   30
For well the soul, if stout within,
Can arm impregnably the skin,
And polar frost my frame defied,
Made of the air that blows outside.'

With glad remembrance of my debt,
I homeward turn; farewell, my pet!
When here again thy pilgrim comes,
He shall bring store of seeds and crumbs.
5   Doubt not, so long as earth has bread,
Thou first and foremost shalt be fed;
The Providence that is most large
Takes hearts like thine in special charge,
Helps who for their own need are strong,
10   And the sky dotes on cheerful song.
Henceforth I prize thy wiry chant
O'er all that mass and minster vaunt;
For men mis-hear thy call in Spring,
As 'twould accost some frivolous wing,
15   Crying out of the hazel copse, *Phe-be!*
And, in winter, *Chic-a-dee-dee!*
I think old Cæsar must have heard
In northern Gaul my dauntless bird,
And, echoed in some frosty wold,
20   Borrowed thy battle-numbers bold.
And I will write our annals new,
And thank thee for a better clew,
I, who dreamed not when I came here
To find the antidote of fear,
25   Now hear thee say in Roman key,
Pæan! Veni, vidi, vici.

FORBEARANCE

Hast thou named all the birds without a gun?
Loved the wood-rose, and left it on its stalk?
At rich men's tables eaten bread and pulse?
30   Unarmed, faced danger with a heart of trust?
And loved so well a high behavior,
In man or maid, that thou from speech refrained,
Nobility more nobly to repay?
Oh, be my friend and teach me to be thine!

THE SNOW-STORM

Announced by all the trumpets of the sky,
Arrives the snow; and, driving o'er the fields,
Seems nowhere to alight; the whited air
Hides hills and woods, the river, and the heaven,
And veils the farm-house at the garden's end.   5
The sled and traveler stopped, the courier's feet
Delayed, all friends shut out, the housemates sit
Around the radiant fireplace, inclosed
In a tumultuous privacy of storm.

THE RHODORA

ON BEING ASKED WHENCE IS THE FLOWER

In May, when sea winds pierced our solitudes,   10
I found the fresh Rhodora in the woods,
Spreading its leafless blooms in a damp nook,
To please the desert and the sluggish brook.
The purple petals, fallen in the pool,
Made the black water with their beauty gay;   15
Here might the redbird come his plumes to cool,
And court the flower that cheapens his array.
Rhodora! if the sages ask thee why
This charm is wasted on the earth and sky,
Tell them, dear, that if eyes were made for seeing,   20
Then Beauty is its own excuse for being:
Why thou wert there, O rival of the rose!
I never thought to ask, I never knew:
But, in my simple ignorance, suppose
The self-same Power that brought me there brought you.   25

THE HUMBLE-BEE

Burly, dozing humble-bee,
Where thou art is clime for me.
Let them sail for Porto Rique,
Far-off heats through seas to seek;

I will follow thee alone,
Thou animated torrid zone!
Zigzag steerer, desert cheerer,
Let me chase thy waving lines;
5   Keep me nearer, me thy hearer,
Singing over shrubs and vines.

Insect lover of the sun,
Joy of thy dominion!
Sailor of the atmosphere;
10   Swimmer through the waves of air;
Voyager of light and noon;
Epicurean of June;
Wait, I prithee, till I come
Within earshot of thy hum,—
15   All without is martyrdom.

When the south wind, in May days,
With a net of shining haze
Silvers the horizon wall,
And with softness touching all,
20   Tints the human countenance
With the color of romance,
And infusing subtle heats,
Turns the sod to violets,
Thou, in sunny solitudes,
25   Rover of the underwoods,
The green silence dost displace
With thy mellow, breezy bass.

Hot midsummer's petted crone,
Sweet to me thy drowsy tone
30   Tells of countless sunny hours,
Long days, and solid banks of flowers;
Of gulfs of sweetness without bound
Of Indian wildernesses found;

Of Syrian peace, immortal leisure,
Firmest cheer, and birdlike pleasure.

Aught unsavory or unclean
Hath my insect never seen;
But violets and bilberry bells,   5
Maple-sap and daffodils,
Grass with green flag half-mast high,
Succory to match the sky,
Columbine with horn of honey,
Scented fern and agrimony,   10
Clover, catchfly, adder's tongue
And brier-roses dwelt among;
All beside was unknown waste,
All was picture as he passed.

Wiser far than human seer,   15
Yellow-breeched philosopher!
Seeing only what is fair,
Sipping only what is sweet,
Thou dost mock at fate and care,
Leave the chaff and take the wheat.   20
When the fierce northwestern blast
Cools sea and land so far and fast,
Thou already slumberest deep;
Woe and want thou canst outsleep;
Want and woe, which torture us,   25
Thy sleep makes ridiculous.

GOOD–BYE

Good-bye, proud world! I'm going home:
Thou art not my friend, and I'm not thine.
Long through thy weary crowds I roam;
A river-ark on the ocean brine,   30
Long I've been tossed like the driven foam;
But now, proud world! I'm going home.

Good-bye to Flattery's fawning face;
To Grandeur with his wise grimace;
To upstart Wealth's averted eye;
To supple Office, low and high;
5   To crowded halls, to court and street;
To frozen hearts and hasting feet;
To those who go, and those who come;
Good-bye, proud world! I'm going home.

I am going to my own hearthstone,
10   Bosomed in yon green hills alone,—
A secret nook in a pleasant land,
Whose groves the frolic fairies planned;
Where arches green, the livelong day,
Echo the blackbird's roundelay,
15   And vulgar feet have never trod
A spot that is sacred to thought and God.

Oh, when I am safe in my sylvan home,
I tread on the pride of Greece and Rome;
And when I am stretched beneath the pines,
20   Where the evening star so holy shines,
I laugh at the lore and the pride of man,
At the sophist schools and the learned clan;
For what are they all, in their high conceit,
When man in the bush with God may meet?

DAYS

25   Daughters of Time, the hypocritic Days,
Muffled and dumb like barefoot dervishes,
And marching single in an endless file,
Bring diadems and fagots in their hands.
To each they offer gifts after his will,
30   Bread, kingdoms, stars, and sky that holds them all.

I, in my pleached garden, watched the pomp,
Forgot my morning wishes, hastily
Took a few herbs and apples, and the Day
Turned and departed silent. I, too late,
Under her solemn fillet saw the scorn.   5

WORKS AND DAYS[1]

[Extracts]

A farmer said, "he should like to have all the land that
joined his own." Bonaparte, who had the same appetite, endeavored to make the Mediterranean a French lake. Czar
Alexander was more expansive, and wished to call the Pacific
my ocean; and the Americans were obliged to resist his at- 10
tempts to make it a close sea. But if he had the earth for his
pasture, and the sea for his pond, he would be a pauper still.
He only is rich who owns the day. There is no king, rich
man, fairy, or demon who possesses such power as that. The
days are ever divine as to the first Aryans. They are of the 15
least pretension, and of the greatest capacity, of anything
that exists. They come and go like muffled and veiled figures,
sent from a distant friendly party; but they say nothing;
and if we do not use the gifts they bring, they carry them as
silently away.   20

.   .   .   .

One of the illusions is that the present hour is not the critical, decisive hour. Write it on your heart that every day is
the best day in the year. No man has learned anything
rightly, until he knows that every day is Doomsday. 'Tis
the old secret of the gods that they come in low disguises. 25
'Tis the vulgar great who come dizened with gold and jewels.
Real kings hide away their crowns in their wardrobes, and
affect a plain and poor exterior. In the Norse legend of our
ancestors, Odin dwells in a fisher's hut, and patches a boat.

---

[1] Reprinted by permission of Houghton Mifflin Company, publishers.

In the Hindu legends, Hari dwells a peasant among peasants. In the Greek legend, Apollo lodges with the shepherds
of Admetus; and Jove liked to rusticate among the poor
Ethiopians. So, in our history, Jesus is born in a barn, and
5 his twelve peers are fishermen.

THE AMERICAN SCHOLAR

I

The first in time and the first in importance of the influences upon the mind is that of nature. Every day, the sun;
and, after sunset, night and her stars. Ever the winds blow;
ever the grass grows. Every day, men and women, convers-
10 ing, beholding and beholden. The scholar is he of all men
whom this spectacle most engages. He must settle its value
in his mind. What is nature to him? There is never a beginning, there is never an end, to the inexplicable continuity
of this web of God, but always circular power returning into
15 itself. Therein it resembles his own spirit, whose beginning,
whose ending, he never can find,—so entire, so boundless.
Far, too, as her splendors shine, system on system shooting
like rays, upward, downward, without center, without circumference,—in the mass and in the particle, nature hastens
20 to render account of herself to the mind. Classification begins. To the young mind everything is individual, stands
by itself. By and by, it finds how to join two things, and see
in them one nature; then three, then three thousand; and so,
tyrannized over by its own unifying instinct, it goes on tying
25 things together, diminishing anomalies, discovering roots
running underground, whereby contrary and remote things
cohere and flower out from one stem. It presently learns,
that, since the dawn of history, there has been a constant
accumulation and classifying of facts. But what is classifi-
30 cation but the perceiving that these objects are not chaotic,
and are not foreign, but have a law which is also a law of the
human mind? The astronomer discovers that geometry, a

pure abstraction of the human mind, is the measure of planetary motion. The chemist finds proportions and intelligible method throughout matter; and science is nothing but the finding of analogy, identity, in the most remote parts. The ambitious soul sits down before each refractory fact; one after another, reduces all strange constitutions, all new powers, to their class and their law, and goes on forever to animate the last fiber of organization, the outskirts of nature, by insight.

Thus to him, to this schoolboy under the bending dome of day, is suggested that he and it proceed from one root; one is leaf and one is flower; relation, sympathy, stirring in every vein. And what is that root? Is not that soul of his soul? A thought too bold,—a dream too wild. Yet when this spiritual light shall have revealed the law of more earthly natures,—when he has learned to worship the soul, and to see that the natural philosophy that now is, is only the first gropings of its gigantic hand, he shall look forward to an ever expanding knowledge as to a becoming creator. He shall see that nature is the opposite of the soul, answering to it part for part. One is seal, and one is print. Its beauty is the beauty of his own mind. Its laws are the laws of his own mind. Nature then becomes to him the measure of his attainments. So much of nature as he is ignorant of, so much of his own mind does he not yet possess. And, in fine, the ancient precept, "Know thyself," and the modern precept, "Study nature," become at last one maxim.

II

The next great influence into the spirit of the scholar is the mind of the Past,—in whatever form, whether of literature, of art, of institutions, that mind is inscribed. Books are the best type of the influence of the past; and perhaps we shall get at the truth,—learn the amount of this influence more conveniently,—by considering their value alone.

The theory of books is noble. The scholar of the first age received into him the world around; brooded thereon'; gave it the new arrangement of his own mind, and uttered it again. It came into him, life; it went out from him, truth. It came
5 to him, short-lived actions; it went out from him, immortal thoughts. It came to him, business; it went from him, poetry. It was dead fact; now, it is quick thought. It can stand, and it can go. It now endures, it now flies, it now inspires. Precisely in proportion to the depth of mind from
10 which it issued, so high does it soar, so long does it sing.

Or, I might say, it depends on how far the process had gone, of transmuting life into truth. In proportion to the completeness of the distillation, so will the purity and imperishableness of the product be. But none is quite perfect.
15 As no air-pump can by any means make a perfect vacuum, so neither can any artist entirely exclude the conventional, the local, the perishable from his book, or write a book of pure thought, that shall be as efficient, in all respects, to a remote posterity, as to contemporaries, or rather to the second
20 age. Each age, it is found, must write its own books; or rather, each generation for the next succeeding. The books of an older period will not fit this.

Yet hence arises a grave mischief. The sacredness which attaches to the act of creation,—the act of thought,—is trans-
25 ferred to the record. The poet chanting was felt to be a divine man: henceforth the chant is divine also. The writer was a just and wise spirit: henceforward it is settled, the book is perfect; as love of the hero corrupts into worship of his statue. Instantly, the book becomes noxious: the guide
30 is a tyrant. The sluggish and perverted mind of the multitude, slow to open to the incursions of Reason, having once so opened, having once received this book, stands upon it, and makes an outcry if it is disparaged. Colleges are built on it. Books are written on it by thinkers, not by Man Thinking;
35 by men of talent, that is, who start wrong, who set out from accepted dogmas, not from their own sight of principles. Meek

young men grow up in libraries, believing it their duty to accept the views which Cicero, which Locke, which Bacon, have given, forgetful that Cicero, Locke, and Bacon were only young men in libraries, when they wrote these books.

. . . .

Undoubtedly there is a right way of reading, so it be 5 sternly subordinated. Man Thinking must not be subdued by his instruments. Books are for the scholar's idle times. When he can read God directly, the hour is too precious to be wasted in other men's transcripts of their readings. But when the intervals of darkness come, as come they must,— 10 when the sun is hid, and the stars withdraw their shining,—we repair to the lamps which were kindled by their ray, to guide our steps to the East again, where the dawn is. We hear, that we may speak. The Arabian proverb says, "A fig tree, looking on a fig tree, becometh fruitful." 15

LITERARY ETHICS

[Conclusion of an Address delivered before the Literary Societies of Dartmouth College, July 24, 1838]

Gentlemen, I have ventured to offer you these considerations upon the scholar's place, and hope, because I thought, that, standing, as many of you now do, on the threshold of this College, girt and ready to go and assume tasks, public and private, in your country, you would not be sorry to be 20 admonished of those primary duties of the intellect, whereof you will seldom hear from the lips of your new companions. You will hear every day the maxims of a low prudence. You will hear that the first duty is to get land and money, place and name. "What is this Truth you seek? what is this 25 Beauty?" men will ask, with derision. If, nevertheless, God have called any of you to explore truth and beauty, be bold, be firm, be true. When you shall say, "As others do, so will I: I renounce, I am sorry for it, my early visions; I must eat the good of the land, and let learning and romantic expecta- 30 tions go, until a more convenient season;"—then dies the man in you; then once more perish the buds of art, and poetry, and science, as they have died already in a thousand thousand men. The hour of that choice is the crisis of your history; and see that you hold yourself fast by the intellect. It is this domineering temper of the sensual world that creates the extreme need of the priests of science; and it is the office and right of the intellect to make and not take its estimate. Bend to the persuasion which is flowing to you from every object in nature, to be its tongue to the heart of man, and to show the besotted world how passing fair is wisdom. Forewarned that the vice of the times and the country is an excessive pretension, let us seek the shade, and find wisdom in neglect. Be content with a little light, so it be your own. Explore, and explore. Be neither chided nor flattered out of your position of perpetual inquiry. Neither dogmatize, nor accept another's dogmatism. Why should you renounce your right to traverse the star-lit deserts of truth, for the premature comforts of an acre, house, and barn? Truth also has its roof, and bed, and board. Make yourself necessary to the world, and mankind will give you bread, and if not store of it, yet such as shall not take away your property in all men's possessions, in all men's affections, in art, in nature, and in hope.

You will not fear that I am enjoining too stern an asceticism. Ask not, Of what use is a scholarship that systematically retreats? or, Who is the better for the philosopher who conceals his accomplishments, and hides his thoughts from the waiting world? Hides his thoughts! Hide the sun and moon. Thought is all light, and publishes itself to the universe. It will speak, though you were dumb, by its own miraculous organ. It will flow out of your actions, your manners, and your face. It will bring you friendships. It will impledge you to truth by the love and expectation of generous minds. By virtue of the laws of that Nature, which is one and perfect, it shall yield every sincere good that is in the soul to the scholar beloved of earth and heaven.

NATHANIEL HAWTHORNE

MOSSES FROM AN OLD MANSE

THE OLD MANSE

Between two tall gateposts of rough-hewn stone (the gate itself having fallen from its hinges at some unknown epoch) we beheld the gray front of the old parsonage terminating the vista of an avenue of black ash-trees. It was now a twelvemonth since the funeral procession of the venerable 5 clergyman, its last inhabitant, had turned from that gateway towards the village burying-ground. The wheel-track leading to the door, as well as the whole breadth of the avenue, was almost overgrown with grass, affording dainty mouthfuls to two or three vagrant cows and an old white 10 horse who had his own living to pick up along the roadside. The glimmering shadows that lay half asleep between the door of the house and the public highway were a kind of spiritual medium, seen through which the edifice had not quite the aspect of belonging to the material world. Cer- 15 tainly it had little in common with those ordinary abodes which stand so imminent upon the road that every passer-by can thrust his head, as it were, into the domestic circle. From these quiet windows the figures of passing travelers looked too remote and dim to disturb the sense of privacy. In its 20 near retirement and accessible seclusion it was the very spot for the residence of a clergyman,—a man not estranged from human life, yet enveloped in the midst of it with a veil woven of intermingled gloom and brightness. It was worthy to have been one of the time-honored parsonages of England in 25 which, through many generations, a succession of holy occupants pass from youth to age, and bequeath each an inheritance of sanctity to pervade the house and hover over it as with an atmosphere.

Nor, in truth, had the Old Manse ever been profaned by a 30 lay occupant until that memorable summer afternoon when

I entered it as my home. A priest had built it; a priest had
succeeded to it; other priestly men from time to time had
dwelt in it; and children born in its chambers had grown up
to assume the priestly character. It was awful to reflect how
5 many sermons must have been written there. The latest inhabitant alone—he by whose translation to paradise the dwelling was left vacant—had penned nearly three thousand
discourses, besides the better, if not the greater, number that
gushed living from his lips. How often, no doubt, had he
10 paced to and fro along the avenue, attuning his meditations
to the sighs and gentle murmurs, and deep and solemn peals
of the wind among the lofty tops of the trees! In that
variety of natural utterances he could find something ac-
cordant with every passage of his sermon, were it of tender-
15 ness or reverential fear. The boughs over my head seemed
shadowy with solemn thoughts as well as with rustling
leaves. I took shame to myself for having been so long a
writer of idle stories, and ventured to hope that wisdom
would descend upon me with the falling leaves of the ave-
20 nue, and that I should light upon an intellectual treasure
in the Old Manse well worth those hoards of long-hidden
gold which people seek for in moss-grown houses. Profound
treatises of morality; a layman's unprofessional and therefore unprejudiced views of religion; histories (such as Ban-
25 croft might have written had he taken up his abode here as
he once purposed) bright with picture, gleaming over a
depth of philosophic thought,—these were the works that
might fitly have flowed from such a retirement. In the hum-
blest event I resolved at least to achieve a novel that should
30 evolve some deep lesson and should possess physical substance enough to stand alone.

In furtherance of my design, and as if to leave me no pre-
text for not fulfilling it, there was in the rear of the house the
most delightful little nook of a study that ever afforded its
35 snug seclusion to a scholar. It was here that Emerson wrote
Nature; for he was then an inhabitant of the Manse, and

used to watch the Assyrian dawn and Paphian sunset and
moonrise from the summit of our eastern hill. When I first
saw the room its walls were blackened with the smoke
of unnumbered years, and made still blacker by the grim
prints of Puritan ministers that hung around. These worthies 5
looked strangely like bad angels, or at least like men who
had wrestled so continually and so sternly with the devil
that somewhat of his sooty fierceness had been imparted to
their own visages. They had all vanished now; a cheerful
coat of paint and golden-tinted paper-hangings lighted up 10
the small apartment; while the shadow of a willow-tree that
swept against the overhanging eaves attempered the cheery
western sunshine. In place of the grim prints there was the
sweet and lovely head of one of Raphael's Madonnas and
two pleasant little pictures of the Lake of Como. The only 15
other decorations were a purple vase of flowers, always fresh,
and a bronze one containing graceful ferns. My books (few,
and by no means choice; for they were chiefly such waifs as
chance had thrown in my way) stood in order about the
room, seldom to be disturbed.   20

The study had three windows, set with little, old-fashioned
panes of glass, each with a crack across it. The two on the
western side looked, or rather peeped, between the willow
branches down into the orchard, with glimpses of the river
through the trees. The third, facing northward, commanded 25
a broader view of the river at a spot where its hitherto
obscure waters gleam forth into the light of history. It was
at this window that the clergyman who then dwelt in the
Manse stood watching the outbreak of a long and deadly
struggle between two nations; he saw the irregular array of 30
his parishioners on the farther side of the river and the
glittering line of the British on the hither bank. He awaited
in an agony of suspense the rattle of the musketry. It came,
and there needed but a gentle wind to sweep the battle smoke
around this quiet house.   35

Perhaps the reader, whom I cannot help considering as my

guest in the Old Manse and entitled to all courtesy in the
way of sight-showing,—perhaps he will choose to take a
nearer view of the memorable spot. We stand now on the
river's brink. It may well be called the Concord, the river
5 of peace and quietness; for it is certainly the most unex-
citable and sluggish stream that ever loitered imperceptibly
towards its eternity—the sea. Positively, I had lived three
weeks beside it before it grew quite clear to my perception
which way the current flowed. It never has a vivacious as-
10 pect except when a northwestern breeze is vexing its surface
on a sunshiny day. From the incurable indolence of its nature, the stream is happily incapable of becoming the slave
of human ingenuity, as is the fate of so many a wild, free
mountain torrent. While all things else are compelled to
15 subserve some useful purpose, it idles its sluggish life away
in lazy liberty, without turning a solitary spindle or affording
even water-power enough to grind the corn that grows upon
its banks. The torpor of its movement allows it nowhere a
bright, pebbly shore, nor so much as a narrow strip of glisten-
20 ing sand, in any part of its course. It slumbers between
broad prairies, kissing the long meadow grass, and bathes
the overhanging boughs of elder bushes and willows or the
roots of elms and ash-trees and clumps of maples. Flags and
rushes grow along its plashy shore; the yellow water-lily
25 spreads its broad flat leaves on the margin; and the fragrant
white pond-lily abounds, generally selecting a position just
so far from the river's brink that it cannot be grasped save
at the hazard of plunging in.

It is a marvel whence this perfect flower derives its loveli-
30 ness and perfume, springing as it does from the black mud
over which the river sleeps, and where lurk the slimy eel and
speckled frog and the mud turtle, whom continual washing
cannot cleanse. It is the very same black mud out of which
the yellow lily sucks its obscene life and noisome odor. Thus
35 we see, too, in the world that some persons assimilate only
what is ugly and evil from the same moral circumstances

which supply good and beautiful results—the fragrance of
celestial flowers—to the daily life of others.

. . . .

Blessed was the sunshine when it came again at the close
of another stormy day, beaming from the edge of the western
horizon; while the massive firmament of clouds threw down 5
all the gloom it could, but served only to kindle the golden
light into a more brilliant glow by the strongly contrasted
shadows. Heaven smiled at the earth, so long unseen, from
beneath its heavy eyelid. To-morrow for the hill-tops and
the wood paths. 10

Or it might be that Ellery Channing came up the avenue to
join me in a fishing excursion on the river. Strange and happy
times were those when we cast aside all irksome forms and
strait-laced habitudes, and delivered ourselves up to the free
air, to live like the Indians or any less conventional race dur- 15
ing one bright semicircle of the sun. Rowing our boat against
the current, between wide meadows, we turned aside into the
Assabeth. A more lovely stream than this, for a mile above
its junction with the Concord, has never flowed on earth,—
nowhere, indeed, except to lave the interior regions of a 20
poet's imagination. It is sheltered from the breeze by woods
and a hillside; so that elsewhere there might be a hurricane,
and here scarcely a ripple across the shaded water. The
current lingers along so gently that the mere force of the
boatman's will seems sufficient to propel his craft against it. 25
It comes flowing softly through the midmost privacy and
deepest heart of a wood which whispers it to be quiet; while
the stream whispers back again from its sedgy borders, as if
river and wood were hushing one another to sleep. Yes; the
river sleeps along its course and dreams of the sky and of the 30
clustering foliage, amid which fall showers of broken sunlight, imparting specks of vivid cheerfulness, in contrast with
the quiet depth of the prevailing tint. Of all this scene, the
slumbering river has a dream picture in its bosom. Which,
after all, was the most real—the picture, or the original?— 35

the objects palpable to our grosser senses, or their apotheo-
sis in the stream beneath? Surely the disembodied images
stand in closer relation to the soul. But both the original and
the reflection had here an ideal charm, and, had it been a
thought more wild, I could have fancied that this river had
strayed forth out of the rich scenery of my companion's inner
world; only the vegetation along its banks should then have
had an Oriental character.

Gentle and unobtrusive as the river is, yet the tranquil
woods seem hardly satisfied to allow it passage. The trees
are rooted on the very verge of the water, and dip their
pendent branches into it. At one spot there is a lofty bank,
on the slope of which grow some hemlocks, declining across
the stream with outstretched arms, as if resolute to take the
plunge. In other places the banks are almost on a level with
the water; so that the quiet congregation of trees set their
feet in the flood, and are fringed with foliage down to the
surface. Cardinal flowers kindle their spiral flames and illu-
minate the dark nooks among the shrubbery. The pond-lily
grows abundantly along the margin—that delicious flower,
which, as Thoreau tells me, opens its virgin bosom to the first
sunlight and perfects its being through the magic of that
genial kiss. He has beheld beds of them unfolding in due
succession as the sunrise stole gradually from flower to flower
—a sight not to be hoped for unless when a poet adjusts his
inward eye to a proper focus with the outward organ. Grapevines here and there twine themselves around shrub and tree
and hang their clusters over the water within reach of the
boatman's hand. Oftentimes they unite two trees of alien
race in an inextricable twine, marrying the hemlock and the
maple against their will, and enriching them with a purple
offspring of which neither is the parent. One of these ambitious parasites has climbed into the upper branches of a
tall, white pine, and is still ascending from bough to bough,
unsatisfied till it shall crown the tree's airy summit with a
wreath of its broad foliage and a cluster of its grapes.

The winding course of the stream continually shut out the scene behind us, and revealed as calm and lovely a one before. We glided from depth to depth, and breathed new seclusion at every turn. The shy kingfisher flew from the withered branch close at hand to another at a distance, uttering a shrill cry of anger or alarm. Ducks that had been floating there since the preceding eve were startled at our approach, and skimmed among the glassy river, breaking its dark surface with a bright streak. The pickerel leaped from among the lily-pads. The turtle, sunning itself upon a rock or at the root of a tree, slid suddenly into the water with a plunge. The painted Indian who paddled his canoe along the Assabeth three hundred years ago could hardly have seen a wilder gentleness displayed upon its banks and reflected in its bosom than we did. Nor could the same Indian have prepared his noontide meal with more simplicity. We drew up our skiff at some point where the overarching shade formed a natural bower, and there kindled a fire with the pine cones and decayed branches that lay strewn plentifully around. Soon the smoke ascended among the trees, impregnated with a savory incense, not heavy, dull, and surfeiting, like the steam of cookery within doors, but sprightly and piquant. The smell of our feast was akin to the woodland odors with which it mingled: there was no sacrilege committed by our intrusion there: the sacred solitude was hospitable, and granted us free leave to cook and eat in the recess that was at once our kitchen and banqueting hall. It is strange what humble offices may be performed in a beautiful scene without destroying its poetry. Our fire, red gleaming among the trees, and we beside it, busied with culinary rites and spreading out our meal on a mossgrown log, all seemed in unison with the river gliding by and the foliage rustling over us. And, what was strangest, neither did our mirth seem to disturb the propriety of the solemn woods; although the hobgoblins of the old wilderness and the will-of-the-wisps that glimmered in the marshy places might have come trooping to share our table talk, and

have added their shrill laughter to our merriment. It was the very spot in which to utter the extremest nonsense or the profoundest wisdom, or that ethereal product of the mind which partakes of both, and may become one or the other, in
5 correspondence with the faith and insight of the auditor.

So amid sunshine and shadow, rustling leaves and sighing waters, up gushed our talk like the babble of a fountain. The evanescent spray was Ellery's; and his, too, the lumps of golden thought that lay glimmering in the fountain's bed and
10 brightened both our faces by the reflection. Could he have drawn out that virgin gold and stamped it with the mint mark that alone gives currency, the world might have had the profit, and he the fame. My mind was the richer merely by the knowledge that it was there. But the chief profit of
15 those wild days to him and me lay, not in any definite idea, not in any angular or rounded truth, which we dug out of the shapeless mass of problematical stuff, but in the freedom which we thereby won from all custom and conventionalism and fettering influences of man on man. We were so free
20 to-day that it was impossible to be slaves again to-morrow. When we crossed the threshold of the house or trod the thronged pavements of a city, still the leaves of the trees that overhang the Assabeth were whispering to us, "Be free! be free!" Therefore along that shady river-bank there are spots,
25 marked with a heap of ashes and half-consumed brands, only less sacred in my remembrance than the hearth of a household fire.

And yet how sweet, as we floated homeward adown the golden river at sunset,—how sweet was it to return within the
30 system of human society, not as to a dungeon and a chain, but as to a stately edifice, whence we could go forth at will into statelier simplicity! How gently, too, did the sight of the Old Manse, best seen from the river, overshadowed with its willow and all environed about with the foliage of its orchard
35 and avenue,—how gently did its gray, homely aspect rebuke the speculative extravagances of the day! It had grown

sacred in connection with the artificial life against which we inveighed; it had been a home for many years in spite of all; it was my home too; and, with these thoughts, it seemed to me that all the artifice and conventionalism of life was but an impalpable thinness upon its surface, and that the depth be- 5 low was none the worse for it. Once, as we turned our boat to the bank, there was a cloud, in the shape of an immensely gigantic figure of a hound, couched above the house, as if keeping guard over it. Gazing at this symbol, I prayed that the upper influences might long protect the institutions that 10 had grown out of the heart of mankind.

. . . .

LADY ELEANORE'S MANTLE

Not long after Colonel Shute had assumed the government of Massachusetts Bay, now nearly a hundred and twenty years ago, a young lady of rank and fortune arrived from England, to claim his protection as her guardian. He was her 15 distant relative, but the nearest who had survived the gradual extinction of her family; so that no more eligible shelter could be found for the rich and high-born Lady Eleanore Rochcliffe than within the Province House of a transatlantic colony. The consort of Governor Shute, moreover, had been 20 as a mother to her childhood, and was now anxious to receive her, in the hope that a beautiful young woman would be exposed to infinitely less peril from the primitive society of New England than amid the artifices and corruptions of a court. If either the Governor or his lady had especially con- 25 sulted their own comfort, they would probably have sought to devolve the responsibility on other hands; since, with some noble and splendid traits of character, Lady Eleanore was remarkable for a harsh, unyielding pride, a haughty consciousness of her hereditary and personal advantages, which 30 made her almost incapable of control. Judging from many traditionary anecdotes, this peculiar temper was hardly less than a monomania; or, if the acts which it inspired were those

of a sane person, it seemed due from Providence that pride so sinful should be followed by as severe a retribution. That tinge of the marvelous which is thrown over so many of these half-forgotten legends has probably imparted an additional
5 wildness to the strange story of Lady Eleanore Rochcliffe.

The ship in which she came passenger had arrived at Newport, whence Lady Eleanore was conveyed to Boston in the Governor's coach, attended by a small escort of gentlemen on horseback. The ponderous equipage, with its four black
10 horses, attracted much notice as it rumbled through Cornhill, surrounded by the prancing steeds of half a dozen cavaliers, with swords dangling to their stirrups and pistols at their holsters. Through the large glass windows of the coach, as it rolled along, the people could discern the figure of Lady
15 Eleanore, strangely combining an almost queenly stateliness with the grace and beauty of a maiden in her teens. A singular tale had gone abroad among the ladies of the province, that their fair rival was indebted for much of the irresistible charm of her appearance to a certain article of dress,—an
20 embroidered mantle,—which had been wrought by the most skillful artist in London, and possessed even magical properties of adornment. On the present occasion, however, she owed nothing to the witchery of dress, being clad in a riding-habit of velvet, which would have appeared stiff and ungrace-
25 ful on any other form.

The coachman reined in his four black steeds, and the whole cavalcade came to a pause in front of the contorted iron balustrade that fenced the Province House from the public street. It was an awkward coincidence that the bell
30 of the Old South was just then tolling for a funeral; so that, instead of a gladsome peal, with which it was customary to announce the arrival of distinguished strangers, Lady Eleanore Rochcliffe was ushered by a doleful clang, as if calamity had come embodied in her beautiful person.

35   "A very great disrespect!" exclaimed Captain Langford, an English officer, who had recently brought dispatches to

Governor Shute. "The funeral should have been deferred, lest Lady Eleanore's spirits be affected by such a dismal welcome."

"With your pardon, sir," replied Dr. Clarke, a physician, and a famous champion of the popular party, "whatever the heralds may pretend, a dead beggar must have precedence of a living queen. King Death confers high privileges."

These remarks were interchanged while the speakers waited a passage through the crowd, which had gathered on each side of the gateway, leaving an open avenue to the portal of the Province House. A black slave in livery now leaped from behind the coach, and threw open the door; while at the same moment Governor Shute descended the flight of steps from his mansion, to assist Lady Eleanore in alighting. But the Governor's stately approach was anticipated in a manner that excited general astonishment. A pale young man, with his black hair all in disorder, rushed from the throng, and prostrated himself beside the coach, thus offering his person as a footstool for Lady Eleanore Rochcliffe to tread upon. She held back an instant; yet with an expression as if doubting whether the young man were worthy to bear the weight of her footstep, rather than dissatisfied to receive such awful reverence from a fellow-mortal.

"Up, sir," said the Governor sternly, at the same time lifting his cane over the intruder. "What means the Bedlamite by this freak?"

"Nay," answered Lady Eleanore playfully, but with more scorn than pity in her tone, "your Excellency shall not strike him. When men seek only to be trampled upon, it were a pity to deny them a favor so easily granted—and so well deserved."

Then, though as lightly as a sunbeam on a cloud, she placed her foot upon the cowering form, and extended her hand to meet that of the Governor. There was a brief interval, during which Lady Eleanore retained this attitude; and never, surely, was there an apter emblem of aristocracy and heredi-

tary pride trampling on human sympathies and the kindred
of nature than these two figures presented at that moment.
Yet the spectators were so smitten with her beauty, and so
essential did pride seem to the existence of such a creature,
5 that they gave a simultaneous acclamation of applause.

"Who is this insolent young fellow?" inquired Captain
Langford, who still remained beside Dr. Clarke. "If he be in
his senses, his impertinence demands the bastinado. If mad,
Lady Eleanore should be secured from further inconvenience,
10 by his confinement."

"His name is Jervase Helwyse," answered the Doctor; "a
youth of no birth or fortune, or other advantages, save the
mind and soul that nature gave him; and, being secretary to
our colonial agent in London, it was his misfortune to meet
15 this Lady Eleanore Rochcliffe. He loved her,—and her scorn
has driven him mad."

"He was mad so to aspire," observed the English officer.

"It may be so," said Dr. Clarke, frowning as he spoke.
"But I tell you, sir, I could well-nigh doubt the justice of
20 the heaven above us, if no signal humiliation overtake this
lady, who now treads so haughtily into yonder mansion. She
seeks to place herself above the sympathies of our common
nature, which envelops all human souls. See, if that nature
do not assert its claim over her in some mode that shall bring
25 her level with the lowest!"

"Never!" cried Captain Langford indignantly; "neither
in life, nor when they lay her with her ancestors."

Not many days afterwards the Governor gave a ball in
honor of Lady Eleanore Rochcliffe. The principal gentry of
30 the colony received invitations, which were distributed to
their residences, far and near, by messengers on horseback,
bearing missives sealed with all the formality of official dispatches. In obedience to the summons, there was a general
gathering of rank, wealth, and beauty; and the wide door of
35 the Province House had seldom given admittance to more
numerous and honorable guests than on the evening of Lady

Eleanore's ball. Without much extravagance of eulogy, the
spectacle might even be termed splendid; for, according to
the fashion of the times, the ladies shone in rich silks and
satins, outspread over wide-projecting hoops; and the gentlemen glittered in gold embroidery, laid unsparingly upon the 5
purple, or scarlet, or sky-blue velvet, which was the material
of their coats and waistcoats. The latter article of dress was
of great importance, since it enveloped the wearer's body
nearly to the knees, and was perhaps bedizened with the
amount of his whole year's income, in golden flowers and 10
foliage. The altered taste of the present day—a taste symbolic of a deep change in the whole system of society—would
look upon almost any of those gorgeous figures as ridiculous;
although that evening the guests sought their reflections in
the pier-glasses, and rejoiced to catch their own glitter amid 15
the glittering crowd. What a pity that one of the stately
mirrors has not preserved a picture of the scene, which, by
the very traits that were so transitory, might have taught us
much that would be worth knowing and remembering.

Would, at least, that either painter or mirror could convey 20
to us some faint idea of a garment, already noticed in this
legend,—the Lady Eleanore's embroidered mantle,—which
the gossips whispered was invested with magic properties, so
as to lend a new and untried grace to her figure each time that
she put it on! Idle fancy as it is, this mysterious mantle has 25
thrown an awe around my image of her, partly from its
fabled virtues, and partly because it was the handiwork of a
dying woman and, perchance, owed the fantastic grace of its
conception to the delirium of approaching death.

After the ceremonial greetings had been paid, Lady 30
Eleanore Rochcliffe stood apart from the mob of guests,
insulating herself within a small and distinguished circle, to
whom she accorded a more cordial favor than to the general
throng. The waxen torches threw their radiance vividly over
the scene, bringing out its brilliant points in strong relief; 35
but she gazed carelessly, and with now and then an expres-

sion of weariness or scorn, tempered with such feminine grace
that her auditors scarcely perceived the moral deformity of
which it was the utterance. She beheld the spectacle, not
with vulgar ridicule, as disdaining to be pleased with the
provincial mockery of a court festival, but with the deeper
scorn of one whose spirit held itself too high to participate in
the enjoyment of other human souls. Whether or no the recollections of those who saw her that evening were influenced
by the strange events with which she was subsequently connected, so it was that her figure ever after recurred to them
as marked by something wild and unnatural; although, at the
time, the general whisper was of her exceeding beauty, and
of the indescribable charm which her mantle threw around
her. Some close observers, indeed, detected a feverish flush
and alternate paleness of countenance, with a corresponding
flow and revulsion of spirits, and once or twice a painful and
helpless betrayal of lassitude, as if she were on the point of
sinking to the ground. Then, with a nervous shudder, she
seemed to arouse her energies, and threw some bright and
playful, yet half-wicked sarcasm into the conversation. There
was so strange a characteristic in her manners and sentiments that it astonished every right-minded listener; till,
looking in her face, a lurking and incomprehensible glance
and smile perplexed them with doubts both as to her serious-
ness and sanity. Gradually, Lady Eleanore Rochcliffe's circle
grew smaller, till only four gentlemen remained in it. These
were Captain Langford, the English officer before mentioned;
a Virginian planter, who had come to Massachusetts on some
political errand; a young Episcopal clergyman, the grandson
of a British Earl; and, lastly, the private secretary of Governor Shute, whose obsequiousness had won a sort of tolerance from Lady Eleanore.

At different periods of the evening the liveried servants of
the Province House passed among the guests, bearing huge
trays of refreshments, and French and Spanish wines. Lady
Eleanore Rochcliffe, who refused to wet her beautiful lips

even with a bubble of champagné, had sunk back into a large
damask chair, apparently overwearied either with the excitement of the scene or its tedium; and while, for an instant, she
was unconscious of voices, laughter, and music a young man
stole forward, and knelt down at her feet. He bore a salver   5
in his hand, on which was a chased silver goblet, filled to the
brim with wine, which he offered as reverentially as to a
crowned queen, or rather with the awful devotion of a priest
doing sacrifice to his idol. Conscious that someone touched
her robe, Lady Eleanore started, and unclosed her eyes   10
upon the pale, wild features and disheveled hair of Jervase
Helwyse.

"Why do you haunt me thus?" said she, in a languid tone,
but with a kindlier feeling than she ordinarily permitted herself to express. "They tell me that I have done you harm."   15

"Heaven knows if that be so," replied the young man
solemnly. "But, Lady Eleanore, in requital of that harm,
if such there be, and for your own earthly and heavenly welfare, I pray you to take one sip of this holy wine, and then
to pass the goblet round among the guests. And this shall   20
be a symbol that you have not sought to withdraw yourself
from the chain of human sympathies,—which whoso would
shake off must keep company with fallen angels."

"Where has this mad fellow stolen that sacramental vessel?" exclaimed the Episcopal clergyman.   25

This question drew the notice of the guests to the silver
cup, which was recognized as appertaining to the communion
plate of the Old South Church; and for aught that could be
known, it was brimming over with the consecrated wine.

"Perhaps it is poisoned," half whispered the Governor's   30
secretary.

"Pour it down the villain's throat!" cried the Virginian
fiercely.

"Turn him out of the house!" cried Captain Langford,
seizing Jervase Helwyse so roughly by the shoulder that the   35
sacramental cup was overturned, and its contents sprinkled

upon Lady Eleanore's mantle. "Whether knave, fool, or Bedlamite, it is intolerable that the fellow should go at large."

"Pray, gentlemen, do my poor admirer no harm," said Lady Eleanore, with a faint and weary smile. "Take him out of my sight, if such be your pleasure; for I can find in my heart to do nothing but laugh at him: whereas, in all decency and conscience, it would become me to weep for the mischief I have wrought."

But while the bystanders were attempting to lead away the unfortunate young man, he broke from them, and, with a wild, impassioned earnestness, offered a new and equally strange petition to Lady Eleanore. It was no other than that she should throw off the mantle, which, while he pressed the silver cup of wine upon her, she had drawn more closely around her form, so as almost to shroud herself within it.

"Cast it from you!" exclaimed Jervase Helwyse, clasping his hands in an agony of entreaty. "It may not yet be too late! Give the accursed garment to the flames!"

But Lady Eleanore, with a laugh of scorn, drew the rich folds of the embroidered mantle over her head, in such a fashion as to give a completely new aspect to her beautiful face, which—half hidden, half revealed—seemed to belong to some being of mysterious character and purposes.

"Farewell, Jervase Helwyse!" said she. "Keep my image in your remembrance, as you behold it now."

"Alas, lady!" he replied, in a tone no longer wild, but sad as a funeral bell. "We must meet shortly, when your face may wear another aspect, and that shall be the image that must abide within me."

He made no more resistance to the violent efforts of the gentlemen and servants, who almost dragged him out of the apartment, and dismissed him roughly from the iron gate of the Province House. Captain Langford, who had been very active in this affair, was returning to the presence of Lady Eleanore Rochcliffe, when he encountered the physician,

Dr. Clarke, with whom he had held some casual talk on the day of her arrival. The Doctor stood apart, separated from Lady Eleanore by the width of the room, but eying her with such keen sagacity that Captain Langford involuntarily gave him credit for the discovery of some deep secret.

"You appear to be smitten, after all, with the charms of this queenly maiden," said he, hoping thus to draw forth the physician's hidden knowledge.

"God forbid!" answered Dr. Clarke, with a grave smile; "and if you be wise, you will put up the same prayer for yourself. Woe to those who shall be smitten by this beautiful Lady Eleanore! But yonder stands the Governor, and I have a word or two for his private ear. Good night!"

He accordingly advanced to Governor Shute, and addressed him in so low a tone that none of the bystanders could catch a word of what he said; although the sudden change of his Excellency's hitherto cheerful visage betokened that the communication could be of no agreeable import. A very few moments afterwards, it was announced to the guests that an unforeseen circumstance rendered it necessary to put a premature close to the festival.

The ball at the Province House supplied a topic of conversation for the colonial metropolis for some days after its occurrence, and might still longer have been the general theme, only that a subject of all-engrossing interest thrust it, for a time, from the public recollection. This was the appearance of a dreadful epidemic, which in that age, and long before and afterwards, was wont to slay its hundreds and thousands on both sides of the Atlantic. On the occasion of which we speak, it was distinguished by a peculiar virulence, insomuch that it has left its traces—its pit-marks, to use an appropriate figure—on the history of the country, the affairs of which were thrown into confusion by its ravages. At first, unlike its ordinary course, the disease seemed to confine itself to the higher circles of society, selecting its victims from among the proud, the well-born, and the wealthy; entering

unabashed into stately chambers, and lying down with the
slumberers in silken beds. Some of the most distinguished
guests of the Province House—even those whom the haughty
Lady Eleanore Rochcliffe had deemed not unworthy of her
5 favor—were stricken by this fatal scourge. It was noticed,
with an ungenerous bitterness of feeling, that the four gentlemen—the Virginian, the British officer, the young clergyman,
and the Governor's secretary—who had been her most devoted attendants on the evening of the ball, were the foremost
10 on whom the plague-stroke fell. But the disease, pursuing
its onward progress, soon ceased to be exclusively a prerogative of aristocracy. Its red brand was no longer conferred .
like a noble's star, or an order of knighthood. It threaded
its way through the narrow and crooked streets, and entered
15 the low, mean, darksome dwellings, and laid its hand of death
upon the artisans and laboring classes of the town. It compelled rich and poor to feel themselves brethren, then; and
stalking to and fro across the Three Hills, with a fierceness
which made it almost a new pestilence, there was that mighty
20 conqueror—that scourge and horror of our forefathers—the
Small-Pox!

We cannot estimate the affright which this plague inspired
of yore, by contemplating it as the fangless monster of the
present day. We must remember, rather, with what awe we
25 watched the gigantic footsteps of the Asiatic cholera, striding
from shore to shore of the Atlantic, and marching like destiny
upon cities far remote, which flight had already half depopu-
lated. There is no other fear so horrible and unhumanizing
as that which makes man dread the hand of a brother or
30 friend, lest the grip of the pestilence should clutch him. Such
was the dismay that now followed in the track of the disease,
or ran before it throughout the town. Graves were hastily
dug, and the pestilential relics as hastily covered, because the
dead were enemies of the living, and strove to draw them
35 headlong, as it were, into their own dismal pit. The public
councils were suspended, as if mortal wisdom might relin-

quish its devices, now that an unearthly usurper had found
his way into the ruler's mansion. Had an enemy's fleet been
hovering on the coast, or his armies trampling on our soil,
the people would probably have committed their defense to
that same direful conqueror who had wrought their own
calamity, and would permit no interference with his sway.
This conqueror had a symbol of his triumphs. It was a blood-
red flag, that fluttered in the tainted air over the door of
every dwelling into which the Small-Pox had entered.

Such a banner was long since waving over the portal of the
Province House; for thence, as was proved by tracking its
footsteps back, had all this dreadful mischief issued. It had
been traced back to a lady's luxurious chamber,—to the
proudest of the proud,—to her that was so delicate, and
hardly owned herself of earthly mold,—to the haughty one,
who took her stand above human sympathies,—to Lady
Eleanore! There remained no room for doubt that the contagion had lurked in that gorgeous mantle, which threw so
strange a grace around her at the festival. Its fantastic splendor had been conceived in the delirious brain of a woman
on her death-bed, and was the last toil of her stiffening
fingers, which had interwoven fate and misery with its golden
threads. This dark tale, whispered at first, was now bruited
far and wide. The people raved against the Lady Eleanore,
and cried out that her pride and scorn had evoked a fiend,
and that, between them both, this monstrous evil had been
born. At times, their rage and despair took the semblance
of grinning mirth; and whenever the red flag of the pestilence
was hoisted over another and yet another door, they clapped
their hands and shouted through the streets in bitter mockery,
"Behold a new triumph for the Lady Eleanore!"

One day, in the midst of these dismal times, a wild figure
approached the portal of the Province House, and, folding
his arms, stood contemplating the scarlet banner, which a
passing breeze shook fitfully, as if to fling abroad the contagion that it typified. At length, climbing one of the pillars

by means of the iron balustrade, he took down the flag, and
entered the mansion, waving it above his head. At the foot
of the staircase he met the Governor, booted and spurred,
with his cloak drawn around him, evidently on the point of
5 setting forth upon a journey.

"Wretched lunatic, what do you seek here?" exclaimed
Shute, extending his cane to guard himself from contact.
"There is nothing here but Death. Back,—or you will meet
him!"

10   "Death will not touch me, the banner-bearer of the pestilence!" cried Jervase Helwyse, shaking the red flag aloft.
"Death and the Pestilence, who wears the aspect of the Lady
Eleanore, will walk through the streets to-night, and I must
march before them with this banner!"

15   "Why do I waste words on the fellow?" muttered the
Governor, drawing his cloak across his mouth. "What matters his miserable life, when none of us are sure of twelve
hours' breath? On, fool, to your own destruction!"

He made way for Jervase Helwyse, who immediately
20 ascended the staircase, but, on the first landing-place, was
arrested by the firm grasp of a hand upon his shoulder.
Looking fiercely up, with a madman's impulse to struggle
with and rend asunder his opponent, he found himself power-
less beneath a calm, stern eye, which possessed the mysterious
25 property of quelling frenzy at its height. The person whom
he had now encountered was the physician, Dr. Clarke, the
duties of whose sad profession had led him to the Province
House, where he was an infrequent guest in more prosperous
times.

30   "Young man, what is your purpose?" demanded he.

"I seek the Lady Eleanore," answered Jervase Helwyse
submissively.

"All have fled from her," said the physician. "Why do
you seek her now? I tell you, youth, her nurse fell death-
35 stricken on the threshold of that fatal chamber. Know ye
not that never came such a curse to our shores as this lovely

Lady Eleanore?—that her breath has filled the air with poison?—that she has shaken pestilence and death upon the land, from the folds of her accursed mantle?"

"Let me look upon her!" rejoined the mad youth more wildly. "Let me behold her, in her awful beauty, clad in the regal garments of the pestilence! She and Death sit on a throne together. Let me kneel down before them!"

"Poor youth!" said Dr. Clarke; and, moved by a deep sense of human weakness, a smile of caustic humor curled his lip even then. "Wilt thou still worship the destroyer, and surround her image with fantasies the more magnificent, the more evil she has wrought? Thus man doth ever to his tyrants! Approach, then! Madness, as I have noted, has that good efficacy that it will guard you from contagion; and perchance its own cure may be found in yonder chamber."

Ascending another flight of stairs, he threw open a door, and signed to Jervase Helwyse that he should enter. The poor lunatic, it seems probable, had cherished a delusion that his haughty mistress sat in state, unharmed herself by the pestilential influence which, as by enchantment, she scattered round about her. He dreamed, no doubt, that her beauty was not dimmed, but brightened into superhuman splendor. With such anticipations, he stole reverentially to the door at which the physician stood, but paused upon the threshold, gazing fearfully into the gloom of the darkened chamber.

"Where is the Lady Eleanore?" whispered he.

"Call her," replied the physician.

"Lady Eleanore!—Princess!—Queen of Death!" cried Jervase Helwyse, advancing three steps into the chamber. "She is not here! There, on yonder table, I behold the sparkle of a diamond which once she wore upon her bosom. There,"—and he shuddered,—"there hangs her mantle, on which a dead woman embroidered a spell of dreadful potency. But where is the Lady Eleanore?"

Something stirred within the silken curtains of a canopied bed; and a low moan was uttered, which, listening intently,

Jervase Helwyse began to distinguish as a woman's voice, complaining dolefully of thirst. He fancied, even, that he recognized its tones.

"My throat!—my throat is scorched," murmured the voice. "A drop of water!"

"What thing art thou?" said the brain-stricken youth, drawing near the bed and tearing asunder its curtains. "Whose voice hast thou stolen for thy murmurs and miserable petitions, as if Lady Eleanore could be conscious of mortal infirmity? Fie! Heap of diseased mortality, why lurkest thou in my lady's chamber?"

"O Jervase Helwyse," said the voice,—and, as it spoke, the figure contorted itself, struggling to hide its blasted face, —"look not now on the woman you once loved! The curse of Heaven hath stricken me, because I would not call man my brother, nor woman sister. I wrapped myself in *pride* as in a *mantle*, and scorned the sympathies of nature; and therefore has nature made this wretched body the medium of a dreadful sympathy. You are avenged,—they are all avenged,—nature is avenged,—for I am Eleanore Rochcliffe!"

The malice of his mental disease, the bitterness lurking at the bottom of his heart, mad as he was, for a blighted and ruined life, and love that had been paid with cruel scorn, awoke within the breast of Jervase Helwyse. He shook his finger at the wretched girl, and the chamber echoed, the curtains of the bed were shaken, with his outburst of insane merriment.

"Another triumph for the Lady Eleanore!" he cried. "All have been her victims! Who so worthy to be the final victim as herself?"

Impelled by some new fantasy of his crazed intellect, he snatched the fatal mantle and rushed from the chamber and the house. That night, a procession passed, by torchlight, through the streets, bearing in the midst the figure of a woman, enveloped with a richly embroidered mantle; while in advance stalked Jervase Helwyse, waving the red flag of the pestilence. Arriving opposite the Province House, the mob

burned the effigy, and a strong wind came and swept away
the ashes. It was said that, from that very hour, the pestilence abated, as if its sway had some mysterious connection,
from the first plague-stroke to the last, with Lady Eleanore's
Mantle. A remarkable uncertainty broods over that unhappy 5
lady's fate. There is a belief, however, that, in a certain
chamber of this mansion, a female form may sometimes be
duskily discerned, shrinking into the darkest corner, and
muffling her face within an embroidered mantle. Supposing
the legend true, can this be other than the once proud Lady 10
Eleanore?

HENRY TIMROD

THE ARCTIC VOYAGER[1]

Shall I desist, twice baffled? Once by land,
And once by sea, I fought and strove with storms,
All shades of danger, tides, and weary calms;
Head-currents, cold and famine, savage beasts,   15
And men more savage; all the while my face
Looked northward toward the pole; if mortal strength
Could have sustained me, I had never turned
Till I had seen the star which never sets
Freeze in the Arctic zenith. That I failed   20
To solve the mysteries of the ice-bound world,
Was not because I faltered in the quest.
Witness those pathless forests which conceal
The bones of perished comrades, that long march,
Blood-tracked o'er flint and snow, and one dread night   25
By Athabasca, when a cherished life
Flowed to give life to others. This, and worse,
I suffered—let it pass—it has not tamed
My spirit nor the faith which was my strength.

[1] This selection is reprinted from the Memorial Edition through the
courtesy of the holder of the copyright, Johnson Publishing Company,
Richmond, Virginia.

Despite of waning years, despite the world
Which doubts, the few who dare, I purpose now—
A purpose long and thoughtfully resolved,
Through all its grounds of reasonable hope—
5   To seek beyond the ice which guards the Pole,
A sea of open water; for I hold,
Not without proofs, that such a sea exists,
And may be reached, though since this earth was made
No keel hath plowed it, and to mortal ear
10   No wind hath told its secrets. . . . With this tide
I sail; if all be well, this very moon
Shall see my ship beyond the southern cape
Of Greenland, and far up the bay through which,
With diamond spire and gorgeous pinnacle,
15   The fleets of winter pass to warmer seas.
Whether, my hardy shipmates! we shall reach
Our bourne, and come with tales of wonder back,
Or whether we shall lose the precious time,
Locked in thick ice, or whether some strange fate
20   Shall end us all, I know not; but I know
A lofty hope, if earnestly pursued,
Is its own crown, and never in this life
Is labor wholly fruitless. In this faith
I shall not count the chances—sure that all
25   A prudent foresight asks we shall not want,
And all that bold and patient hearts can do
Ye will not leave undone. The rest is God's!

HARK TO THE SHOUTING WIND[1]

Hark to the shouting Wind!
Hark to the flying Rain!
30   And I care not though I never see
A bright blue sky again.

[1] This selection is reprinted from the Memorial Edition through the courtesy of the holder of the copyright, Johnson Publishing Company, Richmond, Virginia.

There are thoughts in my breast to-day
    That are not for human speech;
But I hear them in the driving storm,
    And the roar upon the beach.

And oh, to be with that ship   5
    That I watch through the blinding brine!
O Wind! for thy sweep of land and sea!
    O Sea! for a voice like thine!

Shout on, thou pitiless Wind,
    To the frightened and flying Rain!   10
I care not though I never see
    A calm blue sky again.

PAUL HAMILTON HAYNE

THE AX AND THE PINE[1]

All day, on bole and limb the axes ring,
And every stroke upon my startled brain
Falls with the power of sympathetic pain;   15
I shrink to view each glorious forest king
Descend to earth, a wan, discrownèd thing.
Ah, Heaven! beside these foliaged giants slain,
How small the human dwarfs whose lust for gain
Hath edged their brutal steel to smite and sting!   20
Hark! to those long-drawn murmurings, strange and drear!
The wail of Dryads in their last distress;
O'er ruined haunts and ravished loveliness
Still tower those brawny arms; tones coarsely loud
Rise still beyond the greenery's waning cloud,   25
While falls the insatiate steel, sharp, cold and sheer!

[1] Reprinted by permission of Lothrop, Lee & Shepard Co., publishers.

THE TEMPTER IN THE HOUSE[1]

The sky is dark with a cloudy pall,
   And the earth is dim with rain,
And the ghastly pine trees toss and moan
   By the side of the moaning main;
5   And around the eaves of the desolate Hall
   The shrill March winds complain.

But a darker pall has shrouded the light
   Of the Household Hopes within,
For the troubled hearts that toss and moan
10   By the terrible verge of sin
Are sorely beset by the Tempter's might,
   And the Devil is sure to win!

ABRAM J. RYAN

LINES[2]

The death of men is not the death
Of rights that urged them to the fray;
15   For men may yield
   On battlefield
A noble life with stainless shield,
   And swords may rust
   Above their dust,
20   But still, and still
   The touch and thrill
Of freedom's vivifying breath
   Will nerve a heart and rouse a will
   In some hour, in the days to be,
25   To win back triumphs from defeat;
And those who blame us then will greet
   Right's glorious eternity.

[1] Reprinted by permission of Lothrop, Lee & Shepard Co., publishers.
[2] Reprinted by permission of P. J. Kenedy & Sons, publishers.

For right lives in a thousand things;
 Its cradle is its martyr's grave,
Wherein it rests awhile until
 The life that heroisms gave
Will rise again, at God's own will,   5
  And right the wrong
  Which long and long
Did reign above the true and just;
And through the songs the poet sings,
Right's vivifying spirit rings;   10
  Each simple rhyme
  Keeps step and time
With those who marched away and fell,
  And all his lines
  Are humble shrines   15
Where love of right will love to dwell.

BAYARD TAYLOR

BEDOUIN SONG[1]

From the Desert I come to thee
 On a stallion shod with fire;
And the winds are left behind
 In the speed of my desire.   20
Under thy window I stand,
 And the midnight hears my cry:
I love thee, I love but thee,
 With a love that shall not die
  Till the sun grows cold,   25
  And the stars are old,
  And the leaves of the Judgment
   Book unfold!

Look from thy window and see
 My passion and my pain;   30

[1]Reprinted by permission of G. P. Putnam's Sons, publishers.

I lie on the sands below,
   And I faint in thy disdain.
Let the night-winds touch thy brow
   With the heat of my burning sigh,
And melt thee to hear the vow
   Of a love that shall not die
     Till the sun grows cold,
     And the stars are old,
     And the leaves of the Judgment
      Book unfold!

My steps are nightly driven,
   By the fever in my breast,
To hear from thy lattice breathed
   The word that shall give me rest.
Open the door of thy heart,
   And open thy chamber door,
And my kisses shall teach thy lips
   The love that shall fade no more
     Till the sun grows cold,
     And the stars are old,
     And the leaves of the Judgment
      Book unfold!

THE NATIONAL ODE[1]

[Extract]

II (3)

Bow down!
Doff thine æonian crown!
   One hour forget
The glory, and recall the debt:
   Make expiation,
   Of humbler mood,
For the pride of thine exultation
O'er peril conquered and strife subdued!

---

[1]Reprinted by permission of G. P. Putnam's Sons, publishers.

But half the right is wrested
   When victory yields her prize,
And half the marrow tested
   When old endurance dies.
In the sight of them that love thee,   5
Bow to the Greater above thee!
   He faileth not to smite
The idle ownership of Right,
Nor spares to sinews fresh from trial,
And virtue schooled in long denial,   10
   The tests that wait for thee
In larger perils of prosperity.
   Here, at the Century's awful shrine,
   Bow to thy Fathers' God—and thine!

HARRIET BEECHER STOWE

THE PEARL OF ORR'S ISLAND

CHAPTER XXXV. THE TOOTHACRE COTTAGE

Aunt Roxy and Aunt Ruey Toothacre lived in a little one-   15
story gambrel-roofed cottage, on the side of Harpswell Bay,
just at the head of the long cove which we have already described. The windows on two sides commanded the beautiful
bay and the opposite shores, and on the other they looked out
into the dense forest, through whose deep shadows of white   20
birch and pine the silver rise and fall of the sea daily revealed
itself.

The house itself was a miracle of neatness within, for the
two thrifty sisters were worshipers of soap and sand, and these
two tutelary deities had kept every board of the house-floor   25
white and smooth, and also every table and bench and tub of
household use. There was a sacred care over each article,
however small and insignificant, which composed their slender household stock. The loss or breakage of one of them
would have made a visible crack in the hearts of the worthy   30

sisters,—for every plate, knife, fork, spoon, cup, or glass was as intimate with them, as instinct with home feeling, as if it had a soul; each defect or spot had its history, and a cracked dish or article of furniture received as tender and considerate
5 medical treatment as if it were capable of understanding and feeling the attention.

It was now a warm, spicy day in June,—one of those which bring out the pineapple fragrance from the fir-shoots, and cause the spruce and hemlocks to exude a warm, resinous
10 perfume. The two sisters, for a wonder, were having a day to themselves, free from the numerous calls of the vicinity for twelve miles round. The room in which they were sitting was bestrewn with fragments of dresses and bonnets, which were being torn to pieces in a most wholesale way, with a
15 view to general rejuvenescence. A person of unsympathetic temperament, and disposed to take sarcastic views of life, might perhaps wonder what possible object these two battered and weather-beaten old bodies proposed to themselves in this process,—whether Miss Roxy's gaunt black-straw hel-
20 met, which she had worn defiantly all winter, was likely to receive much luster from being pressed over and trimmed with an old green ribbon which that energetic female had colored black by a domestic recipe; and whether Miss Roxy's rusty bombazette would really seem to the world any fresher
25 for being ripped, and washed, and turned, for the second or third time, and made over with every breadth in a different situation. Probably after a week of efficient labor, busily expended in bleaching, dyeing, pressing, sewing, and ripping, an unenlightened spectator, seeing them come into the
30 meeting-house, would simply think, "There are those two old frights with the same old things on they have worn these fifty years." Happily the weird sisters were contentedly ignorant of any such remarks, for no duchesses could have enjoyed a more quiet belief in their own social position, and
35 their semiannual spring and fall rehabilitation was therefore entered into with the most simple-hearted satisfaction.

"I'm a-thinkin', Roxy," said Aunt Ruey, considerately turning and turning on her hand an old straw bonnet, on which were streaked all the marks of the former trimming in lighter lines, which revealed too clearly the effects of wind and weather,—"I'm a-thinkin' whether or no this 'ere mightn't as well be dyed and done with it as try to bleach it out. I've had it ten years last May, and it's kind o' losin' its freshness, you know. I don't believe these 'ere streaks will bleach out."

"Never mind, Ruey," said Miss Roxy, authoritatively, "I'm goin' to do Mis' Badger's leg'orn, and it won't cost nothin'; so hang your'n in the barrel along with it,—the same smoke'll do 'em both. Mis' Badger she finds the brimstone, and next fall you can put it in the dye when we do the yarn."

"That ar straw is a beautiful straw!" said Miss Ruey, in a plaintive tone, tenderly examining the battered old head-piece.—"I braided every stroke on it myself, and I don't know as I could do it ag'in. My fingers ain't quite so limber as they was! I don't think I shall put green ribbon on it ag'in; 'cause green is such a color to ruin, if a body gets caught out in a shower! There's these green streaks come that day I left my amberil at Captain Broad's, and went to meetin'. Mis' Broad she says to me, 'Aunt Ruey, it won't rain.' And says I to her, 'Well, Mis' Broad, I'll try it; though I never did leave my amberil at home but what it rained.' And so I went, and sure enough it rained cats and dogs, and streaked my bonnet all up; and them ar streaks won't bleach out, I'm feared."

"How long is it Mis' Badger has had that ar leg'orn?"

"Why, you know, the Cap'n he brought it home when he came from his voyage from Marseilles. That ar was when Phebe Ann was born, and she's fifteen year old. It was a most elegant thing when he brought it; but I think it kind o' led Mis' Badger on to extravagant ways,—for gettin' new trimmin' spring and fall so uses up money as fast as new bonnets; but Mis' Badger's got the money, and she's got a right

to use it if she pleases; but if I'd a-had new trimmin's spring
and fall, I shouldn't a-put away what I have in the bank."

"Have you seen the straw Sally Kittridge is braidin' for
Mara Lincoln's weddin' bonnet?" said Miss Ruey. "It's
jist the finest thing ever you did see,—and the whitest. I was
a-tellin' Sally that I could do as well once myself, but my
mantle was a-fallin' on her. Sally don't seem to act a bit like
a disap'inted gal. She is as chipper as she can be about
Mara's weddin', and seems like she couldn't do too much.
But laws, everybody seems to want to be a-doin' for her.
Miss Emily was a-showin' me a fine double damask table-
cloth that she was goin' to give her; and Mis' Pennel, she's
been a-spinnin' and layin' up sheets and towels and table-
cloths all her life,—and then she has all Naomi's things.
Mis' Pennel was talkin' to me the other day about bleachin'
'em out 'cause they'd got yellow a-lyin'. I kind o' felt as if
'twas unlucky to be a-fittin' out a bride with her dead
mother's things, but I didn't like to say nothin'."

"Ruey," said Miss Roxy impressively, "I hain't never
had but jist one mind about Mara Lincoln's weddin',—it's
to be,—but it won't be the way people think. I hain't nussed
and watched and sot up nights sixty years for nothin'. I can
see beyond what most folks can,—her weddin' garments is
bought and paid for, and she'll wear 'em, but she won't be
Moses Pennel's wife,—now you see."

"Why, whose wife will she be then?" said Miss Ruey,
"'cause that ar Mr. Adams is married. I saw it in the paper
last week when I was up to Mis' Badger's."

Miss Roxy shut her lips with oracular sternness and went
on with her sewing.

"Who's that comin' in the back door?" said Miss Ruey,
as the sound of a footstep fell upon her ear. "Bless me," she
added, as she started up to look, "if folks ain't always nearest
when you're talkin' about 'em. Why, Mara; you come down
here and catched us in all our dirt! Well now, we're glad to
see you, if we be," said Miss Ruey.

HERMAN MELVILLE

MOBY DICK

Chapter CXXXIII. The Chase—First Day

That night, in the mid-watch, when the old man—as his wont at intervals—stepped forth from the scuttle in which he leaned, and went to his pivot-hole, he suddenly thrust out his face fiercely, snuffing up the sea air as a sagacious ship's dog will, in drawing nigh to some barbarous isle. He declared that a whale must be near. Soon that peculiar odor, sometimes to a great distance given forth by the living sperm whale, was palpable to all the watch; nor was any mariner surprised when, after inspecting the compass, and then the dog-vane, and then ascertaining the precise bearing of the odor as nearly as possible, Ahab rapidly ordered the ship's course to be slightly altered, and the sail to be shortened.

The acute policy dictating these movements was sufficiently vindicated at daybreak, by the sight of a long sleek on the sea directly and lengthwise ahead, smooth as oil, and resembling, in the pleated watery wrinkles bordering it, the polished metallic-like marks of some swift tide-rip, at the mouth of a deep, rapid stream.

"Man the mastheads! Call all hands!"

Thundering with the butts of three clubbed handspikes on the forecastle deck, Daggoo roused the sleepers with such judgment claps that they seemed to exhale from the scuttle, so instantaneously did they appear with their clothes in their hands.

"What d'ye see?" cried Ahab, flattening his face to the sky.

"Nothing, nothing, sir!" was the sound hailing down in reply.

"T'gallant-sails!—stunsails! alow and aloft, and on both sides!"

All sail being set, he now cast loose the lifeline, reserved

for swaying him to the main-royal masthead, and in a few
moments they were hoisting him thither, when, while but
two thirds of the way aloft, and while peering ahead through
the horizontal vacancy between the main-topsail and top-
5 gallant-sail, he raised a gull-like cry in the air, "There she
blows!—there she blows! A hump like a snow-hill! It is
Moby Dick!"

Fired by the cry which seemed simultaneously taken up by
the three lookouts, the men on deck rushed to the rigging
10 to behold the famous whale they had so long been pursuing.
Ahab had now gained his final perch, some feet above the
other lookouts, Tashtego standing just beneath him on the
cap of the top-gallant-mast, so that the Indian's head was
almost on a level with Ahab's heel. From this height the
15 whale was now seen some mile or so ahead, at every roll of
the sea revealing his high sparkling hump, and regularly jet-
ting his silent spout into the air. To the credulous mariners
it seemed the same silent spout they had so long ago beheld
in the moonlit Atlantic and Indian Oceans.

20   "And did none of ye see it before?" cried Ahab, hailing
the perched men all around him.

"I saw him almost that same instant, sir, that Captain
Ahab did, and I cried out," said Tashtego.

"Not the same instant; not the same—no, the doubloon is
25 mine, Fate reserved the doubloon for me. *I* only; none of ye
could have raised the White Whale first. There she blows!
there she blows!—there she blows! There again!—there
again!" he cried, in long-drawn, lingering, methodic tones,
attuned to the gradual prolongings of the whale's visible
30 jets. "He's going to sound! In stunsails! Down top-gallant-
sails! Stand by three boats. Mr. Starbuck, remember, stay
on board, and keep the ship. Helm there! Luff, luff a point!
So; steady, man, steady! There go flukes! No, no; only
black water! All ready the boats there? Stand by, stand by!
35 Lower me, Mr. Starbuck; lower, lower,—quick, quicker!"
and he slid through the air to the deck.

"He is heading straight to leeward, sir," cried Stubb, "right away from us; cannot have seen the ship yet."

"Be dumb, man! Stand by the braces! Hard down the helm!—brace up! Shiver her!—shiver her! So; well that! Boats, boats!"

Soon all the boats but Starbuck's were dropped; all the boat-sails set—all the paddles plying; with rippling swiftness, shooting to leeward; and Ahab heading the onset. A pale death-glimmer lit up Fedallah's sunken eyes, a hideous motion gnawed his mouth.

Like noiseless nautilus shells, their light prows sped through the sea; but only slowly they neared the foe. As they neared him, the ocean grew still more smooth; seemed drawing a carpet over its waves; seemed a noon-meadow, so serenely it spread. At length the breathless hunter came so nigh his seemingly unsuspecting prey, that his entire dazzling hump was distinctly visible, sliding along the sea as if an isolated thing, and continually set in a revolving ring of finest, fleecy, greenish foam. He saw the vast, involved wrinkles of the slightly projecting head beyond. Before it, far out on the soft Turkish-rugged waters, went the glistening white shadow from his broad, milky forehead, a musical rippling playfully accompanying the shade; and behind, the blue waters interchangeably flowed over into the moving valley of his steady wake; and on either hand bright bubbles arose and danced by his side. But these were broken again by the light toes of hundreds of gay fowl softly feathering the sea, alternate with their fitful flight; and like to some flag-staff rising from the painted hull of an argosy, the tall but shattered pole of a recent lance projected from the white whale's back; and at intervals one of the cloud of soft-toed fowls hovering, and to and fro skimming like a canopy over the fish, silently perched and rocked on this pole, the long tail feathers streaming like pennons.

A gentle joyousness—a mighty mildness of repose in swiftness, invested the gliding whale. Not the white bull Jupiter

swimming away with ravished Europa clinging to his graceful horns; his lovely, leering eyes sideways intent upon the maid; with smooth bewitching fleetness, rippling straight for the nuptial bower in Crete; not Jove, not that great majesty
5 Supreme! did surpass the glorified White Whale as he so divinely swam.

On each soft side—coincident with the parted swell that, but once leaving him, then flowed so wide away—on each bright side, the whale shed off enticings. No wonder there had
10 been some among the hunters who, namelessly transported and allured by all this serenity, had ventured to assail it; but had fatally found that quietude but the vesture of tornadoes. Yet calm, enticing calm, oh, whale! thou glidest on, to all who for the first time eye thee, no matter how many in that
15 same way thou may'st have bejuggled and destroyed before.

And thus, through the serene tranquillities of the tropical sea, among waves whose hand-clappings were suspended by exceeding rapture, Moby Dick moved on, still withholding from sight the full terrors of his submerged trunk, entirely
20 hiding the wrenched hideousness of his jaw. But soon the fore part of him slowly rose from the water; for an instant his whole marbleized body formed a high arch, like Virginia's Natural Bridge, and warningly waving his bannered flukes in the air, the grand god revealed himself, sounded, and went
25 out of sight. Hoveringly halting, and dipping on the wing, the white sea-fowls longingly lingered over the agitated pool that he left.

With oars apeak, and paddles down, the sheets of their sails adrift, the three boats now stilly floated, awaiting Moby
30 Dick's reappearance.

"An hour," said Ahab, standing rooted in his boat's stern; and he gazed beyond the whale's place, towards the dim blue spaces and wide wooing vacancies to leeward. It was only an instant; for again his eyes seemed whirling round in his head
35 as he swept the watery circle. The breeze now freshened; the sea began to swell.

"The birds!—the birds!" cried Tashtego.

In long Indian file, as when herons take wing, the white birds were now all flying towards Ahab's boat; and when within a few yards began fluttering over the water there, wheeling round and round, with joyous, expectant cries. Their vision was keener than man's; Ahab could discover no sign in the sea. But suddenly as he peered down and down into its depths, he profoundly saw a white living spot no bigger than a white weasel, with wonderful celerity uprising, and magnifying as it rose, till it turned, and then there were plainly revealed two long crooked rows of white, glistening teeth, floating up from the undiscoverable bottom. It was Moby Dick's open mouth and scrolled jaw; his vast, shadowed bulk still half blending with the blue of the sea. The glittering mouth yawned beneath the boat like an open-doored marble tomb; and giving one sidelong sweep with his steering oar, Ahab whirled the craft aside from this tremendous apparition. Then, calling upon Fedallah to change places with him, went forward to the bows, and seizing Perth's harpoon, commanded his crew to grasp their oars and stand by to stern.

Now, by reason of this timely spinning round the boat upon its axis, its bow, by anticipation, was made to face the whale's head while yet under water. But as if perceiving this stratagem, Moby Dick, with that malicious intelligence ascribed to him, sidelingly transplanted himself, as it were, in an instant, shooting his pleated head lengthwise beneath the boat.

Through and through; through every plank and each rib, it thrilled for an instant, the whale obliquely lying on his back, in the manner of a biting shark, slowly and feelingly taking its bows full within his mouth, so that the long, narrow, scrolled lower jaw curled high up into the open air, and one of the teeth caught in a rowlock. The bluish pearl-white of the inside of the jaw was within six inches of Ahab's head, and reached higher than that. In this attitude the

White Whale now shook the slight cedar as a mildly cruel cat her mouse. With unastonished eyes Fedallah gazed, and crossed his arms; but the tiger-yellow crew were tumbling over each other's heads to gain the uttermost stern.

5   And now, while both elastic gunwales were springing in and out, as the whale dallied with the doomed craft in this devilish way; and from his body being submerged beneath the boat, he could not be darted at from the bows, for the bows were almost inside of him, as it were; and while the
10 other boats involuntarily paused, as before a quick crisis impossible to withstand, then it was that monomaniac Ahab, furious with this tantalizing vicinity of his foe, which placed him all alive and helpless in the very jaws he hated, frenzied with all this, he seized the long bone with his naked hands,
15 and wildly strove to wrench it from its gripe. As now he thus vainly strove, the jaw slipped from him; the frail gunwales bent in, collapsed, and snapped, as both jaws, like an enormous shears, sliding further aft, bit the craft completely in twain, and locked themselves fast again in the sea, midway
20 between the two floating wrecks. These floated aside, the broken ends drooping, the crew at the stern-wreck clinging to the gunwales, and striving to hold fast to the oars to lash them across.

At that preluding moment, ere the boat was yet snapped,
25 Ahab, the first to perceive the whale's intent, by the crafty upraising of his head, a movement that loosed his hold for the time; at that moment his hand had made one final effort to push the boat out of the bite. But only slipping further into the whale's mouth, and tilting over sideways as it
30 slipped, the boat had shaken off his hold on the jaw; spilled him out of it, as he leaned to the push; and so he fell flat-faced upon the sea.

Ripplingly withdrawing from his prey, Moby Dick now lay at a little distance, vertically thrusting his oblong white
35 head up and down in the billows; and at the same time slowly revolving his whole spindled body; so that when his

vast wrinkled forehead rose—some twenty or more feet out
of the water—the now rising swells, with all their confluent
waves, dazzlingly broke against it; vindictively tossing their
shivered spray still higher into the air. So, in a gale, the
but half baffled Channel billows only recoil from the base of 5
the Eddystone, triumphantly to overleap its summit with
their scud.

But soon resuming his horizontal attitude, Moby Dick
swam swiftly round and round the wrecked crew; sideways
churning the water in his vengeful wake, as if lashing him- 10
self up to still another and more deadly assault. The sight
of the splintered boat seemed to madden him, as the blood
of grapes and mulberries cast before Antiochus's elephants
in the book of Maccabees. Meanwhile Ahab half smothered
in the foam of the whale's insolent tail, and too much of a 15
cripple to swim,—though he could still keep afloat, even in
the heart of such a whirlpool as that; helpless Ahab's head
was seen, like a tossed bubble which the least chance shock
might burst. From the boat's fragmentary stern, Fedallah
incuriously and mildly eyed him; the clinging crew, at the 20
other drifting end, could not succor him; more than enough
was it for them to look to themselves. For so revolvingly
appalling was the White Whale's aspect, and so planetarily
swift the ever-contracting circles he made, that he seemed
horizontally swooping upon them. And though the other 25
boats, unharmed, still hovered hard by; still they dared not
pull into the eddy to strike, lest that should be the signal for
the instant destruction of the jeopardized castaways, Ahab
and all; nor in that case could they themselves hope to
escape. With straining eyes, then, they remained on the 30
outer edge of the direful zone, whose center had now become
the old man's head.

Meantime, from the beginning all this had been descried
from the ship's mastheads; and squaring her yards, she had
borne down upon the scene; and was now so nigh, that Ahab 35
in the water hailed her;—"Sail on the"—but that moment

a breaking sea dashed on him from Moby Dick, and whelmed him for the time. But struggling out of it again, and chancing to rise on a towering crest, he shouted,—"Sail on the whale!—Drive him off!"

5   The *Pequod's* prows were pointed; and breaking up the charmed circle, she effectually parted the white whale from his victim. As he sullenly swam off, the boats flew to the rescue.

    Dragged into Stubb's boat with blood-shot, blinded eyes, 10 the white brine caking in his wrinkles; the long tension of Ahab's bodily strength did crack, and helplessly he yielded to his body's doom: for a time, lying all crushed in the bottom of Stubb's boat, like one trodden under foot of herds of elephants. Far inland, nameless wails came from him, as 15 desolate sounds from out ravines.

    But this intensity of his physical prostration did but so much the more abbreviate it. In an instant's compass, great hearts sometimes condense to one deep pang the sum total of those shallow pains kindly diffused through feebler men's 20 whole lives. And so, such hearts, though summary in each one suffering, still, if the gods decree it, in their lifetime aggregate a whole age of woe, wholly made up of instantaneous intensities; for even in their pointless centers, those noble natures contain the entire circumferences of inferior 25 souls.

    "The harpoon," said Ahab, halfway rising, and draggingly leaning on one bended arm—"is it safe?"

    "Aye, sir, for it was not darted; this is it," said Stubb, showing it.

30   "Lay it before me;—any missing men?"

    "One, two, three, four, five;—there were five oars, sir, and here are five men."

    "That's good.—Help me, man; I wish to stand. So, so I see him! there! there! going to leeward still; what a leap- 35 ing spout!—Hands off from me! The eternal sap runs up in Ahab's bones again! Set the sail; out oars; the helm!"

It is often the case that when a boat is stove, its crew, being picked up by another boat, help to work that second boat; and the chase is thus continued with what is called double-banked oars. It was thus now. But the added power of the boat did not equal the added power of the whale, for he seemed to have treble-banked his every fin; swimming with a velocity which plainly showed, that if now, under these circumstances, pushed on, the chase would prove an indefinitely prolonged, if not a hopeless one; nor could any crew endure for so long a period, such an unintermitted, intense straining at the oar; a thing barely tolerable only in some one brief vicissitude. The ship itself, then, as it sometimes happens, offered the most promising intermediate means of overtaking the chase. Accordingly, the boats now made for her, and were soon swayed up to their cranes—the two parts of the wrecked boat having been previously secured by her— and then hoisting everything to her side, and stacking her canvas high up, and sideways outstretching it with stunsails, like the double-jointed wings of an albatross; the *Pequod* bore down in the leeward wake of Moby Dick. At the well known, methodic intervals, the whale's glittering spout was regularly announced from the manned mastheads; and when he would be reported as just gone down, Ahab would take the time, and then pacing the deck, binnacle-watch in hand, so soon as the last second of the allotted hour expired, his voice was heard.—"Whose is the doubloon now? D'ye see him?" and if the reply was, No, sir! straightway he commanded them to lift him to his perch. In this way the day wore on; Ahab, now aloft and motionless; anon, unrestingly pacing the planks.

As he was thus walking, uttering no sound, except to hail the men aloft, or to bid them hoist a sail still higher, or to spread one to a still greater breadth—thus to and fro pacing, beneath his slouched hat, at every turn he passed his own wrecked boat, which had been dropped upon the quarterdeck, and lay there reversed; broken bow to shattered stern.

At last he paused before it; and as in an already overclouded sky fresh troops of clouds will sometimes sail across, so over the old man's face there now stole some such added gloom as this.

5 Stubb saw him pause; and perhaps intending, not vainly, though, to evince his own unabated fortitude, and thus keep up a valiant place in his Captain's mind, he advanced, and eying the wreck exclaimed—"The thistle the ass refused; it pricked his mouth too keenly, sir; ha! ha!"

10 "What soulless thing is this that laughs before a wreck? Man, man! did I not know thee brave as fearless fire (and as mechanical) I could swear thou wert a poltroon. Groan nor laugh should be heard before a wreck."

"Aye, sir," said Starbuck drawing near, "'tis a solemn 15 sight; an omen, and an ill one."

"Omen? omen?—the dictionary! If the gods think to speak outright to man, they will honorably speak outright; not shake their heads, and give an old wives' darkling hint.— Begone! Ye two are the opposite poles of one thing; Star- 20 buck is Stubb reversed, and Stubb is Starbuck; and ye two are all mankind; and Ahab stands alone among the millions of the peopled earth, nor gods nor men his neighbors! Cold, cold—I shiver!—How now? Aloft there! D'ye see him? Sing out for every spout, though he spout ten times a 25 second!"

The day was nearly done; only the hem of his golden robe was rustling. Soon, it was almost dark, but the lookout men still remained unset.

"Can't see the spout now, sir;—too dark"—cried a voice 30 from the air.

"How heading when last seen?"

"As before, sir,—straight to leeward."

"Good! he will travel slower now 'tis night. Down royals and top-gallant-stunsails, Mr. Starbuck. We must not run 35 over him before morning; he's making a passage now, and may heave-to awhile. Helm there! keep her full before the

wind!—Aloft! come down!—Mr. Stubb, send a fresh hand
to the fore-masthead, and see it manned till morning."—
Then advancing towards the doubloon in the main-mast—
"Men, this gold is mine, for I earned it; but I shall let it
abide here till the White Whale is dead; and then, whoso- 5
ever of ye first raises him, upon the day he shall be killed,
this gold is that man's; and if on that day I shall again raise
him, then, ten times its sum shall be divided among all of ye!
Away now!—the deck is thine, sir."

And so saying, he placed himself halfway within the 10
scuttle, and slouching his hat, stood there till dawn, except
when at intervals rousing himself to see how the night
wore on.

JOHN ESTEN COOKE

LEATHER STOCKING AND SILK

CHAPTER XVIII. HOW THEY RAN FOR THE BOTTLE

The wedding morning dawned clear and auspicious, with
a laughing sun above the evergreen pines, and on the many- 15
colored woods of later fall; and a bracing freshness in the
wandering wind that gently caressed the cheek, and brightened every eye. The stream danced along the valley with a
gayer music than its wont; the golden leaves seemed laughing
and chuckling privately to themselves; the small white clouds 20
came slowly floating from the east and west with the veering
wind, and pausing just above the home of hunter John, were
plainly interested equally with stream, and leaf, and tree, in
this the wedding-day of the valley's "darling!"

Noon was approaching when an echoing shout—flying 25
and gamboling like a schoolboy on a holiday—came down
the valley, and gave warning that the company were drawing on.

In five minutes the dell seemed alive with horsemen, who,
galloping as though a rushing flood greater than ever broke 30

through Holland dikes was at their heels, flew onward toward
the house of hunter John. With hair streaming—caps waved
madly over their heads—and heels dug violently into the
sides of their flying coursers, they came more recklessly than
5 ever yet the riders in any steeple-chase, toward the hill.
For there awaited them old hunter John—a mighty, ribbon-
ornamented bottle in his hand. Why need we add, those
rushing roaring mountain youths were "running for the
bottle!"

10   Among the foremost, mounted on his gallant sorrel, and
thundering along with careless rein and hand upon his thigh,
was Doctor Thomas. The doctor was clad with unusual elegance. He wore a laced velvet coat, a many-colored vest,
and his silk stockings and white-topped boots were marvels
15 of taste and richness. You hardly looked at the rider nevertheless—so fine a sight was the noble sorrel, with arched neck
and glossy coat, flying onward to the merrymaking, as though
he too knew the meaning of it all.

    Behind the valiant doctor came a dozen other horsemen,
20 all at full speed, with coats streaming, hats waved madly over
head, and merry shouts; behind, for though the speed of the
mountain horses was great, the sorrel kept before them all.

    Suddenly, with a burst of jocund laughter all drew up,
checking their foaming horses, and yielding in the contest.
25 Doctor Thomas had reached the hill, sped up to the door,
and received from hunter John the famous bottle. A shout
greeted this performance, and the horsemen coming up, the
victor was congratulated by all. He handed the bottle to a
young mountaineer, on a swift black mare; and in a moment
30 the young man was on his way back at full speed. Barry and
the wedding party were to drink of "Black Bess"—so they
called it—before they came on to the mansion.

    By noon the guests had all arrived—among the rest father
Von Horn, and Nina, and—to the profound astonishment
35 of all—Mrs. Courtlandt! That lady was not clad, as Doctor Thomas had threatened, in her singular home costume of

moccasins and coat, but in a plain dark dress, which set off well her calm and refined countenance. Hunter John expressed some consternation on her arrival—mounted on the little white pony all knew well—but soon this passed, and the merrymaking commenced. The bride had not as yet made her appearance; but soon her door was thrown open, and the "darling" of the valley issued forth.

HENRY DAVID THOREAU

WALDEN

THE PONDS

Sometimes, having had a surfeit of human society and gossip, and worn out all my village friends, I rambled still farther westward than I habitually dwell, into yet more unfrequented parts of the town, "to fresh woods and pastures new," or, while the sun was setting, made my supper of huckleberries and blueberries on Fair Haven Hill, and laid up a store for several days. The fruits do not yield their true flavor to the purchaser of them, nor to him who raises them for the market. There is but one way to obtain it, yet few take that way. If you would know the flavor of huckleberries, ask the cowboy or the partridge. It is a vulgar error to suppose that you have tasted huckleberries who never plucked them. A huckleberry never reaches Boston; they have not been known there since they grew on her three hills. The ambrosial and essential part of the fruit is lost with the bloom which is rubbed off in the market cart, and they become mere provender. As long as Eternal Justice reigns, not one innocent huckleberry can be transported thither from the country's hills.

Occasionally, after my hoeing was done for the day, I joined some impatient companion who had been fishing on the pond since morning, as silent and motionless as a duck or a floating leaf, and, after practicing various kinds of

philosophy, had concluded commonly, by the time I arrived,
that he belonged to the ancient sect of Cenobites. There was
an older man, an excellent fisher and skilled in all kinds of
woodcraft, who was pleased to look upon my house as a build-
5 ing erected for the convenience of fishermen; and I was
equally pleased when he sat in my doorway to arrange his
lines.   Once in a while we sat together on the pond, he at one
end of the boat, and I at the other; but not many words
passed between us, for he had grown deaf in his later years,
10 but he occasionally hummed a psalm, which harmonized well
enough with my philosophy.   Our intercourse was thus altogether one of unbroken harmony, far more pleasing to remember than if it had been carried on by speech.   When, as
was commonly the case, I had none to commune with, I used
15 to raise the echoes by striking with a paddle on the side of
my boat, filling the surrounding woods with circling and
dilating sound, stirring them up as the keeper of a menagerie
his wild beasts, until I elicited a growl from every wooded
vale and hillside.

20   In warm evenings I frequently sat in the boat playing the
flute, and saw the perch, which I seemed to have charmed,
hovering around me, and the moon traveling over the ribbed
bottom, which was strewed with the wrecks of the forest.
Formerly I had come to this pond adventurously, from time
25 to time, in dark summer nights, with a companion, and making a fire close to the water's edge, which we thought attracted the fishes, we caught pouts with a bunch of worms
strung on a thread, and when we had done, far in the night,
threw the burning brands high into the air like skyrockets,
30 which, coming down into the pond, were quenched with a
loud hissing, and we were suddenly groping in total darkness.   Through this, whistling a tune, we took our way to
the haunts of men again.   But now I had made my home
by the shore.

35   Sometimes, after staying in a village parlor till the family
had all retired, I have returned to the woods, and, partly with

a view to the next day's dinner, spent the hours of midnight
fishing from a boat by moonlight, serenaded by owls and
foxes, and hearing, from time to time, the creaking note of
some unknown bird close at hand. These experiences were
very memorable and valuable to me,—anchored in forty feet 5
of water, and twenty or thirty rods from the shore, surrounded sometimes by thousands of small perch and shiners,
dimpling the surface with their tails in the moonlight, and
communicating by a long flaxen line with mysterious noc-
turnal fishes which had their dwelling forty feet below, or 10
sometimes dragging sixty feet of line about the pond as I
drifted in the gentle night breeze, now and then feeling a
slight vibration along it, indicative of some life prowling
about its extremity, of dull uncertain blundering purpose
there, and slow to make up its mind. At length you slowly 15
raise, pulling hand over hand, some horned pout squeaking
and squirming to the upper air. It was very queer, especially
in dark nights, when your thoughts had wandered to vast
and cosmogonal themes in other spheres, to feel this faint
jerk, which came to interrupt your dreams and link you to 20
Nature again. It seemed as if I might next cast my line
upward into the air, as well as downward into this element
which was scarcely more dense. Thus I caught two fishes as
it were with one hook.

The scenery of Walden is on a humble scale, and, though 25
very beautiful, does not approach to grandeur, nor can it
much concern one who has not long frequented it or lived by
its shore; yet this pond is so remarkable for its depth and
purity as to merit a particular description. It is a clear and
deep green well, half a mile long and a mile and three quar- 30
ters in circumference, and contains about sixty-one and a
half acres; a perennial spring in the midst of pine and oak
woods, without any visible inlet or outlet except by the clouds
and evaporation. The surrounding hills rise abruptly from
the water to the height of forty to eighty feet, though on the 35

southeast and east they attain to about one hundred and one hundred and fifty feet respectively, within a quarter and a third of a mile. They are exclusively woodland. All our Concord waters have two colors at least, one when viewed at a distance, and another, more proper, close at hand. The first depends more on the light, and follows the sky. In clear weather, in summer, they appear blue at a little distance, especially if agitated, and at a great distance all appear alike. In stormy weather they are sometimes of a dark slate color. The sea, however, is said to be blue one day and green another without any perceptible change in the atmosphere. I have seen our river, when, the landscape being covered with snow, both water and ice were almost as green as grass. Some consider blue "to be the color of pure water, whether liquid or solid." But, looking directly down into our waters from a boat, they are seen to be of very different colors. Walden is blue at one time and green at another, even from the same point of view. Lying between the earth and the heavens, it partakes of the color of both. Viewed from a hilltop it reflects the color of the sky, but near at hand it is of a yellowish tint next the shore where you can see the sand, then a light green, which gradually deepens to a uniform dark green in the body of the pond. In some lights, viewed even from a hilltop, it is of a vivid green next the shore. Some have referred this to the reflection of the verdure, but it is equally green there against the railroad sand-bank, and in the spring, before the leaves are expanded, and it may be simply the result of the prevailing blue mixed with the yellow of the sand. Such is the color of its iris. This is that portion, also, where in the spring the ice being warmed by the heat of the sun reflected from the bottom, and also transmitted through the earth, melts first and forms a narrow canal about the still frozen middle. Like the rest of our waters, when much agitated, in clear weather, so that the surface of the waves may reflect the sky at the right angle, or because there is more light mixed with it, it appears at a little distance of a darker blue than the sky itself; and at such a time, being on its surface, and looking with divided vision, so as to see the reflection, I have discerned a matchless and indescribable light blue, such as watered or changeable silks and sword blades suggest, more cerulean than the sky itself, alternating with the original 5 dark green on the opposite sides of the waves, which last appeared but muddy in comparison. It is a vitreous greenish blue, as I remember it, like those patches of the winter sky seen through cloud vistas in the west before sundown. Yet a single glass of its water held up to the light is as colorless 10 as an equal quantity of air. It is well known that a large plate of glass will have a green tint, owing, as the makers say, to its "body," but a small piece of the same will be colorless. How large a body of Walden water would be required to reflect a green tint I have never proved. The water 15 of our river is black or a very dark brown to one looking directly down on it, and, like that of most ponds, imparts to the body of one bathing in it a yellowish tinge; but this water is of such crystalline purity that the body of the bather appears of an alabaster whiteness, still more unnatural, 20 which, as the limbs are magnified and distorted withal, produces a monstrous effect, making fit studies for a Michael Angelo.

The water is so transparent that the bottom can easily be discerned at the depth of twenty-five or thirty feet. Paddling 25 over it, you may see many feet beneath the surface the schools of perch and shiners, perhaps only an inch long, yet the former easily distinguished by their transverse bars, and you think that they must be ascetic fish that find a subsistence there. Once, in the winter, many years ago, when I 30 had been cutting holes through the ice in order to catch pickerel, as I stepped ashore I tossed my ax back on to the ice, but, as if some evil genius had directed it, it slid four or five rods directly into one of the holes, where the water was twenty-five feet deep. Out of curiosity, I lay down on the 35 ice and looked through the hole, until I saw the ax a little on one side, standing on its head, with its helve erect and gently swaying to and fro with the pulse of the pond; and there it might have stood erect and swaying till in the course of time the handle rotted off, if I had not disturbed it. Making another hole directly over it with an ice chisel which I had, and cutting down the longest birch which I could find in the neighborhood with my knife, I made a slip-noose, which I attached to its end, and, letting it down carefully, passed it over the knob of the handle, and drew it by a line along the birch, and so pulled the ax out again.

The shore is composed of a belt of smooth rounded white stones, like paving stones, excepting one or two short sand beaches, and is so steep that in many places a single leap will carry you into water over your head; and were it not for its remarkable transparency, that would be the last to be seen of its bottom till it rose on the opposite side. Some think it is bottomless. It is nowhere muddy, and a casual observer would say that there were no weeds at all in it; and of noticeable plants, except in the little meadows recently overflowed, which do not properly belong to it, a closer scrutiny does not detect a flag nor a bulrush, nor even a lily, yellow or white, but only a few small heart-leaves and potamogetons, and perhaps a water-target or two; all which however a bather might not perceive; and these plants are clean and bright like the element they grow in. The stones extend a rod or two into the water, and then the bottom is pure sand, except in the deepest parts, where there is usually a little sediment, probably from the decay of the leaves which have been wafted on to it so many successive falls, and a bright green weed is brought up on anchors even in midwinter.

.   .   .   .

FRANCIS PARKMAN

LA SALLE AND THE DISCOVERY OF THE GREAT WEST[1]

[Extracts]

When last he had passed here, all was solitude; but now the scene was changed. The boundless waste was thronged with life. He beheld that wondrous spectacle, still to be seen at times on the plains of the remotest West, and the memory of which can quicken the pulse and stir the blood after the lapse of years. Far and near, the prairie was alive with buffalo, now like black specks dotting the distant swells; now trampling by in ponderous columns, or filing in long lines, morning, noon, and night, to drink at the river,—wading, plunging, and snorting in the water; climbing the muddy shores, and staring with wild eyes at the passing canoes. It was an opportunity not to be lost. The party landed and encamped for a hunt. Sometimes they hid under the shelving bank, and shot them as they came to drink; sometimes, flat on their faces, they dragged themselves through the long dead grass, till the savage bulls, guardians of the herd, ceased their grazing, raised their huge heads, and glared through tangled hair at the dangerous intruders; their horns splintered and their grim front scarred with battles, while their shaggy mane, like a gigantic lion, well-nigh swept the ground. The hunt was successful. In three days, the hunters killed twelve buffalo, besides deer, geese, and swans. They cut the meat into thin flakes, and dried it in the sun or in the smoke of their fires. The men were in high spirits, delighting in the sport, and rejoicing in the prospect of relieving Tonty and his hungry followers with a bounteous supply.

They embarked again, and soon approached the great town of the Illinois. The buffalo were far behind; and once more the canoes glided on their way through a voiceless solitude. No hunters were seen; no saluting whoop greeted their ears.

[1] Reprinted by permission of Little, Brown & Company, publishers.

They passed the cliff afterwards called the Rock of St. Louis,
where La Salle had ordered Tonty to build his stronghold;
but as he scanned its lofty top, he saw no palisades, no
cabins, no sign of human hand, and still its primeval crest of
5 forests overhung the gliding river. Now the meadow opened
before them where the great town had stood. They gazed,
astonished and confounded: all was desolation. The town
had vanished, and the meadow was black with fire. They
plied their paddles, hastened to the spot, landed; and, as
10 they looked around, their cheeks grew white, and the blood
was frozen in their veins.

.   .   .   .

After touching at several other towns of this people [the
Arkansas], the voyagers resumed their course, guided by two
of the Arkansas; passed the sites, since become historic, of
15 Vicksburg and Grand Gulf; and, about three hundred miles
below the Arkansas, stopped by the edge of a swamp on the
western side of the river. Here, as their two guides told them,
was the path to the great town of the Taensas. Tonty and
Membré were sent to visit it. They and their men shouldered
20 their birch canoe through the swamp, and launched it on a
lake which had once formed a portion of the channel of the
river. In two hours they reached the town, and Tonty gazed
at it with astonishment. He had seen nothing like it in
America: large square dwellings, built of sun-baked mud
25 mixed with straw, arched over with a dome-shaped roof of
canes, and placed in regular order around an open area. Two
of them were larger and better than the rest. One was the lodge
of the chief; the other was the temple, or house of the Sun.
They entered the former, and found a single room, forty feet
30 square, where, in the dim light, for there was no opening but
the door, the chief sat awaiting them on a sort of bedstead,
three of his wives at his side, while sixty old men, wrapped in
white cloaks woven of mulberry-bark, formed his divan.
When he spoke, his wives howled to do him honor; and the
35 assembled councilors listened with the reverence due to a

potentate for whom, at his death, a hundred victims were to
be sacrificed. He received the visitors graciously, and joy-
fully accepted the gifts which Tonty laid before him. This
interview over, the Frenchmen repaired to the temple,
wherein were kept the bones of the departed chiefs. In con-   5
struction it was much like the royal dwelling. Over it were
rude wooden figures, representing three eagles turned towards
the east. A strong mud wall surrounded it, planted with
stakes, on which were stuck the skulls of enemies sacrificed
to the Sun; while before the door was a block of wood, on   10
which lay a large shell surrounded with the braided hair of
the victims. The interior was rude as a barn, dimly lighted
from the doorway, and full of smoke. There was a structure
in the middle which Membré thinks was a kind of altar; and
before it burned a perpetual fire, fed with three logs laid end   15
to end, and watched by two old men devoted to this sacred
office. There was a mysterious recess, too, which the strangers
were forbidden to explore, but which, as Tonty was told,
contained the riches of the nation, consisting of pearls from
the Gulf, and trinkets obtained, probably through other   20
tribes, from the Spaniards and other Europeans.

The chief condescended to visit La Salle at his camp; a
favor which he would by no means have granted, had the
visitors been Indians. A master of ceremonies, and six attendants, preceded him, to clear the path and prepare the   25
place of meeting. When all was ready, he was seen advancing, clothed in a white robe, and preceded by two men bearing white fans; while a third displayed a disk of burnished
copper, doubtless to represent the Sun, his ancestor; or, as
others will have it, his elder brother. His aspect was mar-   30
velously grave, and he and La Salle met with gestures of
ceremonious courtesy. The interview was very friendly; and
the chief returned well pleased with the gifts which his entertainer bestowed on him, and which, indeed, had been the
principal motive of his visit.   35

· · · · · · · · · ·

And now they neared their journey's end. On the sixth
of April, the river divided itself into three broad channels.
La Salle followed that of the west, and D'Autray that of the
east; while Tonty took the middle passage. As he drifted
5 down the turbid current, between the low and marshy shores,
the brackish water changed to brine, and the breeze grew
fresh with the salt breath of the sea. Then the broad bosom
of the great Gulf opened on his sight, tossing its restless
billows, limitless, voiceless, lonely, as when born of chaos,
10 without a sail, without a sign of life.

La Salle, in a canoe, coasted the marshy borders of the
sea; and then the reunited parties assembled on a spot of dry
ground, a short distance above the mouth of the river. Here
a column was made ready, bearing the arms of France, and
15 inscribed with the words,—

> Louis Le Grand, Roy de France et de Navarre, Règne;
> le Neuvième Avril, 1682

THE ALL-AMERICA PERIOD

BRET HARTE

TENNESSEE'S PARTNER[1]

I do not think that we ever knew his real name. Our
ignorance of it certainly never gave us any social inconvenience, for at Sandy Bar in 1854 most men were christened
anew. Sometimes these appellatives were derived from some
distinctiveness of dress, as in the case of "Dungaree Jack"; 5
or from some peculiarity of habit, as shown in "Saleratus
Bill," so called from an undue proportion of that chemical
in his daily bread; or from some unlucky slip, as exhibited in
"The Iron Pirate," a mild, inoffensive man, who earned that
baleful title by his unfortunate mispronunciation of the 10
term "iron pyrites." Perhaps this may have been the beginning of a rude heraldry; but I am constrained to think that
it was because a man's real name in that day rested solely
upon his own unsupported statement. "Call yourself Clifford, do you?" said Boston, addressing a timid newcomer 15
with infinite scorn; "hell is full of such Cliffords!" He then
introduced the unfortunate man, whose name happened to be
really Clifford, as "Jaybird Charley,"—an unhallowed inspiration of the moment that clung to him ever after.

But to return to Tennessee's Partner, whom we never knew 20
by any other than this relative title; that he had ever existed
as a separate and distinct individuality we only learned later.
It seems that in 1853 he left Poker Flat to go to San Francisco, ostensibly to procure a wife. He never got any farther
than Stockton. At that place he was attracted by a young 25

[1] Reprinted by permission of Houghton Mifflin Company, publishers.

person who waited upon the table at the hotel where he took his meals. One morning he said something to her which caused her to smile not unkindly, to somewhat coquettishly break a plate of toast over his upturned, serious, simple face, and to retreat to the kitchen. He followed her, and emerged a few moments later, covered with more toast and victory. That day week they were married by a Justice of the Peace, and returned to Poker Flat. I am aware that something more might be made of this episode, but I prefer to tell it as it was current at Sandy Bar,—in the gulches and bar-rooms,—where all sentiment was modified by a strong sense of humor.

Of their married felicity but little is known, perhaps for the reason that Tennessee, then living with his partner, one day took occasion to say something to the bride on his own account, at which, it is said, she smiled not unkindly and chastely retreated,—this time as far as Marysville, where Tennessee followed her, and where they went to housekeeping without the aid of a Justice of the Peace. Tennessee's Partner took the loss of his wife simply and seriously, as was his fashion. But to everybody's surprise, when Tennessee one day returned from Marysville, without his partner's wife,—she having smiled and retreated with somebody else,—Tennessee's Partner was the first man to shake his hand and greet him with affection. The boys who had gathered in the cañon to see the shooting were naturally indignant. Their indignation might have found vent in sarcasm but for a certain look in Tennessee's Partner's eye that indicated a lack of humorous appreciation. In fact, he was a grave man, with a steady application to practical detail which was unpleasant in a difficulty.

Meanwhile a popular feeling against Tennessee had grown up on the Bar. He was known to be a gambler; he was suspected to be a thief. In these suspicions Tennessee's Partner was equally compromised; his continued intimacy with Tennessee after the affair above quoted could only be accounted for on the hypothesis of a copartnership of crime. At last Tennessee's guilt became flagrant. One day he overtook

a stranger on his way to Red Dog. The stranger afterward related that Tennessee beguiled the time with interesting anecdote and reminiscence, but illogically concluded the
interview in the following words: "And now, young man, I'll
trouble you for your knife, your pistols, and your money. 5
You see your weppings might get you into trouble at Red
Dog, and your money's a temptation to the evilly disposed.
I think you said your address was San Francisco. I shall
endeavor to call." It may be stated here that Tennessee had
a fine flow of humor, which no business preoccupation could 10
wholly subdue.

This exploit was his last. Red Dog and Sandy Bar made
common cause against the highwayman. Tennessee was
hunted in very much the same fashion as his prototype, the
grizzly. As the toils closed around him, he made a desperate 15
dash through the Bar, emptying his revolver at the crowd
before the Arcade Saloon, and so on up Grizzly Cañon; but
at its farther extremity he was stopped by a small man on a
gray horse. The men looked at each other a moment in
silence. Both were fearless, both self-possessed and inde- 20
pendent, and both types of a civilization that in the seventeenth century would have been called heroic, but in the
nineteenth simply "reckless." "What have you got there?—
I call," said Tennessee, quietly. "Two bowers and an ace,"
said the stranger, as quietly, showing two revolvers and a 25
bowie-knife. "That takes me," returned Tennessee; and,
with this gambler's epigram, he threw away his useless pistol,
and rode back with his captor.

It was a warm night. The cool breeze which usually sprang
up with the going down of the sun behind the *chaparral-* 30
crested mountain was that evening withheld from Sandy Bar.
The little cañon was stifling with heated resinous odors, and
the decaying driftwood on the Bar sent forth faint, sickening
exhalations. The feverishness of day and its fierce passions
still filled the camp. Lights moved restlessly along the bank 35

of the river, striking no answering reflection from its tawny
current. Against the blackness of the pines the windows
of the old loft above the express-office stood out staringly
bright; and through their curtainless panes the loungers below could see the forms of those who were even then deciding
the fate of Tennessee. And above all this, etched on the dark
firmament, rose the Sierra, remote and passionless, crowned
with remoter passionless stars.

The trial of Tennessee was conducted as fairly as was con-
sistent with a judge and jury who felt themselves to some
extent obliged to justify, in their verdict, the previous irregu-
larities of arrest and indictment. The law of Sandy Bar was
implacable, but not vengeful. The excitement and personal
feeling of the chase were over; with Tennessee safe in their
hands they were ready to listen patiently to any defense,
which they were already satisfied was insufficient. There being no doubt in their own minds, they were willing to give the
prisoner the benefit of any that might exist. Secure in the
hypothesis that he ought to be hanged, on general principles,
they indulged him with more latitude of defense than his
reckless hardihood seemed to ask. The Judge appeared to
be more anxious than the prisoner, who, otherwise uncon-
cerned, evidently took a grim pleasure in the responsibility
he had created. "I don't take any hand in this yer game,"
had been his invariable but good-humored reply to all questions. The Judge—who was also his captor—for a moment
vaguely regretted that he had not shot him "on sight," that
morning, but presently dismissed this human weakness as unworthy of the judicial mind. Nevertheless, when there was
a tap at the door, and it was said that Tennessee's Partner
was there on behalf of the prisoner, he was admitted at once
without question. Perhaps the younger members of the jury,
to whom the proceedings were becoming irksomely thoughtful, hailed him as a relief.

For he was not, certainly, an imposing figure. Short and
stout, with a square face, sunburned into a preternatural red-

ness, clad in a loose duck "jumper" and trousers streaked and splashed with red soil, his aspect under any circumstances would have been quaint, and was now even ridiculous. As he stooped to deposit at his feet a heavy carpet-bag he was carrying, it became obvious, from partially developed legends and inscriptions, that the material with which his trousers had been patched had been originally intended for a less ambitious covering. Yet he advanced with great gravity, and after shaking the hand of each person in the room with labored cordiality, he wiped his serious, perplexed face on a red bandanna handkerchief, a shade lighter than his complexion, laid his powerful hand upon the table to steady himself, and thus addressed the Judge:

"I was passin' by," he began, by way of apology, "and I thought I'd just step in and see how things was gittin' on with Tennessee thar,—my pardner. It's a hot night. I disremember any sich weather before on the Bar."

He paused a moment, but nobody volunteering any other meteorological recollection, he again had recourse to his pocket-handkerchief, and for some moments mopped his face diligently.

"Have you anything to say on behalf of the prisoner?" said the Judge, finally.

"Thet's it," said Tennessee's Partner, in a tone of relief. "I come yar as Tennessee's pardner,—knowing him nigh on four year, off and on, wet and dry, in luck and out o' luck. His ways ain't allers my ways, but thar ain't any p'ints in that young man, thar ain't any liveliness as he's been up to, as I don't know. And you sez to me, sez you,—confidential-like, and between man and man,—sez you, 'Do you know anything in his behalf?' and I sez to you, sez I,—confidential-like, as between man and man,—'What should a man know of his pardner?'"

"Is this all you have to say?" asked the Judge impatiently, feeling, perhaps, that a dangerous sympathy of humor was beginning to humanize the court.

"Thet's so," continued Tennessee's Partner. "It ain't for me to say anything agin' him. And now, what's the case? Here's Tennessee wants money, wants it bad, and doesn't like to ask it of his old pardner. Well, what does Tennessee do? He lays for a stranger, and he fetches that stranger; and you lays for *him*, and you fetches *him*; and the honors is easy. And I put it to you, bein' a far-minded man, and to you, gentlemen all, as far-minded men, ef this isn't so."

"Prisoner," said the Judge, interrupting, "have you any questions to ask this man?"

"No! no!" continued Tennessee's Partner hastily. "I play this yer hand alone. To come down to the bed-rock, it's just this: Tennessee, thar, has played it pretty rough and expensive-like on a stranger, and on this yer camp. And now, what's the fair thing? Some would say more; some would say less. Here's seventeen hundred dollars in coarse gold and a watch,—it's about all my pile,—and call it square!" And before a hand could be raised to prevent him, he had emptied the contents of the carpet-bag upon the table.

For a moment his life was in jeopardy. One or two men sprang to their feet, several hands groped for hidden weapons, and a suggestion to "throw him from the window" was only overridden by a gesture from the Judge. Tennessee laughed. And apparently oblivious of the excitement, Tennessee's Partner improved the opportunity to mop his face again with his handkerchief.

When order was restored, and the man was made to understand, by the use of forcible figures and rhetoric, that Tennessee's offense could not be condoned by money, his face took a more serious and sanguinary hue, and those who were nearest to him noticed that his rough hand trembled slightly on the table. He hesitated a moment as he slowly returned the gold to the carpet-bag, as if he had not yet entirely caught the elevated sense of justice which swayed the tribunal, and was perplexed with the belief that he had not offered enough. Then he turned to the Judge, and saying, "This yer is a

lone hand, played alone, and without my pardner," he bowed
to the jury and was about to withdraw, when the Judge called
him back. "If you have anything to say to Tennessee, you
had better say it now." For the first time that evening the
eyes of the prisoner and his strange advocate met. Tennessee
smiled, showed his white teeth, and saying, "Euchred, old
man!" held out his hand. Tennessee's Partner took it in his
own, and saying, "I just dropped in as I was passin' to see
how things was gettin' on," let the hand passively fall, and
adding that "it was a warm night," again mopped his face
with his handkerchief, and without another word withdrew.

The two men never again met each other alive. For the
unparalleled insult of a bribe offered to Judge Lynch—who,
whether bigoted, weak, or narrow, was at least incorruptible
—firmly fixed in the mind of that mythical personage any
wavering determination of Tennessee's fate; and at the break
of day he was marched, closely guarded, to meet it at the top
of Marley's Hill.

How he met it, how cool he was, how he refused to say
anything, how perfect were the arrangements of the committee, were all duly reported, with the addition of a warning
moral and example to all future evil-doers, in the *Red Dog
Clarion*, by its editor, who was present, and to whose vigorous
English I cheerfully refer the reader. But the beauty of that
midsummer morning, the blessed amity of earth and air and
sky, the awakened life of the free woods and hills, the joyous
renewal and promise of Nature, and, above all, the infinite
serenity that thrilled through each, was not reported, as not
being a part of the social lesson. And yet, when the weak
and foolish deed was done, and a life, with its possibilities
and responsibilities, had passed out of the misshapen thing
that dangled between earth and sky, the birds sang, the
flowers bloomed, the sun shone, as cheerily as before; and
possibly the *Red Dog Clarion* was right.

Tennessee's Partner was not in the group that surrounded
the ominous tree. But as they turned to disperse, attention

was drawn to the singular appearance of a motionless donkey-cart halted at the side of the road. As they approached, they at once recognized the venerable Jenny and the two-wheeled cart as the property of Tennessee's Partner,—used by him in 5 carrying dirt from his claim; and a few paces distant the owner of the equipage himself, sitting under a buckeye tree, wiping the perspiration from his glowing face. In answer to an inquiry, he said he had come for the body of the "diseased," "if it was all the same to the committee." He didn't 10 wish to "hurry anything"; he could wait. He was not working that day; and when the gentlemen were done with the "diseased" he would take him. "Ef thar is any present," he added, in his simple, serious way, "as would care to jine in the fun'l, they kin come." Perhaps it was from a sense of humor, 15 which I have already intimated was a feature of Sandy Bar,—perhaps it was from something even better than that; but two thirds of the loungers accepted the invitation at once.

It was noon when the body of Tennessee was delivered into the hands of his partner. As the cart drew up to the fatal tree, 20 we noticed that it contained a rough oblong box,—apparently made from a section of sluicing,—and half filled with bark and the tassels of pine. The cart was further decorated with slips of willow, and made fragrant with buckeye-blossoms. When the body was deposited in the box, Tennessee's Partner 25 drew over it a piece of tarred canvas, and gravely mounting the narrow seat in front, with his feet upon the shafts, urged the little donkey forward. The equipage moved slowly on, at that decorous pace which was habitual with Jenny even under less solemn circumstances. The men—half curiously, 30 half jestingly, but all good-humoredly—strolled along beside the cart; some in advance, some a little in the rear, of the homely catafalque. But, whether from the narrowing of the road or some present sense of decorum, as the cart passed on, the company fell to the rear in couples, keeping step, and 35 otherwise assuming the external show of a formal procession. Jack Folinsbee, who had at the outset played a funeral march in dumb show upon an imaginary trombone, desisted, from a lack of sympathy and appreciation,—not having, perhaps, your true humorist's capacity to be content with the enjoyment of his own fun.

The way led through Grizzly Cañon, by this time clothed in funereal drapery and shadows. The redwoods, burying their moccasined feet in the red soil, stood in Indian-file along the track, trailing an uncouth benediction from their bending boughs upon the passing bier. A hare, surprised into helpless inactivity, sat upright and pulsating in the ferns by the road-side, as the *cortège* went by. Squirrels hastened to gain a secure outlook from higher boughs; and the blue-jays, spreading their wings, fluttered before them like outriders, until the outskirts of Sandy Bar were reached, and the solitary cabin of Tennessee's Partner.

Viewed under more favorable circumstances, it would not have been a cheerful place. The unpicturesque site, the rude and unlovely outlines, the unsavory details, which distinguish the nest-building of the California miner, were all here, with the dreariness of decay superadded. A few paces from the cabin there was a rough inclosure, which, in the brief days of Tennessee's Partner's matrimonial felicity, had been used as a garden, but was now overgrown with fern. As we approached it we were surprised to find that what we had taken for a recent attempt at cultivation was the broken soil about an open grave.

The cart was halted before the inclosure; and rejecting the offers of assistance with the same air of simple self-reliance he had displayed throughout, Tennessee's Partner lifted the rough coffin on his back, and deposited it unaided, within the shallow grave. He then nailed down the board which served as a lid, and mounting the little mound of earth beside it, took off his hat, and slowly mopped his face with his handkerchief. This the crowd felt was a preliminary to speech; and they disposed themselves variously on stumps and bowlders, and sat expectant.

"When a man," began Tennessee's Partner slowly, "has been running free all day, what's the natural thing for him to do? Why, to come home. And if he ain't in a condition to go home, what can his best friend do? Why, bring him home! And here's Tennessee has been running free, and we brings him home from his wandering." He paused, and picked up a fragment of quartz, rubbed it thoughtfully on his sleeve, and went on: "It ain't the first time that I've packed him on my back, as you see'd me now. It ain't the first time that I brought him to this yer cabin when he couldn't help himself; it ain't the first time that I and Jinny have waited for him on yon hill, and picked him up and so fetched him home, when he couldn't speak, and didn't know me. And now that it's the last time, why"—he paused, and rubbed the quartz gently on his sleeve—"you see it's sort of rough on his pardner. And now, gentlemen," he added abruptly, picking up his long-handled shovel, "the fun'l's over; and my thanks, and Tennessee's thanks, to you for your trouble."

Resisting any proffers of assistance, he began to fill in the grave, turning his back upon the crowd, that after a few moments' hesitation gradually withdrew. As they crossed the little ridge that hid Sandy Bar from view, some, looking back, thought they could see Tennessee's Partner, his work done, sitting upon the grave, his shovel between his knees, and his face buried in his red bandanna handkerchief. But it was argued by others that you couldn't tell his face from his hand- kerchief at that distance; and this point remained undecided.

In the reaction that followed the feverish excitement of that day, Tennessee's Partner was not forgotten. A secret investigation had cleared him of any complicity in Tennes- see's guilt, and left only a suspicion of his general sanity. Sandy Bar made a point of calling on him, and proffering various uncouth but well-meant kindnesses. But from that day his rude health and great strength seemed visibly to de- cline; and when the rainy season fairly set in, and the tiny grass-blades were beginning to peep from the rocky mound above Tennessee's grave, he took to his bed.

One night, when the pines beside the cabin were swaying in the storm, and trailing their slender fingers over the roof, and the roar and rush of the swollen river were heard below, Tennessee's Partner lifted his head from the pillow, saying, "It is time to go for Tennessee; I must put Jinny in the cart"; and would have risen from his bed but for the restraint of his attendant. Struggling, he still pursued his singular fancy: "There, now, steady, Jinny,—steady, old girl. How dark it is! Look out for the ruts,—and look out for him, too, old gal. Sometimes, you know, when he's blind drunk, he drops down right in the trail. Keep on straight up to the pine on the top of the hill. Thar! I told you so!—thar he is, coming this way, too,—all by himself, sober, and his face a-shining. Tennessee! Pardner!"

And so they met.

GEORGE WASHINGTON CABLE

MADAME DÉLICIEUSE[1]

Just adjoining the old Café de Poésie on the corner, stood the little one-story, yellow-washed tenement of Dr. Mossy, with its two glass doors protected by batten shutters, and its low, weed-grown tile roof sloping out over the sidewalk. You were very likely to find the Doctor in, for he was a great student and rather negligent of his business—as business. He was a small, sedate, Creole gentleman of thirty or more, with a young-old face and manner that provoked instant admiration. He would receive you—be you who you may—in a mild, candid manner, looking into your face with his deep blue eyes, and reassuring you with a modest, amiable smile, very sweet and rare on a man's mouth.

[1] Reprinted from *Old Creole Days* by permission of Charles Scribner's Sons, publishers.

To be frank, the Doctor's little establishment was dusty and disorderly—very. It was curious to see the jars, and jars, and jars. In them were serpents and hideous fishes and precious specimens of many sorts. There were stuffed birds on
5 broken perches; and dried lizards, and eels, and little alligators, and old skulls with their crowns sawed off, and ten thousand odd scraps of writing-paper strewn with crumbs of lonely lunches, and interspersed with long-lost spatulas and rust-eaten lancets.

10 All New Orleans, at least all Creole New Orleans, knew, and yet did not know, the dear little Doctor. So gentle, so kind, so skillful, so patient, so lenient; so careless of the rich and so attentive to the poor; a man, all in all, such as, should you once love him, you would love him forever. So very
15 learned, too, but with apparently no idea of how to *show himself* to his social profit,—two features much more smiled at than respected, not to say admired, by a people remote from the seats of learning, and spending most of their esteem upon animal heroisms and exterior display.

20 "Alas!" said his wealthy acquaintance, "what a pity; when he might as well be rich."

"Yes, his father has plenty."

"Certainly, and gives it freely. But intends his son shall see none of it."

25 "His son? You dare not so much as mention him."

"Well, well, how strange! But they can never agree—not even upon their name. Is not that droll?—a man named General Villivicencio, and his son, Dr. Mossy!"

"Oh, that is nothing; it is only that the Doctor drops the
30 *de Villivicencio.*"

"Drops the *de Villivicencio?* but I think the *de Villivicencio* drops him, ho, ho, ho,—*diable!* "

Next to the residence of good Dr. Mossy towered the narrow, red-brick-front mansion of young Madame Délicieuse,
35 firm friend at once and always of those two antipodes, General Villivicencio and Dr. Mossy. Its dark, covered carriage-

way was ever rumbling, and, with nightfall, its drawing-rooms
always sent forth a luxurious light from the lace-curtained
windows of the second-story balconies.

It was one of the sights of the Rue Royale to see by night
its tall, narrow outline reaching high up toward the stars, 5
with all its windows aglow.

The Madame had had some tastes of human experience;
had been betrothed at sixteen (to a man she did not love,
"being at that time a fool," as she said); one summer day
at noon had been a bride, and at sundown—a widow. Acci- 10
dental discharge of the tipsy bridegroom's own pistol. Pass
it by! It left but one lasting effect on her, a special detesta-
tion of quarrels and weapons.

The little maidens whom poor parentage has doomed to sit
upon street door-sills and nurse their infant brothers have a 15
game of "choosing" the beautiful ladies who sweep by along
the pavement; but in Rue Royale there was no choosing;
every little damsel must own Madame Délicieuse or nobody,
and as that richly adorned and regal favorite of old General
Villivicencio came along they would lift their big, bold eyes 20
away up to her face and pour forth their admiration in a
universal—"Ah-h-h-h!"

But, mark you, she was good Madame Délicieuse as well
as fair Madame Délicieuse: her principles, however, not constructed in the austere Anglo-Saxon style, exactly (what need, 25
with the lattice of the Confessional not a stone's-throw off?).
Her kind offices and beneficent schemes were almost as
famous as General Villivicencio's splendid alms; if she could
at times do what the infantile Washington said he could not,
why, no doubt she and her friends generally looked upon it 30
as a mere question of enterprise.

She had charms, too, of intellect—albeit not such a sinner
against time and place as to be an "educated woman"—
charms that, even in a plainer person, would have brought
down the half of New Orleans upon one knee, with both 35
hands on the left side. *She* had the *whole* city at her feet,

and, with the fine tact which was the perfection of her character, kept it there contented. Madame was, in short, one of the kind that gracefully wrest from society the prerogative of doing as they please, and had gone even to such ex-
5 travagant lengths as driving out in the *Américain* faubourg, learning the English tongue, talking national politics, and similar freaks whereby she provoked the unbounded worship of her less audacious lady friends. In the center of the cluster of Creole beauties which everywhere gathered about her, and,
10 most of all, in those incomparable companies which assembled in her own splendid drawing-rooms, she was always queen lily. *Her* house, *her* drawing-rooms, etc.; for the little brown aunt who lived with her was a mere piece of curious furniture.

There was this notable charm about Madame Délicieuse,
15 she improved by comparison. She never looked so grand as when, hanging on General Villivicencio's arm at some gorgeous ball, these two bore down on you like a royal barge lashed to a ship-of-the-line. She never looked so like her sweet name, as when she seated all her prettiest lady adorers
20 close around her, and got them all a-laughing.

Of the two balconies which overhung the *banquette* on the front of the Délicieuse house, one was a small affair, and the other a deeper and broader one, from which Madame and her ladies were wont upon gala days to wave handkerchiefs and
25 cast flowers to the friends in the processions. There they gathered one Eighth of January morning to see the military display. It was a bright blue day, and the group that quite filled the balcony had laid wrappings aside, as all flower-buds are apt to do on such Creole January days, and shone
30 resplendent in spring attire.

The sightseers passing below looked up by hundreds and smiled at the ladies' eager twitter, as, flirting in humming-bird fashion from one subject to another, they laughed away the half-hours waiting for the pageant. By and by they fell
35 a-listening, for Madame Délicieuse had begun a narrative concerning Dr. Mossy. She sat somewhat above her listeners,

her elbow on the arm of her chair, and her plump white hand
waving now and then in graceful gesture, they silently attending with eyes full of laughter and lips starting apart.

"*Vous savez*," she said (they conversed in French of course),
"you know it is now long that Dr. Mossy and his father have
been in discord. Indeed, when have they not differed? For
when Mossy was but a little boy, his father thought it hard
that he was not a rowdy. He switched him once because he
would not play with his toy gun and drum. He was not *so*
high when his father wished to send him to Paris to enter the
French army; but he would not go. We used to play often
together on the *banquette*—for I am not so very many years
younger than he, no indeed—and, if I wanted some fun, I
had only to pull his hair and run into the house; he would
cry, and monsieur papa would come out with his hand spread
open and"—

Madame gave her hand a malicious little sweep, and joined
heartily in the laugh which followed.

"That was when they lived over the way. But wait! you
shall see; I have something. This evening the General"—

The houses of Rue Royale gave a start and rattled their
windows. In the long, irregular line of balconies the beauty
of the city rose up. Then the houses jumped again and the
windows rattled; Madame steps inside the window and gives
a message which the housemaid smiles at in receiving. As
she turns the houses shake again, and now again; and now
there comes a distant strain of trumpets, and by and by the
drums and bayonets and clattering hoofs, and plumes and
dancing banners; far down the long street stretch out the
shining ranks of gallant men, and the fluttering, overleaning
swarms of ladies shower down their sweet favors and wave
their countless welcomes.

In the front, towering above his captains, rides General
Villivicencio, veteran of 1814–1815, and, with the gracious
pomp of the old-time gentleman, lifts his cocked hat, and
bows, and bows.

Madame Délicieuse's balcony was a perfect maze of waving kerchiefs. The General looked up for the woman of all women; she was not there. But he remembered the other balcony, the smaller one, and cast his glance onward to it.
5 There he saw Madame and one other person only. A small blue-eyed, broad-browed, scholarly-looking man whom the arch lady had lured from his pen by means of a mock professional summons, and who now stood beside her, a smile of pleasure playing on his lips and about his eyes.

10 "*Vite!*" said Madame, as the father's eyes met the son's. Dr. Mossy lifted his arm and cast a bouquet of roses. A girl in the crowd bounded forward, caught it in the air, and, blushing, handed it to the plumed giant. He bowed low, first to the girl, then to the balcony above; and then, with a
15 responsive smile, tossed up two splendid kisses, one to Madame, and one, it seemed—

"For what was that cheer?"

"Why, did you not see? General Villivicencio cast a kiss to his son."

.   .   .   .

THOMAS NELSON PAGE

MEH LADY[1]

[Extract]

20 "Well, one night a curisome thing happen. We had done got mighty lean, what wid our mens an' Yankees an' all; an' de craps ain' come in, an' de team done gone, an' de fences done bu'nt up, an' things gettin' mighty down, I tell you. And dat night I wuz settin' out in de yard, jes' done finish
25 smokin', and studyin' 'bout gwine to bed. De sky wuz sort o' thick, an' meh mine wuz runnin' on my horses, an' pres'n'y, suh, I heah one on 'em gallopin' tobucket, tobucket, tobucket,

---

[1] Reprinted from *In Ole Virginia*, by permission of Charles Scribner's Sons, publishers.

right swif' 'long de parf' cross de fiel', an' I thought to myself,
I know Romilus' gallop; I set right still, an' he come 'cross
de branch and stop to drink jes' a moufful, an' den he come
up de hill, tobucket, tobucket, tobucket. I say, 'Dat hoss
got heap o' sense; he know he hot, an' he ain' gwine to hu't 5
hese'f drinkin', don' keer how thusty he is. He gwine up to
de stable now,' I say, 'an' I got to go up dyah an' le' him in;'
but 'stid o' dat, he tu'n 'roun' by de laundry, an' come close
roun' de house to whar I settin', an' stop, an' I wuz jes'
sayin', 'Well, ef dat don' beat any horse ever wuz in de wull; 10
how he know I heah?' when somebody say, 'Good-evenin'.'
Um-h! I sut'n'y wuz disapp'inted; dyah wuz a man settin'
dyah in de dark on a gre't black horse, an' say he wan' me to
show him de way th'oo de place. He ax me ef I warn' sleep,
an' I tell him, 'Nor, I jes' studyin';' den he ax me a whole 15
parecel o' questions 'bout Mistis and Marse Phil an' all, an'
say he kin to 'em an' he used to know Mistis a long time ago.
Den I ax him to 'light, an' tell him we'd all be mighty glad to
see him; but he say he 'bleeged to git right on; an' he keep
on axin' how dee wuz an' how dee been, an' ef dee sick an' all, 20
an' so 'quisitive; pres'n'y I ain' tell him no mo' 'sep' dat dee
all well 'skusin' Mistis; an' den he ax me to show him de way
th'oo, an' when I start, he ax me cyarn he go th'oo de yard,
dat de 'rection he warn' go, an' I tell him 'Yes,' an' le' him
th'oo de back gate, an' he ride 'cross de yard on de grahss. 25
As he ride by de rose-bush nigh de gate, he lean over, an' I
thought he breck a switch off, an' I tell him not to breck dat;
dat Meh Lady' rose-bush, whar she set mo' sto' by den all de
res'; an' he say, ''Tis a rose-bush, sho' 'nough,' an' he come
'long to de gate, holdin' a rose in he hand. Dyah he ax me 30
which is Mistis' room, an' I tell him, 'De one by de po'ch,'
an' he say he s'pose dee don' use upstyars much now de
fam'bly so small; an' I tell him, 'Nor,' dat Meh Lady' room
right next to Mistis' dis side, an' he stop an' look at de winder
good; den he come 'long to de gate, an' when I ax him which 35
way he gwine, he say, 'By de hewn-tree ford.' An' blessed

Gord! ef de wud ain' bring up things I done mos' forgit—dat gener'l ridin' up to de gate, an' Meh Lady standin' dyah, shadin' her eyes, wid de rose de Cap'n done gi' her off dat same bush, an' de gener'l say he envy him he prison. I see
5 him jes' plain as ef he standin' dyah befo' me, an' heah him axin' de way to de hewn-tree ford; but jes' den I heah some'n jingle, an' he jes' over an' poke some'n heavy in my hand, an' befo' I ken say a wud he gone gallopin' in de dark. And when I git back to de light, I find six gre't big yaller gold
10 pieces in meh hand, look like gre't pats o' butter, an' ef 't hadn' been for dat I'd 'mos' 'a' believe' 'twuz a dream; but dyah de money, an' dyah de horse-track, an' de limb done pull off Meh Lady' rose-bush.

"I hide de money in a ole sock onder de j'ice, and I p'int to
15 tell Meh Lady 'bout it; but Hannah, she say I ain' know who 'tis—(and so I ain' den); and I jes' gwine 'sturb Mistis wid folks ridin' 'bout th'oo de yard at night, and so I ain' say nuttin'; but when I heah Meh Lady grievin' bout somebody done breck her rose-bush an' steal one of her roses, I mighty
20 nigh tell her, an' I would, on'y I don't orn' aggrivate Hannah. You know 'twon't do to aggrivate women-folks.

"Well, 'twarn' no gre't while after dat de war broke; 'twuz de nex' spring 'bout plantin'-corn time, on'y we ain' plant much 'cause de team so weak; stealin' an' Yankee teckin'
25 together done clean us up, an' Mistis an' Meh Lady had to gi' a deed o' struss on de lan' to buy a new team dat spring, befo' we could breck up de corn-land, an' hadn' git mo' 'n half done fo' Richmon' fall an' de folks wuz all free; den de army parse th'oo an' some on 'em come by home, an' teck
30 ev'y blessed Gord's horse an' mule on de place, 'sep' one ole mule—George, whar wuz ole an' bline, an' dee won' have him. Dem wuz turrible times, an' ef Meh Lady an' Mistis didn' cry! not 'cause dee teck de horses an' mules—we done get use' to dat, an' dat jes' meck 'em mad and high-sperited—
35 but 'cause Richmon' done fall an' Gener'l Lee surrendered. Ef dee didn' cry! When Richmon' fall dee wuz 'stonished, but

dee say dat ain' meck no diffunce, Gener'l Lee gwine whip 'em yit; but when dee heah Gener'l Lee done surrender dee gin up; fust dee wouldn' b'lieve it, but dee sut'n'y wuz strusted. Dee grieve 'bout dat 'mos' much as when Marse Phil die. Mistis she ain' nuver rekiver. She wuz al'ays sickly and in bed after dat, and Meh Lady and Hannah dee use' to nuss her.

"After de fust year or so mos' o' de folks went away. Meh Lady she tell 'em dee better go, dat dee'l fine dem kin do mo' for 'em 'en she kin now; heap on 'em say dee ain' gwine 'way, but after we so po' dee went 'way, dthough Meh Lady sell some Mistis' diamonds to buy 'em some'n to eat while dee dyah.

"Well, 'twan' so ve'y long after dis, or maybe 'twuz befo', 'twuz jes' after Richmon' fall, Mistis get a letter fum de Cun'l—dat's Cap'n Wilton; he done Cun'l den,—tellin' her he want her to le' him come down an' see her an' Meh Lady, an' he been love Meh Lady all de time sence he wounded heah in de war, an' al'ays will love her, an' won' she le' him help her any way; dat he owe Mistis an' Meh Lady he life. Hannah heah 'em read it. De letter 'sturb Mistis might'ly, an' she jes' put it in Meh Lady' han's an' tu'n 'way widout a wud.

"Meh Lady, Hannah say, set right still a minute an' look mighty solemn; den she look at Mistis sort o' sideways, an' den she say, 'Tell him, No.' An' Mistis went over an' kiss her right sorf.

"An' dat evenin' I cyar de letter whar Mistis write to de office.

"Well, 'twarn' so much time after dat dee begin to sue Mistis on Marster's debts. We heah dee suin' her in de co't, an' Mistis she teck to her bed reg'lar wid so much trouble, an' say she hope she won' nuver live to see de place sold, an' Meh Lady she got to byah ev'ything. She used to sing to Mistis an' read to her an' try to hearten her up, meckin' out dat 'tain' meck no diffunce. Hit did do', an' she know it,

'cause we po' now, sho' 'nough; an' dee wuz po'er 'n Hannah an' me, 'cause de lan' ain' got nobody to wuck it an' no team to wuck it wid, an' we ain' know who it b'longst to, an' hit done all grow up in bushes an' blackberry briers; ev'y year
5 hit grow up mo' an' mo', an' we gittin' po'er an' po'er. Mistis she boun' to have flour, ain' been use' to nuttin' but de fines' bread, jes' as white as you' shu't, an' she so sickly now she got to have heap o' things, tell Meh Lady fyar at her wits' een to git 'em. Dat's all I ever see her cry 'bout, when she
10 ain' got nuttin' to buy what Mistis want. She use' to cry 'bout dat dthough. But Mistis ain' know nottin' 'bout dat: she think Meh Lady got heap mo' 'n she is, bein' shet up in her room now all de time. De doctor say she got 'sumption, an' Meh Lady doin' all she kin to keep 't fum her how po'
15 we is, smilin' an' singin' fur her. She jes' whah herse'f out wid it, nussin' her, wuckin' fur her, singin' to her. Hit used to hu't me sometimes to heah de chile singin' of a evenin' things she use' to sing in ole times, like she got ev'ything on uth same as befo' de war, an' I know she jes' singin' to ease
20 Mistis' mine, an' maybe she hongry right now.

"'Twuz den I went an' git de rest o' de money de Cap'n gi' me dat night fum onder de j'ice (I had done spend right smart chance on it gittin' things, meckin' b'lieve I meck it on de farm), an' I put it in meh ole hat an' cyar it to Meh Lady,
25 'cause it sort o' hern anyways, an' her face sort o' light up when she see de gold shinin', 'cause she sut'n'y had use for it, an' she ax me whar I git so much money, an' I tell her some-body gi' 't to me, an' she say what I gwine do wid it. An' I tell her it hern, an' she say how, an' I tell her I owe it to her
30 for rent, an' she bu'st out cryin' so she skeer me. She say she owe me an' her mammy ev'ything in de wull, an' she know we jes' stayin' wid 'em 'cause dee helpless, an' sich things, an' she cry so I upped an' tole her how I come by de money, an' she stop an' listen good. Den she say she cyarn'
35 tech a cent o' dat money, an' she oodn', mon, tell I tell her I wan' buy de mule; an' she say she consider him mine now,

an' ef he ain' she gi' him to me, an' I say, nor, I wan' buy him.
Den she say how much he wuth, an' I say, he wuth a hundred
dollars, but I ain' got dat much right now, I kin owe her de
res'; an' she breck out laughin', like when she wuz a little
girl an' would begin to laugh ef you please her, wid de tears 5
on her face an' dress, sort o' April-like. Hit gratify me so, I
keep on at it, but she say she'll teck twenty dollars for de
mule, an' no mo', an' I say I ain' gwine disqualify dat mule
wid no sich price; den pres'n'y we 'gree on forty dollars, an'
I pay it to her, an' she sont me up to Richmon' next day to git 10
things for Mistis, an' she al'ays meck it a p'int after dat to
feed George a little some'n' ev'y day.

"Den she teck de school; did you know 'bout dat? Dat
de school-house right down de road a little piece. I reckon
you see it as you come 'long. I ain' b'lieve it when I heah 15
'em say Meh Lady gwine teach it. I say, 'She teach niggers!
dat she ain'! not my young mistis.' But she laugh at me an'
Hannah, an' say she been teachin' de colored chil'n all her
life, ain' she? an' she wan' Hannah an' me to ease Mistis'
min' 'bout it ef she say anything. I sut'n'y was 'posed to 20
it, do'; an' de colored chil'n she been teachin' wuz diffunt—
dee b'longst to her. But she al'ays so sot on doin' what she
gwine do, she meck you b'lieve she right don' keer what 'tis;
an' I tell her pres'n'y, all right, but ef dem niggers impident
to her, jes' le' me know an' I'll come down dyah an' wyah 25
'em out. So she went reg'lar, walk right 'long dis ve'y parf
wid her books an' her little basket. An' sometimes I'd bring
de mule for her to ride home ef she been up de night befo'
wid Mistis; but she wouldn' ride much, 'cause she think
George got to wuck.   30

"Tell 'long in de spring Meh Lady she done breck down,
what wid teachin' school, an' settin' up, and bein' so po',
stintin' for Mistis, an' her face gittin' real white 'stid o' pink
like peach-blossom, as it used to be, on'y, her eyes dee bigger
an' prettier 'n ever, 'sep' dee look tired when she come out o' 35
Mistis' chahmber an' lean 'g'inst de do', lookin' out down de

lonesome road; an' de doctor whar come from Richmon' to
see Mistis, 'cause de ain' no doctor in the neighborhood sence
de war, tell Hannah when he went 'way de larst time 'tain' no
hope for Mistis, she mos' gone, an' she better look mighty
5 good after Meh Lady too; he say she mos' sick as Mistis, an'
fust thing she know she'll be gone too. Dat 'sturb Hannah
might'ly. Well, so 'twuz tell in de spring. I had done plant
meh corn, an' it hed done come up right good; 'bout mos'
eight acres, right below the barn whar de lan' strong (I
10 couldn' put in no mo' 'cause de mule he wuz mighty ole);
an' come a man down heah one mornin', riding a sway-back
sorrel horse, an' say dee gwine sell de place in 'bout a mon'.
Meh Lady hed gone to school, an' I ain' le' him see Mistis,
nor tell him whar Meh Lady is nuther; I jes' teck de message
15 an' call Hannah so as she kin git it straight; an' when Meh
Lady come home dat evenin' I tell her. She sut'n'y did tu'n
white, an' dat night she ain' sleep a wink. After she put her
ma to sleep, she come out to her mammy' house, an' fling
herself on Hannah' bed an' cry an' cry. 'Twuz jes' as ef her
20 heart gwine breck; she say 'twould kill her ma, an' hit did.

"Mistis she boun' to heah 'bout it, 'cause Meh Lady
'bleeged to breck it to her now; and at fust it 'peared like
she got better on it, she teck mo' noticement o' ev'ything, an'
her eyes look bright and shiny. She ain' know not yit 'bout
25 how hard Meh Lady been had to scuffle; she say she keep on
after her to git herse'f some new clo'es, a dress an' things, an'
she oont; an' Meh Lady would jes' smile, tired like, an' say
she teachin' now, and don' want no mo' 'n she got, an' her
smile meck me mos' sorry like she cryin'.

30 "So hit went on tell jes' befo' de sale. An' one day Meh
Lady she done lef' her ma settin' in her cheer by de winder,
whar she done fix her good wid pillows, an' she done gone to
school, an' Hannah come out whar I grazin' de mule on de
ditch-bank, an' say Mistis wan' see me toreckly. I gi' Han-
35 nah de lines, an' I went an' knock at de do', an' when Mistis
ain' heah, I went an' knock at de chamber do' an' she tell me

to come in; an' I ax her how she is, an' she say she ain' got
long to stay wid us, an' she wan' ax me some'n, and she
wan' me tell her de truth, an' she say I al'ays been mighty
faithful an' kind to her an' hern, an' she hope Gord will
erward me an' Hannah for it, an' she wan' me now to tell her   5
de truth. When she talk dat way, hit sut'n'y hu't me, an' I
tole her I sut'n'y would tell her faithful. Den she went on
an' ax me how we wuz gettin' on, an' ef we ain' been mighty
po', an' ef Meh Lady ain' done stint herse'f more 'n she ever
know; an' I tell her all 'bout it, ev'ything jes' like it wuz—   10
de fatal truth, 'cause I done promised her; an' she sut'n'y
was grieved, I tell you, an' the tears roll down an' drap off
her face on de pillow; an' pres'n'y she say she hope Gord
would forgive her, an' she teck out her breast dem little rocks
Marster gi' her when she married, whar hed been old Mistis',   15
an' she say she gin up all the urrs, but dese she keep to
gi' Meh Lady when she married, an' now she feared 'twuz
pride, an' Gord done punish her, lettin' her chile starve, but
she ain' know hit 'zactly, an' ign'ance he forgive; an' she
went on an' talk 'bout Marster an' ole times when she fust   20
come home a bride, an' 'bout Marse Phil an' Meh Lady,
tell she leetle mo' breck my heart, an' de tears rain down my
face on de flo'. She sut'n'y talk beautiful. Den she gi' me de
diamonds, an' dee shine like a handful of lightning-bugs! an'
she tell me to teck 'em an' teck keer on 'em, an' gi' 'em to   25
Meh Lady some time after she gone, an' not le' nobody else
have 'em; an' wouldn' me an' Hannah teck good keer o' her,
an' stay wid her, and not le' her wuck so hard, an' I tell her
we sut'n'y would do dat. Den her voice mos' gin out an' she
'peared mighty tired, but hit look like she got some'n still on   30
her min', an' pres'n'y she say I mus' come close, she mighty
tired; an' I sort o' ben' todes her, an' she say she wan' me
after she gone, as soon as I kin, to get the wud to Meh Lady's
cousin whar wuz heah wounded indurin' o' de war dat *she*
dead, an' dat ef he kin help her chile, an' be her pertector,   35
she know he'll do it; an' I ain' to le' Meh Lady know nuttin'

'bout it, not nuttin' 't all, an' to tell him he been mighty good
to her, an' she lef' him her blessin'. Den she git so faint, I
run an' call Hannah, an' she come runnin' an' gi' her some
sperrits, an' tell me to teck de mule an' go after Meh Lady

5 toreckly, an' so I did. When she got dyah, do', Mistis done
mos' speechless; Hannah hed done git her in de bed, which
wan't no trouble, she so light. She know Meh Lady, do';
an' try to speak to her two or th'ee times, but dee ain' meck
out much mo' 'n Gord would bless her and teck keer on her;

10 an' she die right easy jes' befo' mornin'. An' Meh Lady ax me
to pray, an' I did. She sut'n'y die peaceful, an' she look jes'
like she smilin' after she dead; she sut'n'y wuz ready to go.

"Well, Hannah and Meh Lady lay her out in her bes'
frock, an' she sho'ly look younger 'n I ever see her look sence

15 Richmon' fell, ef she ain' look younger 'n she look sence
befo' de war; an' de neighbors, de few dat's lef', an' de black
folks roun' cum, an' we bury her de evenin' after in the
gyardin' right side Marse Phil, her fust-born, whar we know
she wan' be; an' her mammy she went in de house after dat

20 to stay at night in the room wid Meh Lady, an' I sleep on the
front po'ch to teck keer de house. 'Cause we sut'n'y wuz
'sturbed 'bout de chile; she ain' sleep an' she ain' eat an' she
ain' cry none, an' Hannah say dat ain' reasonable, which
'tain't, 'cause womens dee cry sort o' natchel.

25 "But so 'twuz; de larst time she cry wuz dat evenin' she
come in Hannah' house, an' fling herse'f on de bed, an' cry
so grievous 'cause dee gwine sell de place, an' 'twould kill
her ma. She ain' cry no mo'!

"Well, after we done bury Mistis, as I wuz sayin', we

30 sut'n'y wuz natchelly tossified 'bout Meh Lady. Hit look
like what de doctor say wuz sut'n'y so, an' she gwine right
after her ma.

"I try to meck her ride de mule to school, an' tell her I
ain' got no use for him, I got to thin de corn: but she oodn't;

35 she say he so po' she don' like to gi' him no mo' wuck 'n
necessary; an' dat's de fact, he wuz mighty po' 'bout den,

'cause de feed done gi' out an' de grass ain' come good yit,
and when mule bline an' ole he mighty hard to git up; but
he been a good mule in he time, an' he a good mule yit.

"So she'd go to school of a mornin', an' me or Hannah
one'd go to meet her of a evenin' to tote her books, 'cause she 5
hardly able to tote herse'f den; an' she do right well at school
(de chil'un all love her); 'twuz when she got home she so
sufferin'; den her mind sort o' wrastlin' wid itself, an' she
jes' set down an' think an' study an' look so grieved. Hit
sut'n'y did hu't me an' Hannah to see her settin' dyah at de 10
winder o' Mistis' chahmber, leanin' her head on her han' an'
jes' lookin' out all de evenin' so lonesome, and she look beautiful too. Hannah say she grievin' herself to death.

"Well, dat went on for mo' 'n six weeks, and de chile jes'
settin' dyah ev'y night all by herse'f wid de moonlight shinin' 15
all over her, meckin' her look so pale. Hannah she tell me
one night I got to do some'n, an' I say, 'What 'tis?' An' she
say I got to git de wud dat Mistis say to de Cap'n, dat de
chile need a pertector, an' I say, 'How?' And she say I got
to write a letter. Den I say, 'I cyarn' neither read nor write, 20
but I can get Meh Lady to write it;' an' she say, nor I cyarn',
'cause ain' Mistis done spressify partic'lar Meh Lady ain' to
know nuttin' 'bout it? Den I say, 'I kin git somebody at de
post-office to write it, an' I kin pay 'em in eggs;' an' she say
she ain' gwine have no po' white folks writin' an' spearin' 25
'bout Mistis' business. Den I say, 'How I gwine do den?'
An' she study a little while, an' den she say I got to teck de
mule an' go fine him. I say, 'Hi! Good Gord! Hannah, how
I gwine fine him? De Cap'n live 'way up yander in New
York, or somewhar or nuther, an' dat's further 'n Lynch- 30
bu'g, an' I'll ride de mule to death befo' I git dyah; besides
I ain' got nothin' to feed him.'

"But Hannah got argiment to all dem wuds; she say I got
tongue in meh head, an' I kin fine de way; an' as to ridin' de
mule to death, I kin git down an' le' him res', or I kin lead 35
him, an' I kin graze him side de road ef nobody oon le' me

graze him in dee pahsture. Den she study little while, an'
den say she got it now—I must go to Richmon' an' sell de
mule, an' teck de money an' git on de kyars an' fine him.
Hannah, I know, she gwine wuck it, 'cause she al'ays a power-
5 ful han' to 'ravel anything. But it sut'n'y did hu't me to part
wid dat mule, he sich a ambitious mule, an' I tell Hannah I
ain' done sidin' meh corn; an' she say dat ain' meck no
diff'unce, she gwine hoe de corn after I gone, and de chile
grievin' so she feared she'll die, an' what good sidin' corn
10 gwine do den? she grievin' mo' 'n she 'quainted wid, Hannah
say. So I wuz to go to Richmon' nex' mornin' but one, befo'
light, an' Hannah she wash meh shu't nex' day, an' cook meh
rations while Meh Lady at school. Well, I knock off wuck
right early nex' evenin' 'bout two hours be sun, 'cause I wan'
15 rest de mule, an' after grazin' him for a while in de yard, I put
him in he stall, an' gi' him a half-peck o' meal, 'cause dat de
lahst night I gwine feed him; and soon as I went in wid de
meal, he swi'ch his tail an' hump hese'f jes' like he gwine
kick me; dat's de way he al'ays do when he got anything
20 'g'inst you, 'cause you sich a fool or anything, 'cause mule
got a heap o' sense when you know 'em. Well, I think he
jes' aggrivated 'cause I gwine sell him, an' I holler at him
right ambitious like I gwine cut him in two, to fool him ef
I kin, an' meck him b'lieve 'tain' nothin' de matter.

25 "An' jes' den I heah a horse steppin' 'long right brisk, an'
I stop an' listen, an' de horse come 'long de pahf right study
an' up todes de stable. I say, 'Hi! who dat?' an' when I
went to de stall do', dyah wuz a gent'man settin' on a strange
horse wid two white foots, an' a beard on he face, an' he hat
30 pulled over he eyes to keep de sun out'n 'em; an' when he
see me, he ride on up to de stable, an' ax me is Meh Lady at
de house, an' how she is, an' a whole parcel o' questions; an
he so p'inted in he quiration I ain' had time to study ef I
ever see him befo', but I don' think I is. He a mighty straight,
35 fine-lookin' gent'man do', wid he face right brown like he
been wuckin', an' I ain' able to fix him no ways. Den he

tell me he heah o' Mistis' death, an' he jes' come 'cross de
ocean, an' he wan' see Meh Lady partic'lar; an' I tell him she
at school, but it mos' time for her come back; an' he ax
whichaways, an' I show him de pahf, an' he git down an' ax
me ef I cyarn' feed he horse, an' I tell him of co'se, do' Gord 5
knows I ain' got nuttin' to feed him wid 'sep' grahss; but I
ain' gwine le' him know dat, so I ax him to walk to de house
an' teck a seat on de po'ch tell Meh Lady come, an' I teck
de horse and cyar him in de stable like I got de corn-house
full o' corn. An' when I come out I look, an' dyar he gwine 10
stridin' 'way 'cross de fiel' 'long de pahf whar Meh Lady
comin'.

"Well, I say, 'Hi! now he gwine to meet Meh Lady, an' I
ain' know he name nur what he want,' an' I study a little
while wherr I should go an' fin' Hannah or hurry myse'f an' 15
meet Meh Lady. Not dat I b'lieve he gwine speak out de
way to Meh Lady, 'cause he sut'n'y wuz quality, I see dat;
I know hit time I look at him settin' dyah so straight on he
horse, 'mindin' me of Marse Phil, and he voice hit sholy wuz
easy when he name Meh Lady' name and Mistis'; but I ain' 20
know but what he somebody wan' to buy de place, an' I know
Meh Lady ain' wan' talk 'bout dat, an' ain' wan' see strangers
no way; so I jes' lip out 'cross de fiel' th'oo a nigher way to
hit de pahf at dis ve'y place whar de gap wuz, an' whar I
thought Meh Lady mighty apt to res' ef she tired or grievin'. 25

"An' I hurry 'long right swift to git heah befo' de white
gent'man kin git heah, an' all de time I tu'nnin' in meh min'
whar I heah anybody got voice sound deep an' cl'ar like dat,
an' ax questions ef Meh Lady well, dat anxious, an' I cyarn'
git it. An' by dat time I wuz done got right to de tu'n in de 30
pahf dyah, mos' out of breaf, an' jes' as I tu'nned round dat
clump o' bushes I see Meh Lady settin' right dyah on de
'bankment whar de gap use' to be, wid her books by her side
on de groun', her hat off at her feet, an' her head leanin'
for'ard in her han's, an' her hyah mos' tumble down, an' de 35
sun jes' techin' it th'oo de bushes; an' hit all come to me in a

minute, jes' as clear as ef she jes' settin' on de gap dyah
yistidy wid de rose-leaves done shatter all on de groun' by
her, an' Cap'n Wilton kissin' her han' to comfort her, an'
axin' her oon' she le' him come back some time to love her.
An' I say, 'Dyah! 'fo' Gord! ef I ain' know him soon as I lay
meh eyes on him! De pertector done come!' Den I know
huccome dat mule act so 'sponsible.

"An' jes' den he come walkin' long down de pahf, wid he
hat on de back o' he head an' he eyes on her right farst, an'
he face look so tender hit look right sweet. She think hit me,
an' she ain' move nor look up tell he call her name; den she
mos' jump out her seat, and look up right swift, an' give a
sort o' cry, an' her face light up like she tu'n 't to de sun, an'
he retch out bofe he han's to her; an' I slip' back so he
couldn' see me, an' come 'long home right quick to tell
Hannah."

HELEN HUNT JACKSON

RAMONA[1]

Chapter XIV

[Alessandro's Return]

It was sunset of the eighteenth day since Alessandro's departure. Ramona had lain for four days well-nigh motionless on her bed. She herself began to think she must be going
to die. Her mind seemed to be vacant of all thought. She
did not even sorrow for Alessandro's death; she seemed tor-
pid, body and soul. Such prostrations as these are Nature's
enforced rests. It is often only by help of them that our
bodies tide over crises, strains, in which, if we continued
to battle, we should be slain.

As Ramona lay half conscious,—neither awake nor yet
asleep,—on this evening, she was suddenly aware of a vivid

[1] Copyrighted by Little, Brown & Company, publishers.

impression produced upon her; it was not sound, it was not
sight. She was alone; the house was still as death; the warm
September twilight silence reigned outside. She sat up in
her bed, intent—half alarmed—half glad—bewildered—alive.
What had happened? Still there was no sound, no stir. The 5
twilight was fast deepening; not a breath of air moving.
Gradually her bewildered senses and faculties awoke from
their long-dormant condition; she looked around the room;
even the walls seemed revivified; she clasped her hands, and
leaped from the bed. "Alessandro is not dead!" she said 10
aloud; and she laughed hysterically. "He is not dead!" she
repeated. "He is not dead! He is somewhere near!"

With quivering hands she dressed, and stole out of the
house. After the first few seconds she found herself strangely
strong; she did not tremble; her feet trod firm on the ground. 15
"Oh, miracle!" she thought, as she hastened down the garden-
walk; "I am well again! Alessandro is near!" So vivid was
the impression, that when she reached the willows and found
the spot silent, vacant, as when she had last sat there, hopeless, broken-hearted, she experienced a revulsion of disap- 20
pointment. "Not here!" she cried; "not here!" and a swift
fear shook her. "Am I mad? Is it this way, perhaps, people
lose their senses, when they are as I have been!"

But the young, strong blood was running swift in her veins.
No! this was no madness; rather a newly discovered power; 25
a fullness of sense; a revelation. Alessandro was near.

Swiftly she walked down the river road. The farther she
went, the keener grew her expectation, her sense of Alessandro's nearness. In her present mood she would have walked
on and on, even to Temecula itself, sure that she was at each 30
step drawing nearer to Alessandro. As she approached the
second willow copse, which lay perhaps a quarter of a mile
west of the first, she saw the figure of a man, standing, leaning against one of the trees. She halted. It could not be
Alessandro. He would not have paused for a moment so 35
near the house where he was to find her. She was afraid to

go on. It was late to meet a stranger in this lonely spot. The figure was strangely still; so still that, as she peered through the dusk, she half fancied it might be an optical illusion. She advanced a few steps, hesitatingly, then stopped. As she did so, the man advanced a few steps, then stopped. As he came out from the shadows of the trees, she saw that he was of Alessandro's height. She quickened her steps, then suddenly stopped again. What did this mean? It could not be Alessandro. Ramona wrung her hands in agony of suspense. An almost unconquerable instinct urged her forward; but terror held her back. After standing irresolute for some minutes, she turned to walk back to the house, saying, "I must not run the risk of its being a stranger. If it is Alessandro, he will come."

But her feet seemed to refuse to move in the opposite direction. Slower and slower she walked for a few paces, then turned again. The man had returned to his former place, and stood as at first, leaning against the tree.

"It may be a messenger from him," she said; "a messenger who has been told not to come to the house until after dark."

Her mind was made up. She quickened her pace to a run. A few moments more brought her so near that she could see distinctly. It was—yes, it was Alessandro. He did not see her. His face was turned partially away, his head resting against the tree; he must be ill. Ramona flew, rather than ran. In a moment more, Alessandro had heard the light steps, turned, saw Ramona, and, with a cry, bounded forward, and they were clasped in each other's arms before they had looked in each other's faces. Ramona spoke first. Disengaging herself gently, and looking up, she began: "Alessandro—" But at the first sight of his face she shrieked. Was this Alessandro, this haggard, emaciated, speechless man, who gazed at her with hollow eyes, full of misery, and no joy! "O God," cried Ramona, "you have been ill! you are ill! My God, Alessandro, what is it?"

Alessandro passed his hand slowly over his forehead, as if trying to collect his thoughts before speaking, all the while keeping his eyes fixed on Ramona, with the same anguished look, convulsively holding both her hands in his.

"Señorita," he said, "my Señorita!" Then he stopped. His tongue seemed to refuse him utterance; and this voice, —this strange, hard, unresonant voice,—whose voice was it? Not Alessandro's.

"My Señorita," he began again, "I could not go without one sight of your face; but when I was here, I had not courage to go near the house. If you had not come, I should have gone back without seeing you."

Ramona heard these words in fast-deepening terror. What did they mean? Her look seemed to suggest a new thought to Alessandro.

"Heavens, Señorita!" he cried, "have you not heard? Do you not know what has happened?"

"I know nothing, love," answered Ramona. "I have heard nothing since you went away. For ten days I have been sure you were dead; but to-night something told me that you were near, and I came to meet you."

At the first words of Ramona's sentence, Alessandro threw his arms around her again. As she said "love," his whole frame shook with emotion.

"My Señorita!" he whispered, "my Señorita! how shall I tell you! How shall I tell you!"

"What is there to tell, Alessandro?" she said. "I am afraid of nothing, now that you are here, and not dead, as I thought."

But Alessandro did not speak. It seemed impossible. At last, straining her closer to his breast, he cried: "Dearest Señorita! I feel as if I should die when I tell you,—I have no home; my father is dead; my people are driven out of their village. I am only a beggar now, Señorita; like those you used to feed and pity in Los Angeles convent!" As he spoke the last words, he reeled, and, supporting himself against the tree, added: "I am not strong, Señorita; we have been starving."

Ramona's face did not reassure him. Even in the dusk he could see its look of incredulous horror. He misread it.

"I only came to look at you once more," he continued. "I will go now. May the saints bless you, my Señorita, always. I think the Virgin sent you to me to-night. I should never have seen your face if you had not come."

While he was speaking, Ramona had buried her face in his bosom. Lifting it now, she said, "Did you mean to leave me to think you were dead, Alessandro?"

"I thought that the news about our village must have reached you," he said, "and that you would know I had no home, and could not come, to seem to remind you of what you had said. Oh, Señorita, it was little enough I had before to give you! I don't know how I dared to believe that you could come to be with me; but I loved you so much, I had thought of many things I could do; and—" lowering his voice and speaking almost sullenly—"it is the saints, I believe, who have punished me thus for having resolved to leave my people, and take all I had for myself and you. Now they have left me nothing;" and he groaned.

"Who?" cried Ramona. "Was there a battle? Was your father killed?" She was trembling with horror.

"No," answered Alessandro. "There was no battle. There would have been, if I had had my way; but my father implored me not to resist. He said it would only make it worse for us in the end. The sheriff, too, he begged me to let it all go on peaceably, and help him keep the people quiet. He felt terribly to have to do it. It was Mr. Rothsaker, from San Diego. We had often worked for him on his ranch. He knew all about us. Don't you recollect, Señorita, I told you about him,—how fair he always was, and kind too? He has the biggest wheat-ranch in Cajon; we've harvested miles and miles of wheat for him. He said he would have rather died, almost, than have had it to do; but if we resisted, he would have to order his men to shoot. He had twenty men with him. They thought there would be trouble; and well they might,—turning a whole village full of men and women and children out of their houses, and driving them off like foxes. If it had been any man but Mr. Rothsaker, I would have shot him dead, if I had hung for it; but I knew if he thought we must go, there was no help for us."

"But, Alessandro," interrupted Ramona, "I can't understand. Who was it made Mr. Rothsaker do it? Who has the land now?"

"I don't know who they are," Alessandro replied, his voice full of anger and scorn. "They're Americans,—eight or ten of them. They all got together and brought a suit, they call it, up in San Francisco; and it was decided in the court that they owned all our land. That was all Mr. Rothsaker could tell about it. It was the law, he said, and nobody could go against the law."

"Oh," said Ramona, "that's the way the Americans took so much of the Señora's land away from her. It was in the court up in San Francisco; and they decided that miles and miles of her land, which the General had always had, was not hers at all. They said it belonged to the United States Government."

"They are a pack of thieves and liars, every one of them!" cried Alessandro. "They are going to steal all the land in this country; we might all just as well throw ourselves into the sea, and let them have it. My father has been telling me this for years. He saw it coming; but I did not believe him. I did not think men could be so wicked; but he was right. I am glad he is dead. That is the only thing I have to be thankful for now. One day I thought he was going to get well, and I prayed to the Virgin not to let him. I did not want him to live. He never knew anything clear after they took him out of his house. That was before I got there. I found him sitting on the ground outside. They said it was the sun that had turned him crazy; but it was not. It was his heart breaking in his bosom. He would not come out of his house, and the men lifted him up and carried him out by force, and threw him on the ground; and then they threw out all the furniture we had; and when he saw them doing that, he put his hands up to his head, and called out, 'Alessandro! Alessandro!' and I was not there! Señorita, they said it was a voice to make the dead hear, that he called with; and nobody could stop him. All that day and all the night he kept on calling. God! Señorita, I wonder I did not die when they told me! When I got there, someone had built up a little booth of tule over his head, to keep the sun off. He did not call any more, only for water, water. That was what made them think the sun had done it. They did all they could; but it was such a dreadful time, nobody could do much; the sheriff's men were in great hurry; they gave no time. They said the people must all be off in two days. Everybody was running hither and thither. Everything out of the houses in piles on the ground. The people took all the roofs off their houses too. They were made of the tule reeds; so they would do again. Oh, Señorita, don't ask me to tell you any more! It is like death. I can't!"

Ramona was crying bitterly. She did not know what to say. What was love, in face of such calamity? What had she to give to a man stricken like this?

"Don't weep, Señorita," said Alessandro, drearily. "Tears kill one, and do no good."

"How long did your father live?" asked Ramona, clasping her arms closer around his neck. They were sitting on the ground now, and Ramona, yearning over Alessandro, as if she were the strong one and he the one to be sheltered, had drawn his head to her bosom, caressing him as if he had been hers for years. Nothing could have so clearly shown his enfeebled and benumbed condition, as the manner in which he received these caresses, which once would have made him beside himself with joy. He leaned against her breast as a child might.

"He! He died only four days ago. I stayed to bury him, and then I came away. I have been three days on the way; the horse, poor beast, is almost weaker than I. The Americans took my horse," Alessandro said.

"Took your horse!" cried Ramona, aghast. "Is that the 5 law, too?"

"So Mr. Rothsaker told me. He said the judge had said he must take enough of our cattle and horses to pay all it had cost for the suit up in San Francisco. They didn't reckon the cattle at what they were worth, I thought; but they said 10 cattle were selling very low now. There were not enough in all the village to pay it, so we had to make it up in horses; and they took mine. I was not there the day they drove the cattle away, or I would have put a ball into Benito's head before any American should ever have had him to ride. But 15 I was over in Pachanga with my father. He would not stir a step for anybody but me; so I led him all the way; and then after he got there he was so ill I never left him a minute. He did not know me any more, nor know anything that had happened. I built a little hut of tule, and he lay on the ground 20 till he died. When I put him in his grave, I was glad."

"In Temecula?" asked Ramona.

"In Temecula!" exclaimed Alessandro, fiercely. "You don't seem to understand, Señorita. We have no right in Temecula, not even to our graveyard full of the dead. Mr. Rothsaker 25 warned us all not to be hanging about there; for he said the men who were coming in were a rough set, and they would shoot any Indian at sight, if they saw him trespassing on their property."

"Their property!" ejaculated Ramona. 30

"Yes; it is theirs," said Alessandro, doggedly. "That is the law. They've got all the papers to show it. That is what my father always said,—if the Señor Valdez had only given him a paper! But they never did in those days. Nobody had papers. The American law is different." 35

"It's a law of thieves!" cried Ramona.

"Yes, and of murderers too," said Alessandro. "Don't you call my father murdered just as much as if they had shot him? I do! And, O Señorita, my Señorita, there was José! You recollect José, who went for my violin? But, my beloved one, I am killing you with these terrible things! I will speak no more."

"No, no, Alessandro. Tell me all, all. You must have no grief I do not share. Tell me about José," cried Ramona, breathlessly.

"Señorita, it will break your heart to hear. José was married a year ago. He had the best house in Temecula, next to my father's. It was the only other one that had a shingled roof. And he had a barn too, and that splendid horse he rode, and oxen, and a flock of sheep. He was at home when the sheriff came. A great many of the men were away, grape-picking. That made it worse. But José was at home; for his wife had a little baby only a few weeks old, and the child seemed sickly and not like to live, and José would not leave it. José was the first one that saw the sheriff riding into the village, and the band of armed men behind him, and José knew what it meant. He had often talked it over with me and with my father, and now he saw that it had come; and he went crazy in one minute, and fell on the ground all froth at his mouth. He had had a fit like that once before; and the doctor said if he had another, he would die. But he did not. They picked him up, and presently he was better; and Mr. Rothsaker said nobody worked so well in the moving the first day as José did. Most of the men would not lift a hand. They sat on the ground with the women, and covered up their faces, and would not see. But José worked; and, Señorita, one of the first things he did, was to run with my father's violin to the store, to Mrs. Hartsel, and ask her to hide it for us; José knew it was worth money. But before noon the second day he had another fit, and died in it,—died right in his own door, carrying out some of the things; and after Carmena—that's his wife's name—saw he was dead, she never spoke, but sat rocking back and forth on the ground, with the baby in her arms. She went over to Pachanga at the same time I did with my father. It was a long procession of us."

"Where is Pachanga?" asked Ramona.   5

"About three miles from Temecula, a little sort of cañon. I told the people they'd better move over there; the land did not belong to anybody, and perhaps they could make a living there. There isn't any water; that's the worst of it."

"No water!" cried Ramona.   10

"No running water. There is one little spring, and they dug a well by it as soon as they got there; so there was water to drink, but that is all. I saw Carmena could hardly keep up, and I carried the baby for her on one arm, while I led my father with the other hand; but the baby cried, so she took it 15 back. I thought then it wouldn't live the day out; but it did live till the morning of the day my father died. Just a few hours before he died, Carmena came along with the baby rolled up in her shawl, and sat down by me on the ground, and did not speak. When I said, 'How is the little one?' 20 she opened her shawl and showed it to me, dead. 'Good, Carmena!' said I. 'It is good! My father is dying too. We will bury them together.' So she sat by me all that morning, and at night she helped me dig the graves. I wanted to put the baby on my father's breast; but she said, no, it must 25 have a little grave. So she dug it herself; and we put them in; and she never spoke, except that once. She was sitting there by the grave when I came away. I made a cross of two little trees with the boughs chopped off, and set it up by the graves. So that is the way our new graveyard was begun,— 30 my father and the little baby; it is the very young and the very old that have the blessed fortune to die. I cannot die, it seems!"

"Where did they bury José?" gasped Ramona.

"In Temecula," said Alessandro. "Mr. Rothsaker made 35 two of his men dig a grave in our old graveyard for José. But

I think Carmena will go at night and bring his body away.
I would! But, my Señorita, it is very dark, I can hardly see
your beloved eyes. I think you must not stay longer. Can
I go as far as the brook with you, safely, without being seen?
5 The saints bless you, beloved, for coming. I could not have
lived, I think, without one more sight of your face;" and,
springing to his feet, Alessandro stood waiting for Ramona
to move. She remained still. She was in a sore strait. Her
heart held but one impulse, one desire,—to go with Alessan-
10 dro; nothing was apparently farther from his thoughts than
this. Could she offer to go? Should she risk laying a burden
on him greater than he could bear? If he were indeed a
beggar, as he said, would his life be hindered or helped by
her? She felt herself strong and able. Work had no terrors
15 for her; privations she knew nothing of, but she felt no fear
of them.

"Alessandro!" she said, in a tone which startled him.

"My Señorita!" he said tenderly.

"You have never once called me Ramona."

20 "I cannot, Señorita!" he replied.

"Why not?"

"I do not know. I sometimes think 'Ramona,'" he added
faintly; "but not often. If I think of you by any other name
than as my Señorita, it is usually by a name you never heard."

25 "What is it?" exclaimed Ramona, wonderingly.

"An Indian word, my dearest one, the name of the bird
you are like,—the wood-dove. In the Luiseno tongue that is
Majel; that was what I thought my people would have called
you, if you had come to dwell among us. It is a beautiful
30 name, Señorita, and is like you."

Alessandro was still standing. Ramona rose; coming close
to him, she laid both her hands on his breast, and her head
on her hands, and said: "Alessandro, I have something to
tell you. I am an Indian. I belong to your people."

35 Alessandro's silence astonished her. "You are surprised,"
she said. "I thought you would be glad."

"The gladness of it came to me long a⸍
said. "I knew it!"

"How?" cried Ramona. "And ⸍
Alessandro!"

"How could I?" he replied. "I d
it was, told me."

"Juan Canito!" said Ramona, musingly. "ᴴ⸍
have known?" Then in a few rapid words she told Aless⸍
dro all that the Señora had told her. "Is that what Juan
Can said?" she asked.   10

"All except the father's name," stammered Alessandro.

"Who did he say was my father?" she asked.

Alessandro was silent.

"It matters not," said Ramona. "He was wrong. The
Señora, of course, knew. He was a friend of hers, and of the 15
Señora Ortegna, to whom he gave me. But I think, Ales-
sandro, I have more of my mother than of my father."

"Yes, you have, my Señorita," replied Alessandro, tenderly. "After I knew it, I then saw what it was in your
face had always seemed to me like the faces of my own 20
people."

"Are you not glad, Alessandro?"

"Yes, my Señorita."

What more should Ramona say? Suddenly her heart gave
way; and without premeditation, without resolve, almost 25
without consciousness of what she was doing, she flung herself on Alessandro's breast, and cried: "Oh, Alessandro, take
me with you! take me with you! I would rather die than
have you leave me again!"

MARY E. WILKINS FREEMAN

THE DEBTOR[1]

[A Formal Call]

"Did you ring the bell?" asked Mrs. Van Dorn, anxiously.

"I thought I did. I pressed the button very hard."

"I didn't hear it. I think you had better ring again."

Mrs. Lee obediently pressed the bell again, and then both
5 ladies heard distinctly the far-away tinkle in the depths of
the house.

"I heard that," said Mrs. Lee.

"Yes, so did I. It rang that time."

Then the ladies waited again.

10 "Suppose you ring again," said Mrs. Van Dorn, and
Mrs. Lee rang again. Then they waited again, straining
their ears for the slightest sound in the house.

"I am afraid they are out," said Mrs. Van Dorn.

"So am I. It is such a lovely afternoon."

15 Mrs. Van Dorn, after they had waited a short time, put
out her hand with a decisive motion, and rang the bell yet
again.

"I'm going to make sure they are not at home," said she,
"for I don't know when I shall get out calling again, and I
20 always feel as if it was my duty to call on newcomers in the
village pretty soon after they move in."

Then they waited again, but no one came. Once Mrs. Lee
started and said she was sure she heard someone coming, but
it was only the rumble of a train at a station two miles away.

25 "Shall we leave our cards?" said Mrs. Lee. "I don't suppose there is much use in waiting any longer, or ringing
again."

Mrs. Van Dorn, who had been staring intently at the door,
looked quickly at her companion with a curious expression.
30 Her face had flushed.

---

[1] Reprinted by permission of Harper & Brothers, publishers.

"What is it?" asked Mrs. Lee. "You don't suppose anyone is in there and not coming to the door?" Mrs. Lee had a
somewhat suspicious nature.

"No; I don't think there is a soul in that house, but—"

"But what?"   5

"Nothing, only—"

"Only what?"

"Why, don't you see what they have done?"

"I am afraid I don't quite know what you mean," Mrs. Lee
returned, in a puzzled way. It was quite evident that   10
Mrs. Van Dorn wished her to grasp something which her
own mind had mastered, that she wished it without further
explanation, and Mrs. Lee felt bewilderedly apologetic that
she could not comply.

"Don't you see that they have gone off and left the front   15
door unlocked?" said Mrs. Van Dorn, with inflections of embarrassment, eagerness, and impatience. If she and Mrs. Lee
had been, as of yore, school children together, she would certainly have said, "You ninny!" to finish.

"Why!" returned Mrs. Lee, with a sort of gasp. She saw   20
then that the front door was not only unlocked, but slightly
ajar. "Do you suppose they really are not at home?" she
whispered.

"Of course they are not at home."

"Would they go away and leave the front door un-   25
locked?"

"They have."

"They might be in the back part of the house, and not have
heard the bell," Mrs. Lee said, with a curious tone, as if she
replied to some unspoken suggestion.   30

"I know this house as well as I do my own. You know how
much I used to be here when the Ranger girls were alive.
There is not a room in this house where anybody with ears
can't hear the bell."

Still, Mrs. Van Dorn spoke in that curiously ashamed and   35
indignant voice. Mrs. Lee contradicted her no further.

"Well, I suppose you must be right," said she. "There can't be anybody at home; but it is strange they went off and did not even shut the front door."

"I don't know what the Ranger girls would have said, if they knew it. They would have had a fit at the bare idea of going away for ever so short a time, and leaving the house and furniture alone and the door unlocked."

"Their furniture is here now, I suppose?"

"Yes, I suppose so—some of it, anyway, but I don't know how much furniture these people bought, of course."

"Mr. Lee said he heard they had such magnificent things."

"I heard so, but you hear a good deal that isn't so in Banbridge!"

"That is true. I suppose you knew the house and the Ranger girls' furniture so well that you could tell at a glance what was new and what wasn't?"

"Yes, I could."

As with one impulse both women turned and peered through a green maze of trees and bushes at Samson Rawdy, several yards distant.

"Can you see him?" whispered Mrs. Lee.

"Yes. I think he's asleep. He is sitting with his head all bent over."

"He is—not—looking?"

"No."

Mrs. Lee and Mrs. Van Dorn regarded each other. Both looked at once ashamed and defiant before the other, then into each pair of eyes leaped a light of guilty understanding and perfect sympathy. There are some natures for whom curiosity is one of the master passions, and the desire for knowledge of the affairs of others can become a lust, and Mrs. Lee and Mrs. Van Dorn were of the number. Mrs. Van Dorn gave her head in her best calling-bonnet a toss, and the violets, which were none too securely fastened, nodded loosely; then she thrust her chin forward, she sniffed like a hunting-hound on the scent, pushed open the front door, and

entered, with Mrs. Lee following. As Mrs. Van Dorn entered, the violets on her bonnet became quite detached and
fell softly to the floor of the porch, but neither of the ladies
noticed.

Mrs. Lee, in particular, had led a monotonous life, and she
had a small but intense spirit which could have weathered
extremes. Now her faculties seemed to give a leap; she was
afraid, but there was distinct rapture in her fear. She had
not been so actively happy since she was a child and had
been left at home with the measles one Sunday when the
rest of the family had gone to church, and she had run
away and gone wading in the brook, at the imminent risk
not only of condign punishment, but of the measles striking
in. She felt now just as then, as if something terrible and
mysterious were striking in, and she fairly smacked her soul
over it.

Mrs. Lee no longer shrank; she stood up straight; she also
thrust her chin forward; her nose sharpened, her blue eyes
contracted under her light brows. She even forgot her rôle
of obligation, and did not give Mrs. Van Dorn the precedence; she actually pushed before her. Mrs. Van Dorn had
closed the front door very softly, and they stood in a long,
narrow hall, with an obsolete tapestry carpet, and large-
figured gold and white paper revealing its gleaming scrolls
in stray patches of light. Mrs. Lee went close to an old-
fashioned black-walnut hat-tree, the one article of furniture
besides a chair in the hall.

"Was this theirs?" she whispered to Mrs. Van Dorn.

Mrs. Van Dorn nodded.

Mrs. Lee deliberately removed the nice white kid glove
from her right hand, and extending one small taper forefinger,
rubbed it over the surface of the black-walnut tree; then she
pointed meaningly at the piece of furniture, which plainly,
even in the half-light, disclosed an unhousewifely streak.
She also showed the dusty forefinger to the other lady, and
they both nodded with intense enjoyment.

Then Mrs. Lee folded her silk skirts tightly around her and lifted them high above her starched white petticoat lest she contaminate them in such an untidy house; Mrs. Van Dorn followed her example, and they tiptoed into the double par-
5 lors. They were furnished, for the most part, with the pieces dating back to the building of the house, in one of the ugliest eras of the country, both in architecture and furniture. The ceilings in these rather small square rooms were so lofty that one was giddy with staring at the elaborate cornices and
10 the plaster centerpieces. The mantels were all of massively carved marble, the windows were few and narrow, the doors multitudinous, and lofty enough for giants. The parlor floor was carpeted with tapestry in enormous designs of crimson roses, in deliriums of arabesques, though there were a few
15 very good Eastern rugs. The furniture was black-walnut, upholstered in crimson plush; the tables had marble tops; the hangings were lace under heavily fringed crimson lambre-quins dependent from massive gilt moldings. There were a bronze clock and a whatnot and a few gilt-framed oil-
20 paintings of the conventional landscape type, contemporary with the furniture in American best parlors. Still, there were a few things in the room which directly excited comment on the part of the visitors. Mrs. Lee pointed at some bronzes on the shelf.
25   "Those are theirs, aren't they?" said she.
"Yes, the Ranger girls had some very handsome Royal Worcester vases. I guess James Ranger saw to it that those weren't left here."
Mrs. Van Dorn eyed the bronzes with outward respect,
30 but she did not admire them. Banbridge ladies, as a rule, unless they posed, did not admire bronzes. She also viewed with some disapproval a number of exquisite little Chinese ivory carvings on the whatnot. "Those are theirs," said she.
"The Ranger girls had some handsome bound books and a
35 silver card-receiver, and a bust of Clytie on top of the what-not. I suppose these are very expensive; I have always

heard so. I never priced any, but it always seemed to me that they hardly showed the money."

"I suppose they have afternoon tea," said Mrs. Lee, regarding a charming little inlaid tea-table, decked with Dresden.

"Perhaps so," replied Mrs. Van Dorn, doubtfully. "But I have noticed that when tea-tables are so handsome, folks don't use them. They are more for show. That cloth is beautiful."

"There is a tea-stain on it," declared Mrs. Lee, pointing triumphantly.

"That is so," assented Mrs. Van Dorn. "They must use it." She looked hard at the stain on the tea-cloth. "It's a pity to get tea on such a cloth as that," said she. "It will never come out."

"Oh, I don't believe that will trouble them much," said Mrs. Lee, with soft maliciousness. She indicated with the pointed toe of her best calling-shoe, a hole in the corner of the resplendent Eastern rug.

"Oh," returned Mrs. Van Dorn.

"I know it is considered desirable to have these Oriental things worn," said Mrs. Lee, "but there is no sense in letting an expensive rug like this wear out, and no good house-keeper would."

"Well, I agree with you," said Mrs. Van Dorn.

Presently they passed on to the other rooms. They made a long halt in the dining-room.

"That must be their solid silver," said Mrs. Van Dorn, regarding rather an ostentatious display on the sideboard.

"The idea of going away and leaving all that silver, and the doors unlocked!" said Mrs. Lee.

"Evidently they are people so accustomed to rich things that they don't think of such risks," said Mrs. Van Dorn, with a curious effect of smacking her lips over possessions of her own, instead of her neighbors. She in reality spoke from the heights of a small but solid silver service, and a noble supply of spoons, and Mrs. Lee knew it.

"I suppose they must have perfectly beautiful table-linen," remarked Mrs. Lee, with a wistful glance at the sideboard drawers.

"Yes, I suppose so," assented Mrs. Van Dorn, with a half-sigh. Her eyes, also on the closed drawers of the sideboard, were melancholy, but there was a line which neither woman could pass. They could pry about another woman's house in her absence, but they shrank from opening her drawers and investigating her closets. They respected all that was covered from plain sight. Upstairs it was the same. Things were strewn about rather carelessly, therefore they saw more than they would otherwise have done, but the closet doors and the bureau drawers happened to be closed, and those were inviolate.

"If all their clothes are as nice as these, they must have wardrobes nicer than any ever seen in Banbridge," said Mrs. Lee, fingering delicately a lace-trimmed petticoat flung over a chair in one of the bedrooms. "This is real lace, don't you think so, Mrs. Van Dorn?"

"I don't think. I know," replied Mrs. Van Dorn. "They must have elegant wardrobes, and they must be very wealthy people. They—" Suddenly Mrs. Van Dorn cut her remarks short. She turned quite pale and clutched at her companion's silk-clad arm. "Hush!" she whispered. "What was that?"

Mrs. Lee, herself ashy white, looked at her. Both had distinctly heard a noise. Now they heard it again. The sound was that of footsteps, evidently those of a man, in the lower hall.

"What shall we do? Oh, what shall we do?" said Mrs. Lee, in a thin whisper. She trembled so that she could scarcely stand.

Mrs. Van Dorn, trying to speak, only chattered. She clutched Mrs. Lee harder.

"Is there a back staircase? Oh, is there?" whispered Mrs. Lee. "Is there?" The odor of a cigar stole softly through the house. "I can smell his cigar," whispered Mrs. Lee, in agony.

Mrs. Van Dorn pulled herself together. She nodded, and began pulling Mrs. Lee towards the door.

"Oh," panted Mrs. Lee, "anything except being caught upstairs in their bedrooms! They might think—anything."

"Hurry!" hissed Mrs. Van Dorn. They could hear the footsteps very distinctly, and the cigar-smoke made them want to cough. Holding their silk skirts like twisted ropes around them so they should not rustle, still clinging closely one to the other, the two women began slowly moving, inch by inch, through the upper hall, towards the back stairs. These they descended in safety, and emerged on the lower hall.

They were looking for a rear door, with the view of a stealthy egress and a skirting of the bushes on the lawn unobserved until they should gain the shelter of the carriage, when there was a movement at their backs, and a voice observed, "Good-afternoon, ladies," and they turned, and there was Captain Arthur Carroll. He was a man possibly well over forty, possibly older than that, but his face was as smooth as a boy's, and he was a man of great stature, with nevertheless a boyish cant to his shoulders. Captain Arthur Carroll was a very handsome man, with a viking sort of beauty. He was faultlessly dressed in one of the lightest of spring suits and a fancy waistcoat, and he held quite gracefully the knot of violets which had fallen from Mrs. Van Dorn's bonnet.

The two stood before him, gasping, coloring, trembling. For both of them it was horrible. All their lives they had been women who had held up their heads high in point of respectability and more. None was above them in Banbridge, no shame of wrongdoing or folly had ever been known by either of them, and now both their finely bonneted heads were in the dust. They stood before this handsome, courteously smiling gentleman and were conscious of a very nakedness of spirit. Their lust of curiosity was laid bare, they were caught in the act. Mrs. Van Dorn opened her mouth, she tried to speak, but she only made a strange, croaking sound. Her face was now flaming. But Mrs. Lee was pale, and she stood rather unsteadily.

5   Arthur Carroll at first looked merely bewildered. "Aren't the ladies at home?" said he. "Have you seen the ladies?" He glanced at Mrs. Van Dorn's deflowered bonnet, and extended the bunch of violets. "Yours, I think," he said. Mrs. Van Dorn took them with an idiotic expression, and he
10 asked again if they had seen the ladies.

The spectacle of two elderly, well-dressed females of Banbridge quaking before him in this wise, and of their sudden appearance in his house, was a mystery too great to be grasped at once even by a clever man, and he was certainly
15 a clever man. So he stared for a second, while the two remained standing before him, holding their card-cases in their shaking, white-gloved fingers, and Mrs. Van Dorn with the violets; then suddenly an expression of the most delighted comprehension and amusement overspread his face.

20   "Oh," he said, politely, with a great flourish, as it were of deference, "the ladies are not in. They will be exceedingly sorry to have missed your call. But will you not come in and sit down?"

Mrs. Van Dorn gained voice enough to gasp that she
25 thought they must go. Captain Carroll stood back, and the two women, pressing closely together, tottered through the hall towards the front door.

Captain Carroll followed, beaming with delighted malice. "I hope you will call again, when the ladies are home," he
30 said to Mrs. Van Dorn, whom he recognized as the leader.

She made an inarticulate attempt at "Thank you." She was making for the door, like a scared hare to the entrance of its cover.

"But I have not your names, ladies, that I may inform
35 Mrs. Carroll who has called?" said Captain Carroll, in his stingingly polite voice.

Both women looked over their shrinking shoulders at him at that. Suddenly the hideous consequences of it all, the afterclap, sounded in their ears. That was the end of their fair fame in Banbridge, in their world. Life for them was over. Their faces, good, motherly, elderly village faces, after all, were pitiful; the shame in them was a shame to see, so ignominious was it. They stood convicted of such a mean fault, that the shame was the meaner also.

Suddenly Mr. Carroll's face changed. It became broadly comprehensive, so generously lenient that it was fairly grand. A certain gentleness also was evident, his voice was kind.

"Never mind, ladies," said Arthur Carroll. "There is really very little use in your telling me your names, because my memory is so bad. I remember neither names nor faces. If I should meet you on the street, and should fail to recognize you on that account, I trust that you will pardon me. And—" said Captain Carroll, "on that account, I will not say anything about your call to the ladies of my family; I should be sure to get it all wrong. We will wait, and trust that you will find them at home the next time you call. Good-afternoon, ladies." Captain Carroll had further mercy. He allowed the ladies to leave the house unattended and to dive desperately into the waiting coach.

"Home at once," Mrs. Von Dorn cried, hoarsely, to Samson Rawdy, waking from his nap in some bewilderment.

Captain Carroll was standing on the porch with a compound look of kindest pity and mirth on his face when the Carroll ladies came strolling round that way from the pond. He kissed them all, as was his wont; then he laughed out inconsequently.

"What are you laughing at, dear?" asked Amy.

"At my thoughts, sweetheart."

"What are your thoughts, daddy?" asked Charlotte.

"Thoughts I shall never tell anybody, honey," he replied, with another laugh. And Captain Arthur Carroll never did tell.

HAMLIN GARLAND

A SON OF THE MIDDLE BORDER[1]

WHEAT AND THE HARVEST

As I look back over my life on that Iowa farm the song of
the reaper fills large place in my mind. We were all worshipers of wheat in those days. The men thought and talked
of little else between seeding and harvest, and you will not
5 wonder at this if you have known and bowed down before
such abundance as we then enjoyed.

Deep as the breast of a man, wide as the sea, heavy-headed,
supple-stocked, many-voiced, full of multitudinous, secret,
whispered colloquies,—a meeting place of winds and of sun-
10 light,—our fields ran to the world's end.

We trembled when the storm lay hard upon the wheat, we
exulted as the lilac shadows of noonday drifted over it! We
went out into it at noon when all was still—so still we could
hear the pulse of the transforming sap as it crept from cool
15 root to swaying plume. We stood before it at evening when
the setting sun flooded it with crimson, the bearded heads
lazily swirling under the wings of the wind, the mousing hawk
dipping into its green deeps like the eagle into the sea, and
our hearts expanded with the beauty and the mystery of it,
20 —and back of all this was the knowledge that its abundance
meant a new carriage, an addition to the house or a new suit
of clothes.

Haying was over, and day by day we boys watched with
deepening interest while the hot sun transformed the juices
25 of the soil into those stately stalks. I loved to go out into
the fairy forest of it, and lying there, silent in its swaying
deeps, hear the wild chickens peep and the wind sing its
subtle song over our heads. Day by day I studied the barley
as it turned yellow, first at the root and then at the neck

[1] Reprinted from Hamlin Garland's *A Son of the Middle Border*. By
special arrangement with The Macmillan Company, publisher.

(while the middle joints, rank and sappy, retained their blue-green sheen), until at last the lower leaves began to wither and the stems to stiffen in order to uphold the daily increasing weight of the milky berries, and then almost in an hour—lo! the edge of the field became a banded ribbon of green and yellow, languidly waving in and out with every rush of the breeze.

Now we got out the reaper, put the sickles in order, and father laid in a store of provisions. Extra hands were hired, and at last, early on a hot July morning, the boss mounted to his seat on the self-rake "McCormick" and drove into the field. Frank rode the lead horse, four stalwart hands and my-self took "stations" behind the reaper and the battle was on!

Reaping generally came about the 20th of July, the hottest and driest part of the summer, and was the most pressing work of the year. It demanded early rising for the men, and it meant an all-day broiling over the kitchen stove for the women. Stern, incessant toil went on inside and out from dawn till sunset, no matter how the thermometer sizzled. On many days the mercury mounted to ninety-five in the shade, but with wide fields all yellowing at the same moment, no one thought of laying off. A storm might sweep it flat, or if neglected too long, it might "crinkle."

Our reaper in 1874 was a new model of the McCormick self-rake,—the Marsh Harvester was not yet in general use. The Woods Dropper, the Seymour and Morgan hand-rake "contraptions" seemed a long way in the past. True the McCormick required four horses to drag it but it was effec-tive. It was hard to believe that anything more cunning would ever come to claim the farmer's money. Weird tales of a machine on which two men rode and bound twelve acres of wheat in ten hours came to us, but we did not potently believe these reports—on the contrary we accepted the self-rake as quite the final word in harvesting machinery and cheerily bent to the binding of sheaves with their own straw in the good old time-honored way.

No task save that of "cradling" surpassed in severity "binding on a station." It was a full-grown man's job, but every boy was ambitious to try his hand, and when at fourteen years of age I was promoted from "bundle boy" to be one of the five hands to bind after the reaper, I went to my corner with joy and confidence. For two years I had been serving as binder on the corners, (to keep the grain out of the way of the horses) and I knew my job.

I was short and broad-shouldered with large strong hands admirably adapted for this work, and for the first two hours easily held my own with the rest of the crew, but as the morning wore on and the sun grew hotter, my enthusiasm waned. A painful void developed in my chest. My breakfast had been ample, but no mere stomachful of food could carry a growing boy through five hours of desperate toil. Along about a quarter to ten, I began to scan the field with anxious eye, longing to see Harriet and the promised luncheon basket.

Just when it seemed that I could endure the strain no longer she came bearing a jug of cool milk, some cheese and some deliciously fresh fried-cakes. With keen joy I set a couple of tall sheaves together like a tent and flung myself down flat on my back in their shadow to devour my lunch.

Tired as I was, my dim eyes apprehended something of the splendor of the shining clouds which rolled like storms of snow through the deep-blue spaces of sky; and so, resting silently as a clod, I could hear the chirp of the crickets, the buzzing wings of flies, and the faint, fairylike tread of smaller unseen insects hurrying their way just beneath my ear in the stubble. Strange green worms, grasshoppers and shining beetles crept over me as I dozed.

This delicious, dreamful respite was broken by the far-off approaching purr of the sickle, flicked by the faint snap of the driver's whip, and out of the low rustle of the ever-stirring Lilliputian forest came the wailing cry of a baby wild chicken lost from its mother—a falling, thrilling, piteous little pipe.

Such momentary communion with nature seemed all the sweeter for the work which had preceded it, as well as that which was to follow it. It took resolution to rise and go back 5 to my work, but I did it, sustained by a kind of soldierly pride.

At noon we hurried to the house, surrounded the kitchen table and fell upon our boiled beef and potatoes with such ferocity that in fifteen minutes our meal was over. There was no ceremony and very little talking till the hid wolf was 10 appeased. Then came a heavenly half-hour of rest on the cool grass in the shade of the trees, a siesta as luxurious as that of a Spanish monarch—but alas!—this "nooning," as we called it, was always cut short by father's word of sharp command, "Roll out, boys!" and again the big white jugs 15 were filled at the well, the horses, lazy with food, led the way back to the field, and the stern contest began again.

All nature at this hour seemed to invite to repose rather than to labor, and as the heat increased I longed with wordless fervor for the green woods of the Cedar River. At times 20 the gentle wind hardly moved the bended heads of the barley, and the hawks hung in the air like trout sleeping in deep pools. The sunlight was a golden, silent, scorching cataract —yet each of us must strain his tired muscles and bend his aching back to the harvest.   25

Supper came at five, another delicious interval—and then at six we all went out again for another hour or two in the cool of the sunset.—However, the pace was more leisurely now, for the end of the day was near. I always enjoyed this period, for the shadows lengthening across the stubble, and 30 the fiery sun, veiled by the gray clouds of the west, had wondrous charm. The air began to moisten and grow cool. The voices of the men pulsed powerfully and cheerfully across the narrowing field of unreaped grain, the prairie hens led forth their broods to feed; and, at last, father's long-drawn and 35 musical cry, "Turn OUT! All hands TURN OUT!" rang

with restful significance through the dusk. Then, slowly,
with low-hung heads the freed horses moved toward the barn,
walking with lagging steps like weary warriors going into
camp.

JAMES LANE ALLEN

THE REIGN OF LAW[1]

CHAPTER XV

[Gabriella's History]

5   Gabriella's memoirs might be writ large in four parts that
would really be the history of the United States, just as
a slender seam of gold can only be explained through the
geology of the earth. But they can also be writ so small that
each volume may be dropped, like certain minute-books of
10 bygone fashions, into a waistcoat pocket, or even read, as
through a magnifying glass, entire on a single page.

The first volume was the childhood book, covering the
period from Gabriella's birth to the beginning of the Civil
War, by which time she was fourteen years old: it was a
15 fairy tale. These earliest recollections went back to herself
as a very tiny child living with her mother and grandmother
in a big white house with green window-shutters, in Lexington—so big that she knew only the two or three rooms in
one ell. Her mother wore mourning for her father, and was
20 always drawing her to her bosom and leaving tears on her
face or lilylike hands. One day—she could not remember
very well—but the house had been darkened and the servants
never for a moment ceased amusing her—one day the house
was all opened again and Gabriella could not find her mother;
25 and her grandmother, everybody else, was kinder to her than
ever. She did not think what kindness was then, but years
afterward she learned perfectly.

[1] Reprinted from James Lane Allen's *The Reign of Law*. By special
arrangement with The Macmillan Company, publisher.

Very slowly Gabriella's knowledge began to extend over
the house and outside it. There were enormous, high-ceiled
halls and parlors, and bedrooms and bedrooms and bedrooms.
There were verandas front and back, so long that it took her
breath away to run the length of one and return. Upstairs, 5
front and back, verandas again, balustraded so that little
girls could not forget themselves and fall off. The pillars of
these verandas at the rear of the house were connected by a
network of wires, and trained up the pillars and branching
over the wires were coiling twisting vines of wisteria as large 10
as Gabriella's neck. This was the sunny southern side; and
when the wisteria was blooming, Gabriella moved her establishment of playthings out behind those sunlit cascades of
purple and green, musical sometimes with goldfinches.

The front of the house faced a yard of stately evergreens 15
and great tubs of flowers, oleander, crêpe myrtle, and pome-
granate. Beyond the yard, a graveled carriage drive wound
out of sight behind cedars, catalpa, and forest trees, shadowing a turfy lawn. At the end of the lawn was the great entrance gate and the street of the town. Gabriella long knew 20
this approach only by her drives with her grandmother. At
the rear of the house was enough for her: a large yard,
green grazing lots for the stable of horses, and best of all a
high-fenced garden containing everything the heart could
desire: vegetables, and flowers; summerhouses, and arbors 25
with seats; pumps of cold water, and hothouses of plants
and grapes, and fruit trees, and a swing, and gooseberry
bushes—everything.

In one corner, the ground was too shaded by an old apple
tree to be of use: they gave this to Gabriella for her garden. 30
She had attached particularly to her person a little negress
of about the same age—her Milly, the color of a ripe gourd.
So when in spring the gardener began to make his garden,
with her grandmother sometimes standing over him, direct-
ing, Gabriella, taking her little chair to the apple tree,— 35
with some pretended needlework and a real switch,—would

set Milly to work making hers. Nothing that they put into
the earth ever was heard of again, though they would sometimes make the same garden over every day for a week. So
that more than once, forsaking seed, they pulled off the tops
5 of green things near by, planted these, and so had a perfect
garden in an hour.

   .   .   .   .

The time came when Gabriella began to extend her knowledge to the country, as she drove out beside her grandmother
in the balmy spring and early summer afternoons.

10 "What is that, grandmother?" she would say, pointing
with her small forefinger to a field by the turnpike.

"That is corn."

"And what is that?"

"That is wheat."

15 "And what is that?"

"Oats, Gabriella."

"Oh, grandmother, what is *that*?"

"Tut, tut, child! Don't you know what that is? That's
hemp. That is what bales all our cotton."

20 "Oh, grandmother, smell it!"

After this, sometimes Gabriella would order the driver to
turn off into some green lane about sunset and press on till
they found a field by the way. As soon as they began to pass
it, over into their faces would be wafted the clean, cool-
25 ing, velvet-soft, balsam breath of the hemp. The carriage
would stop, and Gabriella, standing up and facing the field,
would fill her lungs again and again, smiling at her grandmother for approval. Then she would take her seat and say
quietly: "Turn round, Tom, and drive back. I have smelt
30 it enough."

These drives alone with her grandmother were for spring
and early summer only. Full summer brought up from their
plantations in Louisiana, Arkansas, and Mississippi, her
uncles and the wives and children of some of them. All the
35 bedrooms in the big house were filled, and Gabriella was

nearly lost in the multitude, she being the only child of the
only daughter of her grandmother. And now what happy
times there were. The silks, and satins, and laces! The
plate, the gold, the cut glass! The dinners, the music, the
laughter, the wines! 5

Later, some of her uncles' families might travel on with
their servants to watering places farther north. But in September all were back again under the one broad Kentucky
roof, stopping for the beautiful Kentucky fair, then celebrated all over the land; and for the races,—those days of the 10
thoroughbred only; and until frost fall should make it safe
to return to the swamps and bayous, loved by the yellow
fever.

When all were departed, sometimes her grandmother, closing the house for the winter, would follow one of her sons to 15
his plantation; thence later proceeding to New Orleans, at
that time the most brilliant of American capitals; and so
Gabriella would see the Father of Waters, and the things that
happened in the floating palaces of the Mississippi; see the
social life of the ancient French and Spanish city. 20

All that could be most luxurious and splendid in Kentucky
during those last deep, rich years of the old social order,
was Gabriella's: the extravagance, the gayety, the pride,
the lovely manners, the selfishness and cruelty in its terrible, unconscious, and narrow way, the false ideals, the 25
aristocratic virtues. Then it was that, overspreading land
and people, lay the full autumn of that sowing, which had
moved silently on its way toward its fateful fruits for over
fifty years. Everything was ripe, sweet, mellow, dropping,
turning rotten. 30

O ye who have young children, if possible give them happy
memories! Fill their earliest years with bright pictures! A
great historian many centuries ago wrote it down that the
first thing conquered in battle are the eyes: the soldier flees
from what he sees before him. But so often in the world's 35
fight we are defeated by what we look back upon; we are

whipped in the end by the things we saw in the beginning
of life. The time arrived for Gabriella when all the gorgeous
fairy tale of her childhood was all that she had to sustain her:
when it meant consolation, courage, fortitude, victory.

5　　A war volume, black, fiery, furious, awful—this comprised
the second part of her history: it contained the overthrow of
half the American people, and the downfall of the child
princess Gabriella. An idea—how negative, nerveless, it
looks printed! A little group of four ideas—how should they
10 have power of life and death over millions of human beings!
But say that one is the idea of the right of self-government—
much loved and fought for all round the earth by the Anglo-
Saxon race. Say that a second is the idea that with his own
property a man has a right to do as he pleases: another no-
15 tion that has been warred over, world without end. Let
these two ideas run in the blood and passions of the Southern
people. Say that a third idea is that of national greatness
(the preservation of the Union), another idol of this nation-
building race. Say that the fourth idea is that of evolving
20 humanity, or, at least, that slaveholding societies must be
made nonslaveholding—if not peaceably, then by force of
arms. Let these two ideas be running in the blood and passions of the Northern people. Bring the first set of ideas and
the second set together in a struggle for supremacy. By all
25 mankind it is now known what the result was for the nation.
What these ideas did for one little girl, living in Lexington,
Kentucky, was part of that same sad, sublime history.

They ordered the grandmother across the lines, as a
wealthy sympathizer and political agent of the Southern
30 cause; they seized her house, confiscated it, used it as officers'
headquarters: in the end they killed her with grief and care;
they sent her sons, every man of them, into the Southern
armies, ravaged their plantations, liberated their slaves, left
them dead on the fields of battle, or wrecked in health, hope,
35 fortune. Gabriella, placed in a boarding-school in Lexington
at that last hurried parting with her grandmother, stayed

there a year. Then the funds left to her account in bank were gone; she went to live with near relatives; and during the remaining years of the war was first in one household, then another, of kindred or friends all of whom contended for the privilege of finding her a home. But at the close of 5 the war, Gabriella, issuing from the temporary shelters given her during the storm, might have been seen as a snow-white pigeon flying lost and bewildered across a black cloud covering half the sky.

The third volume—the Peace Book in which there was no 10 Peace: this was the beginning of Gabriella, child of the Revolution. She did not now own a human being except herself; could give orders to none but herself; could train for this work, whip up to that duty, only herself; and if she was still minded to play the mistress—firm, kind, efficient, 15 capable—must be such a mistress solely to Gabriella.

By that social evolution of the race which in one country after another had wrought the overthrow of slavery, she had now been placed with a generation unique in history: a generation of young Southern girls, of gentle birth and breed- 20 ing, of the most delicate nature, who, heiresses in slaves and lands at the beginning of the war, were penniless and un- recognized wards of the federal government at its close, their slaves having been made citizens and their plantations laid waste. On these unprepared and innocent girls thus fell 25 most heavily not only the mistakes and misdeeds of their own fathers and mothers but the common guilt of the whole nation, and particularly of New England, as respects the original traffic in human souls. The change in the lives of these girls was as sudden and terrible as if one had entered 30 a brilliant ballroom and in the voice of an overseer ordered the dancers to go as they were to the factories.

To the factories many of them went, in a sense: to hard work of some sort—to wage-earning and wage-taking: some- times becoming the mainstay of aged or infirm parents, the 35 dependence of younger brothers and sisters. If the history of it all is ever written, it will make pitiful, heroic, noble reading.

The last volume of Gabriella's memoirs showed her in this field of struggle—of new growth to suit the newer day. It was
5 so unlike the first volume as to seem no continuation of her own life. It began one summer morning about two years after the close of the war—an interval which she had spent in various efforts at self-help, at self-training.

On that morning, pale and trembling, but resolute, her
10 face heavily veiled, she might have been seen on her way to Water Street in Lexington—a street she had heard of all her life and had been careful never to enter except to take or to alight from a train at the station. Passing quickly along until she reached a certain ill-smelling little stairway which
15 opened on the foul sidewalk, she mounted it, knocked at a low black-painted door, and entered a room which was a curiosity shop. There she was greeted by an elderly gentleman, who united in himself the offices of superintendent of schools, experimental astronomer, and manufacturer of a
20 high grade of mustard. She had presented herself to be examined for a teacher's certificate.

Fortunately for Gabriella this kindly old sage remembered well her grandmother and her uncles: they had been connoisseurs; they had for years bought liberally of his mustard.
25 Her uncles had used it first on their dinner tables as a condiment and afterward on their foreheads and stomachs as a plaster. They had never failed to praise it to his face—both for its power to draw an appetite and for its power to withdraw an ache. In turn he now praised them and asked the
30 easiest questions. Gabriella, whose knowledge of arithmetic was as a grain of mustard seed, and who spoke beautiful English, but could not have parsed, "John, come here!"— received a first-class certificate for the sake of the future and a box of mustard in memory of the past.

35 Early in that autumn she climbed, one morning, into an old yellow-red, ever muddied stagecoach (the same that

David had ridden in) and set out to a remote neighborhood, where, after many failures otherwise, she had secured a position to teach a small country school. She was glad that it was distant; she had a feeling that the farther away it was from Lexington, the easier it would be to teach.   5

MARK TWAIN

LIFE ON THE MISSISSIPPI[1]

CHAPTER IX. CONTINUED PERPLEXITIES

There was no use in arguing with a person like this. I promptly put such a strain on my memory that by and by even the shoal water and the countless crossing-marks began to stay with me. But the result was just the same. I never could more than get one knotty thing learned before another 10 presented itself. Now I had often seen pilots gazing at the water and pretending to read it as if it were a book; but it was a book that told me nothing. A time came at last, however, when Mr. Bixby seemed to think me far enough advanced to bear a lesson on water-reading. So he began: 15

"Do you see that long, slanting line on the face of the water? Now, that's a reef. Moreover, it's a bluff reef. There is a solid sand-bar under it that is nearly as straight up and down as the side of a house. There is plenty of water close up to it, but mighty little on top of it. If you were to hit it, 20 you would knock the boat's brains out. Do you see where the line fringes out at the upper end and begins to fade away?"

"Yes, sir."

"Well, that is a low place; that is the head of the reef. You can climb over there, and not hurt anything. Cross over, 25 now, and follow along close under the reef—easy water there —not much current."

[1] Reprinted with the permission of the estate of Samuel L. Clemens, Mark Twain Company, and Harper & Brothers, publishers, with a full reservation of all copyright privileges.

I followed the reef along till I approached the fringed end. Then Mr. Bixby said:

"Now get ready. Wait till I give the word. She won't want to mount the reef; a boat hates shoal water. Stand by
5 —wait—*wait*—keep her well in hand. *Now* cramp her down! Snatch her! Snatch her!"

He seized the other side of the wheel and helped to spin it around until it was hard down, and then we held it so. The boat resisted, and refused to answer for a while, and next she
10 came surging to starboard, mounted the reef, and sent a long, angry ridge of water foaming away from her bows.

"Now watch her; watch her like a cat, or she'll get away from you. When she fights strong and the tiller slips a little, in a jerky, greasy sort of way, let up on her a trifle; it is the
15 way she tells you at night that the water is too shoal; but keep edging her up, little by little, toward the point. You are well up on the bar now; there is a bar under every point, because the water that comes down around it forms an eddy and allows the sediment to sink. Do you see those fine lines
20 on the face of the water that branch out like the ribs of a fan? Well, those are little reefs; you want to just miss the ends of them, but run them pretty close. Now look out—look out! Don't you crowd that slick, greasy-looking place; there ain't nine feet there; she won't stand it. She begins to smell it;
25 look sharp, I tell you! Oh, blazes, there you go! Stop the starboard wheel! Quick! Ship up to back! Set her back!"

The engine bells jingled and the engines answered promptly, shooting white columns of steam far aloft out of the 'scape-pipes, but it was too late. The boat had "smelt" the bar in
30 good earnest; the foamy ridges that radiated from her bows suddenly disappeared, a great dead swell came rolling forward, and swept ahead of her, she careened far over to larboard, and went tearing away toward the shore as if she were about scared to death. We were a good mile from where we
35 ought to have been when we finally got the upper hand of her again.

During the afternoon watch the next day, Mr. Bixby asked me if I knew how to run the next few miles. I said:

"Go inside the first snag above the point, outside the next one, start out from the lower end of Higgins's wood-yard, make a square crossing, and—"   5

"That's all right. I'll be back before you close up on the next point."

But he wasn't. He was still below when I rounded it and entered upon a piece of river which I had some misgivings about. I did not know that he was hiding behind a chimney 10 to see how I would perform. I went gayly along, getting prouder and prouder, for he had never left the boat in my sole charge such a length of time before. I even got to "set-ting" her and letting the wheel go entirely, while I vain-gloriously turned my back and inspected the stern marks and 15 hummed a tune, a sort of easy indifference which I had pro-digiously admired in Bixby and other great pilots. Once I inspected rather long, and when I faced to the front again my heart flew into my mouth so suddenly that if I hadn't clapped my teeth together I should have lost it. One of those 20 frightful bluff reefs was stretching its deadly length right across our bows! My head was gone in a moment; I did not know which end I stood on; I gasped and could not get my breath; I spun the wheel down with such rapidity that it wove itself together like a spider's web, the boat answered 25 and turned square away from the reef, but the reef followed her! I fled, but still it followed, still it kept—right across my bows! I never looked to see where I was going, I only fled. The awful crash was imminent. Why didn't that villain come? If I committed the crime of ringing a bell I might get 30 thrown overboard. But better that than kill the boat. So in blind desperation I started such a rattling "shivaree" down below as never had astounded an engineer in this world be-fore, I fancy. Amidst the frenzy of the bells the engines be-gan to back and fill in a furious way, and my reason forsook 35 its throne—we were about to crash into the woods on the

other side of the river. Just then Mr. Bixby stepped calmly into view on the hurricane deck. My soul went out to him in gratitude. My distress vanished; I would have felt safe on the brink of Niagara with Mr. Bixby up on the hurricane
5 deck. He blandly and sweetly took his toothpick out of his mouth between his fingers, as if it were a cigar,—we were just in the act of climbing an overhanging big tree, and the passengers were scudding astern like rats,—and lifted up these commands to me ever so gently!

10   "Stop the starboard! Stop the larboard! Set her back on both!"

The boat hesitated, halted, pressed her nose among the boughs a critical instant, then reluctantly began to back away.

15   "Stop the larboard! Come ahead on it! Stop the starboard! Come ahead on it! Point her for the bar!"

I sailed away as serenely as a summer's morning. Mr. Bixby came in and said with mock simplicity:

"When you have a hail, my boy, you ought to tap the big
20 bell three times before you land, so that the engineers can get ready."

I blushed under the sarcasm, and said I hadn't had any hail.

"Ah! Then it was for wood, I suppose. The officer of the
25 watch will tell you when he wants to wood up."

I went on consuming, and said I wasn't after wood.

"Indeed? Why, what could you want over here in the bend, then? Did you ever know of a boat following a bend up-stream at this stage of the river?"

30   "No, sir—and I wasn't trying to follow it. I was getting away from a bluff reef."

"No, it wasn't a bluff reef; there isn't one within three miles of where you were."

"But I saw it. It was as bluff as that one yonder."

35   "Just about. Run over it!"

"Do you give it as an order?"

"Yes. Run over it!"

"If I don't, I wish I may die."

"All right; I am taking the responsibility."

I was just as anxious to kill the boat, now, as I had been to
save it before. I impressed my orders upon my memory, to
be used at the inquest, and made a straight break for the reef.
As it disappeared under our bows I held my breath; but we
slid over it like oil.

"Now, don't you see the difference? It wasn't anything
but a *wind* reef. The wind does that!"

"So I see. But it is exactly like a bluff reef. How am I
ever going to tell them apart?"

"I can't tell you. It is an instinct. By and by you will
just naturally *know* one from the other, but you never will
be able to explain why or how you know them apart."

It turned out to be true. The face of the water, in time,
became a wonderful book—a book that was a dead language
to the uneducated passenger, but which told its mind to
me without reserve, delivering its most cherished secrets as
clearly as if it uttered them with a voice. And it was not a
book to be read once and thrown aside, for it had a new
story to tell every day. Throughout the long twelve hundred
miles there was never a page that was void of interest, never
one that you could leave unread without loss, never one that
you would want to skip, thinking you could find higher enjoyment in some other thing. There never was so wonderful
a book written by man; never one whose interest was so
absorbing, so unflagging, so sparklingly renewed with every
re-perusal. The passenger who could not read it was charmed
with a peculiar sort of faint dimple on its surface (on the
rare occasions when he did not overlook it altogether); but
to the pilot that was an *italicized* passage; indeed, it was
more than that, it was a legend of the largest capitals, with
a string of shouting exclamation points at the end of it, for
it meant that a wreck or a rock was buried there that could
tear the life out of the strongest vessel that ever floated. It

is the faintest and simplest expression the water ever makes, and the most hideous to a pilot's eye. In truth the passenger who could not read this book saw nothing but all manner of pretty pictures in it, painted by the sun and shaded by the clouds, whereas to the trained eye these were not pictures at all, but the grimmest and most dead-earnest of reading matter.

Now when I had mastered the language of this water, and had come to know every trifling feature that bordered the great river as familiarly as I knew the letters of the alphabet, I had made a valuable acquisition. But I had lost something, too. I had lost something which could never be restored to me while I lived. All the grace, the beauty, the poetry, had gone out of the majestic river! I still kept in mind a certain wonderful sunset which I witnessed when steamboating was new to me. A broad expanse of the river was turned to blood; in the middle distance the red hue brightened into gold, through which a solitary log came floating, black and conspicuous; in one place a long, slanting mark lay sparkling upon the water; in another the surface was broken by boiling, tumbling rings, that were as many-tinted as an opal; where the ruddy flush was faintest, was a smooth spot that was covered with graceful circles and radiating lines, ever so delicately traced; the shore on our left was densely wooded, and the somber shadow that fell from this forest was broken in one place by a long, ruffled trail that shone like silver; and high above the forest wall a clean-stemmed dead tree waved a single leafy bough that glowed like a flame in the unobstructed splendor that was flowing from the sun. There were graceful curves, reflected images, woody heights, soft distances; and over the whole scene, far and near, the dissolving lights drifted steadily, enriching it every passing moment with new marvels of coloring.

I stood like one bewitched. I drank it in, in a speechless rapture. The world was new to me, and I had never seen anything like this at home. But as I have said, a day came

when I began to cease from noting the glories and the charms
which the moon and the sun and the twilight wrought upon
the river's face; another day came when I ceased altogether
to note them. Then, if that sunset scene had been repeated,
I should have looked upon it without rapture, and should 5
have commented upon it, inwardly, after this fashion: "This
sun means that we are going to have wind to-morrow; that
floating log means that the river is rising, small thanks to it;
that slanting mark on the water refers to a bluff reef which
is going to kill somebody's steamboat one of these nights, if 10
it keeps on stretching out like that; those tumbling 'boils'
show a dissolving bar and a changing channel there; the
lines and circles in the slick water over yonder are a warning
that that troublesome place is shoaling up dangerously; that
silver streak in the shadow of the forest is the 'break' from 15
a new snag, and he has located himself in the very best place
he could have found to fish for steamboats; that tall dead
tree, with a single living branch, is not going to last long, and
then how is a body ever going to get through this blind place
at night without the friendly old landmark?"   20

No, the romance and the beauty were all gone from the
river. All the value any feature of it had for me now was
the amount of usefulness it could furnish toward compassing
the safe piloting of a steamboat. Since those days, I have
pitied doctors from my heart. What does the lovely flush in 25
a beauty's cheek mean to a doctor but a "break" that ripples
above some deadly disease? Are not all her visible charms
sown thick with what are to him the signs and symbols of
hidden decay? Does he ever see her beauty at all, or doesn't
he simply view her professionally, and comment upon her 30
unwholesome condition all to himself? And doesn't he sometimes wonder whether he has gained most or lost most by
learning his trade?

HUCKLEBERRY FINN[1]

CHAPTER IX

[The Cavern]

Jim said if we had the canoe hid in a good place, and had all the traps in the cavern, we could rush there if anybody was to come to the island, and they would never find us without dogs. And, besides, he said them little birds had said it was going to rain, and did I want the things to get wet?

So we went back and got the canoe, and paddled up abreast of the cavern, and lugged all the traps up there. Then we hunted up a place close by to hide the canoe in, amongst the thick willows. We took some fish off of the lines and set them again, and begun to get ready for dinner.

The door in the cavern was big enough to roll a hogshead in, and on one side of the door the floor stuck out a little bit, and was flat and a good place to build a fire on. So we built it there and cooked dinner.

We spread the blankets inside for a carpet, and eat our dinner in there. We put all the other things handy at the back of the cavern. Pretty soon it darkened up, and begun to thunder and lighten; so the birds was right about it. Directly it begun to rain, and it rained like all fury, too, and I never see the wind blow so. It was one of these regular summer storms. It would get so dark that it looked all blue-black outside, and lovely; and the rain would thrash along by so thick that the trees off a little ways looked dim and spider-webby; and here would come a blast of wind that would bend the trees down and turn up the pale underside of the leaves; and then a perfect ripper of a gust would follow along and set the branches to tossing their arms as if they was just wild; and next, when it was just about the bluest

and blackest—*fst*! it was as bright as glory, and you'd have
a little glimpse of tree-tops a-plunging about away off yonder
in the storm, hundreds of yards further than you could see
before; dark as sin again in a second, and now you'd hear the
thunder let go with an awful crash, and then go rumbling, 5
grumbling, tumbling down the sky towards the underside of
the world, like rolling empty barrels downstairs—where it's
long stairs and they bounce a good deal, you know.

"Jim, this is nice," I says. "I wouldn't want to be nowhere
else but here. Pass me along another hunk of fish and some 10
hot corn-bread."

"Well, you wouldn't a ben here 'f it hadn't a ben for Jim.
You'd a ben down dah in de woods widout any dinner, en
gittin' mos' drownded, too; dat you would, honey. Chickens
knows when it's gwyne to rain, en so do de birds, chile." 15

The river went on raising and raising for ten or twelve
days, till at last it was over the banks. The water was three
or four foot deep on the island in the low places and on the
Illinois bottom. On that side it was a good many miles wide,
but on the Missouri side it was the same old distance across 20
—a half a mile—because the Missouri shore was just a wall
of high bluffs.

Daytimes we paddled all over the island in the canoe.
It was mighty cool and shady in the deep woods, even if
the sun was blazing outside. We went winding in and out 25
amongst the trees, and sometimes the vines hung so thick we
had to back away and go some other way. Well, on every
old broken-down tree you could see rabbits and snakes and
such things; and when the island had been overflowed a day
or two they got so tame, on account of being hungry, that 30
you could paddle right up and put your hand on them if you
wanted to; but not the snakes and turtles—they would slide
off in the water. The ridge our cavern was in was full of
them. We could a had pets enough if we'd wanted them.

One night we catched a little section of a lumber-raft— 35
nice pine planks. It was twelve foot wide and about fifteen

or sixteen foot long, and the top stood above water six or
seven inches—a solid, level floor. We could see saw-logs go
by in the daylight sometimes, but we let them go; we didn't
show ourselves in daylight.

EDMUND CLARENCE STEDMAN

ALICE OF MONMOUTH

[Extract]

5 They two, the boy and the grandsire, lived at the manor-
    house, and grew,
The one to all manly arts apace, the other a youth anew—
Pleased with the boy's free spirit, and teaching him, step by
    step, to wield
The mastery over living things, and the craft of flood and field.

Apt, indeed, was the scholar; and born with a subtle spell
    to gain
10 The love of all dumb creatures at will; now lifting himself,
    by the mane,
Over the neck of the three-year colt, for a random bareback
    ride;
Now chasing the waves on the rifted beach at the turn of the
    evening tide.

Proud, in sooth, was the master: the youngster, he oft and
    roundly swore,
Was fit for the life a gentleman led in the lusty days of yore!
15 And he took the boy wherever he drove—to a county fair or race;
Gave him the reins and watch'd him guide the span at a
    spanking pace;

Taught him the sportsman's keen delight: to swallow the
    air of morn,
And start the whistling quail that hides and feeds in the
    dewy corn;

Or in clear November underwoods to bag the squirrels, and
  flush
The brown-winged mottled partridge awhir from her nest in
  the tangled brush;

Taught him the golden harvest laws, and the signs of sun
  and shower,
And the thousand beautiful secret ways of graft and fruit
  and flower;
Set him straight in his saddle, and cheer'd him galloping
  over the sand;   5
Sail'd with him to the fishing-shoals and placed the helm in
  his hand.

Often the yacht, with all sail spread, was steer'd by the
  fearless twain,
Around the beacon of Sandy Hook, and out in the open main;
Till the great sea-surges rolling in, as south-by-east they
  wore,
Lifted the bows of the dancing craft, and the buoyant hearts
  she bore.   10

But in dreamy hours, which young men know, Hugh loved
  with the tide to float
Far up the deep, dark-channel'd creeks, alone in his two-oar'd
  boat;
While a fiery woven tapestry o'erhung the waters low,
The warp of the frosted chestnut, the woof with maple and
  birch aglow;

Picking the grapes which dangled down; or watching the
  autumn skies,   15
The osprey's slow imperial swoop, the scrawny bittern's rise;
Nursing a longing for larger life than circled a rural home,
An instinct of leadership within, and of action yet to come.

THOMAS BAILEY ALDRICH

SONNET XX

Books and Seasons [1]

Because the sky is blue; because blithe May
Masks in the wren's note and the lilac's hue;
Because—in fine, because the sky is blue
I will read none but piteous tales to-day.
5   Keep happy laughter till the skies be gray,
And the sad season cypress wears, and rue;
Then, when the wind is moaning in the flue,
And ways are dark, bid Chaucer make us gay.
But now a little sadness! All too sweet
10 This springtide riot, this most poignant air,
This sensuous world of color and perfume.
So listen, love, while I the woes repeat
Of Hamlet and Ophelia, and that pair
Whose bridal bed was builded in a tomb.

SONNET XXI

Outward Bound [1]

15 I leave behind me the elm-shadowed square
And carven portals of the silent street,
And wander on with listless, vagrant feet
Through seaward-leading alleys, till the air
Smells of the sea, and straightway then the care
20 Slips from my heart, and life once more is sweet.
At the lane's ending lie the white-winged fleet.
O restless Fancy, whither wouldst thou fare?
Here are brave pinions that shall take thee far—
Gaunt hulks of Norway; ships of red Ceylon;

[1] Reprinted by permission of Houghton Mifflin Company, publishers.

Slim-masted lovers of the blue Azores!
'Tis but an instant hence to Zanzibar,
Or to the regions of the Midnight Sun;
Ionian isles are thine, and all the fairy shores!

JOAQUIN MILLER

DAWN AT SAN DIEGO[1]

[Extract]

'Twas night, and still it seemed not night.   5
Yet, far down in the cañon deep,
Where night had housed all day, to keep
Companion with the wolf, you might
Have hewn a statue out of night.

The shrill coyote loosed his tongue   10
Deep in the dark arroyo's bed;
And bat and owl above his head
From out their gloomy caverns swung;
A swoop of wings, a catlike call,
A crackle sharp of chaparral!   15

Then sudden, fitful winds sprang out,
And swept the mesa like a broom;
Wild, saucy winds, that sang of room!
That leapt the cañon with a shout
From dusty throats, audaciously   20
And headlong tore into the sea,
As tore the swine with lifted snout.

Some birds came, went, then came again
From out the hermit's wood-hung hill;
Came swift, and arrowlike, and still,   25
As you have seen birds, when the rain—

[1] From *Songs of the Sierras*. Permission granted by the Harr Wagner
Publishing Company, publisher of Joaquin Miller's complete works.

The great, big, high-born rain, leapt white
And sudden from a cloud like night.

And then a dove, dear, nunlike dove,
With eyes all tenderness, with eyes
5   So loving, longing, full of love,
That when she reached her slender throat
And sang one low, soft, sweetest note,
Just one, so faint, so far, so near,
You could have wept with joy to hear.

VAQUERO[1]

10   His broad-brimmed hat pushed back with careless air,
The proud vaquero sits his steed as free
As winds that toss his black abundant hair.
No rover ever swept a lawless sea
With such a haught and heedless air as he
15   Who scorns the path, and bounds with swift disdain
Away, a peon born, yet born to be
A splendid king; behold him ride, and reign.

How brave he takes his herds in branding days,
On timber'd hills that belt about the plain;
20   He climbs, he wheels, he shouts through winding ways
Of hiding ferns and hanging fir; the rein
Is loose, the rattling spur drives swift; the mane
Blows free; the bullocks rush in storms before;
They turn with lifted heads, they rush again,
25   Then sudden plunge from out the wood, and pour
A cloud upon the plain with one terrific roar.

Now sweeps the tawny man on stormy steed,
His gaudy trappings toss'd about and blown
About the limbs as lithe as any reed;

[1] From *Songs of the Sierras*. Permission granted by the Harr Wagner
Publishing Company, publisher of Joaquin Miller's complete works.

The swift long lasso twirl'd above is thrown
From flying hand; the fall, the fearful groan
Of bullock toil'd and tumbled in the dust—
The black herds onward sweep, and all disown
The fallen, struggling monarch that has thrust   5
His tongue in rage and roll'd his red eyes in disgust.

JAMES WHITCOMB RILEY

WHEN THE FROST IS ON THE PUNKIN[1]

When the frost is on the punkin and the fodder's in the shock,
And you hear the kyouck and gobble of the struttin' turkey-
    cock,
And the clackin' of the guineys, and the cluckin' of the hens,
And the rooster's hallylooyer as he tiptoes on the fence;   10
O, it's then's the times a feller is a-feelin' at his best,
With the risin' sun to greet him from a night of peaceful rest,
As he leaves the house, bareheaded, and goes out to feed the
    stock,
When the frost is on the punkin and the fodder's in the shock.

They's something kind o' harty-like about the atmosphere   15
When the heat of summer's over and the coolin' fall is here—
Of course we miss the flowers, and the blossoms on the trees,
And the mumble of the hummin'-birds and buzzin' of the
    bees;
But the air's so appetizin'; and the landscape through the
    haze
Of a crisp and sunny morning of the airly autumn days   20
Is a pictur' that no painter has the colorin' to mock—
When the frost is on the punkin and the fodder's in the shock.

The husky, rusty rustle of the tossels of the corn,
And the raspin' of the tangled leaves, as golden as the morn;
The stubble in the furries—kind o' lonesome-like, but still
A-preachin' sermons to us of the barns they growed to fill;
5 The strawstack in the medder, and the reaper in the shed;
The hosses in theyr stalls below—the clover overhead!—
O, it sets my heart a-clickin' like the tickin' of a clock,
When the frost is on the punkin and the fodder 's in the shock!

CELIA THAXTER

CHANTICLEER [1]

    I wake! I feel the day is near;
10   I hear the red cock crowing!
    He cries "'Tis dawn!" How sweet and clear
    His cheerful call comes to my ear,
        While light is slowly growing.

    The white snow gathers, flake on flake;
15   I hear the red cock crowing!
    Is anybody else awake
    To see the winter morning break,
        While thick and fast 'tis snowing?

    I think the world is all asleep;
20   I hear the red cock crowing!
    Out of the frosty pane I peep;
    The drifts are piled so wide and deep,
        And wild the wind is blowing!

    Nothing I see has shape or form;
25   I hear the red cock crowing!
    But that dear voice comes through the storm
    To greet me in my nest so warm,
        As if the sky were glowing!

[1] Reprinted by permission of Houghton Mifflin Company, publishers.

A happy little child, I lie
  And hear the red cock crowing.
The day is dark. I wonder why
His voice rings out so brave and high,
  With gladness overflowing.   5

THE SANDPIPER[1]

Across the narrow beach we flit,
  One little sandpiper and I
And fast I gather, bit by bit,
  The scattered driftwood, bleached and dry,
The wild waves reach their hands for it,   10
  The wild wind raves, the tide runs high,
As up and down the beach we flit,—
  One little sandpiper and I.

Above our heads the sullen clouds
  Scud black and swift across the sky;   15
Like silent ghosts in misty shrouds
  Stand out the white lighthouses high.
Almost as far as eye can reach
  I see the close-reefed vessels fly,
As fast we flit along the beach,—   20
  One little sandpiper and I.

I watch him as he skims along
  Uttering his sweet and mournful cry.
He starts not at my fitful song,
  Or flash of fluttering drapery.   25
He has no thought of any wrong;
  He scans me with a fearless eye.
Stanch friends are we, well tried and strong,
  The little sandpiper and I.

[1] Reprinted by permission of Houghton Mifflin Company, publishers.

Comrade, where wilt thou be to-night
  When the loosed storm breaks furiously?
My driftwood fire will burn so bright!
  To what warm shelter canst thou fly?
I do not fear for thee, though wroth
  The tempest rushes through the sky:
For are we not God's children both,
  Thou, little sandpiper, and I?

EDWARD ROWLAND SILL

THE FOOL'S PRAYER[1]

The royal feast was done; the King
  Sought some new sport to banish care,
And to his jester cried: "Sir Fool,
  Kneel now, and make for us a prayer!"

The jester doffed his cap and bells,
  And stood the mocking court before;
They could not see the bitter smile
  Behind the painted grin he wore.

He bowed his head, and bent his knee
  Upon the monarch's silken stool;
His pleading voice arose: "O Lord,
  Be merciful to me, a fool!

"No pity, Lord, could change the heart
  From red with wrong to white as wool:
The rod must heal the sin; but, Lord,
  Be merciful to me, a fool!

"'Tis not by guilt the onward sweep
  Of truth and right, O Lord, we stay;
'Tis by our follies that so long
  We hold the earth from heaven away.

[1] Reprinted by permission of Houghton Mifflin Company, publishers.

"These clumsy feet, still in the mire,
 Go crushing blossoms without end;
These hard, well-meaning hands we thrust
 Among the heart-strings of a friend.

"The ill-timed truth we might have kept—   5
 Who knows how sharp it pierced and stung!
The word we had not sense to say—
 Who knows how grandly it had rung!

"Our faults no tenderness should ask,
 The chastening stripes must cleanse them all;   10
But for our blunders—oh, in shame
 Before the eyes of heaven we fall.

"Earth bears no balsam for mistakes;
 Men crown the knave, and scourge the tool
That did his will; but thou, O Lord,   15
 Be merciful to me, a fool!"

The room was hushed; in silence rose
 The King and sought his gardens cool,
And walked apart, and murmured low,
 "Be merciful to me, a fool!"   20

EMILY DICKINSON

THE STORM[1]

There came a wind like a bugle;
It quivered through the grass,
And a green chill upon the heat
So ominous did pass
We barred the windows and the doors   25
As from an emerald ghost;
The doom's electric moccason
That very instant passed.

[1] Reprinted by permission of Little, Brown & Company, publishers.

On a strange mob of panting trees,
And fences fled away,
And rivers where the houses ran
The living looked that day.
The bell within the steeple wild
The flying tidings whirled.
How much can come
And much can go
And yet abide the world !

A BOOK[1]

He ate and drank the precious words,
His spirit grew robust;
He knew no more that he was poor,
Nor that his frame was dust.
He danced along the dingy days,
And this bequest of wings
Was but a book. What liberty
A loosened spirit brings!

EMMA LAZARUS

VENUS OF THE LOUVRE[2]

Down the long hall she glistens like a star,
The foam-born mother of Love, transfixed to stone,
Yet none the less immortal, breathing on.
Time's brutal hand hath maimed but could not mar.
When first the enthralled enchantress from afar
Dazzled mine eyes, I saw not her alone,
Serenely poised on her world-worshiped throne,
As when she guided once her dove-drawn car,—

[1] Reprinted by permission of Little, Brown & Company, publishers.
[2] Reprinted by permission of Mrs. Annie Humphreys Johnstone.

But at her feet a pale, death-stricken Jew,
Her life adorer, sobbed farewell to love.
Here *Heine* wept!   Here still he weeps anew,
Nor ever shall his shadow lift or move,
While mourns one ardent heart, one poet-brain,   5
For vanished Hellas and Hebraic pain.

LUCY LARCOM

WHEN THE WOODS TURN BROWN[1]

How will it be when the roses fade
Out of the garden and out of the glade?
When the fresh pink bloom of the sweet-brier wild,
That leans from the dell like the cheek of a child,   10
Is changed for dry hips on a thorny bush?
Then scarlet and carmine the groves will flush.

How will it be when the autumn flowers
Wither away from their leafless bowers?
When sun-flower and star-flower and goldenrod   15
Glimmer no more from the frosted sod,
And the hillside nooks are empty and cold?
Then the forest-tops will be gay with gold.

How will it be when the woods turn brown,
Their gold and their crimson all dropped down,   20
And crumbled to dust?   Oh, then, as we lay
Our ear to Earth's lips, we shall hear her say,
"In the dark, I am seeking new gems for my crown:"—
We will dream of green leaves, when the woods turn brown.

[1] Reprinted by permission of Houghton Mifflin Company, publishers.

THE WATER–LILY [1]

From the reek of the pond the lily
  Has risen, in raiment white,
A spirit of air and water,
  A form of incarnate light.
5   Yet, except for the rooted stem
     That steadies her diadem,
Except for the earth she is nourished by,
Could the soul of the lily have climbed to the sky?

EUGENE FIELD

THE SINGING IN GOD'S ACRE [2]

Out yonder in the moonlight, wherein God's Acre lies,
10 Go angels walking to and fro, singing their lullabies.
Their radiant wings are folded, and their eyes are bended low,
As they sing among the beds whereon the flowers delight to
    grow,—
     "Sleep, oh, sleep!
     The Shepherd guardeth his sheep.
15   Fast speedeth the night away,
     Soon cometh the glorious day;
     Sleep, weary ones, while ye may,
     Sleep, oh, sleep!"

The flowers within God's Acre see that fair and wondrous
    sight,
20 And hear the angels singing to the sleepers through the night;
And, lo! throughout the hours of day those gentle flowers
    prolong
The music of the angels in that tender slumber-song,—

---

[1] Reprinted by permission of Houghton Mifflin Company, publishers.
[2] Reprinted by permission of Charles Scribner's Sons, publishers.

"Sleep, oh, sleep!
The Shepherd loveth his sheep.
He that guardeth his flock the best
Hath folded them to his loving breast;
So sleep ye now, and take your rest,—   5
Sleep, oh, sleep!"

From angel and from flower the years have learned that
    soothing song,
And with its heavenly music speed the days and nights along;
So through all time, whose flight the Shepherd's vigils glorify,
God's Acre slumbereth in the grace of that sweet lullaby,—   10

"Sleep, oh, sleep!
The Shepherd loveth his sheep.
Fast speedeth the night away,
Soon cometh the glorious day;
Sleep, weary ones, while ye may,—   15
Sleep, oh, sleep!"

THE EXPLORER'S WOOING[1]

Oh, come with me to the arctic seas
    Where the blizzards and icebergs grow,
And dally awhile with the polar breeze
    In the land of the Eskimo.   20
We will fish for seal and the great white bears
    In their caves on the frozen shores;
We will spread our nets in the frigid lairs
    Of the walrus that snorts and roars.

When the rest of creation swoons with heat   25
    All pleasant and chipper we'll be;
'Twould be hard to find a summer retreat
    As cool as the arctic sea.

[1] Reprinted by permission of Charles Scribner's Sons, publishers.

We will ramble along in some snowy glade
  With never a sultry sigh,
Or loll at ease in the grateful shade
  Of an iceberg four miles high.

5 So come with me to the arctic pole—
    To the land of the walrus and bear,
  Where the glaciers wave and the blizzards roll,
    And victuals are frequently rare.
  You are plump and fat—with such a mate
10   In my iceberg I would dwell,
  In the pleasing hope I could baffle fate
    By eating you *au naturel*.

MARION CRAWFORD

VIA CRUCIS[1]

Chapter X

[An Ambush]

June was upon Italy, as a gossamer veil and a garland on
the brow of a girl bride. The first sweet hay was drying in
15 Tuscan valleys; the fig leaves were spreading, and shadowing
the watery fruit that begins to grow upon the crooked twigs
before the leaves themselves, and which the people call "fig-
blossoms," because the real figs come later; the fresh and
silvery olive shoots had shed a snow-flurry of small white
20 stars; the yellow holy thorn still blossomed in the rough
places of the hills, and the blending of many wild flowers
was like a maiden blush on the earth's soft bosom.

At early morning Gilbert rode along the crest of a low and
grassy hill that was still sheltered from the sun by the high
25 mountains to eastward, and he drank in the cool and scented

---

[1] Reprinted from Marion Crawford's *Via Crucis*. By special arrangement with The Macmillan Company, publisher.

air as if it had been water of paradise, and he a man saved
out of death to life by the draught. There was much peace in
his heart, and a still security that he had not felt yet since he
had seen his father lying dead before him. He knew not how
it was, but he was suddenly sure that Beatrix loved him and
had escaped to the court of France in the hope of finding him,
and was waiting for him day by day. And he was also sure
that the Church would not cut him off from her in the end,
let the churchmen say what they would. Was not the Queen
of France his friend? She would plead his case, and the
Pope would understand and take away the bar. He thought
of these things, and he felt his hopes rising bright, like the
steady sun.

He reached the end of the crest and drew rein before descending, and he looked down into the broad valley and the
river winding in and out among trees, gleaming like silver out
there in the sun beyond the narrowing shadow, then dark
blue, and then, in places, as black as ink. The white road,
broad and dusty, winding on to Florence, followed the changing river. Gilbert took his cap from his head and felt the
coolness of the morning on his forehead and the gentle breath
of the early summer in his fair hair; and then, sitting there
in the deep silence, bareheaded, it seemed to him that he was
in the very holy place of God's cathedral.

"The peace of God, which passeth all understanding," he
repeated softly and almost involuntarily.

"Now the God of peace be with you all, amen," answered
Dunstan.

But there was a tone in his voice that made Gilbert look at
him, and he saw in the man's face a quiet smile, as if something amused him, while the black eyes were fixed on a sight
far away. Dunstan was pointing to what he saw; so Gilbert
looked, too, and he perceived a gleaming, very far off, that
moved slowly on the white road beside the shining river.

"They are expecting a fight to-day," said Gilbert, "for they
are in mail and their mule-train is behind them."

"Shall we turn aside and ride up the mountain, to let them pass?" asked Dunstan, who could fight like a wildcat, but had also the cat's instinctive caution.

"It would be a pity not to see the fight," answered Gilbert, and he began to ride forward down the descent.

The track was worn down to the depth of a man's height by the hoofs of the beasts that had trodden it for ages; and in places it was very narrow, so that two laden mules could hardly pass each other. Young chestnut shoots of three or four years' growth sprang up in thick green masses from the top of the bank on each side, and now and then the branches of nut trees almost joined their broad leaves across the way, making a deep shade that was cool and smelt of fresh mold and green things. A little way down the hill a spring of water trickled into a little pool hollowed out by travelers, and the water overflowed and made thick black mud of the earth churned up with last year's dead leaves.

Gilbert let his horse stop to drink, and his men waited in single file to take their turn.

"Psst!" The peculiar hiss which Italians make to attract attention came sharp and distinct from the low growth of the chestnut shoots.

Gilbert turned his head quickly in the direction of the sound. A swarthy face appeared, framed in a close leathern cap on which small rings of rusty iron were sewn strongly, but not very regularly. Then a long left arm, clad in the same sort of mail, pushed the lower boughs aside and made a gesture in the direction whence Gilbert had come, which was meant to warn him back—a gesture of the flat hand, held across the breast with thumb hidden, just moving a little up and down.

"Why should I go back?" asked Gilbert, in his natural voice.

"Because yes," answered the dark man, in the common Italian idiom, and in a low tone. "Because we are waiting for the Florentines, certain of us of Pistoja, and we want no travelers in the way. And then—because, if you will not—"

The right arm suddenly appeared, and in the hand was a spear, and the act was a threat to run Gilbert through, unmailed as he was, and just below his adversary. But as Gilbert laid his hand upon his sword, looking straight at the man's eye, he very suddenly saw a strange sight; for there was a long arrow sticking through the head, the point out on one side and the feather on the other; and for a moment the man still looked at him with eyes wide open. Then, standing as he was, his body slowly bent forward upon itself as if curling up, and with a crash of steel it rolled down the bank into the pool of water, where the lance snapped under it.

For little Alric, the Saxon groom, had quietly slipped to the ground and had strung his bow, suspecting trouble, and had laid an arrow to the string, waiting; and little Alric's aim was very sure; it was also the first time that he had shot a man, and he came of men who had been bowmen since Alfred's day, and before that, and had killed many, for generations, so that it was an instinct with them to slay with the bow.

"Well done, boy!" cried Gilbert.

But his horse reared back, as the dead body fell splashing into the pool, and Alric quietly unstrung his bow again and remounted to be ready. Then Gilbert would have ridden on, but Dunstan hindered him.

"This fellow was but a sentinel," he said. "A little further on you will find these woods filled with armed men waiting to surprise the riders we saw from above. Surely, I will die with you, sir; but we need not die like rats in a corn-bin. Let us ride up a little way again, and then skirt the woods and take the road where it joins the river, down in the valley."

"And warn those men of Florence that they are riding into an ambush," added Gilbert, turning his horse.

So they rode up the hill; and scarcely were they out of sight of the spring when a very old woman and a ragged little

boy crept out of the bushes, with knives, and began to rob
the dead man of his rusty mail and his poor clothes.

Gilbert reached the road a long stone's-throw beyond the
last chestnut shoots, and galloped forward to meet the advancing knights and men-at-arms. He drew rein suddenly,
a dozen lengths before them, and threw up his open right
hand. They were riding leisurely, but all in mail, some having surcoats with devices embroidered thereon, and most of
them with their heads uncovered, their steel caps and hoods
of mail hanging at their saddle-bows.

"Sirs," cried Gilbert, in a loud, clear voice, "you ride to an
ambush! The chestnut woods are full of the men of Pistoja."

A knight who rode in front, and was the leader, came close
to Gilbert. He was a man not young, with a dark, smooth
face, as finely cut as a relief carved upon a shell, and his hair
was short and iron-gray.

Gilbert told him what had happened in the woods, and
the elderly knight listened quietly and thoughtfully, while
examining Gilbert's face with half-unconscious keenness.

"If you please," said the young man, "I will lead you by
the way I have ridden, and you may enter the bushes from
above, and fight at better advantage."

But the Florentine smiled at such simple tactics. To feel
the breeze, he held up his right hand, which issued from a slit
in the wrist of his mail, so that the iron mitten hung loose;
and the wind was blowing toward the woods. He called to
his squire.

"Take ten men, light torches, and set fire to those young
trees."

The men got a cook's earthenware pot of coals, fed all day
long with charcoal on the march, lest there should be no fire
for the camp at night; and they lit torches of pitched hemp-
rope, and presently there was a great smoke and a crackling
of green branches. But the leader of the Florentines put on
his steel cap and drew the mail hood down over his shoulders,
while all the others who were bareheaded did the same.

"Sir," said the knight to Gilbert, "you should withdraw behind us, now that you have done us this great service. For presently there will be fighting here, and you are unmailed."

"The weather is overwarm for an iron coat," answered Gilbert, with a laugh. "But if I shall not trespass upon the 5 courtesies of your country by thrusting my company upon you, I will ride at your left hand, that you may the more safely slay with your right."

"Sir," answered the other, "you are a very courteous man. Of what country may you be?" 10

"An Englishman, sir, and of Norman blood." He also told his name.

"Gino Buondelmonte, at your service," replied the knight, naming himself.

"Nay, sir," laughed Gilbert, "a knight cannot serve a 15 simple squire!"

"It is never shame for gentle-born to serve gentle-born," answered the other.

But now the smoke was driving the men of Pistoja out of the wood, and the hillside down which Gilbert had ridden 20 was covered with men in mail, on horseback, and with footmen in leather and such poor armor as had been worn by the dead sentinel. Buondelmonte thrust his feet home in his wide stirrups, settled himself in the saddle, shortened his reins, and drew his sword, while watching all the time the 25 movements of the enemy. Gilbert sat quietly watching them, too. As yet he had never ridden at a foe, though he had fought on foot, and he unconsciously smiled with pleasure at the prospect, trying to pick out the man likely to fall by his sword. In England, or in France, he would certainly have 30 put on the good mail which was packed on the sumpter mule's back; but here in the sweet Italian spring, in the morning breeze full of the scent of wild flowers, and the humming of bees and the twittering of little birds, even fighting had a look of harmless play, and he felt as secure in his 35 cloth tunic as if it had been of woven steel.

The position of the Florentines was the better, for they had the broad homeward road behind them, in case of defeat; but the men of Pistoja, driven from the woods by the thick smoke and the burning of the undergrowth, were obliged to scramble down a descent so steep that many of them were forced to dismount, and they then found themselves huddled together in a narrow strip of irregular meadow between the road and the foot of the stony hill. Buondelmonte saw his advantage. His sword shot up at arm's length over his head, and his high, clear voice rang out in a single word of command.

In a moment the peace of nature was rent by the scream of war. Hoofs thundered, swords flashed, men yelled, and arrows shot through the great cloud of dust that rose suddenly as from an explosion. In the front of the charge the Italian and the Norman rode side by side, the inscrutable black eyes and the calm olive features beside the Norman's terrible young figure, with its white glowing face and fair hair streaming on the wind, and wide, deep eyes like blue steel, and the quivering nostrils of the man born for fight.

Short was the strife and sharp, as the Florentines spread to right and left of their leader and pressed the foe back against the steep hill in the narrow meadow. Then Buondelmonte thrust out straight and sure, in the Italian fashion, and once the mortal wound was in the face, and once in the throat, and many times men felt it in their breasts through mail and gambeson and bone. But Gilbert's great strokes flashed like lightnings from his pliant wrist, and behind the wrist was the Norman arm, and behind the arm the relentless pale face and the even lips, that just tightened upon each other as the death-blows went out, one by one, each to its place in a life. The Italian destroyed men skillfully and quickly, yet as if it were distasteful to him. The Norman slew like a bright destroying angel, breathing the swift and silent wrath of God upon mankind.

Blow upon blow, with clash of steel, thrust after thrust as

the darting of serpents, till the dead lay in heaps, and the horses' hoofs churned blood and grass to a green-red foam, till the sword-arm waited high and then sank slowly, because there was none for the sword to strike, and the point rested among the close-sewn rings of mail on Buondelmonte's foot, and the thin streams of blood trickled quietly down the dimmed blade.

"Sir," said Buondelmonte, courteously, "you are a marvelous fine swordsman, though you fence not in our manner, with the point. I am your debtor for the safety of my left side. Are you hurt, sir?"

"Not I!" laughed Gilbert, wiping his broad blade slowly on his horse's mane for lack of anything better.

Then Buondelmonte looked at him again and smiled.

"You have won yourself a fair crest," he laughed, as he glanced at Gilbert's cap.

"A crest?" Gilbert put up his hand, and uttered an exclamation as it struck against a sharp steel point.

A half-spent arrow had pierced the top of his red cloth cap and was sticking there, like a woman's long hairpin. He thought that if it had struck two inches lower, with a little more force, he should have looked as the man in the woods did, whom Alric had killed. He plucked the shaft from the stiff cloth with some difficulty, and, barely glancing at it, tossed it away. But little Alric, who had left the guide to take care of the mules and had followed the charge on foot, picked up the arrow, marked it with his knife and put it carefully into his leathern quiver, which he filled with arrows he picked up on the grass till it would hold no more. Dunstan, who had ridden in the press with the rest, was looking among the dead for a good sword to take, his own being broken.

"Florence owes you a debt, sir," said Buondelmonte, an hour later, when they were riding back from the pursuit. "But for your warning, many of us would be lying dead in that wood. I pray you, take from the spoil, such as it is, whatsoever you desire. And if it please you to stay with us, the archbishop shall make a knight of you, for you have won knighthood to-day."

But Gilbert shook his head, smiling gravely.

5 "Praised be God, I need nothing, sir," he answered. "I thank you for your courteous hospitality, but I cannot stay, seeing that I ride upon a lady's bidding. And as for a debt, sir, Florence has paid hers largely in giving me your acquaintance."

10 "My friendship, sir," replied Buondelmonte, not yielding in compliment to the knightly youth.

So they broke bread together and drank a draught, and parted. But Buondelmonte gave Dunstan a small purse of gold and a handful of silver to little Alric and the muleteer, 15 and Gilbert rode away with his men, and all were well pleased.

Yet when he was alone in the evening, a sadness and a horror of what he had done came over him; for he had taken life that day as a man mows down grass, in swaths, and he 20 could not tell why he had slain, for he knew not the men who fought on the two sides, nor their difference. He had charged because he saw men charging, he had struck for the love of strife, and had killed because it was of his nature to kill. But now that the blood was shed, and the sun which had risen 25 on life was going down on death, Gilbert Warde was sorry for what he had done, and his brave charge seemed but a senseless deed of slaughter, for which he should rather have done penance than received knighthood.

"I am no better than a wild beast," he said, when he had 30 told Dunstan what he felt. "Go and find out a priest to pray for those I have killed to-day."

He covered his brow with his hand as he sat at the supper table.

"I go," answered the young man. "Yet it is a pleasant 35 sight to see the lion weeping for pity over the calf he has killed."

"The lion kills that he may eat and himself live," answered Gilbert. "And the men who fought to-day fought for a cause. But I smote for the wanton love of smiting that is in all our blood, and I am ashamed. Bid the priest pray for me also."   5

MAURICE THOMPSON

A MARSH-LAND INCIDENT[1]

A schooner, listing sharply to a fragrant breeze, gives me the motion that I best like, when I stand well forward, feeling the kiss of chill spray over the bow. The delight is emphatic after a long rain (alternating shower and fog), during which nothing better than a swarm of mosquitoes has offered relief   10 from the lifeless monotony of a breathless sea. Indeed, it was like magic when I awoke and felt the swell under me. I sat up in my little musty bunk, rubbing my eyes, then hurried on with my clothes. No sooner was my head above deck, as I mounted the narrow ladder, than I smelled as well as felt   15 the weather's change. Half the sky was already clear; the breeze had the fog going, while our little schooner flew after it like a bird.

Two swarthy, wrinkled sailors were mopping the deck, one of them whistling contentedly a lugubrious tune, so his looks   20 suggested, while the other grumbled in mongrel patois. Right ahead of us, under the lifting fog, I saw a marsh, beyond which a forest of live-oaks was dimly outlined. As my skipper had told me that we were off the west shore of Borgne, I at once recognized the place, and gave orders that the schooner   25 should be sailed into a bight at the mouth of a little bayou coming through the marsh from the distant hummock-lands. In fact, we sailed up the bayou for a mile or more, and lay to, the men lowering a boat in which I was to be rowed to the live-oaks.   30

[1] Reprinted by permission of The Century Company, publishers.

It was interesting to observe the silent, almost stupid curiosity with which the old water-dogs furtively gazed at my archery tackle, but they asked no questions, leaning to their oars vigorously. The bayou narrowed, as we ascended
5 its winding water, until there was in places scant room for a full sweep of the oars. Two or three marsh-hens showed themselves for a moment on the mud at the edge of the stream, then darted into the tall grass. Gulls flew overhead, their wings shining like snow against the blue sky.

10 The prospect of a whole day alone in the wood toward which I was going by a flight so lively made my blood tingle; and when at last, an hour after sunrise, I stood on shore, waving good speed to the returning boat, I was as happy as any bird. In the distance lay the schooner, as if on the
15 marsh itself, her wide sails curling gently. Behind me, less than a bow-shot away, the oak-foliage and the gray-green moss twinkled in the breeze. I heard bird-voices, a red-cockaded woodpecker's most distinctly, in the first fringe of the wood.

20 Swinging my bag of luncheon over my shoulder, and making sure that I had all of my tackle, I went splashing through a bit of rushy marsh direct to the nearest trees, where there was a little bluff marking the hummock's limit. Pretty soon I hung the luncheon-bag on a bough and marked the place.
25 The breeze here was strong enough to make way with all of the gnats and mosquitoes in the open parts of the wood, and the magnificent wide-armed live-oaks and water-oaks looked like immense apple-trees—an orchard of the gods.

I stood still, looking all around. But what had become of
30 the birds heard awhile ago? Not a sound could I hear, save the multitudinous rustlings of the wind. No wing-shine flashed across the aisles. The impression of solitude was perfect. Of course, I had not expected to find a swarming wood in midwinter; but I well knew that this utter silence
35 and stillness could not last; so I strolled on deeper into the shadows, and the first sign of animal life to attract my atten-

tion was a tiny brown creeper going spirally up a big tree,
amid the lichens and ferns. I stopped to make a note of this,
according to habit; and while I was putting away my book
and pencil a large bird flew along close to me and lit on a
branch not twenty yards distant, but amid the leaves and 5
moss, so that I could not see it. From the merest glimpse, as
it went by, I supposed it to be some species of hawk. To
ascertain I drove an arrow to the spot, guessing at the proper
place. It clipped keenly through the tangle, with a whack
upon a tree-bole beyond, and out rushed the bird, which 10
proved to be a golden-winged woodpecker.

My arrow's stroke seemed to shock the whole wood suddenly into life. I saw a dozen birds in the next ten seconds:
blue jays, woodpeckers, a mocking-bird, and several small
species that I could not identify. Upon all of these I used 15
my field-glass, not my bow. It was not the season of song,
but many voices chirped and whistled cheerily as I passed
slowly and noiselessly along. What I most wished to come
upon was one of the small deer said to abound in the place.
But this was not to be; nor did I find any game larger than a 20
woodcock during the day. The event which made my tramp
worth special record (wherefore this paper) began after I
had walked entirely through the wood and emerged upon a
marsh-prairie, covered with low grass in the main, but dotted
irregularly with tufts or tussocks of high weeds and rushlike 25
plants—a plashy area half covered with water.

I had stretched myself on a big log to rest, my back to the
wood, my face to the marsh and the sea beyond, and had lain
thus for half an hour, when a small object moving slyly at the
edge of a tussock caught my eye. A peculiar satiny gleam be- 30
trayed it, and then I saw the form of a heron. Out came my
field-glass, and in a moment a beautiful egret was stalking
apparently almost under my nose. It was the Louisiana
egret, a rare bird now, so many have been killed for their
beautiful plumes. Of course it was not in full feather; but 35
it was lovely even without its fine purple trail, and every

movement displayed a tint of color exquisitely delicate. I
saw that it was feeding upon what it got by stabbing the mud
with its bill, probably some kind of grub or marsh insect.
Its eyes flashed with a reddish light and had a singularly
5 cruel expression. The purple of its neck-feathers and crest
shimmered softly in the sunlight.

While I was looking the bird suddenly quit eating, crouched
in a frightened way, then skulked into the tall growth of the
tussock. After half an hour had elapsed, and while I was
10 writing in my notebook, it reappeared and stood with its
neck stretched almost perpendicularly to its full length. I
watched it for a long time before it moved in the slightest,
then it resumed its feeding. It was uneasy, however, and I
noticed that it frequently gazed upward as if half expecting
15 some calamity from on high. I looked to the sky for a sign
of danger, for I thought that a hawk might be circling overhead; but all was clear.

A few minutes later the heron suddenly flattened itself
upon the mud, its wings slightly spread, its neck drawn close
20 to its body, and at the same time a peculiar noise, a low,
whizzing roar, fell from above. I glanced up, and at first saw
nothing; but the sound rapidly increased, and then I caught
sight of a large hawk rushing almost vertically down. It was
still very high; its wings were almost close shut, and its
25 velocity was doubling momently. As it neared the ground,
I could scarcely follow its movement with my eyes; but I
saw that it was not swooping upon the heron. What it did
strike was a meadow-lark, a hundred yards farther away
from me, which it bore off to the woods.

30 As for the heron, it lay quite motionless for a long time,
evidently in a very trance of terror. I observed it closely
with my glass, and do not think a single feather on it stirred.
Indeed, the bird lay there as if dead, save that its cruel red
eyes burned like live coals. After a while I tried a shot at it.
35 The arrow fell about a foot short, but flung mud all over the
sheeny plumage of the heron's back and neck. That was too

much; the trance was broken, and away flew the beautiful thing far across the marsh.

When I went to recover my shaft, some snipe flashed swiftly out of the grass, with their rasping cry: "Scaipe! scaipe!" I marked them down and followed; but they would not lie until I got near enough for a shot; so I returned to the wood's edge, where now the birds of song were noisy, piping each in his own key. Luck a few minutes later gave me a great opportunity, as I find it recorded in a weather-stained notebook to which I confided much more than mere entries of shots and their results, and maybe the flavor of an archer's log will not be bad. At a venture I will transcribe a page:

Had crept for some distance under cover of a magnolia-bush,—trying to approach a log-cock,—when by some chance an indirect ray of vision fell upon a much larger bird standing in the oozy mud beside a little black puddle. It was a wood-ibis, shining white in the gloomy place. I think it the finest specimen I ever saw.

You will see that the note in its last sentence bears the inference of a successful shot. I recollect it well: sixty yards, and a small rift in a thicket to shoot through—a very trying piece of work for an archer. The flat trajectory of a rifle-ball eliminates such a difficulty; but an arrow at sixty yards rises five or more feet above the line of sight,—of course, I speak of heavy hunting-shafts,— and this often causes serious interference with the shot where the trees, branches, and undergrowth are thick. A nice calculation must be made in an instant, and the factors are many, each one absolutely important. In the present case I had plenty of time; for the bird did not see me or even suspect danger from any quarter.

Have you ever heard a bow-shot in a lonely forest, when the wind was still and nothing but wild bird-voices broke the primeval silence? It is a memorable sound; not a "twang," as the poets say, nor yet a dead "flap," but rather a subdued yet ringing noise (like that from a smitten tambourine

muffled in cotton), and followed by the low "whish-sh" of
the flying arrow; then the stroke. It is all one phrase of
three notes. You may think it would not impress you;
but I tell you that few natures are proof against it. It
5 is an elementary, an aboriginal voice, with singular power
in it.

A friend of mine who had been, in his youth, a tireless
woodsman in the far West, told me about lying, once upon a
time, half asleep at the root of a tree. For many days he had
10 been wandering all alone. It was high noon, and he felt the
need of rest. The great forest was still, silent, gloomy. Suddenly a sound, "chuff!" fifty yards away, was followed by a
sharp whisper, and then "whack!" an arrow struck into the
tree's bole an inch above his head! A lordly savage, who
15 was a poor archer, had taken a chance shot at him from behind a rock. "Well," said my friend, shaking his head in
memory of the "close call," and smiling reminiscently, "an
arrow sounds scarier 'n any bullet!"

To this moment that shot at the ibis is a fresh line on a
20 page of my experience, and I can scarcely realize that it was
years ago that I loosed the shaft. I hear the bow's sturdy
recoil, the keen sibilation of the arrow, the dull, successful
stroke. Doubtless the joy of an archer comes from a deeper
well than that of the man who shoots with a gun. I have
25 tried both weapons. It is almost infinitely easier to take
game with a fowling-piece than with a bow; but the demand
which the old implement makes upon one's patience, wari-
ness, stealth, skill, is of itself an endless fascination; and
when, at last, the successful shot is delivered, something
30 strangely and inexplicably thrilling comes out of it. Moreover, the simple fact that shots are many and killings few
may account for the greater part of sylvan archery's fascination. The archer shoots for the joy of shooting, not for the
bag's weight.

35   I have read old Roger Ascham's *Toxophilus* in many an
ancient wood, while resting and waiting for the wild things to

show themselves. Ascham was no sylvan bowman, nor is his
little book adequate to the needs of one who aspires to successful wild-wood shooting; but it is a quaint style he wields,
an ancient and moss-covered diction, so that nosing over
Toxophilus in a wild forest nook has its justification and 5
its comfort. By my notebook I am reminded that after I
had secured the ibis, and duly taken its dimensions for
ornithology's sake, I sat down, with the great bird on one
side of me and my bow on the other, to read awhile, as is
my way. "Got Ascham out of my pocket," runs the note, 10
"and read him for an hour—the stilted old scamp! In my
opinion, he was but a book-archer, shooting poorly even with
his pen; yet somehow he managed to get into the current of
eternity, and here he is." Yes, sure enough; there he was,
archaic spelling and all, telling me how to "shote."   15

But, curiously enough, neither Ascham nor the magnificent
ibis, neither the fine shooting at herons, a little later, nor the
exhilarating walk back to the boat against a freshening
breeze, could affect me as had the little egret when it flattened itself on the ground in deadly fear of the downward 20
swooping hawk.

WILLIAM HAMILTON GIBSON

PASTORAL DAYS[1]

SPRING

As far as the eye can reach the snow lies in a deep mantle
over the cheerless landscape. I look out upon a dreary moor,
where the horizon melts into the cold gray of a heavy sky.
The restless wind sweeps with pitiless blast through shivering 25
trees and over bleak hills, from whose crests, like a great
white veil, the clouds of hoary flakes are lifted and drawn
along by the gale. Down the upland slope, across the un-

dulating field, the blinding drift, like a thing of life, speeds
in its wild caprice, now swirling in fantastic eddies around
some isolated stack, half hidden in its chill embrace, now
winding away over bare-blown wall and scraggy fence, and
through the sighing willows near the frozen stream; now with
a wild whirl it flies aloft, and the dark pines and hemlocks
on the mountainside fade away in its icy mist. Again, yonder
it appears trailing along the meadow, until, flying like some
fugitive spirit chased from earth by the howling wind, it
vanishes in the sky. On every side these winged phantoms
lead their flying chase across the dreary landscape, and fence
and barn and house upon the hill in turn are dimmed or lost
to sight.

Who has not watched the strange antics of the driving snow
whirling past the window on a blustering winter's day? But
this is not a winter's day. This is the advent of a New
England spring.

Fortunate are we that its promises are not fulfilled, for the
ides of March might as oft betoken the approach of a tem-
pestuous winter as of a balmy spring. Consecrated to Mars
and Tantalus, it is a month of contradictions and disappoint-
ments, of broken promises and incessant warfare. It is the
struggle of tender awakening life against the buffeting of
rude and blighting elements. No man can tell what a day
may bring forth. Now we look out verily upon bleak December; to-morrow—who knows?—we may be transported into
May, and, with aspirations high, feel our ardor cooled by a
blast of ice and a blinding fall of snow. But this cannot always
last, for soon the southern breezes come and hold their sway
for days, and the north wind, angry in its defeat, is driven
back in lowering clouds to the region of eternal ice and snow.
Then comes a lovely day, without even a cloud—all blue
above, all dazzling white below. The sun shines with a glowing warmth, and we say unto ourselves, "This is, indeed, a
harbinger of spring." The sugar maples throb and trickle
with the flowing sap, and the lumbering ox-team and sled

wind through the woods from tree to tree to relieve the overflowing buckets. The boiling caldron in the sugar-house near
by receives the continual supply, and gives forth that sweet-
scented steam that issues from the open door, and comes
to us in occasional welcome whiffs across the snow. Long 5
"wedges" of wild-geese are seen cleaving the sky in their
northward flight. The little pussies on the willows are coaxed
from their winter nest, and creep out upon the stem. The
solitary bluebird makes his appearance, flying along the
thickets and stone walls with little hesitating warble, as if it 10
were not yet the appointed time to sing; and down among
the bogs, that cautious little pioneer, the swamp-cabbage
flower, peers above the ground beneath his purple-spotted
hood. He knows the fickle month which gives him birth, and
keeps well under cover. 15

Such days in March are too perfect to endure, and at night
the sky is overcast and dark. Then follows a long warm rain
that unlocks the ice in all the streams. The whiteness of the
hills and meadows melts into broad contracting strips and
patches. One by one, as mere specks upon the landscape, 20
these vanish in turn, until the last vestige of winter is washed
from the face of the earth to swell the tide of the rushing
stream. Even now, from the distant valley, we hear a continuous muffled roar, as the mighty freshet, impelled by an
irresistible force, plows its tortuous channel through the 25
lowlands and ravines. The quiet town is filled with an unusual commotion. Excited groups of townspeople crowd the
village store, and eager voices tell of the havoc wrought by
the fearful flood. We hear how the old toll-bridge, with toll-
man's house and all, was lifted from its piers like a pile of 30
straw, and whirled away upon the current. How its floating
timbers, in a great blockade, crushed into the old mill-pond;
how the dam had burst, and the rickety red sawmill gone
to pieces down the stream. Farmer Nathan's barn had gone,
and his flat meadows were like a whirling sea, strewn with 35
floating rails and driftwood. Every hour records its new

disaster as some eager messenger returns from the excited
crowds which line the river-bank.

. . . .

The tepid rain has penetrated deep into the yielding
ground, and with the winter's frost now coming to the sur-
5 face, the roads are well-nigh impassable with their plethora
of mud. For a full appreciation of *mud* in all its glory, and
in its superlative degree, one should see a New England
highway "when the frost comes out of the ground." The
roads are furrowed with deep grimy ruts, in which the be-
10 dabbled wheels sink to their hubs as in a quicksand, and the
hoofs of the floundering horse are held in the swampy depths
as if in a vise. For a week or more this state of things continues, until at length, after warm winds and sunny days, the
ground once more packs firm beneath the tread. This marks
15 the close of idle days. The junk pile in the barn is invaded,
and the rusty plow abstracted from the midst of rakes and
scythes and other farming tools. The old white horse thrusts
his long head from the stall near by, and whinnies at the
memories it revives, and with pricked-up ears and whisking
20 tail tells plainly of the eagerness he feels.

. . . .

Little did we suspect the mission of those rainy days, so
dreary and dismal without, or the sweet surprise preparing
for us in the myriad mysteries of life beneath the sod, where
every root and threadlike rootlet in the thirsty earth was
25 drinking in that welcome moisture, and numberless sleeping
germs, dwelling in darkness, were awakening into life to seek
the light of day, waiting only for the glory of a sunny dawn
to burst forth from their hiding-places! That sunny morning does come at last, and in its beams it sheds abroad a
30 power that stirs the deepest root. It is, indeed, a glorious
day. The clustered buds upon the silver-maples burst in
their exuberance, and fringe the graceful branches with their
silken tassels. The restless crocus, for months an unwilling
captive in its winter prison, can contain itself no longer, and

with its little overflowing cup lifts up its face to the blue
heaven. Golden daffodils burst into bloom on drooping stems,
and exchange their little nods right and left. The air is filled
with a faint perfume, in which the very earth mold yields its
fragrance—that wild aroma only known to spring. Our little 5
feathered friends, so few and far between as yet, are full of
song. The bluebird woos his mate with a loving warble,
full of tender sweetness, as they flit among the swaying twigs,
or pry with diligent search for some snug nesting-place among
the hollow crannies of the orchard trees. The noisy black- 10
birds hold high carnival in the top of the old pine-tree, the
woodpecker taps upon the hollow limb his resonant tattoo,
and the hungry crows, like a posse of tramps, hang around
the great oak-tree upon the knoll, and watch to see what they
can steal. Down through the meadow the gurgling stream 15
babbles as of old, and along its fretted banks the alder
thickets are hanging full with drooping catkins swinging at
every breeze. The glossy willow-buds throw off their coat
of fur, and plume themselves in their wealth of inflorescence,
lighting up the brookside with a yellow glow, and exhaling 20
a fresh, delicious perfume. Here, too, we hear the rattling
screech of the swooping kingfisher, as with quick beats of
wing he skims along the surface of the stream, and with an
ascending glide settles upon the overhanging branch above
the ripples. All these and a thousand more I vividly recall 25
from the memory of that New England spring; but the
sweetest of all its manifold surprises was that crowning con-
summation, that miracle of a single night, bringing on countless wings through the early morning mist the welcome chorus
of the returning flocks of birds. How they swarm the orchard 30
and the elms, where but yesterday the bluebird held his
sway! Now we see the fiery oriole in his gold and jetty velvet flashing in the morning sun, and robins without number
swell their ruddy throats in a continuous roundelay of song.
The pert catbird in his Quaker garb is here, and with flip- 35
pant jerk of tail and impertinent mew bustles about among

the arbor vitæs, where even now are remnants of his last
year's nest. The puffy wrens, too, what saucy sputtering little
bursts of glee are theirs as they strut upon the rustic boxes in
the maples! The fields are vocal with their sweet spring
5 melody, in which the happy carols of the linnets and the song
sparrows form a continuous pastoral. Now we hear the mellow bell of the wood thrush echoing from some neighboring
tree, and all intermingled with the chatter and the gossip of
the martens on their lofty house. Birds in the sky, birds in
10 the trees and on the ground, birds everywhere, and not a
silent throat among them; but from far and near, from
mountainside and meadow, from earth and sky, uniting in
a happy choral of perpetual jubilee.

JOHN FISKE

THE TOWN-MEETING[1]

[Extract]

The most primitive self-governing body of which we have
15 any knowledge is the village-community of the ancient Teutons, of which such strict counterparts are found in other
parts of the Aryan world as to make it apparent that in its
essential features it must be an inheritance from prehistoric
Aryan antiquity. In its Teutonic form the primitive village-
20 community (or rather, the spot inhabited by it) is known as
the *Mark*,—that is, a place defined by a boundary-line. One
characteristic of the mark-community is that all its free
members are in theory supposed to be related to each other
through descent from a common progenitor; and in this re-
25 spect the mark-community agrees with the *gens*, γένος, or
clan. The earliest form of political union in the world is one
which rests, not upon territorial contiguity, but upon blood-

---

[1] Reprinted from *American Political Ideas Viewed from the Standpoint
of Universal History*, by permission of Houghton Mifflin Company,
publishers.

relationship, either real or assumed through the legal fiction
of adoption. . . . Though individual freedom was by no
means considerable, the legal existence of the individual
being almost entirely merged in that of his clan, the mark-
community was a completely self-governing body. The as-   5
sembly of the markmen, or members of the community,
allotted land for tillage, determined the law or declared the
custom as to methods of tillage, fixed the dates for sowing
and reaping, voted upon the admission of new families into
the village, and in general transacted what was then regarded   10
as the public business of the community. In all essential
respects this village assembly or *mark-mote* would seem to
have resembled the town-meetings of New England.

.   .   .   .

In England . . . the free village-community, though perhaps nowhere found in its primitive integrity, has neverthe-   15
less survived in partially transfigured forms which have
played no unimportant part in the history of the English
people. In one shape or another the assembly of freemen for
purposes of local legislation has always existed. The Puritans who colonized New England, therefore, did not invent   20
the town-meeting. They were familiar already with the proceedings of the vestry-meeting and the manorial courts, but
they were severed now from church and from aristocracy.
So they had but to discard the ecclesiastical and lordly ter-
minology, with such limitations as they involved, and to   25
reintegrate the separate jurisdictions into one,—and forthwith the old assembly of the township, founded in imme-
morial tradition, but revivified by new thoughts and purposes
gained through ages of political training, emerged into fresh
life and entered upon a more glorious career.   30

It is not to an audience which speaks the English language
that I need to argue the point that the preservation of local
self-government is of the highest importance for the maintenance of a rich and powerful national life. As we contem-
plate the vicissitudes of local self-government in the various   35

portions of the Aryan world, we see the contrasted fortunes of France and England illustrating for us most forcibly the significance of this truth. For the preservation of local self-government in England various causes may be assigned; but
5 of these there are two which may be cited as especially prominent. In the first place, owing to the peculiar circumstances of the Teutonic settlement of Britain, the civilization of England previous to the Norman Conquest was but little affected by Roman ideas or institutions. In the second place
10 the thrusting down of the old thegnhood by the Norman Conquest . . . checked the growth of a *noblesse* or *adel* of the continental type,—a nobility raised above the common people like a separate caste. For the old thegnhood, which might have grown into such a caste, was pushed down into a
15 secondary position, and the peerage which arose after the Conquest was something different from a *noblesse*. It was primarily a nobility of office rather than a rank or privilege. The peers were those men who retained the right of summons to the Great Council, or Witenagemote, which has survived
20 as the House of Lords. The peer was therefore the holder of a legislative and judicial office, which only one of his children could inherit, from the very nature of the case, and which none of his children could share with him. Hence the brothers and younger children of a peer were always com-
25 moners, and their interests were not remotely separated from those of other commoners. Hence after the establishment of a House of Commons, their best chance for a political career lay in representing the interests of the people in the lower house. Hence between the upper and lower strata of
30 English society there has always been kept up a circulation or interchange of ideas and interests, and the effect of this upon English history has been prodigious. While on the continent a sovereign like Charles the Bold could use his nobility to extinguish the liberties of the merchant towns of
35 Flanders, nothing of the sort was ever possible in England. Throughout the Middle Ages, in every contest between the

people and the crown, the weight of the peerage was thrown
into the scale in favor of popular liberties. But for this
peculiar position of the peerage we might have had no Earl
Simon; it is largely through it that representative government and local liberties have been preserved to the English 5
race.

In France the course of events has brought about very
different results. . . . The slow conversion of the feudal
monarchy of the early Capetians into the absolute despotism
of Louis XIV was accomplished by the king gradually *con-* 10
quering his vassals one after another, and adding their domains to his own. As one vassal territory after another was
added to the royal domain, the king sent prefects, responsible
only to himself, to administer its local affairs, sedulously
crushing out, so far as possible, the last vestiges of self- 15
government. The nobles, deprived of their provincial rule,
in great part flocked to Paris to become idle courtiers. The
means for carrying on the gigantic machinery of centralized
administration, and for supporting the court in its follies,
were wrung from the groaning peasantry with a cynical in- 20
difference like that with which tribute is extorted by barbaric
chieftains from a conquered enemy. And thus came about
that abominable state of things which a century since was
abruptly ended by one of the fiercest convulsions of modern
times.   25

The prodigious superiority—in respect to national vitality
—of a freely governed country over one that is governed by
a centralized despotism, is nowhere more brilliantly illus-
trated than in the contrasted fortunes of France and England
as *colonizing* nations. . . . The French colony in Canada 30
was one of the most complete examples of a despotic government that the world has ever seen. All the autocratic and
bureaucratic ideas of Louis XIV were here carried out without let or hindrance. It would be incredible, were it not
attested by such abundant evidence, that the affairs of any 35
people could be subjected to such minute and sleepless super-

vision as were the affairs of the French colonists in Canada.
A man could not even build his own house, or rear his own
cattle, or sow his own seed, or reap his own grain, save under
the supervision of prefects acting under instructions from the
5 home government. No one was allowed to enter or leave the
colony without permission, not from the colonists but from
the king. No farmer could visit Montreal or Quebec without
permission. No Huguenot could set his foot on Canadian
soil. No public meetings of any kind were tolerated, nor
10 were there any means of giving expression to one's opinions
on any subject. The details of all this, which may be read in
Mr. Parkman's admirable work on *The Old Régime in
Canada*, make a wonderful chapter of history. Never was
a colony, moreover, so loaded with bounties, so fostered,
15 petted, and protected. The result was absolute paralysis,
political and social. When after a century of irritation and
skirmishing the French in Canada came to a life-and-death
struggle with the self-governing colonists of New England,
New York, and Virginia, the result for the French power
20 in America was instant and irretrievable annihilation. The
town-meeting pitted against the bureaucracy was like a Titan
overthrowing a cripple. The historic lesson owes its value
to the fact that this ruin of the French scheme of colonial
empire was due to no accidental circumstances, but was in-
25 volved in the very nature of the French political system.
Obviously it is impossible for a people to plant beyond sea a
colony which shall be self-supporting, unless it has retained
intact the power of self-government at home. It is to the
self-government of England, and to no lesser cause, that we
30 are to look for the secret of that boundless vitality which has
given to men of English speech the uttermost parts of the
earth for an inheritance.

WILLIAM DEAN HOWELLS

LITERARY FRIENDS AND ACQUAINTANCE[1]

The White Mr. Longfellow

We had expected to stay in Boston only until we could find a house in Old Cambridge. This was not so simple a matter as it might seem; for the ancient town had not yet quickened its scholarly pace to the modern step. Indeed, in the spring of 1866 the impulse of expansion was not yet visibly felt anywhere; the enormous material growth that followed the civil war had not yet begun. In Cambridge the houses to be let were few, and such as there were fell either below our pride or rose above our purse. I wish I might tell how at last we bought a house; we had no money, but we were rich in friends, who are still alive to shrink from the story of their constant faith in a financial future which we sometimes doubted, and who backed their credulity with their credit. It is sufficient for the present record, which professes to be strictly literary, to notify the fact that on the first day of May, 1866, we went out to Cambridge and began to live in a house which we owned in fee if not in deed, and which was none the less valuable for being covered with mortgages. Physically, it was a carpenter's box, of a sort which is readily imagined by the Anglo-American genius for ugliness, but which it is not so easy to impart a just conception of. A trim hedge of arbor vitæ tried to hide it from the world in front, and a tall board fence behind; the little lot was well planted (perhaps too well planted) with pears, grapes, and currants, and there was a small open space which I lost no time in digging up for a kitchen-garden. On one side of us were the open fields; on the other a brief line of neighbor-houses; across the street before us was a grove of stately oaks, which I never could persuade Aldrich had painted leaves on them in the fall. We were really in a poor suburb of a suburb;

[1] Reprinted by permission of Harper & Brothers, publishers.

but such is the fascination of ownership, even the ownership of a fully mortgaged property, that we calculated the latitude and longitude of the whole earth from the spot we called ours. In our walks about Cambridge we saw other places
5 where we might have been willing to live; only, we said, they were too far off. We even prized the architecture of our little box, though we had but so lately lived in a Gothic palace on the Grand Canal in Venice, and were not uncritical of beauty in the possessions of others. Positive beauty we could not have
10 honestly said we thought our cottage had as a whole, though we might have held out for something of the kind in the brackets of turned wood under its eaves. But we were richly content with it; and with life in Cambridge, as it began to open itself to us, we were infinitely more than content. This
15 life, so refined, so intelligent, so gracefully simple, I do not suppose has anywhere else had its parallel.

I

It was the moment before the old American customs had been changed by European influences among people of easier circumstances; and in Cambridge society kept what was best
20 of its village traditions, and chose to keep them in the full knowledge of different things. Nearly everyone had been abroad; and nearly everyone had acquired the taste for olives without losing a relish for native sauces; through the intellectual life there was an entire democracy, and I do not
25 believe that since the capitalistic era began there was ever a community in which money counted for less. There was little show of what money could buy: I remember but one private carriage (naturally, a publisher's); and there was not one livery, except a livery in the larger sense kept by
30 the stableman Pike, who made us pay now a quarter and now a half dollar for a seat in his carriages, according as he lost or gathered courage for the charge. We thought him extortionate, and we mostly walked through snow and mud of amazing depth and thickness.

The reader will imagine how acceptable this circumstance was to a young literary man beginning life with a fully mortgaged house and a salary of untried elasticity. If there were distinctions made in Cambridge they were not against literature, and we found ourselves in the midst of a charming society, indifferent, apparently, to all questions but those of the higher education which comes so largely by nature. That is to say, in the Cambridge of that day (and, I dare say, of this) a mind cultivated in some sort was essential, and after that came civil manners, and the willingness and ability to be agreeable and interesting; but the question of riches or poverty did not enter. Even the question of family, which is of so great concern in New England, was in abeyance. Perhaps it was taken for granted that everyone in Old Cambridge society must be of good family, or he could not be there, perhaps his mere residence tacitly ennobled him; certainly his acceptance was an informal patent of gentility. To my mind, the structure of society was almost ideal, and until we have a perfectly socialized condition of things I do not believe we shall ever have a more perfect society. The instincts which governed it were not such as can arise from the sordid competition of interests; they flowed from a devotion to letters, and from a self-sacrifice in material things which I can give no better notion of than by saying that the outlay of the richest college magnate seemed to be graduated to the income of the poorest.

In those days, the men whose names have given splendor to Cambridge were still living there. I shall forget some of them in the alphabetical enumeration of Louis Agassiz, Francis J. Child, Richard Henry Dana, Jun., John Fiske, Dr. Asa Gray, the family of the Jameses, father and sons, Lowell, Longfellow, Charles Eliot Norton, Dr. John G. Palfrey, James Peirce, Dr. Peabody, Professor Parsons, Professor Sophocles. The variety of talents and of achievements was indeed so great that Mr. Bret Harte, when fresh from his Pacific slope, justly said, after listening to a partial re-

hearsal of them, "Why, you couldn't fire a revolver from
your front porch anywhere without bringing down a two-
volumer!" Everybody had written a book, or an article, or
a poem; or was in the process or expectation of doing it, and
doubtless those whose names escape me will have greater
difficulty in eluding fame. These kindly, these gifted folk
each came to see us and to make us at home among them;
and my home is still among them, on this side and on that
side of the line between the living and the dead, which in-
visibly passes through all the streets of the cities of men.

II

We had the whole summer for the exploration of Cambridge before society returned from the mountains and the
seashore, and it was not till October that I saw Longfellow.
I heard again, as I heard when I first came to Boston, that he
was at Nahant, and though Nahant was no longer so far
away, now, as it was then, I did not think of seeking him out
even when we went for a day to explore that coast during the
summer. It seems strange that I cannot recall just when
and where I saw him, but early after his return to Cambridge
I had a message from him asking me to come to a meeting of
the Dante Club at Craigie House.

Longfellow was that winter (1866–1867) revising his translation of the *Paradiso*, and the Dante Club was the circle of
Italianate friends and scholars whom he invited to follow
him and criticize his work from the original, while he read
his version aloud. Those who were most constantly present
were Lowell and Professor Norton, but from time to time
others came in, and we seldom sat down at the nine-o'clock
supper that followed the reading of the canto in less number
than ten or twelve.

.   .   .   .

When Longfellow read verse, it was with a hollow, with a
mellow resonant murmur, like the note of some deep-throated
horn. His voice was very lulling in quality, and at the Dante

Club it used to have early effect with an old scholar who sat
in a cavernous armchair at the corner of the fire, and who
drowsed audibly in the soft tone and the gentle heat. The
poet had a fat terrier who wished always to be present at the
meetings of the Club, and he commonly fell asleep at the same 5
moment with that dear old scholar, so that when they began
to make themselves heard in concert, one could not tell which
it was that most took our thoughts from the text of the
Paradiso. When the duet opened, Longfellow would look up
with an arch recognition of the fact, and then go gravely on 10
to the end of the canto. At the close he would speak to his
friend and lead him out to supper as if he had not seen or
heard anything amiss.

III

In that elect company I was silent, partly because I was
conscious of my youthful inadequacy, and partly because I 15
preferred to listen. But Longfellow always behaved as if I
were saying a succession of edifying and delightful things,
and from time to time he addressed himself to me, so that I
should not feel left out. He did not talk much himself, and
I recall nothing that he said. But he always spoke both 20
wisely and simply, without the least touch of pose, and with
no intention of effect, but with something that I must call
quality for want of a better word; so that at a table where
Holmes sparkled, and Lowell glowed, and Agassiz beamed,
he cast the light of a gentle gayety, which seemed to dim all 25
those vivider luminaries. While he spoke you did not miss
Fields's story or Tom Appleton's wit, or even the gracious
amity of Mr. Norton, with his unequaled intuitions.

The supper was very plain: a cold turkey, which the host
carved, or a haunch of venison, or some braces of grouse, or 30
a platter of quails, with a deep bowl of salad, and the sympathetic companionship of those elect vintages which Longfellow loved, and which he chose with the inspiration of
affection. We usually began with oysters, and when some-

one who was expected did not come promptly, Longfellow invited us to raid his plate, as a just punishment of his delay. One evening Lowell remarked, with the cayenne poised above his blue-points, "It's astonishing how fond these fellows are 5 of pepper."

The old friend of the cavernous armchair was perhaps not wide enough awake to repress an "Ah?" of deep interest in this fact of natural history, and Lowell was provoked to go on. "Yes, I've dropped a red pepper pod into a barrel of 10 them, before now, and then taken them out in a solid mass, clinging to it like a swarm of bees to their queen."

"Is it possible?" cried the old friend; and then Longfellow intervened to save him from worse, and turned the talk.

I reproach myself that I made no record of the talk, for I 15 find that only a few fragments of it have caught in my memory, and that the sieve which should have kept the gold has let it wash away with the gravel. I remember once Dr. Holmes's talking of the physician as the true seer, whose awful gift it was to behold with the fatal second sight 20 of science the shroud gathering to the throat of many a doomed man apparently in perfect health, and happy in the promise of unnumbered days. The thought may have been suggested by some of the toys of superstition which intellectual people like to play with.

25 I never could be quite sure at first that Longfellow's brother-in-law, Appleton, was seriously a spiritualist, even when he disputed the most strenuously with the unbelieving Autocrat. But he really was in earnest about it, though he relished a joke at the expense of his doctrine, like some clerics 30 when they are in the safe company of other clerics. He told me once of having recounted to Agassiz the facts of a very remarkable séance, where the souls of the departed outdid themselves in the athletics and acrobatics they seem so fond of over there, throwing large stones across the room, moving 35 pianos, and lifting dinner-tables and settling them a-twirl under the chandelier. "And now," he demanded, "what do you

say to that?" "Well, Mr. Appleton," Agassiz answered, to Appleton's infinite delight, "*I say that it did not happen.*"

One night they began to speak at the Dante supper of the unhappy man whose crime is a red stain in the Cambridge an- nals, and one and another recalled their impressions of Pro- fessor Webster. It was possibly with a retroactive sense that they had all felt something uncanny in him, but, apropos of the deep salad-bowl in the center of the table, Longfellow remembered a supper Webster was at, where he lighted some chemical in such a dish and held his head over it, with a handkerchief noosed about his throat and lifted above it with one hand, while his face, in the pale light, took on the livid ghastliness of that of a man hanged by the neck.

Another night the talk wandered to the visit which an Eng- lish author (now with God) paid America at the height of a popularity long since toppled to the ground, with many an- other. He was in very good humor with our whole continent, and at Longfellow's table he found the champagne even sur- prisingly fine. "But," he said to his host, who now told the story, "it cawn't be *genuine*, you know!"

Many years afterwards this author revisited our shores, and I dined with him at Longfellow's, where he was anxious to constitute himself a guest during his sojourn in our neighbor- hood. Longfellow was equally anxious that he should not do so, and he took a harmless pleasure in outmaneuvering him. He seized a chance to speak with me alone, and plotted to deliver him over to me without apparent unkindness, when the latest horse-car should be going in to Boston, and begged me to walk him to Harvard Square and put him aboard. "Put him aboard, and don't leave him till the car starts, and then watch that he doesn't get off."

These instructions he accompanied with a lifting of the eyebrows, and a pursing of the mouth, in an anxiety not altogether burlesque. He knew himself the prey of anyone who chose to batten on him, and his hospitality was subject to frightful abuse. Perhaps Mr. Norton has somewhere told how, when he asked if a certain person who had been out-staying his time was not a dreadful bore, Longfellow answered, with angelic patience, "Yes; but then you know I have been bored so often!"

. . . .

IV

. . . .

5 The study where the Dante Club met, and where I mostly saw Longfellow, was a plain, pleasant room, with broad paneling in white painted pine; in the center before the fireplace stood his round table, laden with books, papers, and proofs; in the farthest corner by the window was a high desk
10 which he sometimes stood at to write. In this room Washington held his councils and transacted his business with all comers; in the chamber overhead he slept. I do not think Longfellow associated the place much with him, and I never heard him speak of Washington in relation to it except once,
15 when he told me with peculiar relish what he called the true version of a pious story concerning the aide-de-camp who blundered in upon him while he knelt in prayer. The father of his country rose and rebuked the young man severely, and then resumed his devotions. "He rebuked him," said Long-
20 fellow, lifting his brows and making rings round the pupils of his eyes, "by throwing his scabbard at his head."

BOOKS AND WRITERS OF THE PRESENT DAY

EDITH WHARTON

THE DEBT[1]

[*Synopsis of Parts I and II*. Professor Lanfear, the most brilliant
biologist of his generation, finds in Galen Dredge, an awkward, penniless lad whom his son Archie has brought home from college, an
unusually promising student. He befriends Dredge, directs his studies,
and takes him into his household, to the great inconvenience of his   5
family, especially Mrs. Lanfear and their daughter Mabel, for Dredge
is as obtuse and uncouth in the drawing-room as he is keen and skillful in the laboratory. Dogged, patient, persistent, Dredge slowly
develops into a young scientist whose work attracts the attention of
older men, while Archie Lanfear, quick, clever, superficial, drifts from 10
biology to music, from music to physics, thence by way of the drama
to archæology. Dredge returns from study abroad, without the awk-
wardness of his youth, but with unchanged devotion to the Lanfears,
to become Professor Lanfear's assistant and loyal disciple. When a
magnificent laboratory for research is named in honor of Professor 15
Lanfear, Dredge, though still young for so great a post, is named as
its chief. Professor Lanfear dies in happy confidence that Dredge
will carry on his work; and for two years this work is continued
without a break.]

III

The third winter I was off collecting in Central America, 20
and didn't get back till Dredge's course had been going for a
couple of months. The very day I turned up in town Archie
Lanfear descended on me with a summons from his mother.
I was wanted at once at a family council.

[1] From *Tales of Men and Ghosts*; copyright, 1910, by Charles Scribner's Sons. By permission of the publishers.

I found the Lanfear ladies in a state of explosive distress, which Archie's own indignation hardly made more intelligible. But gradually I put together their fragmentary charges, and learned that Dredge's lectures were turning into an organized assault on his master's doctrine.

"It amounts to just this," Archie said, controlling his women with the masterful gesture of the weak man. "Galen has simply turned round and betrayed my father."

"Just for a handful of silver he left us," Mabel sobbed in parenthesis, while Mrs. Lanfear tearfully cited Hamlet.

Archie silenced them again. "The ugly part of it is that he must have had this up his sleeve for years. He must have known when he was asked to succeed my father what use he meant to make of his opportunity. What he's doing isn't the result of a hasty conclusion: it means years of work and preparation."

Archie broke off to explain himself. He had returned from Europe the week before, and had learned on arriving that Dredge's lectures were stirring the world of science as nothing had stirred it since Lanfear's *Utility and Variation*. And the incredible affront was that they owed their success to the fact of being an attempted refutation of Lanfear's great work.

I own that I was staggered: the case looked ugly, as Archie said. And there was a veil of reticence, of secrecy, about Dredge, that always kept his conduct in a half-light of uncertainty. Of some men one would have said off-hand: "It's impossible!" But one couldn't affirm it of him.

Archie hadn't seen him as yet; and Mrs. Lanfear had sent for me because she wished me to be present at the interview between the two men. The Lanfear ladies had a touching belief in Archie's violence: they thought him as terrible as a natural force. My own idea was that if there were any broken bones they wouldn't be Dredge's; but I was too curious as to the outcome not to be glad to offer my services as moderator.

First, however, I wanted to hear one of the lectures; and
I went the next afternoon. The hall was jammed, and I saw,
as soon as Dredge appeared, what increased security and ease
the sympathy of his audience had given him. He had been
clear the year before, now he was also eloquent. The lecture 5
was a remarkable effort: you'll find the gist of it in Chapter VII of *The Arrival of the Fittest*. Archie sat at my
side in a white rage; he was too intelligent not to measure
the extent of the disaster. And I was almost as indignant as
he when we went to see Dredge the next day.   10

I saw at a glance that the latter suspected nothing; and it
was characteristic of him that he began by questioning me
about my finds, and only afterward turned to reproach Archie
for having been back a week without letting him know.

"You know I'm up to my neck in this job. Why in the 15
world didn't you hunt me up before this?"

The question was exasperating, and I could understand
Archie's stammer of wrath.

"Hunt you up? Hunt you up? What the deuce are you
made of, to ask me such a question instead of wondering 20
why I'm here now?"

Dredge bent his slow calm scrutiny on his friend's agitated
face; then he turned to me.

"What's the matter?" he said simply.

"The matter?" shrieked Archie, his fist hovering excitedly 25
above the desk by which he stood; but Dredge, with un-
wonted quickness, caught the fist as it descended.

"Careful—I've got a *Kallima* in that jar there." He
pushed a chair forward, and added quietly: "Sit down."

Archie, ignoring the gesture, towered pale and avenging in 30
his place; and Dredge, after a moment, took the chair himself.

"The matter?" Archie reiterated. "Are you so lost to all
sense of decency and honor that you can put that question in
good faith? Don't you really *know* what's the matter?"

Dredge smiled slowly. "There are so few things one really 35
knows."

"Oh, damn your scientific hair-splitting! Don't you know you're insulting my father's memory?"

Dredge thoughtfully turned his spectacles from one of us to the other.

5 "Oh, that's it, is it? Then you'd better sit down. If you don't see at once it'll take some time to make you."

Archie burst into an ironic laugh.

"I rather think it will!" he retorted.

"Sit down, Archie," I said, setting the example; and he
10 obeyed, with a gesture that made his consent a protest.

Dredge seemed to notice nothing beyond the fact that his visitors were seated. He reached for his pipe, and filled it with the care which the habit of delicate manipulations gave to all the motions of his long knotty hands.

15 "It's about the lectures?" he said.

Archie's answer was a deep scornful breath.

"You've only been back a week, so you've only heard one, I suppose?"

"It was not necessary to hear even that one. You must
20 know the talk they're making. If notoriety is what you're after—"

"Well, I'm not sorry to make a noise," said Dredge, putting a match to his pipe.

Archie bounded in his chair. "There's no easier way of
25 doing it than to attack a man who can't answer you!"

Dredge raised a sobering hand. "Hold on. Perhaps you and I don't mean the same thing. Tell me first what's in your mind."

The question steadied Archie, who turned on Dredge a
30 countenance really eloquent with filial indignation.

"It's an odd question for you to ask; it makes me wonder what's in *yours*. Not much thought of my father, at any rate, or you couldn't stand in his place and use the chance he's given you to push yourself at his expense."

35 Dredge received this in silence, puffing slowly at his pipe.

"Is that the way it strikes you?" he asked at length.

"God! It's the way it would strike most men."

He turned to me. "You too?"

"I can see how Archie feels," I said.

"That I am attacking his father's memory to glorify myself?"

"Well, not precisely: I think what he really feels is that, if your convictions didn't permit you to continue his father's teaching, you might perhaps have done better to sever your connection with the Lanfear lectureship."

"Then you and he regard the Lanfear lectureship as having been founded to perpetuate a dogma, not to try and get at the truth?"

"Certainly not," Archie broke in. "But there's a question of taste, of delicacy, involved in the case that can't be decided on abstract principles. We know as well as you that my father meant the laboratory and the lectureship to serve the ends of science, at whatever cost to his own special convictions; what we feel—and you don't seem to—is that you're the last man to put them to that particular use; and I don't want to remind you why."

A slight redness rose through Dredge's sallow skin. "You needn't," he said. "It's because he pulled me out of my hole, woke me up, made me, shoved me off from the shore. Because he saved me ten or twenty years of muddled effort, and put me where I am at an age when my best working years are still ahead of me. Everyone knows that's what your father did for me, but I'm the only person who knows the time and trouble it took."

It was well said, and I glanced quickly at Archie, who was never closed to generous emotions.

"Well, then—?" he said, flushing also.

"Well, then," Dredge continued, his voice deepening and losing its nasal edge, "I had to pay him back, didn't I?"

The sudden drop flung Archie back on his prepared attitude of irony. "It would be the natural inference—with most men."

"Just so. And I'm not so very different. I knew your father wanted a successor—someone who'd try and tie up the loose ends. And I took the lectureship with that object."

"And you're using it to tear the whole fabric to pieces!"

5   Dredge paused to relight his pipe. "Looks that way," he conceded. "This year anyhow."

"*This year*—?" Archie echoed.

"Yes. When I took up the job I saw it just as your father left it. Or rather, I didn't see any other way of going on with 10 it. The change came gradually, as I worked."

"Gradually? So that you had time to look round you, to know where you were, to see that you were fatally committed to undoing the work he had done?"

"Oh, yes—I had time," Dredge conceded.

15   "And yet you kept the chair and went on with the course?"

Dredge refilled his pipe, and then turned in his seat so that he looked squarely at Archie.

"What would your father have done in my place?" he asked.

20   "In your place—?"

"Yes: supposing he'd found out the things I've found out in the last year or two. You'll see what they are, and how much they count, if you'll run over the report of the lectures. If your father'd been alive he might have come across the 25 same facts just as easily."

There was a silence which Archie at last broke by saying: "But he didn't, and you did. There's the difference."

"The difference? What difference? Would your father have suppressed the facts if he'd found them? It's *you* who 30 insult his memory by implying it! And if I'd brought them to him, would he have used his hold over me to get me to suppress them?"

"Certainly not. But can't you see it's his death that makes the difference? He's not here to defend his case."

35   Dredge laughed, but not unkindly. "My dear Archie, your father wasn't one of the kind who bother to defend their

case. Men like him are the masters, not the servants, of
their theories. They respect an idea only as long as it's of
use to them; when its usefulness ends they chuck it out. And
that's what your father would have done."

Archie reddened. "Don't you assume a good deal in taking
it for granted that he would have had to do so in this particular case?"

Dredge reflected. "Yes: I was going too far. Each of us
can only answer for himself. But to my mind your father's
theory is refuted."

"And you don't hesitate to be the man to do it?"

"Should I have been of any use if I had? And did your
father ever ask anything of me but to be of as much use as
I could?"

It was Archie's turn to reflect. "No. That was what he
always wanted, of course."

"That's the way I've always felt. The first day he took
me away from East Lethe I knew the debt I was piling up
against him, and I never had any doubt as to how I'd pay it,
or how he'd want it paid. He didn't pick me out and train
me for any object but to carry on the light. Do you suppose
he'd have wanted me to snuff it out because it happened to
light up a fact *he* didn't fancy? I'm using *his* oil to feed my
torch with: yes, but it isn't really his torch or mine, or his
oil or mine: they belong to each of us till we drop and hand
them on."

Archie turned a sobered glance on him. "I see your point.
But if the job had to be done I don't see that you need have
done it from his chair."

"There's where we differ. If I did it at all I had to do it
in the best way, and with all the authority his backing gave
me. If I owe your father anything, I owe him that. It would
have made him sick to see the job badly done. And don't
you see that the way to honor him, and show what he's done
for science, was to spare no advantage in my attack on him—
that I'm proving the strength of his position by the desperate-

ness of my assault?" Dredge paused and squared his loung-
ing shoulders. "After all," he added, "he's not down yet,
and if I leave him standing I guess it'll be some time before
anybody else cares to tackle him."

5   There was a silence between the two men; then Dredge
continued in a lighter tone: "There's one thing, though, that
we're both in danger of forgetting: and that is how little, in
the long run, it all counts either way." He smiled a little at
Archie's indignant gesture. "The most we can any of us do
10   —even by such a magnificent effort as your father's—is to
turn the great marching army a hair's breadth nearer what
seems to us the right direction; if one of us drops out, here
and there, the loss of headway's hardly perceptible. And
that's what I'm coming to now."

15   He rose from his seat, and walked across to the hearth;
then, cautiously resting his shoulder-blades against the
mantel-shelf jammed with miscellaneous specimens, he bent
his musing spectacles on Archie.

       "Your father would have understood why I've done what
20   I'm doing; but that's no reason why the rest of you should.
And I rather think it's the rest of you who've suffered most
from me. He always knew what I was *there for*, and that
must have been some comfort even when I was most in the
way; but I was just an ordinary nuisance to you and your
25   mother and Mabel. You were all too kind to let me see it
at the time, but I've seen it since, and it makes me feel that,
after all, the settling of this matter lies with you. If it hurts
you to have me go on with my examination of your father's
theory, I'm ready to drop the lectures to-morrow, and trust
30   to the Lanfear Laboratory to breed up a young chap who'll
knock us both out in time. You've only got to say the word."

       There was a pause while Dredge turned and laid his ex-
tinguished pipe carefully between a jar of embryo sea-urchins
and a colony of regenerating planarians.

35   Then Archie rose and held out his hand.
       "No," he said simply; "go on."

O. HENRY

A SERVICE OF LOVE[1]

When one loves one's Art no service seems too hard.

That is our premise. This story shall draw a conclusion from it, and show at the same time that the premise is incorrect. That will be a new thing in logic, and a feat in story-telling somewhat older than the great wall of China.   5

Joe Larrabee came out of the post-oak flats of the Middle West pulsing with a genius for pictorial art. At six he drew a picture of the town pump with a prominent citizen passing it hastily. This effort was framed and hung in the drug store window by the side of the ear of corn with an uneven number 10 of rows. At twenty he left for New York with a flowing necktie and a capital tied up somewhat closer.

Delia Caruthers did things in six octaves so promisingly in a pine-tree village in the South that her relatives chipped in enough in her chip hat for her to go "North" and "finish." 15 They could not see her f——, but that is our story.

Joe and Delia met in an atelier where a number of art and music students had gathered to discuss chiaroscuro, Wagner, music, Rembrandt's works, pictures, Waldteufel, wall paper, Chopin and Oolong.   20

Joe and Delia became enamored one of the other, or each of the other, as you please, and in a short time were married —for (see above), when one loves one's Art no service seems too hard.

Mr. and Mrs. Larrabee began housekeeping in a flat. It 25 was a lonesome flat—something like the A sharp way down at the left-hand end of the keyboard. And they were happy, for they had their Art, and they had each other. And my advice to the rich young man would be—sell all thou hast, and give it to the poor—janitor for the privilege of living in a 30 flat with your Art and your Delia.

[1] From *The Four Million*, reprinted by permission of Doubleday, Page & Company, publishers.

Flat-dwellers shall indorse my dictum that theirs is the only true happiness. If a home is happy it cannot fit too close—let the dresser collapse and become a billiard table; let the mantel turn to a rowing machine, the escritoire to a spare bedchamber, the washstand to an upright piano; let the four walls come together, if they will, so you and your Delia are between. But if home be the other kind, let it be wide and long—enter you at the Golden Gate, hang your hat on Hatteras, your cape on Cape Horn and go out by the Labrador.

Joe was painting in the class of the great Magister—you know his fame. His fees are high; his lessons are light—his high-lights have brought him renown. Delia was studying under Rosenstock—you know his repute as a disturber of the piano keys.

They were mighty happy as long as their money lasted. So is every—but I will not be cynical. Their aims were very clear and defined. Joe was to become capable very soon of turning out pictures that old gentlemen with thin side-whiskers and thick pocketbooks would sandbag one another in his studio for the privilege of buying. Delia was to become familiar and then contemptuous with Music, so that when she saw the orchestra seats and boxes unsold she could have sore throat and lobster in a private dining-room and refuse to go on the stage.

But the best, in my opinion, was the home life in the little flat—the ardent, voluble chats after the day's study; the cozy dinners and fresh, light breakfasts; the interchange of ambitions—ambitions interwoven each with the other's or else inconsiderable—the mutual help and inspiration; and— overlook my artlessness—stuffed olives and cheese sandwiches at 11 P.M.

But after a while Art flagged. It sometimes does, even if some switchman doesn't flag it. Everything going out and nothing coming in, as the vulgarians say. Money was lacking to pay Mr. Magister and Herr Rosenstock their prices. When one loves one's Art no service seems too hard. So,

Delia said she must give music lessons to keep the chafing dish bubbling.

For two or three days she went out canvassing for pupils. One evening she came home elated.

"Joe, dear," she said, gleefully, "I've a pupil. And, oh, the loveliest people. General—General A. B. Pinkney's daughter —on Seventy-first street. Such a splendid house, Joe—you ought to see the front door! Byzantine, I think you would call it. And inside! Oh, Joe, I never saw anything like it before.

"My pupil is his daughter Clementina. I dearly love her already. She's a delicate thing—dresses always in white; and the sweetest, simplest manners! Only eighteen years old. I'm to give three lessons a week; and, just think, Joe! Five dollars a lesson. I don't mind it a bit; for when I get two or three more pupils I can resume my lessons with Herr Rosenstock. Now, smooth out that wrinkle between your brows, dear, and let's have a nice supper."

"That's all right for you, Dele," said Joe, attacking a can of peas with a carving knife and a hatchet, "but how about me? Do you think I'm going to let you hustle for wages while I philander in the regions of high art? Not by the bones of Benvenuto Cellini! I guess I can sell papers or lay cobblestones, and bring in a dollar or two."

Delia came and hung about his neck.

"Joe, dear, you are silly. You must keep on at your studies. It is not as if I had quit my music and gone to work at something else. While I teach I learn. I am always with my music. And we can live as happily as millionaires on fifteen dollars a week. You mustn't think of leaving Mr. Magister."

"All right," said Joe, reaching for the blue scalloped vegetable dish. "But I hate for you to be giving lessons. It isn't Art. But you're a trump and a dear to do it."

"When one loves one's Art no service seems too hard," said Delia.

"Magister praised the sky in that sketch I made in the park," said Joe. "And Tinkle gave me permission to hang two of them in his window. I may sell one if the right kind of a moneyed idiot sees them."

5 "I'm sure you will," said Delia, sweetly. "And now let's be thankful for General Pinkney and this veal roast."

During all of the next week the Larrabees had an early breakfast. Joe was enthusiastic about some morning-effect sketches he was doing in Central Park, and Delia packed him 10 off breakfasted, coddled, praised and kissed at seven o'clock. Art is an engaging mistress. It was most times seven o'clock when he returned in the evening.

At the end of the week Delia, sweetly proud but languid, triumphantly tossed three five-dollar bills on the eight by ten 15 (inches) center table of the eight by ten (feet) flat parlor.

"Sometimes," she said, a little wearily, "Clementina tries me. I'm afraid she doesn't practice enough, and I have to tell her the same things so often. And then she always dresses entirely in white, and that does get monotonous. 20 But General Pinkney is the dearest old man! I wish you could know him, Joe. He comes in sometimes when I am with Clementina at the piano—he is a widower, you know —and stands there pulling his white goatee. 'And how are the semiquavers and the demisemiquavers progressing?' he 25 always asks.

"I wish you could see the wainscoting in that drawing-room, Joe! And those Astrakhan rug portières. And Clementina has such a funny little cough. I hope she is stronger than she looks. Oh, I really am getting attached to her, she 30 is so gentle and high bred. General Pinkney's brother was once Minister to Bolivia."

And then Joe, with the air of a Monte Cristo, drew forth a ten, a five, a two and a one—all legal tender notes—and laid them beside Delia's earnings.

35 "Sold that watercolor of the obelisk to a man from Peoria," he announced overwhelmingly.

"Don't joke with me," said Delia—"not from Peoria!"

"All the way. I wish you could see him, Dele. Fat man with a woolen muffler and a quill toothpick. He saw the sketch in Tinkle's window and thought it was a windmill at first. He was game, though, and bought it anyhow. He ordered another—an oil sketch of the Lackawanna freight depot—to take back with him. Music lessons! Oh, I guess Art is still in it."

"I'm so glad you've kept on," said Delia, heartily. "You're bound to win, dear. Thirty-three dollars! We never had so much to spend before. We'll have oysters to-night."

"And filet mignon with champignons," said Joe. "Where is the olive fork?"

On the next Saturday evening Joe reached home first. He spread his eighteen dollars on the parlor table and washed what seemed to be a great deal of dark paint from his hands.

Half an hour later Delia arrived, her right hand tied up in a shapeless bundle of wraps and bandages.

"How is this?" asked Joe after the usual greetings. Delia laughed, but not very joyously.

"Clementina," she explained, "insisted upon a Welsh rabbit after her lesson. She is such a queer girl. Welsh rabbits at five in the afternoon. The General was there. You should have seen him run for the chafing dish, Joe, just as if there wasn't a servant in the house. I know Clementina isn't in good health; she is so nervous. In serving the rabbit she spilled a great lot of it, boiling hot, over my hand and wrist. It hurt awfully, Joe. And the dear girl was so sorry! But General Pinkney!—Joe, that old man nearly went distracted. He rushed downstairs and sent somebody—they said the furnace man or somebody in the basement—out to a drug store for some oil and things to bind it up with. It doesn't hurt so much now."

"What's this?" asked Joe, taking the hand tenderly and pulling at some white strands beneath the bandages.

"It's something soft," said Delia, "that had oil on it. Oh, Joe, did you sell another sketch?" she had seen the money on the table.

"Did I?" said Joe; "just ask the man from Peoria. He got his depot to-day, and he isn't sure but he thinks he wants another parkscape and a view on the Hudson. What time this afternoon did you burn your hand, Dele?"

"Five o'clock, I think," said Dele plaintively. "The iron —I mean the rabbit came off the fire about that time. You ought to have seen General Pinkney, Joe, when—"

"Sit down here a moment, Dele," said Joe. He drew her to the couch, sat beside her and put his arm across her shoulders.

"What have you been doing for the last two weeks, Dele?" he asked.

She braved it for a moment or two with an eye full of love and stubbornness, and murmured a phrase or two vaguely of General Pinkney; but at length down went her head and out came the truth and tears.

"I couldn't get any pupils," she confessed. "And I couldn't bear to have you give up your lessons; and I got a place ironing shirts in that big Twenty-fourth street laundry. And I think I did very well to make up both General Pinkney and Clementina, don't you, Joe? And when a girl in the laundry set down a hot iron on my hand this afternoon I was all the way home making up that story about the Welsh rabbit. You're not angry, are you, Joe? And if I hadn't got the work you mightn't have sold your sketches to that man from Peoria."

"He wasn't from Peoria," said Joe, slowly.

"Well, it doesn't matter where he was from. How clever you are, Joe—and—kiss me, Joe—and what made you ever suspect that I wasn't giving music lessons to Clementina?"

"I didn't," said Joe, "until to-night. And I wouldn't have then, only I sent up this cotton waste and oil from the engine room this afternoon for a girl upstairs who had her hand

burned with a smoothing-iron. I've been firing the engine in
that laundry for the last two weeks."

"And then you didn't—"

"My purchaser from Peoria," said Joe, "and General Pinkney are both creations of the same art—but you wouldn't 5
call it either painting or music."

And then they both laughed, and Joe began:

"When one loves one's Art, no service seems—"

But Delia stopped him with her hand on his lips. "No,"
she said—"just 'When one loves.'"   10

SARA TEASDALE

A PRAYER [1]

When I am dying, let me know
That I loved the blowing snow
    Although it stung like whips;
That I loved all lovely things
And I tried to take their stings   15
    With gay unembittered lips;
That I loved with all my strength,
To my soul's full depth and length,
    Careless if my heart must break,
That I sang as children sing   20
Fitting tunes to everything,
    Loving life for its own sake.

PIERROT [2]

Pierrot stands in the garden
    Beneath a waning moon,
And on his lute he fashions   25
    A fragile silver tune.

[1] Reprinted from Sara Teasdale's *Flame and Shadow*. By special arrangement with The Macmillan Company, publisher.

[2] Reprinted from Sara Teasdale's *Love Songs*. By special arrangement
with The Macmillan Company, publisher.

Pierrot plays in the garden,
  He thinks he plays for me,
But I am quite forgotten
  Under the cherry tree.

5   Pierrot plays in the garden,
  And all the roses know
That Pierrot loves his music,—
  But I love Pierrot.

THE GARDEN[1]

My heart is a garden tired with autumn,
10   Heaped with bending asters and dahlias heavy and dark,
In the hazy sunshine, the garden remembers April,
  The drench of rains and a snow-drop quick and clear as
    a spark;

Daffodils blowing in the cold wind of morning,
  And golden tulips, goblets holding the rain—
15 The garden will be hushed with snow, forgotten soon,
    forgotten—
  After the stillness, will spring come again?

RED MAPLES[1]

In the last year I have learned
How few men are worth my trust;
I have seen the friend I loved
20   Struck by death into the dust,
And fears I never knew before
Have knocked and knocked upon my door—
"I shall hope little and ask for less,"
I said, "There is no happiness."

---

[1] Reprinted from Sara Teasdale's *Flame and Shadow*. By special arrangement with The Macmillan Company, publisher.

I have grown wise at last—but how
Can I hide the gleam on the willow-bough,
Or keep the fragrance out of the rain
Now that April is here again?
When maples stand in a haze of fire   5
What can I say to the old desire,
What shall I do with the joy in me
That is born out of agony?

THE COIN[1]

Into my heart's treasury
　　I slipped a coin   10
That time cannot take
　　Nor a thief purloin,—
Oh, better than the minting
　　Of a gold-crowned king
Is the safe-kept memory   15
　　Of a lovely thing.

MARGARET WIDDEMER

OLD BOOKS[2]

The people up and down the world that talk and laugh
　　and cry,
They're pleasant when you're young and gay, and life is all
　　to try,
But when your heart is tired and dumb, your soul has need
　　of ease,
There's none like the quiet folk who wait in libraries—   20
The counselors who never change, the friends who never go,
The old books, the dear books that understand and know!

[1] Reprinted from Sara Teasdale's *Flame and Shadow*. By special arrangement with The Macmillan Company, publisher.
[2] From *The Old Road to Paradise*, reprinted by permission of Henry
Holt and Company, publishers.

"Why, this thing was over, child, and that deed was
    done,"
They say, "when Cleopatra died, two thousand years
    agone,
And this tale was spun for men and that jest was told
When Sappho was a singing-lass and Greece was very old,
5 And this thought you hide so close was sung along the wind
The day that young Orlando came a-courting Rosalind!"

The foolish thing that hurt you so your lips could never tell,
Your sister out of Babylon, she knows its secret well,
The merriment you could not share with any on the earth
10 Your brother from King Francis' court he leans to share your
    mirth,
For all the ways your feet must fare, the roads your heart
    must go,
The old books, the dear books, they understand and know!

You read your lover's hid heart plain beneath some dead
    lad's lace,
And in a glass from some Greek tomb you see your own wet
    face,
15 For they have stripped from out their souls the thing they
    could not speak
And strung it to a written song that you might come to
    seek,
And they have lifted out their hearts when they were beating
    new
And pinned them on a printed page and given them to you.

The people close beside you, all their hearts are dumb and
    young,
20 The kindest word they try to say it stumbles on the tongue,
Their hearts are only questing hearts, and though they strive
    and try,

Their softest touch may hurt you sore, their best word make
    you cry.
But still through all the years that come and all the dreams
    that go
The old books, the dear books, they understand and know!

TO YOUTH AFTER PAIN[1]

What if this year has given
    Grief that some year must bring,   5
What if it hurt your joyous youth,
    Crippled your laughter's wing?
You always knew it was coming,
    Coming to all, to you,
They always said there was suffering—   10
    Now it is done, come through.

Even if you have blundered,
    Even if you have sinned,
Still is the steadfast arch of the sky
    And the healing veil of the wind . . .   15
And after only a little,
    A little of hurt and pain,
You shall have the web of your own old dreams
    Wrapping your heart again.

Only your heart can pity   20
    Now, where it laughed and passed,
Now you can bend to comfort men,
    One with them all at last,
You shall have back your laughter,
    You shall have back your song,   25
Only the world is your brother now,
    Only your soul is strong!

[1] From *The Old Road to Paradise*, reprinted by permission of Henry
Holt and Company, publishers.

EDWIN ARLINGTON ROBINSON

OCTAVES[1]

I

To get at the eternal strength of things,
And fearlessly to make strong songs of it,
Is, to my mind, the mission of that man
The world would call a poet. He may sing
But roughly, and withal ungraciously;
But if he touch to life the one right chord
Wherein God's music slumbers, and awake
To truth one drowsed ambition, he sings well.

THE WILDERNESS[1]

Come away! come away! there's a frost along the marshes,
And a frozen wind that skims the shoal where it shakes the
 dead black water;
There's a moan across the lowland and a wailing through the
 woodland
Of a dirge that sings to send us back to the arms of those
 that love us.
There is nothing left but ashes now where the crimson chills
 of autumn
Put off the summer's languor with a touch that made us glad
For the glory that is gone from us, with a flight we cannot
 follow,
To the slopes of other valleys and the sounds of other shores.

Come away! come away! you can hear them calling, calling,
Calling us to come to them, and roam no more.
Over there beyond the ridges and the land that lies between us,
There's an old song calling us to come!

[1] Reprinted from *The Children of the Night*, by permission of Charles
Scribner's Sons, publishers.

Come away! come away!—for the scenes we leave behind us
Are barren for the lights of home and a flame that's young
    forever;
And the lonely trees around us creak the warning of the night-
    wind,
That love and all the dreams of love are away beyond the
    mountains.
The songs that call for us to-night, they have called for men
    before us,   5
And the winds that blow the message, they have blown ten
    thousand years;
But this will end our wander-time, for we know the joy that
    waits us
In the strangeness of home-coming, and a woman's waiting
    eyes.

Come away! come away! there is nothing now to cheer us—
Nothing now to comfort us, but love's road home:—   10
Over there beyond the darkness there's a window gleams to
    greet us,
And a warm hearth waits for us within.

Come away! come away!—or the roving-fiend will hold us,
And make us all to dwell with him to the end of human
    faring:
There are no men yet may leave him when his hands are
    clutched upon them,   15
There are none will own his enmity, there are none will call
    him brother.
So we'll be up and on the way, and the less we boast the better
For the freedom that God gave us and the dread we do not
    know:—
The frost that skips the willow-leaf will again be back to
    blight it,
And the doom we cannot fly from is the doom we do not see. 20

Come away! come away! there are dead men all around us—
Frozen men that mock us with a wild, hard laugh
That shrieks and sinks and whimpers in the shrill November
    rushes,
And the long fall wind on the lake.

VACHEL LINDSAY

ABRAHAM LINCOLN WALKS AT MIDNIGHT[1]

5   It is portentous, and a thing of state
That here at midnight, in our little town
A mourning figure walks, and will not rest,
Near the old court-house pacing up and down,

Or by his homestead, or in shadowed yards
10   He lingers where his children used to play,
Or through the market, on the well-worn stones
He stalks until the dawn-stars burn away.

A bronzed, lank man! His suit of ancient black,
A famous high-top hat and plain worn shawl
15   Make him the quaint great figure that men love,
The prairie lawyer, master of us all.

He cannot sleep upon his hillside now.
He is among us:—as in times before!
And we who toss and lie awake for long
20   Breathe deep, and start, to see him pass the door.

His head is bowed. He thinks on men and kings.
Yea, when the sick world cries, how can he sleep?
Too many peasants fight, they know not why,
Too many homesteads in black terror weep.

---

[1] Reprinted from Vachel Lindsay's *The Congo and Other Poems.* **By**
special arrangement with The Macmillan Company, publisher.

The sins of all the war-lords burn his heart.
He sees the dreadnaughts scouring every main.
He carries on his shawl-wrapped shoulders now
The bitterness, the folly and the pain.

He cannot rest until a spirit-dawn   5
Shall come;—the shining hope of Europe free:
The league of sober folk, the Workers' Earth,
Bringing long peace to Cornland, Alp and Sea.

It breaks his heart that kings must murder still,
That all his hours of travail here for men   10
Seem yet in vain. And who will bring white peace
That he may sleep upon his hill again?

NIAGARA [1]

I

Within the town of Buffalo
Are prosy men with leaden eyes.
Like ants they worry to and fro,   15
(Important men, in Buffalo.)
But only twenty miles away
A deathless glory is at play:
Niagara, Niagara.

The women buy their lace and cry:—   20
"O such a delicate design,"
And over ostrich feathers sigh,
By counters there, in Buffalo.
The children haunt the trinket shops,
They buy false faces, bells, and tops,   25
Forgetting great Niagara.

---

[1] Reprinted from Vachel Lindsay's *The Chinese Nightingale*. By special
arrangement with The Macmillan Company, publisher.

Within the town of Buffalo
Are stores with garnets, sapphires, pearls,
Rubies, emeralds aglow,—
Opal chains in Buffalo,
5   Cherished symbols of success.
They value not your rainbow dress:—
Niagara, Niagara.

The shaggy meaning of her name
This Buffalo, this recreant town,
10   Sharps and lawyers prune and tame:
Few pioneers in Buffalo;
Except young lovers flushed and fleet
And winds hallooing down the street:
"Niagara, Niagara."

15   The journalists are sick of ink:
Boy prodigals are lost in wine,
By night where white and red lights blink,
The eyes of Death, in Buffalo.
And only twenty miles away
20   Are starlit rocks and healing spray:—
Niagara, Niagara.

Above the town a tiny bird,
A shining speck at sleepy dawn,
Forgets the ant-hill so absurd,
25   This self-important Buffalo.
Descending twenty miles away
He bathes his wings at break of day—
Niagara, Niagara.

II

What marching men of Buffalo
30   *Flood the streets in rash crusade?*
Fools-to-free-the-world, they go,
Primeval hearts from Buffalo.

Red cataracts of France to-day
Awake, three thousand miles away
An echo of Niagara,
The cataract Niagara.

THE LIGHT O' THE MOON[1]

The Beggar Speaks

"What Mister Moon Said to Me"

Come, eat the bread of idleness,   5
Come, sit beside the spring:
Some of the flowers will keep awake,
Some of the birds will sing.

Come, eat the bread no man has sought
For half a hundred years: 10
Men hurry so they have no griefs,
Nor even idle tears:

They hurry so they have no loves:
They cannot curse nor laugh—
Their hearts die in their youth with neither   15
Grave nor epitaph.

My bread would make them careless,
And never quite on time—
Their eyelids would be heavy,
Their fancies full of rhyme: 20

Each soul a mystic rose-tree,
Or a curious incense tree:
        .   .   .   .   .

Come, eat the bread of idleness,
Said Mister Moon to me.

[1] Reprinted from Vachel Lindsay's *General William Booth Enters into Heaven*. By special arrangement with The Macmillan Company, publisher.

EDITH M. THOMAS

"CLEAVE TO THINE ACRE"[1]

My neighbor was a forester
    And ranged with bow and spear;
I was a simple gardener,
    And delved the whole round year.

5   Time came when both a-weary were,
    And both resolved on change;
So he became a gardener,
    And I the woods did range.

The seed springs never to the light,—
10   He chides the soil, the air!
The forest genii, in despite,
    Adrift mine arrows bear!

Folk say the woods be full of deer,
    The wild-flowers praise the soil:
15   But flower nor game, the whole round year,
    Rewards our alien toil.

GEORGE EDWARD WOODBERRY

ALBERT OF BELGIUM[2]

True victor thou, heroic Belgian King,
    Albert, who wouldst not traffic in thy crown!
    A Kingdom's heirloom goes thy glory down,
20 And with thy people's praise all countries ring;
Thee and thy folk shall unborn poets sing,
    And age to age repeat thy just renown,
    Who held the peril of an empire's frown,
With thy land's honor matched, an idle thing.

---

[1] Reprinted from *Cassia and Other Poems*, copyrighted 1905.
[2] From *The Roamer*, published 1920, Harcourt, Brace and Company, Inc.

But rather of the crown that grows not old
   Thy thought, who others saved, saving thine own,
   And left this wisdom to thy little state:
Put not thy trust in armies nor in gold,
   Nor on proud navies set the people's throne,   5
   But by the justice of thy cause be great!

KATHARINE LEE BATES

YELLOW WARBLERS[1]

The first faint dawn was flushing up the skies
When, dreamland still bewildering mine eyes,
I looked out to the oak that, winter-long,
—A winter wild with war and woe and wrong—   10
Beyond my casement had been void of song.

And lo! with golden buds the twigs were set,
Live buds that warbled like a rivulet
Beneath a veil of willows. Then I knew
Those tiny voices, clear as drops of dew,   15
Those flying daffodils that fleck the blue,

Those sparkling visitants from myrtle isles,
Wee pilgrims of the sun, that measure miles
Innumerable over land and sea
With wings of shining inches. Flakes of glee,   20
They filled that dark old oak with jubilee,

Foretelling in delicious roundelays
Their dainty courtships on the dipping sprays,
How they should fashion nests, mate helping mate,
Of milkweed flax and fern-down delicate   25
To keep sky-tinted eggs inviolate.

[1] Copyright, 1918, by E. P. Dutton & Company.

Listening to those blithe notes, I slipped once more
From lyric dawn through dreamland's open door,
And there was God, Eternal Life that sings
Eternal joy, brooding all mortal things,
5   A nest of stars beneath untroubled wings.

ALAN SEEGER

I HAVE A RENDEZVOUS WITH DEATH[1]

I have a rendezvous with Death
At some disputed barricade,
When Spring comes round with rustling shade
And apple blossoms fill the air.
10   I have a rendezvous with Death
When Spring brings back blue days and fair.

It may be he shall take my hand
And lead me into his dark land
And close my eyes and quench my breath;
15   It may be I shall pass him still.
I have a rendezvous with Death
On some scarred slope of battered hill,
When Spring comes round again this year
And the first meadow flowers appear.

20   God knows 'twere better to be deep
Pillowed in silk and scented down,
Where love throbs out in blissful sleep,
Pulse nigh to pulse, and breath to breath,
Where hushed awakenings are dear.
25   But I've a rendezvous with Death
At midnight in some flaming town,
When Spring trips north again this year,
And I to my pledged word am true,
I shall not fail that rendezvous.

[1] Reprinted by permission of Charles Scribner's Sons, publishers.

ROBERT FROST

MENDING WALL[1]

Something there is that doesn't love a wall,
That sends the frozen-ground-swell under it,
And spills the upper bowlders in the sun;
And makes gaps even two can pass abreast.
The work of hunters is another thing: 5
I have come after them and made repair
Where they have left not one stone on a stone,
But they would have the rabbit out of hiding,
To please the yelping dogs. The gaps I mean,
No one has seen them made or heard them made,   10
But at spring mending-time we find them there.
I let my neighbor know beyond the hill;
And on a day we meet to walk the line
And set the wall between us once again.
We keep the wall between us as we go.   15
To each the bowlders that have fallen to each.
And some are loaves and some so nearly balls
We have to use a spell to make them balance:
"Stay where you are until our backs are turned!"
We wear our fingers rough with handling them.   20
Oh, just another kind of outdoor game,
One on a side. It comes to little more:
There where it is we do not need the wall:
He is all pine and I am apple orchard.
My apple trees will never get across   25
And eat the cones under his pines, I tell him.
He only says, "Good fences make good neighbors."
Spring is the mischief in me, and I wonder
If I could put a notion in his head:
"*Why* do they make good neighbors? Isn't it   30
Where there are cows? But here there are no cows.

[1] From *North of Boston*, reprinted by permission of Henry Holt and
Company, publishers.

Before I built a wall I'd ask to know
What I was walling in or walling out
And to whom I was like to give offense.
Something there is that doesn't love a wall,
That wants it down." I could say "Elves" to him,
But it's not elves exactly, and I'd rather
He said it for himself. I see him there
Bringing a stone grasped firmly by the top
In each hand, like an old-stone savage armed.
He moves in darkness as it seems to me,
Not of woods only and the shade of trees.
He will not go behind his father's saying,
And he likes having thought of it so well
He says again, "Good fences make good neighbors."

AFTER APPLE–PICKING[1]

My long two-pointed ladder's sticking through a tree
Toward heaven still,
And there's a barrel that I didn't fill
Beside it, and there may be two or three
Apples I didn't pick upon some bough.
But I am done with apple-picking now.
Essence of winter sleep is on the night,
The scent of apples: I am drowsing off.
I cannot rub the strangeness from my sight
I got from looking through a pane of glass
I skimmed this morning from the drinking trough
And held against the world of hoary grass.
It melted, and I let it fall and break.
But I was well
Upon my way to sleep before it fell,
And I could tell
What form my dreaming was about to take.

[1] From *North of Boston*, reprinted by permission of Henry Holt and Company, publishers.

Magnified apples appear and disappear,
Stem end and blossom end,
And every fleck of russet showing clear.
My instep arch not only keeps the ache,
It keeps the pressure of a ladder-round.   5
I feel the ladder sway as the boughs bend.
And I keep hearing from the cellar bin
The rumbling sound
Of load on load of apples coming in.
For I have had too much   10
Of apple-picking: I am overtired
Of the great harvest I myself desired.
There were ten thousand thousand fruit to touch,
Cherish in hand, lift down, and not let fall.
For all   15
That struck the earth,
No matter if not bruised or spiked with stubble,
Went surely to the cider-apple heap
As of no worth.
One can see what will trouble   20
This sleep of mine, whatever sleep it is.
Were he not gone,
The woodchuck could say whether it's like his
Long sleep, as I describe its coming on,
Or just some human sleep.   25

AMY LOWELL

THE COAL PICKER[1]

He perches in the slime, inert,
Bedaubed with iridescent dirt.
The oil upon the puddles dries
To colors like a peacock's eyes,

[1] From *Sword Blades and Poppy Seed*, reprinted by permission of Houghton Mifflin Company, publishers.

And half-submerged tomato-cans
Shine scaly, as leviathans
Oozily crawling through the mud.
The ground is here and there bestud
With lumps of only part-burned coal.
His duty is to glean the whole,
To pick them from the filth, each one,
To hoard them for the hidden sun
Which glows within each fiery core
And waits to be made free once more.
Their sharp and glistening edges cut
His stiffened fingers. Through the smut
Gleam red the wounds which will not shut.
Wet through and shivering he kneels
And digs the slippery coals; like eels
They slide about. His force all spent,
He counts his small accomplishment.
A half-a-dozen clinker coals
Which still have fire in their souls.
Fire! And in his thought there burns
The topaz fire of votive urns.
He sees it fling from hill to hill,
And still consumed, is burning still.
Higher and higher leaps the flame,
The smoke an ever-shifting frame.
He sees a Spanish Castle old,
With silver steps and paths of gold.
From myrtle bowers comes the plash
Of fountains, and the emerald flash
Of parrots in the orange trees,
Whose blossoms pasture humming bees.
He knows he feeds the urns whose smoke
Bears visions, that his master-stroke
Is out of dirt and misery
To light the fire of poesy.

He sees the glory, yet he knows
That others cannot see his shows.
To them his smoke is sightless, black,
His votive vessels but a pack
Of old, discarded shards, his fire 5
A peddler's; still to him the pyre
Is incensed, an enduring goal!
He sighs and grubs another coal.

JOSEPHINE PRESTON PEABODY

MEN HAVE WINGS AT LAST[1]

[The Air-Raid]

'Wolf, wolf,—stay-at-home,
Prowler,—scout, 10
Clanless and castaways,
And ailing with the drought!
Out from your hidings, hither to the call;
Lift up your eyes to the high wind-fall;
Lift up your eyes from the stagnant spring; 15
Overhead, overhead! The dragon thing,
What should it bring?—
Poising on the wing?'

'Wolf, wolf, old one,—I saw it, even I;
Yesterday, yesterday, the Thing came by.— 20
Prowling at the outpost of the last lean wood,
By the gray waste ashes where the minster stood,
And out through the cloister, where the belfry fronts
The market place, and the town was, once.

[1] From *Harvest Moon*, reprinted by permission of Houghton Mifflin
Company, publishers.

High, high, above the bright wide square,
And the folk all flocking together, unaware,
The thing with the wings came there.
    Brother Vulture saw it,
      And called me as it passed:
    "Look and see, look and see,
      Men have wings at last!"

'By the eyeless belfry I saw it, overhead,
Poise like a hawk,—like a storm unshed.
Near the huddled doves there, from a shattered cote,
I watched too.—And it smote.

'Not a threat of thunder, not an armèd man,
Where the fury struck, and the fleet fire ran.
But girl-child, man-child, mothers and their young,
New-born of woman with milk upon its tongue;
Nursling where it clung!

'Not a talon reached they, then, the lords of prey!
But left the red dregs there, rent and cast away;—
Fled from the spoil there, scattered things accurst!
    It was not for hunger;
    It was not for thirst.

    'From the eyeless belfry,
      Brother Vulture laughed:
    "This is all we have to see
      For his master-craft?
    Old ones,—lean ones,
      Never now to fast,
      Men have wings at last!"

'Brought they any tidings for us from the Sun?'
    'No, my chief, not one.'
'Left they not a road-mark, how the way was won?'
    'No, my chief, none.

'But girl-child, man-child, creature yet unborn,
Doe and fawn together so, weltering and torn,
New-born of woman where the flag-stones bled:
(Better can the vultures do, for the shamèd dead!)
Road-dust, sobbing, where the lightnings burst!   5
    It was not for hunger;
    It was not for thirst.'

'Brought they not some token that the stars look on?'
    'No, my chief, none.'
'Never yet a message from the highway overhead?'   10
    'Brother, I have said.'

'Old years, gray years, years of growing things,
We have toiled and kept the watch with our wonderings,
But to see what thing should be, when that men had wings.

'Sea-mark, sea-wall, ships above the tide: 15
Mine and mole-way under-earth, to have its hidden pride,
Not enough; not enough; more and more beside.

'Bridle for our proud of mane; then the triple yoke;
Ox-goad and lash again, and bonded fellow-folk!
Not enough; not enough;—for his master stroke.   20

'Thunder trapped and muttering and led away for thrall,
Lightnings leashed together then, at his beck and call;
Not enough; not enough, for his wherewithal!

    'He must look with evil eye
    On the spaces of the sky;   25
    He must scheme and try!
    While all we, with dread and awe,
    Sheathing and unsheathing claw,
    Watch apart, and prophesy
        That we never saw.—   30

'Wings, to seek his more-and-more,
　　Where we knew us blind;
Wings, to make him conqueror
　　With his master-mind;
'5　　Wings, that he outwatch, outsoar
　　　Eagle and his kind!

'Lo, the dream fulfilled at last!　And the dread outgrown,
Broken, as a bird's heart; fallen, as a stone.
　　What was he, to make afraid?—
10　　Hating all that he had made,
　　　Hating all his own!

'Scatter to your strongholds, till the race is run.
(Doe and fawn together so, soon it will be done.)
Never now, never now, ship without a mast,
15　In the harbor of the sun, do you make fast!
　　But the floods shall cleanse again
　　Every blackened trail of men,
　　　Men with wings, at last!'

JOYCE KILMER

HOLY IRELAND[1]

We had hiked seventeen miles that stormy December day
20 —the third of a four days' journey.　The snow was piled high
on our packs, our rifles were crusted with ice, the leather of
our hob-nailed boots was frozen stiff over our lamed feet.
The weary lieutenant led us to the door of a little house in a
side street.

25　　"Next twelve men," he said.　A dozen of us dropped out of
the ranks and dragged ourselves over the threshold.　We
tracked snow and mud over a spotless stone floor.　Before an

---

[1] "Holy Ireland," from *Joyce Kilmer*.　Edited by Robert Cortes Holliday.　Copyright, 1916, 1917, 1918, George H. Doran Company, publishers.

open fire stood Madame and the three children—a girl of
eight years, a boy of five, a boy of three. They stared with
round frightened eyes at *les soldats Américains*, the first they
had ever seen. We were too tired to stare back. We at once
climbed to the chill attic, our billet, our lodging for the night. 5
First we lifted the packs from one another's aching shoulders;
then, without spreading our blankets, we lay down on the
bare boards.

For ten minutes there was silence, broken by an occasional
groan, an oath, the striking of a match. Cigarettes glowed 10
like fireflies in a forest. Then a voice came from the corner:

"Where is Sergeant Reilly?" it said. We lazily searched.
There was no Sergeant Reilly to be found.

"I'll bet the old bum has gone out after a pint," said the
voice. And with the curiosity of the American and the en- 15
thusiasm of the Irish we lumbered downstairs in quest of
Sergeant Reilly.

He was sitting on a low bench by the fire. His shoes were
off and his bruised feet were in a pail of cold water. He was
too good a soldier to expose them to the heat at once. The 20
little girl was on his lap and the little boys stood by and
envied him. And in a voice that twenty years of soldiering
and oceans of whisky had failed to rob of its Celtic sweetness,
he was softly singing: "Ireland Isn't Ireland Any More."
We listened respectfully.   25

"They cheer the King and then salute him," said Sergeant
Reilly.

"A regular Irishman would shoot him," and we all joined
in the chorus, "Ireland Isn't Ireland Any More."

"Ooh, la, la!" exclaimed Madame, and she and all the 30
children began to talk at the top of their voices. What
they said Heaven knows, but the tones were friendly, even
admiring.

"Gentlemen," said Sergeant Reilly from his post of honor,
"the lady who runs this billet is a very nice lady indeed. 35
She says yez can all take off your shoes and dry your socks

by the fire. But take turns and don't crowd or I'll turn yez all upstairs."

Now Madame, a woman of some forty years, was a true bourgeoise, with all the thrift of her class. And by the terms of her agreement with the authorities she was required to let the soldiers have for one night the attic of her house to sleep in—nothing more; no light, no heat. Also, wood is very expensive in France—for reasons that are engraven in letters of blood on the pages of history. Nevertheless—

"Asseyez-vous, s'il vous plaît," said Madame. And she brought nearer to the fire all the chairs the establishment possessed and some chests and boxes to be used as seats. And she and the little girl, whose name was Solange, went out into the snow and came back with heaping armfuls of small logs. The fire blazed merrily—more merrily than it had blazed since August, 1914, perhaps. We surrounded it, and soon the air was thick with steam from our drying socks.

Meanwhile Madame and the Sergeant had generously admitted all eleven of us into their conversation. A spirited conversation it was, too, in spite of the fact that she knew no English and the extent of his French was "du pain," "du vin," "cognac" and "bonjour." Those of us who knew a little more of the language of the country acted as interpreters for the others. We learned the names of the children and their ages. We learned that our hostess was a widow. Her husband had fallen in battle just one month before our arrival in her home. She showed us with simple pride and affection and restrained grief his picture. Then she showed us those of her two brothers—one now fighting at Salonica, the other a prisoner of war—of her mother and father, of herself dressed for First Communion.

This last picture she showed us somewhat shyly, as if doubting that we would understand it. But when one of us asked in halting French if Solange, her little daughter, had yet made her First Communion, then Madame's face cleared.

"Mais oui!" she exclaimed. "Et vous, ma foi, vous êtes Catholiques, n'est-ce pas?"

At once rosary beads were flourished to prove our right to answer this question affirmatively. Tattered prayer-books and somewhat dingy scapulars were brought to light. Madame and the children chattered their surprise and delight to each other, and every exhibit called for a new outburst.

"Ah, le bon S. Benoit! Ah, voilà, la Conception Immaculée! Ooh la la, le Sacré Cœur!" (which last exclamation sounded in no wise as irreverent as it looks in print).

Now other treasures, too, were shown—treasures chiefly photographic. There were family groups, there were Coney Island snapshots. And Madame and the children were a gratifyingly appreciative audience. They admired and sympathized; they exclaimed appropriately at the beauty of every girl's face, the tenderness of every pictured mother. We had become the intimates of Madame. She had admitted us into her family and we her into ours.

Soldiers—American soldiers of Irish descent—have souls and hearts. These organs (if the soul may be so termed) had been satisfied. But our stomachs remained—and that they yearned was evident to us. We had made our hike on a meal of hardtack and "corned willy." Mess call would sound soon. Should we force our wet shoes on again and plod through the snowy streets to the temporary mess-shack? We knew our supply wagons had not succeeded in climbing the last hill into town, and that therefore bread and unsweetened coffee would be our portion. A great depression settled upon us.

But Sergeant Reilly rose to the occasion.

"Boys," he said, "this here lady has got a good fire going, and I'll bet she can cook. What do you say we get her to fix us up a meal?"

This proposal was received joyously at first. Then someone said:

"But I haven't got any money." "Neither have I—not a

damn sou!" said another. And again the spiritual temperature of the room fell.

Again Sergeant Reilly spoke:

"I haven't got any money to speak of, meself," he said.
5 "But let's have a show-down. I guess we've got enough to buy somethin' to eat."

It was long after pay-day, and we were not hopeful of the results of the search. But the wealthy (that is, those who had two francs) made up for the poor (that is, those who had
10 two sous). And among the coins on the table I noticed an American dime, an English half-crown and a Chinese piece with a square hole in the center. In negotiable tender the money came in all to eight francs.

It takes more money than that to feed twelve hungry sol-
15 diers these days in France. But there was no harm in trying. So an ex-seminarian, an ex-bookkeeper and ex-street-car conductor aided Sergeant Reilly in explaining in French that had both a brogue and a Yankee twang that we were hungry, that this was all the money we had in the world, and that we
20 wanted her to cook us something to eat.

Now Madame was what they call in New England a "capable" woman. In a jiffy she had the money in Solange's hand and had that admirable child cloaked and wooden-shod for the street and fully informed her as to what she was to
25 buy. What Madame and the children had intended to have for supper I do not know, for there was nothing in the kitchen but the fire, the stove, the table, some shelves of dishes and an enormous bed. Nothing in the way of a food cupboard could be seen. And the only other room of the house was
30 the bare attic.

When Solange came back she carried in a basket bigger than herself these articles: (1) two loaves of war-bread; (2) five bottles of red wine; (3) three cheeses; (4) numerous potatoes; (5) a lump of fat; (6) a bag of coffee. The whole
35 represented, as was afterward demonstrated, exactly the sum of ten francs, fifty centimes.

Well, we all set to work peeling potatoes. Then with a veritable French trench-knife Madame cut the potatoes into long strips. Meanwhile Solange had put the lump of fat into the big black pot that hung by a chain over the fire. In the boiling grease the potatoes were placed, Madame standing by with a big ladle punched full of holes (I regret that I do not know the technical name for this instrument) and keeping the potato-strips swimming, zealously frustrating any attempt on their part to lie lazily at the bottom of the pot.

We forgot all about the hike as we sat at supper that evening. The only absentees were the two little boys, Michael and Paul. And they were really absent only from our board —they were in the room, in the great built-in bed that was later to hold also Madame and Solange. Their little bodies were covered by the three-foot thick mattresslike red silk quilt, but their touseled heads protruded and they watched us unblinkingly all the evening.

But just as we sat down, before Sergeant Reilly began his task of dishing out the potatoes and starting the bottles on their way, Madame stopped her chattering and looked at Solange. And Solange stopped her chattering and looked at Madame. And they both looked rather searchingly at us. We didn't know what was the matter, but we felt rather embarrassed.

Then Madame began to talk, slowly and loudly, as one talks to make foreigners understand. And the gist of her remarks was that she was surprised to see that American Catholics did not say grace before eating, like French Catholics.

We sprang to our feet at once. But it was not Sergeant Reilly who saved the situation. Instead, the ex-seminarian (he is only temporarily an ex-seminarian; he'll be preaching missions and giving retreats yet if a bit of shrapnel doesn't hasten his journey to Heaven) said, after we had blessed ourselves: "Benedicite; nos et quae sumus sumpturi benedicat Deus, Pater et Filius et Spiritus Sanctus. Amen."

Madame and Solange, obviously relieved, joined us in the
Amen, and we sat down again to eat.

It was a memorable feast. There was not much conversation—except on the part of Madame and Solange—but there
5 was plenty of good cheer. Also there was enough cheese and
bread and wine and potatoes for all of us—half starved as we
were when we sat down. Even big Considine, who drains a
can of condensed milk at a gulp, and has been known to eat
an apple pie without stopping to take breath, was satisfied.
10 There were toasts, also, all proposed by Sergeant Reilly—
toasts to Madame, and to the children, and to France, and to
the United States, and to the Old Gray Mare (this last toast
having an esoteric significance apparent only to illuminati
of Sergeant Reilly's circle).

15   The table cleared and the "agimus tibi gratias" duly said,
we sat before the fire, most of us on the floor. We were warm
and happy and full of good food and good wine. I spied a
slip of paper on the floor by Solange's foot and unashamedly
read it. It was an accounting for the evening's expenditures
20 —totaling exactly ten francs and fifty centimes.

Now when soldiers are unhappy—during a long, hard hike
for instance—they sing to keep up their spirits. And when
they are happy, as on the evening now under consideration,
they sing to express their satisfaction with life. We sang
25 "Sweet Rosie O'Grady." We shook the kitchen-bedroom
with the echoes of "Take Me Back to New York Town." We
informed Madame, Solange, Paul, Michael, in fact, the whole
village, that we had never been a wanderer and that we
longed for our Indiana home. We grew sentimental over
30 "Mother Machree." And Sergeant Reilly obliged with a
reel—in his socks—to an accompaniment of whistling and
handclapping.

Now, it was our hostess's turn to entertain. We intimated
as much. She responded, first by much talk, much consulta-
35 tion with Solange, and finally by going to one of the shelves
that held the plans and taking down some paper-covered books.

Then there was more consultation, whispered this time, and much turning of pages. Then, after some preliminary coughing and humming, the music began—the woman's rich alto blending with the child's shrill but sweet notes. And what they sang was "Tantum ergo Sacramentum."   5

Why she should have thought that an appropriate song to offer this company of rough soldiers from a distant land I do not know. And why we found it appropriate it is harder still to say. But it did seem appropriate to all of us—to Sergeant Reilly, to Jim (who used to drive a truck), to Larry (who 10 sold cigars), to Frank (who tended a bar on Fourteenth Street). It seemed, for some reason, eminently fitting. Not one of us then or later expressed any surprise that this hymn, familiar to most of us since our mothers first led us to the Parish Church down the pavements of New York or across 15 the Irish hills, should be sung to us in this strange land and in these strange circumstances.

Since the gracious Latin of the Church was in order and since the season was appropriate, one of us suggested "Adeste Fideles" for the next item on the evening's program. Madame 20 and Solange and our ex-seminarian knew all the words and the rest of us came in strong with "Venite, adoremus Dominum."

Then, as if to show that piety and mirth may live together, the ladies obliged with "Au Clair de la Lune" and other 25 simple ballads of old France. And after taps had sounded in the street outside our door, and there was yawning, and wrist-watches were being scanned, the evening's entertainment ended, by general consent, with patriotic selections. We sang —as best we could—the "Star-Spangled Banner," Solange 30 and her mother humming the air and applauding at the con-clusion. Then we attempted "La Marseillaise." Of course, we did not know the words. Solange came to our rescue with two little pamphlets containing the song, so we looked over each other's shoulders and got to work in earnest. Madame 35 sang with us, and Solange. But during the final stanza

Madame did not sing. She leaned against the great family
bedstead and looked at us. She had taken one of the babies
from under the red comforter and held him to her breast.
One of her red and toil-scarred hands half covered his fat
little back. There was a gentle dignity about that plain,
hard-working woman, that soldier's widow—we all felt it.
And some of us saw the tears in her eyes.

There are mists, faint and beautiful and unchanging, that
hang over the green slopes of some mountains I know. I
have seen them on the Irish hills and I have seen them on the
hills of France. I think that they are made of the tears of
good brave women.

Before I went to sleep that night I exchanged a few words
with Sergeant Reilly. We lay side by side on the floor, now
piled with straw. Blankets, shelterhalves, slickers and over-
coats insured warm sleep. Sergeant Reilly's hard old face
was wrapped round with his muffler. The final cigarette of
the day burned lazily in a corner of his mouth.

"That was a pretty good evening, Sarge," I said. "We
sure were in luck when we struck this billet."

He grunted affirmatively, then puffed in silence for a few
minutes. Then he deftly spat the cigarette into a strawless
portion of the floor, where it glowed for a few seconds before
it went out.

"You said it," he remarked. "We were in luck is right.
What do you know about the lady, anyway?"

"Why," I answered, "I thought she treated us pretty
white."

"Joe," said Sergeant Reilly; "do you realize how much
trouble that woman took to make this bunch of roughnecks
comfortable? She didn't make a damn cent on that feed,
you know. The kid spent all the money we give her. And
she's out about six francs for firewood, too—I wish to God I
had the money to pay her. I bet she'll go cold for a week
now, and hungry, too.

"And that ain't all," he continued, after a pause broken only by an occasional snore from our blissful neighbors. "Look at the way she cooked them pomme de terres and fixed things up for us and let us sit down there with her like we was her family. And look at the way she and the little Sallie there sung for us.

"I tell you, Joe, it makes me think of old times to hear a woman sing them church hymns to me that way. It's forty years since I heard a hymn sung in a kitchen, and it was my mother, God rest her, that sang them. I sort of realize what we're fighting for now, and I never did before. It's for women like that and their kids.

"It gave me a turn to see her a-sitting there singing them hymns. I remembered when I was a boy in Shanagolden. I wonder if there's many women like that in France now— telling their beads and singing the old hymns and treating poor traveling men the way she's just after treating us. There used to be lots of women like that in the Old Country. And I think that's why it was called 'Holy Ireland.'"

NOTES

Heavy figures refer to pages, and light figures refer to lines. For diacritical marks see Key to Pronunciation preceding the Index

1 William Bradford: a signer of the *Mayflower* Compact; he succeeded John Carver as governor of the Plymouth Colony. He was remarkably successful in dealing with the Indians: the peace made with Massasoit continued not only for twenty-four years, as stated by Bradford in 1645, but actually until 1675. During the Revolution, when the Old South Church in Boston was used as a riding-school by British soldiers, the manuscript of Bradford's *History of Plymouth Plantation* disappeared from the library in the steeple. It was found in the library of Fulham Palace, in England, in 1858, and was returned to Massachusetts in 1898.—1 **All this while:** the first winter after the landing of the Pilgrims at Plymouth, December, 1620.

2 6 Afterwards they . . . began to plant: in April, after the sailing of the *Mayflower* for England.—**as many as were able:** More than half the Colonists died during the first winter; and few of the survivors escaped serious illness as a result of hardship, exposure, and poor food.—10 **fish:** alewives, very common along the north Atlantic coast, but of poor quality as food. They go up the streams to spawn several weeks before the shad. —30 **Christmas-day:** The early settlers of New England were very conscientious, even rigid, in their observance of Sunday, but paid no attention to other holy days observed in the Old World. As late as the middle of the nineteenth century some of their descendants made no observance of Christmas.—32 **new company:** mostly young men, who arrived in November, 1621, without provisions or even adequate clothing for the winter.

3 *The History of the Dividing Line:* the account of an expedition made in order to settle the disputed boundary between Virginia and North Carolina. As a large part of the way was through pathless, snake-infested swamps, the undertaking was both difficult and dangerous. To this undertaking William Byrd went from his beautiful and luxurious estate at Westover, where he was born and where he died. He was educated in England, and had one of the largest libraries in the Colonies at that period.

4 8 Edenton: the county seat of Chowan County, North Carolina. Mr. Eden was governor of North Carolina early in the eighteenth century.—26 **Norfolk or Nansemond:** Elsewhere in this book Byrd says, "Norfolk has most the air of a town of any in Virginia." "Nansemond" is an Indian name. Besides the town, there are Nansemond River and

Nansemond County, the latter extending from Hampton Roads to the North Carolina border.—29 **Muscovy:** Russia.—32 **Lubberland:** an imaginary land of abundance and laziness.

7 Michael Wigglesworth: born in Yorkshire, England, in 1631; came to America in 1638; died in Malden, Massachusetts, in 1705. Besides being a clergyman and a poet he was skilled in medicine. He was compelled by ill health to decline the presidency of Harvard College in 1684.— 22 **mauger:** in spite of.

8 Anne Bradstreet: daughter of Thomas Dudley, second in command to John Winthrop, the first governor, and later himself governor of the Massachusetts Bay Colony; married the future Colonial governor Simon Bradstreet in 1628 and came with him to New England in 1630. She was the mother of eight children, and wrote in the leisure which was left her from the household duties of a pioneer wife and mother.

9 Thomas Godfrey: born in Philadelphia; died near Wilmington, North Carolina.—**Parthia:** a country southeast of the Caspian Sea; an imperial power often at war with Rome, and finally conquered by the Persian dynasty of the Sassanidæ about A.D. 226.

10 John Williams: born in Roxbury, Massachusetts, in 1664; died in Deerfield, Massachusetts, in 1729. He graduated from Harvard in 1683. He was minister of the church in Deerfield at the time of the Indian raid here described, February 29, 1704. He was taken to Canada, where he was treated humanely and courteously by the French, was redeemed, and returned to Boston November 21, 1706, with two of his six children who had been carried off with him. His daughter Eunice, ten years old, was left in Canada and later married an Indian.—11 **Maquas:** an old name for the Iroquois Indians.

12 16 **laid down:** a correct form at the time Williams wrote.

13 Cotton Mather: born in Boston; graduated at Harvard College at fifteen. He taught school and, giving up studying for the ministry because of an impediment in his speech, studied medicine. Later, having conquered his stammering, he finished his theological studies and became first (at the age of seventeen) assistant and then colleague to his father, who was pastor of the largest church in New England, the North Church in Boston. When his father went to England on business for the colony, Mather, then twenty-five years old, was left in charge of the church. He was a scholar and a linguist, and kept his interest in scientific matters, being the first American elected to membership in the Royal Society of London. He stood boldly with Dr. Boylston in favor of inoculation for smallpox, in the face of great opposition on the part of both doctors and the general public; in 1721 the first operation of this sort was performed in Boston.— *Magnalia Christi Americana:* "Wonders of Christ in America."—**Nehemias Americanus:** "The American Nehemiah." Nehemiah was governor of Judea under Artaxerxes, in the fifth century before Christ. He was active in rebuilding Jerusalem and in restoring the Temple. Mather likens John Winthrop, the first governor of the Massachusetts Bay Colony, to this Hebrew patriot. —24 **Moses:** the leader of the Hebrews out of servitude in Egypt toward freedom in the Promised Land.

14 6 **disagreeable:** unsuitable.

15 Jonathan **Edwards:** graduated at the Collegiate School (which later became Yale College) in 1720, as valedictorian of a class of ten. He was minister of the church in Northampton, Massachusetts (then considered the most important church in the colony outside of Boston), from 1729 to 1750, when, partly as a result of controversy over conditions of admission to communion, he was dismissed by the church. From Northampton he went to Stockbridge, Massachusetts, as missionary to the Indians, and during his seven years there he produced most of his writings. In 1757 he became president of the college at Princeton, but soon after going there died from inoculation for smallpox.

19 1 I **now took a fancy:** while Franklin, as a boy, was serving his apprenticeship in his brother's printing office.—8 **Grub-street:** a shabby street in London, inhabited by poor, unsuccessful authors.

20 28 the *Spectator*: one of the forerunners of the modern literary magazine. It was founded in London in 1711. The Sir Roger de Coverley papers and other essays by Addison and Steele first appeared in the *Spectator*.

22 1 **Socratic method:** The method of Socrates was to ask a series of questions, leading his opponent from one point to another, until ultimately it was the opponent who uttered the truth Socrates wished to prove.

23 5 **Pope says:** in his "Essay on Criticism."—8 **And now I set on foot:** about 1731. This was one of the first circulating libraries in America, and became the first public library of Philadelphia.—10 **scrivener:** one whose business is the preparation of contracts and other documents.—11 **Junto:** a group of men combined for a special purpose, usually political. This junto was a club for mutual improvement, discussion, and debate, and was started by Franklin not long after his return from England in 1726. Ultimately it grew into the American Philosophical Society.—12 **forty shillings:** probably about $6.66.—**ten shillings:** probably about $1.66.

25 17 **three-and-twenty shillings:** probably about $3.82.

26 6 **Alexander's name:** Alexander the Great was king of Macedon in the fourth century before Christ.

28 James **Otis** (1725–1783): graduated at Harvard in 1743; became a lawyer. As advocate-general under the crown in 1761, it would have been his duty to appear in behalf of the Writs of Assistance. He resigned the post in order to plead the cause of the people against these writs, which would have given the customs officers power to search houses for smuggled goods without naming either the houses or the goods. Otis published a book on the *Rudiments of Latin Prosody*, and wrote a similar book on Greek prosody, which was never published for lack of facilities for printing it in the Colonies.

29 17 **greatest monarch upon earth:** George III.—22 **one King of England:** Charles I.—23 **and another his throne:** James II.

30 Patrick Henry (1736–1799): born in Studley, Virginia; practiced law in Virginia. As a member of the Virginia House of Burgesses in 1765, he was the author of the "Virginia Resolutions" against the Stamp Act. His speech in favor of these resolutions ended with the famous sentence "Tarquin and Cæsar had each his Brutus; Charles the First, his Cromwell; and George the Third [cries of 'Treason' interrupted him] and George the Third may profit by their example. If *this* be treason, make the most of it." The speech on Arming the Colony was delivered in the Virginia convention in March, 1775.

31 Alexander Hamilton (1757–1804): born in the West Indies. He was sent to New York in 1772 to be educated and entered King's College (later Columbia University) in 1774; but his course was cut short by the breaking-out of the Revolution, into which he threw himself, serving four years as secretary and aide to Washington, and later holding a field command and distinguishing himself at Yorktown. As Secretary of the Treasury under Washington he was constantly in opposition to Jefferson as Secretary of State; and from this opposition grew the first two political parties in this country, the Federalists of Hamilton and the Democratic-Republicans of Jefferson. He was killed in a duel with Aaron Burr.

35 Thomas Jefferson (1743–1826): born at Shadwell, in Albemarle County, Virginia; studied at William and Mary College; then studied and practiced law. While practicing law he made a collection of early Virginia statutes. He was a member of the House of Burgesses from 1769 to 1775, when he entered the Continental Congress. In the next Congress he wrote the Declaration of Independence; but he refused reappointment to Congress, in order to return to Virginia to aid in revising the laws of the state in the direction of democracy. From 1779 to 1781 he was governor of Virginia; from 1784 to 1789 he was in France, first to aid in negotiating commercial treaties, and then as minister to France. In 1789 he was invited to help draft a constitution for France, but declined because of his official position. On his return to America he was made Secretary of State under Washington. As president of the United States he was democratic in practice as in theory. When a student he was an expert musician and athlete, and he kept all his life his fondness for outdoor life, for horses and gardening, making many experiments with seeds and plants and in the application of mechanical principles to farm tools.—20 **the remissness of Congress:** in 1783.

36 11 **Directory of France:** the body of five men which, under the constitution of 1795, held the executive power from 1795 to 1799.

37 22 **deliberate bodies:** deliberative bodies.—25 **Bonaparte's dumb legislature:** Soon after taking control of the government of France, in the autumn of 1799, Napoleon Bonaparte gave France a new constitution, which provided four assemblies: one to propose laws, another to discuss them, a third to vote on them after having listened in silence to the first two, and a fourth to decide whether or not they were constitutional. As a matter of fact, Napoleon, as First Consul, kept in his own hands practically all real power. Between 1799 and 1804 he put through an administrative system under which the French Republic is still governed, and a revision of the civil laws, called the *Code Napoléon*, which is in use to-day in France and, with modifications, in Holland, Belgium, Italy, parts of Germany, and the state of Louisiana.

38 16 **Themistocles:** statesman and general; induced the Athenians to build a navy to meet the invasion of the Persians, and then by his strategy in placing the fleet in the straits between the island of Salamis and the mainland enabled the Greeks to win a decisive victory over the vastly larger fleet of the Persians, 480 B.C.—**Thomas Paine:** born (1737) in Norfolk County, England. In 1774 he met Franklin, who gave him letters to Colonial leaders. With these letters he came to America, and aided the Colonists not only with his writings, but in the field as a volunteer aid to General Greene. He returned to England in 1787, and engaged in controversial writing there, his first effort being to bring about friendly relations between England and France. The last seven years of his life he spent in America, dying in New York in 1809.

43 Abigail Adams (1744–1818): Abigail Smith was born in Weymouth, Massachusetts. She was educated at home, as she was not strong enough to go to school. In 1764, against the wishes of her father, she married John Adams, who became the second president of the United States. At the time of the first letter Mr. Adams was in France on a diplomatic mission with their eldest son, John Quincy Adams, who became the sixth president. The officers and ships mentioned in this letter were part of the forces sent by France to aid the Colonies.

47 John Woolman: born in Northampton, New Jersey, in 1720. From the age of twenty-one he was a speaker in meetings of the Society of Friends. Though supporting his family first as a bookkeeper and then as a tailor, he made many preaching tours in various parts of the Colonies, and one to England, where he died in 1772. The part of the diary from which this extract is taken tells of a self-imposed mission to the Indians on the Susquehanna.—21 **sixth month:** June. The Quakers, or Friends, designate the days of the week and the months by numbers: Sunday is "first day."

48 33 **under which we purposed to lay:** see note on **12** 16.

50 28 **matchcoat:** a mantle worn by the Indians, originally of fur, later of a coarse woolen cloth called matchcloth.

52 26 **Moravian:** one of a denomination of Christians, called also the United Brethren.

53 11 **below a branch:** of the river.

54 Charles Brockden Brown: born in Philadelphia. A delicate boy, unfitted for active life, he overtaxed his strength in studying between the ages of eleven and sixteen years, but at sixteen he had gained a substantial literary education and had made extensive plans for writing. He wrote essays as well as romances, and he founded two magazines, the second of which he maintained for five years.

56 22 **Lennilennapee:** Delaware Indian.

59 Fitz-Greene Halleck: born in Guilford, Connecticut, in 1790; died there in 1867. He was descended from John Eliot, the "Apostle to the Indians." As a boy he worked in a country store, and then became a clerk in a bank in New York, where he remained twenty years. Then he became confidential agent of John Jacob Astor, who made him one of the first trustees of the Astor Library. After "Marco Bozzaris" the poem for which he is best known is the one he wrote on the death of his friend Joseph Rodman Drake.— 13 **Suliote:** The Suliotes were a people of mixed Greek and Albanian origin who fled to the Suli Mountains in Epirus, in the seventeenth century, to escape the Turks.— 18 **Platæa:** a ruined city of Bœotia, in Greece, where the Persians were defeated, 479 B.C.

62 Joseph Rodman Drake: born in New York in 1795; died there in 1820. He was left an orphan when very young, and had a hard struggle for an education, but obtained his degree in medicine in 1816, the same year in which he wrote "The Culprit Fay." Two years later he went to Europe. On his return he wrote a series of satires in verse for the New York *Evening Post*, which he signed "Croaker." When Fitz-Greene Halleck began to collaborate with Drake in these satires, he signed his work "Croaker, Jr.," at first; later they both used the signature "Croaker and Company."

63 William Gilmore Simms: a native of Charleston, South Carolina, where he lived most of his life. As his mother died when he was a baby and his father became an Indian fighter, he was brought up by his grandmother. For a time he was a clerk. Then he studied law, and was admitted to the bar at Charleston in 1827; but he soon gave up law for literature. In 1829 he became editor and part owner of the Charleston *City Gazette*, which failed in 1833. Later he was editor of the *Southern Quarterly Review*.— **The Yemassee:** a powerful Indian tribe. During the Yemassee War, 1714–1715, four hundred South Carolinians were killed in one battle.

64 12 **Manneyto:** Manito, one of the spirits controlling the forces of nature.

65 Richard Henry Wilde: born in Dublin, Ireland, in 1789. At the age of twelve he came to the United States with his parents. He studied law in Georgia, and was admitted to the bar there in 1809. He was Attorney-General of Georgia, and for three terms represented the state in Congress. After five years in Europe, he settled in New Orleans, where he practiced law and taught constitutional law (in Louisiana State University), and where he died in 1847.

66 John Pendleton Kennedy: born in Baltimore, Maryland, in 1795; died in Newport, Rhode Island, in 1870. He graduated at Baltimore College in 1812, and served as a volunteer in the ranks in 1814. He was ad-

NOTES

mitted to the bar in 1816, and practiced law successfully for twenty years.
He was a member of the Maryland House of Delegates, 1820–1823, and a
member of Congress, 1839–1845. In 1852 he became Secretary of the Navy.
In 1818 he and a friend began a fortnightly publication, called the *Red
Book*, which they maintained for two years. His first novel, *Swallow Barn*,
was published in 1832; other works are *Horseshoe Robinson, a Tale of
Tory Ascendancy*; *Rob of the Bowl*, telling of Maryland under the second
Lord Baltimore; *Life of William Wirt*; *Annals of Quodlibet*; *Mr. Am-
brose's Letters on the Rebellion*. He was a friend of Thackeray, and
collaborated on the fourth chapter of the second volume of *The Vir-
ginians*.

67 9 **Tivoli:** a town in Italy, famous for the lofty falls of the river
Anio. These falls to-day supply the electricity which lights Rome and
drives its street cars.—30 **Tartarus:** the infernal regions, according to
Homer as far below Hades as heaven is above the earth.

69 22 **Hendrick Hudson:** Henry Hudson, an English explorer. In
1609 he discovered the river which was named for him. Irving uses the
Dutch form of his Christian name.

70 1 **Hessian:** one of the mercenaries from Hesse, Germany, who
formed a large part of the British armies in the American Revolution.

72 1 **anaconda:** a boa, a large snake which crushes its prey and de-
vours it whole.

77 3 **adamant:** stone of unimaginable hardness.—22 **Herculean:** like
Hercules, extraordinarily large or strong.—34 **rantipole:** wild, unruly.

79 36 **Mercury:** the messenger of the gods, often represented wearing
a close-fitting cap with little wings.

80 4 **Mynheer** (mĭn hār′): Dutch for "Mister."

84 13 **Major André:** a British officer, sent to treat with Benedict
Arnold for the surrender of West Point. He was captured and executed as
a spy.

93 3 **Ten Pound Court:** a petty court in which cases involving not
more than ten pounds (twenty-five dollars) might be tried.

102 9 **yards:** long spars used to support and extend the sails.—
15 **courses:** the lowest sails.—18 **hand:** furl.

103 24 **ketch:** a two-masted vessel, differing from the yawl in that the
small mizzenmast is stepped forward of the rudderpost instead of abaft
it. When used for bombing, as the *Vesuvius* was, the mainmast was
stepped in about the middle of the vessel, and there were square sails on
one or both masts.

104 18 **studding-sails:** light sails set at the sides of the principal
square sails to increase the speed of a vessel.

106 25 **mizzen-channels:** ledges bolted to the outside of the ship to
increase the spread of the shrouds (ropes which lead to the top of the mizzenmast in order to support it).

107 10 **main-rigging:** the rigging of the mainmast.

108 28 **log:** the record of the ship's voyage.—36 **waist:** the middle part of the ship.

109 8 **rattlings:** ratlines, small transverse ropes attached to the shrouds to make the steps of a ladder.

111 5 **levin:** lightning.—6 **Pleiads:** Pleiades, the constellation named for the seven daughters of Atlas and Pleione. Merope, the seventh, hides herself for shame at having loved a mortal.—19 **Houri** (hoo'rĭ): one of the beautiful nymphs of the Moslem paradise.

113 8 **Nicæan:** Critics differ as to whether this is a reference to ancient Nicæa, the present city of Nice in France; a misspelling of "Nyseian," from the island of Nysa off the coast of Libya; or a substitution for "Phæacian." In this last case the weary, wayworn wanderer is Ulysses.— 13 **hyacinth hair:** This has been taken to mean hair as beautiful as that of Hyacinthus, the beautiful youth beloved by Apollo, or curly hair, or hair of a deep red-brown color, perhaps in reference to the mineral, hyacinth.— 14 **Naiad:** nymphlike. The naiads of Greek mythology were water nymphs. —**Maelström** (māl'strŏm): a famous whirlpool in the Arctic Ocean near the Lofoden (lŏ fō'dĕn) Islands, off the northwest coast of Norway, called also the Moskoeström. Poe in describing this whirlpool drew partly on his imagination, partly on early accounts, which were greatly exaggerated. The Lofoden Islands are ruggedly mountainous, with no wood and little agriculture, the mean annual temperature being 38.5 F. The chief industry is cod fishing, in which many lives are lost because of the sudden storms.

122 **"Giotto's Tower":** Giotto was a painter and architect, who lived and worked in Florence in the late thirteenth and the early fourteenth century.—20 **Paraclete:** the Comforter, the Holy Spirit.

124 24 **Master:** of the shipyard.—32 **wold:** open country.

126 8 **shores and spurs:** timbers which support the ship during construction.

127 10 **Master:** Washington.—11 **Workmen:** the fathers of the Republic.

134 3 **Roumili:** Rumelia, the Turkish possessions in the Balkan peninsula.—8 **Pillars of Hercules:** the promontories forming the Strait of Gibraltar.—20 **Istamboul** (ē stäm bool'): Constantinople.—**Lucknow:** a city of India, a center of the Sepoy Mutiny, relieved by General Havelock in September, 1857.

136 11 **Goomtee:** Gumti, a river in India, five hundred miles long, tributary to the Ganges.

137 **"Telling the Bees":** According to a superstition brought to New England from old England, it was necessary to tell the bees promptly of a death in the family and to drape the hives in mourning; otherwise the bees would leave their hives and seek a new home.

141 2 **Pisa's leaning miracle:** the beautiful bell tower of Pisa (in Tuscany, Italy), begun in 1174. It is 179 feet high, and leans 13 feet from the perpendicular.—27 **Amun**: Amon, the ram-headed deity of the ancient Egyptians.

144 25 **Boar's Head**: a high bluff near Hampton Beach, New Hampshire, opposite the Isles of Shoals.

147 1 **Pindus ... Olympus**: mountains in Greece, the latter the fabled home of the gods.—**Arachthus**: now the Arta River.

149 28 **Mainote**: The Mainotes were a wild, warlike tribe, living in an inaccessible mountainous district of southern Greece. Ypsilanti led them in their struggle for independence against the Turks.

155 13 **Sybaris** (sĭb'á rĭs): an ancient Greek city in southern Italy, noted for its luxury.

157 7 **Bloomfield**: Robert Bloomfield, an English poet (1766–1823).—18 **Dr. Johnson's**: Samuel Johnson (1709–1784) was an English author, noted chiefly for his conversation and his dictionary.—31 **Argos**: in Greece.

158 1 **spies, as did the Jews**: The Hebrew spies brought back fruits, including a bunch of grapes so large that it was carried on a staff between two men.—6 **Wellington's**: Arthur Wellesley (1769–1852), Duke of Wellington, was commander in the Peninsular War against Napoleon. Though he never had adequate transport, and though in consequence his troops were sometimes on the verge of starvation, yet he won the confidence of the civilian inhabitants and the dislike of his soldiers by his stern repression of plundering.—**"Old Ironsides"**: The *Constitution*, thanks to Holmes, may still be seen at its wharf in the Charlestown Navy Yard.

159 3 **harpies**: destructive monsters, in classical mythology represented as partly woman and partly bird.

161 **"Chambered Nautilus"**: The nautilus is a shellfish of the Indian and South Pacific oceans. It occupies the outer chamber of its spiral shell, and was supposed to have a membrane which served as a sail.—23 **Siren**: one of the sea nymphs who, by their singing, led sailors to shipwreck.

162 16 **Triton**: a demigod of the sea, represented always with a trumpet made from a conch shell.

164 18 **Indiaman**: a ship in the India trade.

165 6 **Behemoth** (bē'hĕ mŏth): a very large, strong animal, perhaps the hippopotamus, mentioned in the Book of Job.—12 **Elysian**: heavenly. In classical mythology Elysium was the home of the happy dead.—18 **in chancery**: an expression used in boxing, when one has his antagonist's head securely under his arm,—an allusion to the helplessness of persons involved in the courts of chancery.—29 **thrid**: an old form of "thread."

166 6 **Gramercy**: an interjection expressing thankfulness, here with a scornful turn.

167 21 **Cleopatra**: queen of Egypt in the first century before Christ. The Roman triumvir Antony expressing surprise at the luxury and costliness of a banquet, Cleopatra dissolved a pearl in acid, and drank the liquid to his health, saying, "My draught to Antony shall exceed in value the whole banquet."

169 "The Man-of-War Bird": the frigate bird, a large marine bird.

174 19 wold: wood (obsolete). See note on **124** 32.—26 *Veni, vidi, vici*: "I came, I saw, I conquered," Cæsar's laconic message announcing his suppression, in five days, of a revolt in Asia Minor.

175 11 Rhodora: a shrub related to the rhododendron, found in Canada and New England. The vivid pink flowers appear before the leaves in spring.

178 24 bush: the bush which burned and was not consumed, from which Moses heard the voice of God, as told in the Book of Exodus.—26 **dervishes:** members of various Moslem societies, who take vows of poverty and austerity.

179 1 pleached: fenced or shaded by interwoven boughs.—8 **Czar Alexander:** Alexander I, Czar of Russia, 1801–1825.—15 **Aryans:** Indo-Europeans, persons who speak any of the Indo-European languages.—24 **Doomsday:** day of judgment.—29 **Odin:** the chief god of the Norse peoples, as Jove was of the Romans.

180 1 Hari: Harischandra, twenty-eighth king of the Solar dynasty, celebrated for justice, generosity, and piety.—2 **Apollo:** god of music, healing, and prophecy, of manly sports and arts, protector of flocks and herds.—3 **Admetus:** a king in Thessaly.—4 **Ethiopians:** inhabitants of the valley of the Nile above the first cataract.

183 2 Cicero: Marcus Tullius Cicero, a Roman lawyer and politician of the first century before Christ, famous as a poet, philosopher, letter-writer, and especially as an orator.—**Locke:** John Locke (1632–1704), an English philosopher.—**Bacon:** Francis Bacon (1561–1626), an English statesman and philosopher.

185 Manse: the residence of a parish minister.

187 1 Assyrian . . . Paphian: from Assyria, the ancient empire of the Euphrates valley, and Paphos, an ancient city of Cyprus, used here simply to suggest oriental gorgeousness.—15 **Como:** one of the loveliest of the Italian Lakes.

189 11 Ellery Channing: William Ellery Channing (1818–1901), an American poet, nephew of the preacher of this name.

193 19 Province House: in Boston, the official residence of the governors appointed by the crown.

194 10 Cornhill: now Washington Street.—30 **Old South:** Old South Church. See note on *William Bradford*, p. 401. This building has been restored as nearly as possible to its original appearance, and is used as a museum and as a place for civic meetings.

195 25 Bedlamite: madman. "Bedlam" is a corruption of "Bethlehem." As early as 1402 the hospital of St. Mary of Bethlehem in London, which was founded as a priory in 1247, was used as an asylum for the insane.

196 8 bastinado: a beating on the soles of the feet.

202 18 Three Hills: Boston was called originally Trimontane, from the three hills which stood on the peninsula, the highest being Beacon Hill, the others Fort Hill and Copp's Hill.

207 Henry Timrod: born in Charleston, South Carolina, in 1829; died in Columbia, South Carolina, in 1867. He was educated at the University of Georgia, studied law, and then was tutor in private families, using his leisure for writing verse. At the outbreak of the Civil War he became a newspaper correspondent, and in 1864 assistant editor of the *South Carolinian* at Columbia.—26 **Athabasca:** Athabaska, a lake in northwestern Canada.

209 Paul Hamilton Hayne: born in Charleston, South Carolina, in 1830; died in Groveton, Georgia, in 1886. He was a nephew of Robert Young Hayne, the defender of the doctrine of states' rights, who educated him. After graduating at the College of Charleston, Hayne studied law, and then went into literary work and became a magazine editor. He served in the Confederate army until his health failed.—22 **Dryads:** In classical mythology a dryad is a nymph whose life is bound up with that of a tree.

210 Abram J. Ryan: born in Norfolk, Virginia, in 1839; died in Louisville, Kentucky, in 1886. Soon after being ordained to the priesthood of the Roman Catholic Church he entered the Confederate army as chaplain and served until the end of the war. Later he combined clerical and editorial work in New Orleans, Louisiana, and Augusta, Georgia.

211 Bayard Taylor: born in Kennett Square, Pennsylvania, in 1825. At the age of fifteen, while a schoolboy, he wrote a poem which was printed in the *Saturday Evening Post*. At nineteen he published a small book of poems, and started for Europe with about a hundred dollars in money and with promises from newspapers in Philadelphia and New York to pay for letters he might send them to print. With his knapsack he tramped through Europe for two years, learning Italian, German, and French, and arrived in London almost in rags and with thirty cents in his pocket. There he found work, and then returned to the United States. All his life he was a traveler, and many of his poems, as well as his prose works, have to do with far countries. In 1878 he was appointed United States minister to Germany, and died in Berlin a few months after his arrival there.

213 Harriet Beecher Stowe: Harriet Elizabeth Beecher, daughter of Lyman Beecher, the theologian, and sister of Henry Ward Beecher, was born in Litchfield, Connecticut. She was a student and then a teacher in her sister's school in Hartford. In 1836 she married Calvin E. Stowe. She wrote *Uncle Tom's Cabin* in Brunswick, Maine, while her husband was professor in Bowdoin College, 1850–1852.

214 32 **weird sisters:** in humorous reference to the Fates and to the witches in *Macbeth*.

216 7 **mantle:** Elijah the prophet left his disciple Elisha his mantle as a token of the transmission to him of the prophetic gift.

217 Herman Melville: born in New York City, where he died. His grandfather was the original of Holmes's "The Last Leaf." At the age of eighteen, after the death of his father, who had been in business as an importer, Melville made his first voyage as a cabin boy. On his return he

taught school for a while, and then, in 1841, went on a whaling voyage
from New Bedford. A year later he escaped from the ship to one of the
Marquesas and ultimately was rescued from this island by an Australian
whaler.— *Moby Dick :* the name of the White Whale. Ahab, the captain of
the whaler *Pequod*, had lost a leg in a previous adventure with a whale,
and used an artificial leg carved from the jawbone of a whale. On the
quarterdeck he steadied this bone leg in a hole bored in the planking,
spoken of as the pivot-hole. Ahab and the mates, Starbuck, Stubb, and
Flask, were Americans. The crew came from all parts of the world : Tashtego was an American Indian from Gay Head; Daggoo, an African negro;
the mysterious Fedallah, an Oriental.— 10 **dog-vane:** a small, light vane
carried on a ship's rail to show the direction of the wind.— 29 **T'-gallant-
sails:** The top-gallant-sail is the sail above the topsail and below the royal,
the royal being ordinarily the highest sail on a square-rigged ship; if there
is one higher, it is usually a skysail.— **stunsails:** a shortened form of
"studding-sails." See note on **104** 18.

218 1 **main-royal masthead:** the top of the main-royal mast. A
square-rigged ship has foremast, mainmast, and mizzenmast. Above the
mainmast is the main topmast; above the main topmast, the main top-
gallant mast; above that, the main-royal mast; highest of all is the main
skysail mast.— 24 **doubloon:** the gold coin which earlier in the voyage
Captain Ahab had nailed to the mainmast, promising it to the member of
the crew who should first raise (catch sight of) the White Whale.—
30 **sound:** dive suddenly toward the bottom.— 32 **luff a point:** turn the
head of the ship one of the thirty-two points of the compass nearer the
wind.— 33 **flukes:** the lobes of the whale's tail.

219 29 **argosy:** a very large merchant ship.— 36 **Jupiter ... Europa:**
Jupiter loved Europa, daughter of a Phœnician king, and, in the guise of
a white bull, carried her off to Crete.

227 **John Esten Cooke:** born in Winchester, Virginia. He studied law,
but soon turned his attention to literature, and published several books
before he was twenty-five. During the Civil War he was an officer in
the Confederate army, serving on the staffs of Stonewall Jackson and
J. E. B. Stuart. After the war he returned to his writing and continued it
steadily until his death.

229 **Henry David Thoreau:** born and died in Concord, Massachusetts;
graduated at Harvard in 1837. He taught school for a time, but soon gave
up teaching, preferring to pick up his modest living by odd jobs and to
keep his time for his own purposes. He gave occasional public lectures,
made excellent pencils, wrote for magazines, and worked as surveyor, boat-
builder, etc.

230 2 **Cenobites** (sĕn'ô bīts) : members of a religious order, living in a
convent community.

231 19 **cosmogonal** (kŏz mŏg'o nȧl): having to do with the origin of
the universe.

234 22 **potamogetons** (pŏt′à mŏ jē′tŏnz): pond weeds.

235 Francis Parkman: born in Boston. He was a delicate boy and spent much time with his grandfather in Medford, close to the Middlesex Fells, where he lived outdoors, trapping animals, shooting birds with arrows, and making collections of eggs, insects, etc. He graduated at Harvard in 1844 and then studied for two years in the Harvard Law School. Early in his college course he had decided on his life work, the writing of the history of the American forest. In 1842 he went to Italy for his health and lived for some time in a Passionist monastery, studying monastic life for its bearing on history. Soon after leaving Harvard he spent five months among the Dakotas and other Indian tribes for the sake of gaining first-hand information about Indian life and character. The hardships of this trip undermined his health and injured his eyes so seriously that he never recovered. For ten years, 1853–1863, he was unable to do any historical work and set himself to gardening, so successfully that he was made professor of horticulture in the Bussey Institute of Harvard University. His *Book of Roses* is still an authority. Often he was unable. to work for more than a few minutes at a time, but a year before he died he finished the historical work he had set himself to do.—1 **When last he had passed here:** La Salle, who had been forced to return to Canada for supplies, leaving a small garrison at Fort Crèvecœur, near what is now Peoria, Illinois, was going back toward the Mississippi along the Kankakee and upper Illinois rivers.—25 **Tonty:** Henri de Tonty, an Italian officer, La Salle's loyal lieutenant, who had been left in charge at Fort Crèvecœur. In the Sicilian wars Tonty had lost a hand, and used one of iron, usually gloved, with which once or twice he struck disorderly Indians blows which to them seemed supernatural. In spite of this handicap and a constitution far from robust he overcame hardships and difficulties which vanquished men apparently better fitted than he for life in the wilderness.

236 18 **Taensas** (tä ĕn′säz): a tribe of Indians, which probably merged later into the Choctaws or Creeks.—19 **Membré** (mäɴ brä′): Father Zenobius Membré, a missionary friar, who joined La Salle in 1679.

238 3 **D'Autray** (dō trä′): Jean Bourdon, Sieur d'Autray, one of La Salle's most trusted followers.—16 **Louis Le Grand . . . 1682:** Louis the Great, King of France and of Navarre, Rules; April 9, 1682.

239 (Francis) Bret Harte: born in Albany, New York. At the age of seventeen, his father having died, he went with his mother to California, and at first taught school. Then he tried mining, was unsuccessful, and entered a printing office, being in 1857 a compositor on the San Francisco *Golden Era*. He was successively express messenger, secretary of the mint in San Francisco, and editor, becoming editor of the first important magazine on the Pacific coast, the *Overland Monthly*, at its foundation in 1868. For one year he was professor at the University of California, and then went to New York City, where he lived from 1871 to 1878. He was United States consul at Crefeld, Germany, 1878–1880, and at Glasgow, 1880–1885.

From 1885 he lived and wrote in London.—5 **Dungaree:** a coarse cotton cloth made in India; in the plural, trousers or clothing made of dungaree, usually worn by sailors.—11 **pyrites** (pǐ rī'tēz): disulphide of iron, yellow in color, with a metallic sheen, and called fool's gold.

240 10 **gulches:** ravines.—24 **cañon:** a very deep, steep-sided valley.

241 24 **bowers:** in euchre the knave of the trump suit and the other knave of the same color, these two being the highest cards ordinarily used. —31 *chaparral* (chăp á răl'): a thicket of stiff, thorny bushes.

245 6 **Euchred:** defeated in a hand at euchre; hence defeated in an undertaking.

249 **George Washington Cable:** born in New Orleans in 1844. When he was fourteen his father died, and he went to work as clerk in a shop to support his mother and sisters. From 1863 to 1865 he served in the cavalry of the Confederate army. After the war he went first into engineering and then into newspaper work in New Orleans. As a writer he first attracted attention by the stories of Creole life in New Orleans which were collected later in *Old Creole Days*.—24 **Creole:** a white American, descended from the French (or Spanish) settlers of Louisiana and other Gulf states.

252 5 **faubourg** (fō boōr'): the French for "suburb."—21 *banquette* (bäɴ kĕt'): sidewalk.

253 4 *Vous savez* (voō sȧ vä'): You know.

254 10 *Vite* (vēt): Quick.—**Thomas Nelson Page:** born in Hanover County, Virginia, in 1853. His great-grandfathers, John Page and Thomas Nelson, for whom he was named, were both governors of Virginia, and the latter was a signer of the Declaration of Independence. He studied at Washington and Lee University, and in 1874 graduated in law at the University of Virginia. He practiced in Virginia until 1893, when he gave up the law to devote his time to writing and lecturing. He was United States ambassador to Italy from 1913 to 1919.—26 **my horses:** The time is that of the Civil War; and the plantation, lying in the path of the armies, has been raided by both sides, and all the horses have been taken. The speaker is the old negro servant.

255 3 **branch:** brook.—16 **Mistis:** Meh Lady's mother. Marse Phil was Meh Lady's brother, an officer in the Confederate army, who had been killed in battle.

257 16 **Cap'n Wilton:** Meh Lady's cousin, an officer in the Northern army, who had been wounded at a battle in the neighborhood early in the war and nursed back to health by Meh Lady and Mistis.

266 **Helen Hunt Jackson:** Helen Maria Fiske, daughter of a professor in Amherst College, was born in Amherst, Massachusetts, in 1831. In 1852 she married Lieutenant E. B. Hunt of the United States Engineers. After his death, in 1863, she began writing prose and verse for the magazines, usually signing her work "H. H." In 1875 she married William S. Jackson, a banker in Colorado Springs. In 1881 she published *A Century of Dishonor*, arraigning the treatment of the Indians by the whites, and two years later she was made a member of a special commission which investigated the condition and the needs of the Mission Indians in California. *Ramona* was published in 1884.

278 19 Mary E. Wilkins Freeman: Mary Eleanor Wilkins was born in Randolph, Massachusetts, in 1862. She was educated at Mount Holyoke Seminary, and was for many years secretary to Oliver Wendell Holmes. In 1902 she married Charles M. Freeman. Her short stories of New England life first attracted attention in 1886.

280 19 Samson Rawdy: a driver from the village livery stable, hired for the afternoon's calling expedition.

288 Hamlin Garland: born at West Salem, near La Crosse, Wisconsin, in 1860. His father had the spirit of the pioneer, growing restless as he achieved the beginnings of comfort, and moving out to new, unbroken land. Hamlin Garland went to school in Iowa, taught school in Illinois and Dakota, and worked on farms in various states. In 1884 he went to Boston to write and study, and lived there until 1893, when he returned to the West. More recently he has made his home in New York City.

289 12 Frank: the younger brother; Harriet was their sister.

290 36 Lilliputian (lĭl ĭ pū'shȧn): diminutive; from the land of Lilliput in *Gulliver's Travels*, by Swift, where everything was on a very small scale.

292 James Lane Allen: born near Lexington, Kentucky, in 1849. He was educated at Transylvania University, taught school in Kentucky and Missouri, and then taught in Kentucky University and in Bethany College, West Virginia. From 1886 he devoted himself to writing.

299 Mark Twain (Samuel Langhorne Clemens): born at Florida, Missouri. In 1848 he was apprenticed to a printer, and later worked at the printer's trade in Philadelphia and New York. This extract from *Life on the Mississippi* tells something of his experience in learning to be a pilot on the Mississippi River. He gave up this occupation to become secretary to his brother, who had been appointed secretary of the Territory of Nevada. Then he was a fortune-seeker in the mines of Nevada and California, a reporter, and a newspaper editor. He began lecturing after a trip to Hawaii in 1866. On his marriage he settled in Hartford, Connecticut.—
6 a person like this: Bixby, the pilot who was his teacher.

300 10 starboard: the right-hand side of a vessel as one faces the bow; the larboard, or port, side is the left.

301 32 shivaree: a corruption of "charivari," a mock serenade.

302 24 wood: The Mississippi River steamboats used wood as fuel and often had to stop for supplies—to "wood up."

306 1 Jim: a runaway slave. Huckleberry Finn, who tells the story, is a white boy who has escaped to this island in the Mississippi River from the abuse of a drunken father.

308 Edmund Clarence Stedman: born in Hartford, Connecticut. He studied at Yale, then wrote for New York papers, and during part of the

Civil War was the Washington correspondent of the New York *World*. From 1869 to 1900 he was in business in New York, and a member of the stock exchange.

310 Thomas Bailey Aldrich: born in Portsmouth, New Hampshire. His father died as he was about to enter college, and he went to work in a newspaper office in New York. Then he worked on N. P. Willis's *Home Journal*. From 1881 to 1890 he was editor of the *Atlantic Monthly*.— 6 cypress . . . and rue: the symbols of mourning and regret.—13 that pair . . . tomb: Romeo and Juliet.

311 Joaquin Miller (Cincinnatus Heine Miller): born in the Wabash district of Indiana. He went with his family to Oregon when a boy, but when thirteen years old ran away from home and drove cattle in Mexico and washed gold in California. On his way from Oregon, and again in returning, he was seriously wounded in encounters with Indians, but both times he was rescued and cared for by friendly Indians. He graduated at Columbia College, Oregon, in 1858, studied law, and tried, unsuccessfully, to practice it in Idaho. He became an express messenger, and later an editor. Then he returned to the law and from 1866 to 1870 was a judge. He obtained the name of "Joaquin" through his defense of the Mexican bandit Joaquin Murietta.—10 coyote: the prairie wolf.—11 arroyo's bed: bed of a watercourse or gully cut by water.—15 chaparral: see note on 241 31. —17 mesa (mä′sä): a plateau with steeply sloping sides.—22 swine: In the Gospels a herd of swine ran down a steep place into the Sea of Galilee and perished in its waters.

312 "Vaquero": cowboy.—14 haught: archaic form for "haughty." —16 peon: a common laborer; the term is applied to the hands on large estates in Latin America.

313 James Whitcomb Riley (1853–1916): born in Greenfield, Indiana. At sixteen he went to work for a house-painter. Finding that he had some skill in drawing and lettering, he became an itinerant sign-painter, then joined a wandering minstrel show. Afterward he worked on a country newspaper and began to write poetry. He always kept his fondness for traveling about the country, and as he became known he went about reading his poems.

314 Celia Thaxter: Celia Leighton was born in Portsmouth, New Hampshire, in 1835. When she was five years old her father became keeper of the lighthouse at the Isles of Shoals, the group of tiny, rocky islands off the New Hampshire coast. She was always fond of the sea and of wild birds. As a child she used to pick up birds which had hurt themselves by flying against the lighthouse, and care for them until they were able to fly again. After her marriage to Levi Thaxter, who had come to the Isles of Shoals as a missionary to the little fishing settlement there, she often went back to the island home to visit her family. She died in 1894.

316 Edward Rowland Sill: born at Windsor, Connecticut, in 1841; died at Cleveland Falls, Ohio, in 1887. He graduated at Yale in 1861. He tried business, then teaching, and began to study for the ministry before becoming literary critic of the New York *Evening Mail*. Then he taught school in Ohio, and later served as principal of the high school in Oakland, California, and as professor of English in the University of California. In 1883 he returned to Ohio and gave his time to writing.

317 Emily Dickinson (1830–1886): born and died in Amherst, Massachusetts. She lived a very retired life, and little of her work was published until after her death.

318 Emma Lazarus (1849–1887): born in New York City. She was educated at home, and published her first book of poems and translations in 1867. Besides poetry she wrote magazine articles, pleading in *The Century* (1882–1883) the cause of persecuted Russian Jews. When many destitute Jews, driven from Russia, came to New York, she was active in philanthropic work for them.—"**Venus of the Louvre**": The Louvre is an enormous palace in Paris, extending half a mile along the Seine, and now used as an art museum. The statue of Venus de Milo stands in a room by itself, against a dark velvet curtain, at the end of a long corridor.

319 3 *Heine*: Heinrich Heine (hīn′rĭĸ hī′nĕ), a German poet (1797–1856).—**Lucy Larcom**: born in 1826 in Beverly, Massachusetts; died in 1893 in Boston. As a girl she worked in a cotton mill in Lowell and contributed to a literary magazine, called the *Lowell Offering*, conducted by factory workers there. After three years in Monticello Seminary in Illinois, she taught in Wheaton Seminary in Massachusetts. From 1865 to 1874 she was editor in chief of *Our Young Folks*, which was afterward merged with *St. Nicholas*.

320 Eugene Field (1850–1895): born in St. Louis, Missouri. He spent much of his boyhood in Vermont and Massachusetts, and studied at Williams and Knox colleges and at the University of Missouri. When twenty-three years old he entered newspaper work, and at thirty-three began work on the Chicago *News*, for which he conducted a column, "Sharps and Flats," for twelve years. Most of his work, later collected, appeared first in this column.—**9 God's Acre**: burying-ground, graveyard.—**14 Shepherd . . . sheep**: from the Twenty-third Psalm, beginning, "The Lord is my shepherd."

322 12 *au naturel* (ō nà tü rĕl′): plainly cooked.—**(Francis) Marion Crawford**: born in Italy in 1854; died there in 1909; son of an American sculptor, Thomas Crawford, and nephew of Julia Ward Howe. He was a student at St. Paul's School, Concord, New Hampshire; Cambridge University, England; Heidelberg; and Rome. In 1879 he went to India, studied Sanskrit, and edited a newspaper in Allahabad. Then he returned to America, continued at Harvard the study of Sanskrit, wrote for magazines, and in 1882 published his first novel. The next year he returned to Italy and made his home at Sorrento, on the beautiful Bay of Naples. He prepared French versions of two of his books, and in recognition of his quality as a writer was awarded a medal and a prize by the French Academy. In *Via*

Crucis he tells of events which took place just before the middle of the twelfth century.—23 Gilbert: a young Norman from England. A few months before this chapter opens, his father had been treacherously killed in battle by a neighbor, and Gilbert himself, in trying to avenge his father's death, had been wounded and left for dead by the same man. Found and nursed back to health by monks, Gilbert learned that his enemy had obtained possession of his lands and married his mother. In despair he has started on a pilgrimage.

323 5 Beatrix: the daughter of Gilbert's enemy. By the custom of the time the marriage of Beatrix's father and Gilbert's mother made the young people, though actually not at all related, legally brother and sister.— 9 Queen of France: Eleanor, duchess of Aquitaine, was the wife of Louis VII of France; later, by her marriage to Henry II (Plantagenet), she became queen of England.—28 Dunstan: Gilbert's man.

324 36 Pistoja (pĕs tō′yä): a town in Tuscany, twenty-one miles northwest of Florence, to which it was a dangerous enemy at times during the Middle Ages.

326 8 surcoats: long, flowing cloaks worn over armor. Because a man in armor with the visor of his helmet closed was unrecognizable, it was customary to embroider the coat of arms, or some device by which he was known, on the surcoat, as well as to blazon it on the shield.

327 31 sumpter mule's back: pack mule's back.

328 27 gambeson (găm′bĕ zŏn): a quilted garment of cloth or leather.

331 (James) Maurice Thompson (1844–1901): born in Fairfield, Indiana. He was educated in Georgia, and served in the Confederate army. He practiced law and civil engineering in Crawfordsville, Indiana, and from 1885 to 1889 was state geologist and head of the department of natural history in Indiana.—21 mongrel patois (pȧ twä′): a dialect derived from more than one language.—24 Borgne: a lake or bay in southeastern Louisiana.—26 bight (bīt): a bend in a shore or in a mountain chain.— bayou (bī′ōō): an inlet from the Gulf of Mexico or from a large river or a lake.

337 16 Ascham (ăs′kȧm): Roger Ascham (1515–1568), tutor to Queen Elizabeth. His *Toxophilus*, "On the Art of Shooting," was a novelty in that he had "written this Englishe matter in the Englishe tongue for Englishe men," saying that "what the best of the realm think it honest to use" he "ought not to suppose it vile for him to write." In his *Scholemaster*, also in English, he urged that flogging in schools, then everywhere customary, be given up.—William Hamilton Gibson: born in 1850 in Sandy Hook, Connecticut; died in 1896 in Washington, Connecticut. He was a student in Brooklyn Polytechnic Institute when his father, a New York broker, failed in business and then died (1868), and he began to earn his living by life insurance. He had drawn flowers and insects from the time he was eight years old, and soon gave up the insurance business for natural history and illustrating. Besides drawing in black and white and painting in water colors (though he used color little), he became an expert engraver and photographer. He was a popular lecturer on natural history.

338 20 **Mars:** the Roman god of war.—21 **Tantalus:** in Greek mythology, son of Zeus. In the lower world he was placed in water which reached his chin but receded when he tried to drink, with fruit just out of reach above his head.—35 **harbinger:** a messenger who used to precede the king of England when the king was on a journey, to prepare lodgings; hence a forerunner.

342 John Fiske (1842–1901): born in Hartford, Connecticut. He was originally Edmund Fiske Green, but in 1855 took the name of his great-grandfather. He studied and read widely in Greek, Latin, several modern languages, English literature, and history before entering Harvard, at which he graduated in 1863. Two years later he graduated at the Harvard Law School, was admitted to the bar, and opened an office in Boston. He soon gave most of his time to writing for the magazines, having already, as an undergraduate, published in the *National Quarterly Review* an article which attracted attention. He was a lecturer at Harvard and assistant librarian there from 1872 to 1879, and continued to make his home in Cambridge as long as he lived, though he gave courses of lectures at Washington University, in St. Louis, and in England.—15 **Teutons:** the tall, blond race of northern Europe.—17 **Aryan:** see note on **179** 15.

344 6 **peculiar circumstances of the Teutonic settlement of Britain:** The invaders from beyond the North Sea killed off the Romanized Britons or drove them into the mountains, without extensive mingling.— 8 **Norman Conquest:** A.D. 1066.—10 **thegnhood:** or "thanehood," the upper classes of Saxon feudalism.—11 *noblesse . . . adel:* French and German, respectively, for "nobility."—33 **Charles the Bold** (1433–1477): duke of Burgundy.

345 3 **Earl Simon:** Simon de Montfort, earl of Leicester (1208–1265), leader of the barons and townsmen against Henry III. Under his authority representatives of the towns and counties were first summoned to Parliament.—9 **Capetians** (kå pē′shȧnz): the royal family of France for nearly nine hundred years was named Capet (kå pä′).—10 **Louis XIV:** called Louis the Great; king of France from 1643 to 1715. He is famous for the definition attributed to him, *L'état c'est moi* (I am the State).

346 8 **Huguenot:** a French Protestant in the sixteenth and seventeenth centuries.—21 **Titan:** one of the primitive gods of Greek mythology.

347 William Dean Howells (1837–1920): born in Martin's Ferry, Ohio. He began to write verses when a very little boy. His father owned and published daily papers in Ohio, and as a boy Howells learned the printer's trade and the various details of the newspaper business. In 1859, when he was news editor of the *Ohio State Journal*, he brought out his first volume of poems and had some poems published in the *Atlantic Monthly*. In 1860 he wrote a life of Abraham Lincoln, who had just been nominated for the presidency. From 1861 to 1865 he was United States consul at Venice.

Then he worked on New York newspapers, and in 1866 became assistant editor of the *Atlantic Monthly* and in 1872 editor in chief. In 1886, after spending some time abroad, in England and Italy, he became an editor of *Harper's Magazine.*—29 **Aldrich:** see note on **310.**

348 7 **Gothic:** medieval.

349 29 **Louis Agassiz** (ăg'à sē̇) : Jean Louis Rodolphe Agassiz, born in Switzerland in 1807. He came to the United States in 1846. A geologist, biologist, and great teacher, he was made professor of zoölogy at Harvard in 1847, and founded the Summer School of Marine Biology at Penikese Island, in Buzzards Bay, in 1873. See Longfellow's poem "The Fiftieth Birthday of Agassiz," and Whittier's poem "The Prayer of Agassiz."— 30 **Francis J. Child:** scholar and teacher, professor of English at Harvard from 1851 to 1896.— **Richard Henry Dana, Jun.:** author of *Two Years Before the Mast.*—31 **Dr. Asa Gray:** the greatest of American botanists, professor at Harvard from 1842 to 1888.— **Jameses:** Henry James the elder was a clergyman and a writer on religion and morals. His sons were Henry, the novelist and essayist, and William, the psychologist and teacher. —32 **Charles Eliot Norton:** professor of the history of art at Harvard from 1875 to 1900. With Lowell he edited the *North American Review* from 1864 to 1868. The foremost Dante scholar in America, he founded the American Dante Society and made a complete prose translation of Dante.— **Dr. John G. Palfrey:** clergyman and American historian; professor at Harvard, 1830–1839; editor of the *North American Review*, 1835–1843; member of the state legislature; secretary of the Commonwealth of Massachusetts, 1844–1848; member of Congress, 1847–1849; postmaster at Boston, 1861–1867.— 33 **James Peirce:** James Mills Peirce (1834–1906), professor of mathematics at Harvard from 1861.— **Dr. Peabody:** Andrew Preston Peabody (1811–1893), clergyman and writer. He edited the *North American Review* from 1852 to 1861. From 1860 to 1881 he was professor at Harvard.— **Professor Parsons:** Theophilus Parsons (1797–1882), professor in the Harvard Law School from 1847 to 1872. He wrote for the *North American Review*, founded and edited the *United States Literary Gazette*, and wrote well-known legal handbooks and books on the Swedenborgian faith.— **Professor Sophocles:** Evangelinus Apostolides Sophocles, born in Greece in 1807; died in Cambridge, Massachusetts, in 1883; professor of ancient and modern Greek at Harvard.

350 21 **Dante:** Dante Alighieri (dän'tä ä'lē̇ gyâ'rē) (1265–1321), the greatest of Italian poets and one of the greatest writers of the world. The *Divine Comedy*, of which the "Paradiso" forms the third part, is his most important work.— **Craigie House:** where Longfellow made his home in Cambridge. It was Washington's headquarters during the siege of Boston.

351 27 **Fields's story:** James T. Fields was a publisher, author, and lecturer, and editor of the *Atlantic Monthly* from 1862 to 1870. It was the post of assistant editor under Fields that had brought Howells to Cambridge.— **Tom Appleton's wit:** Thomas Gold Appleton (1812–1884), author and artist, brother-in-law of Longfellow, was known as a brilliant talker. He was the author of the saying " Good Americans, when they die, go to Paris."

353 5 **Professor Webster:** John Webster, professor in the Harvard Medical School, in a sudden quarrel struck a friend and, when the blow proved fatal, destroyed the body.

355 Edith Wharton: Edith Newbold Jones was born in New York in 1862. She was educated at home. In 1885 she married Edward Wharton of Boston, and since then has lived much abroad. During the World War she did much for Belgian refugees and other sufferers. In recognition of her services in relief work and in her writings she was made Chevalier of the Legion of Honor (of France) and the Order of Leopold (of Belgium).

356 9 **Just for a handful of silver he left us:** the first line of Browning's poem "The Lost Leader."

357 28 *Kallima* (kăl'ĭ má): a butterfly of southern Asia and the East Indies which, when settled on a twig with folded wings, looks like a dried leaf; consequently called leaf butterfly.

359 11 **dogma:** a teaching which is supported by the authority of the teacher rather than by evidence.

362 33 **embryo:** in the early stages of development.—34 **planarians:** a group of soft-bodied, unsegmented worms, usually aquatic. Some kinds increase by fission, that is, by the division of an individual into two, each of which regenerates the parts it lacks.

363 O. **Henry:** pen name of William Sydney Porter (1862–1910).— 17 **atelier** (à tẽ lyā'): studio.—18 **chiaroscuro** (kyä rō skoo'rō): light and shade.—**Wagner:** Richard Wagner (1813–1883), German composer. —19 **Rembrandt's works:** Rembrandt van Rijn (rĕm'bränt vän rīn') (1606–1669) was a Dutch painter.—**Waldteufel** (vält'toi'fĕl): Emile Waldteufel, born in Strasbourg in 1837; known especially as a composer of waltzes.—20 **Chopin** (shŏ păn'): Frédéric François Chopin (1809–1849), French-Polish composer and pianist.

365 8 **Byzantine** (bĭ zăn'tĭn): characteristic of Byzantium (Constantinople) or the Byzantine Empire.—23 **Benvenuto Cellini** (chĕl lē'nē) (1500–1571): Italian artist, sculptor, and worker in metals.

366 32 **Monte Cristo** (mon'te crĭs'tō): In Dumas's novel *The Count of Monte Cristo* the hero obtains possession of treasure.

367 12 **filet mignon with champignons** (fē lē' mē nyôN', shäN pē nyôN'): tenderloin steak with mushrooms.

369 Sara Teasdale: born in St. Louis, Missouri, in 1884; married Ernst B. Filsinger in 1914. She is of an old American family: an ancestor, Major Simon Willard, was one of the founders of Concord, Massachusetts; ancestors on both sides fought in the Revolution; both families moved to the Middle West in 1850. Her *Love Songs* won the Columbia University prize for the best book of poems published by an American in 1917.— "**Pierrot**": a wandering minstrel in the costume of a buffoon.

371 Margaret Widdemer: born in Doylestown, Pennsylvania; graduated at Drexel Institute Library School in 1909. She began to write as a child. In 1919 her book *The Old Road to Paradise* shared with one of Carl Sandburg's the Pulitzer prize for the best book of poems. She married Robert Haven Schauffler in 1919.

372 2 Cleopatra: queen of Egypt (69–30 B.C.). See also note on **167** 21.—**4 Sappho** (săf'ō): a Greek lyric poetess, who lived about six hundred years before Christ.—**6 Orlando . . . Rosalind:** in Shakespeare's play *As You Like It.*—**10 King Francis' court:** Francis I (1494–1547), king of France, autocratic and pleasure-loving, though caring sincerely for letters and art, developed a court more brilliant than France had known before his time.

374 Edwin Arlington Robinson: born at Head Tide, Maine, in 1869. He was a student at Harvard from 1891 to 1893. Since 1900 he has lived in New York, at first earning his living at various occupations but giving his time mainly to writing poetry. In 1903–1904 he was inspector in the New York subway, then under construction; from 1905 to 1909 he did office work in the New York customhouse, through appointment by President Roosevelt. In 1922 his *Collected Poems* received the Pulitzer prize and the prizes of the Poetry Society and the Authors' Club. Since 1911 he has spent his summers in the MacDowell Colony at Peterboro, New Hampshire.

376 (Nicholas) Vachel Lindsay: born at Springfield, Illinois, in 1879. He studied at Hiram College, Ohio, at the Art Institute of Chicago, and at the New York School of Art. He has given much time to lecturing and to reciting his poems.

380 Edith M. Thomas: born at Chatham, Ohio, in 1854. She was educated at the Normal Institute of Geneva, Ohio. Since 1888 she has lived in New York, and for much of the time has been on the editorial staff of *Harper's Magazine.*—**George Edward Woodberry:** born at Beverly, Massachusetts, in 1855; A. B., Harvard, 1877. He was professor of English literature at the University of Nebraska, 1877–1878 and 1880–1882, and professor of comparative literature at Columbia University, 1891–1904.

381 Katharine Lee Bates: born at Falmouth, Massachusetts, in 1859; A.B., Wellesley College, 1880; A.M., 1891. She is professor of English literature at Wellesley.—**22 roundelays:** A roundelay is a poem or song with a constantly recurring refrain.

382 Alan Seeger (1886–1916): In 1912, on his graduation from Harvard, he went to Paris to study and write. When the World War broke out he joined the French Foreign Legion and served until he was killed in action, July 5, 1916.

383 Robert Frost: born in San Francisco in 1875. Of New England stock, he went to New England to live in 1885. He was a student at Dartmouth, in 1892, and at Harvard, 1897–1899. For five years he was a farmer in Derry, New Hampshire; then he taught English in Pinkerton

NOTES 423

Academy in Derry, and psychology in the State Normal School in Plymouth, New Hampshire. For four years, beginning in 1916, he was professor of English at Amherst College; then he held the fellowship of creative literature at the University of Michigan. In 1923 he was again at Amherst, and then returned to Michigan.

385 Amy Lowell: born in Brookline, Massachusetts, in 1874. She was educated in private schools. Her grandfather was a cousin of James Russell Lowell.

386 2 leviathans: huge aquatic animals, perhaps crocodiles.

387 Josephine Preston Peabody (1874–1922): born in New York. She studied at Radcliffe College from 1894 to 1896, and was instructor in English literature at Wellesley from 1901 to 1903. She married Professor Lionel S. Marks in 1906.—22 **minster:** the church of a monastery. Often the church has continued to be called a minster after the monastery has disappeared; for example, York Minster. The word is used commonly, but improperly, of any large church.—23 **cloister:** a covered passage at the side of a court, usually having a wall on one side and an open colonnade on the other.

390 Joyce Kilmer (1886–1918): born in New Brunswick, New Jersey; A.B., Columbia University, 1908. He taught Latin in the high school of Morristown, New Jersey, 1908–1909, and then engaged in literary and editorial work in New York. He was a soldier in the World War, a sergeant when he was killed in action at the second battle of the Marne.

392 4 bourgeoise (bŏŏr zhwȧz′): a woman of the middle class.— 10 **Asseyez-vous, s'il vous plaît** (à sĕ yä-vŏŏ, sĕl vŏŏ plĕ): Please sit down.—21 **pain . . . vin . . . cognac . . . bonjour** (păɴ, văɴ, kŏ̂ nyȧk′, bôɴ zhŏŏr′): bread . . . wine . . . brandy . . . good day.

393 1 Mais oui! . . . Et vous, ma foi, vous êtes Catholiques, n'est-ce pas? (mĕ wĕ . . . ā vŏŏ, mȧ fwä, vŏŏ zĕt kȧ tŏ̂ lĕk′, nĕs pä): Oh, yes! . . . And you, gracious, you're Catholics, aren't you?—5 **scapulars:** two small squares of cloth connected by cords, worn over the shoulders under the clothing as a matter of devotion, as symbols of or substitutes for monastic habits.

394 1 sou (sŏŏ): cent.—9 **francs:** Before the war a franc was worth about twenty cents. It is divided into one hundred centimes, though the smallest coin is the five-centime piece.—11 **half-crown:** about sixty-one cents.

395 36 Benedicite . . . Sanctus (bā nā dē′chĕ̂ tā; nŏs′ ĕt quā sŏŏ′mŏŏs sŏŏmp tŏŏ′rē bā nā′dĕ cȧt dā′ŏŏs, pä′tĕr ĕt fē′le ŏŏs ĕt spē′rĕ̂ tŏŏs sȧnc′- tŏŏs ä′mĕn)[1]: Bless [the Lord]; may God, the Father, Son, and Holy Spirit bless us and that which we are about to receive.

---

[1] It is well known that different pronunciations of Latin are in use. In the notes on this selection the pronunciation used by the Catholic Church in the United States is intended.

396 13 **esoteric:** private, confidential.—**illuminati** (ĭ lū'mĭ nā'tĭ): enlightened. This term was applied in the early Church to baptized persons, who received each a lighted candle; later it was applied to various religious and political groups.—15 **agimus tibi gratias** (ä'jĕ mŏŏs tē'bē grä'tsĕ äs): we give thee thanks.

397 5 **Tantum ergo Sacramentum** (tän'tŏŏm ĕr'gō sä crä mĕn'tŏŏm): Bowing then in adoration, we this sacrament revere.—19 **Adeste Fideles** (ä däs'tä fē dā'lĕs): Oh come, all ye faithful.—22 **Venite, adoremus Dominum** (vä nē'tä, ä dō̆ rä'mŏŏs 'dō'mĕ nŏŏm): O come, let us adore the Lord.—25 **"Au Clair de la Lune"** (ō clĕr d' lä lün'): By moonlight.

399 14 **Shanagolden:** a town in Limerick County, Ireland.

INDEX AND PRONOUNCING VOCABULARY

KEY TO PRONUNCIATION

ā, as in fate; ă, as in fat; ä, as in arm; á, as in ask; a̤, as in all; a̧, as in what; â, as in care; ȧ, as in sofa
ē, as in mete; ê, as in event; ĕ, as in met; ē, as in maker
ī, as in ice; ĭ, as in it
ō, as in old; ŏ, as in obey; ŏ, as in not; ô, as in horse; ōō, as in food; ŏŏ as in foot
ū, as in use; ŭ, as in up; û, as in fur; ü, French sound of u, as in vue
ou, as in out
ᴋ, like ch in German ich or ach
ɴ, indicating nasalization of preceding vowel, as in bon

NOTE. Titles of books, poems, and essays are in italics. First lines of poetical quotations are indicated by quotation marks. The figures in heavy-faced type refer to the Readings.

Abbott, Charles, 191
Aboard at a Ship's Helm, **169**
Abolitionist party and Whittier, 92, 94
Abraham Davenport, 101
Abraham Lincoln, 223
Abraham Lincoln walks at Midnight, **376**
Adams, Abigail, 22, **43**
Adam's Diary, 178
Adventures of Captain Bonneville, (bŏn'vĭl), 41
Adventures While Preaching the Gospel of Beauty, 216
Afloat and Ashore, 58
After Apple-Picking, **384**
Age of Innocence, The, 204
Agitation, the age of, 76
Albert of Belgium, **380**
Alcott, Louisa M., 160
Aldrich, Thomas Bailey, 185, 173, 174, 184, **310**
Alhambra (ăl hăm'brȧ), *The,* 41
Alhambra group, Irving's works, 37, 40
Alice of Monmouth, **308**
All-America period, the, 169; short stories, 170–174; novels, 174–183; poetry, 183–189; miscellaneous prose, 189–195, **239**; bibliography, 195

All's Well, **150**
Allegory, Hawthorne's, 149
Allen, James Lane, 175, 207, 210, **292**
America the Beautiful, 217
American Ornithology, 190
American Political Ideas, 192, **342**
American Scholar, The, 140, 143, **180**
Among My Books, 109
Anna Christie, 223
Annalists, Colonial, 5
Annie, For, 71
Annie Kilburn, 174, 177
Annuals, literary, 51
Arctic Voyager, The, **207**
Arming the Colony, Speech on, **30**
Art, Colonial, 2–3
Arthur Gordon Pym, Narrative of, 72
"As the bird trims her to the gale," 136
Astoria (ăs tō'rĭ ȧ), 41
Atherton, Gertrude, 208
Atmosphere, stories of, 69
Audubon (ô'dōō bŏn), John James, 190
Austin, Mary, 208
Autobiography, Franklin's, 14, **19**; Jefferson's, 22, **35**
Autocrat of the Breakfast Table, The, 115, 111, 113, 117, **164**
Ax and the Pine, The, **209**

Bacheller, Irving, 206
Bailey, Florence, 191
Ballads, Whittier's variation of, 97–98
Barclay of Ury, 97
Barlow, Joel, 17
Basket Woman, The, 208
Bates, Katharine Lee, 217, **381**
Beauty, Poe's ideal, 66
Bedouin (bĕd´o͞o ĭn) *Song*, **211**
"Behind him lay the gray Azores,"
    28
Belasco, David, 223
Bell of Atri (ä´trē), *The*, 90
Belles-lettres (bel´let´r'), professor-
    ships of, 80
Bells of San Blas (sän bläs´), *The*, 90
Benavente, Jacinto, 221
Beyond the Horizon, 223
Biglow Papers, The, 108, 105
Birds of America, 190
Bivouac of the Dead, The, 75
Black Oxen, 208
Blazed Trail, The, 210
Blithedale Romance, The, 153, 147
Boker, George H., 157
Bolles, Frank, 191
Book, A, **318**
Books and Seasons, **310**
Border Beagles, The, 30
Boy's Will, A, 218
Bracebridge Hall, 35
Bradford, William, 5, 2, 9, 12, **1**
Bradstreet, Anne, 7, 112, **8**
Bravo (brä´vō), *The*, 55, 56
Breakfast Table series, Holmes, 115
Brer Rabbit, 180
Brewster, William, 2
Bridal of Pennacook, The, 96
Brook Farm, 77, 114, 153, 165
Brooks, Maria Gowen, 32
Brown, Charles Brockden, 24, 68, **54**
Brownell, Henry H., 157
Bryant, William Cullen, 44; life, 45;
    poetical works, 47; estimate of, 50;
    compared with Lowell, 107. 8, 82,
    93
Building of the Ship, The, 80, **123**
Bunner, Henry C., 173, 189
Burke, Edmund, 19, 22
Burroughs, John, 191
By the Bivouac's Fitful Flame, **168**
"By the rude bridge that arched the
    flood," 139
Byrd, William, 5, 2, **3**

Cable, George W., 173, **249**
Caliban, 224
California and Oregon Trail, The,
    164, 41
Cambridge Thirty Years Ago, 110
Canterbury Pilgrims, The, 224
Captain Blood, 210
Carleton, Will, 187
Carver, Jonathan, 22
Cassia and Other Verse, 217
Catherwood, Mary Hartwell, 182
Cavalier and Puritan, 5, 119
Cavalry Crossing a Ford, **168**
Cawein, Madison, 189
Celebrated Jumping Frog, The, 178
Centennial Exposition of 1876, 165,
    169
Chambered Nautilus (nạ´ti lus), *The*,
    114, **161**
Channing, William Ellery, 23, 78, 144
Chanticleer, **314**
Charles Egbert Craddock. *See* Murfree
Charleston School, the, 30, 33
Charlotte Temple, 23
Chicago Poems, 220
Child, Mrs. Lydia, 96
Children of the Night, 215
Chinese Nightingale, The, 216
Chingachgook (chin gach´gook), 55, 58
Chopin, Mrs. Kate, 173
Christus : a Mystery, Longfellow, 89
Churchill, Winston, 182, 205
Circuit Rider, The, 159
Citizen literature, 18–20
Civil War, 75, 78
Clarence, 224
Class poems of Holmes, 113
Cleave to Thine Acre, **380**
Clemens, Samuel L. (Mark Twain),
    177, **299**
Coal Picker, The, **385**
Coin, The, **371**
Colleges, early American, 2
Colonial literature, quality of, 1, 3
Colonial period, the, 4; annalists, 5;
    poets, 6; Indian narratives, 9; re-
    ligious writers, 10; summary, 25;
    selections for reading, 26; bibliog-
    raphy, 27; **1**
Columbiad, The, 17
"Come up from the Fields, Father,"
    130
Commemoration Ode, Lowell, 106
Common Sense, 22

Concord Hymn, 139
Condescension in Foreigners, On, 110
Congo, The, 216
Conjuror's House, 210
Connecticut Yankee at King Arthur's Court, A, 178
Conqueror, The, 208
Conquest of Canaan, The, 17
Contemporary history and criticism, 170
Contentment, Holmes, 115
Cooke, John Esten, 159, **227**
Cooke, Rose Terry, 173, 176
Cooper, James Fenimore, 52; life, 53; works, 56; scenes and characters, 59; general characteristics, 26, 9, 25, 29, 31, 44, 71. **102**
Correspondence of Carlyle and Emerson, 135
Courtship of Miles Standish, The, 86, 88
Covered Wagon, The, 203
Crane, Stephen, 179, 209, 210
Crawford, Marion, 182, **322**
Crèvecœur (krĕv kûr'), Hector St. John de, 22
Crisis, The, Paine, 22, **38**; Churchill, 205
Cross of Snow, The, 83
Cross-Currents, 215
Crossing Brooklyn Ferry, 127
Culprit Fay, The, **62**
Curtis, George William, 195

Dana, Richard H., Jr., 158
Dandelion, To the, 107, **154**
Danvis Folk, 179
David Harum (Hâr'ŭm), 206
Dawn at San Diego, **311**
Day of Doom, The, 7
Days, Emerson, 144, **178**
Deacon's Masterpiece, The, 114
Death, Whitman's poems on, 131
Death's Epitaph, **25**
Debt, The, **355**
Debtor, The, **278**
Declaration of Independence, A, 21
Deerslayer, The, 58, 31, 53
Descent into the Maelström, A, **113**
Detectives in fiction, 69
Dickinson, Emily, 189, **317**
Diedrich Knickerbocker, 37, 38
Divine Comedy, Longfellow's translation of the, 83, 89

Dome of Many-Coloured Glass, A, 220
Don Quixote (Spanish, dōn kē hō'tĕ; English, dŏn kwiks'ōt), 111
Drake, Joseph Rodman, 30, **62**
Drama, modern American, 220
Driftwood Essays, Longfellow, 82, 83
Dunbar, Paul Lawrence, 188
Dupin (dü păn'), a fictitious character of Poe's, 69
Dutchman's Fireside, The, 30
Dwight, Timothy, 17

Each and All, 137
Eben Holden, 206
Edgar Huntly, 25, **54**
Edwards, Jonathan, 11, 12, 144, **15**
Eggleston, Edward, 159
Eliot, John, 6, 10, 12
Elsie Venner, 111, 116
Emerson, Ralph Waldo, 133; life, 134; poems, 137; prose works, 139; doctrine of, 141; estimate of, 144; and Carlyle, 135, 140; quoted, 52. 78, 151, **171**
Emperor Jones, The, 223
Enthusiasm of first national period, 28, 29
Erskine Dale, Pioneer, 207
Essays, Lowell, 109, **156**; Emerson, 140, **180, 183**
Eternal Goodness, The, 101, 102
Ethiopia Saluting the Colors, 130
Evangeline (ē văn'jĕ lĭn), 86
Evening Song, **167**
"*Evensong*," poems, 85
Explorer's Wooing, The, **321**

Fable for Critics, A, 108, 105
Factories and Other Poems, 215
Fair Harbor, 207
Fairy Gold, 217
Fall of the House of Usher, The, 69, 70, 72
Farewell Sermon, A, **15**
Farm Ballads, Carleton, 187
Father Abraham's Speech, 16
Faust (foust), Goethe, Taylor's translation of, 157
Federalist, The, 21, **31**
Federalist party, 13
Female Quixotism, 24
Fiction, beginning of American, 23
Field, Eugene, 188, **320**
First Snowfall, The, 107

Fiske, John, 192, **342**
Flame and Shadow, 214
Flint, Timothy, 32
Fool's Prayer, The, **316**
Forbearance, **174**
Ford, Paul Leicester, 182
Forest Hymn, A, 48, 49, 101, **94**
" For this true nobleness I seek in vain," 156
Four Million, The, 213
Fox, John, Jr., 207
Franklin, Benjamin, 14, 33, 144, **19**
Free verse, 219–220
Freedom, Bryant, 51
Freedom of the Will, Edwards, 12
Freeman. *See* Wilkins
French, Alice, 173
Freneau (frē nō'), Philip, 17, 9, **25**
Frost, Robert, 218, **383**

Garden, The, **370**
Garland, Hamlin, 173, **288**
Garrison, William Lloyd, 94, 103
Gentle Boy, The, 151
Gentle Julia, 203
Geoffrey (jĕf'rĭ) Crayon, 37
Gibson, William Hamilton, 191, **337**
Gilder, Richard Watson, 189
Giotto's (jôt'tō) *Tower*, **122**
Godfrey, Thomas, 9, **9**
God's Controversy with New England, **7**
Gold Bug, The, 69, 70
Golden Legend, The, Longfellow, 89
Golden Whales of California, The, 216
Good-Bye, **177**
Goodrich, Samuel, 32
Gookin, Daniel, 10
Gothic novel, the, 25, 68
Grandfather's Chair, Hawthorne, 148
Gray Champion, The, 151
Great Divide, The, 224
Great Stone Face, The, 150
Grey, Zane, 211
Guardian Angel, The, 116

Hale, Edward Everett, 174, 195
Hall, James, 32
Halleck, Fitz-Greene, 30, **59**
Hamilton, Alexander, 20, **31**
Hampton Beach, **151**
Handy Guide for Beggars, A, 216
Hardy, Arthur Sherburne, 183
Hark to the Shouting Wind, **208**
Harris, Joel Chandler, 179–180

Harte, Francis Bret, 172, 169, **239**
Hartford Wits, the, 17
Hawthorne, Nathaniel, 145; life, 145–148; short stories, 148; romances, 151; characteristics, 153. 25, 70, **185**
Hay, John, 184, 189
Hayne, Paul Hamilton, 156, **209**
Hazard of New Fortunes, A, 177
Headsman, The, 55
Hearn (hern), Lafcadio (lăf cä'dĭ ō), 81
Heartsease and Rue, 101
Heidenmauer (hī'den mou er), *The*, 55
Height of the Ridiculous, The, **162**
Hémon (ā mōn'), Louis, 198
Henry, Patrick, 19, **30**
Hiawatha (hī a wạ'thä *or* hē ạ wạ'tä), 88, 86, **127**
Higginson, Thomas Wentworth, 195
Hills of Song, 219
Historical impulse in Colonial writing, 4
Historical romances, modern, 204–205
History, the epic of, 163
History of the Dividing Line, 5, 9, **3**
History of the Navy, Cooper, 56
History of the Pequot Wars, 10
Hobomok (hŏ bōō'mŏk), 96
Holland, Josiah Gilbert, 157
Holmes, Oliver Wendell, 111; life, 111–113; poems, 113; prose works, 115; estimate of, 116. 96, **158**
Holy Grail, the, Lowell's legend of, 108
Holy Ireland, **390**
Home as Found, 55
Hoosier Schoolmaster, The, 158
Hope Leslie, 32
Horror as a motive in fiction, 68
Horseshoe Robinson, 32
Hough (hŭf), Emerson, 203
House of Mirth, The, 204
House of Night, The, **25**
House of the Seven Gables, The, 151, 148
Hovey, Richard, 189
Howard, Blanche Willis, 183
Howells, William Dean, 176, 195, **347**
How Love Looked for Hell, 123
Huckleberry Finn, 178, **306**
Hugh Wynne, Free Quaker, 205, 182
Human nature in Colonial literature, 7–9
Humble-Bee, The, **175**
Humor, American, 39, 43, 111, 114
Hunt, Helen, 181, 9

Hymn of Trust, **159**
Hyperion (hī pē′rǐ on *or* hī per ī′on), Longfellow, 83, 89

Ichabod (ik′à bŏd), 97
Idealism of Emerson, 141
Idyls, American, 86, 97
I Have a Rendezvous (räN′dā vōō) *with Death*, 217, **382**
Iliad (ĭl′ĭ ăd), Bryant's translation of the, 47
"I'm going out to fetch the little calf," 197
Immigrants, The, 224
In Absence, **167**
Indian Burying Ground, The, **26**
Indian narratives, early, 10
Indian-Summer Reverie, An, 107
Indians in literature, 9, 96
Individualism, of Emerson, 142; of Hawthorne, 155; of Thoreau, 160
In the Harbor, Longfellow, 82, 83
Innocents Abroad, The, 178
In Ole Virginia, 179, **254**
Inside of the Cup, The, 205
Irving, Washington, 33; life, 34–37; works, 37–42; estimate of, 43. 30, 71, **68**
Israfel, **110**

Jackson, Helen Hunt, 181, 9, **266**
Jefferson, Thomas, 20, 19, **35**
Jewett, Sarah Orne, 169, 173, 175, 176
John Brent, 159
Johnston, Mary, 182
Jonathan Oldstyle, 37
Josselyn, John, 9, 190
Journal, Woolman's, 23, **47**; Timothy Flint's, 32; Emerson's, 136; Thoreau's, 190
Journal of Julius Rodman, The, 72
Joy, Shipmate, Joy! **171**
June, Bryant, 48
Juvenile Poems, Godfrey, 7

Katherine Walton, 30
Kavanagh (kăv′à nạ), 83
Kennedy, John Pendleton, 31, 32, 65, **66**
Kentucky Warbler, The, 207
Kilmer, Joyce, 217, **390**
King, Grace, 173
Knickerbocker History, The, 38
Knickerbocker School, the, 30, 33
Knoblauch (nŏb′louk), Edward, 224

Lady Eleanore's Mantle, **193**
Lady or the Tiger, The, 174
Lanier (lă nēr′), Sidney, 117; life, 119; works, 122; characteristics, 124; compared with Whittier, 125. **165**
Larcom, Lucy, 188, **319**
La Salle (lä säl) *and the Discovery of the Great West*, 164, **235**
Last Leaf, The, **160**
Last of the Mohicans (mŏ hē′kȧnz), *The*, 58, 9
Laus Deo (lous dē′ō), 95, 96, 102
Lazarus, Emma, 188, **318**
Leatherstocking and Silk, 159, **227**
Leatherstocking Tales, 58
Leaves of Grass, 127
Legend Beautiful, The, 90
Legend of Sleepy Hollow, The, 40, **68**
Legends, 220
Letter from Charleston, **40**
Letters, Adams, **43**
Letters, Jefferson; 22
Letters from an American Farmer, 22
Letters from the West, Hall, 32
Libraries, Colonial, 2
Life of John Winthrop, **13**
Life on the Mississippi, 177, **299**
Life and Song, 123
Life and Times of Columbus, 36
Life of Washington, Irving, 42
Light o' the Moon, The, **379**
Lincoln, Abraham, 77, 80
Lincoln, Joseph, 206
Lindsay, Vachel (vā′chĕl), 216, **376**
Lines, Ryan, **210**
Linwoods, The, 32
Lionel Lincoln, 56, 57
Literary Ethics, **183**
Literary Friends and Acquaintance, **347**
Literary histories, American, 193
"Little I ask, my wants are few," 115
Little Shepherd of Kingdom Come, The, 207
Little Theater, The, 221
"Little thinks, in the field, yon red-cloaked clown," 137
Lives of Distinguished Naval Officers, 56
Local color, stories of, 171, 172
Longfellow, Henry Wadsworth, 81; life, 81–83; minor poems, 84; idyls, 86; miscellaneous works, 89; characteristics, 90. 45, 80, 101, 146, **121**

Long Roll, The, 205
Long Tom Coffin, 57
Lost Occasion, The, 97
Love Songs, Teasdale, 214
Lowell, Amy, 220, **385**
Lowell, James Russell, 104 ; life, 104–106 ; poems, 106–108 ; essays, 109 ; as critic, 110 ; compared with Bryant, 107. 113, 145, **152**
Loyalist or Tory party, 13, 16
Loyalist Poetry of the Revolution, 17
Luck of Roaring Camp, The, 172
Lyceums, American, 77, 136
Lynch Lawyers, 221
Lyrics and Sonnets, 217

M'Fingal (mak fĭng'gᾰl), 17
Mackaye (mᾰ kī'), Percy, 224
Madame Délicieuse (dā lē sē ûz'), **249**
Madame Delphine (del fēn'), 173
Madison, Dolly, 22
Magnalia Christi Americana (mᾰg-nä'lĭ ᾰ kris'tē a mĕr ĭ cä'nᾰ) 11, **13**
Magnificent Ambersons, The, 203
Man Against the Sky, The, 215
Man from Bar-20, The, 211
Man of the Forest, The, 211
Man that Corrupted Hadleyburg, The, 178
Man without a Country, The, 174
Manuscript Found in a Bottle, 64, 71
Marble Faun, The, 152, 148
Marco Bozzaris, **59**
Maria Chapdelaine (mä rē'ä shᾰp dē lĕn'), 198
Marjorie Daw, 174
Mark Twain, 177, **299**
Marshes of Glynn, The, 124, 118
Marsh-Land Incident, A, **331**
Mary-'Gusta, 207
Mason, John, 10
Massachusetts to Virginia, 96
Materialism and idealism, 141
Mather, Cotton, 11, 2, **13**
Maud Muller, 99, 102
Meh Lady, **254**
Melting-pot notion, the, 22
Melville, Herman, 158, 57, **217**
Men Have Wings at Last, **387**
Mending Wall, **383**
Mercedes (mĕr thä'thäs) *of Castile* (kas tēl'), 57
Merlin and the Gleam, 120
Mettle of the Pasture, The, 207

Miles (Myles) Standish, 86, 88
Miller, Joaquin (wä kēn'), 185–186, 28, 169, 184, **311**
Miller, Olive Thorne, 191
Milton, John, 4
Minister's Black Veil, The, 150
Minister's Charge, The, 176
Mitchell, Donald Grant, 195
Mitchell, S. Weir, 182, 205
Mitchell, Samuel L., 38
Moby (mō'bĭ) *Dick,* 158, **217**
Modern Instance, A, 176
Mogg Megone, 96
Monsieur Beaucaire (bō kâr'), 203
Moody, William Vaughn, 189, 224
Moon of the Caribbees, The, 223
Moral quality of Hawthorne, 155
Moralizing in poetry, 50, 138
Mortal Antipathy, A, 116
Morton, Sarah Wentworth, 9, 32
Mosses from an Old Manse, 149, **185**
Motley, John Lothrop, 163
Mountain Interval, 219
Mourt's (moort *or* mŏrt) *Relation,* 5
Muir (mūr), John, 191
Mulford, Clarence Edward, 211
Murders in the Rue Morgue (rü môrg) 69
Murfree, Mary Noailles (nō ĭ'), 173. 175
Music and poetry, 122, 124
My Garden Acquaintance, 110, **156**
My Lady's Dress, 224
My Springs, 119, 122
My Study Windows, 109, **156**
" My terminus near," 132
Mysteries of Udolpho (ū dŏl'fō), *The,* 68

Nation, the new American, 28
National Ode, The, Taylor, **212**
Natty Bumppo, 55, 58, 60
Nature, in Colonial writings, 7 ; two views of, 101
Nature, Emerson, 139, 133, 142
Nature writers, the, 190
Neal, John, 32
Nehemias Americanus, **13**
New England's Prospect, 9
New England's Rarities Discovered, 9
New Nation, Literature of the, 28 ; history of the period, 28 ; literary environment, 29 ; minor writers, 30 ; major writers, 33 ; summary,

72; selections for reading, 73; bibliography, 74. *See also* Cooper, Irving, etc.
Niagara, **377**
Night and Day, 123, **166**
Night Thoughts, 47
Noiseless Patient Spider, A, 131
Norris, Frank, 179, 173, 209
North of Boston, 219
Note-Books, Hawthorne, 147, 153
Notes, Lanier, 122
Novel, The, Crawford, 182
Novelists, recent American, 201
Novels, early American, 23; recent American, 201; of the frontier, 202; of society, 203; historical, 204; of character, 205; social, 209; of adventure, 210

O Captain! My Captain, 130, **170**
O. Henry, 213, **363**
" O, I have passed a miserable night," 223
Octaves, I, Robinson, **374**
Octopus, The, 209, 179
Odyssey (ŏd'ĭ sĭ), Bryant's translation of the, 47
Of Plymouth Plantation, **1**
"Oh, slow to smite and swift to spare," Bryant, 77
O'Hara, Theodore, 75, 156
Old Books, **371**
Old Creole Days, 173
Old Ironsides, 112, **158**
Old Manse, The, **185**
Old Road to Paradise, The, 215
Old Swimmin' Hole, 188
Oldstyle group, Irving's works, 37
Oldtown Folks, 157
Oliver Goldsmith, Irving, 42
O'Neill, Eugene, 223
Oratory in Revolutionary Period, 18
Oregon Trail, The, 164, 41
Otis, James, 19, **28**
Outcasts of Poker Flat, The, 172
Outre Mer (ōōtr mâr), 83
Outward Bound, **310**
Over the Teacups, 113

Page, Thomas Nelson, 173, **254**
Paine, Thomas, 22, **38**
Parkman, Francis, 163–164, **235**
Partisan, The, 31
Party literature in America, 13

Pathfinder, The, 58
Patriot or Whig party, 13, 16
Paulding, James Kirk, 30
Paul Revere's Ride, 90
Peabody, Josephine Preston, 222, **387**
Pearl of Orr's Island, The, **213**
Penrod, 203
Percival, James Gates, 32
Period of Conflict, The, 75; political history, 75; social agitation, 77; literary characteristics, 78; poets, 81; prose writers, 133; secondary writers, 156; summary, 165; selections for reading, 165; bibliography, 166; **121**
Peter Parley, 32
Picture of New York, 38
Pictures of the Floating World, 220
Pierce, Franklin, 146, 148
Pierrot (pyĕ'rō'), **369**
Pike County Ballads, 169, 184
Pilot, The, 57
Pine Tree, The, 93, 96
Pioneers, two views of the, 1
Pioneers, Whitman, 130
Pioneers, The, Cooper, 58, 53
Pioneers of France in the New World, 164
Piper, The, 222
Pipes at Lucknow (lŭk'nou), *The*, 98, **134**
Pirate, The, 57
Pit, The, Norris, 209, 179
Plymouth Plantation, Of, 5
Poe, Edgar Allan, 62; life, 63; poems, 65; tales, 68; estimate of, 70. 24, 25, 81, 109, **110**
Poems Here at Home, 188
Poetry, spirit of recent, 183. *See also* Colonial, Revolutionary, etc.
Poor Richard's Almanac, 15
Pope, Alexander, 16, 17
Porter, William Sydney (O. Henry), 213, **363**
Portygee, The, 207
Prairie, The, Bryant, 50; Cooper, 58
Prayer, A, Teasdale, **369**
Prayer of Agassiz, The, Whittier, 101
Prayer of Columbus, The, Whitman, 132
Preacher, The, 12
Precaution, 54
Prescott, William Hickling, 163
Present Crisis, The, 107

Present-day American literature, introduction, 197; authors and readers, 199; novelists, 201; short stories, 212; poetry, 214; drama, 220; bibliography, 225. **355**
Prince of Parthia (pär'thǐ ä), *The*, 7, **9**
Problem novels, 208
Psalm of Life, A, 84, 92, **121**
Psalm of the West, A, 123
Puritan, the, in Colonial history, 2; in Hawthorne's fiction, 145, 151
Puritan and Cavalier, 119

Quabi (qua̤'bē), *or the Virtues of Nature*, 9
Quality of Mercy, The, 177
Quick, Herbert, 202

Ramona (rǎ mō'nä), 181, 9, **266**
Randall, James Ryder, 156
Randolph of Roanoke, 95, 96
Raven, The, 66, 71
Read, Thomas B., 157
Readers' relation to modern authors, 199
Realism in fiction, 175, 159
Recent literature. *See* All-America Period
Recent poetry, 214
Red Badge of Courage, The, 179, 210
Red Maples, **370**
Red Rover, The, 58, **102**
Redeemed Captive, The, 10, **10**
Reign of Law, The, 210, **292**
Religious motive in Colonial writings, 4, 10
Representative Men, 140
Retinue, The, 217
Return to nature, the, 60, 190
Return of Peter Grimm, The, 223
Return of Youth, The, **93**
Revolution, American, 13
Revolutionary Period, The, 13, **19**; transition to, 14; poets, 16; orators and statesmen, 18; miscellaneous writings, 22; fiction, 23; summary, 25; selections for reading, 26; bibliography, 27. *See also* Freneau, Franklin, etc.
Rhodora, The, **175**
Rhymes of Childhood Days, 188
Richard Carvel, 182, 205
Richardson, Charles F., 195
Richardson, Samuel, 24

Riley, James Whitcomb, 188, 187, **313**
Rip Van Winkle, 40
Rise of Silas Lapham, The, 176
Roamer, The, 217
Robbins, Royal, 30
Robert of Lincoln, **99**
Robinson, Edwin Arlington, 215, **374**
Robinson, Rowland, 173, 179, 191
Roe, Edward Payson, 181
Romances, modern American, 181, 182
" Room, room to turn round in, to breathe and be free," 186
Roughing It, 177
Rowlandson, Mrs. Mary, 10
Rowson, Mrs. Susanna, 23
Russell, Clark, 57
Russell, Irwin, 187
Ryan, Abram J., 156, **210**

Sabatini, Rafael, 210
Saga (sä'gà) *of King Olaf* (ō'läf), *The*, 90
Salmagundi (sǎl mǎ gŭn'dǐ), 30, 37
Sandburg, Carl, 220
Sandpiper, The, **315**
Saxe, John G., 157
Scarlet Letter, The, 153, 147, 148, 151
Schoolcraft, Henry Rowe, 88
Schultz, J. Willard, 208
Science of English Verse, The, 122
Scollard, Clinton, 219
Sea Dream, A, 99
Sedgwick, Catherine, 32
Seeger, Alan, 217, **382**
Service of Love, A, **363**
Seventeen, 203
Short story, the, modern, 170, 212
Sign language, example of the, 87
Silent Places, The, 210
Sill, Edward Rowland, 189, **316**
Simms, William Gilmore, 30, 29, **63**
Singing in God's Acre, The, **320**
Sir Launfal (lạn'fặl), Lowell, 108, 105
Sketch Book, The, 39, 34, 35, 37
Slabs of the Sunburnt West, 220
Snow-Bound, 99, 95, 100, **139**
Snow Image, The, 148, 149
Snow-Storm, The, **175**
Some Verses upon the Burning of Our House, **8**
Son of the Middle Border, A, **288**
Song of Myself, 128
Songs and Ballads of the Revolution, 17

Songs of the Sierras (sĭ ĕr´ăz), 185, 169, 184, **311**

Sonnets, Longfellow, 86; Lowell, 108, **156**; Aldrich, **310**

Southern Literary Messenger, The, 431

Sovereignty and Goodness of God, The, 10

Spanish group, Irving's works, 37, 41

Spanish Student, The, 89

Spider, allegory of the, 130

Splendid Idle Forties, The, 208

Spring, Gibson, **337**

"Spring still makes spring in the mind," 138

Spy, The, 56, 31, 42, 54, 57

Stedman, Edmund Clarence, 183, 92, 184, 194, **308**

Stirrup Cup, The, 122

Stockton, Frank R., 173, 174

Stoddard, Richard H., 157, 195

Storm, The, **317**

Stowe, Harriet Beecher, 157, 79, 158, **213**

Summary View, A, Jefferson, 22

Summer Rose, The, **65**

Sunnyside, house, 36; group of Irving's works, 37

Sunrise, Lanier, 121

Swallow Barn, 32, **66**

Symbolism, Hawthorne's use of, 149, 154

Symphony, The, 123, 119, 124

Tales of the Border, 32

Tales of a Traveller, 35

Tales of a Wayside Inn, 90

Tamerlane and Other Poems, 64

Tampa Robins, **165**

Tanglewood Tales, 148

Tarkington, Booth, 203, 224

Taylor, Bayard, 157, 184, **211**

"Teach me your mood, O patient stars," 144

Teasdale, Sara, 214, **369**

Telling the Bees, 99, 102, **137**

Tennessee's Partner, 172, **239**

Tenney, Tabitha, 24

Tent on the Beach, The, 100

Tenth Muse, The, 7

Terminus, 136

Thanatopsis (than *a* top´sis), 46, 47, 50

Thaxter, Celia, 189, **314**

Theater, the modern, 220

"The death of men is not the death," 210

Thomas, Augustus, 223

Thomas, Edith M., 189, 216, **380**

Thompson, Maurice, 182, 190, **331**

Thoreau (thō´rō), Henry D., 160–162, 190, 191, **229**

"Thou mother with thy equal brood," 132, 169

Threnody (thrĕn´ŏ dĭ), Emerson, 139

Tiger Lilies, 124

Timrod, Henry, 156, 117, **207**

Titmouse, The, **171**

To the Fringed Gentian, **101**

To Have and to Hold, 205, 182

To Helen, 67, **113**

To the Man-of-War Bird, **169**

To One in Paradise, **112**

To a Waterfowl, **98**

To Youth after Pain, **373**

Tom Sawyer, 178

Tories, 13, 16

Torrey, Bradford, 190

Tour on the Prairies, A, 41

Town Down the River, The, 215

Town-Meeting, The, **342**

Trail of the Lonesome Pine, The, 207

Trailing Arbutus, The, **150**

Transcendentalism (trăn sĕn dĕn´tăl-ĭsm), 78

Travels, Carver, 22

Treasure Island, 69

Trees and Other Poems, 218

Trowbridge, John T., 160, 195

Trumbull, John, 17

Twice-Told Tales, 149

Two Years before the Mast, 158

Tyler, Moses Coit, 194

Typee (tĭ´pē), 158

Ulalume (ōōl a lōōm´), 67

Uncle Remus (rē´mus), 179, 169

Uncle Tom's Cabin, 157, 79, 181

Under the Old Elm, **152**

Vandemark's Folly, 202

Vaquero (vä kä´rō), **312**

Venus of the Louvre, **318**

Verne, Jules, 69

Vesper songs, 85

Via Crucis (wī´å krōō´kĭs), **322**

Virginia Comedians, The, 159, 174

Virginian, The, 207

Vision of Sir Launfal, The. See Sir
  Launfal
Voices of Freedom, 96, 102
Voices of the Night, 81, 83

Walden, 162, 117, 139, 190, **229**
Wallace, Lew, 182
Wanderer of the Wasteland, The, 211
Warden of the Cinque (sink) *Ports,
  The*, 90
Water Witch, The, 58
Waterlily, The, **320**
Way to Wealth, The, 16
Webster, Daniel, 76, 97
Wept of Wish-Ton-Wish, The, 57, 61
Westcott, Edward Noyes, 206
Western group, Irving's works, 37, 41
Wharton, Edith, 204, **355**
When the Frost is on the Punkin, **313**
" When lilacs last in the dooryard
  bloomed," 130
When the Woods Turn Brown, **319**
Whigs, 13, 16
White, Stewart Edward, 210
White, William Patterson, 211
White Czar, The, 90, **133**
White Jacket, 158
Whitman, Walt, 126; life, 126; typi-
  cal verse, 127; war poems, 129;
  later poems, 130; Lanier's criticism
  of, 122. **168**
Whittier, John Greenleaf, 92; life,
  93-95; early works, 96; ballads and
  idyls, 97; poems of faith and
  nature, 100; characteristics of, 102;
  compared with Lanier, 125. 9, 79,
  134

" Who are you, dusky woman ? " 130
Widdemer, Margaret, 215, **371**
Wieland (vē'länd), Brown, 25
Wigglesworth, Michael, 7, **7**
Wild Honeysuckle, The, **27**
Wilde, Richard Henry, 31, **65**
Wilderness, The, **374**
Wilderness and Warpath, 32
Wilkins, Mary E., 173, **278**
Wilkinson, Eliza, 22, **40**
William Wilson, 63, 69, 70
Williams, John, 10, **10**
Willis, Nathaniel P., 30
Wilson, Alexander, 190
Wing and Wing, 58
Winthrop, Theodore, 159
Wister, Owen, 207
Witching Hour, The, 223
" With husky-haughty lips, O sea," 130
With Reed and Lyre, 219
Woman's Reason, A, 176
Wonder Book, A, 148
Wonders of the Invisible World, 11
Wood, William, 9
Woodberry, George Edward, 189, 217,
  380
Woodnotes, 133
Woolman, John, 23, **47**
Works and Days, **179**
World Soul, The, 138
Wreck of Rivermouth, The, 97, 101
Writs of Assistance, Speech on, Otis, **28**

Year's Life, A, 106
Yellow Clover, 217
Yellow Warblers, **381**
Yemassee (yĕm a sē'), *The*, 30, 31, **63**